Strategic Management & Organisational Dynamics

Second Edition

Ralph D Stacey

Professor of Management
University of Hertfordshire Business School

London · Hong Kong · Johannesburg · Melbourne
Singapore · Washington DC

PITMAN PUBLISHING
128 Long Acre, London WC2E 9AN

A Division of Pearson Professional Limited

© R D Stacey 1993, 1996

First published in Great Britain 1993
Second edition published in 1996

British Library Cataloguing-in-Publication Data
A catalogue record for this book is available from the
British Library

ISBN 0 273 61375 8

10 9 8 7 6 5 4 3 2 1

Typeset by Pantek Arts, Maidstone, Kent.
Printed in England by Clays Ltd, St Ives plc

Contents

Part One
THE CONCEPTUAL FRAMEWORK
Change, decision-making and control

Part Two

ORDINARY MANAGEMENT CLOSE TO CERTAINTY AND AGREEMENT

Organisational intention and the reinforcement of current strategic direction in the legitimate system

Contents

9   System dynamics far from equilibrium   309

Complex feedback systems coevolving into open-ended evolutionary space

CASE STUDIES

Part Four

EXTRAORDINARY MANAGEMENT FAR FROM CERTAINTY AND AGREEMENT

*Self-organisation and the emergence of new strategic direction
in the shadow system*

10   The nature of an organisation's shadow system and its primary purpose   378

Learning far from certainty and agreement

11 Decision-making and control processes employed in the shadow system   391
Effective and ineffective learning in organisations

12 Extraordinary management in the shadow system   441
How managers create knowledge and intervene far from certainty

CASE STUDIES

Part Five

CREATIVITY AND TENSIONS BETWEEN LEGITIMATE AND SHADOW SYSTEMS

The paradox of ordinary and extraordinary management

Plan of the book

Chapter 1 The nature of strategy

Part One – THE CONCEPTUAL FRAMEWORK

Chapter 2 The nature of change and its implications for decision-making and control	Chapter 3 Ordinary and extraordinary management

Case Studies

Part Two – ORDINARY MANAGEMENT CLOSE TO CERTAINTY AND AGREEMENT

Chapter 4 The nature of an organisation's legitimate system and its primary purpose	Chapter 5 The rational model of strategic management
Chapter 6 The visionary/ideological model of strategic management	Chapter 7 The results of using ordinary management to make long-term strategies

Case Studies

Part Three – ORGANISATIONAL DYNAMICS

Chapter 8 Organisations are feedback systems	Chapter 9 System dynamics far from equilibrium

Case Studies

Part Four – EXTRAORDINARY MANAGEMENT FAR FROM CERTAINTY AND AGREEMENT

Chapter 10 The nature of an organisation's shadow system and its primary purpose	Chapter 11 Decision-making and control processes employed in the shadow system

Chapter 12 Extraordinary management in the shadow system

Case Studies

Part Five – CREATIVITY AND TENSION BETWEEN LEGITIMATE AND SHADOW SYSTEMS

Chapter 13 Strategic management and organisational dynamics in perspective

List of key concepts

List of illustrations

List of figures and exhibits

Preface

Why another strategic management textbook?

Having added to the substantial pile of strategic management texts in the form of the first edition of this book, it is gratifying to find that it has stimulated sufficient interest to require the preparation of a second edition. I hope you will allow me to repeat my reasons for believing that there is a need for yet another textbook in the strategy field – they remain valid and also account for the preparation of this second edition.

At least ninety per cent of the contents of all the textbooks on strategic management that I know of, apart, of course, from this one, are devoted to that part of the management task which is relatively easy – the part that has to do with running the organisational 'machine' in as surprise-free a way as possible. Thus, most textbooks focus heavily on techniques and procedures for long-term planning, on the need for visions and missions, on the importance and the means of securing strongly shared cultures, on the equation of success with consensus, consistency, uniformity and order. This relative emphasis in content terms has the effect of reinforcing a conventional wisdom that today dominates the conscious approach of Western managers to strategic management, namely the belief that the purpose of strategic management is to reduce the level of surprise, to increase the level of predictability, and thereby improve the ability of those at the top to control the long-term destiny of their organisation. These beliefs are promoted and reinforced through the persistent failure of most textbooks to question the most fundamental belief upon which that conventional wisdom is built: namely, the belief that organisations succeed when they operate in states of stability and harmony to adapt intentionally to their environments.

Reflection on why an organisation needs managers at all, however, reveals how exceedingly odd this conventional wisdom is. Organisations need managers primarily to handle the surprises that all organisations must inevitably encounter as they move through time. Managers, from the first supervisory level right up to the chairman of the board, justify their existence when they apply their intuition and judgement to those situations in which the techniques, procedures, rules, structures and so on turn out to be inadequate in some way – a machine may break down, operators may suddenly quarrel, bank loans may be recalled, new market opportunities may appear and so on. If we could rely on the absence of such events, that is if the techniques and prescriptions of the conventional wisdom could be relied on to work, then of course there would be very little need for managers – it would suffice if one or two managers were available to maintain the systems. We need armies of managers because organisational life is inevitably full of ambiguities, uncertainties and surprises and no matter how perfect the techniques and how hard we try this is still so.

The real management task, then, is that of handling the exceptions, rapidly and under pressure, as and when they unexpectedly occur. In other words, the real management task is that of coping with and even using unpredictability, clashing counter-cultures, disensus, contention, conflict, and inconsistency. In short, the task that justifies the existence of all managers has to do with instability, irregularity, difference and disorder — matters that most textbooks devote less than ten per cent of their content to.

Furthermore, there is evidence available that the conventional wisdom – all explanations and prescriptions that encourage managers to focus on uniformity, stability and regularity – leads to failure rather than success in rapidly changing and highly competitive conditions. The evidence suggests that organisations succeed in highly uncertain environments when they sustain states of instability, contradiction, contention and creative tension in order to provoke new perspectives and continual learning. In this manner successful organisations create and discover their own environments and their innovative strategies emerge without prior, organisation-wide intention. In such circumstances no-one can be in control of future direction.

An alternative textbook on strategic management continues, therefore, to be justified, by the need for a critical treatment of today's dominant conventional wisdom, a treatment that juxtaposes the conventional perspective of success as a state of stability with its direct opposite, success flowing from instability. This textbook therefore turns convention on its head and devotes the minor part of its contents to order, stability and lack of surprise, and the major part to the tasks of coping with and using instability and difference.

Organisational dynamics and feedback systems

The concern with real life instability pursued in this book is reflected in the emphasis on the study of the dynamics of organisations: that is, the patterns of change that organisations display as they move through time and the properties of the systems driving those patterns.

To study the dynamics, it is necessary to understand that an organisation is a feedback system. A dynamic study of organisations is a study of the properties and consequences of their feedback system nature. Most textbooks today, however, focus heavily on the static analysis of competitive positions and largely ignore the dynamics. This follows from the fact that they provide almost no explicit examination of the feedback system nature of organisations. This lack is now made particularly serious by the discoveries that mathematicians and natural scientists have made about the dynamics of feedback systems – the properties of chaos, complexity and self-organisation. These discoveries have important implications for how it is possible to manage an organisation strategically.

This alternative textbook on strategic management is therefore required to continue filling the need for a focus on organisational dynamics and thus the feedback system properties of organisations. An understanding of the dynamics leads to greater insight into those processes of strategic management that may lead to success.

The particular concern this book has with the dynamics of feedback systems has methodological consequences. The key point about such systems is that the links between cause and effect may be lost in the detailed behaviour of the system and it therefore follows that a reductionist approach to understanding such systems will prove to be seriously misleading. That is to say, we will develop a defective understanding of the whole organisation if we follow a procedure of splitting it into discrete levels and other parts, then identify cause-and-effect links to understand each part, and finally put it all together again in the expectation of now understanding the whole. Instead, when feedback systems operate in states where cause-and-effect links disappear, we have to try to comprehend the system's functioning in terms of overall patterns in its behaviour across many levels. We have to sacrifice precision and logical rigour to gain more useful qualitative images and insights into how the system evolves.

There is, therefore, in what follows no sequential approach to behaviour at the individual level, building into behaviour at a group and then an organisational level. Instead, the argument is structured into examinations of different kinds of feedback process. One way a feedback system can operate is through negative feedback processes, which, in certain conditions, generate stability. In organisations managers use a whole raft of negative feedback processes to make decisions and control behaviour – I have called this 'ordinary management'. Part One of this book outlines the coneptual framework and explains why this ordinary management can be practised only in conditions close to certainty and agreement. Part Two then examines the process of ordinary management. In Part Three the focus shifts to positive feedback, and to systems that flip between positive and negative feedback. It is argued that this also applies to organisations and is essentially how innovative organisations develop – I have called this process 'extraordinary management' and it is explored in Part Four. That part explores how managers cope with the simultaneous presence of positive and negative feedback in the conditions far from certainty and agreement that they generate – the process of extraordinary management.

In using a number of different theories and models to shed light on the pattern of development that different types of feedback produce, this book shows little concern with presenting those theories in any kind of chronological order. The rationale for what is presented and when it is presented is one of maximising the appreciation of feedback patterns, rather than providing a chronological development of ideas on strategic management. I have been primarily concerned with assisting the reader to keep in mind the essential distinction between conditions close to certainty and agreement where it is possible to practise ordinary management, which includes conventional approaches to strategic management, and conditions far from certainty and agreement where there is no option but to practise extraordinary management, if an organisation is to survive.

Furthermore, because the book is structured around the implications of different types of feedback, it will sometimes happen that a particular topic is dealt with in a number of places. For example, politics and group behaviour may be interpreted by some writers in a manner that implies negative feedback, while others may deal with these matters in a way that uses positive feedback concepts. Although the topic is the same, the feedback implications are different and thus that topic is repeated, but from a different angle.

Prescription and description

Another methodological point relates to the balance between prescription and description. Some textbooks adopt a heavily prescriptive approach; that is, they specify general sets of prescriptions that managers should apply in a wide range of strategic situations if they are to be successful. Others, however, may tilt the balance toward the description of what managers can be observed to do, leaving it to the reader to draw direct conclusions about best practice. This book falls more into the latter category. It is primarily concerned with trying to explain what managers do, why they do it, and what the consequences are in different kinds of decision and control situations. The reason for this is that it is impossible to develop general sets of prescriptions at the cutting edge of strategic management. If it were possible to develop such general prescriptions we would be back to the no-surprise situation discussed at the beginning of this Preface. Instead, managers have to develop unique responses to each unique strategic situation they face. As far as general prescriptions are concerned, therefore, Chapters 5 and 6 present the prescriptions of the conventional wisdom, and Chapter 7 explains why they are inadequate, while at the end of Chapter 12 some rather loose prescriptions for encouraging learning organisations are presented. Elsewhere it is up to readers to extract their own conclusions and prescriptions from the explaining and understanding that develops.

Some readers may want a fuller appreciation of the structure of the argument we are going to pursue, rather than waiting for it to unfold through the book. Such a preview can be acquired by reading Chapters 1 and 13.

Readership and presentation of material

The book is aimed at students in the final year of undergraduate business degrees and at practising managers taking post-experience courses, for example Diploma in Management Studies and Master of Business Administration. It is intended to serve as a textbook for courses on business strategy, business policy, strategic management, change management, managerial decision-making, and organisational behaviour.

Let me make some other points about the presentation of the material in the book. Most chapters identify key concepts, highlighted by placing them in boxes. The rationale behind selecting an idea for inclusion in the list of key concepts is that of underlining the fundamental tools for understanding organisational dynamics. This is why the idea of 'cause and effect' appears as a key concept, while that of 'competitive advantage' does not. There is no intention of saying that one is more important than the other, simply that, in developing an understanding of the dynamics of organising, one is more fundamental than the other. In addition to the key points, the text also highlights case examples and other illustrative material in boxes. At the end of each part there is a set of case studies for use in discussing the concepts developed in the book. Although the cases are given at the end of each part rather than particular chapter, it should be borne in mind that strategic management is a whole, not reducible to some neat compartments – the point about systems and reductionism again. The cases can be used to think about a number of aspects that cover more than one part. A Commentary for Lecturers containing teaching notes on the cases, as well as comments on how the book might be used in teaching, is also available from Pitman Publishing to lecturers adopting this text.

Changes to the second edition and acknowledgements

Now, let me say something about how this edition differs from the first one. Some of the case studies have been changed and some new material, primarily on the science of complexity and on neurotic forms of leadership, has been added. The change in content, then, is relatively small. What I have concentrated on, instead, is a major revision of the structure of the book. I have done this as a result of feedback from a number of teacher and student users of the first edition indicating that it was sometimes difficult to follow. In particular I have benefited from the comments of Dr Ronnie Lessem at City University Business School, and also Dr Dorothea Noble at my own business school. It is really at their suggestion that I have rearranged the material and the central flow of the argument to focus first on ordinary management and then on extraordinary management. I wish to record my thanks to them. Also, the presentation of the section on extraordinary management has been heavily influenced by suggestions from Ronnie Lessem. I also wish to thank Dr Georges Romme of the University of Limburg in Maastricht and Dr Bente Løwendahl of the Norwegion School of Management for the helpful comments and suggestions they made.

Then, I wish to thank the following authors of case studies: Christine Czyzewska, Bengt Johannisson, Keith Randle, Dorothea Noble, Georges Romme, Alan Kitson, Mary Klemm and Michaela Smith. Finally I continue to thank students and colleagues at the University of Hertfordshire Business School, as well as consulting colleagues and clients, for the assistance they perhaps unknowingly provide in the way I come to see things.

RDS
London
December 1995

CHAPTER 1

The nature of strategy

INTRODUCTION

Strategy is a serious, exciting and often bizarre game that managers play every day. It is a game that groups of managers play with other groups in their own and other organisations and with individuals both inside and outside their organisation. The smallest players in the game are individual managers, single-person households and one-person businesses. The largest players are powerful teams of top managers in global corporations and government organisations. Some of the internal players are called departments, others business units, and yet others project teams. Some of the external players are called customers, others suppliers, and yet others competitors, regulators, or financiers.

Honda versus General Motors

A well-known example of the strategy game runs like this. In the late 1950s, Honda's managers made a move into the United States motor cycle market. They tried to get support for this move from MITI, the Japanese trade ministry, but were denied it. They went ahead anyway with their intention of selling large motor cycles in the US but they found that potential customers were not interested. So, the Honda executives displayed their entrepreneurial flare by selling their small 50cc Super Cub range of motor cycles instead and that worked (*Pascale, 1984*).

Managers at General Motors paid no attention to this move. Why should they? They produced automobiles, not motor cycles, and they were the most powerful of the players in the US market with their 50 per cent market share. The arrival of a tiny motor cycle importer on the West Coast was hardly worth noticing.

But competition comes from unexpected quarters in the strategy game and Honda turned out to be one of the tiny changes that would escalate into a transformation of the market. In the 1960s Honda built up its automobile manufacturing capability in Japan,

1

again without the support of MITI, and by the 1970s was exporting cars to the US. By 1978 it had a 2.4 per cent market share and a decade later it had its own US manufacturing capability and a market share of over 7 per cent. Other Japanese manufacturers were developing much the same posture and imports of cars into the US rose from almost nothing in the late 1950s to around 30 per cent of the market by the late 1980s. General Motors' market share fell from 50 per cent to 33 per cent and with its market share, its profits and share price tumbled too – its performance deteriorated markedly. In 1992, General Motors was still deteriorating. That deterioration continued into the 1990s with large declines in profits and major contraction and restructuring.

These changing positions and postures over more than thirty years were clearly the consequences of the strategies that the managers in the different companies were pursuing, that is, of the patterns in their actions. For example, during the 1970s General Motors continued to supply all segments of the market, responding to higher fuel costs and foreign imports of small cars by reducing the size of its vehicles across the whole product range. General Motors' managers called the strategy *downsizing* (Quinn, 1985). Honda on the other hand, after initial difficulties with quality, concentrated on differentiating its products by quality in a relatively narrow range of products (Quinn, 1990). We could label that a strategy of *focused differentiation*. In the late 1970s, 80 per cent of General Motors vehicles were recalled for quality defects while only 20 per cent of Japanese vehicles were. However we label them, one strategy or pattern in actions was clearly leading to success while another was not. It is also clear that both strategies came about through the decision-making processes employed by managers in each organisation. The key to success has to do with the processes of strategic decision-making and action.

Variations on this particular Far Eastern version of the game have, as we all know, been played in a number of other industries in the USA and in Europe too. And this version of the game, in which those from the Far East almost always win, is still being widely played. The game, however, is not confined to such dramatic moves and large players. Managers in a small family business selling fertiliser in East Anglia in the UK have to play the game too, against ICI and Norsk Hydro, if they wish to survive. The same applies to not-for-profit organisations such as Oxfam, hospitals, educational institutions and other bodies in the state sector, where they have to play against each other for the funds that keep them alive.

Why a game?

It is important right at the outset to think of strategy as a game that people play, because when it is discussed more seriously there is a strong tendency to slip into talking about it as a response that 'the organisation' makes to 'an environment'. When we do that, we depersonalise the game and unwittingly slip into understanding it in mechanical terms, where one 'thing' moves in predetermined ways in relation to another 'thing'. The inevitable result is a lack of insight into the real complexities of strategic management, because in reality organisations and their environments are not things, one adapting to the other, but groupings of people interacting one with another. When we think about strategy as a game, therefore, we focus on how success or failure flows from the circular process of moves a player makes that provoke responses from other players, in turn feeding back into counter-responses from the first, and so on from day to day. That is to say, we focus on the feedback process and the dynamics it generates, and this leads to a sharper insight into the nature of strategy.

When managers think in terms of one thing adapting to another, they play the strategy game in unimaginative, predictable ways that are unlikely to lead to winning positions. If, however, they understand the dynamic patterns of interaction between suppliers, competitors and customers, they are much more likely to design successful moves. Our task as students of strategic management is to try to determine which patterns of moves lead to success and which do not, and this means that we too must pay attention to the dynamics.

The **first key question** we will be addressing throughout this book, therefore, is **what can we say about the dynamics of organisations** and the impact this has on how managers make strategies? Let me clarify this point on dynamics and in so doing define the key features of the strategy game.

1.2 DEFINING THE KEY FEATURES OF THE STRATEGY GAME

Some of the most essential features of the dynamic strategy game – the underlying nature of moves like those made by the managers at Honda and at General Motors over many years – can be illustrated in the manner shown in *Figure 1.1*.

The figure depicts a continuing loop over time connecting the actions of people in an organisation to the responses of people outside it, and the reactions to those responses.

Starting at the left-hand side of *Figure 1.1*, we see that people in the environment of Organisation A do something that people in Organisation A discover. People in Organisation A choose how to respond and then act upon that choice. The actions of people in Organisation A also have consequences for people in the environment, for example customers, competitors, suppliers and regulators. Thus, in the above example, Honda discovered that there might be an opportunity in the United States, chose to set up an operation in that country and sold small, high-quality cars. The consequence was a decline in General Motors' market share.

Returning to *Figure 1.1* we can see how it depicts people who are the environment discovering the consequences of Organisation A's actions, choosing how to respond and then acting. For example, General Motors responded to Honda's action by reducing the size of all of its cars but paid little attention to improved quality.

Returning once more to *Figure 1.1* we can see how the actions of people in the environment then have further consequences for people in Organisation A. The latter in turn discover, choose and act. People both within and outside any organisation are therefore continuously moving around feedback loops, that is processes through which they interact to make the decisions and take the actions that control and develop their organisations.

This brings us to the **second key question** that we will be exploring throughout this book: **what do we know about the operation of the feedback systems** that drive an organisation and about the patterns of behaviour those feedback systems produce?

Studying the dynamics

We can look back in time from the present, to in *Figure 1.1*, and, if we are able to perceive a pattern in past actions, we call this pattern the strategy of the organisation.

FIGURE 1.1
The strategy concept

If we are able to look forward to time t_f we might perceive a pattern, or strategy, in future actions. Strategy is a perceived pattern in actions past or yet to come. We cannot touch a strategy or feel it – it is an interpretation we make of what has happened or what we expect to happen next. A strategy is simply a category into which we put certain patterns of action: for example Honda's actions to establish differentiation through superior quality or General Motors' actions to downsize its product line. Strategy is a label applied to patterns in action.

The patterns in action are generated by the circular loop between discovery, choice and action, that is the management process: strategic management is a feedback loop connecting discovery, choice and action. For example, General Motors discovered the likely increase in fuel costs and foreign competition through its analysis of the market. It chose to respond by formulating a plan to downsize its product range and acted by implementing that plan. At the same time Honda was discovering the importance of quality from customer feedback, choosing to focus on quality and acting to improve that quality.

When we seek to understand strategy in terms of patterns over time and strategic management in terms of the feedback processes generating those patterns, we are conducting a study of the dynamics of organisations. In a dynamic study we are concerned with the ebb and flow over time in the game managers in an organisation are playing, and with how they constitute an interactive system. We are concerned with how the players are provoking responses from each other and whether their moves are regular and predictable or not. Dynamics is concerned with the stability or instability of a system and the conditions that produce that stability or instability.

Static analysis

Figure 1.1 also depicts a snapshot at some past point in time, t_p, showing the posture of the organisation and the position it occupied in relation to the actors in its environment at that past time point.

The posture of an organisation refers to matters such as:

- the composition of its activities in terms of product lines and markets operated in;
- the technologies on which those activities are based;
- the manner in which the organisation is structured and controlled;
- the predominant shared behaviours or culture of the people in the organisation.

In other words, the posture of an organisation is a picture of what it looks like, its shape and its capabilities. The *posture* of an organisation is what you see when you stand at the organisational boundary and *look inwards*.

We could describe the position of the organisation in terms of aspects such as:

- market shares in particular segments;
- customer image;
- competence in relation to competitors;
- relative importance to suppliers

Position, then, is a picture of how an organisation relates to the people that are its environment. The *position* is what you see when you stand at the organisational boundary and *look outwards*.

The posture and the position of the organisation are the result of the strategy, the pattern in actions, it has pursued. That posture and position determine its performance at the time and performance refers to:

- financial dimensions such as cost levels, return on capital, profit growth; and
- operational dimensions such as quality and service levels.

When we seek to understand the position, posture and performance of an organisation at a particular point in time, we are concerned with static analysis. Static analysis is about a situation and its determinants at a point in time. So we might understand the General Motors situation in the late 1980s by analysing the structure of the US automobile market and the competitive capability of the firms operating in it. We would describe General Motors' position in terms of its 33 per cent market share, its image for poor quality, and its decline relative to Honda. Its posture could be analysed as that of an operator with a wide product range, hierarchical structures, bureaucratic processes and conservative cultures. Its performance would be measured in terms of profitability and product quality.

Comparative statics

We can also take a snapshot at the present time, t_0 in *Figure 1.1*. This will show the current organisational posture, position and resulting performance. The change in posture, position and performance from t_p to t_0 is the result of the strategy that has been pursued.

When we seek to understand strategy in terms of comparisons between one point in time and another, we are concerned with comparative static analysis. For example, in a comparative static analysis we would compare the 50 per cent General Motors' market share in the late 1970s with its 33 per cent share in the late 1980s and look for the causes of this decline.

The future – uncertainty and ambiguity

We study the dynamics of organisational life, and we analyse the past performance and decision-making processes of large numbers of organisations, because we hope to identify the fundamental laws governing successful organisational development. If we can do this we will be able to prescribe what to do to create and manage organisations that will succeed in the future.

The task of strategic management is that of somehow producing a posture and position for a particular organisation that will yield acceptable performance at some long-term future point, t_f in *Figure 1.1*. To do this it is necessary to determine the pattern in actions (the strategy) that will lead to the required posture and position. And to do that it is necessary to establish the particular feedback processes, the form of strategic management, that will lead to the required patterns. *Figure 1.1* shows the processes of strategic management to be undertaken in the future as dotted feedback loops.

As soon as we approach the task of identifying successful future strategies and strategic management processes, we are confronted by the problems of uncertainty and ambiguity. The strategy game is a turbulent one in which everything keeps changing – people's attitudes, their requirements for goods and services, their tastes and fashions change all the time, as do technologies, government policies and many more factors. Therefore, managers have to make decisions and take actions now that will have uncertain consequences – the world in which managerial actions bear fruit will be different to the one in which they were initiated. At the time of taking a decision managers will not be sure of the meaning of many of the changes they are trying to cope with – these changes will be ambiguous.

For example, at any particular point in time, the managers at General Motors could quite legitimately have attached different meanings to the success that Honda was achieving in the US automobile market. Some of General Motors' managers could have concluded that Honda was being successful because Honda cars were small and therefore low fuel consumers. Other General Motors managers, however, could quite sensibly have argued that Honda's success was due to their lower price. Yet others could have insisted that Honda's success was due to higher quality. The situation would have been ambiguous and the conclusions drawn would have depended upon the shared way in which groups of managers were making sense of their world. That is to say, the explanation most managers accept at any one time depends upon what they together believe is important about their business. During the 1970s the prevailing belief amongst General Motors' managers was that customers were looking for small, fuel-efficient cars. The particular meanings that the most powerful group of General Motors' managers identified and believed in determined what they subsequently did.

The point we have to pay attention to throughout our study of strategic management, therefore, is that of the effect of uncertainty and ambiguity on the behaviour of people as they go about the tasks of deciding and acting strategically. People decide and act in one way when they operate close to certainty but, when they find themselves far from certainty, they have to decide and act in different ways.

The **third key question** that will arise again and again in the following chapters is that of just **what uncertainty and ambiguity mean** for the processes of strategic management.

This discussion about uncertainty and ambiguity also raises the **fourth key question** that will concern us much in what follows, namely the central importance to an understanding of strategic management of **the nature and role of shared ways of understanding the world**. Another word for a shared way of understanding the world is a paradigm and the same meaning is conveyed by the terms 'the conventional wisdom' or the 'company recipe'. A *paradigm* is a set of deeply held, unquestioned beliefs about what makes particular organisations successful, how they should be managed, and what is important about the needs they serve. How managers act in a strategic sense has a great deal to do with the paradigm they share. The views managers and writers of textbooks have on the nature of successful strategic management processes also depends upon their paradigm.

The management process and intention

Most people believe that any order they observe in a human system, such as a society or an organisation, has been put there by a designing mind. They believe that organisations follow the strategies they do because this is what their leaders have decided; the practice of paying large bonuses to chief executives when their organisations improve performance and then firing them as soon as their organisations falter is the practical expression of this belief. Quite consistent with this belief in the designing mind is the belief that the circular process of discovery, choice and action that is strategic management is a deliberate and intentional one. It is most frequently believed to be a process of:

- setting a goal in which the organisation's capability is matched to the requirements of its environment;
- analysing the environment and the capability of the organisation;
- deriving from the analysis those options that will achieve the goal;
- selecting the best option and then implementing it.

This is a model of the strategy process that deals in an analytical, rational way with the questions:

- How did we get here?
- Where do we want to go now?
- How shall we get there?

The important point to bear in mind is that this interpretation of what managers do or should do reflects a particular paradigm: a belief in the importance of intention, stability and regularity for the success of a system. There are, however, other interpretations. The process of discovery, choice and action could be interpreted as a process in which managers:

- discover in an intuitive rather than an analytical way;
- make unconscious, automatic choices rather than consciously intentional ones;
- carry those choices out in a reflexive, automatic way rather than a deliberate one.

They might not ask the questions in the rational model at all. They might:

- discover changes by chance;
- make choices on the basis of emotion and power; and
- carry those choices out in a tentative, trial-and-error way.

In this alternative interpretation, managers are not necessarily going around the loop in a deliberate way and what happens may not be intentional – it may simply emerge and may even be contrary to intention. This second interpretation of how managers might discover, choose and act also flows from a paradigm; this time based on the belief that human systems are so complex that no individual or small group of individuals can understand them fully enough to intend what happens to them. Order may nevertheless emerge despite a lack of intention.

This leads to the **fifth key question** that we will return to frequently as we proceed through the chapters that follow: **to what extent is successful strategy the result of organisational intention** and to what extent does it emerge from the complex interactions between people in organisations?

If we are to develop a deep understanding of strategy and strategic management we have to avoid jumping to immediate conclusions about the nature of the successful process. The nature of the successful process is what we have to explore carefully, not what we have to start off assuming. We need to try to expose the paradigms that lead to different views on the nature of successful strategic management processes. It is for this reason that I have used the words 'discovery', 'choice' and 'action'. They are intentionally vague and general enough to be open to many different interpretations. The posture, position and level of performance that discovery, choice and action lead to could all be intentional, or they could all just emerge. Our task in studying strategy is to identify the conditions that must be satisfied for it to be possible to make intentional strategies and the conditions within which there is no choice but to encourage emergent strategy. That task is far from easy, as we shall see in the next section.

1.3 DIFFICULTIES IN STUDYING STRATEGIC MANAGEMENT

Strategy is a deadly serious game because the livelihood, and indeed the lives, of all of us depend upon how and with what results it is played. Strategy is also a challenging and exciting game because it is so uncertain and fast moving, with extreme outcomes ranging from great success to catastrophic failure. Furthermore, it is in many ways an amusingly bizarre, Alice-in-Wonderland kind of game because it is so often extremely difficult to work out what the players are doing and why they are doing it. Simply asking them what they are doing, and why, is frequently of little use because they often act in skilled automatic ways that they find difficult, or even embarrassing, to explain. It is this sometimes bizarre aspect that makes the game so interesting to reflect upon and so difficult to draw conclusions about.

Saying one thing and doing another

For example, ask a sample of managers what they do and they will usually tell you something along these lines: organising and planning the work of others to achieve the organisation's goals. Managers still say this with great frequency despite the research evidence (*Mintzberg, 1975; Stewart, 1983*) showing that they dash around under great pressure, spending a few minutes on each task, with very little visible sign of organising and planning.

Or, ask the members of a board of directors of a large company what the role of that board is. They will almost certainly say that the role is one of formulating the strategy of their company and overseeing its implementation. If you sit and watch them at work in the boardroom, however, you will observe that they usually spend 90 per cent of their time together reviewing past results against budget, legitimising decisions already taken, and attending to administrative matters, in that order of importance. This leaves less than 10 per cent of the time for what all board members say is their principal function.

As they play the strategy game, managers frequently say they are doing one thing when they are really doing another. It is often rather difficult to explain why they are doing this and even harder to change what they are doing. This clearly makes the study of strategic management a tricky business – all may not be as it seems.

This tendency to say one thing while doing another is particularly noticeable when people become anxious, and few things arouse anxiety and conflict as much as the uncertain and the ambiguous. Any realistic study of strategic management will therefore have to take account of how people discover, choose and act when they become anxious and conflict with each other.

The **sixth key question** that we will keep returning to in later chapters is therefore to do with the **behaviour of people in groups** and the impact this has on the way they choose and act strategically. The importance of the behavioural aspect is reinforced when you consider the frequency with which myths grow up in organisations.

Myths

To make the study of strategic management even more difficult, myths often grow up around how things happened. Sometimes the managers themselves come to believe the myths but sometimes they do 'remember' how it 'actually' happened if they are asked the right questions.

Take the entry of Honda into the USA. It is usually described in terms of carefully laid plans by top Honda executives to do with global domination; or in terms of strong strategic intent, or vision, to build core competences in engines and a global presence in the automobile market (*Hamel & Prahalad, 1989*). We also often hear that Japanese companies win because they are backed by their government. These, however, appear to be myths.

Interviews with the Honda executives involved in the US market entry reveal a different story (*Pascale, 1984*). A small group of Honda executives was despatched to San Francisco on a trial basis. No market research had been carried out and there was no long-term plan; the executives concerned simply thought that there might be a market for large motor cycles in the United States. After many months of failing to sell those large motor cycles, the executives were on the verge of withdrawal, when by chance they noticed that people were interested in the small 50cc Super Cub that they were using for their own personal transport to save on scarce foreign currency. So they abandoned the idea of selling large motor cycles for a time and concentrated on selling Super Cubs instead – they had enough determination and initiative to use chance when it arrived. Also, we saw above that the Japanese government refused to back Honda; they did it on their own.

Few managers, however, describe the realisation of their strategies in such opportunistic terms, preferring to give more rational, even if mythical accounts. Again these tendencies create problems for the serious study of strategic management and therefore for deriving prescriptions on how to do it successfully. When you ask managers how they manage strategically you have to be careful about the myths. They may in reality not be using the visible formal organisation where they implement plans; they may be acting instead through the shadowy informal organisation that consists of a network of personal contacts where decisions are made on intuitive and political grounds.

It is all too easy to focus on the formal, or legitimate, organisation and the myths about its use, and so miss what managers are actually doing when they manage strategically.

This **question of the role of the informal, or shadow, organisation is the seventh key one** that we will visit many times in the chapters that follow.

Winners and losers

The Alice-in-Wonderland quality of the strategy game is particularly evident when it comes to judging which organisations are winning and which are losing: we keep changing our minds about who is a success and who is a failure. During the mid-1980s UK commentators hailed the business folk heroes of the Thatcher era; for example, Ralph Halpern of Burtons, George Davies of Next, and Alan Sugar who built up the Amstrad consumer electronics empire. Some ten years later, Burtons and Next together with their principal architects are seen as 'has-beens'. Alan Sugar and Amstrad come in for periodic criticism.

In the USA, Ford Motor Company is praised for its business skill during some periods and written off in others. General Electric is held up as a model for all to follow in some periods and then knocked down as an overweight conglomerate during others. In the early 1980s IBM was regarded as an excellent company, then it was widely judged to be 'dead', and by the late 1980s it was once again being acclaimed as an example to the rest of the business world. In 1995, it was going through another difficult period. Clearly, we judge success to be a state of steady performance – a state of stability – but that state seems to be an extremely elusive one.

This raises **key question number eight** that we will pose a number of times in later chapters: is **success to be found in states of stability**, consistency, and consensus, or does it have more to do with instability, contradiction, and conflict?

This leads to the **ninth key question** that will occupy our attention as we move through the book, namely that to do with **paradox**. We will see that organisational success is not a matter of *either* stability *or* instability, but one of *both* stability *and* instability. In other words, real organisations have to deal with the simultaneous presence of completely opposed forces, that is a paradox. This does not apply to questions of stability and instability alone but to many other aspects of organisational life. For example, organisations have to achieve both low prices and high quality; and people want both to be individuals and to lose themselves in a group.

1.4 OUTLINE OF THE BOOK

To summarise, the strategies of any organisation are the *perceived patterns*, over a long time period, in the sequences of actions undertaken by people in that organisation. They are categories into which we can sort typical patterns in action; they are labels we can apply to experience.

These patterns in action flow from the circular feedback *processes* of discovery, choice and action employed by people in organisations. The strategic management processes may be deliberate ones that produce intentional outcomes. On the other hand, those processes may not be deliberate and so produce unintended, emergent outcomes. Or they may be quite deliberate processes that produce unexpected and unintended outcomes. The processes may be the visible ones of the formal, legitimate organisation, or the much less visible ones of the informal, shadow organisation, and it is quite possible that managers may be using the latter without being all that aware of it.

Strategic actions have widespread, long-term consequences that establish the *posture* (that is, the internal shape and capability) of an organisation and its *position* (that is, its relationship to customers, competitors, suppliers, regulators, and financiers). The organisation's posture and position determine its *performance*. Today's posture, position and performance feed back into the process of strategic management to determine the next unfolding of patterns in action.

The strategy is the pattern in actions. The source of the strategy is the circular feedback process of strategic management employed. The result of the strategy is the posture and position of the organisation. Together posture and position determine performance and they provide the platform from which further patterns in action are developed. Every organisation is what it is because of the precise detail of its history, the result of all the choices its members made and also all the choices they did not make, as well as the choices of others that impacted upon them.

The definitions say nothing about the presence or absence of stability, regularity or predictability in the patterns in action, positions, postures and performance levels. The definitions say nothing about the sources and nature of uncertainty and ambiguity, or about their impact on people and processes. Nor do the definitions say anything about the presence or absence of organisational intention. All these matters, and the connection between them and success, are what we need to explore through the study of strategic management. We have to avoid making assumptions about these matters before we embark on the study.

Key concerns

We have identified six important aspects of strategy, all made to start with the letter P (after *Mintzberg, 1987*) because that is a fashionable thing to do in management books! These six Ps establish a broad but rather empty framework that is to be filled in with meaning as we study strategic management in the chapters that follow. The key questions we will need to keep posing to fill in the meaning have to do with:

1 The dynamics or patterns of change in organisational development, their stability and predictability or otherwise.
2 The circular feedback process of discovery, choice and action that generates the dynamics.
3 The effect of uncertainty and ambiguity on that circular feedback process.
4 The central part played by shared beliefs and shared ways of making sense of the world in determining management actions.
5 The role of shared intention in driving organisational strategy as opposed to the possibility of emergent strategies.
6 The impact of group behavioural dynamics on the choices and actions of managers.
7 The role of formal and informal systems, the tension between legitimate and shadow systems, in the successful management of an organisation.
8 The relationship between success and stability.
9 The presence of paradox and how managers cope with it.

We have also identified three different approaches to understanding all of this. One is the dynamic route that focuses on patterns and circular processes over time. The other two are forms of static analysis that focus on the determinants of postures, positions and performance at particular points in time. As we examine the different views of writers in the chapters that follow we will seek to identify the form of analysis they use and the manner in which they take account of the dynamics.

The whole point of studying strategic management is to find out what managers need to do to develop an organisational posture and position that will yield successful performance at some point in the future. In other words, we study strategic management quite simply because we are looking for the recipe for success, that is for general prescriptions we can apply to many different strategic situations. The trouble is that in matters as complex as strategic management there may be no reliable general recipes for success that managers can use in a wide variety of strategic situations. To the extent that strategic situations are unique and exceptional, managers will have to develop a unique way to handle each strategic situation as they face it. In such circumstances, general sets of prescriptions will be misleading and far more useful will be explanations of how things work, patterns of the kinds of general things that tend to happen, that can be used in a loose way to design custom-made responses to unique situations as they crop up. This book will argue that the approach of understanding systems and seeing patterns is far more useful than trying to set out lists of generic prescriptions. The matter of general prescriptions is dealt with in Chapters 5 and 6 and some prescriptions are presented at the end of Chapter 12, but the rest of the book is concerned with explanation and descriptive material that aids in explanation. Armed with insight and understanding of the dynamics, managers may cope far better with the ambiguous and uncertain than they will if all they have is sets of general prescriptions that cannot by definition apply to unique situations.

The chapters that follow are grouped into parts, each part representing a major step in the argument that the book conducts and the chapters in each Part seeking to explain that step.

So, Part One sets out the fundamental concepts that are required to follow the chain of reasoning about strategic management that it is the purpose of this book to present. The primary task of a manager is that of handling change in some way, that is, making decisions and engaging in some kind of controlled behaviour so that continuing joint action can be taken by members of an organisation. To put it another way, the role of a manager is to promote, in whatever manner proves to be possible, the performance of an organisation's primary tasks. The key argument upon which the whole of the rest of the book is built is this: when they take up their roles, managers are confronted by different kinds of change and this absolutely requires them to make decisions and practise control in fundamentally different ways.

Chapter 2 sets this argument out in some detail. It describes the spectrum of change situations that managers, indeed all of us, face. At one end of the spectrum we find ourselves operating close to certainty about the connections between our actions and their outcomes, and close to agreement with each other about what we jointly want to achieve and how we should go about achieving it. In those circumstances, and only in those circumstances, we can and should make decisions in a technically rational manner and practise control in its monitoring form; we can and we should plan our future and that future will be what we intend it to be if we are competent.

As we move some way away from certainty and agreement we find it more and more difficult to plan, and so we resort to expressing long-term intention in the form of visions and we practise the control that comes from adhering to a shared ideology.

Then, if we behave in a conforming enough manner, we will often be able to realise our jointly shared long-term intended outcomes, although we will have to discover how to do so along the way.

However, at the other end of the spectrum of change situations, when we find ourselves operating very far indeed from certainty and agreement with each other, then it is absolutely impossible either to plan or to realise visions of the long-term future. In such circumstances we have no option but to create and discover our future through engaging with each other in complex interactions of a political and learning nature. In all logic, the form of strategic management we practise has to change as we move further and further away from certainty and agreement. If managers proclaim that they are practising methods appropriate to the certain end of the spectrum when they are in fact at the uncertain end, then we can be sure that they are defending themselves against the anxiety which uncertainty arouses by using the basic defence of denying that uncertainty. A group of people cannot, by definition, plan or envision the future state that will materialise if they are currently highly uncertain about the link between their action and its outcomes and if they cannot agree amongst themselves what they want to achieve. Instead of planning and visioning they have to do something else – they have to learn their way into an open-ended future.

It is quite pointless to do what most strategic management approaches do, which is, in effect, to tell people that they should identify the links between action and outcome and that they should agree with each other – if they could do these things then they would be rather close to certainty and agreement, not very far from it. What we are trying to understand is what we all do when we do not know what we are doing and we cannot agree with each other on where we are going or what we want to achieve. It is no use whatsoever to say: 'Well, you should not be like this in the first place. You should not be uncertain and you should not disagree. So stop it.' This is of no help to anyone because it does not tell them how to 'stop it'. If they could, they would, because it is not all that pleasant not knowing and not agreeing. These points are, of course, blindingly obvious tautologies and yet they are widely ignored by managers, consultants and writers alike in what appears to be a massive cover-up to defend ourselves against the anxiety of not knowing what the future holds and not being in control of the outcome.

On this perfectly logical, in fact tautological basis, Chapter 3 presents a number of widely accepted concepts in the management literature that lead us to a distinction between what I have called ordinary and extraordinary management. The difference between these conceptualisations of management is very simple: ordinary management is the same process as simple single-loop learning which leads to the more and more efficient performance of current primary tasks. Extraordinary management is the process by which groups of people change their shared mental models that drive ordinary management. Extraordinary management is thus the same as complex double-loop learning. Chapter 3 shows how ordinary management is the appropriate form for conditions close to certainty and agreement, while extraordinary management is the only way in which it is possible to cope with conditions very far from certainty and agreement.

The central point that this book seeks to make is this: managers have no option but to confront conditions both far from and near to certainty and agreement. This is a fact of organisational life. It follows that managers have no option but simultaneously to practise both ordinary and extraordinary management if their organisation is to survive. The difficulty is that these two forms of management are direct opposites and the need to practise both therefore generates continuing tension – but the tension can be creative. This too is an existential fact of organisational life. Chapter 3 ends by pointing to the dangers, in terms of organisational survival, of trying to practise only one form of management.

The rest of the book explores the nature of both ordinary and extraordinary management. Part Two is devoted to ordinary management, that is, the forms of decision-making and control that are appropriate for conditions close to certainty and agreement. When managers practise ordinary management they do so within the legitimate system of their organisation, that is, within the hierarchy and bureaucracy designed by the most powerful and within the ideology that those powerful approve of. The practice of ordinary management within the legitimate system in conditions close to certainty and agreement enables managers to actualise their shared intentions about their organisation's future. Ordinary management is vital for the efficient performance of an organisation's current primary task, its day-to-day business.

In Part Two, Chapter 4 explores two different aspects of ordinary management. First, it describes the technically rational decision-making process and the monitoring form of control that can be practised only when conditions are very close to certainty and agreement. Then it goes on to discuss the role of visions in guiding political forms of decision making and the practice of control through ideological conformity, all of which is appropriate in conditions somewhat further from certainty and agreement. The nature of leadership and the role of groups in ordinary management is also explored.

Chapter 5 considers the nature of long-term planning and shows how it is an extension of ordinary management processes. This approach is appropriate for reinforcing existing strategic directions in conditions rather close to certainty, but contributes little to the development of new strategic direction, to creativity and innovation. Chapter 6 reviews proposals for using the visionary/ideological processes of ordinary management to make strategies. These too can only reinforce existing strategic direction rather than generate creative, innovative new directions.

To end Part Two, Chapter 7 considers what happens when managers try to apply the processes of ordinary management to make strategies far from certainty and agreement. There is no reliable evidence that such a procedure is beneficial and I believe that this in itself is persuasive evidence for arguing that the result is simply to trap organisations in the stable state which was the reason for their success some time previously, but which has become increasingly inappropriate as the world changed.

Part Three focuses on what it means to be close to and far from certainty and agreement. The point is to understand how the internal dynamic of the organisational system, that is, the nature of the interaction between members of an organisation, determines this change spectrum. The internal dynamic is generated by the iterative feedback interaction between members of an organisation. Sometimes that feedback is negative, in which case the organisation tends to stability. At other times the feedback is positive so that an organisation moves to instability or disintegration. However, the modern science of complexity shows that there is a phase transition as a system moves from stability to instability, a state that has been called the edge of chaos, the edge of disintegration.

Complexity scientists conjecture that systems are creative when they operate at the edge of chaos, at the edge of disintegration. They demonstrate how the future is radically unpredictable when a system operates at the edge of disintegration and how systems are, therefore, driven by self-organisation to produce emergent outcomes. In organisational terms self-organisation is the same as complex double-loop learning, and it is through this process that managers and members of organisations produce emergent new strategic direction. Emergence means that an outcome is realised not through prior shared intention, not through some blueprint, but through the local interaction of members of the organisation.

Once we understand something about the dynamics of those human systems we call organisations, then we are in a position to understand something about the nature of extraordinary management. Part Four goes on to explore this.

First, Chapter 10 describes how managers practise extraordinary management in the shadow system, as opposed to the legitimate system, of their organisation. The shadow system is the network of informal social contacts people self-organise amongst themselves. The shadow system can also be understood as communities of practice in which people learn. An organisation's shadow system is, therefore, the system managers and members of an organisation use to learn in complex ways, but also the system they also use to block that complex learning. We all seek to block complex learning because it is both creative and destructive: it creates new ways of perceiving and being in the world but to do so it also destroys old ways of perceiving and being. To defend ourselves against the anxiety to which such destruction gives rise, we use defensive mechanisms, such as denial, to avoid the learning. The shadow system has both harmful and beneficial aspects, but it is the only instrument we have, in practice, for dealing with conditions very far from certainty and agreement.

Chapter 11 then examines what managers and members of organisations 'get up to' when they take up roles in their shadow system. In other words, the chapter considers what decision-making and control processes are operative in the shadow system. What we find are very complex modes of interaction between people. The state of being far from certainty and agreement arouses fears of failure that are defended against by all manner of game-playing and covert politics. That state also arouses deep anxiety that is protected against by unconscious group processes of one kind and another. The effect of covert politics and unconscious processes may be to block completely the kind of complex learning required for survival when a group is far from certainty and agreement. That will trap an organisation in the processes of ordinary management, which in turn trap it in a state of stability in which it is incapable of developing new strategic directions. The effective practice of extraordinary management is thus predominantly about containing the fear of failure and the anxiety of not knowing the outcome and not being in control. This leads to an understanding of how the roles of leadership and groups are completely different in extraordinary management terms to what they are in ordinary management terms.

Effective practice of extraordinary management in the shadow system creates new knowledge and leads to the emergence of new strategic direction. Chapter 12 explores this and makes a few tentative suggestions about creating the leadership and group conditions in which anxiety and fear may be contained enough to enable the generation of new knowledge.

Part Five is very short, taking the form of a summary of the argument presented in the book and a synthesis in which it is stressed that managers must practise both ordinary and extraordinary management, conceptually separable but in practice intimately intertwined, if their organisation is to survive. This means in essence that, although they have roles in the legitimate system, they must also take up roles in a shadow system that operates in tension with the legitimate system and seeks to undermine and replace it. The shadow system is subversive of the legitimate system and it is through this subversion that an organisation transforms itself and develops new direction. The tension between the legitimate system and its shadow may be creative.

The pattern of organisational development is such that innovation arising in the shadow system, eventually replaces all, or parts, of the legitimate system, so itself becoming institutionalised. The new institution, the new legitimate system, however, spawns another shadow which seeks to undermine it once more. When this dynamic process and the tension it both generates and is generated by come to an end, the organisation approaches its demise.

The result is a population of organisations consisting of large numbers of small, recently founded organisations, most of which die in their infancy; young vigorously growing ones with a lower death rate; and a number of larger organisations, most of which are in the stability trap and are slowly, and sometimes not so slowly, approaching death. In this population the average life expectancy is about 40 years and there are, worldwide, only a very few organisations (probably not more than 30 to 40 according to unpublished research by Shell) that last into an old age of more than 100 years. Those very few have all substantially transformed themselves a number of times, often moving into completely different areas of operation.

Perhaps the purpose of studying the dynamics of organisational life and death, as well as the processes of strategic management, is to increase the number of organisations capable of longevity. On the other hand, we might argue that we are going to all the trouble of understanding organisational life so that we can promote greater creativity amongst the population of organisations as a whole without necessarily increasing average life expectancy or longevity. Either way, we need to understand the dynamics of human systems and the wide range of decision-making and control processes we employ if we want to improve the way we manage things.

References

Hamel, G. & Prahalad, C. K. (1989), Strategic intent, *Harvard Business Review*, May–June, pp. 63–76.

Mintzberg, H. (1975), The manager's job: fact and folklore, *Harvard Business Review*, July–Aug.

Mintzberg, H. (1987), Five Ps for strategy, *California Management Review* (Fall).

Pascale, R. T. (1984), Perspectives on strategy: the real story behind Honda's success, *California Management Review*, vol. XXVI, no. 3, pp. 47–72.

Quinn, J. B. (1985), General Motors Corporation: the downsizing decision, in Mintzberg, H., Quinn, J. B. & James, R. M. (Eds.) (1988), *The Strategy Process: Concepts, Contexts, Cases*, Englewood Cliffs, NJ: Prentice-Hall.

Quinn, J. B. (1990), The Honda Motor Company, in Mintzberg, H. & Quinn, J. B. (Eds.), *The Strategy Process: Concepts, Contexts, Cases*, Englewood Cliffs, NJ: Prentice-Hall.

Stewart, R. (1983), *The Reality of Management*, 2nd edn, London: Heinemann.

PART ONE

The conceptual framework

Change, decision-making and control

The purpose of this part of the book is to set out the most fundamental concepts that we are going to use to make sense of
organisational dynamics and strategic management.

Management is the task of handling change in some way, and so I
am going to describe what we face when we face change.
Management is about making decisions, taking action and controlling
behaviour in situations of change, and so I am going to review the
main models of decision-making and control in organisations and
show how different change situations call for different modes of
decision-making and control. Management is about making sense of
life in organisations and about making sense of the process of
management itself. So we are going to consider the ways in which
we make sense of our world and how we cope with it. A distinction
of great importance will be drawn between simple single-loop
learning and complex double-loop learning. This distinction will form
the basis of a differentiation I am going to make between what I
have called ordinary management and extraordinary management.

The principal message of this part is this: ordinary management
processes are the appropriate ones to apply in situations close to
certainty, and extraordinary management is the only form that it is
possible to apply far from certainty.

</br>

CHAPTER 2

The nature of change and its implications for decision-making and control

Different change situations require different processes

</br>

2.1   INTRODUCTION

In Chapter 1 we defined strategic management in a very general way as a feedback process in which members of an organisation:

- discover what the other organisations and people it interacts with are doing or expected to do;
- choose how they should respond to this information;
- act; and then
- feed back information on what they discover about the consequences of their action into their next choice.

As they continually move around this feedback loop, essentially a process of decision-making, control and learning, members of an organisation generate a sequence of actions in which they and others can usually perceive a pattern and it is this pattern that they and we call a strategy. Through this pattern in a sequence of actions, through this strategy, members of an organisation establish a posture and position for their organisation. This posture and position, in relation to the postures and positions of the other organisations and people being interacted with, is what determines the performance of their organisation and it is this that determines whether their organisation survives or not, and if it does survive how well.

</br>

</br>

</br>

What we have then is a continuing, interactive game in which organisations and people are adjusting their strategies, changing the rules of the game as it were, so as to render themselves fitter for survival and success. In playing this game together, people and organisations are generating continual change: it is the members of organisations themselves who are determining the rules of the games they play and so generating the changes they must cope with. The key feature of the strategy game is thus change, and the need for management arises almost entirely because there is change of a surprising kind. If the strategy game were a perfectly predictable routine then it would be completely systematised and there would be no need for managers. Managers are needed because organisations do not run according to a given set of rules: organisations keep producing surprises because their members and the members of organisations they interact with keep changing the rules.

So, if we want to understand the strategy game we must be clear about the key features of the change that this game generates and what that change means for the nature of the discovery, choice and action process itself. In other words, we must understand the nature of change and the contexts it creates which call for different modes of decision-making and control. I am first going to introduce the notion of qualitatively different kinds of change and then show how the management literature has quite clearly recognised such a distinction, at least 35 years ago. That literature points to the different kinds of decision-making and control that different change situations call for.

Why should you plough through the review of this literature? The answer is that most people keep forgetting that there are different kinds of change and that they require different management approaches. Most people keep talking as if it is possible to extend the same approach to management, more or less precisely, to all kinds of situations. They keep on talking about strategic management as if it can only mean the formulation and implementation of long-term plans, or some other equally orderly and conformist process. In doing this, they keep losing sight of the fact that there are situations in which it is completely meaningless to talk about planning, or even shared intention, as the process driving management action. It is therefore, in my view, a matter of great importance to go through the reasoning about the need for different management processes in different change situations and to hold on to the notion of this distinction, at least throughout the rest of this book and it is to be hoped out into real-life management too. That is the task of this chapter. To embark on this task, consider first the nature of change that organisations face.

2.2 CHANGE SITUATIONS

As we stand in the present, we all face, as individuals living a life or as managers managing an organisation, the need to design our next action. We have to act in the here and now, knowing some consequences of our proposed action but not knowing many others. The problem is how to design our next action effectively in a situation that is a mixture of the known and the unknown. Consider the following purely descriptive model of this situation, one that distinguishes between three rather different kinds of change that we all must deal with (*Stacey, 1990, 1991*).

Closed change

When we look back at the history of an organisation, there are some sequences of events that we can clearly recount in a manner commanding the widespread agreement of the members involved. We are able to say what happened, why it happened, and what the consequences were. We are also able to explain in a widely accepted way how such a sequence of events and actions will continue to affect the future course of the business. We will call this a closed change situation.

Such closed change would normally apply to the continuing operation of an existing business. For example, consider a business that supplies pop records and tapes to the teenage market. Managers in that business are able to say with some precision how the number of customers in what market has changed over the past and furthermore how it will change for the next fifteen years or so. Those customers already exist. The managers can establish fairly clear-cut relationships between the number of customers and the number of records and tapes they have bought and will buy.

Closed change is depicted in *Figure 2.1* as the darkly shaded area under curve A. This curve shows how the sequence of actions and events began at some point in the past, time t_{-1} on the horizontal axis, and then how the consequences developed to the present t_0, and will proceed into the future.

Contained change

Other sequences of events and actions flowing from the past are less clear-cut. Here we find that we are able to say only what probably happened, why it probably happened, and what its probable consequences were. The impact of such a sequence of events upon the future course of the business has similarly to be qualified by probability statements

For example, the supplier of records and tapes will find it harder to explain why particular kinds of records and tapes sold better than others. That supplier will find it somewhat difficult to forecast what kinds of tapes and records will sell better in the future; but market research, life style studies and statistical projections will enable reasonably helpful forecasts for at least the short term.

It is reasonable to think of causality here as approximate or statistical, that is taking the form of probability statements. We will call this contained change. It is represented in *Figure 2.1* as the lightly shaded area under curve B.

Open-ended change

There are yet other sequences of events and actions arising from the past and continuing to impact on the future where explanations do not command anything like widespread acceptance by those involved.

The company supplying records and tapes may have decided in the past to diversify into video film distribution, by acquiring another company already in that business. That acquisition may then become unprofitable and the managers involved could well subscribe to conflicting explanations of why this is so. Some may claim that the market for video films is too competitive. Others that the diversification was a wrong move because it meant operating in a different market with which they were not familiar. Others may say that it is due to a temporary decline in demand and that

FIGURE 2.1

The consequences of past change

Source: R. Stacey (1992), *Managing Chaos*, London: Kogan Page

the market will pick up in the future. Yet others may ascribe it to poor management of the acquisition, or to a failure to integrate it properly into the business, or to a clash of cultures between the two businesses. What that team of managers does next to deal with low profitability obviously depends upon the explanation of past failure they subscribe to.

We will call this open-ended change. Here we do not know with any clarity what caused the change, why the change occurred, or what its consequences were and will be. It is depicted in *Figure 2.1* as the blank area under the dotted curve C. That curve ends with a question mark because managers do not know what the consequences of the particular sequence of events and actions will be in the future.

The present and the future

As they stand in the here and now, at time t_0 in *Figure 2.1,* managers face three different kinds of change situation arising from sequences of events and actions that have already occurred.

There are, however, also sequences of events and actions that are starting up now, in the present. Some of these will approximate to contained change – an existing customer places a much larger order for an existing product line. Some sequences of events and actions will approximate to contained change – a new customer places orders for a modified range of products. And others will be open-ended change – setting up a new activity in Poland.

Yet other sequences of events and actions will be initiated at future points. Each of these sequences will also have closed, contained and open-ended components. *Figure 2.1* is completed in *Figure 2.2* by the addition of curves representing these present and future consequences. (The vertical axis measures the magnitude of the consequences without distinguishing between negative and positive. The diagram is drawn this way simply for visual clarity.) The point the diagram makes is this. As they stand in the here and now, the managers and members in any organisation face a spectrum of change situations in every time frame, from the past through the present to the future. At each point, that spectrum stretches from predictable closed change, through statistically predictable contained change, into unknown open-ended

FIGURE 2.2
Change situations

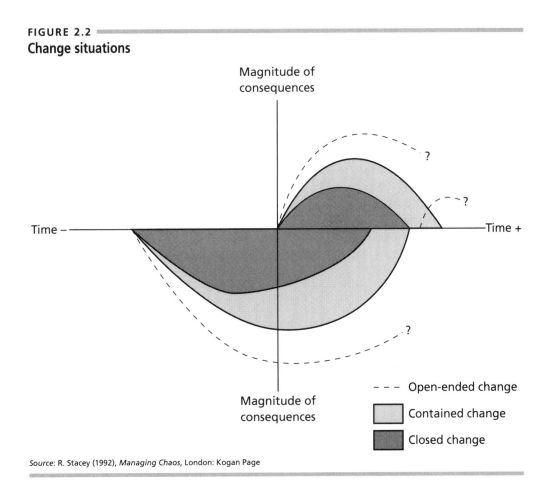

Source: R. Stacey (1992), *Managing Chaos*, London: Kogan Page

Close to certainty

An organisation is close to certainty when its members face closed and contained change, that is, when they face repetitions of what has happened before. This makes it possible for them to make a useful forecast of what is likely to happen for at least a short time ahead: past experience is sufficient to enable some reasonably clear links between cause and effect to be identified.

change. The past and the short-term future are dominated by closed and contained change, but the long-term future is predominantly open-ended. The pattern of change situations alters as we look through time.

What we have then is a spectrum of change situations that stretches from those close to certainty (closed and contained change) to those very far from certainty (open-ended change) – see *Key Concepts 2.1* and *2.2*. This spectrum applies to all time frames and most of the time we have little choice but to cope with most of the spectrum – we cannot choose to live entirely in closed or entirely in open-ended situations simply because other people keep presenting us with the part of the spectrum we think we do not want. Note that this is simply a description of what we all face – no-one has ever, to my knowledge, claimed that this description does not apply to them. Such a perfectly uncontentious description is, therefore, hardly of much interest in itself. What is interesting is why such a spectrum exists in the first place: what does it reflect about the dynamics of that system which we call an organisation, for example? What is also interesting is what such a spectrum means for human behaviour and the kinds of decision-making and control processes it is possible to deploy: how do you discover, choose and act when you are far from certainty and how does this differ from when you are close to certainty, for example?

We will be returning to the first of these questions, the one about dynamics, in Part Three. Now, however, we go on to explore the question that has to do with the implications for human behaviour and the processes of decision-making and control.

Far from certainty

An organisation is far from certainty when its members face open-ended change situations, that is, when they must act in unique circumstances that they have never before encountered. Without the benefit of similar past experience they are not able to make reliable connections between cause and effect and, therefore, they cannot predict the outcome of their actions over the long term.

2.3 BEHAVIOUR AND CHANGE SITUATIONS

Close to certainty

Close to certainty there are clear-cut links between causes and effects, and the consequences of actions can be forecast to a reasonably useful degree of accuracy.

This means that the problems and opportunities facing managers are reasonably clear. Any difficulties lie in finding the answers, not in identifying the questions to ask in the first place. The situation is not characterised by ambiguity and competent managers do not therefore behave in an equivocal manner. If they conflict, there is a substantial possibility of settling the conflict by rational argument, or through exerting hierarchical authority, or bargains of one sort or another. People know what they are doing close to certainty and they will often have decided what to do before any change occurs. The behaviour of groups of people and the models they use in common to design their actions are all understandable and reasonably predictable in these situations. Close to certainty people find it relatively easy to reach and sustain agreement with each other. In other words, it is relatively easy for them to operate close to agreement with each other.

Far from certainty

However, when managers confront open-ended change far from certainty the situation is completely different in every respect. They are faced with actions and events past, present and future that have unknown long-term consequences. The key difficulty, then, is that of identifying what the problems and opportunities are. The prime difficulty is not that of finding answers, but identifying what *questions to ask*. The situation is ambiguous and the responses of managers are equivocal.

Far from certainty there is, inevitably, conflict around how to interpret what is going on and how to design actions to deal with it. Predetermined rules and authority structures become useless as effective means of settling the conflicts, because they presuppose that someone had made a decision and knows what to do. If that were so, however, then such a group of people would no longer be far from certainty.

The unpredictability of specific events within fuzzy categories, which is the hallmark of open-ended change, leads to ambiguity and confusion. The manner in which people interact with each other then becomes a vital part of the decision-making process they employ. We cannot understand what they decide to do without understanding the impact of their personalities and the group dynamic on their decision-making processes. In open-ended change situations, people typically feel insecure and become anxious and the dynamic of their interaction becomes much more complex and can quite often be bizarre. There is a strong tendency to apply inappropriate processes. The key point is that when they have to operate far from certainty, members of organisations are also likely to find themselves far from agreement with each other. *Illustration 2.1* indicates what it means in practice to be close to and far from certainty.

We now consider what these different change situations mean for the mode of decision-making it is possible for managers to apply to their business. We will see that managers have no option but to change the way they make decisions as the level of uncertainty, ambiguity and anxiety is tuned up.

Illustration 2.1

Mövenpick Unternehmungen

Mövenpick was set up by Ueli Präger in 1948 in Zurich, Switzerland. By 1977 it consisted of 56 restaurants, 7 hotels and 11 production and trading units dealing in food. In the mid-1970s Mövenpick set up an operation in Egypt. This is how Ueli Präger describes that decision:

> There are certain strategic decisions which are based on thorough analysis and planning. But there are also events which happen to you. Our international expansion falls into the latter category . . . Our project in Egypt happened in this way. There is a publishing house in Zurich, they print souvenir books with photos of Egyptian treasures. They approached us with the proposal that it might be a good idea if the tourists in Egypt, tired from their visits to the museums, could rest in a Mövenpick restaurant. We were willing to entertain the idea, the Egyptians sent some plane tickets, and we went over to discuss the possibility of a restaurant in a museum. While we were there, I made a courtesy call to the Egyptian organization of tourism. The official in charge and I liked each other instantaneously, the way it sometimes happens when you meet somebody new. After a few minutes he posed the question: 'Do you want to build a hotel near the Pyramids?' I was not prepared for this question, but it was the beginning of a very successful cooperation.
>
> I had never planned to have a hotel near the Pyramids, but that's the way it goes, you open yourself gradually to such ideas and then comes the opportunity. Japan was similar. I had never had a long-range plan to expand in Japan; but then one day some Japanese businessman walked into our office with the idea of opening a chain of restaurants in Japan. ■

Source: Wiechmann & Gillespie, 1978

2.4   THE RELATIONSHIP BETWEEN CHANGE SITUATIONS AND DECISION-MAKING MODES

Thompson and Tuden (1959) relate the mode of decision-making to the type and level of uncertainty and agreement in the following way. They identify different types of uncertainty in terms of:

- the lack of clarity in causal relationships;
- the lack of agreement over objectives.

Where there is very little clarity over causal relationships, and where there is little agreement on objectives, we have the change situation I have called open-ended. The opposite gives us closed change and the other possibilities fit what I have called contained change. In *Figure 2.3*, Thompson and Tuden show how managers shift from one mode of making decisions to others as they move from handling issues in closed change situations to handling issues in open-ended situations.

Where causal connections are clear and objectives shared, the conditions exist for managers to take decisions in a rational-logical way. As they move away from these conditions it becomes impossible to apply rational-logic and so they have to use some other approach.

Thus, when causal connections are clear but managers conflict then the decision has

FIGURE 2.3

Models of decision-making: types of uncertainty

Cause and effect

	Clear	Unclear
Conflict	Compromise + Negotiation	Unprogrammable – 'outcomes' rather than 'solutions'
Objectives		
Shared or Agreed	Rational-logical	Judgement of feasibility – 'will it work?'

Source: R. Turton (1991), *Behaviour in a Business Context*, London: Chapman & Hall

to be made in a political manner – those with the greatest power will prevail. The decision-making process here will be one in which managers build coalitions (*Cyert & March, 1963; Child, 1972 & 1984; Pfeffer, 1981*) a matter to be discussed in Chapter 4, 5 and 11.

When managers are agreed on what they should be trying to achieve but the causal connections make it unclear how to do so, then they will have to use judgemental, or intuitive, modes of making a decision. They will have to reason by analogy; they will have to think laterally and use trial-and-error decision-making processes. We will discuss this approach later in this Chapter as well as in Chapters 5 and 11.

The most difficult situation is where causality is unclear and objectives conflict – the truly open-ended situation. Here managers will have to decide in a way that combines intuitive individual judgements with political interactions in a group.

Duncan's approach

Other writers have also highlighted the connection between levels of uncertainty and modes of making decisions. *Duncan (1972)*, for example, relates modes of decision-making to degrees of environmental complexity and stability as depicted in Figure 2.4.

He distinguishes environments that are static form those that are dynamic, where dynamic means that the frequency, rate and extent of change are all high. He also categorises environments into those that are simple and those that are complex. In simple

FIGURE 2.4
Dimensions of the environment

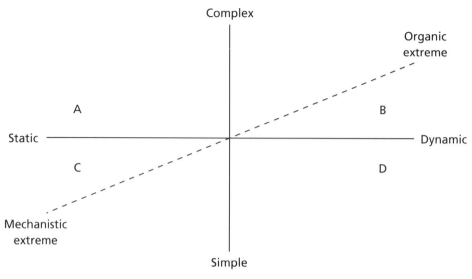

Source: R. Turton (1991), *Behaviour in a Business Context*, London: Chapman & Hall

environments there are only a small number of variables that may change, while in complex environments there are many interconnected variables that may change. The two measures create four archetypal environments. The simplest archetype is the static and simple environment where the appropriate organisational system is the mechanistic one with its rational modes of decision-making. In the most demanding of these environmental archetypes, the complex dynamic one, it is only organic organisational systems that will survive, those with flexible, political, intuitive modes of making decisions. In between, some pragmatic combination of the mechanistic and the organic is required.

Perrow's model

Then, *Perrow (1972)* provides a model of the technology appropriate to different conditions, which makes much the same point. This is shown in *Figure 2.5*. The vertical axis depicts a spectrum of problem-solving procedures. At one end of the spectrum we have problem-solving procedures available that are analysable: they can be broken down into prearranged steps or rules of a logical kind. At the other end the only procedures available in a particular situation are unanalysable or unprogrammable. This means that the problem is such that we have to use some unique method of solving it, unique to that particular problem. Then on the horizontal axis we have the problem-solving situation classified in terms of the number of exceptions. Few exceptions mean that there is little variability in the situation in which decisions have to be made. Actions and responses required are familiar and repetitive. At the other end of the spectrum there are many exceptions calling for different, unique responses.

FIGURE 2.5

The Perrow model of technology

Source: R. Turton (1991), *Behaviour in a Business Context*, London: Chapman & Hall

In situations where there are few exceptions and analysable problem-solving techniques are available, then routine technology is appropriate. The decision-making mode here is clearly the technically rational one. As the situation and the problem-solving techniques become more complex the required technology has a higher skill content – engineering and craft skills are required. The corresponding decision-making mode calls for more judgement, but can still be reduced to step-to-step rules and procedures even though they may become very complex. But when the situation becomes complex and the techniques for solving problems become non-routine and unique, then the required technology is that of research and development. Here the decision-making mode involves unique methods of identifying new problems and finding unique solutions. Technically rational modes of decision-making become inadequate.

What emerges from all these analyses of decision situation and appropriate decision-making mode is this. Making a decision in a technically rational manner is only a possibility in the most restrictive of conditions. It will not be possible in conditions of disagreement, ambiguity and uncertainty. That is to say, it will not be possible when the change being faced is open-ended.

This is a very important point which we will return to on a number of occasions in later chapters. It is, therefore, very important to be clear on exactly what it means to be rational (see *Key Concept 2.3*) Unfortunately rationality can mean many things and that is why I use the term 'technical rationality' to convey a rather precise meaning.

Key Concept 2.3 sets out the different senses in which the word rationality will be used throughout the rest of this book.

Key Concept 2.3

Rationality

The word 'rational' can be used in a number of different ways and its use can cause confusion in discussions about management processes. It is important to distinguish one meaning from another. There are three common meanings of the world 'rational':

1 *Sensible, reasonable in the circumstances, sane, not foolish, absurd or extreme. Rationality here is behaving and deciding in a manner connected to reality and judged likely to bring about desired, intended consequences. Irrationality consists of fantasy-driven behaviour, while rationality involves testing for reality where that reality may well be of an emotional, ideological or cultural kind. I will use the term reality-testing for this kind of rationality and keep the word 'rational' for its next meaning.*

2 *Rejecting that which cannot be tested by reason applied to objective facts. Rationality here is behaving and deciding only on the basis of propositions that can be consciously reasoned about, rather than on the basis of customs, norms, emotions and beliefs. Irrationality here consists not only of fantasy, but also of behaviour driven by emotions and beliefs even if they are connected to an emotional and ideological reality. I will use the word rational in this sense throughout the book.*

3 *A method of deciding that involves setting clear objectives, gathering the facts, generating options, and choosing one that maximises or satisfices (i.e approximately satisfies) the objective. Irrationality here is any behaviour whatsoever that is not preceded by fixing objectives and weighing up options based on observable facts. I will refer to this as technical rationality.*

It is quite possible, indeed highly likely, that reality-testing will lead to the conclusion that technical rationality should be avoided. That is, it may be quite 'rational' in sense 1 to avoid being rational in sense 3. So, in a totally unpredictable environment, under strict time pressures, it would not be logical or sensible to try to make decisions in a painstaking manner that could never anyhow succeed in meeting all the criteria of rationality in its sense 3 meaning. (These criteria will be discussed below in the section on models of decision making far from certainty.)

It could also be rational in terms of meaning 1 (reality-testing) to avoid meaning 2. You may achieve a better response from others if you base your behaviour on emotion and belief in certain circumstances. To do so would therefore be rational in sense 1 but not in sense 2.

It is quite clear, then, that in conditions far from certainty managers have no choice but to apply significantly different decision-making modes to those required in conditions close to certainty (see *Illustration 2.1*). In the next two sections we will examine in more detail what these different modes of decision-making are.

2.5 MODELS OF DECISION-MAKING IN CONDITIONS CLOSE TO CERTAINTY

There are three very well known models of decision-making that can quite clearly be employed only in conditions close to certainty, that is in closed or contained change situations. These are technical rationality; bounded rationality, bureaucracies and dominant coalitions; and trial-and-error or logical incrementalism. This section examines each of these modes.

Technical rationality

When managers know what their objectives are and agree upon them in a closed change situation, then the effective mode of making a decision is that of technical rationality. Managers then discover how their environment and the capability of their organisation are changing by gathering the facts through a continuing process of scanning, research and monitoring. They analyse the facts using the step-by-step rules of logical reasoning to generate all the options open to achieve their objectives. They calculate the effects of carrying out each option on their objectives, choose that option which maximises their objectives, and then act to implement that option. What managers are doing or should be doing is explained in terms of pure rationality, the foundation of scientific management originating in the writings of Fredrick Taylor back in the early part of this century (*Taylor, 1911*).

We have seen in the previous section how a number of writers have shown that this is possible only when the dynamics are stable, that is, when members of an organisation are both close to certainty and close to agreement. Even then, however, the limits on human cognition make pure technical rationality impossible for the following reasons.

Given clear agreed objectives in relation to clear-cut problems, pure rationality requires the decision-maker to perceive the relevant objective facts in a direct manner. Perceiving directly means that we are not seeing the facts through some kind of lens or other means that could open up the possibility of distortion. Having perceived the facts directly, the purely rational person would then have to store them in an exact form so that they could be processed later on without distortion. This would mean storing facts in categories that are precisely defined – we put a fact into a category, if and only if it satisfies all the characteristics of that category. Having memorised the facts in this fashion and having memorised in much the same way the processing techniques required to manipulate them, the rational person would then process the facts in a step-by-step fashion according to the rules of logic and select the action option that maximises the objective. The choice is predetermined by the facts and the problem is simply one of calculation.

However, as we shall see in the next chapter, humans do not perceive in this manner and they cannot therefore decide using a pure technically rational mode. As we shall see, humans use selective models of reality, models they socially construct among themselves and share with each other. The models are constructed around categories of phenomena that have fuzzy, irregular patterns in common.

Bounded rationality, bureaucracy and dominant coalitions

Recognising the restrictive circumstance in which pure technical rationality could be applied, Herbert Simon developed the concept of bounded rationality (*Simon, 1960*). Bounded rationality is thus the weak form of what I have been calling technical rationality. He argued that managers could be rational only within boundaries imposed by resource availability, experience and knowledge of the range of options available for action. The collection, analysis and exchange of information all use resources, impose costs, and are time consuming. It will therefore never be possible, or even sensible, to gather all the information and examine all the options.

Limited economic resources and the nature of an individual brain's processing capacity together impose constraints on communication and flows of information through an organisation. All of this makes it impossible for managers to use the exhaustive process of pure technical rationality. Instead of screening all the facts and generating all the action options before making a choice, managers, in common with all humans, take short cuts. They employ trial-and-error search procedures to identify the most important bits of information in particular circumstances; they identify a limited range of the most important options revealed by the search; and then they act knowing only some of the potential outcomes of their actions. This means that they cannot take the action which maximises their objective. Instead they satisfice: they achieve the first satisfactory outcome they can in the circumstances. What they do then depends upon the sequence in which they discover changes, make choices, and take actions.

Limited resources and the nature of the brain's processing capacity are also compensated for by the use of bureaucratic procedures (*March & Simon, 1958; Cyert & March, 1963; Simon, 1960*). As managers act together they develop rules of action and standard operating procedures in order to cut down on the need to make decisions afresh each time. Precedents are established and subsequent decisions are taken without having to repeat the search process anew. Decisions and actions come to be outputs of standard patterns of behaviour. For example, next year's budget is often determined largely by uprating this year's spend. New alternatives tend to be sought only when a problem is detected, that is, some discrepancy between what is expected and what happens. Once such a discrepancy is detected, a trail-and-error search for a new solution is undertaken. Since all possible outcomes are not known, the tendency will be to make incremental decisions, that is, decisions with consequences as small and containable as possible. By relying on bureaucratic roles, and incremental decision-making, managers are able to reduce the levels of uncertainty they have to face. What the organisation learns will be embodied in its rules and procedures and these are used not to optimise outcomes, but to reduce uncertainty.

The lack of realism of the pure rationality model was recognised in other ways as well (*Cyert & March, 1963*). Although decisions and actions may flow from bureaucratic rules and precedent for most of the time, there are numerous occasions on which objectives and interests conflict. Which objectives are pursued will then depend on what the most powerful coalition of managers want.

The above paragraphs indicate how and why bounded-rationality/bureaucratic explanations of how managers discover, choose and act differ from pure technical rationality. But there are also similarities. Both kinds of rationality do not see problem-framing as the major difficulty. Bounded rationality is still about solving problems, even though they may not be as clearly framed. The processes described are still step-by-step or algorithmic procedures, differing from those of pure rationality only in that they are heuristic, that is, involving rules of thumb to proceed by trial and error. An organisation is still seen as searching for satisfactory attainment of known objectives according to known criteria for success and failure.

What the bounded-rationality/bureaucratic explanations do is recognise economic constraints and take a more complicated view of human cognition; they recognise the limitations of human brain processing capacity. However, they do not see the process of discovery or choice as problematic in any sense other than that of limited processing capacity. All forms of planning and budgeting in organisations employ this weak form of technical rationality as the decision-making process. Since it requires that the outcomes of different possible action options be roughly known, this decision-making process can be used only in conditions close to certainty.

Trial and error – logical incrementation

Quinn's (1980) research into the decision-making process of a number of companies revealed that most strategic decisions are made outside formal planning systems, that is, outside the bounded rationality mode of decision-making. He found that managers purposely blend behavioural, political and formal analytical processes together to improve the quality of decisions and implementation. Effective managers accept the high level of uncertainty and ambiguity they have to face and do not plan everything. They preserve the flexibility of an organisation to deal with the unforeseen as it happens. The key points that Quinn made about the strategic decision-making mode are as follows:

1 Effective managers do not manage strategically in a piecemeal manner. They have a clear view on what they are trying to achieve, where they are trying to take the business. The destination is thus intended.
2 But the route to that destination, the strategy itself, is not intended from the start in any comprehensive way. Effective managers know that the environment they have to operate in is uncertain and ambiguous. They therefore sustain flexibility by holding open the method of reaching the goal.
3 The strategy itself then emerges from the interaction between different groupings of people in the organisation, different groupings with different amounts of power, different requirements for and access to information, different time spans and parochial interest. These different pressures are orchestrated by senior managers. The top is always reassessing, integrating and organising.
4 The strategy emerges or evolves in small incremental, opportunistic steps. But such evolution is not piecemeal or haphazard because of the agreed purpose and the role of top management in reassessing what is happening. It is this that provides the logic in the incremental action.

5 The result is an organisation that is feeling its way to a known goal, opportunistically learning as it goes.

In Quinn's model of the strategy process, the organisation is driven by central intention with respect to the goal, but there is no prior central intention as to how that goal is to be achieved; the route to the goal is discovered through a logical process of taking one small step at a time. In logical incrementalism, overall strategy emerges from step-by-step trial-and-error actions occurring in a number of different places in an organisation; for example, some may be making an acquisition while others are restructuring the reporting structure. These separate initiatives are pushed by champions, each attacking a class of strategic issue. The top executives manage the process, orchestrating it and sustaining some logic in it. It is this that makes it a purposeful, proactive technique. Urgent, interim, piecemeal decisions shape the organisation's future, but they do so in an orderly logical way. No-one fully understands all the implications of what they are all doing together, but they are consciously preparing to move opportunistically (see *Illustration 2.2*).

Illustration 2.2

Exxon Europe

Quinn (1978) illustrates his concept of strategies being developed through a process of logical incrementalism as follows:

When Exxon began its regional decentralization on a worldwide basis, the Executive Committee placed a senior officer and board member with a very responsive management style in a vaguely defined 'coordinative role' vis-à-vis its powerful and successful European units. Over a period of two years this man sensed problems and experimented with voluntary coordinative possibilities on a pan-European basis. Only later, with greater understanding by both corporate and divisional officers, did Exxon move to a more formal line relationship for what became Exxon Europe. Even then the move had to be coordinated in other areas of the world. All of these changes together led to an entirely new power balance toward regional and non-US concerns and to a more responsive worldwide posture for Exxon. ■

Source: Quinn, 1978 p. 102

Since in this model it is assumed to be possible to decide in advance where the organisation is going, it too can apply only in conditions rather close to certainty. The degree of order and logic it describes is not possible in truly open-ended situations.

2.6 MODELS OF DECISION-MAKING IN CONDITIONS FAR FROM CERTAINTY

In open-ended change situations, managers are by definition ignorant even of the outcomes that might possibly flow from a decision they make and an action they take.

They do not know how their actions may be related in a cause-and-effect sense to the outcomes of those actions. In genuinely new situations it is not possible to assign probabilities to outcomes. In this section we are going to review models of decision-making that do not assume knowledge either of the final destination or outcome aimed for, or of the route to that destination or outcome. These, therefore, are the modes that can be applied in open-ended situations.

The search for error

Collingridge (1980) argues that effective decision-making in this situation is a search for error and a willingness to respond to its discovery. Instead of searching for the right decision as you would when using a technically rational mode close to certainty, you need to choose an option that can most easily be found to be in error, error that can most easily be corrected. In this way fewer options are closed off; you get more opportunities to adjust what you have done when the circumstances change.

For example, if you can forecast future electricity demand reliably, the right solution to increased demand may be to build one large power station now. If, however, the future demand for electricity is highly uncertain it would be better to build a number of small power stations, spread over a few years. That way you will find it easier to check for error in your forecast of future demand and easier to correct for mistakes. You may only have to close a small power station instead of running a large one at low capacity.

This kind of approach requires a considerable psychological adjustment. Most of us are used to being judged on whether we made the right choice. If it turns out to be wrong we devote much energy to concealing this fact, or in justifying our original decision. Applying technical rationality in conditions of great uncertainty leads us intentionally to avoid the search for error and to delay its recognition. If we abandon technical rationality in these circumstances and search for error instead, we would have to admit mistakes as soon as possible and avoid trying to justify them. Here we are talking about a mature recognition that being wrong is a valuable learning exercise.

The Mintzberg decision process model

Mintzberg, Theoret & Raisinghani (1976) analysed twenty-five decision-making processes and formulated a descriptive model as follows. The decision-making situations they analysed were characterised by novelty, complexity and open-endedness. The research showed that a final choice was made in such situations only after lengthy periods that involved many difficult discontinuous and recursive steps.

They divided the decision process into three basic stages:

- identification
- development
- selection.

Within each of the stages a number of routines were identified. We will now examine each stage and the routines it involves.

The identification stage

It is a feature of open-ended change situations that the issues which have to be attended to, the problems and opportunities requiring a decision, are not at all obvious or clear. The need to make a decision therefore has to be identified or prompted by signals from the environment or from the working of the organisation. The stimulus for a decision may be the voluntary recognition of a problem or an opportunity, or the result of some pressure or mild crisis, or the consequence of a major crisis that forces a decision. Many small stimuli may need to build up to some threshold before a decision need is identified and a decision triggered. In this regard the frame of reference of the manager is important (*Johnson, 1987*). If the stimuli for a decision fall outside the currently shared wisdom on what the business is about and how it should be conducted, then managers will ignore the stimuli. It will probably require a crisis to force a decision. Where managers identify a problem to which there is no clear solution there will be a tendency to ignore it. Problems for which there are matching solutions will tend to be dealt with.

Note how the routine for recognising a problem depends upon the behaviour of individuals, is culturally conditioned, and involves political interaction.

Once managers have recognised a problem, the diagnosis routine is activated. Old information channels are tapped and new ones opened. The diagnosis may be formal or it may be very informal. It may be skipped altogether. What managers are doing here is trying to shape or structure the problems so that they may decide how to deal with them.

The development stage

The development stage takes up most of the time and resources in the decision-making process. It involves search routines and design routines.

The search routine is an attempt to discover a ready-made solution. These routines include simply waiting for an alternative to materialise, searching the memory of the organisation, that is, the solutions to problems that have worked before, scanning alternatives, hiring consultants and so on. Search is a step-by-step or incremental process beginning with the easiest search routine.

The design routine consists of the steps taken to design a solution to the problem. Mintzberg et al. found that organisations avoid custom-made routines for making a decision because they are expensive and require many steps. In other words, they tend not to consider large numbers of alternatives but to select one promising alternative, one that they have tried before. There is then a natural tendency to avoid innovative approaches to strategic decision-making.

Selection

Selection is often intertwined with the development stage and involves the routines of screening, evaluative choice and authorisation. The screen routine is used to screen out options that are clearly not viable. It is a superficial routine. The evaluation choice routine was not found to be one that involved the use of analytical techniques in the study that Mintzberg et al. conducted. The evaluation criteria were normally based on judgement and intuition. Managers dealt with information overload by using precedent, imitation or tradition. They made judgements on a proposal according to the reliability of the proposer rather than the project, on the track record of the manager.

The final routine is that of authorisation and legitimation of the choices that individuals and groups have made.

The decision-making process identified here is a number of routines that have behavioural, political and learning aspects. The routines are affected by interruptions caused by environmental factors, by scheduling and timing delays as well as speed-ups generated by those involved in the process, by feedback delays as people wait for information and authorisation, and by cycling back to earlier stages in the process.

A simplified version of this model is depicted in *Figure 2.6*.

Dialectical enquiry

Schwenck & Thomas (1983) also address the process of decision-making in open-ended situations. They identify three procedures for formulating problems and selecting outcomes:

- *Brainstorming.* Here a small group of people work together to produce as many ideas as they can on what problems they should be addressing and how they should deal with them. The ideas generated can then be ranked and subjected to further study and consideration.
- *The devil's advocate.* Here one or more persons play the role of trying to tear a proposal apart. They are performing the important function of identifying and questioning the tacit assumptions that are being made.
- *Dialectical enquiry.* This is similar to the devil's advocate approach but involves groups of people. Two opposing groups enter into a debate on a proposed solution to a problem. Again, this focuses attention on tacit assumptions being made. From the two conflicting options being debated, a third, a synthesis of the two, may emerge.

These forms of stimulating the creative identification and handling of problems are illustrated in *Figure 2.7*.

Muddling through, organised anarchy, and garbage-can decision-making

Lindblom (1959) also describes the process of strategic decision-making as incremental, but to him it is a form of 'muddling through'. His observations are derived from decision-making in state sector organisations, but they are relevant to private sector organisations too. Because in complex situations it is not possible to identify all the objectives of different groups of people affected by an issue, policies are chosen directly. Instead of working from a statement of desired ends to the means required to achieve it, managers choose the ends and the means simultaneously. In other words, two different managers may choose the same policy or solution for different reasons.

This means that we cannot judge a policy according to how well it achieves a given end. Instead we judge a policy according to whether it is itself desirable or not. A good policy is thus simply one that gets widespread support. It is then carried out in incremental stages, preserving flexibility to change it as conditions change. The policy

FIGURE 2.6
The Mintzberg et al. model of the strategic management process

Source: Reprinted from 'The structure of "unstructured" decision processes' by H. Mintzberg, A. Théorêt & D. Raisinghani (1976) published in *Administrative Science Quarterly*, vol. 21, no. 2, pp. 246–75, by permission of *Administrative Science Quarterly*.

FIGURE 2.7

Techniques for identifying, formulating and resolving problems

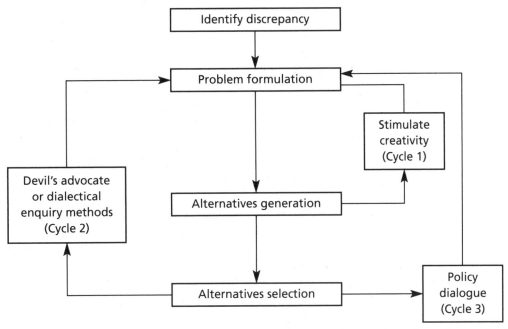

Source: C. Schwenk & H. Thomas (1983), 'Formulating the mess: the role of decision and problem formulation', *Omega: The International Journal of Management Science*, vol. 11, no. 3, pp. 239–52

is pursued in stages of successive limited comparisons. In this approach, dramatically new policies are not considered. New policies have to be close to existing ones and limited comparisons are made. This makes it unnecessary to undertake fundamental enquiries. The procedure also involves ignoring important possible consequences of policies, a necessary evil perhaps if anything is to be done. But serious lasting mistakes can be avoided because the changes are being made in small steps.

Cohen, March & Ohlsen (1972) have carried this kind of analysis of state sector organisations further. They describe many of these organisations as organised anarchies and their decision-making process as garbage-can decision-making.

In their research, they found that universities and some state bodies are characterised by widely distributed power and complex, unclear hierarchical structures. The hierarchical structure is such that just about any issue can be taken to just about any forum, by just about anyone. These institutions are noted for widespread participation in decision-making, for ambiguous and intersecting job definitions, and a lack of shared cultural values across the whole organisation. What is found in the conditions prevailing at universities and some state bodies is the following:

- Individuals and sub-units do not have clear goals.
- No individual has much power and the distribution of power is not stably determined by sanctions, interdependence and contribution. It fluctuates with the context within which decisions are being made and consequently:
- the distribution of power over time is not constant and neither is:

- the distribution of power over issue. And furthermore:
- choices are often avoided, deferred, made by oversight, or never implemented.

Such organisations face open-ended change not only, or even primarily, because their environments are changing but because of the uncertainty of their technology. It is far from certain what good teaching is, for example, or what good medical care is. Such organisations therefore have to be collections of relatively free professionals. This leads to a form that the authors call organised anarchy. Here decisions and their outcomes occur largely by chance. The flow of choices over time is erratic and haphazard. There is a continuing flow of problems, opportunities, solutions and choices coming together in a largely haphazard manner. This happens because there is no simple and clear hierarchy and because the distribution of power is close to equality.

Where power is widely dispersed so that there are no powerful actors who can enforce their wills; where power is therefore unstable over time and issue; where there is little sharing of values; where there are heavy workloads on individuals and meetings; where participation in decision-making is open and fluid; where access to choice situations and participation structures are open and unclear; then choice will be determined largely by chance. The choice will depend entirely upon the context in which it is attended to. It will depend upon the level of attention paid to it in the light of all the other issues; upon who was present and participated; upon how they participated and how others interpreted that participation. Looking back it will not be possible to say that the choice occurred because some individual or group intended it. In this sense intention or purpose is lacking in the choice process. There is no overall rhythm to the process and the specific sequence of choices is random and without any pattern. The sequence of specific choices can shoot just anywhere because important constraints provided by unequal power, clear hierarchies and job descriptions have been removed. Action is then the result of habit, custom or the unpredictable influence of others. It is impossible to predict the choice without knowing all the small details of the context. Intention is lost in the flow of events and goals are the product of sense-making activities after the event.

These studies have shown that where participation is widespread and power equally distributed; where job assignments are unclear and hierarchies complex; where values are not strongly shared; then we get sequences of choices that depend largely on chance.

Politics and agenda building

Political processes, the use of persuasion and negotiation to obtain desired outcomes where there is disagreement, also clearly constitute a decision-making mode. Since open-ended change is characterised by disagreement, the political mode is of great importance.

Huff (1988) identifies the role of politics in strategic choice in the following terms:

- Organisational politics provides an arena for identifying and assessing new strategic alternatives which draw upon the varied experience of organisation members.
- Politics challenges organisation leaders to clarify and modify their thinking about strategic issues. In general, politics is more effective at this task than formal planning systems.

- Organisational politics identifies the individual and group commitments necessary for designing and implementing new strategy.
- Political diversity facilitates the succession of individual leaders, and promotes adaptations in the practices and beliefs which contribute to organisational culture.
- While organisation politics can be disruptive, routined decision cycles can channel potentially disrupting differences of opinion into manageable cycles of debate.

Dutton (1988) presents a model of decision-making in conditions of uncertainty and ambiguity which he calls an issue-building process. This is depicted in Figure 2.8. In this model, issues attract attention if they conform to the strategy and culture of the organisation. If the issue is important and simple enough it will attract attention, otherwise the tendency will be to postpone it. This is much the same point as that made in the garbage-can model. To sustain attention an issue must be sponsored and this brings in the political process. Coalitions have to be built around the issue. Whether the issue gets onto the agenda or not will depend upon context, the other matters pressing for attention for example.

FIGURE 2.8
Issue agenda building

Source: L. Pondy, R. Boland & H Thomas (Eds) (1988), *Managing Ambiguity and Change*, New York: John Wiley & Sons

Management is about more than making a decision and taking action – it is also about evaluating the outcome of the decision and its consequent action. In other words, it is also about control and about learning from the consequences of behaviour. We turn now, therefore, to models of control in organisations and explore how different forms of control apply to different kinds of change situation.

2.7   MODELS OF CONTROL IN CONDITIONS CLOSE TO AND FAR FROM CERTAINTY

Hofstede (1981) defines the situation in which control is to be exerted in terms of:

- the degree of ambiguity in the objectives to be achieved;
- the measurability of the performance to be controlled;
- the extent to which the outcomes of actions are known;
- the extent to which the activity being controlled is repetitive.

Different combinations of these four factors require alternative forms of control and Hofstede distinguishes six of these, shown in *Figure 2.9*, which also indicates the control situation to which each is appropriate.

The six main forms of control Hofstede identifies are as follows.

1 Routine control. This applies only when there is no ambiguity in objectives, the consequences of performance are accurately measurable, the causal links are clear cut so that the outcomes of actions are known, and the activity being controlled is repetitive. The form of control in this situation is automatic negative feedback, in which information about a deviation between some desired and some actual outcome is fed back into the decision-making process to remove the deviation. An automated system to control inventory levels is an example of this.

2 Expert control. If we relax the last requirement to do with repetitive activities then we can no longer practise routine, that is, fully automatic control. But we can come pretty close to it, if we create the possibility of expert intervention at certain points. This is the planning/monitoring form of control in which actual outcomes are reported against projections and managers then discuss the variances, identifying what to do to remove them.

3 Trial-and-error control. Suppose now that the only condition we set for routine control that is not met is that the outcomes of actions are not known. Then, because we cannot predict, we cannot practise routine or expert control; instead we will have to discover the effects of our interventions through a process of trial and error which is possible because actions are repetitive. This is control through trial-and-error learning about the consequences of our actions.

4 Intuitive control. What if the situation in which control is to be exerted becomes even more difficult in that, although objectives are unambiguous and performance is measurable, actions are not repetitive and their outcomes are not known? Then trial and error will not help much because in effect you will get only one chance to take a particular action – it is unique. In these circumstances Hofstede talks about control as intuitive, as an art rather than a science, where there are few rules to guide managers.

5 Judgemental control. If the control situation becomes even more difficult so that activity is not repetitive, its outcomes are unknown and now also not measurable, but objectives are still clear, then control has to take a subjective, judgemental form.

FIGURE 2.9

Hofstede's approach to control

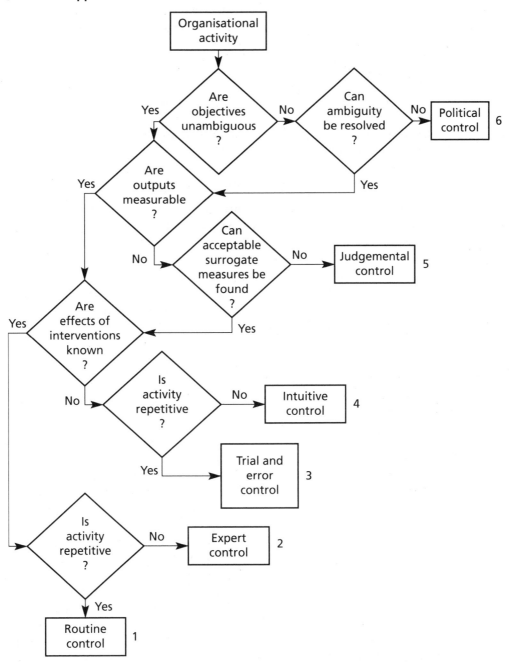

Source: G. Hofstede (1981), 'Management control of public and not-for-profit activities', *Accounting, Organisations and Society*, vol. 6, no. 3, pp. 193–211

6 Political control. Finally, suppose that managers face unique situations in which the objectives to be achieved are unclear and the outcomes of actions are neither measurable nor known. Then the only form of control that it is possible to apply is political control. This relies on the use of power, negotiation, persuasion and manipulation, often expressed in rituals and symbols.

Hofstede's analysis can quite easily be recast into the terminology we have been using in this chapter. When all of his six factors defining the control situation are present, then we have closed change (clear objectives, repetitive actions, measurable and known outcomes). Contained change occurs when there are clear objectives, repetitive actions, imperfectly measurable and largely unknown outcomes. Open-ended change means that there are ambiguous and conflicting objectives, unique actions, non-measurable and unknowable outcomes. These change situations determine what form of control it is possible to apply:

- In conditions near to certainty, control can take forms close to the routine and expert; that is, the planning and monitoring form of control.
- In conditions a little way from certainty, control can take the form of shared cultures, political processes and trial-and-error action.
- In conditions far from certainty, however, control will be possible only in its intuitive, judgemental and political forms. We will see in Chapters 9 and 10 how we can develop these notions into an understanding of self-organisation as a form of control.

2.8 SUMMARY

We started this chapter by describing the nature of the changes that we must deal with in some way as members and managers of an organisation. In very simple and very obvious terms, we can locate this change along a spectrum stretching from that which is close to certainty to that which is far from certainty. The spectrum is present in all time frames, but the further out we look into the future the more the balance of the spectrum shifts away from that close to certainty to that far from certainty.

We then considered the most obvious behavioural implications for members and managers of organisations as they stand in the here and now, and find that they must make decisions and exercise control in relation to a future that tends to be primarily close to certainty in the short term and primarily far from certainty in the long term. We saw that human beings tend to experience higher levels of anxiety the further from certainty is the context in which they must decide and control. That anxiety can be reduced if they can act jointly in agreement with each other about objectives and actions. However, often they find that they must somehow find a way to act jointly even when they are far from agreement with each other, and this state of disagreement is also more likely to pertain the further they are from certainty. Conflict and anxiety are consequently likely to be important factors in influencing behaviour and thus decision-making and control processes when people operate far from agreement and certainty. In fact, if a group of people find themselves further from agreement and certainty than they can bear, then they may either avoid such anxiety-provoking situations altogether and thus be at the mercy of change, or they may disintegrate into full-scale anarchy.

We then went on to see how these factors, degrees of closeness to certainty and agreement, create the context that determines what mode of decision-making and control it is possible for members and managers of organisations to deploy. This is summarised in *Figure 2.10*.

FIGURE 2.10

The relationship between change context and decision-making/control modes

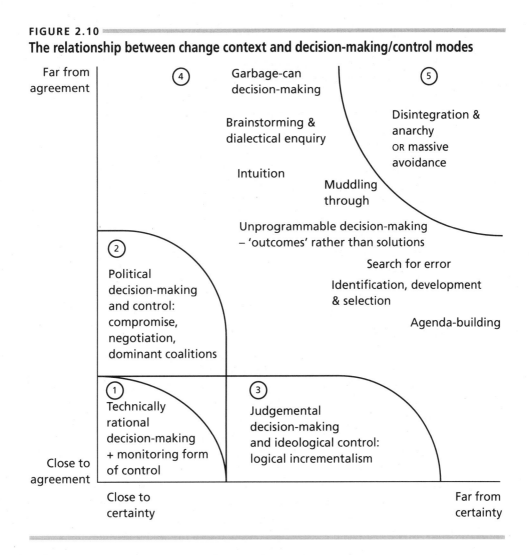

What *Figure 2.10* makes clear is this: it is only in situations close to certainty and agreement (area 1 in the diagram) that it is possible for the members and managers of an organisation to plan their future. Only when they are close to both certainty and agreement can they utilise a technically rational mode of decision-making and a monitoring form of control, the essential elements without which an organisation cannot be said to be following a planned path to a planned future. This indicates that planning is a decision-making/control process that can be applied only over a relatively short time span into the future. The period over which experience shows that members and managers have the ability to make reasonably accurate forecasts determines the period for which they can plan. In all other circumstances there is no option but to employ some other mode of management.

Figure 2.10 also depicts what all the writers reviewed above have made clear about situations close to certainty but some way away from agreement (area 2 in the diagram) – political processes are the only ways in which both decision-making and control can be practised. On the other hand, in situations close to agreement but far from certainty (area 3 in the diagram), both decision-making and control are ideologically driven, with decisions based on judgement and control based on conformity.

The writers surveyed in this chapter have also pointed out that when managers and members of organisations have to operate far from both certainty and agreement (area 4 in the diagram), then decision-making tends to be rather intuitive and unprogrammed and control tends to be based on group pressures. As they move further and further away from certainty and agreement we find managers and members using 'garbage-can' methods of making decisions and 'muddling through'. Finally, at some point the possibility of coherent, constructive joint action breaks down altogether (area 5 in the diagram).

The picture is one in which strategies can be intentional and deliberate in conditions close to certainty and agreement, but there is no option but for them to be emergent when people operate far from certainty and agreement. If we are to understand the nature of strategic management in a manner that is at all realistic, then we are going to have to understand both intentional and emergent strategies and we are going to have to understand in much more depth the whole range of decision-making and control processes that produce them.

Before proceeding with this, however, you should note an important fact that has already been referred to in Chapter 1: the ubiquitous tendency of people in organisations to say that they are doing one thing when they are doing another. Nowhere does this apply more than to the processes of strategic management. Although it has been clear for decades that planning processes can be applied only close to certainty and agreement and that the truly strategic situations are not like this, nevertheless, the majority of managers, consultants and academics carry on talking about strategic outcomes primarily as the consequence of conscious intentions. It is hoped that referral every now and again to the picture drawn in *Figure 2.10* will persuade you not to do this so readily.

Note too that it is possible to be rather clear and explicit about how people should proceed in areas 1, 2 and 3 in the diagram in *Figure 2.10*, but how vague the descriptions of the writers reviewed become when they talk about what people do, or should do, in area 4 of the diagram. The tendency has quite naturally, therefore, been to focus attention on areas 1, 2 and 3 and largely ignore area 4 as if there is not much useful that can be said about it. It is the intention in this book to devote most of the attention to material that ultimately, I hope, will help us to understand area 4 more clearly. It is because we have developed rather few ideas of how to talk about area 4 that Part Four of this book takes a diversion into the natural sciences to look for analogies, metaphors and a language that might help us to get more insight into what we do in area 4.

Further reading

Turton (1991) contains excellent summaries of decision-making modes. For even further detail on particular decision-making modes turn to Quinn (1978), Mintzberg, Théorêt & Raisinghani (1976) and Cohen, March & Ohlsen (1972).

References

Child, J. (1972), Organisational structure, environment and performance: the role of strategic choice, *Sociology*, vol. 6, no. 1, pp. 1–21.

Child. J. (1984), *Organisation*, London: Harper & Row.

Cohen, M. D., March, J. G. & Ohlsen, J. P. (1972), A garbage can model of organizational choice, *Administrative Science Quarterly*, vol. 17, pp. 1–25.

Collingridge, D. (1980), *The Social Control of Technology*, Open University Press.

Cyert, R. M. & March, J. G. (1963), *A Behavioural Theory of the Firm*, Englewood Cliffs: Prentice-Hall.

Duncan, R. (1972), Characteristics of organisational environments and perceived uncertainty, *Administrative Science Quarterly*, vol. 17, pp. 313–27.

Dutton, J. E. (1988), Understanding strategic agenda building and its implications for managing change, in Pondy, L R., Boland, J. R. & Thomas, H. (Eds.) (1988), *Managing Ambiguity and Change*, New York: John Wiley.

Hofstede, G. (1981), Management control of public and not-for-profit activities, *Accounting, Organisations and Society*, vol. 6, no. 3, pp. 193–211.

Huff, A. S. (1988), Politics and arguments as a means of coping with ambiguity and change, in Pondy, L. R., Borland, J. R. & Thomas, H. (Eds.) (1988), *Managing Ambiguity and Change*, New York: John Wiley.

Johnson, G. (1987), *Strategic Change and the Management Process*, Oxford: Blackwell.

Lindblom, L. (1959), The science of muddling through, *Public Administration Review*, vol. 19, pp. 79–88.

March, J. G. & Simon, H. A. (1958), *Organizations*, New York: John Wiley.

Mintzberg, H., Théorêt, A. & Raisinghani, D. (1976), The structure of the unstructured decision making process, *Administrative Science Quarterly*, vol. 21, no. 2, pp. 246–75.

Perrow, C. (1972), *Complex Organizations*, Scott-Forsman.

Pfeffer, J. (1981), *Power in Organizations*, Cambridge, Ma.: Ballinger Publishing Company.

Quinn, J. B. (1978), Strategic change: logical incrementalism, *Sloan Management Review*, vol. 1, no. 20, Fall, pp. 7–21.

Quinn, J. B. (1980), *Strategic Change: Logical Incrementalism*, Homewood, Ill.: Richard D. Irwin.

Schwenk, C. & Thomas, H. (1983), Formulating the mess: the role of decision and problem formulation, *Omega: The International Journal of Management Science*, vol. 11, no. 3, pp. 239–52.

Simon, H. A. (1960), *The New Science of Management Decisions*, New York: Harper Brothers.

Stacey, R. (1990), *Dynamic Strategic Management for the 1990s*, London: Kogan Page.

Stacey, R. (1991), *The Chaos Frontier: Creative Strategic Control for Business*, Oxford: Butterworth-Heinemann.

Stacey, R. (1992), *Managing the Unknowable: The Strategic Boundaries Between Order and Chaos*, San Francisco: Jossey Bass. Also published in the UK as *Managing Chaos*, London: Kogan Page.

Taylor, F. (1911), *Scientific Management*, New York: Harper Brothers.

Thompson, J. D. & Tuden, A. (1959), Strategies, structures and processes of organisational decisions, in Thompson, J. D. et al. (Eds.), *Comparative Studies in Administration*, Pittsburgh: University of Pittsburgh Press.

Turton, R. (1991), *Behaviour in a Business Context*, London: Chapman & Hall.

Wiechmann, U. & Gillespie, K. (1978), Mövenpick Unternehmungen, in Buzzell, R. D. & Quelch, J. A. (1988), *Multinational Marketing Management*, Reading, Ma.: Addison-Wesley.

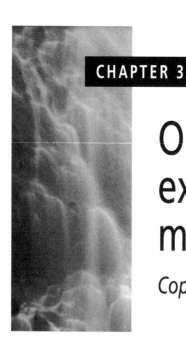

CHAPTER 3

Ordinary and extraordinary management

Coping with both certainty and uncertainty

INTRODUCTION

In the last chapter we saw how managers, in fact all members of organisations, have no choice but to deal with events impacting upon them and the consequences of their own actions that together create conditions ranging from those close to certainty and agreement to those far from certainty and agreement. We have seen how this absolutely requires different modes of decision-making and control ranging from the implementation of shared intentions, through political, intuitive and unprogrammed behaviour that is not at all well defined, to muddling through, and ultimately to the impossibility of taking constructive joint action at all.

The management literature has been dominated, for the past 30 years at least, by prescriptions for, and studies of, the implementation of shared intentions. It is this that also dominates public discussion by practising managers when they say what they do, or should do, in the matter of strategic management. However, there is also an important descriptive literature, admittedly much smaller, that identifies the importance in practice of emergent strategy, that is, patterns in action that emerge over the long term from complex interactions between people without prior shared intention, without any prior blueprint. When it actually comes to doing as opposed to saying, therefore, practising managers frequently find it impossible to realise any prior shared intention they might have articulated and do something else that produces emergent strategies instead.

There is little in the way of management and organisation theory to explain such strategic emergence, and as we have seen the processes that lead to emergence are not at all well defined, simply being defined as intuitive or unprogrammed. It is the purpose of this chapter to suggest a distinction between ordinary and extraordinary management that is capable of providing a theoretical basis for clarifying and understanding the processes that lead to emergent strategy. The distinction I have in mind leads to a clear understanding of just what is meant by the intuitive and unprogrammed decision-making and control processes that result in such emergent strategy. In this chapter, then, I want to explore further how we might make sense of, how we might identify the essential features of, decision-making and control in conditions close to and far from certainty and agreement.

The first step in this sense-making will be to consider how we make sense of anything, in general, and then how we use that sense-making to learn and make further sense of what is happening to us and what we are doing, in general. In other words, we will be examining some theories of cognition and of learning and of how these enable us to cope with the paradoxes of life, including life in organisations. We will be examining how we use paradigms, or mental models. A very important distinction will be drawn between simple single-loop learning, which is the adaptation of behaviour in the light of its consequences without any change in mental model, and complex double-loop learning, which is the adaptation of mental models and thence the adaptation of behaviour. This distinction enables us to differentiate between two conceptually different kinds of management, namely, ordinary management which is conducted within a given mental model and extraordinary management which is the process of changing mental models.

Appreciation of the importance of this distinction between ordinary and extraordinary management requires that we understand the systemic nature of an organisation, particularly the fact that any group of people, and that obviously includes organisations, constitutes a feedback system. Feedback can take either a negative form, in which case information about the consequences of behaviour is fed back to dampen out deviations from some intended pattern of behaviour, or positive, in which case information about the consequences of an action is fed back to amplify deviations from an original intention. Ordinary management is the utilisation of negative feedback in organisations to secure the realisation of prior intention, while extraordinary management utilises the positive feedback processes in organisations to disturb the status quo, a development that is absolutely required if an organisation is to change in any significant way. The systemic nature of organisations, the importance of positive and negative feedback and how they give insight into ordinary and extraordinary management, will be the focus of Part Three of this book. In this chapter we now turn to questions of cognition and learning and see how they lead to concepts of ordinary and extraordinary management.

3.2   HOW PARADIGMS GOVERN WHAT WE SEE AND DO

What every one of us sees, understands and does in any situation depends upon the perspective from which we view that situation. Such a perspective is called a paradigm, a very general way that each of us uses to make sense of the particular world we are operating in. The term is explained in *Key Concept 3.1.* How teachers, researchers and consultants understand the strategy game and therefore advise on it, how managers understand it and therefore play it, all depend in the end upon their paradigm.

Key Concept 3.1

Paradigm

A paradigm is the set of preconceptions we bring from our past to each new situation we have to deal with. The paradigm is, as it were, the lens through which we look at the world and it therefore determines what we perceive. A paradigm is a set of beliefs or assumptions we make about the world, normally beneath the level of awareness and therefore mostly never questioned. As we live and work with other people we come to share a particular way of focusing on the world and that shared paradigm determines what explanations we develop and agree upon amongst ourselves. The origins of all our explanations of everything, therefore, lie in the process of socialisation, in the shared cultures formed by people in groups. The paradigm flows from shared past experience and is reflected in our skilled behaviour, that is, the rapid actions we take automatically to perform complex tasks without thinking about how, and often why, we are performing them.

I can perhaps make clearer what I mean by the importance of paradigms by asking you to look at *Figure 3.1*, which you have no doubt seen before, and construct a story around what you see. If you focus on the white space, seeing the black as unimportant background, you will see a container. Your story will have something to do with a cup, or a vase, and what it might be used for. If you focus on the black spaces, seeing the white as unimportant background, you will see two people facing each other. Your story will have to do with who they are, why they are looking at each other, and what they might do next.

How you focus (the equivalent of your paradigm) determines what you see, and what you see determines what you do, in this case the story you tell. And as you tell your story, the telling itself provokes new thoughts to be added to that story.

In the terminology introduced in Chapter 1, how and what you *discover* (your paradigms and the perceptions they lead you to) directly affects what you *choose* to do since you cannot choose what you have not perceived, and that choice in turn determines your *actions*. And it is through your actions that you make further discoveries, leading to other choices and actions in a continuing feedback loop. Even when you do something as simple as look at *Figure 3.1* and construct a story around it, you are in effect following a feedback loop in which one discovery or action leads to others, just as was the case in the strategic management process illustrated in *Figure 1.1* of Chapter 1. Furthermore, it is your paradigm, how you focus, that determines how you go around the feedback loop. How you go around the loop determines the patterns of change in the behaviour you generate, that is, the dynamics of your behaviour. The paradigms that the managers of an organisation share will therefore determine how they practise strategic management and what strategies they pursue.

To see this, consider what happens if, as in *Figure 3.1*, you focus on the white space of stability, consistency, harmony and adaptation. You will then tell a tale of strategic

FIGURE 3.1
Perception

management that has to do with objectives and visions, plans and shared ideologies. Instability and contradiction will be unimportant background. In other words, you will focus your attention on situations close to certainty and agreement and therefore on management processes that have to do with planning and stabilising politics and ideology. The story you choose to tell will drive much of what you actually do and so you will establish planning systems to deal with your strategic problems, or you will try to set out visions for the future. This will encourage you to follow stable patterns of behaviour that inevitably build on your existing strengths and repeat successful behaviour from the past. In an age where survival depends upon innovation, exclusive reliance on this form of behaviour might be disastrous.

If, however, you focus on the direct opposite, on the black space of instability, contradiction, conflict and creative interaction, then you will tell a tale of strategic management that has to do with challenging and provoking political interactions, personalities, group dynamics and learning. If your story is one of politics and learning you may try to create conditions in which people will develop new perspectives. This will mean unstable patterns of behaviour, conflict and tension, but such behaviour might produce innovation.

Our paradigm, then, ultimately determines what we do in every sphere of life – it comes before any visions we may form and it is prior to any rational analysis. For example, the development of every science is conditioned by the paradigm that a particular community of scientists shares *(Kuhn, 1970)*. In the same way, the paradigm shared by scholars, students and practitioners of strategic management also determines the explanations and prescriptions they put forward on organisational success. It will help us to understand the nature of strategic management, therefore, if we examine Thomas Kuhn's explanation of how paradigms relate to the development of a science.

Kuhn on scientific revolutions

In the framework that Thomas Kuhn uses to explain the development of the natural sciences, he draws a distinction between what he calls normal science and extraordinary science.

Normal science is what most scientists spend most of their lives doing. It is conducted within a paradigm that the great majority of those in a particular discipline share. That paradigm is a set of shared assumptions, that are largely tacit, that is, below the level of consciousness and therefore hardly ever questioned. The paradigm consists of the beliefs that a community of scientists share about:

- what their world of study consists of;
- what the core generalisations on the functioning of that world are;
- what the key problems confronting them are;
- what is acceptable as solutions to the problems;
- what methods are to be employed to study the field and carry out experiments;
- what examples are regarded as typical of the phenomena being dealt with.

The paradigm is therefore far more general than a set of rules or procedures; rather, it constitutes a whole way of thinking that conditions how normal science is carried out.

Normal science

Normal science does not try to invent or discover something completely new; it is not a search for novelty or surprise, but rather the methodical activity of solving puzzles posed by the paradigm, using criteria and rules of procedure that are set by the paradigm. Puzzles have known solutions; it is the method of solving them that is unknown and the challenge is to achieve the anticipated in a new way. The method for doing this is rational argument backed up by evidence and it is the paradigm that sets the ground rules for this rational argument – people can only have a rational argument when they share a paradigm. Examples of normal science and its dependence on a paradigm are given in *Illustration 3.1*.

Every paradigm, however, is a simplification of reality and therefore the conduct of normal science will eventually uncover anomalies that undermine the paradigm. In other words, scientific experiments will inevitably produce discrepancies that cannot be explained within the beliefs of the paradigm and the rules and procedures for conducting experiments that are derived from it. *Illustration 3.1* also gives examples of how normal science produces anomalies.

Thus, normal science is about avoiding surprises and certainly does not set out to undermine and change the paradigm. However, the more diligent the conduct of normal science, the more rapid the build-up of the anomalies that will lead some to question the paradigm.

In a field where the paradigm is being questioned, most of the scientists in that field will at first resist the threats to the paradigm because belief in the paradigm is vital to the continuing conduct of normal science. What is vital to normal science then becomes the enemy of further scientific development.

Extraordinary science

Eventually, however, as more and more anomalies come to light, they generate a crisis in which there is no widely shared paradigm in the field of study. Instead there is a battle between competing paradigms seeking to substitute for the now discredited one. Only when a new paradigm is once again shared can normal science be resumed. This crisis period of paradigm destruction and new paradigm creation is a scientific revolution and this is how all major scientific advances occur.

Illustration 3.1

Relativity and X-rays

During the 19th century scientists believed that light was a wave that moved through a substance called ether and scientists therefore deduced that light was governed by Newton's laws of physical mechanics. So, theories of light were simply extensions of Newtonian theory. If ether did exist, however, it should have been possible to detect the drift of planets through the ether, that is, the way in which the ether slowed their movement; in the course of normal science, expensive equipment was built to detect this drift. No such drift was detected but, despite this, scientists continued to conduct their normal scientific experiments on the assumption that ether existed.

Then in the last two decades of the 19th century Maxwell developed his electromagnetic theory. He continued to believe that light and electricity were displacements of the ether governed by Newton's laws – his normal scientific work continued to be governed by the ether paradigm. However, the theory he had developed did not include ether drag and it proved impossible to incorporate it. Many attempts were made to detect ether drag in electricity, but they failed. Thus the anomalies that could not be explained within the ether paradigm built up and eventually created a crisis for Newtonian theory's assumptions of absolute time and space. It was this crisis that led Einstein to develop his relativity theories and they resulted in a change in paradigm, a switch in perception from Newton's absolute classical mechanics to a relativist view of the world.

Another example is provided by the accidental discovery of X-rays. While conducting a normal experiment with cathode rays, Roentgen noticed that a barium platino-cyanide screen at some distance from his shielded apparatus glowed during the experiment. Further investigation indicated that the cause of the glow was X-rays, which could of course pass through the shielding around Roentgen's apparatus. This discovery was greeted with shock by other scientists and some said it was a hoax. At that time, the design of laboratory equipment and procedures, as well as the rules for interpreting results, were all based on the assumption that a phenomenon such as X-rays did not exist. Consequently, if the existence of X-rays was to be accepted, equipment and procedures would have to be changed and experiments repeated because previous results could have been due to, or at least affected by, X-rays of which the experimenters were ignorant. ∎

It is important to understand the process through which one paradigm comes to substitute for another – it is a process that is very different from what most people understand by the term 'scientific'.

Normal science is conducted through logical argument against rational criteria backed up with evidence. In case of conflict it will be possible for the arguments of one scientist to prevail over those of another on purely rational grounds. This is possible because they share the paradigm and this means that they in effect agree to follow the same rules of argument and accept the same items of evidence. But when it comes to changing the paradigm, this rational process can no longer apply because that which provides the commonly shared rules is no longer shared.

Two scientists arguing about a paradigm have no prior set of concepts or higher intellectual authority to whom they may appeal to settle the argument. Kuhn (1970, p. 199) puts it as follows:

> Debates over [paradigm] choice cannot be cast in a form that resembles logical or mathematical proof. In the latter, premises and rules of inference are stipulated from the start. If there is disagreement about conclusions, the parties to the ensuing debate can retrace their steps one by one, checking each against prior stipulation. At the end of that process one must concede that he has made a mistake, violated a previously accepted rule. After that concession he has no recourse and his opponent's proof is then compelling. Only if the two discover instead that they differ about the meaning or application of stipulated rules, that their prior agreement provides no sufficient basis for proof, does the debate continue in the form it inevitably does during scientific revolutions. That debate is about premises, and its recourse is to persuasion as a prelude to the possibility of proof.

So, when trying to establish a new paradigm, strictly logical, rational ways of resolving any conflict break down. They break down because rationality and logic require the prior existence of some shared set of rules that people agree to abide by and not question. As soon as they do question the paradigm they remove the basis of rationality. A new paradigm can eventually come to be shared only through a political process of persuasion and conversion:

- Some individual or small group of individuals perceives a new paradigm through some process of intuition prompted by the build-up of anomalies under the preceding paradigm.
- That new paradigm champion then uses political processes to persuade the group of scientific colleagues to share it.

Note how the processes used in revolutionary or extraordinary science are completely different to those used in normal science and in many ways are diametrically opposed to them – much the same conclusion as the one we reached in the last chapter about managers operating far from as opposed to close to certainty and agreement. Yet the conduct of science involves both normal and revolutionary science and indeed the latter is prompted by, and leads to, improvements in the former. Without revolutionary paradigm-destroying science there would be no real advance in scientific knowledge, that is, there would be no innovation. Note how extraordinary science is the enemy of normal science, and how normal science necessarily seeks to block the extraordinary, and yet how progress requires this paradox, this contradiction. Again, this is reminiscent of the conclusion we reached in the last chapter – managers must deal both with the normal everyday situations close to certainty and agreement and with the more extraordinary situations far from certainty and agreement.

Kuhn's views, and his research into the history of science to back them up, are of great importance because they make untenable the traditional view that science is a purely rational activity based on observable facts. From the traditional perspective, science is the activity of progressively uncovering the immutable laws of nature through a process of formulating hypotheses about phenomena in a particular area and testing them by experiment. If the testing of the hypothesis predictions against observed fact fails to falsify the hypothesis, then that hypothesis is accepted until such time as it might be falsified and replaced by a better one.

Science, on this view, was held to be free of any distortions due to human perceptions, beliefs, values or cultures. What Kuhn so convincingly demonstrates is that this is not so. At any one time, the laws of science reflect the perceptions, the paradigm of the scientific community, and a paradigm is a culturally conditioned, shared way of understanding the world that arises through social processes and is changed by political activity.

Simply accepting the laws of any science at face value is therefore unwise. What we need to do instead is understand the paradigm, the set of unquestioned assumptions, that underlie, those scientific laws. This applies to managing and organising too. If we are to think of management as a science then we must understand it in terms of the socially constructed paradigms that govern it, and we must also comprehend how we change such paradigms and develop new ones. In other words, we need to understand the process that managers, in common with all human beings, use to make sense of their world and to learn.

3.3 SIMPLE AND COMPLEX LEARNING

Research on human cognitive ability shows that we are capable of retaining only up to seven bits of information in the short-term memory at any one time. A bit is a digit, or a letter of the alphabet, or some chunk of them such as a word. The new information-processing capacity of the human brain is thus very limited. The capacity of the long-term memory is apparently infinite, but it takes seconds to store new information in that long-term memory. Our ability to absorb and process new information is therefore painfully slow, much slower than computers. However, our ability to recognise patterns in information and to extract new meaning from them is considerably greater than that of computers.

Humans are therefore compelled by their limited brain capacity for processing new information to simplify everything they observe; we are unable to know reality itself; all we can do is construct simplifications, that is, mental models of reality. What we discover and therefore what we choose and how we act, all depend upon the mental model we bring to the task. When we look at a particular situation, we see it through the lens provided by the mental models we have built up through past experience and education. We approach each situation every day with a mindset, a recipe we have acquired from the past, that we use to understand the present in order to design our actions to cope with it. When we find that we are taking actions that fail to have the desired result, we often find that the reason lies in the way we perceived the problem in the first place. The remedy is to amend the mental model, the perspective, the mind-set, the paradigm with which we are approaching the task.

The methods we use to store mental models and how we use what we have stored for subsequent discovery and choice have important implications. Research on cognitive ability shows that we do not normally store what we have previously observed and processed in any detailed form. We only store items and recall them in exact detail in exceptional circumstances, for example when we learn the lines of a play or prepare for certain kinds of examination. Normally we store and recall only some important category features of items we have observed. It is as if we label items according to the category they belong to, according to the strength of association they have with other similar items. We store schemas, frames or scenes and we particularly note exceptions. In other words, we store and recall according to degrees of similarity and irregularity, not according to the principles of sameness or regularity. The category features we use are rather vague and fuzzy. Mental models are sketchy, incomplete constructs used in a feedback way to affect what we discover next *(Baddeley, 1990)*. When we confront some situation we do not observe its complete detail. We select certain items and fill in others using our previously stored frames or scenes. Experiments have shown that we can be quite convinced that we have witnessed an event, even though it has not occurred, simply because that event normally occurred in a particular situation the experimenter now presents us with *(Baddeley, 1990)*.

These points about how we build partial, loose, flexible mental models based on similarities and irregularities in the patterns of events we observe, and then use them later partially to reconstruct what we then observe, are of great importance to our understanding of management. These points mean that managers will not simply observe a given environment and a given organisational capability – the facts. They, like all other humans, will sometimes inevitably invent what they observe. The whole process of simplifying and selecting means that the environment is in a real sense the invention and the creation of the managers observing it. It will then only be possible for managers to make sense of what they are doing after they have done it *(Weick, 1969/79)*. In highly complex and uncertain situations, then, explanations of strategic management need to take account of the possibility that environments may be invented or created in managers' minds and that they can often only make sense of what they are doing with hindsight.

Mental models

So far, a number of ways in which humans compensate for their limited brain-processing capacity have been referred to. We simplify complex reality by constructing mental models of that reality in which data are classified in loose, fuzzy categories. We store those models and use them later to understand the next situation and indeed to fill in some of the detail of the next situation. We do not always use algorithmic step-by-step reasoning, but sometimes make intuitive jumps. In this way we can handle far greater levels of complexity and uncertainty, as well as far faster rates of change, than a straight-forward use of our processing capacity would allow. But the consequence of this way of operating is that we may invent the reality around us. In some circumstances this may be a cost, while in others it may be the benefit of creativity.

In addition to all this there are two further means of great importance that we use to compensate for the limited capacity of the brain to process new information in a complex world. First, we automate our mental models, so speeding up the process of recall and application to a new situation. Second, we share those automated models with each other to cut down on the need to communicate before we act together.

Experts and unconscious mental models

A person would function very slowly if for every action that person had consciously to retrieve and examine large numbers of previously acquired mental models and then choose an appropriate one. Experts therefore push previously acquired models below the level of awareness into the unconscious mind. One aspect of learning is through repetition of an action in order to make the design of later similar actions an automatic process. The expert seems to use some form of recognisable pattern in a new situation automatically to trigger the use of past models developed in relation to analogous previous situations. Experts do not examine the whole body of their expertise when they confront a new situation. Instead they detect recognisable similarity in the qualitative patterns of what they observe and automatically produce models which they modify to meet the new circumstances.

For example, an expert chess player differs from a novice in terms of the richness of his or her mental store of patterns and relationships between the pieces on a chess board. On being confronted with some new juxtaposition of pieces, the expert perceives patterns missed by the novice. It is from these perceptions that the expert derives superiority. This conclusion is supported by the fact that the expert is no better than the novice in deciding what to do when the pieces have been set out randomly. It is not therefore that the expert has a better short-term memory or can process information faster. The expert's superiority arises because models of the moves appropriate to different patterns are stored in the expert's memory and drawn on as required through some form of analogous reasoning.

Analogy has been found to pervade thought. We use analogies to make the novel seem familiar by relating it to prior knowledge. We use analogies to make the familiar seem strange by viewing it from a new perspective. These are fundamental aspects of human intelligence used to construct new scientific theories, design experiments, and solve new problems in terms of old ones (*Gick & Holyoak, 1983*). Furthermore, paradox plays a crucial role in developing new insight.

One form of learning, then, is that which uses some form of repetition to push mental models into the unconscious where they can be recalled and used very rapidly. The richer the store of unconscious models the more expert the person. We can call this simple or single-loop learning. Each time we act we learn from the consequences of the action to improve the next action, without having consciously to retrieve and examine the unconscious models we are using to design the action.

But expert behaviour based on single-loop learning and unconscious mental models brings not only benefits; it carries with it significant dangers. The fact that the mental models being used to design actions are unconscious means that we are not questioning them. The more expert we are, the more rapidly we use unconscious models, and therefore the more easily we take for granted the assumptions and simplifications upon which they are inevitably built. This is highly efficient in stable circumstances but when those circumstances change rapidly it becomes highly dangerous – in other words, it is an appropriate way to learn in conditions close to certainty and agreement, but more and more dangerous the further we move away from certainty and agreement. Mental models used without question can rapidly become inappropriate in rapidly changing conditions. The possibility of skilled incompetence *(Argyris, 1990)* then arises. The more expert we are, the more skilled we are in designing certain actions, the greater the risk we run that we will not question what we are doing, the more we are likely to become skilled incompetents. This gives rise to the need for double-loop or complex learning. Here we learn not only in the sense of adjusting our actions in the light of their consequences, but in the sense also of questioning and adjusting the unconscious mental models we are using to design those actions in the first place.

Teams and shared models

Managers do not choose and act as isolated individuals. They interact with each other, choosing and acting in teams or groups. Simply by being part of a group, individuals learn to share the mental models they use to discover, choose and act. In this way they cut down on the communication and information flows that are required before they can act together. In particular, the more they share those implicit, expert models that have been pushed into the unconscious, the less they need to communicate in order to secure cohesive action. This sharing of implicit models is what we mean by the culture of the group or the organisation. Groups and organisations develop cultures, company

---

Key Concept 3.2

Mental models, feedback and skilled incompetence

Mental models are the simplifications that humans construct and store in their brains of the world they encounter. These models are the lenses through which we perceive the world we have to operate in, the constructions we make to explain how it and we are behaving, the structures we use to design our actions. These models are based on loose flexible categories of information, where categories appear to be defined in fuzzy terms of similarity and irregularity. In totally new situations, we use processes of analogous reasoning to construct new mental models using those already stored. Coping with the world can be seen as a continuing feedback from one set of models to another.

We automate our mental models by pushing them into the unconscious – this is the process of becoming an expert. Some models, the expert ones, are therefore implicit and hardly ever questioned while others are explicit and are more likely to be questioned. The latter are the explanations of what we are doing that we articulate. We share the expert unconscious models when we work together in a group. Automation and sharing lead to the strong possibility of expert incompetence and groupthink when conditions are changing rapidly. In the literature a number of words are used to mean much the same thing as mental models – paradigms, mindsets, frames of reference, company and industry recipes, schemas, scripts. Note that the culture of a group is its shared mental model.

and industry recipes or retained memories, as they perform together, in order to speed up their actions. This is exactly what Kuhn was referring to as the paradigm that governs the conduct of ordinary science (see the last section of this chapter).

Individuals who are part of any group are put under strong pressure by group processes to conform, that is, to share the mental models of the other members. While this may have great benefits in terms of efficient action in stable conditions, it becomes a serious liability when conditions are changing rapidly. It then becomes necessary to question the implicit, unconscious group models that are being used to design actions. As conditions change the unquestioned models may well become inappropriate. The powerful pressures that grow up within groups of experts to accept rather than question very fundamental values opens up the strong possibility of skilled incompetence in group behaviour, of groupthink. Once again, note how it is appropriate for managers to share mental models, that is, move close to agreement, when they are close to certainty, but not when they are far from certainty.

Espoused models and models in use

We overcome our very limited physical brain working capacity to produce unlimited mental capacity by simplifying and selecting, building models, automating those models by pushing them below the level of awareness, and learning to share them with others in our group. We use qualitative similarities and dissimilarities between one situation and another when we develop more appropriate models in new situations. Managers design their expert actions in this way, just as physicians and physicists do. The more expert an individual or a group the more actions are designed in ways determined by unconscious, implicit models. Because the assumptions underlying those models are not surfaced and questioned it is quite possible that experts will articulate one model while designing their actions according to another. There may well be a difference between espoused models and models in use *(Argyris and Schon, 1978)*. Experts are quite likely to say one thing and do another. The more expert people become in working together as a group the more prone they are to do this too. Ask managers what they do and most will say that they organise and plan. Observe what managers actually do and we see them dashing from one task to another in a manner which is not all that planned or organised. You will recall from Chapter 1 that it is this tendency to say one thing while doing another which makes it rather difficult to identify just what strategic management is.

When we recognise that there are frequent differences between what expert managers say they are doing and what they are actually doing, differences which they themselves are not usually aware of, we can see how easy it is for managers to play games and build organisational defences against facing up to what is really happening *(Argyris, 1990)*. For example, most managers espouse a rational model of action and believe that they should uncover the facts and consider a sensible range of options before they take action. Most espouse free and open discussions because that is a rational position to take. But at the same time there is a widespread norm in our organisations requiring subordinates to withhold the truth from their superiors, especially if they believe that the superior will find the truth unwelcome and accuse them of being negative. Games of deception and cover-up are therefore played. All know they are being played but none openly discuss what is happening, despite espousal of rational behaviour. We say one thing, do the direct opposite, and rarely find this strange. Add to this the existence of skilled incompetence and you can see how very difficult it will be to change these games and break down these defences. Attempts to explain how strategic management is actually carried out and attempts to prescribe how to do it better will be misleading and perhaps dangerous unless they explicitly recognise the existence of skilled incompetence, the difference between espoused models and models in use, and the behavioural dynamics these lead to. These are matters that we will deal with in more detail in Chapter 11. We turn now, however, to how mental models are used and changed, that is, the process of learning. It is important to distinguish between simple and complex learning and this distinction will form the basis of the two rather different categories of management already mentioned at the end of Chapter 2. This distinction between ordinary and extraordinary management will set the framework for the rest to this book.

Key Concept 3.3

Espoused models and models in use

Espoused mental models are those that we articulate and put forward to explain how we are behaving. Models in use are those mental models that actually drive our behaviour. The espoused modes are simple to identify – they are what people say they are. The models in use are difficult to identify – they have to be reconstructed from what people are actually doing. Since models in use are often going to be those that are being unconsciously used, the actor using them will also have difficulty in identifying them. Experts have considerable difficulty in articulating their models in use.

The difference in espoused models and models in use means that we may well say one thing and do another. This is not necessarily intentional hypocrisy, since we may well be unaware of our models in use which we will normally hardly ever question.

Simple and complex learning

The simple form of learning can be illustrated by the activity of reviewing a budget and taking corrective action. There is a monitoring, or discovery, step in which an actual profit outcome is compared with the desired outcome set in the budget. If actual is below budget, the reason is discovered, a choice of corrective action is made, and action is taken. That action affects profit in the next period as do external changes, leading to the need for the next round of discovery, choice and action. Managers involved in this single loop are controlling and they are also learning. They are discovering the consequences of their actions and amending their behaviour according to what they discover. This kind of learning is simple or single loop because managers are not questioning what they are doing in any fundamental sense. The budget, for example, is not questioned. Taking another example, General Motors thought that high fuel costs and therefore smaller cars were the key issues and Japanese competence in offering small cars the key reason for their success in the 1970s. General Motors' managers focused on this explanation, never questioning their assumptions. This kind of single-loop learning is depicted in *Figure 3.2*.

FIGURE 3.2
Simple single-loop learning

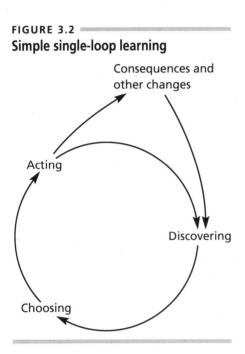

Now consider what these managers would do if they were to learn in a complex or double-loop way. When they analyse why profit is coming in below budget, that is, when they discover, they do so using their expertise, that is, the implicit unconscious mental models they have built up through past experience and have come to share through working together. They have a recipe on how their organisation and its industry or environment work. The reasons they produce to account for poor profit performance will be determined by these unconscious shared mental models. Consequently their choice and their action will also depend on these mental models. In the single-loop case they did not surface what the model was or question it; they simply used it. In double-loop complex learning they would, as part of the discovery stage, surface and question that model. They would be discovering not only what is changing outside and what the consequences of their actions are, but also what this all means for the unconscious models they are using, for their recipes and received wisdom. This simultaneous journey around two loops is depicted in *Figure 3.3*.

Complex learning, then, involves changing a mental model, a recipe, a mindset, a frame of reference, or a paradigm. It is a very difficult process to perform simply because we are trying to examine assumptions we are not normally even aware we are making. We will therefore keep slipping into single-loop learning because that is easier. But it is important to encourage double-loop learning since it is this that produces innovation. Kuhn (1970) has explained how most science is conducted within a

FIGURE 3.3
Complex double-loop learning

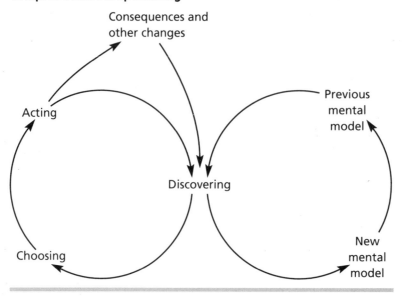

given paradigm that scientists rarely question –– a form of single-loop learning. Every now and then, however, increasing discrepancies between what a science is explaining and what is happening lead to paradigm shifts in which the world comes to be perceived in a different way – double-loop learning. Such shifts are associated with major new discoveries. One such shift is associated with the work of Newton and some believe that today is witnessing another such shift as the implications of complex system dynamics come to be understood. Managers who would innovate need constantly to be shifting, breaking and creating paradigms – they must engage in double-loop learning.

In this section we have seen how managing close to certainty and agreement is essentially a single-loop learning process, while managing far from certainty and agreement must take the form of double-loop learning if an organisation is to survive. However, to perform single-loop learning managers must sustain their existing shared mental models, but to perform double-loop learning they must question those models, destroying at least parts of them and replacing them with others. In a most fundamental way, therefore, management is a paradox, or contradiction, and before we proceed any further it is vital to understand the nature of paradox.

3.4   PARADOX AND HOW WE NORMALLY DEAL WITH IT

There are a number of different definitions of a paradox. First, it may mean an apparent contradiction, a state in which two apparently conflicting elements appear to be operating at the same time. Paradox in this sense can be removed or resolved: by

Key Concept 3.4

Simple and complex learning

Simple or single-loop learning is where we learn from the consequences of previous actions to amend the next action. It is a feedback process from action to consequence to subsequent action, without questioning the mental model driving the action.

Complex learning involves another feedback loop. It occurs when the consequences of actions lead to a questioning of the mental model, the underlying assumptions, that have been driving the actions. That questioning may lead to the amendment of the mental model, the reframing of the problem or opportunity, before action is amended. There is a double loop in which not only are actions amended, but the model driving the actions is too. Complex learning requires destruction – old ways of viewing the world have to be destroyed. Complex learning also involves creation – new ways of viewing the world have to be developed. Complex learning is the shifting, breaking and creating of paradigms.

- *Simple forms of organisational learning take the form of single negative feedback loops in which groups of people review and learn from the actions they have just undertaken.*
- *Simple forms of learning are conducted within a given paradigm and sustain the group learning in a state of stability, moving toward the realisation of a vision or the achievement of a goal.*
- *Complex learning is a double-loop phenomenon, partly the negative feedback learning about the consequences of actions, but also partly an amplifying, positive feedback loop of questioning the underlying assumptions.*
- *Complex learning is therefore essentially destabilising and revolutionary, but it is vitally necessary for innovation and creativity.*

choosing one element above the other all the time; or by reframing the problem to remove the apparent contradiction.

Second, it may mean a state in which two diametrically opposing forces are simultaneously present, neither of which can ever be removed. The choice is not therefore between one or the other, both must be accommodated, and this can be done only by continually rearranging them (*Quinn & Cameron, 1988*).

To see what paradox means return to *Figure 3.1*. You can look at that figure in a manner which involves switching your focus: one second you see the container and the next you see the people. Alternatively you could sustain both perceptions at the same time. This is somewhat harder to do, but if you succeed then you will tell a more complex tale of containers and people. Instead of your story being about *either* containers or people, it will be a more sophisticated tale about *both* containers *and* people. If you can sustain contradictory notions you will be capable of working with sophisticated both/and perceptions as opposed to simple either/or ones (*Weick, 1969/79*).

When it comes to a world that is much more complex than Figure 3.1, the world or organisational strategy, it becomes much more difficult to switch focus from one paradigm to another and even more difficult to see your world in two different ways at once. But if you succeed in this, then you will develop a much more complex understanding and practice of strategy: one that is not the simple either/or choice between stability and instability; one that is instead a sophisticated both/and choice combining stability and instability in appropriate and creative ways.

This is a matter of major importance for Western managers. Western culture, Western scientific traditions and forms of education have strongly encouraged the either/ or way of thinking. The major competitors in the Far East, however, are far more accustomed to both/and thinking, to paradoxes and dilemmas (*Pascale, 1990; Hampden-Turner, 1990*). If Western managers are to compete they will have to learn to see the world of organisations in this more sophisticated both/and way.

Key Concept 3.5

Paradox

As it is used in this book, the word paradox means the presence together at the same time of self-contradictory, essentially conflicting forces, none of which can be removed. The word is not used in the sense of a dilemma, that being a situation where a choice must be made between two equally undesirable possibilities. Dilemmas are solved by making an either/or choice. Paradoxes are resolved or orchestrated by making both/and choices. A state of contention is thus the consequence of a paradox in a human system. Contention is positively expressed as dialogue around the paradoxical forces and negatively expressed as unresolvable conflict. Paradoxes are mutually exclusive and simultaneously present, for example the requirement that control systems should be loose–tight. Neither side can win and the result is creative tension. Creative people wrestle with the irreconcilable until they discover a new frame of reference and only then is the creative tension released. Pascale (1990, p. 110) puts it thus:

> *Paradox has had a pervasive role in creative activities of all types. One pioneering investigation into the essence of creativity studied the milestone contributions of fifty eight famous scientists and artists, including Einstein, Picasso, and Mozart. They shared a common pattern: all breakthroughs occurred 'when two or more opposites were conceived simultaneously, existing side by side – as equally valid, operative and true.' The research report continues: 'In apparent defiance of logic or physical possibility, the creative person consciously embraced antithetical elements and developed these into integrated entities and creations.'*

A paradox forces people to think outside the current paradigm, to transcend the contradiction and see things in a new way (Rothenburg, 1979).

Organisations are paradoxical

Any human organisation is quite clearly paradoxical for the following reasons.

In even the simplest human system we find it necessary for efficiency reasons to divide up the tasks that need to be done. We develop specialisations. But as soon as we do that we create the problem of integrating the divided tasks back into a whole again; we create the problem of control. There is no choice between *either* task division *or* task integration. We have to choose *both* task division *and* task integration if we are to succeed. Paradoxes require both/and choices; either/or choices are not possible.

Each individual in an organisation has a paradoxical desire for freedom and the excitement that goes with chance and uncertainty, while at the same time fearing the unknown and wanting order and discipline. This is the paradoxical human need to fuse into a group and yet remain an individual. There are many other examples of such paradoxes. Businesses have to produce at the lowest cost, but they have to increase costs to provide quality. Organisations have to control what their employees do, but they have to give them freedom if they want to retain them and if they want them to deal with rapidly changing circumstances. All of these examples require both/and rather than either/or choices.

Today's conventional wisdom emphasises either/or choices. It prescribes either stability and success, or instability and failure. It usually does not recognise paradox as fundamental and, when it does, it prescribes some kind of harmonious, equilibrium balance between the paradoxical forces. In this way the paradox is in effect removed; its existence is a nuisance that is not fundamental to success. We normally deal with paradox by seeking to remove it, to find the solution so as to reach equilibrium.

The way we perceive paradox says much about the way we understand organisational dynamics. The idea that paradoxes must be resolved, and the tension they cause must be released if we are to be successful, is part of the paradigm that equates success with the dynamics of stability, regularity and predictability. The notion that paradoxes can never be resolved, only endlessly rearranged, leads to a view of organisational dynamics couched in terms of continuing tension-generating behaviour patterns that are irregular, unstable and unpredictable, but lead to creative novelty.

According to Pascale, successful organisations are characterised by a paradox that is not resolved, but continually rearranged. On the one hand, he argues, organisations have to achieve *fit*. By fit, Pascale means a state of coherence, centralisation, tight central control, synergy and fit between the 7Ss (see the section on configuration in Chapter 5) of the organisation. But successful organisations also require *split*. By split, Pascale means breaking apart, decentralising, differentiating, variety and rivalry. They require split because without it they cannot develop new perspectives and innovative actions. Developing new perspectives means shattering old paradigms and changing old structures – creativity requires destruction. The need for an organisation simultaneously to display fit and split creates tension. But this is creative tension that provokes inquiry and questioning. It is this tension that leads to the learning organisation with its continual dialogue between contradicting points of view. Pascale stresses the importance of dialogue as opposed to argument.

Key Concept 3.6

Dialectics and dialogue

The word dialectic describes the process through which paradoxes are arranged, or orchestrated, to yield a transcending new configuration. It is a process characterised by constructive tension. For example, in an organisation it is necessary to concentrate power in order to operate efficiently. It is simultaneously necessary to distribute power in order to cope with high levels of uncertainty in a rapidly changing environment. Making an either/or choice will not do – it will sacrifice either efficiency or flexibility and we need both. An effective organisation may continually cope with the paradox through shifting patterns of power concentrated for some purposes at some times and dispersed for other purposes at other times. This would be a dialectic process. Note that this resolution through a shifting pattern is not a solution; it throws up its own problems of continuing contention that need to be resolved, so that there is never a solution.

Dialogue is where two parties exchange views about paradoxical situations, each having the intention of modifying their position in the light of the views and evidence presented by the other. Each participant is open to being influenced by the other. Argument is simply stating positions without any intention of moving. Dialogue is thus the required process for dialectics.

Note the connection between the concepts of paradox, contention, creative tension, dialectics and dialogue.

Tension leads to what Pascale calls *contend* (see *Illustration 3.2*), the positive use of tension and conflict to create and generate new perspectives. Through this clash of opposites the organisation *transcends* to a new constellation of fit and split. This view of organisational development is a dialectical one (see *Key Concept 3.6*) in which opposites produce, through learning, a new synthesis consisting of more complex forms of strategy and structure. Organisations use fit and split at the same time to produce sudden jumps to new positions and postures. Pascale stresses the need to orchestrate rather than balance, to preserve the tension rather than move to stable equilibrium. The choices facing an organisation are both/and, not either/or. It is necessary to avoid the extremes of split and fit because they lead to excess and failure. Instead organisations have to use both ends of the fit/split spectrum at once.

Another point made by Pascale is that organisations fail because they are not good at perceiving weak signals from the environment. The concern here is that many of the most important changes start off in a small, almost unnoticeable way. Those small changes can escalate to have major consequences for the organisation. So it becomes a matter of importance to pay attention to small changes and the weak signals they send, before the organisation is engulfed by major consequences (see Chapter 8).

Illustration
3.2

The vectors of contention

Pascale (1990) puts forward seven contentions (based on the 7S framework) that lead to the disequilibrium and creative tension that prompts inquiry. Inquiry and dialogue lead to the new. The seven contentions are:

- planned versus opportunistic strategy
- elitist versus pluralist structures
- mandatory versus discretionary systems
- managerial versus transformational style
- individuality versus collegiality in the treatment of staff
- hard minds versus soft hearts in terms of shared values
- maximise (making more efficient, earning more profit from doing the same thing better) versus 'meta-mise' (transforming the problem or opportunity into the creatively new). ∎

3.5 ORDINARY AND EXTRAORDINARY MANAGEMENT

We are now in a position to pull together the concepts of paradigm/mental model, simple/complex learning, paradox, dialogue and dialectics into two qualitatively different concepts of management – the ordinary and the extraordinary. It should always be remembered, however, that these are concepts to aid the understanding of practice. In actual practice they are intimately intertwined with each other and we would not normally draw this distinction as we act.

You will recall that normal science is practised when a community of scientists strongly share a common paradigm. But as they practise that normal science within the shared paradigm, anomalies build up and lead to the destruction of the paradigm and its replacement by another – a scientific revolution occurs. Very much the same distinction seems to apply to the manner in which organisations develop strategically – organisations require both what we might call ordinary and extraordinary management.

The normal day-to-day conduct of the existing activities of an organisation, together with the implementation of strategies that build on its existing strengths, is always carried out according to some paradigm that most within the organisation share. The circle at the centre of *Figure 3.4* depicts the organisational paradigm governing the shared perceptions that managers have of their task at any one time. That paradigm sets the agenda for the normal conduct of the organisation's activities and it is embodied in the:

- hierarchical reporting structure of the organisation;
- roles people take up within that structure;
- modes of decision-making they employ;
- forms of control they practise and the systems they use to control;
- culture, as well as the leadership and management styles they adhere to;
- kinds of ideology and forms of persuasion they use;

- way 'missions' and 'visions' are stated;
- rules of the competitive game they attach the most importance to.

The paradigm and its principal embodiments taken together lead almost inevitably to particular objectives, to particular conceptions of competitive advantage, and therefore to particular strategies. The ordinary management task is to solve the puzzle of how to implement the strategies and reach the objectives defined by the paradigm. Ordinary management (see *Key Concept 3.7*) is simply going around the negative, damping feedback loop to the right of the circle representing the paradigm in Figure 3.4.

FIGURE 3.4
Ordinary and extraordinary management

The paradigm, however, is a particular arrangement at a particular point in time of many paradoxes: division versus integration; preserving the status quo versus destroying it and creating the new; low cost versus high quality; and many more (*Hampden-Turner, 1990; Quinn & Cameron, 1988; Kets de Vries, 1980*). The paradigm is an arrangement of contradictory states that most managers in an organisation agree, perhaps only unconsciously, to be useful at a particular point in time. However, the effective practice of ordinary management inevitably uncovers anomalies, challenges

Key Concept 3.7

Ordinary management

Ordinary management is practised when most of the managers in an organisation share the same mental models or paradigm. Cognitive feedback loops then operate in a negative feedback manner so that shared mental models are not questioned. Choices are made according to some approximation to technically rational criteria, and this is possible because there is agreement on what the business is all about and what kind of environment it is having to cope with. Also, control is practised in its planning/monitoring and ideological forms through the instrument of hierarchy and bureaucracy. Ordinary management is about rational processes to secure harmony, fit, or convergence to a configuration, and it proceeds in an incremental manner. Ordinary management can only be practised in closed or contained change situations, and indeed it must be practised in such situations if an organisation is to be able to deliver competitive advantage.

to the current paradigm, that open up the paradox once more. This is inevitable because any given arrangement of paradoxes, of contradictory forces, must by definition be unstable. Once the nature of the paradox is reopened, the obvious contradiction leads to conflict and to pressure for a new synthesis, for a new arrangement of the contradictory forces, for a new paradigm. This paradigm-breaking is the extraordinary management depicted in *Figure 3.4* as the loop to the left of the paradigm circle; the connection with Kuhn's ideas is clear.

The important point is that this extraordinary management is not some separate form of management: it is provoked by and in turn governs ordinary management. In *Figure 3.4* an arrow connects the solving of current puzzles with the raising of anomalies. The very activity of the day-to-day running of the existing business throws up anomalies that undermine the paradigm. The more effectively managers run their existing business, the more they uncover what is not working as well as it might. This uncovering of possibilities for improvement undermines the existing received wisdom. The cutting edge of strategic management is this frame-breaking extraordinary management and it flows from and determines the ordinary day-to-day repetitive management of the existing business, the continuing strategy of building on existing strengths. *Illustration 3.3* provides an example of this intertwining of ordinary and extraordinary management. Furthermore, ordinary and extraordinary management require completely different decision-making modes and control forms, matters we have already discussed, and also completely different institutional and behavioural frameworks through which those decision-making modes and control forms must be applied, matters we go on to discuss in the next two chapters. Finally, it must be stressed that we cannot choose to practise either ordinary or extraordinary management – we have to practise both at the same time.

Extraordinary management

Extraordinary management involves questioning and shattering paradigms, and then creating new ones. It is a process which depends critically upon contradiction and tension. Because it is outside the rules of an existing paradigm, because no-one can know what new paradigms will be shared, because no-one knows what the outcomes will be, rational analysis and argument cannot play much part in the developing of a new paradigm. Instead, frame-breaking extraordinary management is a process of persuasion and conversion, requiring the contributions of champions. It is not about consistency or harmony, rather it is destabilising and irregular. Paradigms cannot be changed incrementally. Instead, after long periods of grappling with anomaly, we seem to reach new paradigms in a sudden flash. The changing of paradigms is a revolutionary rather than an evolutionary process. Furthermore, paradigm changes cannot be organisationally intended. Those holding an existing paradigm do not decide in advance to find a new one. Indeed they resist the new one when it is first mooted. Consequently new paradigms have to emerge from the confusion created by anomalies and the contradiction of the existing paradigm. Ordinary incremental management with competitive trial-and-error experiments is bound to uncover anomalies and so lead to crisis and revolution. That revolution need not, however, be on a grand scale. Any small change in an organisation that requires groups of people to change their mental models qualifies as a revolution in the sense the word is being used here. Such revolutions are probably more prevalent than we might at first imagine.

Extraordinary management, then, is the use of intuitive, political, group learning modes of decision-making and self-organising forms of control in open-ended change situations. It is the form of management that managers must use if they are to change strategic direction and innovate.

3.6   INCREMENTAL AND REVOLUTIONARY CHANGE

The last section has argued that those communities of people which we call organisations evolve in essentially the same manner as those communities of people which we call scientists. Both utilise ordinary processes of operating within a given paradigm and both utilise extraordinary processes to change that paradigm. In other words, both communities of people employ both single- and double-loop learning and there is nothing at all surprising about this. It is also not a surprise, therefore, to discover that organisations evolve in both an incremental and a revolutionary way, just as *Kuhn (1970)* demonstrates that sciences do. In the management literature there has been a debate about whether organisations typically act strategically in a gradual incremental manner, converging in an evolutionary way on some state adapted to the environment, or whether strategic actions occur as sharp frame-breaking revolutions. From

Illustration
3.3

Foster Brothers

Johnson (1987) carried out a study of decision-making at the men's clothing retail chain, Foster Brothers, over a number of years in the 1980s. This company operated at the bottom end of the men's clothing market and its managers shared a number of unquestioned beliefs about the nature of their business: they assumed that competitive advantage flowed from high volumes of sales and low costs to be secured by sourcing in the Far East. Shops were seen as places to dispose of merchandise as quickly as possible and there was little in the way of marketing concepts. Then during the 1980s the company ran into difficulties and experienced declining profits. Some managers pushed for a move up market, a move that would require the company to focus on 'fashion'. Johnson describes how new people were brought in to create the necessary changes, but they never lasted long. Market research reports were re-interpreted so that they supported the shared beliefs that managers were having great difficulty in changing. When more managers did recognise the need to move up into the more fashionable segments, they tried to do so in a way clearly determined by their paradigm. They copied fashion items and had them made cheaply in the Far East, and then distributed them through low-cost channels, shops that paid little attention to ambience. Managers could not abandon ways of thinking that were driven by merchandise concepts and buying-driven responses, instead of design and customer satisfaction considerations. Johnson describes how the structure of the organisation, its culture and the decision-making processes managers used, their avoidance of challenging each other, all helped to perpetuate the paradigm. Eventually the company was acquired by a bigger stores group. ■

the perspective we have developed in this chapter we can now see that this question is not an 'either/or' one but a 'both/and' one.

Incremental strategic change

Based on his study of ten large corporations, *Quinn (1980)* identified a pattern of strategic change which he called logical incrementalism – we have already discussed this in Chapter 2, Section 2.5. Here managers have an intended destination for their organisation, but they discover how to reach it by taking logically connected decisions step by step. They do not make major changes but build incrementally in a consistent manner on what they already have. They sense the changes in their environment and gradually adapt to those changes so maintaining a continuing dynamic equilibrium with their environment. This pattern can be illustrated as in *Figure 3.5*.

Revolutionary frame-breaking strategic change

Other studies however, particularly those by *Mintzberg (1989), Miller & Friesen (1980), Greiner (1972), Johnson (1987)* and *Tushman & Romanelli (1985)*, have identified a different pattern of change. Here managers resist changes that conflict with their predominant way of understanding their organisation and its environment, until some crisis makes it impossible to continue doing so. We therefore get patterns of

FIGURE 3.5
Incremental change

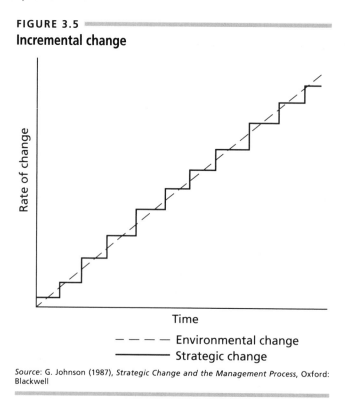

Source: G. Johnson (1987), *Strategic Change and the Management Process*, Oxford: Blackwell

strategic change in which an organisation is driven down the same path by its own momentum, becoming more and more out of line with its environment. This gives rise to strategic drift. In other words, managers and members of such organisations are caught in simple, single-loop learning – they are trapped in their own paradigm and the exclusive practice of ordinary management. When that drift has taken an organisation too far from its environment, it then makes sudden revolutionary adjustments. These inevitably involve breaking the old frames its managers were working within and establishing new ones. In other words, managers and members of such organisations are provoked into the extraordinary processes of double-loop learning that produce revolutionary change. This idea of momentum, drift and revolutionary change is illustrated in *Figure 3.6*.

Greiner's development model

Greiner (1972) presents a model of the typical pattern of development experienced by all companies (see *Figure 3.7*). He holds that all companies must pass through a number of stages if they are to sustain acceptable levels of performance. He describes five phases of growth that are punctuated by crises. In order to make the necessary move from one phase of growth to another, an organisation must pass through a crisis. These phases and their related crises are as follows:

● *Growth through creativity*. In the early stages of its life, when it has simple structures and is small, a company grows through the creative activity of small

FIGURE 3.6

Strategic drift and revolutionary change

Source: G. Johnson (1987), *Strategic Change and the Management Process*, Oxford: Blackwell

close-knit teams. At some point, however, they face the crisis of leadership. As the company increases in size it can no longer be managed in highly personal, informal ways.

● *Growth through direction*. If the leadership crisis is successfully resolved through 'professionalising' the management, specialising its functions and setting up more formal systems, the company proceeds to grow in a centrally directed way. This leads to the crisis of autonomy. As the organisation gets bigger and bigger, employees feel restricted by the hierarchy and the top finds it more and more difficult to maintain detailed control.

● *Growth through delegation*. If the autonomy crisis is successfully resolved through changing formal structures and decentralising, then growth proceeds through delegation. This brings with it a crisis of control. The top feels it is losing control and parochial attitudes develop in the divisions of the company.

● *Growth through coordination*. If the control crisis is successfully resolved through installing systems to bring about greater coordination and cooperation, then the growth of the company proceeds. As it grows larger and more complex it is brought to the crisis of red tape. Increasingly bureaucratic controls create sharp divisions between head office staffs and operating divisions.

● *Growth through collaboration*. Here the crisis of red tape is resolved through strong interpersonal collaboration and control through cultural sharing rather than formal controls. Greiner thinks that this growth stage may lead to a crisis of psychological saturation in which all become exhausted by teamwork. He thinks there may be a sixth growth phase involving a dual organisation: a 'habit' structure for daily work routines and a 'reflective' structure for stimulating new perspectives and personal enrichment.

FIGURE 3.7

Greiner's model of strategic change

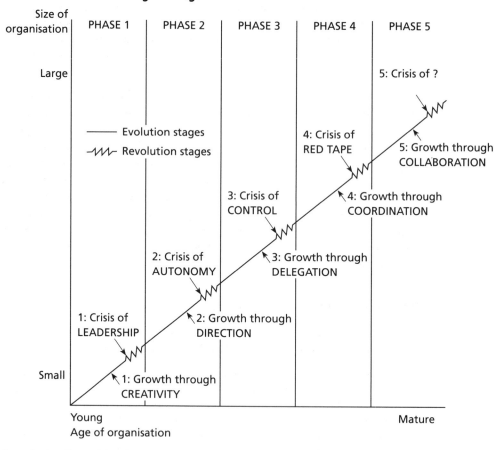

Source: Reprinted by permission of *Harvard Business Review*. An exhibit from 'Evolution and revolution as organizations grow' by L. E. Greiner (July–August 1972). Copyright © 1972 by the President and Fellows of Harvard College. All rights reserved.

We have then two different views about the time path of successful change in an organisation. It is not necessary to claim that either one or the other reflects reality – the ordinary/extraordinary framework we are using here to think about these matters allows us to put them into perspective.

3.7 THE DANGERS OF PRACTISING ONE FORM OF MANAGEMENT ONLY

Mintzberg (1989, p. 97) points out how organisations are rarely simply one thing or another:

We all know the small aggressive entrepreneurial firm, the perfectly machine-like Swiss hotel, the diversified conglomerate, the professional collegial university, the freewheeling intrapreneurial Silicon Valley innovator. But some organisations do not fit, . . and even many that seem to, on closer examination reveal curious anomalies. It is difficult to to imagine a more machine-like organization than McDonald's; why then does it seem to be rather innovative, at least in its own context? And why is it that whenever I mention to an executive group about a 3M or a Hewlett Packard as innovative in form, someone from the audience leaps up to tell me about their tight control systems. Innovative adhocracies are not supposed to rely on tight controls.

It is the consideration of anomalies such as these that demonstrate how organisations do not simply operate with the harmony and consistency of ordinary management, but also with the contradiction and instability of extraordinary management.

Mintzberg (1989), Miller (1990) and *Pascale (1990)* all make the point, backed by empirical research, that the harmony, consistency and fit achieved by a firm that reaches a viable configuration are at one and the same time its strength and its downfall. The tendency is for companies in this position to concentrate on doing better that which they already do well. Their strategies become ones of repetition and excess. Or, in another sense, they become over-adapted to their environment and, when that environment changes, they have great difficulty in changing – the point about strategic drift again.

Trapped in ordinary management

Miller (1990, p. 3) puts it like this. He has researched a number of companies to look for the reasons for failure and finds these in the Icarus paradox.

> The fabled Icarus of Greek mythology is said to have flown so high, so close to the sun, that his artificial wax wings melted and he plunged into the Aegean sea. The power of Icarus's wings gave rise to the abandon that doomed him. The paradox, of course, is that his greatest asset led to his demise. And that same paradox applies to many outstanding companies today: their victories and their strengths often seduce them into excesses that cause their downfall. Success leads to specialization and exaggeration, to confidence and complacency, to dogma and ritual.

Miller detects four trajectories, patterns in action, through which organisations extend and amplify the strategies, policies, attitudes and events that led to their success in the first place:

- The focusing trajectory that take Craftsmen organisations (those with strong engineering and tight operational controls as their major sources of competitive advantage) and turns them into Tinkerers (insular firms whose technocratic culture alienates customers with perfect but irrelevant offerings). By focusing on their quality or cost leadership strategies, their engineering and operational strengths, these companies come to ignore their customers. Periods in the history of Digital, Disney, Caterpillar and Texas Instruments illustrate this path.
- The venturing trajectory converts entrepreneurial Builders (high-growth companies managed by imaginative leaders and creative planning staffs) into Imperialists (companies overtaxing their resources by expanding too rapidly into businesses they know little about). Examples here are provided by ITT, Litton Industries, Gulf and Western, Dome Petroleum.

- The inventing trajectory along which Pioneers (companies with excellent R&D departments, flexible think tank operations, and state of the art products) move to become Escapists (run by cults of scientists who squander resources in the pursuit of grandiose futuristic inventions). Examples here are Federal Express, Wang, Apple, Rolls Royce and Polaroid.
- The decoupling trajectory which transforms Salesmen (companies with developed marketing skills, broad markets and prominent brand names) into Drifters (companies whose sales fetish obscures design issues and who become aimless and bureaucratic producing me-too offerings). Examples here are Procter & Gamble, General Motors and IBM.

Miller makes the point that outstanding organisations are characterised by consistency and harmony – the parts fit together and they constitute typical configurations called builders, craftsman, pioneers and salesmen. Organisations keep extending the central theme of their configuration. They keep building upon, reinforcing and modifying what has made them successful. They do this because of the mental models with which they design their actions and because of the decision-making processes they use. The result of this ordinary management is a momentum for the organisation that suppresses variations and pushes it down typical trajectories that lead to disaster. Momentum is the result of amplifying existing strengths and it leads to a vicious circle of excess. What Miller describes is an example of an amplifying feedback process, that is, a self-reinforcing pattern of circular behaviour that can become either virtuous or vicious. These are important ideas that we will develop later in Chapter 9.

3.8 SUMMARY

This chapter has drawn a crucial distinction between ordinary and extraordinary management that will form the basis of our discussion throughout the rest of this book – see *Figure 3.8.*

Ordinary management is the use of negative feedback processes in an organisation to realise intentions and thus sustain the status quo. It is the form to practise close to certainty and agreement, but it is impossible to practise it far from certainty and agreement. It is single-loop learning, the practice of planning, as well as visionary and ideological forms of decision-making and control. It produces incremental change to realise prior shared intention and improves the efficiency of an organisation. It makes an organisation better and better at what it already does well. Ordinary management consists of the processes applied in what we will call the legitimate system of an organisation, that is, the hierarchy, bureaucracy and officially approved ideology.

Extraordinary management processes are used where it is impossible to apply ordinary management. Extraordinary management is organisational double-loop learning, a process that employs positive feedback to amplify disturbances to the status quo through an organisation so as to produce emergent new strategic directions and change of a revolutionary kind. It changes ways of thinking about what an organisation is doing and is thus the basis of creativity and innovation. Extraordinary management is practised in what we will later define as the shadow system of an organisation, the informal social networks and learning communities that people spontaneously spin amongst themselves in a self-organising manner.

FIGURE 3.8
Learning in context

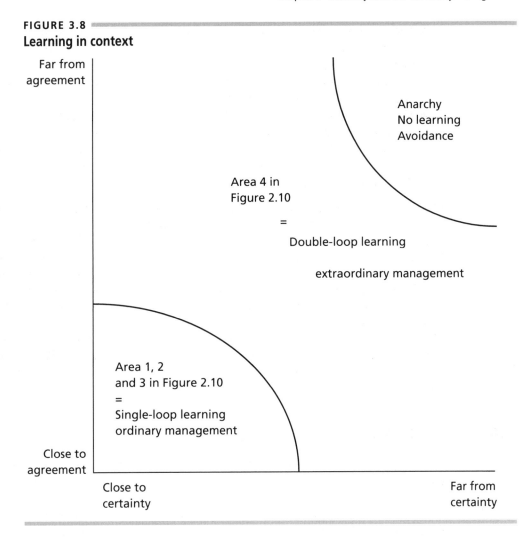

Finally we saw the dangers of applying ordinary management in all situations – the result of employing ordinary management processes in situations far from certainty is to trap an organisation in stability where it is incapable of significant change and thus prey to more imaginative competitors.

However, if an organisation practises ordinary management in an incompetent manner, perhaps channelling most of the energy into extraordinary processes it may display erratic bursts of creativity, but it will fall down on the efficient delivery of its products or services. This too will cause an organisation to fail. Survival, then, requires the simultaneous practice of two contradictory forms of management – a basic paradox of organisational life.

In the next part of this book we are going to survey the nature and processes of ordinary management, and then we are going to reflect upon the dynamics of organisations as systems and what insight this gives us into the nature, particularly, of extraordinary management.

Further reading

It is well worth reading Kuhn (1970), the classic work on paradigms and scientific revolutions. Hampden-Turner (1990) provides an interesting account of how organisations deal with paradoxes and Quinn & Cameron (1988) explore the theoretical issues. It is also well worth reading Pascale (1990) and Miller (1990).

References

Argyris, C. & Schon, D. (1978), *Organizational Learning: A Theory of Action Perspective*, Reading, Ma.: Addision-Wesley.

Argyris, C. 1990, *Overcoming Organizational Defenses: Facilitating Organizational Learning*, Boston: Allyn & Bacon, Prentice-Hall.

Baddeley, A. (1990), *Human Memory: Theory and Practice*, Hove, Sussex: Lawrence Earlbaum Associates.

Gick, M. L. & Holyoak, K. J. (1983), Schema introduction and analogical transfer, *Cognitive Psychology*, vol. 15, pp. 1–38.

Greiner, L. E. (1972), Evolution and revolution as organizations grow, *Harvard Business Review*, July–August.

Hampden-Turner, C. (1990), *Charting the Corporate Mind*, New York: Free Press, Macmillan.

Johnson, G. (1987), *Strategic Change and the Management Process*, Oxford: Blackwell.

Kets de Vries, M. F. R. (1980), *Organizational Paradoxes: Clinical Approaches to Management*, London: Tavistock Publications.

Kuhn, T. S. (1970), *The Structure of Scientific Revolutions*, University of Chicago Press.

Miller, D. & Friesen, P. H. (1980), Momentum and revolution in organizational adaptation, *Academy of Management Journal*, vol. 23, pp. 591–614.

Miller, D. (1990), *The Icarus Paradox: How Excellent Organizations Can Bring About Their Own Downfall*, New York: Harper Business.

Mintzberg. H. (1989), *Mintzberg on Management: Inside Our Strange World of Organisations*, New York: The Free Press.

Pascale, R. T. (1990), *Managing on the Edge: How Successful Companies Use Conflict to Stay Ahead*, London: Viking Penguin.

Quinn, J. B. (1980), *Strategic Change: Logical Incrementalism*, Homewood, Ill.: Richard D. Irwin.

Quinn, R. E. & Cameron, K. S. (1988), *Paradox and Transformation*, New York: Ballinger/Harper & Row.

Rothenburg, D. (1979), *The Emerging Goddess*, Chicago: University of Chicago Press.

Tushman, M. L. & Romanelli, E. (1985), A metamorphosis model of convergence and reorientation, in Straw, B. & Cummings, E. (Eds.), (1985), *Research in Organizational Behavior*, vol. 7, Greenwich, Conn.: JAI Press.

Weick, K. (1969/1979), *The Social Psychology of Organizing*, Reading, Ma.: Addison-Wesley.

Enigma Chemicals (B)

Case Study 9, Enigma Chemicals (A), gives more information on the company but, for the purpose of this Case Study, it is enough to know that Enigma is a rather bureaucratically managed company that has recently moved from a highly centralised functional structure to a more decentralised, divisionalised structure in which the divisions are responsible for profit. This case is concerned specifically with the performance appraisal system that was used for judging people's performance, informing them of what that judgement was and then rewarding them accordingly. The system was also used to design people's training and development needs, as well as to plan their career progression. It was a tool that some found useful in planning management succession.

Before the reorganisation there was a large central personnel function that had unilaterally designed all the personnel systems, including the annual performance-appraisal procedure, and then negotiated their acceptance by the Unions. After the reorganisation many of the personnel staff had been transferred to the divisions and there was now a much smaller Central Personnel function. Managers of this new Central Personnel department believed that the appraisal procedure provided valid data of a detailed kind on managers and staff alike and that this information was particularly vital for top corporate managers to carry out their tasks of planning management succession. One of the personnel managers said, 'Regular updating of information of this kind enables the Chief Executive to plan management succession and move senior managers around for the good of the corporation as a whole. Any change in the system should therefore be small and gradually implemented after careful consultation and negotiation with the Unions.' Central Personnel feared that any major change to the procedure would lead to divisional empire building and to the hoarding of managerial talent at the expense of the corporation as a whole.

A group of divisional managing directors and their personnel managers, however, believed that the

annual appraisal procedure took too long and the forms that had to be completed were too complex and laborious. They argued that the procedure generated a great amount of detailed information that no one wanted or used. They were therefore pressing for a much simpler form and a much less laborious procedure. More specifically, they argued that each division should be free to develop its own procedure subject only to providing certain clearly specified pieces of information that were needed by corporate management. They felt that Central Personnel was trying to hang on to as much of its former power as it could. They argued that substantial change was required and that the divisions needed to develop their own appraisal systems if they really were to manage their own businesses. Furthermore, they maintained that the appraisal system was a matter for managers and that there was no need at all to negotiate its form with the Unions.

This debate between the centre and the operating activities had been going on for years, even before the reorganisation into divisions had occurred. The centre had, from time to time, responded by altering the appraisal form, but there had been little real change. Now, with increased operating activity power through the divisionalised structures, the whole matter was opened up again. The Central Personnel activity also saw quite clearly that some changes would have to be made now that the divisions had increased responsibility.

Both sides to the dispute agreed that the appraisal system was an issue that had to be attended to. Therefore, a committee including representatives of Central Personnel and divisional management was formed to make recommendations to top management on the appraisal system. Before the first meeting, consultants interviewed the representatives from the centre and from the divisions.

In the interviews, the divisional representatives were fairly unanimous in maintaining that Central Personnel were:

- old fashioned bureaucrats unable to adapt to the changing world. They were incapable of understanding modern commercial pressures;
- well meaning people, but they were blind to their own faults and the foolishness of the policy they were trying to preserve. They were really trying to hang on to their own power; and
- seeing divisional managers as potential robber barons. One divisional manager said, 'They believe that if you let the divisional barons loose, those barons will destroy the synergy and corporate identity they [Central Personnel] have worked all their lives to uphold and those barons will destroy the relationship they [Central Personnel] have built up with the Unions over many years.'

The consultants also interviewed the Central Personnel representatives on the Committee. The central staff believed that:

- there was a need to review the procedures but it must be done gradually and in negotiation with the Unions;
- the divisions were overreacting to problems with the present procedure. 'If we are not careful we will undermine the relationship with the Unions and divisional warfare for the best managers will break out. Also we will be undermining the standards of objectivity, rationality and fairness that the present system embodies. They [the divisional managers] will destroy the identity of the corporation'; and that
- the divisions were well-intentioned but they simply did not understand the power of the Unions and the importance of synergy. They were taking the position they took simply because they wanted to grab power. 'And the divisions see us as hopeless bureaucrats who do not understand commercial realities.'

At the first meeting of the Performance Appraisal Procedure Review Committee, divisional representatives proposed that the Committee would proceed faster if it established a working party consisting of lower-level experts to draft new performance appraisal forms. In their presentation to back up this proposal, they kept repeating that although any new appraisal form would certainly not solve all the problems, it would be a step forward. But this step would simply build in a modest way on what was already being done. They said that it would be experimental and it would not threaten anyone. It would certainly not affect the ability to move staff from one division to another. All were in favour of synergy and the use of all senior managers as a corporate resource, not simply a resource for a division, but they did point out how the information generated by the appraisal procedure was used to move staff away from a division to the detriment of that division. There had to be some balance, they said, between the power of the centre to move people about and the power of the division to retain key managers. They recommended that this topic undergo further study and a task force be set up to look at it.

The Central Personnel representatives repeatedly stated how much they supported the ideas of moving carefully and experimentally and trying to make better that which already existed. (The personnel representatives later told the consultant that they saw their approach of selectively agreeing with the divisions as a means of holding them down to gradual change only.) Central representatives also agreed that there was room for improvement but emphasised the importance of regarding senior managers as a group constituting the most important corporate resource. They emphasised the importance of the Unions. They said they would themselves already have made improvements in the procedures but they were overloaded with work due to the reorganisation.

From time to time a central representative made an impassioned plea that they avoid the dangers of disintegration of the corporation; or a divisional representative said that it would be quite impossible to achieve corporate goals unless the procedure was changed. Such pleas were received in embarrassed silence by the other members of the committee until someone introduced a new topic for discussion.

After a number of meetings that continued in much the same fashion, an outline of a new appraisal form was eventually agreed upon and presented to a joint meeting of top corporate managers and Union leaders with the recommendation that it be a guide to divisions but that it should not be imposed upon them. After some argument, the top managers and the Unions agreed that they would appoint a permanent Appraisal Committee with representatives of management and Unions to put 'flesh on the bones' of the form recommended to them and also to administer the new appraisal procedure, and in particular administer any departures from the norm that a specific division might propose. They also set guidelines for this new permanent committee. It had to be fair and objective and provide enough information to enable top managers to plan management succession, but the committee was to avoid costly changes. The meeting ended with a buffet lunch, wine and feelings of cooperation. There was a common feeling that progress had been made.

Green Holdings Ltd

In January 1988, Charles Green, Chairman and majority shareholder of Green Holdings Ltd, appointed consultants to advise him on how to deal with the problems facing his business. Green Holdings Ltd operates as an agricultural merchant, grain trader, seed and fertiliser producer predominantly in Worcestershire and Lincolnshire. The significant profits of the early 1980s had turned into a breakeven position in the financial year June 1986 to May 1987. Although prospects are believed to be improving, Charles does not feel confident that the improvement will be sufficient and therefore wishes to undertake a thorough review of the business. The major bright spot in the situation lies in the value of the company's property assets. Over the years a number of properties had been acquired, largely for the purpose of the business. The expansion of nearby towns, with the consequent increase in traffic, had rendered some of these properties unsuitable for the business of agricultural merchant or seed and fertiliser producer; but they are now ripe for residential development. These properties are probably worth over £4m and negotiations are already proceeding to acquire the necessary planning permissions and to sell them to property developers. The consultants commenced work at the beginning of February. Interviews were held with the members of the Board and with a number of senior managers. The notes made of these discussions follow. The Appendix gives the management accounts for 1986/7.

Notes of meeting with Charles Green

The business was founded by Charles's grandfather, a farmer, in the 1930s and then significantly expanded by his father and uncle. Charles had become the Managing Director in the 1970s and then, three years ago, had concentrated on the role of Chairman, appointing a Managing Director from within the company. This appointment had not proved successful and a new Managing Director, Tony Douglas, had been appointed, also from within the company.

At the present time the business consists of a number of activities. The Seed Division is run by Paul Green, the son of Charles's uncle. Paul has a small shareholding and a seat on the Board. He reports to the Group Managing Director, Tony Douglas, but this reporting relationship is made difficult by personality clashes between the two men. The Division contracts with farmers to grow seed to a certain specification and it then cleans and grades it. This business had been built up since the end of the War under the brand name 'Greenseed'. The branding of seed in this way had been an innovative idea and the brand had made the company's name. The seed is sold direct to farmers in Worcestershire by the Group Sales Force (sales about £1.3m), and in the rest of the country through agricultural merchants. Competitors had long since followed the 'branding' approach and the market is now highly competitive with major companies, like Dalgety, as the market leaders. Greenseed sales amount to around £3m per annum.

The Fertiliser Division is the responsibility of the Group Managing Director, also a member of the Board. Reporting to him are the Commercial Director, David Dunn; the Production Director, Seph Lonsdale; the Sales Director, Richard Oldham, responsible for sales to merchants in the Eastern part of the country; and Nick Foley, responsible for sales to merchants in the Western part of the country. Sales in Worcestershire are made through the Group Sales Force direct to farmers. This business had been developed some years ago by Tony Douglas from the lime quarrying and spreading activity. (Lime quarrying and spreading is now being phased out because farmer requirements have changed and the activity has been losing money for some time – it is not a major part of the business.) The Fertiliser business had also been characterised by innovative ideas. The basic raw materials, phosphate and potassium are purchased from overseas producers and blended to the requirements of the farmers. Tony Douglas had identified an unsatisfied market niche for a specific crop at an early stage. Farming efficiency could be raised by blending a fertiliser (with the addition of sodium) suitable for that specific crop. A soil testing service was provided to determine the most suitable blend and a spreading service was then provided to apply the fertiliser to the land. The product is marketed by Green Fertiliser Ltd under the name 'Greengrow'. Competitors had soon followed and Green now has a market share in Worcestershire of 25 per cent. Greengrow accounts for approximately half the sales of about £4m, the other half being mainly blends for cereal farmers. About 60 per cent of sales go through the Group Sales Force and the rest through merchants in other parts of the country.

The major component of fertiliser is nitrates, a by-product of the activities of the major chemical companies. The market leaders are ICI, Norsk Hydro (a Swedish company who had bought Fisons) and UKF (a Dutch company). These have a market share of about 80 per cent. They sell through agricultural merchants, generally a limited range of products combining nitrates, phosphates and potassium. Over recent years ICI has been trying to undermine the competition provided by the smaller fertiliser blenders such as Green by waging a price war. Margins have therefore been seriously eroded.

Green also operates in the market for crop care and protection chemicals. Some years ago Green had acquired Horchem in Lincolnshire, a company specialising in the merchanting of chemicals primarily for horticultural farmers (about two thirds of their total sales of about £6m, the remainder being of chemicals to arable farmers). The Managing Director of Horchem, Rod New, reports to Tony Douglas. Horchem is profitable but has shown little real growth since its acquisition. Competition in the specialist horticulture market is not all that intense and good margins on sales of around 15 per cent are available. In Worcestershire, sales of chemicals are made through the Group Sales Force and are mainly to arable farmers (around £3m per annum). A small merchant specialising in horticultural chemicals was acquired in late 1987 to augment the limited sales of horticultural chemicals. This activity is the responsibility of Duncan Blacks who reports to Tony Douglas. A further acquisition of a small merchant specialising in arable chemicals was made in early 1988. The former owner of this business (Ike Owl) and his team of two salespeople are now employed to continue their selling activities for the Group. Ike Owl reports to Tony Douglas. Purchasing of the chemicals is, of course, a vitally important function. Tony Douglas conducts the major negotiations with the suppliers – major chemical companies. These negotiations determine likely total annual buy and the associated volume discounts. During the year the detailed negotiations and call off in Lincolnshire are the responsibility of Rod New, and in Worcestershire it is managed by Sammy Vincent, who reports to Tony Douglas. The large national merchants such as Dalgety are the major players in the arable chemicals market and competition is fierce.

In Worcestershire there are four sales centres or depots which are regarded as essential to the ability to sell chemicals. Farmers want to be able to call at the depot and collect chemicals during the spraying season. The sales centres are also important in managing the sales force. An opportunity has been identified in selling sundries (small equipment and clothing and materials required by farmers) from these sales centres and Adam Green, the 26-year-old son of Charles, has been put in charge of developing this.

The final activity of the business is conducted by the Grain Division, located at Warley. This consists of a storage activity (surplus EC grain is stored for the government) and a trading activity. The Group Sales Force identifies sellers of grain and the Grain Division then tests it, negotiates the purchase and sells the grain on to maltsters, bakers and shippers. The Division is run by Herbert Fowler who reports to Tony Douglas and is assisted by Berty Higham. About £1m is tied up in working capital and fixed assets are worth just under £0.5m.

At the Group level the key managers are as follows. Harry Hall, the Sales Director, reports to Tony Douglas and is responsible for the members of the sales force. Tim Davis, Finance Director and member of the Board reports to Tony Douglas. John Green, Charles's brother, is the Personnel Director and a member of the Board.

Looking at the overall competition, most competitors are now making losses. There are a few specialist companies which seem to be doing well. There is a specialist chemicals merchant in Worcestershire called Bakers, who make about £1.5m profit per annum. Sims, a major grain trader, makes about £2m and Nils, a fertiliser blender, with sales about 20 per cent above Green, is also thought to be making good profits. Against the above background Charles sees the need to rethink and reshape the business. The former innovation seems to have disappeared, the market conditions are very difficult and for years now the Green business has not shown any solid or sustainable growth. They seem to be lost between being producers and merchants. They have been acquiring smaller companies and they are now the largest private merchant company in Worcestershire. They are certainly the largest in terms of net assets. There is also the question of when to sell the properties and what to do with the proceeds.

Notes of meeting with Tony Douglas

A major problem facing the Group is the price war that has been going on in the fertiliser market for about three years now, as ICI seeks to regain market share. The price war looks unlikely to end in the foreseeable future. The arable chemicals market is also very competitive and over the last two years Tony has pursued a policy of focusing the sales force on the high margin chemicals. This has meant lower volumes sold, but the total contribution to profit has increased: margins in Worcestershire are up from about 8 per cent to over 15 per cent. Tony keeps very close to the Fertiliser Division and to chemicals – in both of these areas buying is important and Tony has developed very good relationships with the suppliers. Another problem experienced by the Group over the past year was the very bad weather, which hit sales of fertiliser and chemicals.

There had been problems with the sales force but the situation is now improving. Tony is concerned at the diversion which the Grain Division creates for the sales force. Selling chemicals requires a high degree of expertise and it is unrealistic to expect salespeople to develop this expertise, as well as that in seed and fertiliser, and then also identify grain purchasing opportunities. His view is that the Grain Division must stand on its own. He is expecting the Grain Division to make a profit of £100 000 this year.

Another concern is the size of the sales force. Out of a total of 160 employees (16 employed at the fertiliser factory) there are just over 40 sales-people. Is this sufficient for a business of the Green type?

Notes on the meeting with Paul Green

About 550 000 tonnes of seed are produced annually in the country as a whole. The market is dominated by Dalgety with a 30 per cent market share; Green sells just over 7000 tonnes per annum. In Worcestershire they sell through the Group Sales Force (just over 3000 tonnes per annum) and in the rest of the country through other merchants (at a discount on retail price of about 13 per cent, out of which the merchant has to pay transport costs to the customer). A distinction must be drawn between new varieties of seed and speciality seed (this usually means seed treated with chemicals against disease, etc) on the one hand, and basic seed (called C2) on the other hand. The market for new varieties/speciality seed is smaller but higher prices can be charged and higher margins earned. The policy of Green is to focus on the high-margin, high-quality end of the market. The competition in the C2 segment is very fierce with suppliers now selling through merchants at prices that are below cost. The Green policy is to avoid competition on purely price terms. Representatives in the Group Sales Force are given fixed prices and they either sell at these prices or walk away from the sale. Over the past few years the volumes of seed sold through the sales force have been on the decline. Paul is very critical of the sales force. He feels it is not well managed or directed and that there is too much emphasis on training the reps to act as technical advisors to farmers on chemicals, rather than training them on how to close sales.

Notes on the meeting with Harry Hall

Harry Hall is the Group Sales Director. Basically Green is selling crop nutrition, crop care and protection. He outlined some of the history behind the sales force. A few years ago the Group was organised into separate companies. Green Fertiliser produced and sold fertiliser with its own sales force. Green Chem and Frank Green and Sons sold chemicals and seed with their own sales forces. Then about three years ago all the sales forces were amalgamated into one to sell all the Group products in Worcestershire. This had caused problems with the fertiliser salespeople who had to acquire highly technical chemicals product knowledge. To sell chemicals the rep had to be able to walk the farm with the farmer and identify pest and other problems and recommend the best solution. The change also meant that chemical specialists had to acquire fertiliser product knowledge. It is feasible for a rep to be highly expert in one product, very proficient in a second, but only knowledgeable in a third. The tendency therefore is for reps to specialise in either chemicals or fertiliser and relegate seed to third place. In addition, salespeople have to identify grain purchases for the Grain Division. This tends to come very much in fourth place.

After the reorganisation of sales, many of the sales force had left and had been replaced with less expert, younger people. The sales force now tends to be somewhat unbalanced with a number approaching retirement and the remainder being mostly young and relatively inexperienced people. On average the sales per rep in Worcestershire are around £300 000 per annum.

The sales force situation is improving – a good deal of effort has been put into training, concentrating on chemicals product knowledge. However, the training programme is criticised by some of the reps as being too disjointed and 'bitty'. There is an incentive system under which the contribution earned on sales by each rep is compared to his or her salary and if it exceeds salary then incentive payments come into force. However for most, the contribution on sales never exceeds salary and the incentives therefore do not work. The contribution from sales is also used to allocate sales force costs to the producing activities. The formula is such that total costs are never fully allocated and nearly half is left as an unallocated group overhead.

Two years ago the decision had been taken to set up sales centres. These serve as depots for chemicals and also as centres for sales teams. At each centre there is a Team Leader who manages the reps. There is a sales centre at Knutsford run by Bill Sutter with a team of six reps. The location of this centre is very poor because of problems from industrial traffic. But the intention is to sell the land and buildings (the site is also used for the Head Office and the seed factory) and build a new Head Office, sales centre and seed factory on another site owned by the Group. Further north is the Fitter sales centre run by Cain Anderon. This is also the location for Ike Owl's chemicals' sales team. There is a sales centre at Mableham where the Team Leader is Steve Binder, who joined the company six months ago from Norsk Hydro. The fourth sales centre is in Raleigh and is run by Larry Fell. Duncan Blacks, the manager of the horticultural chemicals sales team is located there, but his team of five salespeople is spread around the depots.

Notes on the meeting with Rod New

Rod New is the Managing Director of Green Horchem in Lincolnshire. About two-thirds of his sales are in horticultural chemicals and the rest is in arable chemicals. The latter is a much more competitive market. Chemical reps have to be experts: there is some specialisation between horticultural and arable reps but they do sell to both types of farmers. There are nine reps with sales of about £6m per annum. There are three sales centres. They have a market share of about 60 per cent of horticultural chemicals in Lincolnshire.

Notes on the meeting with David Dunn

David Dunn is the Commercial Director of the Fertiliser Division. He buys, in the main on his own, phosphates and potash from overseas producers. He also buys nitrogen products but Green do not have a UK supplier. They simply sell the nitrogen on to farmers. There is not much margin in this but they do it to be able to provide a complete service to farmers.

He sees some prospect of change in the fertiliser market. The chemical majors may well decide to concentrate on selling nitrogen, their main product. These majors have to buy in phosphates and potash from the same sources as the small blenders such as Green. There is, therefore, nothing very attractive to them in this business. A threat to the market for nitrogen is the environmental pressure to reduce the quantities of nitrates in the water supply.

The Fertiliser Division sells 60 per cent of its product through the Group Sales Force and the remainder through merchants in the rest of the country. The volumes sold through the sales force have been on the decline but there has been an increase so far this year. Steve Binder is now trying to develop sales through other merchants in Worcestershire. They are finding that they have to give these merchants a discount of around 13 per cent on average, out of which the merchant has to pay transport costs to the customer, leaving the merchant with a margin of about 8 per cent. The fertiliser factory is not capacity constrained and could produce 50 per cent more. The obstacle is the state of the market where the demand for fertiliser is not growing. The EC policy of cutbacks on cereal production could lead to declines in the future.

Notes on the meeting with Tim Davis

Tim Davis is the Finance Director. He went through the management accounts and explained some of the items in those accounts which were not clear to the consultant. The item called credit in the group accounts represented charges which were made on the late payment of invoices. Tim did not have much confidence in the forecast profit of the Grain Division. He was doing some work which indicated that there could be a substantial loss.

Other points from meetings

The sales force lacks direction and control and the sales policy is not clear or consistent as far as the reps are concerned. The reps feel they are under attack from the production activities which impose rigid prices on them and then complain about declining volumes. Management style was felt to be dictatorial, with the team leaders of the reps complaining that they are given responsibility without the authority and flexibility to achieve results in a highly competitive marketplace. The reps feel that they are the best people to make detailed judgements on price since they are at the sharp end.

APPENDIX 2A
Financial information on Green Holdings

Group Trading Summary for month of May 1987

	Year to date Actual	Year to date Budget		Year to date Actual	Year to date Budget
Fertiliser – Net trading	−73.9	365.3	Selling costs	−277.7	−105.1
Seed – Net trading	161.9	77.2	Credit	94.7	35.1
Grain – Net trading	−40.3	144.1	Net trading profit	17.4	630.2
Chemical – Net trading	152.7	113.6	Central costs	27.5	20.1
Management & retirement			Cars	6.7	7.2
costs	429.1	360.8	Total costs	226.7	213.7
Finance – bank	106.8	159.3			
Finance – other	2.9	3.1	Added value	257.5	193.1
	566.3	543.1	Group selling	78.6	72.9
Finance charges received	702.1	350.1	Gross contribution	178.9	121.6
			Finance costs	6.1	15.1
Net central cost result	264.2	193.1			
			Net contribution	172.8	106.6
Total trading profit	−246.9	436.9	Central services	46.2	46.2
Other income	33.0	35.0			
Group profit – current year	−213.9	471.9	Other income	35.3	16.8
Group profit – previous year	206.1		Net trading result	161.9	77.2
Department: Fertiliser			**Department: Grain**		
Sales total – units	42425.0	53080.0	Sales total – units	122822.0	128000.0
Sales total – value	4322.1	5984.5	Sales total value	14599.1	15040.1
Costed margin	923.2	1448.1	Costed margin	703.9	801.7
Hauliers	256.1	203.6	Hauliers	199.6	222.7
Adjustment			Adjustment		

	Year to date	
	Actual	*Budget*
Gross margin	666.1	1244.4
Wages	97.3	122.5
Fixed	319.3	346.6
Direct	89.3	469.1
Cars	18.0	18.8
Total costs	523.9	620.1
Added value	142.2	624.4
Group selling	114.1	180.7
Gross contribution	28.1	443.7
Finance costs	57.0	60.1
Net contribution	−28.9	383.7
Central services	42.1	42.1
Other income	−2.9	23.7
Net trading result	−73.9	365.3

Department: Seed

	Actual	*Budget*
Sales total – units	6930.0	7400.0
Sales total – value	2140.1	1896.1
Costed margin	547.6	460.1
Hauliers	63.4	53.4
Adjustment		
Gross margin	500.2	422.7
Wages	44.7	40.1
Fixed	81.1	90.3
Direct	94.3	76.1
Cars	17.3	11.8
Depot costs	51.4	
Total costs	215.2	132.6
Added value	164.2	283.5
Group selling	54.3	179.1
Gross contribution	109.9	104.4
Finance costs	79.0	90.1
Net contribution	30.9	14.5
Central services	42.1	42.1
Other income		
Net trading result	−11.2	−27.6

Department: Horchem

	Actual	*Budget*
Sales total – units		
Sales total – value	5449.1	5850.1
Costed margin	719.1	680.6

	Year to date	
	Actual	*Budget*
Gross margin	504.3	579.1
Wages	15.4	26.2
Fixed	115.9	116.7
Direct	186.9	143.8
Cars	15.1	9.5
Total costs	333.2	296.2
Added value	−52.5	64.6
Group selling	41.1	43.4
Gross contribution	−93.6	21.2
Finance costs	53.1	53.1
Net contribution	−146.7	−31.9
Central services	30.8	42.8
Other income mainly storage	137.1	218.8
Net trading result	−40.4	144.1

Department: Worcestershire Chemicals

	Actual	*Budget*
Sales total – units		
Sales total – value	3194.6	4905.1
Costed margin	422.0	460.5
Hauliers	42.6	
Adjustment		
Gross margin	418.8	460.5
Wages	7.7	7.5
Fixed	25.7	28.6
Direct	113.1	84.7
Hauliers	33.1	30.7
Adjustment		
Gross margin	686.1	649.9
Wages	18.2	18.6
Fixed		
Direct	459.1	497.9
Cars	40.1	45.5
Total costs	517.3	562.1
Added value	168.8	87.9
Group selling		
Gross contribution	168.8	87.9
Finance costs	107.1	140.1
Net contribution	61.7	−52.2
Central services	28.1	28.1
Other income	130.1	221.3
Net trading result	163.7	141.1

Capital employed

	May 1987			December 1987		
	Fixed	*Working*	*Total*	*Fixed*	*Working*	*Total*
Fertiliser	250	600	850	250	85	335
Seed	100	(53)	50	100	27	127
Worcs. Chems.	250	868	1118	250	692	942
Horchem	500	991	1491	500	1093	1593
Grain	200	200	400	200	852	1052
Central	–	–	–	–	–	–
Total Group	1318	2612	3930	1300	2749	4049

Ordinary management close to certainty and agreement

Organisational intention and the reinforcement of current strategic direction in the legitimate system

This Part summarises and reviews the nature and techniques of ordinary management. The determining feature of ordinary management is quite simple: it is management conducted within a mental model, frame of reference or 'recipe', that is, employed largely without significant questioning of the assumptions upon which it is based. It is this ignoring of the anomalies between actual experience and the expectations, largely below the level of awareness, generated by the mental model that enables a group of people in an organisation to employ some mixture of technically rational and visionary driven, political trial-and-error decision-making and some mixture of monitoring and ideological forms of control. Ordinary management is essentially the employment of negative feedback control.

Ordinary management is practised when managers and other members of an organisation take up the roles that they have previously contracted to take up in the legitimate system of their organisation. That legitimate system consists of a hierarchy, a bureaucracy and an officially approved ideology.

When this form of management is practised close to certainty and agreement it enables managers to realise their prior, shared intentions and so improve the efficiency with which the primary tasks of their organisation are conducted. Ordinary management is about team- building, consensus and conformity, and it produces stability, harmony, and adaptation to the environment. It generates progressive, incremental change. ▶

However, when this form of management is practised far from certainty and agreement, the efficiency and stability become a trap that prevents an organisation from adapting to changes in the nature of the game that other organisations are initiating and from initiating its own changes in the game. Ordinary management in adapting an organisation to an environment makes an organisation incapable of coevolving with its environment and it becomes better and better at doing what it already does well, better and better at answering what is turning out to be the wrong question. It is this that absolutely requires the deployment of extraordinary management to generate survival strategies over long time periods, a form of management to be explored in Part Four.

CHAPTER 4

The nature of an organisation's legitimate system and its primary purpose

Efficient performance of current primary tasks

4.1   INTRODUCTION

The really interesting and exciting tasks of management are those that involve creating and coping with the irregular, the exceptional, the ambiguous, the contradictory, the conflicting and the uncertain – in short, extraordinary management. However, while ordinary management may be less interesting and exciting than the creative and innovative process of extraordinary management, it is no less important. No organisation can carry out its day-to-day tasks effectively, no organisation can continue to build on and take advantage of its existing strengths, unless it practises ordinary management with a high degree of skill. It is the purpose of this chapter, and the one following to outline the processes of ordinary management.

In Chapter 2 we have already identified the decision-making processes that are required for ordinary management. There they appeared under the heading of models of decision-making that apply only in conditions close to certainty. You will recall that approximations to technical rationality, bounded rationality, trial-and-error experimentation to achieve a known goal, logical incrementalism, bureaucracy and dominant coalitions were all discussed as modes appropriate in conditions close to certainty. Later on in that chapter we discussed the forms of control that must be practised in ordinary management: planning and monitoring, and ideological conformity. But so far little has been said about the institutional and behavioural frameworks through which the processes of decision-making and control are applied; that is, the reporting structures, the formal groups, the information and communication systems, and the belief systems that go to make up what we might call the legitimate system of an organisation.

This chapter is concerned with such matters – with the instrument managers use to apply the decision-making and control processes of ordinary management, so vital to the orderly conduct of the existing business.

The basis of ordinary management is always some given paradigm that sets the agenda for the ordinary conduct of an organisation's activities. And the current paradigm of an organisation is embodied in its bureaucracy – the bureaucracy reflects and exists to enact and sustain that current paradigm.

Key Concept 4.1

Bureaucracy

A bureaucracy consists of a set of offices or functions arranged in a hierarchy, that is, ascending levels of office-holders where authority increases with upward movement. The office-holders are bound by strict rules that establish the extent of their authority and responsibility. People in a bureaucracy do not owe allegiance to other people, but only to the impersonal duties of the office they occupy. In a bureaucracy, people take up roles under a contract; they are appointed and their functions are carefully specified. Promotion is based on qualifications and there is an established career structure. The term 'bureaucracy' is usually used nowadays in a pejorative sense to mean an overburdensome administrative machine. The term is not used in that sense in this book, but in the sense of a clear reporting structure, accompanied by clear rules, procedures and plans.

When managers act in the ordinary mode they administer the bureaucracy and they bolster it by developing and reinforcing supportive ideologies. In more specific terms:

- They take up roles in formal hierarchies, designed and installed by top managers, that determine status, authority and responsibility for task performance.
- They process information, and they measure and monitor task performance, using the Management Information and Control Systems (MICS) and related reward systems of the organisation. The thought processes required are step-by-step analytical ones.
- They articulate the paradigm. Sometimes managers use mission statements and visions to make explicit some elements of the organisational philosophy that guides the existing business. At other times they express the paradigm in symbols, myths, stories and rituals.
- They use top-down persuasion, exhortation and propaganda to reinforce the paradigm, directing attention to the rules of the competitive game, the timeless values governing behaviour, and other elements of the paradigm judged to be particularly important at any one time. As part of this process they tell stories and develop myths, manifestations of the culture that protect the paradigm, and recruit newcomers as adherents.
- They exert and respond to leadership and they operate in formal groups.

In the sections that follow we will consider these principal tasks of ordinary management. The first aspect to be discussed is the hierarchical reporting structure of the legitimate system and the dialectical way in which it evolves. After that, we will review the techniques of decision-making and control employed in ordinary management and then consider the nature of leadership and the role of groups in relation to the legitimate system.

4.2 HIERARCHICAL STRUCTURES

At any one time, the hierarchical reporting structure of an organisation reflects or embodies its paradigm. The hierarchy represents a particular configuration of the most fundamental of the paradoxes of organising: the paradox created by the force of division on the one hand and that of integration on the other. Structure is a particular way of coping with the tension created by the forces of decentralisation and centralisation.

As an organisation grows in size and complexity, the tension between centralisation and decentralisation increases to a point where any existing structural arrangement can no longer contain that tension. The structure then has to be altered in some way and other mechanisms, for example temporary project teams, have to be added to deal with the complexity. But they, in their turn, bring further tensions. Every structural change or additional mechanism employed to deal with the problems created by the basic paradox, also reflects that paradox. Such changes and mechanisms can therefore only ever provide temporary relief to the tension; soon some other arrangement will be required. This dialectical process is depicted in *Figure 4.1*.

Organisational structure is, therefore, a dynamic evolving phenomenon, unfolding through a dialectical process. For short time periods, however, it provides a stable framework for control.

It is usual to distinguish three different structural arrangements of the paradox of division and integration, three different reflections of typical paradigms:

- simple structure
- functional structure
- divisional structure.

Simple structure

The simple structure resolves the paradox of division and integration by placing the emphasis on centralisation. In this structure, staff and workers report directly to a small number of managers – in most cases one person is very much 'in control'. As you can see from *Figure 4.2*, there is relatively little division of management responsibility and little formal hierarchy.

Because it relies heavily on informal personal contact, the simple structure has the flexibility required to deal with rapid change and high levels of uncertainty. As the size of the organisation expands, however, the vague, overlapping definitions of jobs, the loose reporting relationships, and the typical absence of formal controls increasingly create anomalies: for example, the flexibility makes the system good at acquiring new customers, but the absence of a bureaucracy means that it cannot retain existing ones.

FIGURE 4.1

The dialectic of centralisation and decentralisation

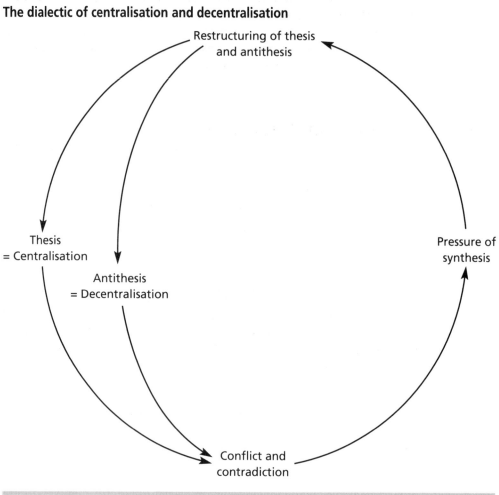

FIGURE 4.2

The simple structure

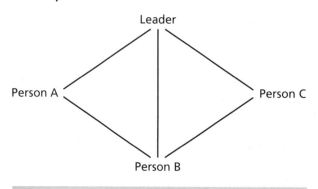

Growth demands the installation of more complex structural forms and more formal systems if control is to be effective; that is, more sophisticated bureaucracies are required.

Failure to recognise the size limitation of this structural form and the need it imposes for an efficient bureaucracy is perhaps the most frequent stumbling block encountered by the entrepreneurial founders of promising businesses.

Functional structure

The simple structure is typically followed by the development of a functional form. This form represents a significant shift from centralisation to decentralisation. Management is divided by primary and support tasks:

- getting the work (sales and marketing);
- carrying the work out (production, delivery);
- getting the raw materials (purchasing, stock control);
- getting, retaining and developing the labour (personnel);
- developing the products and processes (research and development, design, engineering);
- recording the transactions and arranging the finance (accounting and finance).

The integrating function is performed by a superior manager: the managing director, chief executive, or chairman, who acts as the leader of a formally appointed team of managers as shown in *Figure 4.3*.

FIGURE 4.3
The functional structure

The functional form is firmly based on specialisation and standardisation. It allows for:

- a greater injection of expertise and professionalism into the performance of each category of task in the organisation;
- more effective control in complex situations because it decomposes and localises the handling of disturbances to the business.

The functional form reaps the efficiency benefits of task division, but there are prices to be paid for these benefits and they become more evident as an organisation continues to increase in size and diversity. The problems encountered in the functional form centre on:

- role duality
- functional barriers
- overlap
- interdependence
- size and diversity.

These are the typical anomalies that the functional form creates and they eventually lead to contradiction and conflict, forcing a further rearrangement of the paradox of division and integration. Consider how these anomalies are typically dealt with.

Role duality, barriers, interdependence and overlap

As soon as people are divided into separately managed functional units, they are in effect being invited to take up two roles: one in relation to the function they belong to and the other in relation to the organisation as a whole. It is then inevitable that they will develop loyalties to their own particular part of the organisation, apart from, and usually stronger than, their loyalties to the organisation as a whole, so erecting barriers between one function and another. The consequence is usually conflict between functions and a tendency for their members to pursue their own functional goals. The separate functions, however, are all part of the same organisation: they are interdependent, their tasks are interconnected and quite often overlapping. If an organisation as a whole is to be effective, then coordinating devices to soften the impact of the barriers, recognise interdependence and manage overlaps are required.

Coordinating devices

There is a spectrum of coordinating devices:

- At one extreme, coordination is permanent and formally built into the functional structure itself. One example of this is the matrix structure where role duality and interdependence is explicitly and formally recognised by two lines of authority and responsibility which build overlap into the structure (see *Illustration 4.1*). While this structure does deal with overlap, it can lead to confused responsibility, high degrees of conflict, and long decision-making times. It is often accompanied by complex formal committee structures to try to iron out conflicts and monitor performance, the responsibility for which is dispersed among a number of managers.
- At the other extreme, coordination takes a flexible process form. For example, special task forces or specific project teams, which are not a permanent part of the formal hierarchy, may be set up to promote communication and cooperation across functional divides in relation to a specific project.
- In between these extremes we find forms of coordination that contain both structural and process aspects (see *Illustration 4.2*).

The problem of size and diversity

As the functionally structured organisation continues to grow in size without diversifying the range of its activities, the response to growing complexity may be to develop formal structures where there is even greater functional specialisation.

The matrix structure

In the basic functional form, lines of authority and responsibility flow from and to one manager. But the team controlled by that one manager may also be central to the tasks that have been assigned to another manager and that other manager may in turn also require the services of the team under the control of a third manager. One way of dealing with these overlapping requirements is to establish a structural form with dual authority over and responsibility for those teams. This form occurs most frequently in relation to professional or scientific expertise.

For example, the research and development establishment of a major construction company may be organised into permanent sections, each with a manager, according to scientific expertise:

- aggregates section
- concrete section
- plant section
- chemicals testing.

At any one time there will also be a number of development projects, each with its own project manager. Staff will be assigned to the project teams from their sections and they are then accountable to the project manager in respect of their duties on the project team, but accountable to their section manager in respect of professional competence. The section manager would carry out all managerial functions not directly related to the project. ■

FIGURE 4.4
The matrix structure

Illustration
4.2

Brand management

Brand management is a way of dealing with the considerable production facility and market outlet interdependence of different but closely related products. For example, the producer of five different brands of chocolate may use this approach. One manager is given responsibility for the development and marketing of a particular brand but has to secure production from the production function and sales of the product through a sales force that also sells the other brands. Here the brand manager is a permanent part of the formal structure; but there is no dual reporting. Effectiveness depends on the processes the manager applies to persuading and nego-tiating with others. ■

An essentially one-product and one-process business may therefore develop specialist engineering functions that deal with new construction and new plant, while another deals with repair and maintenance. A purchasing empire may well develop, with separate functions for different types of purchases. Separate design or development functions may develop that focus on different processes or stages of production. For example, there may be a research and development function that deals with chemical processes, while another deals with the mechanical processes relevant to the product. All of these departments may also have overlapping responsibilities for quality control and safety.

The possibilities of duplication and overlap between functions may increase dramatically as such an organisation tries to cope with the tensions of division and integration flowing from increased size and complexity. If, in addition to all this, the organisation diversifies its range of activities and the range of markets it operates in, the functional structure will be unable to stand the strain – some other structural form will have to be developed to deal with it.

Divisional structure

In the divisional structure, separate business units are established to:

- serve different market segments;
- provide different products;
- focus on different geographic areas;
- utilise different production processes.

We saw that the move from a simple to a functional organisation represented a move towards the decentralised extreme of the structure spectrum. The move from a functional to a divisionalised form represents a further movement towards that decentralised end of the spectrum. The organisation becomes a collection of separate, decentralised units each of which may then be functionally organised.

The further division of the management task in this way immediately raises the need for other integrative mechanisms. The first of these is provided by the establishment of a corporate head office with its own management structure headed by a chief executive.

FIGURE 4.5
The divisional structure

It does not take long, however, before the anomalies of this divisional structure become apparent. As the number of business units increases, the span of control of the corporate chief executive becomes too great. The response is usually to group business units in some way under a divisional director. These divisions may develop their own management structures with their own divisional functions. In this way, the number of levels in the hierarchy proliferates, creating other centres of power and increasing coordination problems. Tensions grow between the top corporate level, the divisional barons, and the business unit managers. Conflicts on how to define roles, measure performance, allocate costs and capital all increase.

The tensions create three problems:

● Duplication of functional specialisms: corporate, division, and business unit levels tend to develop their own separate functions.
● Role duality, business unit barriers, interdependence and overlap: business units are profit-responsible but they should meet the requirements other units have of them in the interests of the whole corporation.
● Communication and flows of knowledge: knowledge held in one part of the organisation may be required for effective decisions in another part.

Duplication

Each unit in a divisionalised structure might have all of its own functional specialisms or some of them could be located at the corporate or divisional levels and shared by a number of units.

One solution: centralised corporate services

The most common centralised services are the finance and accounting functions, personnel, marketing, purchasing, research and development. The benefits of such centralisation are reduced costs, greater buying power, more marketing strength, better communication, and greater synergy between units. Furthermore, control problems may be eased by these shared services and by the usually large corporate staff.

However, there are also important disadvantages arising from this emphasis on centralisation:

- The autonomy of the business units is restricted and this could lead to inappropriate decisions.
- There is a powerful tendency for the corporate level staff to grow in size, soon offsetting any cost benefits from shared services.
- The number of management layers in the hierarchy tends to expand, increasingly divorcing those at the sharp end of the business from those at the top.
- Centralised staff functions seek to reinforce their own power by establishing vast numbers of rules and procedures. More layers of managers with closely defined and specialised responsibilities, imposing rules and procedures on those at the sharp end of the organisation's activities, slow down responses. The consequence is much slower reaction times and much reduced ability to innovate and to anticipate change.
- Motivation of those at the sharp end is also a casualty of highly centralised structures.

The opposite solution: self-contained business units

The opposite way of dealing with the problem of duplication is to ignore it: that is, to adopt a highly decentralised structure where each business unit is as self-contained as possible with all its own specialist functions.

The benefits of self-contained business units are:

- faster reaction times;
- more innovation;
- greater degree of anticipation of change;
- higher motivation of those at the sharp end of the organisation.

But there are also costs:

- in money terms, arising from the duplication of services in many business units;
- in the loss of synergy between different business units;
- in the increasing difficulties of communication and control of the day-to-day activities;
- in the increased need for formal systems of communication and control.

The holding company

The extreme form of an organisation consisting of independent business units is the holding company. This operates very much as a shareholder and banker. The head office is very small and considerable autonomy is granted to the business units: they are required only to make an adequate return on the capital invested and to seek authority for all capital expenditure. But these 'only' requirements place heavy constraints upon the business units, greatly reducing their scope for strategic manoeuvre.

Control is exerted by regularly monitoring financial performance and in the event of poor performance the holding company will close or sell the unit. Holding companies generally grow by acquisition and are not noted for their organic growth. See *Illustration 4.3*.

Most companies tend to follow cycles of shifting first towards the centralised end of the spectrum and then back again towards the decentralised end. The tension between the requirements of division and integration in the organisation leads to continual change.

Illustration 4.3

Hanson Trust plc

Hanson Trust plc is an acquisitive conglomerate that concentrates on acquiring businesses in basic industries with a clearly defined future. As it is acquired, each business is retained as a separate organisation. The managers of each business are set clear financial objectives and their performance is regularly monitored against these objectives. If they exceed target they are handsomely rewarded and, if they do not, they seek employment elsewhere. Capital investment is tightly controlled, with any unbudgeted item above a few hundred pounds requiring the approval of the Chairman. The corporate head office is very small, consisting of an accounts department to monitor performance against budget and a small acquisitions staff. Each business unit conducts its own affairs and is free to compete with other sister subsidiaries – there is no attempt to manage overlaps between businesses. This kind of company therefore operates very much like a group of separate businesses with only their shareholders in common. ■

4.3 PLANNING AND MONITORING: THE RATIONAL PROCESS OF DECISION-MAKING AND CONTROL

Within any hierarchical structure, managers must plan the activities of their organisation and monitor the implementation and outcomes of their plans. To do this, managers must first identify and agree upon the performance levels, both financial and operational, that they wish to achieve by some point in the future; that is, they must set the quantitative and qualitative objectives that they are going to strive for.

The second step in formulating a plan is the specification of the future organisational posture and position that will produce the performance objectives. You will recall from Chapter 1 that the performance of an organisation at any one time is the consequence of its posture and the position it occupies in its environment at that time. However, before much can be said about an appropriate future position and posture for an organisation, it is necessary to find out something about the future environment in which that position and posture is to be taken; some postures and positions are possible and successful in some environments but not in others. It follows that we cannot plan a position and posture until we know something about what the environment will be.

Finding out about a future environment is a process of analysing the past and the present and then using that analysis as the basis for forecasting. Once managers know something about the nature of their future environment they can then deduce what alternative positions and postures might deliver their performance objectives. For each of these alternatives they will also need to identify the patterns in actions, the plans, that will produce the position and the posture. The range of future positions and postures realistically open to an organisation at some future point, and the appropriate range of actions required to get to those future positions and postures, constitute the organisation's options. Rational criteria must then be applied to evaluate each option and select that option which best achieves the objectives. This becomes the organisation's plan.

The meaning of discovery, choice and action: the rational loop

We can now see how this approach to decision-making and control fills the discovery, choice and action loop with meaning (see *Figure 4.6*). Discovery is a process of systematically gathering objective facts and analysing them. This forms the basis of choice

FIGURE 4.6
Planning and monitoring: the rational loop

and choice is the selecting of performance objectives, the generating of options to achieve them, and the evaluation and selection of an acceptable option as the long-term plan. Action is the implementation of the plan. Since the outcomes of actions will deviate from planned intentions, discovery is also a process of monitoring that feeds deviations back into the choice process, which in turn leads to corrective action to move an organisation back on to plan.

As managers move around this loop they will discover changes that require them to alter their objectives and their plans. Although we have described the process as a step-by-step one running from objectives to options to plans and then to action, it is clearly a circular process and the description could start at any stage.

The most effective forms of planning utilise detailed management information and control systems.

Management information and control systems (MICS)

An efficient MICS (see *Key Concept 4.2*) is built on a painstaking analysis of the precise detail of each step required to perform every task at all levels in the organisation. Standards of performance are established for each task at every level and the information required for the performance of each task and the monitoring of that performance are identified. In addition, the chain of authority and responsibility for carrying out every task and for dealing with variations in performance are clearly set out.

Key Concept 4.2

Management information and control systems (MICS)

The MICS is a set of rules and regulations, procedures and codified traditions that have been built up through past experience and legitimised by those in the relevant hierarchical positions. The primary purpose of the MICS is the setting of objectives and standards for role-holders in the hierarchy and the processing of information on performance compared to standards and objectives, so that responsibility for corrective action can be identified and action taken.

To see what this means in practical terms, consider the formal procedures typically used to control the purchasing of supplies and equipment. This is shown in *Figure 4.7*.

The starting point in that figure is the originator of a purchase: someone in the organisation requires some raw material or some piece of equipment. The originator has to follow a formal procedure to obtain the required item. In the case of raw materials, the originator fills out a requisition form and sends it to Stores. A stock sheet is used to record the raw material supplied and the remaining inventory. If inventories of that item fall below a prearranged level, a preprogrammed response is triggered and a requisition is sent to the Buyer. The procedure the Buyer is to follow is clearly laid out. There is a separate procedure, specifying levels of authorisation, for the procurement of equipment. The processes used here are those of analysis, quantification,

FIGURE 4.7

A purchasing control system

```
                          ( Originator )

                          ( Stores )                              ( Originator )

              ┌──────────────┴──────────────┐                        │
        ┌─────────────┐           ┌─────────────┐            ┌──────────────┐
        │   Stock     │           │   Stock     │            │  Equipment   │
        │   sheet     │           │ requisition │            │ requisition  │
        └─────────────┘           └─────────────┘            └──────────────┘

                                          ┌──────────────┐        │
                                          │  Equipment   │    ( Asst. buyer )
                          ( Buyer )        │ requisition  │
                                          └──────────────┘        │
        ┌──────────────┐          ┌──────────────┐        ┌──────────────┐
        │  Determine   │          │  Return to   │        │    Check     │
        │  material    │          │  originator  │        │  authority   │
        │  purchase    │          └──────────────┘        └──────────────┘
        │ requirements │
        └──────────────┘
                                              No          ◇ Authority ◇
┌──────────┐   ┌──────────────┐  ◀───────────────────────◇   O.K.?   ◇
│ Purchase │──▶│ Pull P.R.card│                            ◇         ◇
│  record  │   │select supplier│                              Yes
│   card   │   └──────────────┘
└──────────┘

         ▽ ┄┄┄ Purchase
              record file        ( Typist )
              by code no.
                        One-off orders ─────┬───── Call-off orders

┌──────────┐  ┌──────────────┐    ┌──────────────┐    ┌──────────┐
│ Purchase │◀─│Type purchase │    │Type call-off │    │ Purchase │
│  record  │  │ order set    │    │  schedule    │    │  record  │
│   card   │  │enter P.R.card│    │enter P.R.card│    │   card   │
└──────────┘  └──────────────┘    └──────────────┘    └──────────┘

                                   ┌──────────┐ 1
                                   │ Call-off │──────▶ To supplier
                                   │ schedule │ 2
                                   └──────────┘
```

106

formal rules, procedures and communication. The intervention required of the higher levels in the hierarchy is minimal.

The intention is to get an organisation working like a machine. But the system will never work as smoothly as planned, because some open-ended change is present in all time frames, including the very short term. More intuitive intervention will occasionally be required to satisfy an unforeseen and urgent demand for some item. Informal rules will replace the formal, and originators will persuade and negotiate directly with the Buyer to secure what they need. In other words, political activity will be deployed to handle change even in the short term – but this is the exception.

This description of a requisition procedure is, of course, an illustration of only one small part of the formal procedures employed by well-run organisations of any size. *Figure 4.8* takes a step higher up the hierarchy and looks at the activities which precede a requisition. Quarterly, weekly and daily despatch schedules for the output of some

FIGURE 4.8
The daily review meeting

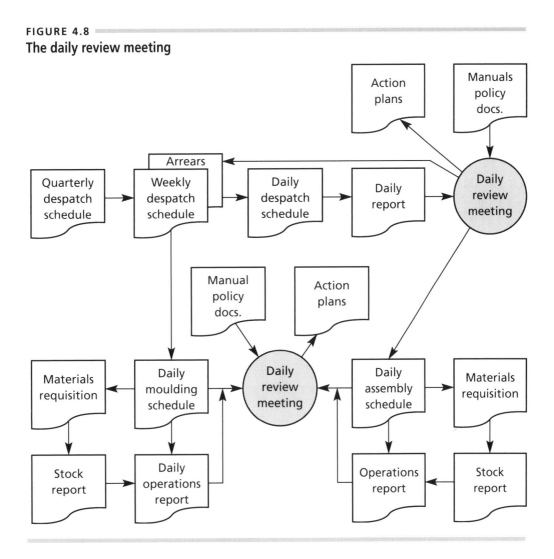

part of the organisation are prepared. These form the basis for production schedules and thus requisitions for materials and equipment. Formal procedures lay down the reports to be prepared on the actual outcomes of despatch and production and the Daily Review Meetings to be held to compare outcomes against plan. Formal rules in policy manuals set out predetermined responses to variances. Formal action plans are prepared and implemented.

The dominant processes at review meetings are likely to be the instructing ones; effective action is usually the outcome of one-to-one contact between superiors in the hierarchy and those reporting to them, or to whom they report. But intuitive and informal negotiating processes are all used when unforeseen events occur.

A further step up the hierarchy reveals what happens to the Daily Reviews: there is a formal pattern according to which Daily Review Meetings lead to Weekly Reports, considered at Weekly Review Meetings by the next level up in the management hierarchy. This in turn is fed into Monthly Review Meetings at higher management levels. Planning, monitoring and corrective action is initiated or legitimised at these meetings. (See *Figure 4.9*.)

Yet a further step up the hierarchy reveals how the formal procedures require each subsidiary to report its activities and actions by means of quarterly reports and budgets to the corporate level. Once again there are formal meetings, quantified budgets, and reports and formal policy documents which to some extent try to set predetermined responses to foreseeable changes. The process culminates in the annual meetings where budgets are set and then formally fed back down through the organisation. This is depicted in *Figure 4.10*.

Note how an efficient bureaucracy is built upon simple hierarchies of managers in which roles are clearly defined. The planning and monitoring functions of the efficient bureaucracy involve the setting of hierarchies of objectives in relation to controlling and developing the existing business and the allocation of authority and responsibility for achieving them. Power in a bureaucracy is clearly derived from the rules, regulations and procedures of the organisation. The focus is therefore on administrative rather than political activity. Communication is institutionalised, rather than informal and spontaneous. Learning is of a simple, single-loop kind, concerned with discovering the outcomes of actions.

Note how MICSs focus on the formal, analytical processes. Leadership takes an instructing, directing form. Power takes the form of authority and the group dynamic is one of compliance and dependence. Discovering, choosing and acting are precisely defined as monitoring, planning and corrective action. Modern information technology is applied. MICSs are about adapting an organisation to its environment to achieve something approaching short-term equilibrium.

The MICS is one of the main forces for stability in an organisation. In one sense it makes it more possible for people in an organisation to handle uncertainty because it provides a secure boundary. At the same time it blocks change because it reinforces the repetition of existing behaviour patterns.

Note how the MICS separates out changes that have a high degree of regularity. It focuses on the repetitive and seeks to automate responses to that regularity.

Note also that the communication arenas, all the meetings and documents shown in *Figures 4.7* to *4.10*, are predetermined. They have already been set up in advance of the change; they are serially arranged with information flowing along prearranged channels from one arena to another. Those who are to participate in the arenas (meeting

FIGURE 4.9

Weekly and monthly review meetings

memberships, document circulation lists) are well defined and stable in the sense that the same group of people always participate.

The functions that each arena is to perform are quite clear. There are restricted membership meetings right at the top of the hierarchy that perform mainly symbolic

FIGURE 4.10
Annual planning

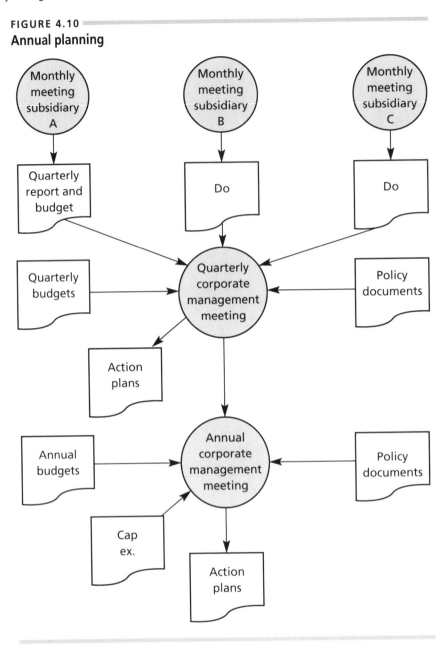

functions (for example, approving budgets and plans, thus giving them legitimacy). Other meetings may perform administrative functions. Many one-to-one meetings perform choice or decision functions from which action flows. Many of the meetings and documents perform rationalisation functions of explaining what has already happened (for example, reviewing performance against budget). The point to note here is the importance of symbolic, legitimising, administrative, explanation of the past functions in these arenas. Making decisions is certainly not the only and may not even be the most important function of the meetings required for the MICS to operate.

An essential element of ordinary management is thus the bureaucracy, of which the hierarchy is a central part. Other aspects of the bureaucracy are the information-processing systems and the controls based on them, as well as the policies, routines and procedures, both written and unwritten but nevertheless officially sanctioned, that govern task performance.

At this point it may be interesting to reflect upon what would happen if we tried to build flexibility into the kinds of system just described: for example, if we were to follow the advice to avoid clear job descriptions and tear up the rule books (*Peters, 1985*). Clearly, the bureaucracy could not function and we might find that we have to sacrifice the benefits of orderly day-to-day conduct of the business that it brings.

4.4   THE VISIONARY/IDEOLOGICAL APPROACH TO DECISION-MAKING AND CONTROL: POLITICAL AND CULTURAL PROCESSES

The technically rational mode of decision-making and the monitoring form of control can be applied only when a group of people find themselves operating rather close to certainty and agreement. We saw in Chapter 2 that as a group of people encounter situations somewhat further away from certainty they have no option but to switch to a decision-making process that involves trial-and-error experimentation, in which the particular trials and the overall goal they seek to achieve are determined by the exercise of power within some shared ideology. An ideology is, of course, some agreed set of values and it also usually involves some agreement as to a vision in the sense of a desirable and achievable future state. It is behavioural interaction between people that then comes to be more important than information-gathering and processing. Consequently, the mental models people are sharing, the process through which they come to share them, the cultures they have evolved through working together, the processes of persuading and converting others to share values and vision, all become important processes of both decision-making and control.

Figure 4.11 summarises how the process of discovery, choice and action are seen from a visionary/ideological perspective. At any one time choice is already embodied in the shared ideology and political system that has come to be through the historical development of an organisation. Action then consists of trial-and-error experiments, a form of searching or single-loop learning aimed at realising the intention embodied in the shared culture or ideology, the shared vision of the future and the balance of power in the political system. Discovery is then the completing link in the learning process, in that it consists of identifying the consequences of the trial-and-error experiment, that is, exploring what the response of the environment is and feeding that information back into the choice process to determine the further direction of trial-and-error experimentation.

The functioning of this mode of decision-making and control depends critically upon the motivation of people to belong to an organisation's belief system. We turn first, then, in exploring further the visionary/ideological form of control, to theories of motivation and then to the nature of mission and vision. This is followed by a consideration of overt political activity in organisations.

FIGURE 4.11
Vision and ideology: the overt political, cultural and cognitive loops

Management theories of motivation

There are a number of different theories of motivation that have been put forward in the management literature on how to secure consensus, cooperation and commitment:

Hertzberg's (1966) extrinsic and intrinsic motivators

Hertzberg pointed out that people are motivated to work in cooperation with others by both extrinsic motivators such as monetary rewards and intrinsic motivators such as recognition for achievement, achievement itself, responsibility, growth and advancement. Intrinsic motivation is the more powerful of the motivators and is increased when jobs are enriched, that is, when jobs are brought up to the skill levels of those performing them.

Maslow's hierarchy of needs (1954)

Maslow distinguished between: basic physiological needs, such as food and shelter; intermediate social needs, such as safety and esteem; and higher self-actualisation needs, such as self-fulfilment. Maslow held that when the conditions are created in which people can satisfy their self-actualisation needs, those people are then powerfully motivated to strive for the good of their organisation.

Schein (1988) and Etzioni's (1961) framework for categorising motivation

These writers distinguished three categories of relationship between the individual and the organisation. The relationship may be coercive, in which case the individual will do only the bare minimum required to escape punishment. The relationship may be a utilitarian one where the individual does only enough to earn the required level of reward. Thirdly, the relationship may take a normative form where individuals value what they are doing for its own sake, because they believe in it and identify with it. In other words, the individual's ideology coincides with an organisation's ideology. This provides the strongest motivator of all for the individual to work for the good of an organisation.

Peters & Waterman (1982): the power of shared ideology as a driver of behaviour

These writers particularly emphasised the emotional content of motivation. They described successful organisations as ones in which people are driven by a sense of excitement and where they have strong feelings of belonging to the organisation.

Pascale & Athos (1981): the importance of organisational culture as a motivator

Their stress on organisational culture resulted from a study into Japanese management. They recognised that people yearn for meaning in their lives and transcendence over mundane things. Cultures that provide this meaning create powerfully motivated employees and managers.

What all these studies point to is this. An organisation succeeds when its people are emotionally engaged in some way, when they believe in what their group and their organisation is doing, when the contribution they make to this organisational activity brings psychological satisfaction of some kind, something more than simple basic rewards. People believe and are emotionally engaged when their organisation has a mission or set of values and when their own personal values match those of the organisation. Organisational missions develop because people search for meaning and purpose and this search includes their work lives (*Campbell & Tawady, 1990*). To win commitment and loyalty and to secure consensus around performing the tasks of ordinary management it becomes necessary to promote a sense of mission. And this is the same thing as the articulation, preaching and propagation of the organisational paradigm itself.

The development of a sense of mission is a central leadership task in the ordinary management of an organisation. It is a vitally important way of gaining commitment to, loyalty for, and consensus around, the nature and purpose of the existing business. An organisation with a sense of mission captures the emotional support of its people, even if only temporarily. In the rest of this section we will first review what a sense of mission means, how it comes about, and how it might be managed.

A sense of mission

A sense of mission is more than a definition of the business, that is the area that an organisation is to operate in. A sense of mission is also to be distinguished from the ideas behind the word 'vision' or 'strategic intent'. The word 'vision' is usually taken to mean a picture of a future state for an organisation, a mental image of a possible and desirable future that is realistic, credible and attractive. The sense in which we are going to use the term mission here differs in that it refers not to the future but to the present. A mission is a way of behaving. Mission is concerned with the way an organisation is managed today, with its purpose or reason for being. Strategic intent is a desired leadership position. It too, therefore, is a desired future state, a goal to do with winning. Mission is to do with here-and-now purpose, the culture, the business philosophy, the paradigm itself.

Key Concept 4.3

A sense of mission

Campbell & Tawady provide a useful definition of a sense of mission (1990). A sense of mission is an emotional response to questions to do with what people are doing, why they are doing it, what they are proud of, what they are enthusiastic about, what they believe in.

The Ashridge mission model sees a mission as consisting of four components, shown in *Figure 4.12*

1 **An inspirational definition of what an organisation is there for.** For some companies the purpose is to make money for shareholders. For example, this is quite clearly the prime purpose of Hanson plc, a purpose frequently enunciated by Lord Hanson and one which quite clearly drives the behaviour of Hanson executives. Other companies have the purpose of satisfying all their stakeholders: shareholders, employees, customers, suppliers and the community. Other companies seek to fulfil a purpose bigger than satisfying stakeholders. For example Steve Jobs' purpose for Apple was to bring computing power to the masses. The purpose of Marks and Spencer has been expressed as that of raising standards for the working man. At the Body Shop the purpose is to sell products that do not hurt animals.

2 **The organisation's strategy.** This is the commercial logic of the business. It defines the area in which the organisation is to operate, the rationale for its operation, the source of competitive advantage it is going to tap, the distinctive competence it is going to provide, the special position it is going to occupy. So one part of the Marks and Spencer business is food retailing in the UK where it seeks to secure a position as the best provider of high-quality food. Competitive advantage comes from dedication to quality.

FIGURE 4.12

The Ashridge mission model

Source: A. Campbell & K. Tawady (1990), *Mission and Business Philosophy: Winning Employee Commitment*, Oxford: Heinemann

3 **The policies and behavioural standards, defining how managers and employees should behave.** These are part of an organisation's way of doing business. For example, one of Marks and Spencer's standards is visible management – managers must be seen in the stores. Another example is given by *Campbell, Devine & Young (1990, p. 30)*:

> British Airways provides a good example of how the company's purpose and strategy have been successfully converted into tangible standards and actions. It promotes itself as the 'world's favourite airline' and its mission statement declares as its aim 'To be the best and most successful company in the airline industry.' The strategy to achieve this is based on providing good value for money and service that overall is superior to its competitors and having friendly, professional managers who are in tune with its staff. These strategic objectives have been translated into policies such as the need for in-flight service to be at least as good as that of competing airlines on the same route, and the requirements that managers should be helpful and friendly at all times.
>
> By translating purpose and strategy into actionable policies and standards, senior managers at British Airways have dramatically changed the performance of the airline. Central to this effort was the training and behaviour change connected with the slogan 'Putting People First'.

4 **The beliefs that constitute an organisation's culture and underpin its management style.** People do things in organisations because there is a strategic logic and because there are moral or value based reasons for doing so.

A strong sense of mission comes about when personal and organisational values match and when the four elements are closely knitted together: when they support and reinforce each other.

Take the clothing retailing activities of Marks and Spencer. The strategy is to produce better-quality classic products through close relationships with manufacturers. By selling these products at normal prices, Marks and Spencer create such a volume of sales that fixed overhead costs are much lower than for competitors and more than compensate for lower retail margins. Linked to this strategy are values based in quality, value for money, service and people care. Behaviour standards such as the company's human relations policies or visible management style tie the strategy and the values together. To sell goods in high volumes, service is critical. By looking after people well and being visibly interested in the operating issues of the business, managers create an atmosphere in which staff want to look after customers and help the business succeed. Finally, these elements of strategy, values and behaviour standards are linked together in an inspiring way by Marks and Spencer's purpose of raising the standards of the working man and woman. (Campbell, Devine & Young, 1990, p. 5.)

The sense of mission is important because it generates trust and belief in the activities in an organisation. It gives meaning to work, motivates people, and brings about consensus and loyalty. It provides the basis for making quick judgemental decisions without having to review things from basics or exchange a great deal of information. For example, a company faced with cash difficulties might dismiss an option of selling off subsidiaries on the grounds that it is there to build businesses, not trade in them. A strong mission provides the criteria for selecting and training people who will fit. It provides self-selecting criteria for conformity. People will leave if they come to realise that they do not fit. In organisations with a strong sense of mission there is conformity, cooperation, trust and consensus.

The research that Campbell carried out on missions in business led to the following conclusions:

- Creating a sense of mission is a long-term project that takes years rather than months. Missions emerge from the way people work together and those that are imposed from the top rarely take root. Top managers who wish to create a sense of mission therefore need to proceed slowly and there is little point in simply writing down intellectual statements of a mission.
- A true consensus at the top of an organisation needs to be developed before a sense of mission can be spread around an organisation.
- A sense of mission is spread through the actions of people at the top, not through their words.
- Top team visibility is essential if its views on mission are to be propagated.
- There must be continuity in the top team if a sense of mission is to be spread through an organisation.
- Any statements of mission need to be inspirational and reflect the personalities of those propounding them.
- Strategies and values should be created together.
- Managers should focus on the link between values and behaviour. Managers create meaning when they assist employees to see the link between tasks and values.

Campbell et al. maintain that a sense of mission can be managed. They draw a distinction between three approaches to managing mission:

- The first is the intellectual approach where managers go away for a weekend and write a mission statement, or they get some consulting expert to do so. The result, according to the research, is almost always a waste of time. No one believes the end product.
- The second approach is where some powerful founder of an organisation develops a business philosophy over a long period of time which takes hold in their

organisation, becoming a set of timeless values that are deeply embedded in people's behaviour.
- The third approach is to focus on particular issues. These are usually rules of the organisational game as it were, values to do with service or quality or cost. People may have lost sight of the importance of these rules or values and the benefit of developing a mission lies in refocusing on them.

Campbell et al. offer this advice for developing and managing a sense of mission:

- Pick the most relevant theme in the particular circumstances, for example quality.
- Place the emphasis on action not words, for example a company-wide training programme, not a mission statement plastered on the walls.
- Focus on behaviour and stress one or two elements of behaviour such as putting people first.
- Expect it to take time.
- Build trust.

To see what this means in practice read *Illustration 4.4.*

Illustration 4.4

British Airways

In November 1983 British Airways introduced a training programme called 'Putting People First'. The aim was to put 12 000 customer-contact people through a two-day course to improve their customer service skills. The programme consisted of a mixture of presentations, exercises and group discussions in which staff reviewed their personal experience as customers of other service organisations. They also examined the implications for British Airways and were pressed to identify what they would do about these implications. The response to the training programme was mixed – some were sceptical, some saw it as a brainwashing exercise, some dropped out, and others were enthusiastic. But top management continued to support the programme, demonstrating their commitment to customer service. Then non-front-line staff began asking to be included and gradually the level of cynicism faded away. Staff began identifying the obstacles, confronting their managers with the fact that resources were insufficient to deliver the levels of customer care called for. The management responded to these issues and so encouraged staff to identify others.

Then in 1984, a programme for managers called 'Managing People First' was launched to change management styles. At the time, management style was perceived to be dominated by roles and procedures and the aim of the training programme was to replace this with something more open and dynamic.

Other changes were made to reinforce the training programmes. For example, quality assurance and performance related reward systems were introduced. The services being offered by the airline were also improved, demonstrating to staff that they would get the resources required to deliver better service.

It was only once the changes in behaviour were starting to show up as better service and greater customer satisfaction that mission statements were formulated in 1986.

Source: Campbell, Devine & Young, 1990. ■

The Campbell & Tawady research also sounds warnings about developing a sense of mission:

- The strategies and values embodied in the mission could become inappropriate as the world changes and continued reinforcement of them would then lead to failure. Over decades the British motor cycle industry stuck to its traditional values and behaviours. This blinded them to the dangers of competition from the Japanese and eventually led to the total destruction of the whole industry.
- Strong belief in a mission leads people in an organisation to resist change and to keep outsiders from occupying positions of any importance.

The authors advise that organisations should not try to develop a strong sense of mission in conditions of rapid change and great uncertainty, where the top team is divided or when the strategy is in a state of flux.

> There are therefore two ways to avoid the risks: avoid creating clear values and discourage employees from becoming emotionally committed to them; or formulate a well-founded mission with values that are timeless and a strategy that can be sustained for decades. The first way of avoiding the risks is appropriate when an organisation faces extreme and temporary uncertainty. In these circumstances it may be better to wait and see how events unfold before developing a mission ... in 12 months time everything is likely to become clearer, making it possible, even advisable, to develop a strategy and build a new organisation, a new mission, around it.
>
> For all other organisations, the pitfalls are best avoided by developing a timeless mission with values that need not change in fundamental ways. (*Campbell & Tawady, 1990, p. 13*)

In support of this conclusion the authors point to Marks and Spencer. Here the principles of good human relations and visible management have not changed, but the policy of buying British has – Marks and Spencer now has a large office in Hong Kong to help source product from the Far East.

The paradox of mission

People in an organisation find themselves pulled in two contradictory directions because of their basic psychological makeup: one force pulls each of them to conformity and consensus and the other pulls them to retain their individuality and difference. The first force leads people to develop a common set of beliefs, a paradigm or mission for their organisation. The second force leads them to pay lip service only to that common mission, or to try to undermine it, or to change it. An organisation's paradigm or mission is itself a temporary arrangement of conflicting motivational drives. The tension this leads to is the source of the dynamics of organisational behaviour, the prompt to the dialectic of continually rearranging the beliefs that constitute the paradigm, and one of the principal sources of both change and of anxiety in organisations.

Argyris (1957) stressed the conflict between the individual and the group. Argyris maintained that there is a conflict between the needs of healthy individuals and the demands of formal organisation. Chains of command and task specialisation require people to be passive and dependent, but psychologically mature individuals seek to be individual and different. The conflict leads to frustration, hostility and rivalry and a focus on a part of the organisation rather than the whole, as well as focus on short-term objectives. To adapt, individuals develop defence routines which then feed back into the organisation and reinforce the adverse effects.

One of the most common defences against anxiety is denial and repression, the result of which is a difference between what we espouse as the reasons for our behaviour and the reasons that actually govern our behaviour. There will then often be a difference between the 'espoused' mission of a group of people and the mission 'in use' (*Argyris & Schon, 1978*). The espoused mission will be very general so that it has more chance of commanding widespread support and not conflicting with individual desires. It will be general enough to encompass a great many of the more specific missions that will actually be driving behaviour. The more effective we are in creating a sense of mission, the more likely we are to arouse the individual motivator to be different, to explore for the new. Missions that are specific enough to drive behaviour are therefore inherently precarious. The more we articulate the timeless, the vague and the general, the more it is likely to last. But then the more it is likely to be the 'espoused' rather than the 'in use'. And the more we succeed in perpetuating a given mission in use, the more difficult we make it for an organisation to change.

Clearly, what is effective for ordinary management is the enemy of extraordinary management. In this chapter we are concerned with the motivating forces that drive to conformity because that is what ordinary management requires. In Chapter 11, we will be concerned with the conflict that is the driving force in extraordinary management.

Orderly overt political activity

Conflict inevitably flows from the development of an organisation: as it differentiates into different functions and different business units, the members of these functions and units identify more closely with each other than with the organisation as a whole. They consequently develop conflicting objectives. Power and politics are resorted to as a means of dealing with such conflict in organisations: overt political activity is a form of negative feedback control as shown in *Figure 4.13*.

So, to the extent that vision and sense of mission fail to sustain conformity, ordinary management resorts to overt politics to restore stability and the status quo. By overt politics we mean the open interplay between vested interests and coalitions of managers and members. Also, as managers face situations some way away from certainty they can no longer select, in advance, that sequence of actions that will realise their objections – they will have to discover appropriate actions through trial and error. Although the paradigm they continue to share still determines the objectives and the boundaries around the kinds of trial and error that are acceptable, it will fall to the exercise of power, to politics, to select particular trial-and-error experiments.

What, then does the literature have to tell us about the practice of politics in organisations, in an ordinary management sense?

Some studies of political activities in organisations have identified broad phases that managers follow as they deal with uncertainty and internal conflict. These conclusions are based on detailed studies over time of individual companies (for example, *Pettigrew, 1985*) and cross-sectional studies of a sample of highly innovative and much less innovative companies in the USA (for example, *Kanter, 1985*).

Galvanising events

The cycle of political activity is triggered by some crisis (*Pettigrew, 1973, 1986*), a galvanising event: departure from tradition, shifts in leadership, upset to existing

FIGURE 4.13
Negative feedback and politics

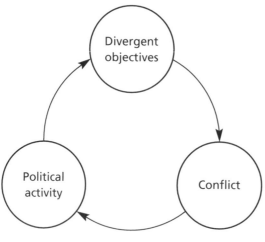

perceptions, non-routine ways of doing things (*Kanter, 1985*). The consequence is some ideological shift, the development of different perceptions and points of view (*Srivasta & Barrett 1986*). This increased uncertainty leads to divergent goals, conflict, and unwillingness and inability to commit to any course of action.

For example at the beginning of the 1980s in the UK, three firms (Metal Box, Nacanco and Francis Packaging) were supplying paint cans to paint manufacturers, amongst whom ICI and Crown Paints were dominant. In the early 1980s, ICI decided to switch the packaging of its emulsion products from tin to plastic containers to increase customer satisfaction. The tin can manufacturers did not respond quickly to this new requirement, so two plastic packaging companies (Mardon Illingworth and Superfos) entered the market and took away a substantial part of the tin can market. In 1985, Francis Packaging was acquired by the conglomerate Suter plc, who removed the managing director and installed a new chief executive. These galvanising events generated great uncertainty and the remaining managers had to develop new perspectives on what their business was all about and how they should change it. They had to deal with the often suppressed conflict which ensued.

Support building

The change in perspectives and the conflict have to be worked through before action can occur (*Pettigrew, 1986*). Particular individuals with vision are prime movers in bringing this about and they do so by developing special interests, making demands and generating support. Individuals or organisational sub-units identify uncertain changes that will affect them in some way and they make demands for particular choices in their own interests. To further these demands they obtain support from other individuals and units (*Pettigrew, 1973*); or, from the observations of other writers, individuals and groups acquire information on what is going on, they define the problems emerging from the questioning of old ways, and build coalitions to gain attention for the problem and their solution to it (*Kanter, 1985; Quinn, 1985; Pfeffer, 1981; Bacharach & Lawler, 1980*). All this support-building and coalition-forming is focused not just on the problems and opportunities generated by change, but also on individual careers and sub-unit positions and aspirations.

This could be detected at Francis Packaging. Coalitions formed around closing some of the plants to respond to the decline in demand and this inevitably affected the career prospects of some of the managers. Others formed coalitions around the issue of updating some of the plant to improve the quality of the remaining business. The new chief executive had to build political support for proposals to develop the business.

Building support is an exercise in building power. Power is the ability of one individual or group to get others to do something against their will. Power involves overcoming resistance (*Pettigrew, 1973; Pfeffer, 1981*). Power is usually distinguished from authority. The latter derives from the structures, rules and procedures of the organisation and the former not. Power in the latter sense is seen by some as illegitimate in organisational terms (*Mayes & Allen, 1977*). Most writers define power as both authority and influence. They see the utilisation of power as an inevitable and necessary process for making organisational choices in conditions of uncertainty and ambiguity. They see it as inevitable because it arises from the very structure of the organisation itself. The division of tasks, the design of separate functions and business units, immediately leads to differing sub-unit goals, in turn generating conflict which can only be resolved by the application of power (*Pettigrew, 1973; Pfeffer, 1981*).

Yet others take an even more favourable view of power as the ability of one individual or group to enable others to do what they could not otherwise have done (*Srivasta & Barrett, 1986*). Here the focus is on cooperation, consensus-seeking and organisational transformation. Power seen as influence is also the ability to enable others to do what they would not otherwise have done because they lacked the information or the perception (*Kanter, 1985*). Here the emphasis is on cooperative discussion to develop ideas. Further, power can take an unobtrusive form in which the decision situation or the cultural norms around decision-making are manipulated to prevent different perceptions, and thus conflict, from emerging (*Pettigrew, 1986*).

Power, then, is a relationship between individuals and groups that determines how one affects or responds to the other in making an organisational choice. The relationships existing now are strongly affected by those which existed and were built up in the past (*Pettigrew, 1973; Pfeffer, 1981*). The choices that an organisation makes are determined by relative power built up over a number of periods. Once the power source of the actors involved has been identified and their relative power positions determined, the choice itself is predictable.

Choice

Once power has been deployed to build enough support, the political cycle moves to its third phase – choice (*Pettigrew, 1973; Pfeffer, 1981*). Some writers describe this as mobilisation and completion, or the acquiring of legitimacy from higher authorities (*Kanter, 1985*). The outcome is the overcoming of conflict, or the avoidance of conflict, or cooperation. For some, this choice is part of an incremental process (*Quinn, 1980*). For others it can be a revolution (*Mintzberg, 1978*).

At Francis Packaging, the power of the Suter board and the individual power of the Francis chief executive resolved important conflicts to do with the closure of some plants, rationalisation and selective investment.

Planned implementation or trial-and-error action

Having made the strategic choice, implementation may be realised by following an agreed plan setting out the action steps required to achieve the chosen goal; or, where the environment is characterised by great uncertainty, that goal may be reached by trial-and-error action. Here the success of each trial step is judged against criteria for success. Such criteria usually relate to the core values of the business and to some logical connection with its existing activities. Francis Packaging decided to invest in some new facilities to produce tin products for segments it had not operated in before. Some of them turned out to be reasonably successful. It also started negotiations with Metal Box to buy those Metal Box subsidiaries that competed with it. This particular trial-and-error action ended up with Metal Box buying the business of Francis Packaging instead. Not long afterwards, Metal Box sold its packaging interests to a French company.

The writers I have been reviewing hold that it is possible to establish conditions in which beneficial political behaviour will occur. This will happen when (*Kanter 1985; Srivasta & Barrett, 1986*):

- People are free and empowered: the required conditions are the wide dispersal of power, local autonomy, and decentralised resources.
- People participate and collaborate with each other, and there is a willingness to share: team-building and the fostering of strongly shared cultures are thus essential.
- There is a culture of commitment and pride in the organisation and its accomplishments: it must also be a culture which values and loves change.
- The cultures, structures, systems and relationships between people are integrative rather than segmentalist.
- There is open communication and networks which operate both informally and are built into the structures.
- Job assignments are ambiguous and non-routine: job definitions are loose and job territories intersecting.
- Leadership is persuasive and visionary, but also sets tough standards.
- There is an orientation to action.

It is postulated that when these conditions are established, people will participate in the kind of discovering, choosing and action that produces innovation. However, I would argue that the negative feedback nature of these models of organisational politics described in *Figure 4.14* leads not to innovation but to sustaining the status quo.

4.5 AN INTEGRATED MODEL OF ORDINARY MANAGEMENT PROCESSES

Figure 4.15 summarises the key decision-making and control processes deployed during the course of ordinary management. In other words, that figure indicates how

FIGURE 4.14

Negative feedback aspects of some models of overt political activity

- Messiness, difficulties, and tendency to regress from cooperative activity are temporary.
- Although disorder and chance may be mentioned in passing, in most explanations of political activity they are in a shadowy background, not at the centre of the stage. Any disorder starts the process off, but does not drive how it unfolds. The impact of group dynamics, and the possibility of dysfunctional group dynamics and neurotic forms of leadership, are not part of the explanation. The interactive impact of personality differences on what choices are made is not incorporated. Thus the dysfunctional politicking, which in practice always accompanies functional political learning, is separated out as 'raw politics' (*Kanter, 1985*) and its impact on what happens is not built into the explanation in an essential way. Chance influences on political outcomes are not incorporated into the explanations.

- These models of political decision-making present an orderly sequential process that occurs to overcome an initial disorderly state of ambiguity and conflict. The outcome is predictable once the sources of power have been identified and measured, once the relative power positions have been determined. Deterministic laws on power relativity yield predetermined outcomes.
- The normal state of the successful organisation is one of commitment, consensus and cooperation.
- Favourable outcomes are assumed to occur if power is widely enough dispersed, and people participate and show continuing commitment and consensus under persuasive, visionary leadership which stresses action. Disorder at an individual level does not contribute to the outcome in any essential way other than to start the whole process off.

discovery, choice and action are defined in an ordinary management sense. At its centre is the rational loop in which, when they are really close to certainty, managers analyse facts about changes in their environment and consequences of their previous actions, evaluate and select options to achieve their objectives, implement their chosen option and then monitor its outcomes. They do all of this in a manner conditioned by a culture and cognition loop which drives them to proceed within a given, shared ideology to which they are inspired and persuaded to conform. They also operate in a manner conditioned by an overt politics loop which reflects vested interests as well as existing coalitions and leadership positions.

When disagreement breaks out, or when the situation confronted moves some way away from certainty, then the culture/cognition and overt politics become more than simply the context within which the rational processes are practised. The culture/cognition and overt politics loops, are, as it were, activated to become themselves processes of decision-making and control. However, in the ordinary management sense, they operate just as the rational loop does, to preserve stability and keep the organisation moving toward its current vision of the future within its current paradigm.

When managers make a choice, that choice will frequently affect the vested interests of some individual or group of people in their organisation, or in other organisations that constitute the environment. Those affected tend to form special interest groups or coalitions to block some choices and foster others. As they attempt to apply rational decision-making and planning/monitoring control, therefore, managers inevitably activate overt political feedback loops. And that political activity in turn affects both the decision-making process and the nature of control. Not only does this loop allow us to incorporate political control into the system, but it also allows for trial-and-error decision-making. It is through the process of champions forming around issues, building coalitions and trying out some responses that an organisation undertakes large numbers of trial actions to explore how to achieve its objectives.

The loop labelled Culture and Cognition in *Figure 4.15* represents the mental models that managers come to share with others as they work together. What managers consider to be irrelevant, what they pay attention to, and therefore what they do at any one time, are all determined by those shared mental models – company and industry recipes (*Johnson, 1987*). Shared mental models determine how managers learn. Mostly managers learn in a simple single-loop way about the consequences of their actions; they then adjust their behaviour according to the outcome of previous behaviour, without questioning their shared mental models. This is what we mean by the process of ordinary management.

The culture and cognition loop in *Figure 4.15* shows that, as managers go about their tasks, they uncover anomalies, contradictions and conflicts that may provoke them to examine and question the mental models that drive their behaviour – double-loop learning – extraordinary management, a matter we will focus on in Part Four of this book. Or managers and members may simply continue to use the same mental models – single-loop learning – ordinary management. The damping, change-resistant nature of the legitimate system and its negative feedback processes make it a highly efficient tool for the efficient conduct of existing primary tasks. However, these strengths make it internally unchangeable and thus incapable of true creativity or innovation. Creativity and innovation are possible only when extraordinary management processes are employed, and these are antithetical to the legitimate system and its ordinary management processes. Since most of the literature on political activity is either about the political choice process of dominant coalitions, or about the disruptive nature of personal politicking, it focuses on the preservation of stability and thus takes an ordinary management perspective.

There are a number of important points to note about the nature of ordinary management. First, it is all about the realisation of organisational intention (see *Key Concept 4.4*). In other words, in the ordinary management process organisations follow sequences of actions that their leaders intend to achieve objectives or visions of future states that their leaders intend. As we shall see in Part Three, indeed as we have already seen in Part One, this is possible only in circumstances reasonably close to certainty. Far from certainty and agreement it is impossible for the intentions of leaders to be realised and then extraordinary management processes produce emergent outcomes. Parts Three and Four will explore this matter in some detail.

FIGURE 4.15
Ordinary management processes

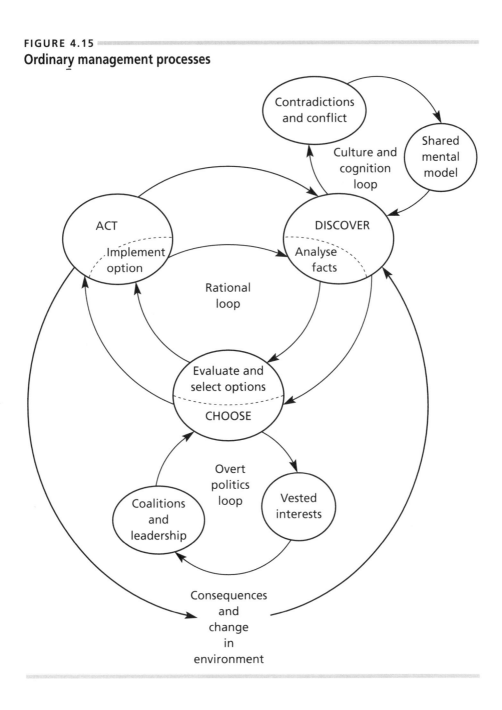

Key Concept 4.4

Organisational intention

In its fullest sense, organisational intention means that: everyone in an organisation, or at least key groups of managers, are deliberately sharing an intention to achieve some future state relating to posture, position and performance; and they are deliberately sharing an intention to achieve that future state through a particular strategy, that is pattern in actions. Organisational intention here has to do with conscious, purposeful, deliberate design of both the future state and the actions leading to that state. It has to do with a concept of predetermined direction shared by the key decision makers if not by all involved.

Few would seriously suggest that an organisation could be controlled and developed over the long term in a fully intentional manner. However, it is the conventional wisdom that it is possible to get close enough to the conditions for intentionality, to make long-term planning an effective approach. This seems to be a natural assumption to make when the only alternative is thought to be haphazard action or short-term reaction. But there is another possible alternative – that of emergence. The practically useful juxtaposition is that of intentionality and emergence. It is perfectly possible for future states and patterns of action to emerge from the continuing interactions between people and groups operating in a complex system. This need not be haphazard.

In his book, Managing on the Edge, *Richard Pascale (1990) describes how Ford transformed itself in the 1980s from a huge loss maker to a profitable and acclaimed excellent company. It is a story of a number of independent initiatives on quality, design, employee participation, executive development, studies on Japanese competitors, management workshops and many more, that somehow came together in a mutually reinforcing way. All of this happened in conditions of conflict and tension and there was no central plan or vision. The outcome emerged from many individual intentions and actions. Pascale describes what happened as the 'coincident unfolding of events' where it is impossible to envision that coincidence without the benefit of hindsight. The idea of no organisational intention and patterns in action emerging from the detail of actions and interactions is therefore not all far-fetched.*

There is then a spectrum of possibilities. At one end of the spectrum all the conditions for full intentionality are satisfied: managers can then establish in advance what the outcome will be and they can identify in advance the pattern of actions necessary to get them there. The mode of strategic management is that of long-term planning (see Chapter 5). At the other end of the spectrum none of the conditions are satisfied; managers then have no idea of what the long-term outcome will be and they can only detect the pattern in what they have done with the benefit of hindsight. In this case the strategy will emerge from the detail of what they do and the mode of strategic management here is a complex form of learning (see Chapter 11). Between these two extremes there is the possibility of intending the final outcome but discovering how to achieve it. The mode of strategic management here is visionary and ideological (see Chapter 6).

The second point to note about ordinary management is this. Because ordinary management is a process of realising the shared intention of leaders, it means that top managers are 'in control': they articulate the belief system; they fix the objectives and the vision for the future. Members of the organisation are inspired and persuaded to believe in the vision and ideology that then constitutes a strongly shared culture. Contained by this belief system, people in an organisation then conduct many experimental actions to discover how to reach the vision. Order is sustained by common culture and common intention and adherence to plans.

Central to the planned and the visionary/ideological modes of controlling and developing the organisation is the leader as a skilled planner and a charismatic political figure who builds and sustains a coalition of supporters. Political activity in this model takes the form of individual product or issue champions who detect, select and build support for particular issues and projects. They use temporary, informal, multidisciplinary teams to develop ideas and try them out in experimental form – but note how they are 'in control' of these teams. To keep this overt political activity stable, vested interests must not be threatened.

So, in ordinary management, the overt political feedback loop is kept stable through the way in which the culture and cognition loop is managed. Strongly shared mental models are promoted and this greatly cuts down on contradiction and conflict. It gives stability to the political system. People are controlled by beliefs as well as by rules and regulations and authority.

The third key point to make about ordinary management is, by now, clear. It is the process by which the status quo is preserved – it secures consensus, conformity, harmony, regularity, stability and order, all in the interests of efficient performance of day-to-day tasks and improvement of current strategies for survival. It is the process an organisation uses for getting better and better at what it already does well.

The fourth key point to note is that ordinary management is a negative feedback process – all its processes involve feeding back information about deviations from the current paradigm as the basis for taking action to dampen down and remove those deviations.

Finally, this means that ordinary management is essentially a single-loop learning process in which learning is done in advance of action and embodied in structures, ideologies, plans, vested interests, policies and routines.

4.6 LEADERSHIP AND THE ROLE OF GROUPS IN ORDINARY MANAGEMENT

The hierarchy, the bureaucracy and the official ideology in effect establish legitimate interconnections between managers and in so doing set up legitimate groupings in which they will be required to work. The key point about these groups is that they have clear tasks defined by the policies and rules of the bureaucracy, or expressed in the legitimate, shared ideology, to do with the day-to-day activities of an organisation and with reinforcing its existing strategic direction. They are legitimate in the sense that they are widely and overtly recognised as directly part of the governance of the organisation. When managers practise ordinary management they take up roles in these legitimate groups. In Chapter 11 we will contrast these roles in the legitimate system with the roles that managers take up in what I have called the shadow system, the vehicle for extraordinary management. But in this section we will consider two key questions relating to ordinary management roles:

- What is the nature of leadership in ordinary management task groups?
- What is the relevance of the group, as opposed to the individual manager, in ordinary management?

The nature of leadership in formal management groups

In an ordinary management context, the primary focus is on the leader as one who:

- translates the directives of those higher up in the hierarchy into the goals and tasks of the group;
- monitors the performance of the task in terms of goal achievement;
- ensures that a cohesive team is built and motivated to perform the task;
- supplies any skills or efforts that are missing in the team;
- articulates purpose and culture, so reducing the uncertainty that team members face.

When leadership is defined in these terms, the concern is with the qualities leaders must possess and the styles they must employ in order to fulfil these functions effectively and efficiently. Those who have put forward explanations on the nature of leadership have differed from each other over whether the effective leader is one who focuses on the task, or one who focuses on relationships with and between people. A related area of concern is whether the effective leader is one who is autocratic, or one who delegates, consults, and invites full participation. The question is which style of leadership motivates people more and thus gets the task done better. Consider three prominent theories.

Fiedler's (1967) Leader-Match Theory

Here managers are placed on a spectrum running from an orientation to the task at one end to an orientation to relationships at the other. Which of these orientations is more effective is said to depend upon the nature of the task, the attitudes of the subordinates, and the power of the leader. Where the task is clearly structured, and the leader has clear hierarchical authority and subordinates are supportive and willing to accept authority, then the task orientation works best. When none of these conditions is present, the task orientation still works best. The reason for this, perhaps surprising, result is that leaders with a relationship orientation would refrain from pressurising people in very unclear situations and thus not get the task done. However, where there is an in-between situation, then relationship-oriented leaders come into their own. The prescription for potential leaders is to discover their orientation and find a situation that fits.

Vroom and Yetton's (1973) Contingency Theory

This theory presents a spectrum of leadership styles from the highly autocratic at one end to the participative at the other. It is claimed that analysis of the problem situation determines which point on this spectrum provides the most effective leadership style for that situation. So, if there is likely to be a best rational solution, if there is sufficient information to reach the solution, if the problem is structured, if acceptance by subordinates is not all that crucial, and anyway they will accept it, then an autocratic style will yield the best results. But if there is unlikely to be a best rational solution, there is insufficient information, the problem is not structured, subordinate acceptance is crucial, goals are shared, but conflict is still likely, then the best style is a highly participative one. In between, various degrees of autocracy and participation would be called for.

Hersey and Blanchard's (1988) Situation Theory

Here, too, style and leader behaviour are to be adapted to the situation and to follower needs if they are to be effective. Task focus and relationship focus are related, however, and instead of being presented as alternatives, four leadership styles are distinguished. Leaders may adopt a 'selling' style, in which they focus heavily on both the task and relationships; or they may use a 'delegation' style, where they put a low emphasis on both task and relationships; or they may emphasise the task heavily and underplay relationships, in which case their style is 'telling'. Finally, they may focus heavily on relationships and underplay the task, in which case their style is 'participating'. The appropriate style depends upon how mature the group is. If maturity is low, then telling is the right style. As the group matures, the leader should move to selling and then to participating and finally to delegating.

Again you can see the importance of paradox: on the one hand the leader needs to focus on the task, while on the other the need is to focus on the people, and these needs must both be met even though they can quite easily be contradictory.

Key Concept 4.5

Roles and leadership in formal groups

Ordinary management is practised in formal groups that require the leader to arrive at the group with particular skills developed beforehand. The required personality, skills and styles (or, as they are sometimes called, competences) can be identified in advance since they depend upon the situation and this is specified by the bureaucracy. Leadership is about motivating people and the concern is with the appropriate role of the leader in securing efficient performance of known tasks.

As we shall see in Chapter 11, the role of the leader in extraordinary management situations is completely different.

The relevance of the group to ordinary management

Ordinary management is practised through a legitimate system consisting of an accepted ideology, a formal hierarchy, a formal set of representative bodies, and a formal administrative bureaucracy. These are all structures that formalise the division and allocation of tasks to individuals and groups of people on the one hand, and the legitimation, integration and control of those tasks through leaders and representative groups on the other. Individuals have roles as leaders and followers, they have roles in groups. But what, if any, distinctive part does the group have to play in how managers exercise their ordinary management role? We will now examine some answers to this question, and in Chapter 11 we will see how very different the role of the group is in extraordinary management which is carried out in the shadow system.

Groups

A group is any number of people who interact with each other, are psychologically aware of each other, and perceive themselves to be a group. The groups of immediate relevance to ordinary management are the formal groups in an organisation. These may be permanent, for example the sales department; or they may be temporary, as is the case when special task forces or multidisciplinary teams are appointed to deal with a particular task. Whether they are temporary or permanent, formal groups have clear goals and tasks; it is the purpose of formal groups to find solutions to structured problems. They usually have appointed leaders – leaders and managers have power given to them. However, they may also be autonomous, self-managing or democratic work groups that elect their own leader and design their own approach to a given structured task. Note that procedures are laid down in advance on how leaders are to be appointed and roles determined. This has sometimes been done to improve motivation and thus efficiency (*Lindblom & Norstedt, 1971*). However, even self-managing groups still have clear structures, tasks, objectives and procedures and so are formal groups, parts of an organisation's legitimate system.

Within, alongside and across the formal groups, there is a strong tendency for informal groups to develop, that is, for a shadow system to emerge. These may be horizontal cliques amongst colleagues on the same hierarchical level, vertical cliques that include people from different hierarchical levels, or random cliques. Informal groups develop primarily because of proximity (*Festinger, Schachter & Back, 1950*): through the contacts people make with each other given their physical location in relation to each other, the nature of their work and the time pressures they are under. From an ordinary management perspective, the immediate concern about these informal groups is whether they will support or counter the operation of formal groups. The concern is with motivating people to cohere into functional teams that will focus on clearly defined tasks, not dissipate energies in destructive informal groups.

From an ordinary management perspective, we are primarily concerned with the authority, responsibility and performance of individual managers in carrying out their pre-assigned tasks. From this perspective, our interest in groups relates to the circumstances in which groups may be more effective than individuals. Groups can:

- accomplish complex interdependent tasks beyond the ability of individuals working alone;
- solve complex problems that require many inputs;
- provide a means of coordinating activities;
- facilitate implementation through generating participation and commitment;

- generate new ideas and creative solutions within the paradigm;
- provide the opportunity of social interaction that improves morale and motivation.

Groups, both formal and informal, meet human needs for affiliation and self-esteem. They provide individuals with a sense of security, they reduce anxiety and the sense of powerlessness, and they provide opportunities for individuals to test reality through discussion with others. But they also create a vehicle for individuals to pursue their own self-interested tasks and problem-solving activities and so can be the enemies of effective ordinary management.

From an ordinary management perspective, then, the central concern in relation to groups is that of motivating people to perform known tasks efficiently. This requires that people should behave in a cohesive manner and develop not counter-productive but supportive informal groups. A number of factors have been identified that determine how groups will behave, how effective and efficient they will be in an ordinary management context. The factors that determine how groups behave in the ordinary management context where they have reasonably clear tasks and well-defined power structures are:

- *Environmental factors.* The nature of the work, the physical location of people and the time pressures they are under determine whether and what kinds of informal groups develop to support the formal groups. Key to the operation of the formal and their informal shadows is the managerial climate. This determines whether the logically designed formal groups can satisfy emotional needs or whether there will be strong pressures to develop alternatives. The conclusion generally reached is that groups designed on purely rational task-centred factors will lead to the emergence of anti-management informal groups. When, however, groups are designed according to social criteria, the result is cohesive teams. But social groups may not be all that logically related to the task, so it is generally thought best if groups are designed on self-actualising criteria. In this way individual motivational factors can be integrated with social factors to lead to cohesive functional teams that are motivated to deal with the task. Thus informal groups in themselves are not seen as relevant to ordinary management; they need to be pre-empted from emerging by the design of formal groups in such a way that those formal groups meet social and psychological needs.
- *Membership factors.* How a group performs will depend upon the personalities of its members, their personal background, status, who they represent and so on. Cohesion is brought about by putting together people with common experience or by creating opportunities for them to develop that common experience.
- *Dynamic factors.* The extent to which members of the group are socialised and sensitive to the group process and the extent to which they have been trained in these.

When it comes to problem solving, groups will generally be better at it than individuals when the problem has multiple parts requiring varied skills and knowledge. The principal reason usually given for using groups to solve problems, however, is that it makes it more likely that they will then implement the solution. Drawbacks are that groups tend to take riskier decisions than individuals (*Stoner, 1968; Davis, Laughin & Komarita 1976*) because responsibility is diluted or because a group may amplify the positive cultural value of taking risks. Another drawback is 'group think' (*Schachter, 1951*). Members with deviant views are pressurised to conform if they are to retain membership. Informal groups have positive aspects too: they relieve the frustration provoked by working in a bureaucracy and they augment the functioning of the bureaucracy when the rules are not appropriate.

As we shall see in Chapter 11, the extraordinary management perspective on groups is very different to this. However, both perspectives are necessary for a fuller understanding of management simply because managers must practise both ordinary and extraordinary management.

4.7 SUMMARY

Ordinary management enables an organisation to build on its strength, deliver competitive advantage, sustain continuity, and carry out the day-to-day activities of an organisation in an orderly and effective manner. It is essentially concerned with repetition and without it an organisation cannot succeed. The paradox, however, is that focusing predominantly on this form of management leads to success only if the organisation is supported by a stable environment or people want to stay the same. If, however, a competitive environment requires an organisation to innovate and change, then focusing predominantly on ordinary management may well lead to failure.

Ordinary management is therefore essentially temporary in nature, taking place within a legitimate system that is also somewhat temporary in nature, except for those institutions for which society sets a primary task of staying the same, preserving the traditional, or providing stability, security and safety. If an organisation is to innovate, then while its managers are acting within the paradigm, they must also be seeking to destroy it. In this sense it is instability that is the essence of success, a matter we will come to in that part of this book which deals with extraordinary management. Before that, we need to consider just how managers are recommended to go about the strategic management of their organisation within the legitimate system and its ordinary management framework that have been outlined in this chapter.

Later on, however, I will argue that the real cutting edge of strategic management is extraordinary management practised is the shadow system – but that is a matter for Part Four of this book.

Further reading

Further information on organisational structures can be found in Mintzberg (1975). For more detail on management information and control systems turn to Rowe, Mason, Dickel & Snyder (1989). Stewart (1983) provides a useful discussion on management roles and Campbell & Tawady (1990) should be referred to for a greater understanding of the mission concept.

References

Argyris, C. (1957), *Personality and Organization*, New York: Harper & Row.

Argyris, C. & Schon, D. (1978), *Organizational Learning: A Theory of Action Perspective*, Reading, Ma.: Addison-Wesley.

Bacharach, S. B. & Lawler, E. J. (1980), *Power and Politics in Organizations*, San Francisco: Jossey-Bass.

Campbell, A., Devine, M. & Young, D. (1990), *A Sense of Mission*, London: Hutchinson.

Campbell, A. & Tawady, K. (1990), *Mission and Business Philosophy: Winning Employee Commitment*, Oxford: Heinemann.

Davis, J. H., Laughin, P. R. & Komarita, S. S. (1976), The social psychology of mixed groups: cooperative and mixed motive interaction, *Annual Review of Psychology*, vol. 27, pp. 501–41.

Etzioni, A. (1961), *Complex Organizations*, New York: Holt, Reinhart & Winston.

Festinger, L., Schachter, S. & Back, K. (1950), *Social Pressures in Informal Groups: A Study of a Housing Project*, New York: Harper & Row.

Fiedler, F. E. (1967), *A Theory of Leadership Effectiveness*, New York: McGraw-Hill.

Hersey, P. & Blanchard, K. (1988), *Organizational Behavior*, Englewood Cliffs, NJ: Prentice-Hall.

Hertzberg, F. (1966), *Work and the Nature of Man*, Cleveland: World Publishing Co.

Johnson, G. (1987), *Strategic Change and the Management Process*, Oxford: Blackwell.

Kanter, R. M. (1985), *The Change Masters: Innovation and Entrepreneurship in the American Corporation*, Englewood Cliffs, NJ: Simon & Schuster.

Kanter, R. M. (1989), *When Giants Learn to Dance: Mastering the Challenge of Strategy Management and Careers in the 1990s*, Englewood Cliffs, NJ: Simon & Schuster.

Lindblom, L. & Norstedt, J. (1971), *The Volvo Report*, Stockholm: Swedish Employers Confederation.

Maslow, A. (1954), *Motivation and Personality*, New York: Harper Brothers.

Mayes, B. T. & Allen, W. R. (1977), Towards a definition of organizational politics, *Academy of Management Review*, vol.2.

Mintzberg, H. (1975), *The Structuring of Organizations*, Englewood Cliffs, NJ: Prentice-Hall.

Mintzberg, H. (1978), Patterns in strategy formation, *Management Science*, vol. 24.

Pascale, R. T. (1990), *Managing on the Edge: How Successful Companies Use Conflict to Stay Ahead*, London: Viking Penguin.

Pascale, R. T. & Athos, A. (1981), *The Art of Japanese Management*, New York: Simon & Schuster.

Peters, T. J. (1985), *Thriving on Chaos*, New York: Macmillan.

Peters, T. J. & Waterman, R. H. (1982), *In Search of Excellence*, New York: Harper & Row.

Pettigrew, A. (1973), *The Politics of Organizational Decision Making*, London: Tavistock Publications.

Pettigrew, A. (1985), *The Awakening Giant*, Oxford: Blackwell.

Pettigrew, A. (1986), Some limits of executive power in creating strategic change, in Srivasta, S. & Associates (Eds.) (1986), *Executive Power*, San Francisco: Jossey-Bass.

Pfeffer, J. (1981), *Power in Organizations*, Cambridge, Ma.: Ballinger Publishing Company.

Quinn, J. B. (1980), *Strategic Change: Logical Incrementalism*, Homewood Ill: Richard D. Irwin.

Rowe, A. J., Mason, R. O., Dickel, K. E. & Snyder, N. H. (1989), *Strategic Management and Business Policy: A Methodological Approach*, Reading, Ma.: Addison-Wesley.

Schachter, S. (1951), Deviation, rejection and communication, *Journal of Abnormal and Social Psychology*, vol. 46, pp. 190–207.

Schein, E. H. (1988), *Organizational Psychology*, Englewood Cliffs, NJ: Prentice-Hall.

Srivasta, S. & Barrett, F. J. (1986), Conclusions: functions of executive power, in Srivasta, S. & Associates (Eds.), *Executive Power*, San Francisco: Jossey-Bass.

Stewart, R. (1983), *The Reality of Management*, 2nd edn, London: Heinemann.

Stoner, J. A. (1968), Risky and cautious shifts in group decisions: the influence of widely held values, *Journal of Experimental Social Psychology*, vol. 4, pp. 442–59.

Vroom, V. H. & Yetton, P. W. (1973), *Leadership and Decision Making*, Pittsburgh: University of Pittsburgh Press.

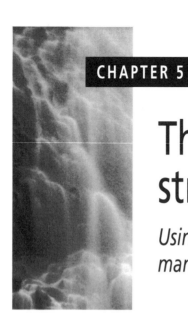

CHAPTER 5

The rational model of strategic management

Using the rational processes of ordinary management to make long-term strategies

5.1 INTRODUCTION

The last chapter summarised the decision-making and control processes of ordinary management. These processes are clearly possible, appropriate and required to manage the short term simply because short-term consequences of actions and events are normally close to certainty and people are normally reasonably close to agreement in such situations. But how are managers and other members of organisations to cope with actions and events having long-term consequences that are much further from certainty and about which they are much further from agreement? In other words, how are we to make long-term strategies in organisations?

The dominant answer to that question, nowadays, is to extend the processes of ordinary management further out into the future, further out into the area far from certainty and far from agreement. We saw in Chapters 2 and 3 that this becomes an increasingly dubious response to the problem of making long-term strategy for purely logical reasons. However, it is the dominant response, and the approaches which it leads to do have some value in thinking about and articulating the history of an organisation and its current position, as well as some limited value for perhaps a little way past the short term. It is, therefore, important to understand what is involved in extending the rational and visionary/ideological models of decision-making and control to the strategic, but it should always be borne in mind that this is an extremely dubious procedure, for purely logical reasons, despite its great popularity. In the next chapter we will review the extension of the visionary/ideological processes of ordinary management to the long term and note the major debate between those advocating the extension of the rational model, to be dealt with in this chapter, and those advocating the extension of the visionary/ideological model. What both have in common is their emphasis on the securing of stability and the realisation of intention. Part Three of this book will demonstrate how and why this is antithetical to creativity and innovation, and Part Four will explain what happens in practice when organisations transform themselves in creative and innovative ways – what they avoid is the extension of ordinary management processes over the long term.

Chapter 7 will then review the results of extending ordinary management processes to the long term. The main point it will make is that it is inappropriate and dangerous to extend the rational and the visionary/ideological models to the area of the strategic. Neither is capable of coping with great uncertainty and neither is about the double-loop learning that underlies creativity and innovation.

Before that, in this chapter, we are going to look carefully at what it means to realise organisational intention over the long term – we have already considered what organisational intention is in general and now we need to understand in a rather precise way what it means over a long time period. We will then examine how it is proposed that technically rational decision-making and monitoring forms of control might realise such long-term intention. What follows falls within ordinary management because it does not explain how a paradigm comes about or how it changes, and it does not effectively prescribe or even describe the process for changing paradigms. It simply assumes that if a paradigm must be changed someone will know what it should be changed to and will be able to persuade others to change without too much bother.

What follows in this chapter is all about general sets of prescriptions that are supposed to be applicable to a wide range of specific situations. It assumes that a leader or some expert has a superior insight through following the prescriptions for analysing and identifying situations and can then persuade others to follow. Let me emphasise again the main point, simply because it is so often brushed aside: you can apply the approaches to be outlined in this chapter only when you are close to certainty and agreement, only when as a group you operate within the same 'recipe' about your world. The techniques that follow are, therefore, inevitably of very restricted use. You will notice that even when one accepts that the techniques outlined in this chapter can be used only close to certainty there are still internal problems with most of them.

The rational prescriptions for making strategies are concerned first of all, with formulating and selecting strategic plans according to given rational criteria. This is a procedure for identifying a specific acceptable strategy for each individual organisation, determined by its own particular circumstances. The first four prescriptions for making strategies (to be explored in the section after the next) are, therefore, concerned with evaluating and selecting long-term plans:

1 Managers should set appropriate long-term goals for their organisations, formulate the right plans to achieve those goals, and then implement their plans. The prescription is for top managers to set the objectives and formulate the plans, or at least approve the plans prepared by subordinates that provide the framework for others to act.

2 Appropriate goals and the right long-term plans are those that produce performance that is acceptable to the most powerful groups of stakeholders in an organisation. The prescription that flows from this is that managers should apply certain well-known analytical techniques to the specific situation of their

organisation to determine in advance whether particular patterns in action are likely to yield acceptable performance.

3 Appropriate goals and the right long-term plans are those that produce performance that is acceptable and patterns in action that are feasible. The prescription here is that managers should identify, through advance analysis, whether they will have the resources and skills to carry out their proposed strategy.

4 Appropriate goals and the right long-term plans are those that produce performance that is acceptable, patterns in actions that are feasible, and what is called 'fit' or suitability. Fit or suitability is the requirement that patterns in action and their consequent positions and postures should be consistent with each other, as well as with long-term goals and with the demands of the environment. This is really saying that organisations are successful when they intentionally achieve internal harmony and external adaptation to their environment. The prescription is for managers to use analytic techniques to identify consistent relationships between the elements of their strategy, their objectives, the capability of their organisation, and the demands of their environment. Managers should analyse their organisation's strengths, weaknesses and opportunities. They should then use the analysis to guide actions that build on their strengths, secure opportunities consistent with those strengths, and avoid threats and activities where they are weak. In short, to be successful, managers should generally stick to what they do best.

Rational approaches to organisational success have focused mainly on selecting the right strategy in advance of action. In much the same way as the visionary/ ideological approach discussed in Chapter 6, this rational approach is also a single-loop learning, ordinary management approach. New paradigms are not developed in an emergent way out of action; instead, any new paradigm has already been developed in a manner not disclosed and then used to guide the analysis and forecasting that leads to a plan. Here we are talking about the realisation of prior shared intention. It has, however, been recognised that the implementation of a selected strategy cannot be taken for granted. This has led to further conclusions and prescriptions (to be explored in a later section of this chapter):

5 Even when managers do follow the prescriptions for selecting long-term strategies, many still fail because of problems with implementing their plans. The prescriptions that follow from this are that managers should analyse an organisation's culture and power structure to identify what the obstacles to implementation will be and then prepare plans to overcome these obstacles in advance of action. Such plans might involve, for example: installing a new management reporting structure; training and developing people; installing new information, control and reward systems; or changing the whole culture of an organisation.

6 Furthermore, managers should monitor the performance of their organisation against their long-term plans and take corrective action to stay on course. In other words, managers should attend as much to the question of control as they do to that of selecting the right plan in the first place.

Finally we will consider some conclusions and prescriptions about the process of strategic management and the overall strategic stance that should be adopted if organisations are successfully to select and implement long-term plans (to be explored in a later section of this chapter):

7   The style of strategic management has to do with the role that managers at different levels – corporate, business unit and functional – play in the strategic management of the whole enterprise so as to cope with the inevitable tensions between short- and long-term objectives, between the parts and the whole of an organisation, and many more tensions. From an ordinary management perspective, an organisation's style has to be appropriate to its nature and to the environment it operates in. Some of the prescriptions that flow from this are as follows. Where an organisation consists of a number of overlapping businesses and has to operate in a highly turbulent environment, then it will succeed if the corporate level adopts a top-down long-term planning style and the other levels implement what the top has decided. On the other hand, where an organisation consists of a number of largely independent, mature businesses operating in stable environments, then it is appropriate for the corporate level to adopt a short-term financial control style of managing the whole organisation and leave the development of strategies to managers in the different business units. There will then be no corporate long-term plans, only business unit ones. Yet other configurations of organisational characteristics and environmental factors lead to other appropriate styles; for example, a style in which top management controls the process of planning but leaves the formulation of the content to managers lower down.

We turn now to an examination of what it means for managers to realise their long-term intentions for their organisation and after that we will return to a detailed exploration of the above seven prescriptions.

5.2   ORGANISATIONAL INTENTION AND WHAT IT MEANS TO REALISE THAT INTENTION

We are so preconditioned to thinking that order in an organisation has to be put in place by a blueprint that most of us tend, at first, to find it very difficult to believe that it might just be possible for order to emerge, that is, to come about without any blueprint – this is a matter that will be explored in some depth in Part Three below. Because of this preconditioning, we loosely slip into thinking and talking about every successful thing that happens to organisations as if it is the realisation of an intention, the result of a plan, when in reality it might simply have emerged from the complex interaction of the people in that organisation. If you are to keep a critical perspective in relation to what follows in this chapter you need to keep reminding yourself in a rather precise way what it means to actualise an intention – you are then more likely to remember that you can only do this when you are close to certainty and agreement. This will keep present in your mind the severe limitations of the prescriptions we will examine in later sections of this chapter and the next.

Criteria for long-term organisational intention

If managers really are to direct their organisation along an intended path over a long time period, and this is what strategic control through long-term planning and monitoring means, then it must be possible for managers to set goals as follows.

Set goals that remain stable over time. Looking back, we will be able to say that managers have controlled their organisation according to an organisational intention if we can show that at the start of some long-term time period, say five years ago, those managers established what the future state (defined as a particular posture, position, performance – see Chapter 1) of their organisation was to be and then kept to that intention in a relatively constant form throughout the period. If the key managers kept changing their intended future state as they proceeded through the time period we are talking about, then they were in effect discovering their long-term intention as they acted. The intention emerged; it was not predetermined.

Set goals that are specific and clear. Looking back, the future state that managers intended to achieve must have been set out in a reasonably specific, unambiguous form so that it is possible to say at a later date whether the managers achieved it or not. If the intended future state was very general and ambiguous, it would usually be possible to provide some rationalisation with hindsight to conclude that an achievement had been intended. If the future state was one of a large number of different possibilities, we would probably be able to select one of them and conclude that managers intentionally achieved the state that actually materialised. Only if one selected future state was spelled out in a reasonably clear form and then realised can we unequivocally say that managers strategically intended what they achieved.

Set goals that are anchored to a future reality. Managers must have related their intended future state to some picture of the environment in which it was to be achieved. The end state must have been anchored in some way to a future reality. This requires a picture of a future market state containing enough information to enable the linking of organisational posture and position to performance. Intended financial objectives may well be stable over time, shared, specific and unambiguous, but on their own they fail the test of being anchored to a future reality unless those financial performance objectives are related to some future posture and position. Only then would it be possible to say whether they had been achieved by chance or not. We have to exclude the possibility of plucking some performance indicators out of thin air and then achieving them by chance, if we want to demonstrate that there was organisational intention.

Set goals that are overarching. Managers must have established a future state that covers the business as a whole. That state must have been overarching and central to the business. If this condition is not satisfied then the future state would relate to a small number of issues among many, rather than the intended direction for the business as a whole. If we find many different, unconnected aims then managers have intended many different specific responses to many different changes, but they will not have intended the future state of the organisation as a whole within a consistent framework, as organisational intention requires.

Share the same goals. If, instead of a shared overarching future state we have a number of individual or sub-unit intentions, then the future state realised will have emerged from the interaction between those individuals and sub-units. That state will not have resulted from organisational intention.

Set unique goals to differentiate themselves from the competition. Managers intend success and, in most markets today, firms survive and succeed when they deliver products that are different in some sense to those of competitors. The intended future state must therefore be a unique one, differentiating the organisation from its competitors. When a future state is defined simply in terms of a required return on capital or a required growth rate in profits or sales, this simply amounts to a restatement of one of the rules of the competition game, namely that a company must make an adequate return on its capital and generate the profit growth required by shareholders. Much the same point applies to long-term performance objectives taking the form of 'beating a prominent competitor' or 'delivering high quality and service levels'. These are simply rules of the competition game that apply to everyone and require no knowledge of a future state. Such aims do not define a state unique enough to provide competitive advantage and it will be left to some unspecified and therefore unintended factors to do this. We can only say that a future state was organisationally intended when the competitive advantage factors were specified in advance.

Connect their goals deliberately to the action required to achieve them. Managers must have deliberately used the intended future state to govern their actions so that connections can be demonstrated between what they did and the state achieved. If this condition is not satisfied, their achievement may have emerged from a number of individual intentions, or even chance events. To meet the criterion of deliberateness, intended posture and position must be linked back to the pattern of actions necessary to produce them. The intended future state must be a guide to the selection and design of a sequence of actions. The aim must be specific enough for managers to screen out some actions and select others. Without this they cannot design actions in advance of the change and so intentionally secure a future state.

Have foresight. It must be possible to decide in advance what pattern of actions will yield the intended future state. This requires an ability to identify cause-and-effect links between the actions of managers in an organisation, the reactions of actors in their environment, and the consequences for the posture and position of their organisation. It must therefore be possible to forecast specific changes in the environment through time to a reasonable degree of accuracy. To establish a useful future goal it is necessary only to be able to forecast a picture at one future point in time. If the actions to reach the goal are to be intended, that is, if there is to be a plan, then the developments leading up to that aimed-for future state must also be reasonably predictable. If we cannot foresee the pattern in actions, then we cannot intend it. It will emerge from the detail of what we do and any pattern will be evident only with hindsight.

It is only when the above eight conditions are satisfied that it will be possible for managers to control their organisation completely according to a shared organisational intention. Those eight conditions can be satisfied only when an organisation is reasonably close to certainty and agreement so that there are clear links between cause and effect and hence the possibility of making reasonably accurate forecasts.

It is also always possible, indeed essential, to apply planning and monitoring forms of decision-making and control over long time periods that are open-ended, but only in a much more limited sense, namely to the execution of a clearly specified project, such as building a new factory. Each step in the construction can, of course, be controlled according to plan, but the commercial outcome cannot be. In other words, the construction process is close to certainty but its long term impact on an organisation will not be.

Despite the slim possibility of being able to satisfy the eight criteria for organisational intention in real-life management in demanding competitive environments over the long term, some managers still continue to believe that they are in control of the strategic direction of their organisation. They believe that it is approximately possible to control their organisation over long time periods in an organisationally intended way, using planning and monitoring forms of control. This will be possible, on purely logical grounds, only if that organisation is simply building on old strengths and repeating and refining what it has already done. In all other circumstances the belief in intentional long-term control must be a fantasy defence to protect managers against the anxiety that uncertainty and ambiguity generate (see *Illustration 5.1*).

The planning and monitoring form of control is, therefore, a restricted, special case view of decision-making and control that can apply only in limited circumstances. This point should always be borne in mind as we now go on to review the prescriptions relating to rational processes for making strategies.

5.3   FORMULATING AND SELECTING STRATEGIC PLANS ACCORDING TO TECHNICALLY RATIONAL CRITERIA

The first prescription of the technically rational approach to strategic management is that managers should formulate a long-term plan.

To do this, managers must first identify and agree upon the performance levels, both financial and operational, that they are going to achieve by some point in the long-term future; that is, they must set the quantitative and qualitative objectives that they are going to strive for. (Note that to be able to do this managers must already have come to share some paradigm, some sense of what is important and unimportant in the world they are operating in.) Those objectives must satisfy the rational criteria of acceptability, feasibility and suitability that we will discuss below.

The second step in formulating a long-term plan is the specification of the future organisational posture and position that will produce the performance objectives. You will recall from Chapter 1 that the performance of an organisation at any one time is the consequence of its posture and the position it occupies in its environment at that time. However, before much can be said about an appropriate future position and posture for an organisation, it is necessary to find out something about the future environment in which that position and posture is to be taken; some postures and positions are possible and successful in some environments but not in others. The requirement for success from an ordinary management perspective, is that an organisation must be adapted to its environment. It follows that we cannot plan a position and posture to do this until we know something about what that environment will be.

Finding out about a future environment is a process of analysing the past and the present and then using that analysis as the basis for forecasting: this makes it clear

Strategy at a chemical company

In 1985, the corporate level of an international chemicals company set growth rate objectives for the particular division with which this illustration will be concerned. it required the division to achieve annual growth rates of 10 per cent in sales and 15 per cent in pretax profits for the next five years. The division carefully examined its product portfolio and concluded that two of its major product lines – call them A and B – would be coming off patent towards the end of the five-year period, opening up the way for inevitable competition and loss of market share. The remaining product lines, C and D, were old ones unlikely to grow at all.

The divisional managers then examined the new product development portfolio and concluded that there was no way in which new products coming on stream, E and F, could compensate for the lack of growth in revenues and profits from the existing product portfolio. It was possible to quantify the negative gap between the corporately set objective for the division and the outcome likely to be generated by existing and new product portfolios by the end of the five-year period in 1990.

Divisional management concluded that in order to plug the gap they would have to adopt a strategy of acquiring products and/or companies. A divisional long-term plan was approved, setting out the objectives, the financial projections, and a general statement that the strategy was to be one of acquisition. The strategy did not specify anything about possible acquisition targets.

What happened between early 1985 and early 1989? At least one reasonably significant new product acquisition was identified and, after careful analysis, a proposal was put forward to the divisional board in mid-1987. But no decision was taken on this and no other significant acquisition was made in the period. Instead, in mid-1987, a merger was announced between the company and another major corporation. That merger was completed by mid-1988.

The two merging companies overlapped in some market segments, but the main effect of the merger was to increase the number of market segments operated in. The merged company was rationalised in a manner that involved some enlargement of the division this illustration is concerned with, but that enlargement by no means resolved the growth gap problem identified back in 1985.

Then in early 1989 the new corporate level set growth objectives for the division covering the five-year period to 1994. The objectives were once again annual growth rates of 10 per cent in sales and 15 per cent in profits. The situation was still one of projected decline in the market shares of the same two major product lines, the lack of compensating new product development, and a similar consequent 'gap'.

Whatever the merger may have done for the corporation as a whole, it had not substantially changed the overall prospects of the division. The divisional plan once again set out the objectives, the projections and the strategy of plugging the gap with acquisitions. A small group of managers was set up to identify suitable acquisitions.

Divisional managers interpreted what they had been doing, and what they were now proposing to do, as the activity of 'planning the long-term future of the division'. They claimed that this was an appropriate interpretation because they all shared clear, long-term, division-wide objectives and they shared a common view on the route to those objectives. They saw the division's future direction as intentional movement towards an identified future state.

When it was pointed out that the objectives, the performance gap and the route to the objectives were all exactly the same as those established nearly five years ago, they replied that the previous five-year plan had not been implemented because of the merger distraction. (Note, however, that this distraction occurred in the second half of the plan period. Even without the distraction, nothing had happened in the first half of the period.) The managers believed that it would be different this time around.

▶

Is this interpretation of what they were doing – that of their organisation moving intentionally towards a predetermined future point – a reasonably realistic one?

The answer is no, because what these managers were doing does not even approximately pass the tests of intentionality. When they set their sales and profit growth targets, they are simply stating one of the rules of the competition game in a quantified form. Note how the rule is exactly the same in 1989 as it was in 1985. There is nothing unique about this at all – all their competitors must be doing much the same thing. They do not need to know anything about a future state to set these targets.

They have not related these aimed-for performance levels to a future posture or shape of the business. They have simply said that today's product portfolio (products A, B, C and D) will generate smaller volumes, new products added to the portfolio (E and F) will not compensate for this, and therefore achievement of performance targets depends upon some yet-to-be-identified acquisition. Nothing is said about that acquisition and the future posture of the business is thus undetermined.

They have also said nothing about the position of the future business in relation to customers and competitors, nor have they said anything about likely future market conditions. The link back from performance to posture and position is absent. The conclusion they have reached from identifying a performance gap is that they will have to do something different in the future to that which they have done over the past four years, but they have said nothing specific about what that something might be.

What they have done is simply stated yet another rule of the competition game. All their competitors are saying much the same thing – they will all probably compete over the same acquisition targets. But, in the end, which of them actually succeeds will depend on which of them does something different to the others.

The future state these managers have identified is therefore not anchored to any reality; nor is there overarching intention since there are many other issues to be dealt with, having little to do with acquisition. For example, there are issues around the effectiveness of the product development process, the productivity of the sales force, new manufacturing technologies and so on. There is also no deliberate connection between a future state and the actions required to achieve it, or any evidence of foresight in relation to those actions.

In this case we cannot point to organisational intention in relation to either the future state or the actions to realise it. It is far more realistic to say that both will emerge from what these managers do from now on. What these managers have done is to identify a key issue – the need for acquisition. That issue is one among many on the agenda. As they move into the future, new issues will be added and some existing ones will be dropped. What they will now do is use a task force to explore and learn about the acquisition issue, so discovering what they might do. Whether anything happens or not will depend upon the extent of political support built up around a particular acquisition proposal. It will depend upon the distractions provided by other issues. Recall why they did not acquire anything over the past few years – they were distracted by the merger issue.

There is intention, but it is intention to explore an issue. Any strategy will emerge from the diverse intentions and actions of key groups of managers, not a single overarching organisational intention. Proposals adopted and actions implemented will have more to do with behavioural interactions between the managers, with other pressures on them, than it will with analyses of potential acquisition targets.

Does it matter whether managers in the division of this chemical company interpret what they are doing as intentional or emergent? It matters very much from a highly practical viewpoint. If those managers interpret what they are doing as intentional planning, their strategic actions will focus on analysis, forecasting, trying to set targets, and allocating responsibilities. But they have been doing this for the past four years, at least, and there has been no acquisition. If instead they understand the emergent nature of what they are doing, they will focus on the effectiveness of their learning and political activities. They will seek to understand why the acquisition issue has received little effective attention. They will ask why they are not developing new products more rapidly because it is this that leads them every few years to the conclusion that they must acquire other companies. ■

why the rational approach to strategic management must be an ordinary one – because it assumes that we are close enough to certainty to be able to forecast. Once managers know something about the nature of their future environment they can then deduce what alternative positions and postures might deliver their performance objectives. For each of these alternatives they will also need to identify the patterns in actions, the plans, that will produce the position and the posture. The range of future positions and postures realistically open to an organisation at some future point, and the appropriate range of actions required to get to those future positions and postures, constitute an organisation's strategic options. The rational criteria of acceptability, feasibility and suitability, to be discussed below, must then be applied to evaluate each option and select that option which best satisfies the criteria. This becomes an organisation's strategy. An example of this kind of prescription is given in *Illustration 5.2*.

Illustration 5.2

Ansoff's strategic success hypothesis

Ansoff (1990) presents a strategic success hypothesis stating that a firm's performance will be optimal when:

- the aggressiveness of the sequence of actions undertaken by the firm matches the level of turbulence in its environment;
- the responsiveness of the firm's capability matches the aggressiveness of its actions;
- the elements of the firm's capability are supportive of one another.

Ansoff defines levels of turbulence in terms of rising levels of unpredictability and complexity and he distinguishes five levels: repetitive, expanding, changing, discontinuous, and surprising.

Strategic aggressiveness is defined in terms of the size of the break with past strategies and the speed with which they are implemented. He identifies five levels of aggressiveness: stable, reactive, anticipatory, entrepreneurial, and creative.

He then distinguishes five levels of capability responsiveness: custodial which is precedent-driven and suppresses change; production-oriented which is efficiency-driven and adapts to change; marketing orientation which is market-driven and seeks familiar change; strategic which is environment-driven and seeks new change; flexible which seeks to create the environment and seeks novel change.

Strategic logic means, for example, that flexible capability and creative action are required in surprising environments. Ansoff maintains that all these levels can be identified in advance of acting by strategic diagnosis. This amounts to a claim that there is no state far from certainty. ∎

Having said something about the nature of planning we turn now to the different kinds of planning that are prescribed for organisations. Since most organisations of any size consist of a collection of different activities organised into units, a distinction is drawn between corporate plans and business unit plans (*Hofer & Schendel, 1978; Porter, 1987*).

The corporate plan

This is concerned with the pattern of actions that is to apply to an organisation as a whole. It is what is supposed to make the whole add up to more than the sum of its parts, a phenomenon known as synergy. The justification for grouping a number of related activities together, rather than having them operate as separate organisations, lies in the value that the corporate level adds. And it adds value by reaping synergies and by coordinating and making the parts consistent.

Corporate strategy is concerned with what activities or businesses the organisation should be involved in and how the corporate level should manage that set of businesses. In other words, corporate strategy is about a portfolio of businesses and what should be done with them. The key question for corporate strategy is: what collection of activities do we need to put together, and how should we manage this collection, to achieve corporate objectives in the end set by shareholders?

Business unit plans

A business unit plan sets out how that business unit is going to build a posture and position that are superior to that of its rivals, so enabling it to achieve the performance objectives set by the corporate level. In other words, business unit strategy is about the means of securing and sustaining competitive advantage. The key question for business unit strategy is: how do we secure competitive advantage so as to achieve the objectives set by the corporation?

Finally, since business units are generally organised on a functional basis – finance, sales, production and research departments, for example – the business unit strategy will have to be translated into functional or operational strategies.

Functional and operational plans

These set out the actions that a function is to take to contribute to the whole strategy of the business unit, just as the business unit strategy contributes to the corporate one. The key question for functional plans is: what actions must we take to contribute our share to the business unit plan?

What we have, then, is a hierarchy of long-term objectives and plans, the corporate creating the framework for the business unit, and the business unit creating the framework for the functional. Furthermore, this collection of long-term plans provides the framework for formulating shorter-term plans and budgets against which an organisation can be controlled in the short term (see *Key Concept 5.1*).

The key question to address now is how managers at whatever level are supposed to select the plans that will lead them to success. The prescribed way of selecting successful plans is to use analytical criteria to evaluate the options.

Evaluation criteria are intended to enable managers to conclude whether or not a particular sequence of actions will lead to a particular position and posture and whether that position and posture will in turn produce some target measure of performance. The criteria are there to enable managers to form judgements about the outcomes of their proposed actions before they take those actions; that is, judgements as to whether a choice of strategy is likely to turn out to be a good one before they do anything at all to implement it. The purpose is to prevent surprises and ensure that an

Key Concept 5.1

Plans and planning

The words 'plans' and 'planning' are often used loosely by managers. For example, managers may say that they have a long-term plan simply because they have set out some long-term financial targets or because they have identified one or two specific actions that they intend to undertake, for example, make an acquisition. As students of strategic management we need to be more precise in using the words 'plans' and 'planning'.

Managers can only be said to be planning the future of their organisation when, as a group, they share a common intention to achieve a particular future posture, position and level of performance for the business (you may wish to refer back to Chapter 1, Figure 1.1); that is, when they select aims and objectives for the business well in advance of acting. In addition to choosing a future state, managers must also share a common intention to pursue a sequence of actions to achieve that chosen future state, if their behaviour is to qualify as planned. Before managers can intentionally choose an intended state and an intended sequence of future actions, however, they have to identify the future environment in which they are to achieve their aims – their intentions must be anchored to a specific future reality. In other words, managers cannot possibly plan unless they can also make reasonably reliable forecasts of the future time period they are planning for. The future must not only be knowable, it must be sufficiently well known in advance of required performance.

In addition, to qualify as controlling and developing an organisation's long-term future in the planning mode, managers must set milestones along the path to the intended future state, couched in terms of results. This will enable the outcomes of actions to be checked and deviations from plan corrected. Action is both implementation of the planned sequence of actions and corrections to keep results on course. Only then is control being exercised in a planned manner. The ability to control by plan depends upon the possibility of establishing organisational intention.

Managers can only be said to be driving their organisation according to a plan over a particular time period when they can be shown to be utilising technically rational decision-making processes and monitoring forms of control in relation to that time period

organisation behaves over long time periods in a manner intended by its members and leaders. There are three very widely proposed sets of criteria for doing this.

Acceptability or desirability

(To be discussed in detail in the next section.) According to this criterion strategies will turn out to be successful only if their consequences are acceptable to the organisation's most powerful stakeholders. These consequences must be acceptable not only in the obvious terms of financial performance but also in terms of meeting other stakeholder expectations, including the impact on their power positions and their cultural beliefs. The stakeholders of an organisation are its owners, managers, employees, customers, suppliers, trade bodies, trades unions, government authorities and community pressure groups. If a pattern of actions is not acceptable to powerful groups from any of the stakeholder categories then the strategy may well fail.

Feasibility

(To be discussed in detail in the section after the next.) This criterion states that a strategy will be a success if it is feasible in the sense that the financial and other resources, the technology and the skills are all available to carry out the strategy. A strategy is feasible when there are no insurmountable obstacles to its implementation. Many strategies have failed and will fail because they require investments of resources, or applications of skill and technology, beyond the capability of the organisation trying to carry them out.

Suitability, appropriateness or fit

(To be discussed in a later section below.) This means that strategies will be successful when they relate to the key features identified by strategic analysis; that is, when the patterns in actions, positions, postures and performance fit with the objectives and the environment of the organisation. The strategy is suitable when it takes advantage of strengths and opportunities, as well as dealing with weaknesses and threats. This then associates success with a strategic logic, or rationale, matching patterns of action to market situations, competitive capability and the culture of the organisation. We can summarise all of this by saying that an organisation fully satisfies the suitability criteria when it is in a stable equilibrium state completely adapted to its environment.

We turn now to the first of the three widely accepted criteria for selecting some future sequence of actions that will make an organisation successful.

Acceptability

There are at least three senses, it is argued, in which strategies have to be acceptable if they are to produce success. First, performance in financial terms must be acceptable to owners and creditors. Second, the consequences of the strategies for the most powerful groupings within an organisation must be acceptable to those groupings in terms of their expectations and the impact on their power positions and cultural beliefs. Third, the consequences of the strategies for powerful groups external to an organisation must be acceptable to those groupings. Consider what each of these senses entails.

1 ACCEPTABLE FINANCIAL PERFORMANCE

If they are to be successful then managers must determine in advance of acting whether their long-term plans are likely to turn out to be financially acceptable. They are supposed to determine this by forecasting the financial consequences of each strategic option open to them: cash flows, capital expenditures and other costs, sales volumes, price levels, profit levels, assets and liabilities including borrowing and other funding requirements. You can see why this procedure is possible only in situations fairly close to certainty – by definition, when you are far from certainty it is not possible to prepare forecasts that are of much use. Next, managers are supposed to use the forecasts to calculate prospective rates of return on sales and capital.

A rate of return is calculated by expressing some measure of profit as a percentage of some measure of the sales that yield that profit or the assets used in generating it. So, if a business earns a profit of £1m from sales of £5m and in order to make these sales it had to use assets of £10m, then the rate of return on sales is 20 per cent and on capital employed it is 10 per cent.

However, complexities arise because it is possible to define profits and assets in many different ways. Managers may be interested in profits before tax or after tax, before allowing for the depreciation of assets or after depreciation, before interest paid on loans or after interest. They may be interested in total assets employed or in net assets employed, that is after deducting amounts owed by the organisation. They may be interested in fixed assets (land, buildings, plant and machinery) or variable assets such as inventories and debtors. There are therefore many different rates of return on sales and capital and the one used depends upon the purpose of use and also on accounting conventions.

No matter what particular rate of return is selected, there will be many difficulties of measurement to be overcome. For example, it may be difficult to measure just how much of an asset has been used up in a particular period of use – the problem of measuring depreciation. Or it is often difficult to know how to allocate the costs of the corporate level of management to the business units.

Once managers have identified what the relevant performance measures are and dealt with the difficulties of measurement, they then have the information they can use to determine the likely financial acceptability of their plans. Financial acceptability rests on a balance between rewards and risks, and we will now discuss how the information on performance can be used to measure rewards and associated risks for those who provide an organisation's funds.

Acceptable financial performance is a relative concept and is defined in terms of the next best opportunity open to the owners of an organisation for using or investing their funds. In the case of state and not-for-profit organisations those alternatives are established through political choices and those choices depend upon the relative power of people interested in the choice.

In 1991, the UK government decided to permit British Rail to build a Channel Tunnel rail link that will pass through east London rather than south London. The reason for choosing an eastern rather than a southern route was most probably because the pressure groups of people living in the east are far less powerful than the pressure groups of the much more affluent inhabitants of the southern parts of the city. Furthermore, the decision to invest government funds in this project constitutes a choice not to use those funds to build, say, a refuge for the homeless. Again that choice reflects the relative power positions of industry that wants the rail link and the homeless who need somewhere to live.

Although the alternative uses of funds in state and not-for-profit bodies are inevitably the result of political decisions, those concerned to apply a more technically rational approach prescribe the use of analytical techniques to identify and compare the costs and benefits of alternative political choices. The argument is that, even if at the end of the day the choice is made on the basis of relative power, those making the choice should at least be aware of what the costs will be of the benefits provided by each option open to them.

Cost/benefit analysis

Cost/benefit analysis (*Rowe, Mason, Dickel & Snyder, 1989; Mirsham, 1980*) attempts to place money values on all the costs and benefits of a particular strategic action option. The difficulty lies in the fact that state bodies and not-for-profit organisations are particularly concerned with intangible, non-traded costs and benefits.

So, for example, an investment in a new road has clear monetary costs relating to its construction, but there are much less clearly measurable costs in terms of the destruction of the countryside, the noise imposed on nearby households and so on. Many of the road's benefits are also not traded, for example the reduction in time wasted in traffic jams. It is therefore difficult to measure and even more difficult to value a great many of the costs and benefits that the particular types of organisations we are talking about get involved in.

The analysis therefore involves many subjective judgements upon which there is likely to be disagreement that cannot be resolved by rational argument in either its technical or reasoned senses (see *Key Concept 2.3* in Chapter 2). In the end the decision has to be made by political processes of persuasion and conversion, or even force. The analysis is there to aid this process by making the factors that need to be taken into account explicit and by creating the appearance of technical and reasoned rationality. This appearance of rationality can be instrumental in persuading people to accept a particular choice and it legitimises the decision, in effect giving it a seal of 'scientific' approval even though such rationality was not actually used to make the choice.

The rest of this section considers organisations in the business sector, where the ability to measure and value costs and benefits is far greater. But bear in mind that, even there, that ability to measure is far from perfect.

Performance benchmarks

For the majority of organisations in the business sector, alternative investment opportunities for owners are established, not by a political system but by the capital markets. Over the long term it is the operators on the capital markets who will judge whether the performance of a business is acceptable or not and they will do so in terms of the financial return on their investment. The exception to this is family-owned private companies, where alternative investment opportunities are also determined by the capital markets, but where the shareholders have the freedom to choose some definition of acceptability other than financial return. However, non-family-owned business organisations will only continue to receive financial backing if capital market operators judge that the rate of return on the assets employed bears some reasonable relationship to long-term interest rates, taking account of likely rates of inflation and different levels of risk. Companies that persistently fail to achieve rates of return on assets and rates of growth in profit levels that are acceptable in these terms, and that are comparable with similar kinds of businesses, will be prime candidates for takeovers. *Illustration 5.3* sets out how benchmark performance measures of this kind can be calculated.

Gap analysis

Benchmark performance measures may be used to perform what is called gap analysis (*Argenti, 1980*). To carry out a gap analysis, the performance of a company is first pro-

Illustration
5.3

Benchmark performance measures

Investors look for income, capital appreciation, or some combination of the two. Acceptable financial performance for a business organisation means some combination of dividend yield and profit growth (the justification for capital appreciation) that is comparable to alternative investment opportunities involving the same level of risk.

Suppose that we were seeking to establish benchmark performance standards for pharmaceutical company A in the UK. If shareholders are to find the shares of this company attractive then it must achieve a performance record at least equal to the industry average. If it consistently underperforms its share price will fall, opening it up to the threat of takeover. The publications of stockbrokers, or reports such as Business Ratios (published by ICC Information Group Limited), provide information on profit growth rates in a wide range of different companies and different business sectors. These reports may show that sales in the pharmaceutical sector have been growing at 8 per cent per annum on average and profit levels at 12 per cent on average. Stockbroker reports may indicate that these growth rates are expected to continue. (Since the rate of return on capital for pharmaceutical companies is regulated by the government, it is profit growth rates that will be the main indicators of performance, but if we were dealing with the electronics industry, we would also be interested in the rate of return on capital.) The top executives of company A would use this comparative information to form a judgement on the sales and profit growth rates their company should be targeting to achieve in order to satisfy shareholders. Achieving more than the sector average will mean a rapidly rising share price and thus protection from takeover threats. So top executives in company A may decide to set targets of 10 per cent per annum growth in sales and 15 per cent per annum growth in profits. These targets would then be communicated to the responsible line managers, who would be judged on how closely they were achieved. ■

jected on the basis that it continues to follow existing policies. The resulting levels of profitability, rates of return and rates of profit growth are then compared with the benchmarks and the gap between them calculated. That gap measures the contribution that will be required from the development of new strategies. It is these new strategies that must fill the gap between what is acceptable and what is likely from continuing to run the business as before. Whether a set of strategies fills the gap or not becomes a criterion for successful strategy selection. *Illustration 5.4* gives an example of how gap analysis is used.

To use gap analysis it is necessary of course to project the profit consequences of continuing to pursue existing policies and the consequences of alternative proposals to fill the gap. This projection and comparison of different courses of action for a firm as a whole is greatly facilitated by the use of computerised corporate financial models. Most companies of any size nowadays have models to forecast future sales volumes and prices. These may be complex and sophisticated regression models or they may be simple rules of thumb. Most companies also have forecasting procedures to form the basis of production scheduling and inventory control. A corporate or financial model

Use of gap analysis

Suppose the corporate level of the pharmaceutical company A referred to in *Illustration 5.3* sets growth rate objectives for one of its divisions. it requires the division to achieve annual growth rates of 10 per cent in sales and 15 per cent in pre-tax profits for the next five years. The division carefully examines its product portfolio and concludes that two of its major product lines – call them X and Z – will be coming off patent towards the end of the five-year period, opening up the way for inevitable competition and loss of market share. The remaining product lines, C and D, are old ones unlikely to grow at all. The divisional managers then examine the new product development portfolio and conclude that there is no way in which new products coming on stream, E and F, could compensate for the lack of growth in revenues and profits from the existing product portfolio. It is now possible to quantify the negative gap between the corporately set objective for the division and the outcome likely to be generated by existing and new product portfolios by the end of the five-year period.

Divisional management conclude that in order to plug the gap they will have to adopt a strategy of acquiring products and/or companies. A divisional long-term plan is put together, setting out the objectives, the financial projections and the general strategy of acquisition. Here analysis of the gap between what is required and what is likely prompts plans to close the gap. ■

combines partial models of this kind with the relationships in the profit and loss account and the balance sheet to constitute a financial model of the corporation as a whole.

Financial models and scenarios

Such corporate models can then be used to simulate the future of the corporation on the basis of different scenarios (*Cooke & Slack, 1984; Shim & McGlade, 1984; Beck, 1982, Rowe, Mason, Dickel & Snyder, 1989*). The use of scenarios involves specifying a number of different possible future environments for a company. Key variables specified by each of these scenarios, for example the rate of growth in the volume of market demand, are then plugged into the corporate model. The performance of the company is thereby simulated for each of the possible scenarios. This is done to assist managers to decide in advance whether a particular set of strategies is likely to result in acceptable performance or not. Simulating the performance of the company in different scenarios for the future allows different calculations of the performance gap. The use of scenarios, simulation and corporate models is illustrated in *Illustration 5.5*.

Investment appraisal techniques

So far, we have been concerned with evaluating the impact of possible strategies on the financial performance of a corporation as a whole. In addition, each of the specific elements of any strategy, that is, each of the investment projects required to put it in place, also have to meet criteria of acceptability. There are a number of techniques of investment appraisal available to test whether individual projects meet the requirements of acceptable return; they are now outlined.

Payback period

This is simply the period of time it takes to pay back the original investment. Thus, if the proposal is to build a new factory to produce concrete building blocks at a cost of £10m, and we estimate that it will take four years for the profits flowing from that factory to add up to £10m, then the payback period is 4. A corporation would set payback targets and require that investment proposals should meet them if they are to be acceptable. So, the target may be a payback of five years or less, in which case our concrete block factory proposal passes the hurdle.

Average rate of return

Here we would estimate what the profit level in the first full year of operation would be and then calculate the rate of return that this represents on the original investment. Thus if the concrete block plant yields a profit of £1.5m in its first year of full operation and it costs £10m, then the rate of return is 15 per cent. A corporation using this method would set a target rate of return, say 12.5 per cent, and reject all investment proposals that fell below this.

Discounted cash flow analysis

The drawback of the payback and the average rate of return methods is that they do not take account of the fact that money in the hand today is worth more than a promise of money tomorrow – if you have money today you can invest it and earn interest on it. Discounted cash flow methods meet this objection by discounting all the cash flows back to the present.

To discount the cash flows, it is necessary to estimate the cash flow for each year in the life of the investment. So, in the case of the concrete block plant, we might decide to calculate cash flows for the next 25 years. The cash flow for the first year would be – £10m because we are spending money on building the plant and getting nothing in return.

Next year we believe that we will make sales of say £12m as we start to attract customers for the plant, but commissioning problems and low capacity usage mean that costs are expected to run at £15m, producing another negative cash flow: –£3m. The year after that we believe that we will double sales and keep costs at the same level, producing a positive cash flow of £9m. Estimates of this kind need to be made for the next 25 years.

Then we use estimates of interest rates to discount each year's cash flow back to the present. For example, suppose today's interest rate is 10 per cent and we invest £7.44m at that rate, then in two years' time it will be worth £9m. So the present value of £9m in two years' time at a discount rate of 10 per cent is £7.44m. When we have performed this calculation for each year's cash flow, we can add them up and if the net result is positive, then the investment is worthwhile in the sense that it will earn more than an investment at today's interest rate. In fact we will want to set a higher discount rate to take account of the fact that investing in a block plant is a great deal riskier than investing in the bank.

The discount rate we set might be, say, 18 per cent when interest rates are 10 per cent. If the net cash flow is still positive at this rate, then we can conclude that it is as good an investment as putting the money in the bank. The discount rate that yields a zero net present value is also clearly the rate of return that the investment will earn.

A corporation using this method of investment appraisal would set a target rate of return and require that investment proposals should meet it. Suppose it sets an 18 per cent discounted cash flow (dcf) rate of return and finds that a proposal yields only 13 per cent, then it would reject it as unacceptable to its shareholders because they could earn more in a risk-adjusted sense by keeping their money in a bank.

The difficulty of forecasting cash flows and interest rates for many years ahead is recognised by those who use that approach. Most therefore make calculations for a number of different scenarios of the environment in which an investment project may operate. A number of different market environments, cost and regulatory regimes are postulated, and the calculations made for each of them. In other words, the future performance of the investment is simulated.

Practical difficulties arise as the number of different scenarios increases. The number of scenarios required in practice to cover the most likely eventualities usually turns out to be so large that managers lose track of what they all mean. The experts preparing the scenarios and simulations end up making literally hundreds of small assumptions about prices, volumes, costs and many other matters. These are so numerous that the line managers who have to take the decision cannot be aware of what they all are. The result can be confusion as to the reasons why an investment is being undertaken. There is also, in common with cost/benefit analysis, the difficulty of incorporating important intangible, difficult-to-measure value elements. So in practice you find that managers include rather arbitrary values to represent the benefits of synergy between the investment they are considering and some other activity. In practice the use of what appear to be highly rational techniques may all too often simply be a rational 'cover-up' for decisions being taken on other bases – this is a matter we will take up in more detail when we come to extraordinary management processes in Chapter 11.

Risk and sensitivity analysis

The use of scenarios and simulations at both total corporate and specific investment project levels allows sensitivity analyses to be performed. The purpose of these analyses is to identify those variables to which performance is particularly sensitive. So a particular company, or a particular investment project, may not be all that sensitive to changes in the exchange rate, but it may be highly sensitive to changes in regulations on pollution control. Sensitivity analysis allows managers to gain some idea of how serious a change in some variable, such as the interest rate, will be for the future performance of an investment or of the corporation as a whole. The manner in which this provides a tool for analysing risk is shown in *Illustration 5.5*.

Financial ratios

There are a number of indicators of the level of financial risk that are used to make judgements about the acceptability or otherwise of performance in financial terms. These indicators take the form of financial ratios and the following are among the most important.

Illustration
5.5

Sensitivity analysis

Suppose a steel production company, the local electricity supply company and a construction company form a consortium to build and operate a small gas turbine power station. The power station is estimated to cost £100 million and in order to provide acceptable financial returns the investors are looking for net profits of £12 million per annum.

The key factors affecting profit levels are the price of gas, the capacity utilisation of the generating plant, and the price of electricity. In order to test the sensitivity of the return on the investment to these three factors we can construct a number of scenarios.

For example, we might assume that plant capacity utilisation will be around 60 per cent and the gas price will remain at a level of 100. We can then calculate the profit levels that will be achieved in these circumstances at different prices of electricity:

at 3.5 pence per unit a profit of £15m is achieved;
at 3.0 pence per unit a profit of £12m is achieved;
at 2.5 pence per unit a profit of £8m is achieved;
at 2.0 pence per unit a loss of £2m is made.

We could then take one of these price levels, say 3 pence per unit, and calculate the effects of higher and lower capacity utilisation and gas price levels. Suppose these showed that profit is even more sensitive to changes in gas prices and capacity utilisation. We might then conclude that we will only undertake the investment if we can secure long-term demand contracts for the electricity and long-term supply contracts for the gas. The main risk, to which profit is highly sensitive, will then be electricity prices. We would then have to consider whether the major generators could afford to allow prices to fall as low as 2 pence per unit. We might decide that they are unlikely to do this and that therefore the risk of price fluctuation is a reasonable one to take; or we might judge that the generators will artificially suppress prices for a time to discourage those who wish to make investments like ours. We might then judge that the proposed investment is too risky. ■

Gearing ratios

A gearing ratio is a measure of how heavily or otherwise an organisation depends on borrowed funds. An organisation can finance its operations using money contributed by its shareholders or it can borrow the money it needs. On that borrowed money it must pay interest whether it earns a profit or not, while on shareholders' funds it pays a dividend only if it earns a profit. Depending on borrowed funds therefore creates risk and it is necessary to make judgements about the level of risk and manage that risk.

A gearing ratio is the ratio of some measure of borrowing to some measure of shareholders' funds. So, if an organisation has borrowings of £50m and shareholders' funds of £100m, then the gearing ratio is 50 per cent. Whether this is too high or too low, and therefore whether it is particularly risky or not, is a matter of judgement. That judgement will be heavily influenced by what is regarded by operators in the capital markets as the norm for companies of a particular type. ICC ratios (already referred to above in *Illustration 5.3*) publish information on gearing ratios and managers can compare the gearing ratio that their plans would produce with that of other companies. If the gearing ratio is judged by investors and lenders to be too high, share prices will fall and lenders will refuse to extend further loans.

Another measure of exposure to borrowing is provided by the ratio of profits to interest paid, a measure known as interest cover. If profits cover interest 20 times, this would probably be judged to be low risk. But, if profits cover interest payments only twice, this would probably be judged to be high risk.

Liquidity ratios

Liquidity ratios provide a measure of how quickly an organisation could realise its assets. Obviously, the faster it can turn its assets into cash the more easily it will be able to deal with any financial crisis that occurs. The most liquid asset is of course cash and therefore the cash ratio is a prime measure of liquidity. This is calculated as the percentage of total assets that are in the form of bank deposits, or capital market instruments such as bonds. Another liquidity ratio would be current assets as a percentage of total assets. Current assets are cash plus inventories plus debtors minus creditors, all reasonably realisable in a short time period.

Inventory turnover

This is a measure of how many times a year the inventories of a business are realised. So, if it takes a year to sell all that is held in inventory, then the inventory turnover is 1. If it takes only a month to sell the whole inventory and replace it, then the turnover is obviously 12. The faster inventories are turned over, that is the more rapidly they can be sold, the safer the business.

So much for determining whether plans will produce financial performance acceptable to shareholders and creditors in terms of both risk and reward levels. Even if plans pass this test, however, they must still pass others – they must meet the expectations of those with power in an organisation.

2 ACCEPTABLE CONSEQUENCES FOR INTERNAL POWER GROUPS

In addition to financial risk and reward, long-term plans have other consequences for people within an organisation. If carried out, strategic plans may well change the way people work, who they work with, what relative power they have, how they are judged by others and so on. Long-term plans could produce consequences that people believe to be morally repugnant or against their customs and beliefs in some other way. If this is the case, those plans are unlikely to succeed because people will do their best to prevent the plan being implemented. Managers must therefore submit their long-term plans to another acceptability test: they must analyse the impact of their plans on the expectations, relative power positions, and cultural beliefs of key individuals and groups within the organisation.

Illustration 5.6 gives an example of how managers rejected what they had calculated to be the most acceptable option in financial terms, because it conflicted with the expectations of some key individuals.

Organisational culture

In order to determine whether a plan is likely to be acceptable in cultural terms it is necessary to analyse the core beliefs that people in an organisation share. Analysis of the culture will reveal whether options being considered fall within that culture or whether they require major cultural change. One would not necessarily reject options that require major cultural change, but then plans to bring this about would have to be formulated – a matter we will discuss in Section 5.4.

The nature of an organisation's culture can be analysed by studying the stories people in that organisation tell. For example, there may be well-known stories about the organisation's founder or other memorable leaders that are always told to new joiners. They may tell the story about the company founder who used to stand at the door each morning to see who was arriving late. The story is a way of emphasising one of the rules that all accept about not being late. In another organisation the leader may wear casual clothing and sit in an open plan office. The leader's clothes are a cultural symbol of a core belief in informal relationships. The culture is revealed by the myths, the heroes, the rituals and symbols that are used. The culture is reflected in leadership and management styles.

When analysing the culture the strategist will identify what the core beliefs are and how strongly people believe in them. Some approaches to classifying cultures will be discussed in the section on implementing strategic plans later on in this chapter.

Key Concept 5.2

The culture of an organisation

The culture of any group of people is that set of beliefs, customs, practices and way of thinking that they have come to share with each other through being and working together. It is a set of assumptions people simply accept without question as they interact with each other. At the visible level the culture of a group of people takes the form of ritual behaviour, symbols, myths, stories, sounds, and artifacts. A culture is much the same as a mental model, or a paradigm. See Key Concepts 3.1 *and* 3.2 *in Chapter 3.*

Power structure

It will also be necessary to analyse the power structure of an organisation to determine whether plans are likely to be acceptable (see *Key Concept 5.3*).

Illustration
5.6

Castings plc

Some 15 months ago Castings plc acquired a company in Colchester which produces castings using three processes:

- sand/Shaw where wooden patterns are used to make ceramic moulds for the casting;
- Lost wax where metal moulds are filled with wax and the ferrous casting subsequently made from the wax shape;
- Lost wax used to manufacture aluminium castings.

The customers for the Colchester factory's products, large companies in the aerospace and general engineering industries, demand high-precision castings at low prices. Demand for product from the lost wax process has been growing rapidly as customers turn to the higher quality and lower cost that this process gives compared to sand/Shaw or machining. Although sand/Shaw is therefore on the wane, it is still cheaper for short runs.

When it acquired the Colchester factory, Castings plc already had another ferrous casting business using lost wax. This is located at Peterborough and it makes higher-volume less-complicated castings than the new acquisition. Another Castings plc business uses lost wax to cast aluminium and it is located at Leicester. These are both very profitable businesses.

Over the first year the newly acquired company with sales of under £2m incurred a £0.5m loss. Losses over the first three months of this financial year have been stemmed, but not reversed. Now the landlord has given notice that the premises occupied by the acquisition must be vacated in 9 months' time.

The board of Castings therefore considered the options open to it. The Finance Director prepared a schedule showing the sales, costs, profits and rates of return of a number of options as follows:

1. Relocating the Colchester factory to a nearby site would yield an average return on capital (ROC) for the next five years of minus 4.8 per cent.
2. Relocating the sand/Shaw business at Colchester to a nearby site, moving the lost wax ferrous business to Peterborough and the aluminium to Leicester would yield a five-year average ROC of 9.1 per cent.
3. Moving everything to Peterborough would yield a five-year average ROC of 20.9 per cent.
4. Closing Colchester down would yield a five-year average ROC of minus 0.1 per cent.

Despite the high rate of return to be gained from concentrating the whole business at Peterborough the board chose option 2. They did this because they knew that the managers of the successful Peterborough business did not want to have to deal with the problem of a declining sand/Shaw business. They would be distracted from their own profitable business. Furthermore, key personnel at Colchester would probably not move and therefore would be lost to the company. Customers too might be disaffected by the change in location. Perhaps most important of all, although it was hardly discussed at the board meeting, was the impact closure would have on operators on the stock market. The closure of Colchester would have to be made public, amounting to an admission of failure on the part of Castings plc board members who had promoted the acquisition in the first place.

The option chosen therefore met a number of people's non-financial expectations, even though it was not the best financial option according to the prescribed way of making that calculation. ∎

Key Concept 5.3

Power

Power flows from relationships, built up over time, between individuals and groups that determine how one affects or responds to another in making organisational choices. Power enables one person or group to force or persuade another to do something that the other does not want to do, or could not otherwise do, or would not otherwise have thought of doing. The sources of power lie in:

- Sanctions. *Power increases with the ability of one person or group to reward or punish another in terms of prestige, status, money or career progression.*
- Interdependence. *One individual or group is relatively more powerful than another if it: controls more resources; has greater access to information; performs critical activities upon which the others depend for their performance; has greater access to communication channels or the more powerful; has control over communication agendas or the decision-making situations.*
- Contribution. *Relative power increases with the personal skills and expertise of particular individuals and their ability to interpret ambiguous situations and so reduce uncertainty for others.*

The source of power has much to do with the form it takes. Power can take the form of authority when it is exercised and consented to because of hierarchical position and because of the rules and regulations of the organisation. Or power can take the form of influence where it is based on interdependence between people and the contributions they make to common endeavours. Or, power can take the form of force.

Having analysed the source and form of power, the strategist has to identify its location and that means identifying the dominant coalitions in the organisation. This may be difficult because the power structure does not necessarily accord with the formal hierarchy – it will be necessary to identify which individuals and groups exercise much influence even though they have less authority. It will be necessary to look for potential alliances between coalitions. *Illustration 5.7* gives some examples of how the power structure affects the acceptability of strategies.

3 ACCEPTABLE CONSEQUENCES FOR EXTERNAL POWER GROUPS

Power groups outside an organisation also determine the acceptability of that organisation's strategies. A community pressure group may find the noise level of a proposed factory expansion unacceptable. Even if the factory itself turns out to be a financially acceptable investment, the total consequences for the image of the corporation could render the strategy unsuccessful. Another example is provided by the electricity and gas industries in the UK. To succeed, strategies of companies in these sectors have to be acceptable to the industry regulators and consumer pressure

Power and the acceptability of strategies

Some strategies will require large injections of funds that can only be obtained by the issue of new shares. This may weaken the control of particularly powerful share-holders, making the strategies unacceptable to them despite acceptable financial performance. Where the ownership of a company is concentrated in the hands of one or two individuals, then acceptability to those individuals in personal power or other terms may count for much more than acceptable performance. So the owner may tolerate below-average performance for years because it is found unacceptable to replace relatives in key positions.

It is not just acceptability to owners that counts. Some strategies may be unac-ceptable to a powerful subsidiary of one division of a corporation because it will undermine that division's power position in the corporation. Suppose a relatively small division proposes to expand its activities from its domestic base to foreign countries. If this is unacceptable to a larger more powerful division already operat-ing in foreign markets, the strategy could well fail for this reason alone. The battles between these two divisions could lead to failure as attention is diverted from the markets. Or, to take another example, for reasons that have little to do with perfor-mance, a powerful chairman may have certain preferences. For example, this chairman may favour the expansion of a house-building subsidiary because his son runs it. Because that subsidiary will require substantial investment, the chairman may be against diversification. Attempts to pursue diversification strategies are then unlikely to succeed. ∎

groups. A further example is where the strategies of one organisation could have dam-aging consequences for the distributors of that organisation's products or for the suppliers to that organisation. Such damage could provoke those distributors and sup-pliers to retaliate in highly detrimental ways, as shown in *Illustration 5.8*.

The reactions of competitors to strategies are also of major importance. Some strat-egies pursued by one company could provoke more than normal competitive responses from competitors. Those competitors may regard the strategies of the first company as unfair competition and this could lead to price wars, hostile mergers, lobbying of the national political institutions, all of which could cause a strategy to fail. For example, North American and European countries have passed laws against imports from Japanese competitors or insisted on voluntary restraints.

Feasibility

Analysis may show that strategies are likely to be acceptable in terms of financial per-formance, and to major power groupings both within and outside an organisation, but yet fail because they are not feasible. To be feasible there must be no insurmountable obstacle to implementing a strategy. Such obstacles could be presented by:

Kitchen Queen

In the 1970s a small company distributing fitted kitchens was set up in Manchester – Kitchen Queen. This company grew rapidly for a number of years because of its policy of advertising and displaying quality fitted kitchens, supporting the product with design and installation services and meeting reliable delivery time criteria. After some years of rapid growth, it was floated on the stock market and then pursued a policy of diversification. It purchased Di Lussio, a firm producing DIY flat-pack fitted kitchens of a high quality. By this move Kitchen Queen diversified into production and the profitability of Di Lussio relied on its distributors, competitors to the original Kitchen Queen business. The distributors were thus an important power group outside Kitchen Queen and the strategy of the latter would have to be in some sense acceptable to those distributors.

The acquisition worked and before long the production activity of the Kitchen Queen Group was generating most of the profit. Then a number of further diversifications were undertaken, including the purchase of a mail order company. The decision was then made to distribute all of Di Lussio's product through the mail order acquisition. When the distributors got wind of this they cancelled all their orders and dumped all their stocks of Di Lussio product onto the market at very low prices. This was one of the major causes of Kitchen Queen's bankruptcy not long afterwards. ■

Source: Kitchen Queen Case Study, Case Clearing House, Cranfield.

- inadequate resources
- resources of insufficient quality
- inappropriate technology
- timing in relation to other events
- competitor strength.

Feasibility and financial resources

One of the immediately obvious resources that must be available if a strategy is to be carried out is the money to finance the strategy over its whole life. If a company gets half-way through a strategy, which is on target to yield acceptable performance, but nevertheless runs out of the funds to continue, then clearly the strategy will fail. The prescription is therefore to carry out a flow-of-funds analysis of the strategy options, before embarking on any of them, to ascertain the probability of running into cash flow problems.

A flow-of-funds analysis identifies the timing and size of the capital expenditures and other costs required for each project that makes up the strategy, and the timing and size of the revenues that those projects will generate. These revenue and expenditure flows then need to be related to projected cash inflows and outflows for the corporation as a whole. The intention would be to identify any potential crisis point in the net flows of cash into the business, well in advance of it occurring.

Normally, an investment project first produces negative cash flows and profit levels – costs are incurred before any revenues can be earned. Later, the cash flows and the profit levels turn positive if the project is a success. The point of change from the negative to the positive is known as *break-even*. A flow of funds analysis makes it possible to calculate this break-even point, where a project, a set of projects constituting a strategy, or a corporation as a whole makes neither a loss nor a profit. An example of break-even analysis is provided in *Illustration 5.9*.

Illustration 5.9

Break-even analysis

In break-even analysis, we identify a few crucial factors upon which success is likely to depend. For example, success may depend heavily on achieving certain volumes of production. These volumes can only be sustained if certain market shares are achieved. So for strategy option A we calculate that we can achieve break-even, that is neither loss nor profit, at a market share of 10 per cent. But for strategy B we discover that we would have to achieve 20 per cent to break even. Given our knowledge of competitor power, we may decide that strategy A is therefore more feasible. ∎

What managers should do, therefore, to establish the feasibility of their strategy is to calculate the flows of funds and the break-even points for different strategic options in different scenarios. This will help them to identify the financing requirements for their strategy, the timing of those requirements, and the key conditions required for the move out of any initial negative cash flow situation.

The flow-of-funds analysis indicates how much money a strategic option will require if it is to be implemented. It may well be that this money cannot be generated by the existing business of a company and it will therefore have to raise more funds from its shareholders, or borrow, if it wishes to proceed. However, there is a limit to the amount of new capital that can be raised from shareholders and there are limits to borrowing. At some point further increases in borrowing will raise the level of risk: the gearing ratio will rise above that regarded as prudent and the stock market will therefore mark the company's shares down; the number of times profit covers interest payments will fall and lenders will be less and less willing to extend further loans.

At some point, then, a strategic option will be feasible only if it generates positive cash flows in some areas to provide the cash requirements of other areas. The prescription is that a strategy must establish a balanced collection, or portfolio, of activities such that the positive profit and cash flow generated by one activity offset the negative flows of others. A balanced portfolio also reduces risk – while the markets for one activity may experience unexpected declines, those for another activity may do unexpectedly well.

The technique available to conduct this test of balance and hence feasibility is called *portfolio analysis*. The building blocks of portfolio analysis are the concepts of the product life cycle and the experience curve. We will first consider these and then see how they can be combined to provide a portfolio analysis.

The product life cycle

This idea is based on the observation that most products follow the typical evolutionary pattern illustrated in *Figure 5.1*:

- An *embryonic* stage in which the product is developed. Here market growth potential may be great but it will be very uncertain; there will be few competitors, little in the way of entry barriers to the market, and perhaps the technology will be new too.
- A *growth* stage in which rapid market growth materialises, attracting other competitors. Competitors develop customer loyalty, so making it harder for more new competitors to enter.
- A *shake-out* stage in which some of the competitors who entered find that they cannot compete and therefore leave.
- A *mature* stage in which growth in the demand for the product slows and a small number of competitors come to dominate the market.
- A *saturation* stage in which demand for the product stabilises and competitors have difficulty in filling their capacity.
- A *decline* stage in which demand begins to switch to substitute products.

These stages in the evolution of a product indicate different general types of strategies – different generic strategies. Which of these generic strategies is appropriate is said to be dependent upon the stage of evolution of the product's market and the competitive strength of the company producing it. So a company with a strong capability should invest heavily in the embryonic stage and establish a position before others arrive. During the growth phase it should continue investing, push for rapid growth, and so defend its strong position against new arrivals. By the time the mature phase is

FIGURE 5.1
The product life cycle

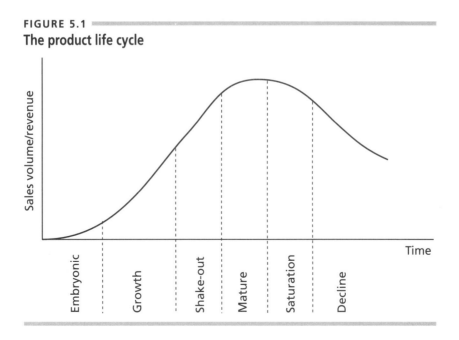

161

reached, this company should have established market leadership and, as the product gets to saturation level, the aging stage, the dominant company should defend its position but withdraw cash from the business. In a declining market it will be able to continue harvesting cash, while weaker competitors withdraw.

Throughout, strong competitors are supposed to follow strategies of cost leadership. The weaker competitors will have to pursue very different strategies, however. In the embryonic stage they will have to identify a niche in the market for the product and occupy that; for example, they may make a luxury, high fashion version of the product and target a particular age or social group. Through the evolution of the market they will have to pursue strategies of making their product different – differentiation – rather than trying to make it cheaper, as the dominant competitors can. In the later stages of product evolution, the weaker competitors will find that they have to withdraw (*Porter, 1980*).

Figure 5.2 illustrates the points made above about the relationship between product stage and strategic option. We now turn to the second block upon which product portfolio techniques are based – the experience curve.

FIGURE 5.2

Generic strategies and the stage of industry development

Stage of 'industry' development

		Growth	*Maturity*	*Decline*
Strategic position of organisation	*Leader*	Keeping ahead of the field	Cost leadership Raise barriers Deter competitors	Redefine scope Divest peripherals Encourage departures
	Follower	Imitation at lower cost Joint ventures	Differentiation Focus	Differentiation New opportunities

Source: M. Porter (1985), *Competitive Advantage: Creating and Sustaining Superior Performance*, New York: The Free Press

The experience curve

The idea of the experience curve is based on the observation that the higher the volume of a particular product that a company produces, the more efficient it becomes at producing it. The cost per unit therefore declines as volume increases, at first rapidly and then more slowly as the learning opportunities for that particular product are exhausted. As a company moves down the learning curve it is in a position to reduce the price it charges customers for the product because its costs are falling. The price curve therefore follows the learning/cost curve as shown in *Figure 5.3*.

From these curves it can be seen that although unit profits are typically high at low volumes, total profits are of course low. As volumes increase, unit profits fall but this is offset by the higher volumes and so total profits increase.

These price and cost curves can be linked to the idea of a product life cycle and the different strategies that strong and weak competitors should pursue. In the early stages of product evolution, a strong competitor will achieve higher volumes than a weak one and so move further down the learning curve. This will enable the strong competitor to reduce prices faster, stimulating demand and so increasing volumes even more to move even faster down the learning curve. Soon, the weaker competitor, or the latecomer, will have no chance of catching up.

FIGURE 5.3
The experience curve

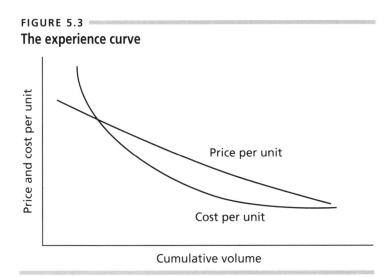

Furthermore, there will be typical patterns in the cash flows and profit levels of companies as a product evolves. At first, all the companies developing a particular product have negative cash flows as they invest and probably incur losses. Later in the growth stage most may still experience negative cash flows as they continue to invest to stay ahead, but the profit levels of the strong competitors will turn positive. Then in the mature stage, investment in the product declines and cash flows run positive for the strong, while profitability becomes less attractive than it was. The weak may be forced to withdraw at this stage. These typical patterns lead to the idea of a product portfolio.

The product portfolio

The earliest and simplest form of product portfolio analysis is the Boston Consulting Group (BCG) growth share matrix (*Henderson, 1970*). To analyse their organisation in this way, managers review their whole business, dividing it up into all its different products, or market segments, or business units. They then calculate the market share they hold for each product, or market segment, or business unit, and then divide it by the share of their nearest rival. This is then the relative market share of that product, segment or business and it is plotted along the horizontal axis of the diagram given in *Figure 5.4*. If the relative share is much greater than 1, then the firm is dominant in that market. If the relative share is well below 1, then the firm is very weak in terms of competitive capability. The relative market share provides a measure of the firm's competitive capability with regard to that product, segment or business unit, because a high market share indicates that the firm is well down the experience curve compared to rivals.

FIGURE 5.4
The BCG product portfolio matrix

Next managers must calculate the rate of growth of the product demand or market segment, represented on the vertical axis of *Figure 5.4*. The rate of growth is held to be a good measure of the attractiveness of the market – the stage in its evolution that it has reached. Rapid rates of growth indicate the entrepreneurial and growth stages of evolution. For each product, market, or business, market share and market growth will therefore be represented by a point plotted on the diagram shown in *Figure 5.4*. Each quadrant of the diagram has a label:

- *Question marks* are products, market segments or business units that are growing rapidly, and the company has a relatively low share. The product life cycle and the experience curve analysis tell us that question marks will require heavy investment, are unlikely to yield profit for some time, and may face strong competitors. They are called question marks because the firm will have to decide how feasible it is to pursue these.
- *Stars* are products, markets or businesses that are growing rapidly, and the firm has a high relative share. Product life cycle and experience curve analysis tell us that these products will require heavy investment (negative cash flow) but may produce high levels of profit. The strategy indicated is one of concentrating effort and money on the stars.

- *Cash cows* are products in mature slow-growth markets in which the firm has a relatively high market share. The prescription is to cut down on investment in these products and harvest the cash. Cash flow will be strongly positive for cows and profit levels rather low.
- *Dogs* are products in slowly growing markets in which the firm has a low share. Both cash flow and profit could be negative. It is in a weak position and should therefore withdraw.

When managers set out all their products, markets or businesses, and the strategic options they are considering, on such a diagram, they can then see how feasible each strategic option will be in financial terms. The feasible options will be those that have some balance between the different quadrants. If a firm has enough cash cows, it will be able to use the money milked from those businesses to support the stars and perhaps try to develop some of the question marks. It can sell dogs and use the money so raised for the same purposes. An unbalanced portfolio – too many stars and not enough cows for example – will mean either that the company has to borrow heavily or it will generate big cash surpluses without knowing what to invest them in.

Criticisms of the BCG matrix

There have been many criticisms of this product portfolio approach (*Slatter, 1980*). First, it is obviously far too simple to equate competitive capability with high market share, large volumes and low cost. This places too great an emphasis on cost; assumes that dominant firms can achieve their position only through low costs when we know that they may well do so by differentiating themselves through the quality they provide. It is also too simple to equate the attractiveness of a market with the growth rate and hence the stage of the product cycle. Even declining markets can provide attractive opportunities for some. Hanson plc has consistently followed a strategy of acquiring businesses that would be classified as cash cows or sometimes even dogs, and yet it has consistently improved its performance.

To overcome the criticism, others have developed more complex product matrices. For example, General Electric developed what it calls the business screen and Shell developed a similar directional policy matrix shown in *Figure 5.5*.

This differs from the BCG matrix in that it does not use simple quantified measures but the judgements of managers as to whether the market is attractive in a number of ways and as to whether they have a strong or a weak position in that market according to a number of criteria. More factors are thus taken into account, but the idea remains that of building a balanced portfolio of businesses to make strategies feasible. The idea is still also that there are generic strategies appropriate for different market conditions and different competitive capabilities.

Even the most complex matrix is still subject to serious drawbacks however. It is all too easy to slip into thinking that the market segments identified for the purpose of the analysis will remain unchanged. For example, in the 1970s General Foods conducted a portfolio analysis and concluded that its coffee business was a cash cow. That business was then starved of funds which were diverted to businesses classified as stars. However, competitors began to segment the coffee market in different ways. They

FIGURE 5.5

A directional policy matrix

developed coffee products suitable for different kinds of coffee – cappuccino, filter coffee, specially ground coffee for espresso, decaffeinated coffee and so on. Because they had differentiated coffee in this way they were able to charge higher prices and attract business away from more traditional coffee suppliers. General Foods became aware of what was happening just in time to prevent the disappearance of its coffee business. Changing the way a market is segmented may thus be more important than applying standardised strategies determined by portfolio analysis.

Furthermore, portfolio analysis makes the assumption that the different products or businesses plotted on the matrix are independent of each other. However, some product that qualifies as a dog may be a crucial component or provide a crucial skill for another product that qualifies as a star. If the standard strategic advice is followed and the dog disposed of, this could damage the competitive position of the star (see *Illustration 5.10*).

Finally, there are those who say that it is the role of the investor to spread risk and balance portfolios by holding a mix of shares in different companies. They claim that it is the role of a company to take risks in a particular business and look to lenders and shareholders for the funds they need.

Some other aspects of feasibility

In addition to financial resources, the availability of the right quality of skilled people will also be a major determinant of the feasibility of strategic options. This makes it necessary for managers to audit the human resources inside their organisation, those available outside, and the availability of training resources to improve the skills of people.

Timing constraints are also important in determining feasibility for obvious reasons. An organisation may have the capability to carry out a strategy and it may have all the skills and resources to do so, but the opportunity the strategy is required to address may be available for only a short time in the near future. This timing constraint may make it impossible for the organisation to mobilise its resources fast enough.

The techniques we have just discussed to identify financial feasibility also clearly have other messages about feasibility too. For example, it will not be feasible to enter a market already dominated by a low-cost producer, unless the focus is to be on a small niche and the strategy is one of differentiation. Product portfolios, life cycles and experience curves indicate relative market power and in doing so say something about feasibility from a market perspective as well as a financial one.

We turn now to the third criterion for the evaluation and selection of successful strategies.

Suitability or fit: adapting to the environment

Having established that their strategies are acceptable and feasible, the next hurdle managers must cross to achieve success is that of demonstrating that those strategies have a *strategic logic*. Strategic logic means that a proposed sequence of actions is consistently related to the objectives of the organisation on the one hand and matches the organisation's capability (including its structure, control systems and culture) to its environment on the other. The idea is that all the pieces of the strategic puzzle should fit together in a predetermined manner – the pieces should be *congruent.* When this happens we can say that the strategies fit, that they are suitable. The prescription is to use analytical techniques to determine the strategic logic of a sequence of actions, how all the pieces do or do not fit together (*Hofer & Schendel, 1978*). The analytic techniques available to do this are briefly summarised in this section.

SWOT analysis

This is a list of an organisation's strengths and weaknesses indicated by an analysis of its resources and capabilities, plus a list of the opportunities and threats that an analysis of its environment identifies. Strategic logic obviously requires that the future pattern of actions to be taken should match strengths with opportunities, ward off threats, and seek to overcome weaknesses.

Life cycle analysis

We have already discussed product life cycles in an earlier section of this chapter as criteria against which to measure the feasibility of strategies. Later in this chapter in

Illustration 5.10

Ciba-Geigy

Ciba-Geigy is a diversified multinational company based in Switzerland and engaged in the production of fine chemicals, dyestuffs and pharmaceuticals. In 1980 Its sales amounted to nearly 12 billion Swiss francs, of which about 3 billion were generated by its Pharmaceuticals Division.

That Division was organised into product groups based on therapeutic areas: cardiovascular, central nervous system, rheuma and pain, infectious diseases, and other therapeutic areas. The last-named product group included dermatological products. In each product group there were product managers for each of the specific lines that the product group consisted of – there were twenty such managers in the Division. In 1981 the Pharmaceuticals Division prepared strategic plans using the company's newly installed portfolio planning system based on the concept of Strategic Business Units (SBUs). One of the main difficulties of this technique lies in how the SBUs are to be defined in practice. In the case of the Pharmaceuticals Division, the product groups were defined as the SBUs. But was this right?

While most managers thought that it was sensible to regard each Division as an SBU, some were doubtful about regarding product areas within the Division as SBUs because they were so interdependent. Medical representatives handled products from a number of product groups, the production facilities and R&D were shared, as were most of the administration costs. To think of the product groups as businesses that could be handled separately might therefore lead to the wrong conclusions. On top of that, each group included specific products that differed from each other in important respects: age, technical maturity and expected growth potential. So if an SBU was defined as a distinctive product grouping, different from others, then perhaps the individual products should be the SBUs. ∎

Source: Buzzell, 1983.

the section on implementing strategies we will discuss the life cycles that have been identified for organisational cultures, and in Chapter 4 the life cycles of organisational structures were explored. Strategic logic demands that a selected sequence of actions for the future should be appropriate to the life cycle in product, structural and cultural terms. So products or markets may be at the mature stage of their life cycle and consistent, matching strategies would probably then have to do with maintaining market share through cost leadership strategies. Or an organisation may have passed through structural stages from the simple structure with a fluid culture to a divisionalised machine bureaucracy with a rather rigid culture. Matching strategies would then consist of many small incremental steps rather than one revolutionary change.

Portfolio analysis

This technique has also been discussed in an earlier section of this chapter as a criterion for feasibility, but it too is concerned with consistency and fit. Strategies that demonstrate strategic logic are those that take an organisation to a more balanced portfolio of activities. According to portfolio analyses, strategic logic requires a company to divest itself of businesses that have low market shares in stagnant markets, to withdraw cash from businesses with high market shares in mature markets, and invest the proceeds in businesses with high market share potential in growth markets.

PIMS

Here statistical relationships have been derived, relating typical performance in a particular market segment back to the causes of that performance. When managers identify the consequences of some strategy option they are considering, say the market share it leads to, they can plug that information into the statistical relationships and calculate the performance it would lead to. In this way the suitability, or strategic logic, of strategy options can be tested (*Buzzell & Gale, 1987*).

Synergy

This is the extra benefit that comes from linking two or more separate activities together. For example, if a corporation can link a business selling financial services to one selling real estate, then it may be possible to reduce costs because only one rather than two retail outlets will be required. Even more important, one business will generate customers for the other – customers arriving to buy a house might also be sold an insurance policy. The prescription then is that the results of potential interconnections between activities should be analysed to identify synergies. Strategic logic requires building in synergies as much as possible.

Industry structure and value chain analysis

These analytical techniques identify key aspects determining the relative market power of an organisation and its ability to sustain excess profits. Strategic logic entails taking actions that are consistent with and match the nature of the organisation's market power. Industry structure is held to determine what the predominant form of competitive advantage, and thus the level of profit, is. Some market structures mean that sustainable competitive advantage can be secured only through cost leadership strategies. Other structures mean that competitive advantage flows from differentiation. Strategic logic means matching actions to those required to secure competitive advantage. Value chain analysis identifies the points in the chain of activity from raw material to consumer that are crucial to competitive advantage. Since these market structure and value chain techniques have attracted widespread attention, they will now be discussed in somewhat greater detail.

Porter's industry structure and generic strategy analysis

Michael Porter (1980 & 1985) has put the classical economic theories of market form into a framework for analysing the nature of competitive advantage in a market and the power of a company in that market.

Defining the market

The first step in analysing industry structure is to define the market (or, as he calls it, the industry). A market is an interaction between a grouping of customers who have similar requirements of a particular good or service on the one hand, and a strategic group of competitors competing to meet those requirements on the other hand. The boundary around a market is defined in terms of similarities in what is demanded and in terms of the closeness of the competition.

For example, when analysing the construction industry managers would be ill advised to regard construction as one market. This is because the 'construction' market contains some very different groupings of customers and competitors. It would be more accurate to talk about a market for private houses because there we can find a reasonably clear group of customers – families who share a similar need for a home – and a relatively constant strategic group of large housebuilders who account for most of the houses built. It might even be necessary to break this market down further, for example into a small-house market for first-time buyers, a market for medium-size homes and a market for luxury homes. In addition, there is a quite separate market for large structures: roads, office blocks and hospitals for example. Here again we find customers looking for much the same thing: organisations with the ability to manage large and complex construction programmes that take long periods of time to complete. We also find that there is a relatively constant group of about 20 or so companies in the UK that compete to fulfil this need. Then there is a market for small structures and repair work. In this market customers are not looking for a management service but for those who will do the work directly. The competitor group is a shifting population of small companies. Each of these markets is very different from the other and therefore different strategies may be appropriate in those different markets. There are no hard and fast rules about drawing the boundaries around a market, but how that boundary is drawn will have a major effect on the analysis.

We have also seen in the General Foods example, discussed in an earlier section in relation to product portfolio analysis, that the boundaries around a market can change quite rapidly. In that example, one homogeneous coffee market split into a number of rather different ones. Managers will therefore have to keep questioning the definitions of the market that they are using to conduct their strategic analysis.

Analysing the five competitive forces

Having defined the market, the next step in the analysis is to identify the structure of that market. We can do this by analysing the five competitive forces that shape the prices firms can charge, the costs they have to bear, and the investment they must undertake to compete and consequently the rate of return they can expect to earn. In other words, the competitive forces determine the relative market power of competitors, the kind of competition they engage in, the factors that give some of them a competitive advantage, and the relative attractiveness of that market compared to others. These competitive forces are depicted in *Figure 5.6* and then summarised below.

1 **The threat of new entrants** New entrants would obviously add production capacity and seek to fill that capacity with volumes competed away from existing

FIGURE 5.6
Porter's five market forces

firms. This would lead to lower prices and hence lower profits. Those already in the market will therefore seek to use or build barriers against the entry of others and if they succeed in this they will be able to hold prices above the minimum level necessary to keep firms in the business. Entry barriers make excess profits possible and so make the market more attractive to firms. Those companies that can shelter behind the barriers come to occupy a powerful market position and the nature of their competitive advantage is tied up with the nature of the entry barrier. One of the most common entry barriers is the need to invest large sums in the production facilities necessary to produce the product.

For example, it is difficult for new firms to enter the automobile market because of the need for large factories. This is not true of the construction markets, but in some of them we still find entry barriers. For example, in the market for large structures it is rare to see new entrants because it takes time to acquire the skills of managing large construction projects. On the other hand, in the market for small structures, the skills are easier to acquire and we therefore find firms coming and going. Some other barriers to entry are provided by brand images, patent laws, and government trade protection policies.

Where the entry barrier is provided by the need to invest large amounts in facilities, we will usually find that a firm's market power, its competitive advantage, lies in its ability to achieve low costs. Where, however, the barriers are provided by brand images or other differentiators such as quality, then we will find that a firm's competitive advantage lies in its ability to differentiate itself from its rivals. Where the entry barriers are low, the threat of new entrants will force firms to compete on cost or try to build a market niche and focus on that.

2 **The threat of substitute goods or services** Another threat that will force competitors to keep their prices low will be that of some substitute for their product or service.

3 **The bargaining power of buyers** Customers have bargaining power if there are few of them. They also have bargaining power if they are buying a product or service to incorporate into something they themselves are producing, and what they buy represents a high proportion of their costs or a critical element of their quality. The importance of what they are buying will make them more demanding customers. A buyer is also powerful when that buyer purchases a significant proportion of a firm's output. Powerful buyers mean that a firm has to keep its prices low.

4 **The bargaining power of suppliers** Suppliers are powerful in relation to a particular firm when they are few in number, if they are supplying a product or service that is not crucial in cost or quality terms to the business of the particular buying firm, or if they are not supplying a major part of their own output to that particular buying firm. Powerful suppliers will mean that a firm's costs will be higher than they otherwise would have been, making profits lower and the market less attractive.

5 **The rivalry among existing competitors** If rivalry is intense, marketing costs are higher or prices lower than they would otherwise have been. Once again the market is less attractive.

Once the competitive forces have been identified, a judgement has to be made on which are the relatively most important because they could be working in different directions. Thus, a firm may face weak buyers but powerful suppliers, or there may be little in the way of entry threats but rivalry amongst those already in the market may be intense. Analysing the forces and making judgements on their relative importance should lead managers to see how they can deal with and influence the forces.

Identifying competitive advantage

The analysis indicates what the source of competitive advantage is. For example, a decade ago the private housing market in the South East of England had weak buyers because there were many families purchasing homes and there was very little threat from substitutes – people mostly live in houses rather than tents or caravans. It was the suppliers of land to build the houses on who were in a powerful position because land is so scarce in the South East of England. Once a house-building company had built up a land bank, that company was in a powerful position because its land bank represented an entry barrier to others. The source of competitive advantage lay primarily in the ability to acquire land. In a less densely populated area, however, the ability to acquire land will not be the source of competitive advantage. Instead it may be the ability to arrange finance for buyers or the ability to build houses at low cost. And currently in the South East competitive advantage may have shifted to those suppliers that can provide cheap finance, given the decline in demand for housing.

When we analyse the structure of a market, we are identifying the position a firm should occupy and the posture it should adopt to generate acceptable performance. The purpose of identifying a market's structure, and the sources of competitive advantage it causes, is to draw conclusions about the strategies that will match or fit the environment. When managers select strategies that are adapted to the environment in this way, then, according to the technically rational, analytical approach, they will be successful.

Porter expresses this relationship between the form of competitive advantage and the matching strategy in the manner shown in *Figure 5.7*. Porter identifies two types of competitive advantage: firms compete either on the basis of lower cost than their rivals, or on the basis of differentiation where they provide some unique and superior value to the buyer allowing them to charge higher prices. Firms can use these competitive advantages in either a broad or a narrow way – their competitive scope. Advantage and scope together create four kinds of strategy.

FIGURE 5.7
Porter's generic strategies

Source: M. Porter (1985), *Competitive Advantage: Creating and Sustaining Superior Performance*, New York: The Free Press

Where the industry structure is such that low cost is the source of competitive advantage, then a firm will succeed only if it takes a broad approach and goes for cost leadership or if it targets narrowly and adopts a strategy of cost focus. For example, producers of standardised silicon chips have to vie for the position of lowest-cost producer – high-cost producers are soon squeezed out. But there is also a market for small numbers of customised chips to be incorporated into large complex pieces of equipment such as body scanners in hospitals. Some chip manufacturers target this small segment and produce at lower cost than the big chip manufacturers because they have more flexible production methods.

Where, however, the industry structure is such that differentiation is the source of competitive advantage, then a firm will succeed only if it takes a broad approach and differentiates its whole range of products from those of its rivals, or if it targets and adopts a strategy of differentiation focus. For example, in the 1970s General Motors supplied cars across the spectrum of demand; it had a car for every price bracket and differentiated itself from rivals in each price bracket through the styling of its cars. Jaguar on the other hand focused on the luxury car segment and sought to create a distinctive image compared to say BMW. Porter's prescriptions for success are:

- Select the strategy that matches the particular market structure your firm faces.
- Make a clear choice between one strategy and another: cost leadership, or differentiation, or focus and avoid the ambivalence of being 'stuck in the middle' with a strategy that is partly cost leadership and partly differentiation.

Having identified the market structure and the matching generic strategy, managers must next identify where costs should be cut and how products and service should be differentiated. To do this they must conduct a value chain analysis.

Porter's value chain analysis

The value chain traces the path a product or service follows right from the raw material stage through production and distribution to the final customer. As it travels along this chain, value is added at each point, accumulating into the combination of values that the customer is looking for. The total value chain therefore consists of a number of firms as illustrated in *Figure 5.8*.

The first stage of the analysis is to identify which links in the chain are the crucial ones for achieving low cost or differentiation. It is these links that will control the whole chain and therefore provide the most attractive opportunities. The kinds of strategy a firm will be able to follow will depend upon the links of the value chain it covers – strategy will have to fit the location in the total value chain.

For example, take the value chain in the market for biscuits: farmers grow the wheat, millers make the flour, biscuit manufacturers produce the biscuits, and supermarkets sell them. The key source of competitive advantage is probably differentiation – taste, variety, attractive packaging are the value that the customer is looking for. The key link in providing these values is the small number of powerful supermarket chains. Each supermarket chain competes with the others on the basis of differentiation and many of the brands of biscuits are sold under a supermarket's own label. They have sufficient power to require the biscuit manufacturers to produce biscuits specified by the supermarket and packaged as the supermarket's product. Biscuit manufacturers will find that they have to compete on the basis of low cost.

By understanding the value chain, managers may be able to change it to the benefit of their company. For example, an ice cream manufacturer, also subject to the power of the supermarkets, may decide to acquire its own retail outlets and promote its own image as Häagen-Dazs ice cream has done.

The notion of a value chain is also relevant to each firm in the total value chain. Every company takes in inputs and uses some process to add value to those inputs, so producing outputs that it passes to the next link in the total value chain. A way of analysing the value chain within a firm is shown in *Figure 5.9*.

FIGURE 5.8
The industry value chain

The value chain consists of primary activities and support activities that together ultimately produce the firm's profit margin. The primary activities consist of:

● *Inbound logistics*: the activities of receiving, storing, handling and distributing the inputs required to produce the product or service, as well as controlling inventories.
● *Operations*: the process of transforming the inputs in some way so that they take on greater value for the ultimate consumer. This would cover making components, testing them, assembling them into a product, and packaging that product.
● *Outbound logistics*: storing the firm's final product and distributing it to the next link in the total value chain.

FIGURE 5.9

The firm's value chain

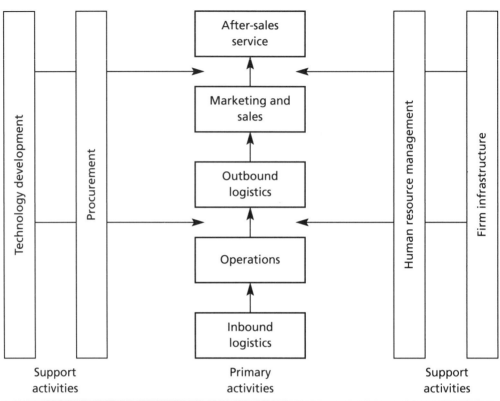

Marketing and sales: making customers aware of the product and ensuring that it is available.

Service: all the activities that enhance or maintain the value of the product such as installation, advice, repairs, spares and so on.

Each of these primary activities has a need for support activities:

- *Procurement*: the administrative activity of ordering the inputs to the primary activities.
- *Technology development*: the activity of researching and developing the processes through which inputs are transformed into outputs.
- *Human resource management*: the activity of recruiting, training, motivating and rewarding the people necessary for the primary activities.
- *Management systems*: the activity of planning, financing and controlling the primary activities.

Having specified their firm's value chain, managers are then in a position to identify which of the primary activities and which of the support activities are the most crucial to providing the competitive advantage either of low cost or of differentiation. To fit or match the situation, a strategy will have to focus particularly on those links. For example, the primary activities of inbound logistics and the support activity of procurement are crucial to keeping the costs of supermarkets competitive. For this reason, supermarkets do not decentralise responsibility for these activities to their store managers. While some specific links will be of particular importance, the value chain must also be managed as a whole system, not simply a collection of separate parts. Reconfiguring the chain, relocating or eliminating activities in the chain, may lead to improved competitive position.

A note of warning. The whole industry structure/value chain analysis is an elaboration of neo-classical economic theory which is firmly based upon the assumption of 'rational economic man' operating in clearing markets that tend to a state of equilibrium. If you take, say, an Austrian or evolutionary economics approach (e.g. Nelson & Winters, 1982) then you would come to different conclusions because this approach to economics is based on the assumptions that economies operate in non-equilibrium states and that firm survival is determined, not by adapting to an industry structure, but by innovating. Firm profitability would then be determined by factors internal to the firm and industry structure would then simply be a statistical consequence of the firms that happened to be in it. Porter's analysis could then be misleading even in the only circumstances to which it can possibly apply, namely, those close to certainty and agreement.

So far in this section, we have been looking in some detail at how managers can use analytical techniques to determine whether the strategic options they are examining satisfy the criterion of suitability or fit. They can use market structure and value chain analysis, for example, to ascertain whether a proposed cost reduction strategy matches the structure of their market and their position in the value chain, or whether some form of differentiation would provide a better match. The suitability criterion is basically saying that whether a strategy is successful or not depends upon, is contingent upon, its capability and its environment. The theoretical justification for this postulated relationship between success and the matching of an organisation to its environment lies in what is called contingency theory. It will be helpful, therefore, briefly to review contingency theory.

Contingency theory

The development of contingency theory (see *Key Concept 5.4*) was a reaction against the idea that there is 'one best way' in management. At the time it was developed that 'one best way' was scientific management, Management By Objectives (MBO) and related sets of prescriptions. Contingency theory substitutes the 'it all depends' approach for the 'one best way'. The approach derives from empirical research (*Burns & Stalker, 1961; Woodward, 1965; Lawrence & Lorsch, 1967*) which showed that success was not correlated with a simple single set of factors. Instead, the effectiveness of a particular organisational structure, culture, or sequence of actions is contingent upon, depends upon, a number of factors. The most important of these contingency factors are usually held to be:

- the environment, particularly the market
- the size of the organisation
- the technology it employs

- the history of the organisation
- the expectations of employees and customers.

The theory states that success will be secured when an organisation secures a good match between its situation and its strategies and structures. For example, mechanistic bureaucracies are said to be appropriate for stable environments, but flexible, organic structures are required for turbulent environments. *Child (1984)* summarises the theory as follows:

> Contingency theory regards the design of an effective organisation as necessarily having to be adapted to cope with the 'contingencies' which derive from the circumstances of environment, technology, scale, resources and other factors in the situation in which the organisation is operating.

Key Concept 5.4

Contingency

Contingency is a theory about the nature of cause and effect. It makes statements like these: if an organisation is operating in an environment that is very complex and changing rapidly, then it requires organic forms of organisation to succeed. If, however, it operates in simple, slow-moving environments, then it requires mechanistic structures to succeed. If an organisation is small, then it requires a simple structure. If an organisation is large, then it requires a divisionalised structure.

Contingency theory postulates a complex web of interconnections between the features of organisations and their environments in which the causal connections are linear in the sense that they run in one direction. It is a particular environment that causes a particular kind of successful strategy and that causes a particular kind of successful structure. The theory does not contemplate circular causation in which the structures of organisations cause them to follow certain strategies which then create certain kinds of environment to which they respond.

Contingency theory is based on the assumption that approximately the same cause will have approximately the same effect. It does not envisage escalation in which a tiny difference between two causes leads to two completely different outcomes. It does not, for example, allow for the possibility that two organisations operating in the same environment may develop in totally different directions simply because one gained a slightly bigger market share than the other in a particular product line at a particular point in time.

By making particular assumptions about the nature of cause and effect, contingency theory is making particular assumptions about the dynamics of organisations. Success is assumed to be a state of equilibrium and, because they are close to equilibrium, the future time paths of successful organisations are predictable. These are all assumptions that are open to question, as we shall see in Chapters 8 and 9.

The contingency concept, and its consequent prescription of consistency and congruence, runs in terms of a large number of different combinations of strategies, structures, cultures and so on, each suited to a particular environment and a particular set of objectives at a particular time. Organisations then adopt whichever of these satisfies the consistency criteria. We have to specify the circumstances rather precisely before we can identify the appropriate combination of strategy, structure and so on. On the other hand, the configuration approach, to which we now turn, tries to identify a relatively small number of typical combinations of strategies, structures and so on, into which we can classify most organisations.

Configuration

The concept of configuration (see *Key Concept 5.5*) is a development of the ideas of contingency and congruence. Whereas contingency theory adopts an 'it all depends' approach, configuration is concerned with 'getting it all together' (*Mintzberg, 1989*).

Key Concept 5.5

Configuration

A configuration is some typical constellation of structural, cultural, strategy pattern, control system features and other organisational factors appropriate to a particular environment. In other words, a particular configuration is one of a limited number of categories, based on many interrelated and mutually supportive features, into which we can classify organisations. A configuration therefore describes a typical or archetypal organisational system.

According to the configuration approach, examples of which are given in *Illustration 5.11*, success flows from selecting and designing an organisation and its strategies from a fairly limited number of archetypes. Empirical studies have been undertaken (reviewed in *Miller, 1986*) to demonstrate the following propositions:

1 There are only a limited number of possible constellations of strategies, structures, cultures and other organisational attributes that are feasible in any environment (*Hannan & Freeman, 1977; Aldrich, 1979; McKelvey, 1981*). Companies following these survive because they are more adapted to the environment, while other less well adapted organisations do not survive. The environment in effect selects out various common constellations of organisational attributes. Success flows from convergence upon a viable configuration. And it is postulated that this convergence will occur in short bursts, after which the successful organisation will display stability. We discussed this point in Chapter 3 in the section on revolutionary change.

2 Organisations are driven toward a few common configurations in order to achieve internal harmony and consistency between structures, cultures, strategies

and contexts. Instead of an infinite number of combinations of elements, organisations tend to pursue one of a relatively small number of central themes that marshal all the elements into a coherent pattern where attributes are complementary and self-reinforcing. So a machine bureaucracy organisation with its highly specialised, routine operating tasks and highly formalised procedures can only function in stable environments in which its inflexibility is not overly limiting; but consistently stable environments enable operating procedures to be formalised, giving the advantage to machine bureaucracies. Machine bureaucracies in stable markets tend to pursue cost leadership strategies; but stable markets encourage growth to a scale that can reap cost benefits. Here the idea of configuration is stressing circular causation, whereas contingency stresses linear causation.

3 Organisations tend to change the elements of their configuration in a manner that either extends a given configuration (incrementally builds on existing strengths), or moves very quickly to a new configuration (strategic revolution) which will then be preserved for a long time. Piecemeal moves to a new configuration will often destroy the complementarities among elements in the configuration and will thus be avoided. Only when a configuration change is absolutely necessary or extremely advantageous will organisations move rapidly to a new configuration. The rest of the time organisations will build on their existing configuration.

A particularly well-known use of the concept of configuration is the 7S framework (*Waterman, Peters & Phillips, 1980*) shown in *Figure 5.10*. This framework indicates how the success or otherwise of an organisation follows from a configuration of seven attributes that are all interconnected, all part of one system. It is no use getting just one or two elements right; since they are all interdependent, they must all fit together and be consistent with each other.

According to a configuration view therefore, the suitability criterion for selecting a sequence of actions is a set of closely interwoven attributes. Elements make sense in terms of the whole. Success flows from selecting patterns of action, positions, postures and performance that all fit together as a puzzle does to produce stability, consistency and regularity, harmony and fit. The criteria for successful choice are provided by a relatively small number of rather standard patterns, not a large number of separate criteria.

Illustration 5.11

Examples of configuration

Miller (1986) describes four configurations:

- Small firms operating in niche markets with simple structures in fragmented industries.
- Large machine bureaucracies operating in stable concentrated industries with high entry barriers pursuing cost leadership strategies.
- Organic adhocracies where the strategy is differentiation through innovation in embryonic or growth industries.
- Large companies pursuing diversification strategies in mature industries with divisionalised conglomerate structures. ∎

FIGURE 5.10
The 7S framework

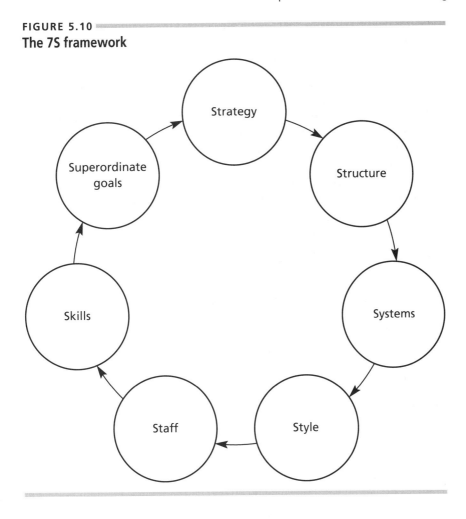

We turn now to the matter of implementing the strategic plan selected and the use of that plan to control an organisation.

5.4 STRATEGY IMPLEMENTATION AND STRATEGIC CONTROL

The main emphasis of technically rational approaches to strategic management has always been on the formulation, evaluation and selection of appropriate strategies.

It is always recognised, however, that none of this analysis is of much use unless the strategies so developed are implemented. It is also often pointed out that in practice managers spend most of their time on implementation rather than formulation and that the failure of strategy is most frequently due, not to poor formulation, but to the difficulties of implementation. Despite the recognition of its importance, however, the question of implementation continues to receive relatively little research attention and some hold that the consequent lack of practical and theoretically sound models to guide managers' actions during implementation is a major cause of implementation failure (*Alexander, 1985*).

When the question is dealt with, successful implementation is held to follow from the installation of a number of key organisational elements. To implement their formulated strategies managers must:

1 Design a hierarchical reporting structure that is appropriate to the strategy they have formulated.
2 Install and operate the management information and control system that will enable them to keep the organisation on its planned path.
3 Install and operate reward systems for people that will provide the monetary incentives for them to carry out the strategy.
4 Change the culture or belief system of people in the organisation to provide the non-monetary motivation for them to carry out the strategy.
5 Develop appropriate social and political behaviour that will not block the implementation of strategy.

We will now consider further each of these elements of implementation.

Installing structures to implement strategy

The structure of an organisation is the formal way of identifying:

- who is to take responsibility for what;
- who is to exercise authority over whom; and
- who is to be answerable to whom.

The structure is a hierarchy of managers and is the source of authority, as well as the legitimacy of decisions and actions. It is normally held that the appropriate structure follows from the strategy that an organisation is pursuing and that organisational structures display typical patterns of development or life cycles (*Chandler, 1962*). Chandler identified four stages in the structure life cycle:

1 Embryonic organisations have very simple structures in which people report rather informally to someone that they accept as their leader. They tend to do whatever needs to be done with relatively little separation of functions. When they embark on a growth strategy, however, they will find it necessary to change the structure to one based on more formal specialisation of functions and identification of authority and responsibility. If this is not done, managers will find it impossible to implement their strategy of growth and the organisation will probably fail.
2 As they pursue their growth strategy, managers will find that they have to carry out strategies of cost reduction to stay ahead and they will be more and more confronted with the problem of integrating specialised functions. The structure will therefore have to be made even more formal with clearer definition of lines of authority and communication. It will also be necessary to systematise and improve the techniques of marketing, manufacturing and materials procurement.
3 Then, as managers pursue strategies of diversification into new products and markets, they find it necessary to set up marketing and manufacturing organisations in different geographic areas: they install additional structures.
4 As they continue their strategy of diversification, the number of additional structures multiplies and they have to restructure to ensure a better 'fit' with the

diversification strategies they are pursuing. They might secure this fit by forming a larger functionally departmentalised structure, with departments at the centre shared by many geographic areas; or by setting up largely independent subsidiaries as divisionalised or holding company structures. Another label for such organisations is the 'machine bureaucracy' (*Mintzberg, 1991*).

Implementation, then, means installing a structure appropriate to the strategy being pursued and this typically results in a life cycle for hierarchical structures. You will recall that in Chapter 4 we took a rather different perspective, seeing the evolution of structure in dialectical rather than life cycle terms.

Systems installation and control

As we saw in Chapter 4, the information and control systems of an organisation are basically procedures, rules and regulations governing:

- what information about the performance of an organisation should flow to whom and when;
- who is required to respond to that information and how they are authorised to respond, in particular what authority they have to deploy the resources of their organisation.

To implement the strategies they have formulated, managers will have to ensure that their information and control systems:

- are adequate enough for the flows of information that implementation requires;
- provide appropriate control mechanisms to enable managers to monitor the outcomes of the strategy implementation and do something if those outcomes are not in accordance with the strategy.

Management control is defined as the process of ensuring that all resources – physical, human and technological – are allocated so as to realise the strategy. It is a process in which a person or a group of people intentionally affects what others do. Control ensures proper behaviour in an organisation and the need for it arises because individuals within the organisation are not always willing to act in the best interests of the organisation (*Wilson, 1991*). The process of control involves setting standards or targets for performance, or expected outcomes of a sequence of actions, then comparing actual performance or outcomes against standards, targets or expectations, and finally taking corrective action to remove any deviations from standard, target or expectation. Control takes a *feedforward* form when corrective action is taken on the basis of predictions with the aim of avoiding deviations from expectations. It takes on a *feedback* form where the predictions cannot be accurate enough. In the *feedback* form, monitoring detects a deviation that has already occurred and then takes action to correct it. Most business control systems are a mixture of feedforward and feedback control.

The principal form taken by the control system in most organisations is that of the annual plan or budget. Strategy implementation is held to depend upon an effective budgeting system. The budget converts strategy into a set of short-term action plans and sets out the financial consequences of those action plans for the year ahead. Control is then a process of regularly comparing what happens to what the budget said would happen. Budgets allocate the resource of an organisation with which different business units and functions are charged to carry out the strategy. Budgets establish the legitimate authority for using the resources of the organisation. The budget will normally be prepared in great detail, showing what people in each business unit and function are required to bring in as revenue, what they are permitted to spend and on what, and therefore what surplus they are required to earn, or deficit they will be allowed to incur.

The budget, however, is a short-term instrument, only the first step in the implementation of the strategy. Some have therefore sought to identify the differences between short-term control and strategic control. For example, *Hurst (1982)* points out that strategic control requires more data from more sources, particularly external sources, and the data must be oriented to a longer-term future. Strategic control is therefore inevitably less precise and less formal than budgetary control. It is concerned more with the accuracy of the premises on which decisions are based and much less with quantitative deviations from standards. Strategic control has to be more flexible and use variable rather than rigidly regular time periods for reporting. The relationships between corrective action and outcome are therefore weaker in strategic control. The conclusion drawn is that although planning and control in a strategic sense is very difficult, a system to compare expectations and outcomes is even more necessary than it is for the short term.

Goold and Quinn's (1990) research shows that very few companies have a strategic control process that is anything like as formal and comprehensive as their budgetary control system. Even where managers do set strategic milestones that would allow them to check on their progress as the strategy was implemented, those milestones take the form of events rather than results. So the milestone might be the completion of a new factory; managers might set this for a period two years hence and then after two years check if the factory is indeed complete. If it is, they may conclude that they are keeping to their strategy. However, since this is an event rather than a result, they will not know if the financial results their strategy was supposed to achieve are in fact being achieved. The reasons for the lack of a proper results-based monitoring and control system was identified as the length of time lags between action and outcome and the risks and uncertainties that long-term plans were subject to. Despite the difficulties, however, Goold and Quinn recommend trying harder to use formal strategic control systems based on milestones for comparison.

Clearly, the technically rational planning approach to strategic management has difficulty with the matters of implementation and strategic control, difficulties that have so far not been satisfactorily resolved. We will be returning to the question of strategic control in the next section of this chapter and again in Chapter 11 but before that we consider the third aspect of strategy implementation.

Installing and operating human resource systems

Effective strategy implementation should occur when the people required to take action to this end are motivated to do so. One of the most powerful motivators is the organisation's reward system (*Galbraith and Kazanian, 1986*). Appropriate rewards stimulate people to make the effort to take actions directly relevant to an organisation's strategy. The way in which people's jobs are graded and the pay scales attached to these grades will affect how people feel about their jobs and the effort they will make. Differentials need to be perceived to be fair if they are not to affect performance adversely. Bonuses, profit-related pay, piecework and productivity schemes are all ways of tying monetary rewards to the actions that strategy implementation requires.

Non-monetary rewards are also of great importance in motivating people. These rewards include promotion, career development, job enrichment, job rotation, training and development. They all help individuals to be more useful to an organisation while developing greater self-fulfilment. Simpler forms of reward are also of great importance, for example praise, recognition and thanks.

Training and development is an important implementation tool, not only because it motivates people, but also because it provides the skills required for strategy implementation (*Hussey, 1991*). The objectives of training and development programmes should be aligned with those of an organisation's strategy and those objectives should consist of measurable changes in corporate performance. *Lorenz (1986)* describes how ICL put 2000 managers through a development programme designed to improve ICL's competitiveness against the Japanese. Such programmes are supposed to allow managers at all levels to develop a comprehensive understanding of what their organisation's strategy actually means.

Culture-change programmes

Just as the reporting structure of an organisation should fit the particular strategy it wishes to pursue, so should its culture, the attitudes and beliefs that people within an organisation share. *Handy (1981)* classifies organisational cultures into four categories:

1 The *power* culture is typically found in small entrepreneurial companies controlled by powerful figures. People in this culture share a belief in individuality and in taking risks. They believe that management should be an informal process with few rules and procedures.

2 The *role* culture is associated with bureaucracies where people's functions are defined in a formal way and they specialise. People here share a belief in the importance of security and predictability. They equate successful management with rules and regulations.

3 The *task* culture is found where people focus on their job, or on a project. People share a belief in the importance of teamwork, expertise and in being adaptable.

4 The *person* culture occurs where people believe that the organisation exists so that they can serve their own personal interest, for example barristers and architects, and many other professionals.

Just as structures need to fit a particular strategy and just as they tend to follow a life cycle from the simple to the functional to the divisional, so too do cultures. The power culture is appropriate to the early stages of a firm's life when its structure is simple. Later it will have to change to the role culture as it grows and installs a functional structure. Then it will have to develop a task culture to fit in with a divisionalised structure.

Implementation may well therefore require that an organisation change its culture and the conventional wisdom prescribes that such change should be planned. The reasons why people might resist a change in culture need to be identified and plans formulated to overcome the resistance. Participation, communication and training are all seen as ways of overcoming resistance. The process of overcoming resistance involves a stage called unfreezing when the existing culture is questioned and is followed by a period of reformulation where people consider what new beliefs they need to develop and share with each other. Finally there is the re-freezing stage where the new culture is fixed in place. We will be returning in Chapter 6 to these matters of planned change in belief systems – the discipline of Organisation Development.

Developing appropriate political behaviour

It is inevitable that people in an organisation will conflict and, when they do, they engage in political behaviour (*Pfeffer, 1981*). As an organisation differentiates into functions and units, those functions and units develop their own objectives, some of which will be different to those of the organisation as a whole. But differentiation brings with it interdependence so that no single function or unit can achieve its objectives on its own. They will have both to compete with each other for scarce resources and to cooperate with each other to reach their objective. Interdependence, heterogeneous goals and scarce resources taken together produce conflict. If the conflict is important and power is distributed enough, then people will use political behaviour, that is persuasion and negotiation, to resolve their conflict. If power is highly centralised then most will simply do as they are told – they will not have enough power to engage in political behaviour.

The kinds of political strategies people employ to come out best from conflict are the selective use of objective criteria, the use of outside experts to support their case, forming alliances and coalitions, sponsoring those with similar ideas, empire building, intentionally doing nothing, suppressing information, making decisions first and using analysis afterwards to justify them, and many more.

The above view of politics as a manipulative process of dubious ethical validity leads to the belief that steps should be taken to reduce the incidence of political behaviour. Such steps are those that reduce the level of conflict and the most powerful of these is to preach and convert people to a common ideology. Creating excess resources should also reduce levels of conflict.

From an ordinary management perspective political activity is seen as a way of managing that is likely to be necessary, but will be a difficult and dangerous task, something to avoid if only it were possible

We now turn to a matter closely connected with strategy implementation and strategic control – strategic management styles.

5.5 INSTALLING STRATEGIC MANAGEMENT STYLES

So far we have discussed the criteria managers are recommended to use to select appropriate strategies, as well as the steps they are recommended to take to implement and control the consequences of those strategies. The question now is: what part should the various levels of management play in the formulation and implementation of strategies and in strategic control? In other words, the question is to do with how managers at various levels add value to the strategy process. It is the manner in which various levels of management contribute to the strategy process that determines what we might call the management style of an organisation. In this section we will consider three well-known ways of categorising the strategic style of an organisation.

Mintzberg's types of strategy

Mintzberg and Waters (1985) distinguish the following eight styles of strategic management:

- *Planned*. Top managers articulate precise intentions and embody these in formal plans that set out what the levels of managers below them are to do. Top management then exert control by monitoring outcomes against plan.
- *Entrepreneunal*. The organisation here is under the personal control of the leader and strategies flow from the unarticulated vision of a single leader.
- *Ideological*. Strategies are the intended patterns in action expressed in collective beliefs. Here top managers articulate inspirational and relatively immutable beliefs that govern the actions of those lower down and so become the strategy. The ideology embodies an organisation's intention and control is through indoctrination and socialisation.
- *Umbrella*. Here the leaders define the overall targets and set the boundaries within which managers lower down actually formulate the content of the strategy. Control is exerted by monitoring achievement against target and behaviour against the boundaries.
- *Process*. The leaders control the process of strategy, for example the reporting structure, the planning timetable and the appointment of managers, and then leave the content to those lower down. Control is exerted through keeping people to timetables and through allocating resources, that is through exercising a final veto.
- *Unconnected*. Here there is either no central intention or groups of people produce strategies in direct contradiction to central intention. The organisation's strategy therefore flows from a collection of unconnected strategies formed by groups within the organisation.
- *Consensus*. People in the organisation converge on a common theme through agreement with each other, without any central managers directing them. Here strategies emerge without prior organisational intention.
- *Imposed*. This occurs where the environment dictates what has to be done.

Mintzberg and Waters (1985) relate these strategic management styles to the kind of environment that managers face. For mature diversified corporations, planned strategic management styles are appropriate for stable environments, but umbrella or process styles will be more suitable in turbulent ones. This corresponds with the distinction usually drawn between top-down and bottom-up planning. For different kinds of organisation in turbulent environments we will tend to find entrepreneurial, unconnected or consensus strategic management styles.

Mintzberg (1991) also distinguished between five types of organisation:

- The *simple structure* in which the entrepreneurial style of management is usually found.

- The *machine bureaucracy* which works according to rules and regulations established by the centre of the organisation. This is appropriate for stable environments and the planned style of strategic management fits with it.
- The *professional bureaucracy* which is bureaucratic but not centralised, such as schools, universities and hospitals. The strategic management style here will normally be of the unconnected type.
- *Divisionalised structures* where the choice of style would lie between planned, process or umbrella.
- *The adhocracy*, which is a highly organic organisation with little in the way of formal structures, rules and procedures. It consists of teams of specialists, for example management consultants. The strategic management style here might be entrepreneurial, consensus or ideological.

Miles and Snow's categories

Miles and Snow (1978) provide another way of categorising strategic management style. They distinguish between the following:

- *Defenders.* Managers in these organisations concentrate on a relatively well-defined market area. They concentrate on increasing their expertise and improving their position in this market, rather than searching for alternative strategies.
- *Prospectors.* Managers here are always searching for new opportunities and they often create change and uncertainty.
- *Analysers.* Managers in this kind of organisation operate in both stable and unstable areas; in the former they use formalised structures while in the latter they adopt a more organic approach.
- *Reactors.* Here managers perceive change and uncertainty but are unable to respond effectively. They lack a consistent strategy and act when the environment forces them to.

Goold and Campbell's strategies and styles

Goold and Campbell (1987) define strategic management styles in terms of the manner in which the corporate level of an organisation resolves a number of tensions. They distinguish between five key tensions:

- *Multiple perspectives versus clear responsibility.* This is the dilemma created when people are given clearly defined jobs in a system that restricts them to those jobs. The result is greater efficiency at the defined job, but it leads to narrow thinking and therefore reduced ability to deal with change. If an organisation moves in the direction of multiple perspectives, however, it suffers a reduction in efficiency.
- *Detailed planning reviews versus entrepreneurial decision making.* This presents an organisation with a similar dilemma. It can secure greater control and higher levels of efficiency if it plans carefully and regularly reviews actions against plan. But this narrows the focus of people and their motivation to act so that many new opportunities will be lost.

- *Strong leadership versus business autonomy.* The dilemma here is that between strong central control with the synergies it brings and local autonomy with the flexibility to deal with unexpected change.
- *Long-term objectives versus short-term objectives.* The tension here occurs because short-term profitability and cash flow is high when a company does not invest in expensive new facilities and research and development, but this failure to invest will reduce long-term profitability.
- *Flexible strategies versus tight controls.* This dilemma is created by the need to set out precisely what people are to do in order to have a firm basis for monitoring their performance. When this is done, however, it removes the flexibility individuals have to handle unexpected changes.

Goold and Campbell argue that successful organisations resolve these tensions in a manner that matches a number of factors internal to the organisation with a number of factors external to it. The internal factors are matters such as the nature of the business portfolio, the extent to which businesses overlap each other, and the skills and personalities of people in the businesses. The external factors include the level of uncertainty the environment presents and the intensity of the competition. A strategic management style is a choice that resolves the tensions to secure equilibrium. The three most important choices of styles they identify are:

The financial control style

One choice is to operate in market segments that are highly stable so that most of the tensions described above are avoided. The organisation can then adopt an uncompromisingly simple, flat, decentralised organisational structure. It can focus firmly on short-term objectives and practise tight short-term control using quantitative management information and control systems. Unforeseen change, the strategic and the long term are all dealt with by the entrepreneurial initiative of the managers closest to the action and/or by an entrepreneurial approach to acquisitions at the corporate level.

The strategic planning style

Here companies adopt complex, centralist structures and practise top-down long-term planning. They place great weight on the achievement of long-term objectives and are tolerant of non-achievement in the short term. They make these choices because they are pursuing interconnections and synergies; they are trying to develop competitive advantage and achieve balance in the portfolio of businesses under their control. This style choice will be appropriate where changes in customer requirements and competitor groupings are turbulent and competition intense. This choice is also appropriate where there are significant interconnections between business units in terms of shared customers or shared operational processes and technology.

The strategic control style

These companies strike a balance between short- and long-term objectives, sacrificing short-term profit where there is a reasonable prospect of this leading to greater long-term profit. They usually choose simple, flat, decentralised organisational structures to allow effective short-term control, but try to promote collaboration to enable some interconnections and synergies to be taken advantage of. They adopt the more facilitating forms of management, relying more on the processes of persuasion and negotiation than on instruction. Planning is then of the bottom-up type. This style choice is far less clear than the other two, but it does offer advantages of flexibility. It is likely to be appropriate where the company consists of businesses that are not significantly interconnected in customer or operational and technology terms, and operates in markets characterised by rapid change arising in contained situations.

If you choose a strategy that focuses on synergy and that requires integrated operational responses and common approaches to customers, then a successful choice is the strategic planning style, with all it means in terms of structures, roles and cultures. If you choose to sacrifice some synergy and operate in rather more independent market segments, which do not have common customer bases and do not require integrated operational responses, then strategic control is the successful choice. This choice also leads to particular structural, cultural, role and systems requirements to fit or match.

5.6 SUMMARY

This chapter has surveyed the manner in which the 'canon' of strategic management literature prescribes the extension of the technically rational decision-making processes and the monitoring forms of control, that is planning, to the management of an organisation over the long term. Plans are, of course, meant to realise prior intention. This chapter started, therefore, by defining just what it means to realise intention over a long time period and it was seen that this requires high degrees of certainty and agreement. Then we went on to consider different types of plan, how it is recommended that they be formulated and what criteria should be used to select action options that are to constitute them. Strategy implementation and control were next considered and we ended by reviewing how the headquarters level of a large firm might add value to that firm according to the style of strategic management it installs. The result is a simple and logically attractive procedure which unfortunately can apply over rather short time periods only, for most organisations in today's turbulent world.

Further reading

To obtain further information on analytical techniques and models for evaluating strategies turn to Hofer & Schendel (1978) as well as Rowe, Mason, Dickel & Snyder (1989). Also Johnson & Scholes (1988) or Bowman & Asch (1987). Also see Ansoff (1990) for a very different perspective to the one presented in this book.

References

Aldrich, H. E. (1979), *Organizations and Environments*, Englewood Cliffs, NJ: Prentice-Hall.

Alexander, L. D. (1985), Successfully implementing strategic decisions, *Long Range Planning*, vol. 18, no. 3, pp. 91–7.

Ansoff, I. (1990), *Implanting Corporate Strategy*, Hemel Hempstead: Prentice-Hall.

Argenti, J. (1980), *Practical Corporate Planning*, London: Allen & Unwin.

Beck, P. W. (1982), Corporate planning for an uncertain future, *Long Range Planning*, vol. 15, no. 4.

Bowman, C. & Asch, D. (1987), *Strategic Management*, London: Macmillan Education.

Burns, T. & Stalker, G. M. (1961), *The Management of Innovation*, London: Tavistock Publications.

Buzzell, R. D. (1983), Ciba-Geigy Pharmaceuticals Division: multinational strategic planning, in Buzzell, R. D. & Quelch, J. A. (Eds.) (1988), *Multinational Marketing Management*, Reading, Ma.: Addison-Wesley.

Buzzell, R. D. & Gale, B. T. (1987), *The PIMS Principle: Linking Strategy to Performance*, New York: Macmillan.

Chandler, A. D. (1962), *Strategy and Structure*, Boston, Ma.: MIT Press.

Child, J. (1984), *Organisation*, London: Harper & Row.

Cooke, S. & Slack, N. (1984), *Making Management Decisions*, Englewood Cliffs, NJ: Prentice-Hall.

Galbraith, J. R. & Kazanian, R. K. (1986), *Strategy Implementation: Structure, Systems and Process*, St. Paul, Minnesota: West Publishing.

Goold, M. & Campbell, A. (1987), *Strategies and Styles*, Oxford: Blackwell.

Goold, M. with Quinn, J. J. (1990), *Strategic Control: Milestones for Long Term Performance*, London: Hutchinson.

Handy, C. B. (1981), *Understanding Organisations*, Harmondsworth: Penguin.

Hannan, M. & Freeman, J. (1977), The population ecology of organizations, *American Journal of Sociology*, vol. 83, pp. 929–64.

Henderson, B. D. (1970), *The Product Portfolio*, Boston Consulting Group.

Hofer, C. W. & Schendel, D. (1978), *Strategy Evaluation: Analytical Concepts*, St. Paul, Minnesota: West Publishing.

Hurst, E. G. (1982), Controlling strategic plans, in Lorange, P. (Ed.) (1982), *Implementation of Strategic Planning*, Englewood Cliffs, NJ: Prentice-Hall.

Hussey, D. E. (1991), Implementing strategy through management education and training, in Hussey, D. E. (Ed.) (1991), *International Review of Strategic Management*, vol. 2, no. 1, Chichester: John Wiley.

Johnson, G. & Scholes, R. (1988), *Exploring Corporate Strategy*, Hemel Hempstead: Prentice-Hall.

Lawrence, P. R. & Lorsch, J. W. (1967), *Organization and Environment*, Cambridge, Ma.: Harvard University Press.

Lorenz, C. (1986), Metamorphosis of a European laggard, London: *Financial Times*, 12 May.

McKelvey, W. (1981), *Organizational Systematics*, Los Angeles, Ca.: University of California Press.

Miles, R. E. & Snow, C. C. (1978), *Organisational Strategy, Structure and Process*, New York: McGraw-Hill.

Miller, D. (1986), Configurations of strategy and structure: towards a synthesis, *Strategic Management Journal*, vol. 7, pp. 233–49a.

Mintzberg, H. (1989), *Mintzberg on Management: Inside Our Strange World of Organizations*, New York: The Free Press.

Mintzberg, H. (1991), The structuring of organizations, in Mintzberg, H. & Quinn, J. B. (Eds.) (1991), *The Strategy Process: Concepts, Contexts, Cases*, Englewood Cliffs, NJ: Prentice-Hall.

Mintzberg, H. & Waters, J. A. (1985), Of strategies deliberate and emergent, *Strategic Management Journal*, vol. 6, pp. 257–72.

Mirsham, E. J. (1980), *Cost/Benefit Analysis*, London: Allen & Unwin

Nelson, R. & Winters, S. (1982), *An Evolutionary Theory of Economic Change*, Cambridge, Mass.: Harvard University Press.

Pfeffer, J. (1981), *Power in Organizations*, Cambridge, Ma.: Ballinger Publishing Company.

Porter, M. (1980), *Competitive Strategy: Techniques for Analyzing Industries and Competitors*, New York: The Free Press.

Porter, M. (1985), *Competitive Advantage: Creating and Sustaining Superior Performance*, New York: The Free Press.

Porter, M. (1987), From competitive advantage to corporate strategy, *Harvard Business Review*, May–June, pp. 43–59.

Rowe, A. J., Mason, R. O., Dickel, K. E. & Snyder, N. H. (1989), *Strategic Management and Business Policy: A Methodological Approach*, Reading, Ma.: Addison-Wesley.

Shim, J. K. & McGlade, R. (1984), The use of corporate planning models: past, present and future, *Journal of Operational Research Science*, vol. 35, no. 10, pp. 885–93.

Slatter (1980), Common pitfalls using the BCG product portfolio matrix, *London Business School Journal*, Winter.

Waterman, R. H., Peters, T. J. & Phillips J. R. (1980), Structure is not organization, *Business Horizons*, June.

Wilson, R. M. S. (1991), Corporate strategy and management control, in Hussey, D. E. (Ed.), (1991), *International Review of Strategic Management*, vol. 2, no. 1, Chichester: John Wiley.

Woodward, J. (1965), *Industrial Organisation: Theory and Practice*, Oxford: Oxford University Press.

CHAPTER 6

The visionary/ideological model of strategic management

Using the visionary/ideological processes of ordinary management to make long-term strategies

6.1   INTRODUCTION

The realisation that the rational model of strategic management can apply only close to certainty and agreement and is, therefore, of very limited value in making long-term strategies has led to the development of another set of prescriptions that have come to constitute a fairly coherent model. This model consists of the extension of the ideological, cultural and political processes of ordinary management over the longer term and in conditions some way away from certainty and agreement. Although these processes are feasible modes of behaving further away from certainty and agreement than is the case for the planning model, they too are restricted by the focus on people in an organisation sharing the same frame of reference. It is this that makes the visionary/ideological approach an ordinary management one that is inapplicable in conditions far from certainty.

In this chapter we are going first to survey those writers who advocate the identification of best practice processes in the most successful organisations and the installing of such 'one best ways' into other organisations. This chapter will also review the prescriptions of Organisation Development, a discipline and a set of prescriptions for installing planned culture changes in organisations in a comprehensive manner.

First, we consider the 'one best way' prescriptions. These are usually derived from studies of excellent organisations that identify the key features those organisations have in common and then conclude that these key features are the sources of excellence. The 'excellence' prescription can be summarised as follows.

An organisation is successful because it possesses a small number of key attributes, primarily leadership and cultural factors, that can be identified by studying how managers in successful organisations behave. These attributes can be imitated by and

installed into other organisations which will then also succeed. The key attributes postulated to be necessary for success relate to behaviour: success follows when groups of
people work together in harmony to adapt to their environment; when they strongly
share the same values and the same vision of the future. The prescription is, therefore,
to install the key attributes: that is, establish a centrally intended vision for the future,
promote internal harmony by encouraging a shared culture, empower people, and
continually adapt to the external environment through trial-and-error action. This is
quite clearly a prescription to install a particular paradigm, a particular kind of shared
mental model, which experts and leaders have identified in advance of action. Any
double-loop learning has, therefore, already been done, away from and in advance of
the action, and we are not told how this has been or is to be done. What is left, then is
the task of single-loop learning, that is the ordinary management process of solving
the puzzles of a paradigm that has already been identified. Strategic management is
seen here, quite clearly, as a process of realising a prior, shared intention.

The excellence approach received a great deal of attention during the 1980s because
of a reaction against the widespread view that success can be secured simply by the
rational formulation and implementation of quantitative long-term plans. The reaction
took the form of emphasising the importance for organisational success of factors that
are the opposite of the rational: for example, vision, emotion, charismatic leadership,
belief, ideology and culture.

However, although this visionary and ideological approach to strategy has had a
powerful impact on the way managers talk and think, the rational formulation and
implementation of long-term plans has continued to be the most widely presented
route to success.

6.2 INSTALLING THE ATTRIBUTES OF EXCELLENCE

In the early 1980s *Peters and Waterman (1982)* published a study of forty-three major
American corporations. The sample included such household names as Disney,
Boeing, IBM, Mars, McDonald's, Dupont, Levi-Strauss, Procter & Gamble, 3M, Cata-
pillar, Hewlett Packard, Kodak, Wang, and Atari. All forty-three companies were
selected because they were judged to be excellent according to six financial yardsticks
and because they had been innovative and adaptable over reasonably long time periods. The study reached the conclusion that the cause of the excellence displayed by
these companies lay in eight prominent attributes they shared in common. The conclusion drawn was that if other companies imitated these eight attributes, they too would
become excellent. The eight attributes are listed below; they are particular characteristics of pattern in actions, position, posture and process.

The attributes of excellence

1 **Stick to the knitting.** This attribute relates to the pattern in sequences of strategic
   actions undertaken by excellent companies. They build on their strengths or core
   competences and they never diversify far away from these. Because successful companies stick to what they know and avoid that which they do not, senior managers
   can have a clear understanding of their business. It is this knowledge and experi-

ence that provides the basis of their management intuition and credibility. For example, McDonald's sticks to fast foods and avoids diversifying into hotels.

2 **Close to the customer.** This attribute relates to the position an excellent company adopts in relation to its environment. Excellent companies actively listen to their customers and place great emphasis on delivering quality, reliability and high levels of service. They set very high standards in these regards and ensure their achievement through reward systems that include emotional rewards, for example reward ceremonies. The excellent companies succeed because by listening to their customers they become better adapted to their environments than their competitors.

3 **Productive through people.** The posture that excellent companies adopt towards their people is one of major importance. They express concern for the feelings of their people and try to foster attitudes in which people perceive themselves as belonging to an extended family.

4 **Autonomy and entrepreneurship.** Excellent companies adopt a posture and process that encourage local initiative and practical risk-taking; they empower people to make decisions about their own jobs. The cultural values are such that people are not penalised for the failures that must sometimes flow from taking risks. Eccentrics are tolerated, provided that they are doers.

5 **Hands on, value driven.** In their decision-making processes, excellent companies place particular emphasis on cultural values and beliefs. The leaders of the company articulate and preach a set of beliefs to which they convert others. It is this strongly shared common culture that is the principal cause of the harmony to be found in excellent companies. The role of the leaders is also to create a strong sense of direction by expressing a vision of the future state the organisation is to occupy. The vision and the core values are not open to question, other than at the fringes. Leaders are inspirational and involved in the activities of their organisation, not superior or aloof monitors of previously planned actions.

6 **Bias for action.** This also refers to the management processes employed by excellent companies. Excellent companies rely heavily on informal communication and employ small, temporary task forces with voluntary membership inspired by visionary product champions to progress many different projects. On this view, organisations make strategic choices in a political manner because the choice depends upon how much support the champion can build for his or her idea.

Excellent companies are interested in tangible results, not lengthy reports; they do not wait for the results of analyses, but rather try ideas out, rapidly one after the other. Their posture and the processes of management they use emphasise fast trial-and-error action through which they learn about their environment.

Note, however, that learning here is of a rather simple kind in which managers are learning about the consequences of their actions. Their learning prompts a change of action, but not a change in beliefs. The previous attribute (all people strongly sharing the same visions and values) means that people will not question basic beliefs and attitudes. This must exclude the more complex forms of learning that takes place when people question the deepest beliefs and assumptions that their views and actions are based upon, and in so doing change them.

7 **Simple form, lean staff.** Excellent companies adopt a structural posture that involves small corporate headquarters with the rest decentralised into small autonomous units. Authority is pushed down the line. Complicated matrix forms of organisation are avoided. People are encouraged to see organisational sub-units as flexible and permeable. Rigid job descriptions are discouraged.

8 **Simultaneous loose–tight properties.** Excellent companies adopt a control posture in which there are two elements. These elements sound contradictory, but the manner in which they are used means that they are not contradictory in practice. On the one hand, excellent companies encourage simple fluid structures with high levels of autonomy and positive attitudes to risk-taking where people are empowered to take their own decisions. On the other hand, excellent companies apply tight short-term financial controls to the performance of all their units and they fiercely guard the core values. But they find it possible to combine individual initiative and enterprise (the loose) with central organisational intention and control (the tight) in a consistent and harmonious way because of the belief system that all strongly share. Harmony and consistency are thus preserved, so solving the apparent contradiction between the tight and the loose.

The conclusion drawn is that if managers install these eight attributes into their organisations then people will be motivated to carry out the trial-and-error actions required to reach the vision shared by all. The top sets the vision and the values and then relies on people in the organisation to find the route to that vision. Peters and Waterman explain that rapid change and high levels of uncertainty make it impossible to forecast enough of what is going to happen to make it possible to prepare stable plans well in advance of acting, that is, to tell people well in advance what they are expected to do. It follows that managers have to discover the route to the future position they wish to occupy through trial-and-error action. The drive to undertake large volumes of trial-and-error action comes from what people believe, hence the heavy emphasis of the eight attributes on ideology, culture and vision – you can see how all of this fits into the definition of discovery, choice and action in *Figure 4.11* in Chapter 4.

Peters and Waterman argued that managers were being misled by a belief that they ought to be rational and were consequently spending too much time on research and analysis that diminished the urge to act – the result was paralysis by analysis. The argument about rationality and the extent to which managers need to use rational criteria to make decisions or to adopt some other approach still continues. Unfortunately, the debate is greatly confused by the fact that rationality has a number of meanings and debaters do not always make it clear which of these meanings they are using, as we saw in Chapter 2 (see *Key Concept 2.3*).

The Peters and Waterman study and the principles it identified have had a very powerful effect on companies throughout the world. During the 1980s many companies cut out layers of management to make their organisations lean and simple. They embarked on major programmes to change the cultures of their organisations and to empower people; they devoted time to forming visions and preparing mission statements; and terms such as vision, values and culture came to occupy a prominent place in the vocabulary of most business people.

The enduring contribution made by the Peters and Waterman study is the attention it focused on the important role that values, culture and beliefs play in organisational success. It also directed attention to the informal aspects of an organisation and the role that organisational politics plays in the process of strategic management by emphasising the role of leaders, product champions, project teams, and task forces. These are much the same kinds of processes that have been observed in studies of political activity in organisations. We have already looked at these in Chapters 4 and 5 and we will return to them in Chapter 11. Informal organisational processes and the implications of empowering people will also be discussed in Chapter 11.

The model of the strategic management process presented by Peters and Waterman in their eight-attribute analysis, with its emphasis on trial-and-error action, is close to Quinn's (1980) logical incrementalism examined in Chapter 2.

Despite the importance of the Peters and Waterman study, however, it has not identified *the* definitive route to success. The eight-attribute plan proved to be a disappointment because, within five years, two-thirds of the companies in the sample had slipped from the pinnacle, some to return later, others to remain in the doldrums. A number of other studies followed (for example, *Goldsmith & Clutterbuck, 1984*), but none so far can be judged to have found the one best way for all companies.

6.3 MANAGING ORGANISATION DEVELOPMENT AND CULTURE CHANGE

Another approach to the visionary/ideological mode of strategy-making is to found in the discipline of Organisation Development. The central concern of those practising this discipline is the planning and management of changes in the beliefs, values, cultures, social interactions and behaviour of people in an organisation in order to improve its effectiveness.

This is clearly an ordinary management approach because it is based upon the assumption that someone, top management or expert consultants, knows what new culture, or paradigm, is to replace the old. The point is this. Although Organisation Development is indeed about changing shared models it is not really a double-loop learning process for the organisation as whole – the top managers and/or the consultants may well have performed double-loop learning some time previously, but now they are simply converting and recruiting to their new paradigm.

Organisation Development (OD) recognises that it is not sufficient to analyse the environment and then set out the planned actions logically required to achieve an organisation's goals in that environment. What actually happens in an organisation does not depend on such rational considerations alone; it depends just as much on the behavioural factors: belief systems, social interactions, cultures, group behaviour and individual psychology. It is not enough to focus on technical or primary task subsystems; it is also necessary to operate on the psycho-social subsystem. Action plans will simply not be implemented if they run counter to the belief system, or if they adversely affect social structures, or if they do not motivate people. For this reason it is necessary to plan changes in beliefs and cultures to support the required actions, according to OD.

OD is therefore a long-term programme of intervention in the social, psychological, cultural and belief systems of an organisation. These interventions are based on certain principles and practices which are assumed to lead to greater organisational effectiveness.

These principles and practices are to do with identifying those beliefs, values and cultures conducive to achieving an organisation's goals – the desired culture – and then designing a systematic and deliberate change programme to move from the current to the desired culture.

One of the pioneers of this line of thinking was *Kurt Lewin (1947, 1951)* and we can explore the main assumptions on organisational dynamics made by OD practitioners if we look briefly at some of the key points he made. His models of the change process in organisations have had an important impact on subsequent thinking. The discipline and practices of OD, with its culture-change programmes, has been heavily influenced by Lewin's thought and is now widely accepted by practising managers.

Lewin (1947) saw social planning as a means of improving the functioning of organisations. He saw such social planning processes in terms of circular feedback in which goals were clarified, paths identified, and actions kept to the path, through the operation of negative feedback (see *Figure 6.1*).

Lewin thought of the organisational change process in the following terms:

- At the beginning of any social change we can think of the organisation as being in a state of stable equilibrium: a state of harmony in which all share the same culture.

FIGURE 6.1
Negative feedback and Organisation Development

- Stable equilibrium means that the forces driving for change and the forces resisting change just balance each other. In other words, driving and restraining forces create what he called a *balanced force field*, illustrated in *Figure 6.2*.
- Then some trigger such as falling profitability, or an announcement of reorganisation, or the setting-up of some programme of planned culture change, upsets the balance between the driving and resisting forces. In other words, some environmental change causes some internal change that unbalances the force field. Consequently, the existing management recipe on what the business is all about and how it should be run is challenged. This is the first stage of organisational change and Lewin called it *unfreezing*.
- When the balance between driving and restraining forces is upset, it causes confusion in which people search for new recipes. This is the second stage of organisational change, called *reformulation*. It comes to an end once a new management recipe has been identified, one that is believed to match the changed environment.
- The third stage is *re-freezing* in which people are converted and persuaded to accept the new recipe. The organisation thus returns once more to the harmony and stability characterised by all sharing the same culture. If the organisation is to survive, this new recipe must be one that is more appropriate to the changed environment.

This is clearly a feedback loop, one that will keep an organisation adapted to its environment, if it functions effectively. To function effectively, the feedback loop must be negative in its operation so as to keep the organisation moving to a desired state established by the environment. The dynamics of successful change are quite clearly to do with the drive to equilibrium and they are characterised by regularity and stability.

Now, the organisational change process could just occur as the environment changed or it could be planned, and OD is based on the belief that such change should be planned along the following lines.

FIGURE 6.2
Lewin's concept of a force field

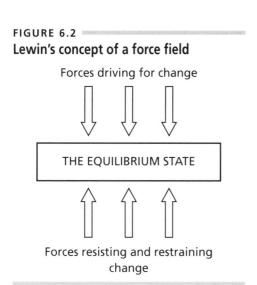

Forces driving for change

THE EQUILIBRIUM STATE

Forces resisting and restraining change

1 The analysis

The first step in planned social change is that of analysing the force field existing at any one time in a specific organisation to identify what the driving forces are and what the resisting forces are.

For example, consider the problems faced by any one of the electricity utilities in the UK in 1989 as they began to prepare to operate as privately owned corporations rather than state bodies. The forces driving change were the new government policies on the ownership of the electricity industry, the European Community Directives on tighter control of pollution, and perhaps the appointment of a new chief executive from the commercial sector to oversee the change. The driving forces were creating a need for a whole new culture, one that focused on profit rather than engineering considerations. The resisting forces were created by the engineering culture of the utility, by the existing beliefs and patterns of work.

Suppose that OD consultants are hired to help with the change process. What would those consultants do? They would first form a clearer picture of the nature of the drivers of and resistances to change. They would do this by holding many discussions with managers and employees. These discussions would surface the main concerns. The consultants would start to form hypotheses about the main resistances to change and then check these by distributing and analysing questionnaires to large samples of managers and employees. The analysis would reveal much about the attitudes, the satisfactions and dissatisfaction of people throughout the organisation, the strengths and weaknesses of the organisation.

2 Developing the plan

The second step in planned social change is to prepare a plan for change that strengthens the favourable driving forces and weakens the blocking resisting forces.

The OD approach to developing such a plan is one that employs process consulting. This means that the consultant does not operate as an expert selling advice to the organisation in response to a need that the organisation has already defined. Nor does the consultant act as the company doctor who diagnoses what is wrong, recommends what to do and then leaves. The process consultant (*Schein, 1987, 1988*) helps the client to perceive and understand what is going on in the environment and within the organisation and then assists the client to develop appropriate responses. The emphasis is on clients helping themselves.

Indeed the OD approach heavily emphasises what it regards as the most effective way for clients to help themselves, namely through widespread participation. The OD process for developing plans for change is one based on an ideology of planned participation and democracy. It focuses very much on the importance of leadership in this process, but leadership of a facilitating, encouraging kind rather than authoritarian, directing kinds.

Typically therefore, OD consultants follow a sequence of activities such as the following:

- A top client group is established consisting of the most senior and politically powerful executives. Sometimes the client is simply the most powerful executive. The analysis of the driving and restraining forces described above is presented to this client and the hypotheses on them discussed. Together the client and the OD consultants identify what changes need to be brought about. So for example, top management and OD consultants in the electricity utilities mentioned above might identify the prime need to change the culture from an engineering to a profit-centred one, to remove the old bureaucracy and cut staff levels. They might agree on a programme of regular meetings at a number of different levels in the hierarchy to set financial and staff reduction targets and then review their part of the business against those targets and take corrective action.

- The top executives might start the process off by going away for a weekend to put together a mission statement setting out what new key values are to drive the business. They might set some broad overall financial targets.
- The next step would then be to 'roll down' the mission statement throughout the organisation. The next most senior level of managers would be formed into a group and a programme of meetings arranged for it. At the first few meetings that group would examine the mission statement prepared by the top team for the whole organisation. They would translate that into a mission for their level.
- Then teams of managers would be established for different business units or for different functions such as sales and production. These teams would then take the mission statements and translate them into mission statements for their own business units and functions.
- As the programmes of meetings continued, members would spend time identifying how to turn the missions into more precise objectives and what plans to prepare to achieve those objectives.

In this way, an orderly hierarchy of management teams pursue a programme of clarifying objectives and roles and preparing plans for change, all in accordance with a broad framework established at the top of the organisation.

3 Implementing the plan

The final step in planned social change is to implement the culture-change plan.

In a sense, implementation is proceeding alongside the development of objectives and plans because managers at many levels in the hierarchy are behaving in a way they did not do before. They are attending planning and reviewing meetings and working collaboratively on developing plans. The process of rolling down the mission statements and the objectives may itself be implementation in so far as the participation motivates people to accept changes in behaviour.

The planned changes in behaviour to more collaborative forms may be specifically reinforced by team-building exercises and training in group skills. So managers may be sent on presentation and assertiveness courses, or they may be sent away in groups for long weekends where they take part in team-building exercises. This may involve playing business games, or taking part in physical activities such as rock climbing, or finding the way through some wilderness. Such exercises are believed to build team spirit and establish bonds between people who have shared hardships or pleasurable activities together.

The top executive team will also probably engage in such team-building activities. These could include exercises in which the executives use questionnaires to identify the personality types to which they belong (*Belbin, 1981; Kiersey & Bates, 1978*). They then explore how these different personality types interact with other types and what impact this has on their working together as a group.

All of these OD interventions are of course a form of social engineering which could have sinister overtones, were it not for the insistence of OD that culture-change programmes will work only if they are collaborative. The culture-change programme must be one that leads the people involved to see for themselves why they should change their culture to a new desired state.

OD is therefore about a comprehensive approach to planning changes in behaviour in organisations. This kind of thinking leads to the rejection of piecemeal culture change as the effective way to alter belief systems. Simply affecting one of the driving or resisting forces is thought unlikely to move the whole system. The whole system must move if the organisation is to change enough. These thoughts lead to the current popularity of the large-scale culture-change programmes adopted by many companies.

Note how OD is built firmly on the idea that negative feedback, planning and reviewing lead to success. Note how the dynamics are described in terms of strong tendencies towards states of stability and harmony. This means that OD can be applied only in conditions reasonably close to certainty and agreement. A summary of OD is given in *Figure 6.3*.

FIGURE 6.3

Organisation Development: a summary

- Organisations are normally in a state of stable equilibrium in terms of cultures and belief systems. The forces driving change and those resisting it balance each other.
- When it becomes necessary, analytical methods can be used to identify some new desirable state for the culture and the belief system. Analysis can also determine which driving and resisting forces to focus on in order to realise the desired change. Someone can know what an appropriate culture is. Specific actions lead to specific changes in beliefs and social structures and small chance events can be prevented from escalating into major changes in beliefs and social interactions – it is possible to prevent chain reactions and bandwagon effects (see Chapter 8, the section on positive feedback and non-linearity in organisations).
- There are collaborative group techniques available to persuade and convert people to the new required belief system. Once rational people of goodwill see why they should change, for the common good, what they believe and how they interact socially, then they will. In other words, OD consultants implicitly assume that it is possible to ignore or overcome deeply buried unconscious group processes which lead people to behave 'irrationally'. (See Chapter 8, the section on Bion's models, which discusses sensitivity training and the Tavistock method. This approach which focuses on unconscious group processes is usually criticised by OD consultants and is very rarely used by them.)
- It is thus possible to install new belief systems and it is possible for someone in an organisation to be in control of the process.
- Once the change process is over, the organisation returns to its normal stable state.
- Successful change is planned, regular, hierarchical. It is secured through harmonious collaboration, the application of negative feedback.

6.4   SUMMARY

This chapter has reviewed two approaches to installing intentional changes in behaviour in a comprehensive manner in organisations. The first involved the identification of best practice processes in the most successful organisations and then the copying of those processes in others to secure success. The second consists of a process for designing and installing a comprehensive set of new beliefs in an organisation. Neither of these approaches has been particularly successful. Organisations remain stubbornly resistant to wholesale cultural engineering.

Further reading

Peters and Waterman (1982) is well worth reading. More detail on Organisation Development can be obtained by reading any of the standard texts on organisational behaviour, for example Robbins (1986).

References

Belbin, R. M. (1981) *Management Teams: Why They Succeed or Fail*, Oxford: Heinemann.

Goldsmith, W. & Clutterbuck, D. (1984), *The Winning Streak*, London: Weidenfeld & Nicolson.

Kiersey, D. & Bates, M. (1978), *Please Understand Me: Character and Temperament Types*, Del Mar, Ca.: Prometheus Nemesis Books.

Lewin, K. (1947), Feedback problems of social diagnosis and action, Part II-B of Frontiers in Group Dynamics, *Human Relations*, vol. 1, pp. 147–53.

Lewin, K. (1951), *Field Theory in Social Science*, New York: Harper & Brothers.

Peters, T. J. & Waterman, R. H. (1982), *In Search of Excellence*, New York: Harper & Row.

Quinn, J. B. (1980), *Strategy Change: Logical Incrementalism*, Homewood, Ill.: Richard D. Irwin.

Robbins, S. P. (1986), *Essentials of Organisational Behaviour*, Hemel Hempstead: Prentice-Hall.

Schein, E. H. (1987), *Process Consultation Volume 1: Its Role in Organization Development*, Reading, Ma.: Addison-Wesley.

Schein, E. H. (1988), *Process Consultation Volume II: Lessons for Managers and Consultants*, Reading, Ma.: Addison-Wesley.

CHAPTER 7

The results of using ordinary management to make long-term strategies

Trapped in stability

7.1 INTRODUCTION

In this chapter we are going to take stock of the position that previous chapters have led us to.

The chain of reasoning we have been following starts with a description of what it is that managers must manage, namely, change. The first link in the chain of reasoning is that as they stand in the here and now, faced with the problem of designing their actions, managers confront change situations in all time frames that cover a spectrum ranging from those close to certainty and agreement to those far from certainty and agreement. Furthermore, the former change situations dominate the short-term future while the latter dominate the long-term future.

The second link in the chain of reasoning is that in situations close to certainty managers are able to operate within a legitimate system consisting of a hierarchy/bureaucracy and an officially approved ideology that is in place before there is a need to take action. This legitimate system embodies a paradigm that is the result of a particular organisation's history – the whole sequence of discoveries, choices and actions of its members since its inception. In this sense the legitimate system of every organisation is unique to it and reflects that part of its lifetime of learning that has been retained in the present. This legitimate system is the stable framework within which managers apply ordinary management processes. These processes are all of a negative feedback, single-loop learning nature. Two types of ordinary management processes have been distinguished from each other to aid our understanding of them. The first consists of the technically rational decision-making and the monitoring control processes, and the second of the visionary/ideological/political processes of decision-making and control. By their very nature these processes dampen down on change and preserve the status quo in the interests of the efficient performance of existing primary tasks. Effective and efficient ordinary management is an absolute requirement if an organisation is to be capable of carrying out its day-to-day activities efficiently and reliably. This is the form of management that makes organisations better and better at doing what they already do well. It is the type of management that groups of managers use to realise their joint intentions formed before they take joint action. It is all about managing change in a progressive incremental manner.

The third link in the chain of reasoning is this. It is possible to employ ordinary management processes only when you are reasonably close to certainty and agreement and it is only appropriate to do so when you are concerned with improving current primary task performance as opposed to changing the rules of the organisational game in a creative and innovative way. The reason for this is quite simple and quite logical – efficient current performance requires sustaining the legitimate system and the paradigm it embodies while changing the rules of the game, being creative and innovative is changing the paradigm and thus the legitimate system. Processes that sustain it cannot also change it – that is a logical impossibility. When managers are concerned with changeability as opposed simply to change, when they are faced with great uncertainty, ambiguity and disagreement, when they seek the effective, the creative and the innovative as opposed to the efficient and the predictable, then they must abandon ordinary management processes and turn to extraordinary ones. In Part Three we will explore further why this is so and in Part Four we will examine what the alternative, extraordinary management, entails.

However, the dominant approach in the strategic management literature when it comes to prescribing what managers should do to manage strategically, as opposed to descriptions of what they actually do, is quite firmly and clearly based on the extension of ordinary management processes into the long-term future. The reasoning we have been employing would lead us to expect such approaches to be of very limited value in a rapidly changing world, and indeed there is evidence that this is the case. It is to this evidence that we turn in this chapter, evidence which suggests that when managers extend ordinary management thinking into truly strategic situations they become trapped in the very stability they seek to create to the point where they cannot respond to changes in the rules of the game that others initiate.

7.2   EVIDENCE OF SUCCESS

Do the conventional strategic management prescriptions actually work?

If we have succeeded in identifying a reliable set of prescriptions for strategic success, then we would expect to find at least a small sample of companies that have mastered those prescriptions. We would expect to find samples of excellent companies that remain successful for long periods of time.

In fact, it seems that no sooner does anyone identify a sample of excellent companies than most of them slip from grace. As we have seen, in the early 1980s, *Peters and Waterman (1982)* identified 43 excellent companies in the USA but within five years two-thirds could no longer be included in the sample. *Goldsmith and Clutterbuck (1984)* carried out a similar analysis of 25 UK companies and the same fate befell their sample. The rankings of the Fortune 500 companies and the *Financial Times* top 100 companies change dramatically over five-year periods.

It is therefore extremely difficult to find a sample of companies that have consistently mastered the task of successful strategic management for a reasonably long period of time. The usual reason given for this difficulty is that the environment is too turbulent to allow continuing success, or that companies fall from the category of excellence because they are incompetently managed. This is, however, a strange response. If the environment is too turbulent to allow the strategic management prescriptions to succeed, then clearly we must abandon them and look for something else. I find it rather difficult to believe that the strategic management prescriptions do not succeed because managers are not applying them competently – surely by now the business schools would have remedied this problem. Or is it possible that business schools are teaching the wrong thing when they teach the dominant view of strategy as an intentional process?

It has also proved very difficult to establish any connection between the existence of formal planning in an organisation and superior performance *(Greenley, 1986)*. That may be because few companies actually use long-term plans as control instruments. A recent survey of large companies in the UK *(Goold & Quinn, 1990)* shows that only 15 per cent of those that do have formal planning systems use them as templates against which to monitor actions. Even those 15 per cent monitor their plans against events such as building a factory rather than by results such as making a profit. It seems that most managers do not use the espoused recipes for success as they are intended to be used; and we cannot establish much of a link between the use of the recipe and success.

Apparently only 20 per cent of Japanese companies practise formal long-term planning *(Argenti, 1984)*. In many other respects these successful global rivals of Western companies seem to do things very differently. *Hamel and Prahalad (1989)* identify the relative success of the Japanese with a superior model in which they do not attempt to adapt to environments but create core competences and build market share. *Hampden-Turner (1990)* describes how Japanese managers are more comfortable with dilemmas and paradoxes than Western managers are. *Nonaka (1988)* describes how Japanese managers intentionally develop the instability of counter-cultures, while the Western approach is to attempt to secure even more conformity.

Today's strategic management prescriptions do not provide reliable answers to the question of how to create and sustain effective and long-lived organisations. Royal Dutch Shell conducted a survey in 1983 and found that the average life-time of the largest industrial corporations was less than forty years *(De Geus, 1988)*. Corporations do not live as long as individual people! That report could only find about 30 corporations, worldwide, that had survived for more than a century and of the 50 per cent of those with reliable enough records all had significantly changed the nature of their activities a number of times. Long-term survivors do not stick to their knitting. Some people are not concerned about this short life-span, holding that the continuous failure of old organisations and creation of new ones is how innovation occurs. This might be an acceptable argument if we knew how to create successful new organisations – the high failure rate of new companies indicates only too forcefully that we do not. Furthermore, securing innovation through allowing the old organisations to die and bringing on the new ones means continually re-experiencing the same problems of turning small companies into large ones. That way we continue to learn old lessons instead of learning how to develop new forms of large organisation. Our failure reliably to create and sustain organisations is therefore an indictment of the conventional wisdom.

The argument, then, is that today's dominant prescriptions for strategic management – the planning, envisioning, controlling and ideology sharing described in the previous two chapters are not leading the corporations of Europe and North America to success. Managers in the Far East see the world through different lenses *(Pascale, 1990; Hampden-Turner, 1990)* and for decades now they have been winning the strategy game. This is certainly not a new conclusion: arguments along these lines have been presented many times over the past few years (for example, *Hayes & Abernathy, 1980; and Hamel & Prahalad, 1989).*

The usual response

This recognition of relative failure normally provokes an intensified effort to improve a selected number of the existing prescriptions. Larger numbers of organisations are researched and the approaches to planning, envisioning, strategically controlling and consensus building are further refined.

For example, the study of large UK companies already referred to identified that only 15 per cent of those who formulated long-term plans subsequently monitored and reviewed action against them *(Goold & Quinn, 1990).* The conclusion drawn by the researchers was that managers were behaving in an ineffective way. Despite the admitted difficulties of doing so, managers were advised to devote more effort to setting strategic milestones and reviewing their actions against those milestones. The implicit assumptions the researchers were making are these:

- Companies will be successful if they formulate consistent long-term plans and then sustain stability by acting in accordance with those plans.
- Such stability can be secured only by reviewing and monitoring action outcomes against milestones.
- Levels of uncertainty are not such as to make all of this completely impossible.

But the managers in the sample of companies knew all about setting milestones and monitoring outcomes. They were doing exactly this when they used budgets for short-term control systems. Why did the majority in the sample not carry the procedure over to the long-term control of their organisation? They all knew about the importance of the long term. Perhaps they did not carry short-term reviewing procedures over to the long term because it did not make much practical sense to do so. Perhaps the level of uncertainty was too high. Repeating advice that has been heeded only superficially for decades now is surely not a useful response to a serious difficulty. But this is exactly what the conventional wisdom predisposes us to do.

Another example of this response is the new book by *Hamel & Prahalad (1994).* It talks about the successful as the ones who 'get to the future' first, so indicating an assumption that the future already exists and the successful discover what it is and then take it for themselves. In fact, the future does not exist yet at all. It is not waiting to be discovered. It will be whatever the players make it. In that case how can anyone identify the competences that will be required to meet it, as Hamel and Prahalad propose?

Is a different response required?

When confronted by the evident failure of strategic management prescriptions to produce consistent organisational success, the conventional wisdom leads us to ascribe this to some combination of environmental turbulence and management incompetence. We then do more research, try to refine the prescriptions further, and exhort managers to try harder. But there is another possibility and this is that there is something fundamentally wrong, namely, that we are trying to apply ordinary strategic management in situations far from certainty and agreement and it is logically impossible for this to work. Futhermore, practitioners actually know this, so most do not actually commit the logical error of practising ordinary strategic management in situations far from certainty and agreement. Instead, they actually practise extraordinary management, but this practice arouses so much anxiety, for reasons we will come to in a later chapter, that they cover this practice up with the pretence of employing the techniques of ordinary strategic management.

What we need, if we are to make sense of this rather complex situation, is a deeper understanding of the assumptions that ordinary management prescriptions are built upon and why they lead to a limited perspective. This will the lead us to some more useful assumptions we can make about organisational life, assumptions that will lead us to an understanding of the nature of extraordinary management. That will be the task of Part Three.

Do comprehensive culture change programmes work any better

Organisation Development (OD) is the intentional change of a culture to be brought about through a systematic, organisation-wide, centrally planned programme of re-education. And this re-education programme has certain specific features: it is education based upon the consent and commitment of the people involved.

OD is based on the assumption that organisations will cope more effectively with change, will implement their strategies more effectively, if the creative potential of their people is unleashed. This is said to require:

- flat organisational structures;
- loose, overlapping job definitions;
- widespread participation in decision-making; and thus
- the dispersion of power as authority to make decisions.

OD is about achieving planned changes in behaviour through empowering people in a particular kind of political system that we may call a democratic, collegial-consensus system (*Greiner & Schein, 1988*). The political system is collegial because it is based on dispersed power and widespread participation. It is a consensus system because it is all held together by strongly shared beliefs and decisions that are taken in a collaborative way. The aim is to move an organisation from a control model to a commitment one.

Despite the end point of dispersed power and consensus decision-making, the OD programme is in fact about reaching that point in a planned manner. Someone has to decide in advance what the change in belief systems is to be; someone is in control of the process. OD is not about changes that emerge or evolve from a pattern of interactions: it is a comprehensive pre-designed programme. And herein lies its danger, for it can all too easily become a propaganda exercise. Herein lies what may be an insuperable obstacle – it is using a control model to install a commitment one. Note the concept of leadership in the OD project: the leader decides in advance what the organisation should do and then facilitates the acceptance of these decisions by others in the organisation. Contrast this with an alternative where leadership takes the form of facilitating a learning experience in which members of the organisation, including the leader, discover what decision to make. That would be a commitment model being used to lead to a commitment one.

Because of its emphasis on planning, OD is based on the unquestioned assumption that an organisation is a feedback system in which negative feedback is the dominant form. It is through the negative feedback of consensus, planning and monitoring that the successful organisation is kept at, or returned to, stable states of consensus around a given culture or belief system, one that can be installed.

How well does this approach work? One study has described a long list of failed efforts at total culture change because of the neglect or lack of support from top management (*Mirvis & Berg, 1977*). Another study of a number of companies (*Beer, Eisenstat & Spector, 1990*) leads to these conclusions:

- Corporate programmes to change the whole culture of a company in a top-down planned manner do not work.
- The most effective change programmes are those that start in a number of small peripheral operations and gradually spread throughout the organisation.
- Changes to formal structures, systems and policies come at the end of successful periods of change, not the beginning. Effective culture change focuses on the tasks people have to do in business units and it spreads not because the top is in control of the spread but because the top creates the right climate for change to spread.

There is therefore, some persuasive evidence indicating that OD programmes simply do not work.

7.3 SUMMARY

This short chapter has considered the usefulness of the dominant way of prescribing for strategic success. It suggests that the question we have to ask about this approach is this: if I take my organisation's current situation can I honestly show that it is what it is because a group of people formulated an intention some 5, 10 or 15 years ago that has now been realised? If I answer 'yes' to that question then I need to ask: is the situation today rather similar to what it was 5, 10 or 15 years ago or is it radically different? My argument is that if it is radically different it will not be possible to say that the situation is the result of some clear, comprehensive intention formed 5, 10 or 15 years previously. It is my experience that when I present this argument to managers in the context of their specific experience of their particular organisation they do not contradict it.

If this is so of the history of organisations, what is it that makes anyone believe that we can now sit down and design and intend a future for an organisation that is radically different from what the current situation is and then expect to be able to realise it, as the dominant received wisdom seeks to persuade us? My belief is that there is no reason at all, and that the dominant approach to strategic management continues to propose this because it is based upon some very fundamental assumptions about the nature of organisations as systems that are simply accepted without question. These assumptions lead those talking and writing about strategy to believe that intentional new strategic directions can be realised. Note that, based on the evidence presented in this chapter, this is a belief, not the kind of scientific fact that some like to claim it is. The purpose of Part Three is to explain why I hold the belief that creative new strategies are not the realisation of intention but are emergent, and why this is more useful than the opposite belief that so dominates current thinking.

Before you dismiss my argument by saying that we may not be able to realise intentions precisely but we can more or less, I ask that you suspend any disbelief until you have worked through Part Three.

So, what conclusion might we reach about the usefulness of the dominant body of strategic management prescriptions reviewed in the last two chapters? If we are dealing with the short term, if we are satisfied that doing better what we already do well will enable us to survive for the next five to ten years, then it is acceptable to use the approach outlined in the last two chapters as those proposing it intend, that is, in a future-oriented manner. And this is a seductive suggestion in many ways. It is a reliable way to avoid the anxiety of creativity and innovation, of fundamental change, and it can serve as an effective cover for all the kinds of covert politics and organisational game-playing that we will discuss in Part Four below.

However, the history of organisational life shows that it is possible for organisations to be creative and innovative and history shows that it is those organisations that succeed in radically transforming themselves a number of times that survive for long periods. To understand this we need to adopt an extraordinary management perspective. That is the task of the rest of this book.

Further reading

Ansoff (1990) is one of the most vociferous supporters of intentional strategy. Good summaries of counter views are to be found in Hurst (1982, 1986), Argyris (1990) and Schein (1988). A more detailed development of the arguments in this chapter may be found in Stacey (1991).

References

Ansoff, I. (1990), *Implanting Corporate Strategy*, Hemel Hempstead: Prentice-Hall.

Argenti, J. (1984), Don't let planners meddle with your strategies, *Accountancy*, April, p. 152.

Argyris, C. 1990, *Overcoming Organizational Defenses: Facilitating Organizational Learning*, Boston: Allyn & Bacon, Prentice-Hall.

Beer, M., Eisenstat, R. A. & Spector, B. (1990), *The Critical Path to Corporate Renewal*, Boston, Ma.: Harvard Business School Press.

De Geus, P. (1988) Planning as learning, *Harvard Business Review*, March–April, pp. 70–4

Goldsmith, W. & Clutterbuck, D. (1984), *The Winning Streak*, London: Weidenfield & Nicolson.

Goold, M. with Quinn, J. J. (1990), *Strategic Control: Milestones for Long Term Performance*, London: Hutchinson.

Greenley, G. E. (1986), Does strategic planning improve performance?, *Long Range Planning*, vol. 19, no. 2, pp. 101–9

Greiner, L. E. & Schein, V. E. (1988), *Power and Organization Development: Mobilizing Power to Implement Change*, Reading, Ma.: Addison-Wesley.

Hamel, G. & Prahalad, C. K. (1989), Strategic intent, *Harvard Business Review*, May–June, pp. 63–76

Hamel, G. & Prahalad, C. K. (1994), *Competing for the Future*, Boston, Ma.: Harvard Business School Press.

Hampden-Turner, C. (1990), *Charting the Corporate Mind*, New York: Free Press, Macmillan.

Hayes, R. & Abernathy, W. (1980), Managing our way to economic decline, *Harvard Business Review*, July–Aug, pp. 11–25.

Hurst, D. K. (1986), Why strategic management is bankrupt, *Organizational Dynamics*, Autumn, pp. 4–77.

Hurst, E. G. (1982), Controlling strategic plans, in Lorange, D. (Ed.) (1982), *Implementation of Strategic Planning*, Englewood Cliffs, NJ: Prentice-Hall.

Mirvis, P. & Berg, D. (1977), *Failures in Organizational Development and Change*, New York: John Wiley.

Nonaka, I. (1988), Creating organizational order out of chaos: self-renewal in Japanese firms, *California Management Review*, Spring, pp. 57–73.

Pascale, R. T. (1990), *Managing on the Edge: How Successful Companies Use Conflict to Stay Ahead*, London: Viking Penguin.

Peters, T. J. & Waterman, R. H. (1982), *In Search of Excellence*, New York: Harper & Row.

Schein, E. H. (1988), *Process Consultation Volume II: Lessons for Managers and Consultants*, Reading, Ma.: Addison-Wesley.

Stacey, R. (1991), *The Chaos Frontier: Creative Strategic Control for Business*, Oxford: Butterworth-Heinemann.

The Suter Packaging Division

In August 1985 Larkfield Management Consultancy Ltd wrote to Francis Packaging Ltd introducing its strategic management service. In late August Larkfield were invited to a meeting with the Francis Chief Executive and in preparation for this meeting one of the Larkfield consultants put together a recent history of Francis Packaging Ltd from published accounts, newspaper reports and discussions with a colleague who had run a production and cost improvement assignment at Francis back in 1982.

The business of Francis Packaging Ltd

Francis Packaging operate in the general line sector of the tinplate packaging market. This market can be divided into a number of sectors which are described in Appendix 3A. Briefly, these are:

- open top cans for beverages and processed food. This is a high volume business and in 1984 sales amounted to over £500m;
- aerosols for a wide variety of uses and total sales of around £80m;
- collapsible tubes for toothpaste and a variety of other uses with sales of about £20m;
- closures, that is the tops, for a wide variety of containers with sales of around £74m;
- general line containers. This category covers many shapes and sizes of container and usually those produced in smaller volumes. Total sales here were about £190m in 1984 (round lever lid cans £60m; rectangular cans about £35m; tinplate drums £20m; others such as biscuit tins, tins for toiletries £75m).

Francis Packaging and its subsidiaries manufacture round cans mainly for the paint industry, rectangular cans for the lubricating and edible oil markets, tinplate drums for a variety of uses and a range of other tinplate containers for tobacco, milk powder, and shortbread. Francis Packaging itself operated from two factories: one at Greenwich, London, which produced paint cans, rectangular cans and drums; the other at Wrexham in Wales which had a similar product range. A subsidiary company, Shemtec Packaging Ltd produced paint cans only at its Leeds factory. Another subsidiary, Drummond Packaging Ltd located in Glasgow, Scotland, produced a variety of tinplate containers for powdered food, tobacco and shortbread as well as 10-litre paint pails.

As a back drop to considering the history of Francis over the 1980s certain key points on the packaging market should be noted:

- after growing more rapidly than the economy as a whole, expenditure on all packaging materials began to grow more slowly than the economy around the turn of the decade;
- the share of tinplate packaging in the total began to decline around the turn of the decade to the benefit of plastic and fibreboard;
- the result was a sharp decline in the volume of materials contained in tinplate.

Strategy over the early 1980s

Going back to 1980, Francis Packaging Ltd had a sales level of £14m on which it earned a profit before tax of £0.3m (see Appendix 3F). At that time, Francis Packaging Ltd was a subsidiary of Francis Industries plc. The other subsidiaries were Clearplas Ltd and Clearplas France SA, manufacturers of plastic products that had nothing to do with packaging; Sagar Richards Ltd; and Lacrinoid Ltd, manufacturers of blow-moulded plastic products, including plastic containers. Francis Industries' sales were nearly £30m on which they earned a profit before tax of £1.8m (see Appendix 3B).

Since 1980 Francis Packaging had adopted a strategy of dealing with the decline in its markets by increasing market share, partly through organic growth and partly through acquisition. Thus in May of 1981 Francis Packaging had acquired Drummond Packaging Ltd from the receiver. The business of Drummond was that of a jobber (short runs, speciality products) rather than a volume producer. The receiver had been called in five months previously, so it took some time to recover customers and build turnover up to £1.8m in 1982. Since that time, however, turnover had shown little growth and profitability had fallen dramatically.

In 1982 Francis Packaging acquired some of the assets and customers of one of its competitors, DKS, who had been making losses in the very difficult market conditions of 1980/1981. The turnover of the businesses whose assets were bought was around £4m. Francis transferred most of the purchased equipment to its factory at Wrexham and a line for producing 10-litre paint pails was transferred to the Greenock factory of Drummond. Then, in 1984 Francis Packaging made a further acquisition, this time of a small family-owned and -run company called Shemtec. This company manufactured round cans mainly for the paint industry and its turnover in 1984 was £4m.

The management at Francis had become increasingly concerned over the years at the penetration of plastic in their markets. The lubricating oil producers switched to plastic for 1-litre containers in the early 1980s – plastic containers of this size were reusable whereas the 1-litre metal containers had a tear off strip which meant that all the contents had to be used at once. The oil producers had drawn this problem to the attention of the tinplate manufacturers but there had been no effective response. Also, some of the paint companies expressed their discontent with rust in the tinplate containers for emulsion paint and in 1981 they drew this to the attention of the tinplate manufacturers. In view of the threat from plastic, the management of Francis gave some consideration to the development or acquisition of a plastics capability, but this never came to anything. In fact, Lacrinoid, the sister company, which did operate in this area, was far from successful and so in 1982 Francis Industries decided to sell it. Some thought was also given to the application of a more effective lacquer to the rim of paint cans, but it was to be some years before this was made available and by that time ICI had already started to pack its emulsion paint in plastic cans.

Mostly as a result of the acquisitions mentioned above, the turnover of the Francis tinplate packaging companies rose from £14m in 1980 to £18.5m in 1983, while the profit increased substantially to £1.5m. The importance of the tinplate companies in Francis Industries had therefore increased considerably (see Appendix 3F).

The Suter takeover

During 1983, Suter plc (see Appendix 3C), an acquisitive conglomerate chaired by David Abell and owning a range of companies in the refrigeration, air conditioning and hairdressing equipment industries, had built up a significant holding of shares in Francis Industries. By January 1984, Suter owned just over 26 per cent of Francis shares and rumours of a takeover bid increased. In March of that year it was announced that preliminary discussions had taken place between Suter and Francis which could lead to an offer being made by Suter. Suter then made a £13.4m bid which was rejected by the Francis Board as inadequate. Francis announced its excellent 1983 results and the Francis Board said that it expected record results for 1984. Suter increased its offer to £14.4m and acquired further shares in Francis, taking its stake to 34 per cent. Through April and May the battle to gain control of Francis continued with the Francis Directors announcing in May that they expected profits to rise 40 per cent to over £2m. Mystery buyers acquired significant numbers of Francis shares and so the matter was referred to the takeover panel by Francis. But no breach of the takeover code was found to have been committed by Suter.

Through May and June, Suter continued to build up its shareholdings and by 5 July it held 42.5 per cent. On 25 July, D M Saunders, Chairman of Francis Industries, resigned from the Board. At the same time D Crosby, the Managing Director of Francis Packaging Ltd, was appointed to the Board. Then in September the Francis Board announced first half results of £1.25m pre-tax profits, in line with the more than £2m which the directors had projected for 1984 as a whole. During October there were a number of false reports of agreement being reached on a new, revised bid. Finally, on 2 November the Francis directors halted dealings in the company's shares after a bid of £18.5m by Suter was agreed. The next day, Suter discovered that Francis would not reach its profit forecast of £2.35m (in fact less than half of this forecast was eventually achieved). By 4 December Suter held almost all of the Francis equity. After taking advice, Suter decided to sue the directors of Francis Industries as well as their merchant bank and accountants for the losses it had suffered as a result of the incorrect forecast. Writs were finally issued in early 1985.

The situation after the takeover

Through the first half of 1985, D Crosby continued as the Managing Director of Francis Packaging, reporting to the Chairman of the Francis Packaging Board, D Burnett, who also remained in office. The other members of the Board and an organisation chart are given in Appendix 3D. The Francis Packaging board remained responsible for Shemtec Packaging Ltd (Managing Director, C Crabtree) and Drummond Packaging Ltd (Managing Director, F Lysons).

By July 1985 D Burnett had left and at the end of July 1985 Suter installed a new Chief Executive, Paton Wallace. Paton Wallace was to take over the packaging companies of the former Francis Group, now to be known as the Suter Packaging Division – other Francis companies such as Clearplas were placed in other Suter Divisions. The Chairman of Suter had appointed Paton Wallace with the clear purpose of achieving an acceptable profit, that being at least 20 per cent on capital employed. The former Managing Director, D Crosby, continued as a consultant to the company and the Production Director left. When Paton Wallace arrived Francis Packaging was forecasting a profit before tax of less than £300,000 compared to the £1m that had been achieved in 1984. Mr Wallace was told that substantial business had been lost for a number of reasons. First, a major competitor, Nacanco, had taken advantage of the situation at Francis to mount a price war and had taken away large contracts with the oil companies. This had a major impact on the volume of sales from the Greenwich and Wrexham factories. Second, an important customer of Shemtec, the paint manufacturer Kalon, had not renewed its contract for reasons which were not clear. Finally, Drummond was suffering from the decline of major customers in the tobacco industry and of a major customer, DCL, who produced yeast.

In late August Larkfield consultants met the new Chief Executive. Mr Wallace outlined the recent history of Francis Packaging and then went on to discuss the problems that he was currently facing. Paton Wallace invited the Larkfield consultant to discuss the problems of the business with colleagues on the Board, a brief summary of which is given in the following paragraphs. He also commissioned the consultants to carry out market research and this is summarised in Appendices 3H to 3M.

A number of points emerged from the discussions that the consultants had with other members of the board. The view was widely held that tinplate would inevitably continue to lose market share to plastic. The conversations centred on the paint market and the dominating position that ICI held in that market. The consultants were told how ICI had taken a policy decision some years before to move to plastic containers for all their emulsion paints. Although solvent-based paints could not be contained in plastic because of the chemical reaction, it was thought that it was only a matter of time before water-based gloss paints would be developed to the point where they would be acceptable substitutes for solvent-based paints. Then ICI, it was felt, would use plastic containers for these paints too. The immediate threat, however, was to the emulsion paint business. ICI had encouraged Mardon Illingworth and Reed Packaging (a subsidiary of Reeds, who also owned Crown Paints) to develop straight-sided plastic cans with the same dimensions and specification as the metal cans. This had been done and ICI was transferring all of its emulsion paint to plastic containers as fast as the production capacity of the plastic can manufacturers would allow. The view at Francis was that, as soon as they could, the other paint producers would follow the ICI lead. In addition, solid emulsion was packaged in a plastic tray and this was also eroding the share of tinplate.

There seemed to be nothing that Francis could do to counter these trends – all the tinplate producers supplying the major paint companies provided a standard can (to Metal Packaging Manufacturer's Association standards) and in the oversupply conditions of the industry there was little scope for price increases.

After completing the discussions with Board members and the market research, the Larkfield consultants then worked on a strategic plan for the Division and its subsidiaries. This plan was prepared in close consultation with the Chief Executive of the Division. Mr Wallace was required to present his strategy to the main Suter Board in December 1985, only five months after taking up the position of Chief Executive. The time constraints were therefore such that it was impossible to involve the other members of the management of the Division.

Towards the end of November the outline of the strategy that Paton Wallace had developed with the consultants was presented to the Managing Directors of the three subsidiaries, the Board of Francis Packaging and two managers whom Paton Wallace had identified for promotion. Initially there was some disagreement on certain points in the market analysis and some reservations on the magnitude of the change which the new strategy represented, but at a second presentation there was a general agreement that it represented the way forward.

APPENDIX 3A
Background note on the packaging industry

Expenditure on packaging materials grew more rapidly than total expenditure in the economy over the second half of the 1970s. Metal packaging was holding its share. Around the turn of the decade there was a sharp change in trend with packaging growing more slowly than the economy and metal packaging losing share within the industry as a whole. These remarks on total value apply even more forcibly to volumes – the packaging industry as a whole and metal packaging in particular had not recovered to 1979 volume levels. Plastic packaging and to a lesser degree fibreboard have been gaining market share from metal and paper and to some extent, glass. Paper prices have risen much faster than inflation generally, as have prices of fibreboard. Metal packaging prices have increased much in line with inflation, but glass and plastic prices have tended to increase more slowly.

Metal packaging accounts for just under one quarter of the total packaging industry and has a total sales level of around £900–1000m. It employs about 21 000 people. The metal packaging industry can be subdivided into segments discussed in the following paragraphs.

Open top cans

These are either three-piece or two-piece. Three-piece is where the body is bent and the tops and bottoms are applied; two-piece is where the body is drawn up from the bottom and a top applied. The two-piece can was introduced in 1973 and currently nearly all beverage cans are of this variety. Here the printing is added to the cylindrical shape while in the case of the three-piece cans the printing is added before the metal is bent. Imports and exports are relatively small, although imports have been tending to rise.

Most open top cans are made of tinplate. Almost all open top cans for food are of tinplate, although about 65 per cent of the ends are made from tin-free steel. About half the beer and soft drink cans are now made of aluminium. The principal technical trends have been towards lighter weight, the use of welded rather than soldered joints and the substitution of aluminium for tinplate. In the past, tinplate cans took market share from glass but future trends are likely to be ones of substitution of tinplate by plastic, composite materials (for example, foil and plastic) and combined forms of packaging such as the bag in the box.

This is a volume production sector – about 9m cans a year. Of these about two-thirds are used by the canned food industry. This demand has been in decline due to the concern for healthier food and the greater demand for frozen food. However, growth in the production of pet food has compensated. Most of the remaining third of open top cans are used in the beverage industry.

The largest producer of open top cans is still Metal Box, but this company has lost market share (now about 50 per cent) to Nacanco (US owned) and American Can (Canadian owned), who together have about 30 per cent of the market. Crown Cork and Continental Can together have about 17 per cent of the market, leaving about 3 per cent for a few small producers. Some food producers manufacture their own cans.

Closures

These are the tops for various kinds of tinplate container. There has been strong substitution in this area by plastic.

Aerosol cans

These containers constitute a sizeable market and are used in a wide variety of applications, particularly in the toiletries and household cleaner markets. The major producer is Metal Box and there are relatively few other producers.

Collapsible aluminium tubes

These are used for tooth paste and ointments. Plastic is increasingly penetrating this sector.

Metal drums

These are made from steel, tinplate and aluminium. About 80 per cent in volume and 25 per cent in value of metal drums are in the 25 litres and less size range and these are predominantly tinplate. Those above 25 litres are made from cold-reduced mild steel. The main end uses of metal drums are as follows:

60% chemicals and petrochemicals;
25% oil products/lubricants and grease;
 5% food, drink and tobacco;
10% other (including paint).

This sector has also been affected by the advent of plastic. Steel and tinplate have a technical advantage in the transport of solvent-based paints, food and oil. Furthermore they are re-usable. But plastic drums are lighter and they have an advantage in the transport of some corrosive liquids and dyestuffs. Bowater has developed blow-moulded plastic drums up to 220 litres.

There are only a few producers of metal drums: Metal Box, Van Leer, Francis, Reads, and Rheem Blagden.

Other general line containers

These are predominantly round cans (mainly used for paint), rectangular cans (main uses being lubricating oil and edible oil) and a wide variety of smaller containers used for toiletries, and gift-ware. Production is characterised by much smaller runs than in the case of open top cans and these production runs are particularly small for the wide variety used in toiletries.

Francis Packaging: Composition of the metal packaging industry

1984		£m
Open top cans		540
Closures		74
Aerosol cans		81
Collapsible aluminium tubes		21
Metal drums		
– 25 litres and smaller	30	
– Above 25 litres	94	124
Other general line		
– Paint cans	50	
– Automotive product cans	15	
– Powdered food	47	
– Tobacco	21	
– Toiletries	19	
– Household	18	170
Total		1011

APPENDIX 3B
Francis Industries plc

Activities: manufacture of packaging and industrial products for petroleum, food, paint and automotive industries.

Subsidiaries: Clearplas Ltd; Clearplas France SA; Drummond Packaging Ltd; F Francis and Sons Ltd; Lacrinoid Products Ltd; Sagar Richards Ltd; Shemtec Packaging Ltd (acquired in 1984).

Extracts from published accounts:
Year ending 31 December (£m)

Year	Turnover	Net profit before tax
1979	32.8	1.9
1980	29.7	1.8
1981	29.9	1.7
1982	32.7	0.0
1983	35.1	0.7

Geographic analysis of turnover (£m):

	1982	1983
UK	28.6	29.8
Rest of Europe	3.5	4.0
America	0.6	1.2

APPENDIX 3C
Suter plc

Activities: Manufacture and wholesaling of commercial refrigeration, air conditioning and hairdressing salon equipment. As a result of the Francis Industries acquisition, Suter also manufactures round and rectangular tinplate containers, die castings, mechanical components and precision injection moulding.

Composition of turnover by activity (£m):

	1983	1984
Hairdressing equipment	3.8	4.8
Refrigeration and air conditioning	27.6	36.2
Francis Industries		3.3*

*results for six months as a related company and one month as a subsidiary

Extracts from published accounts:
Year ending 31 December (£m)

Year	Turnover	Net profit before tax
1980	4.2	0.5
1981	45.0	0.6
1982	58.2	(1.3)
1983	44.9	2.2
1984	47.3	4.1

Geographic analysis of turnover (£m):

	1983	1984
UK	29.0	37.3
France	3.6	4.7
West Germany	1.8	0.8
North America	3.9	0.1

APPENDIX 3D
Francis Packaging Ltd: Organisation chart (May 1985)

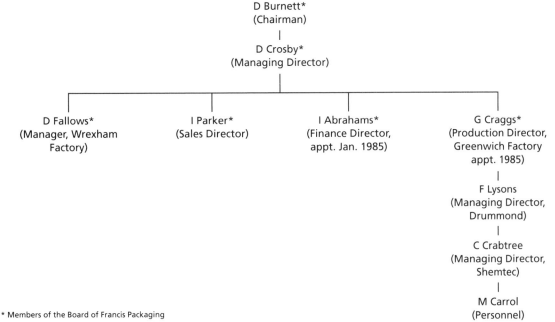

D Burnett*
(Chairman)

D Crosby*
(Managing Director)

D Fallows*
(Manager, Wrexham Factory)

I Parker*
(Sales Director)

I Abrahams*
(Finance Director, appt. Jan. 1985)

G Craggs*
(Production Director, Greenwich Factory appt. 1985)

F Lysons
(Managing Director, Drummond)

C Crabtree
(Managing Director, Shemtec)

M Carrol
(Personnel)

* Members of the Board of Francis Packaging

APPENDIX 3E
Production facilities

Francis Packaging itself operates from two factories, one at Greenwich in London and the other at Wrexham in Wales. The Greenwich and Wrexham factories each have the following production facilities.

- Tinplate printing facility. This is of major importance given the requirement for high print quality for final customer-appeal reasons. The sides of the containers are printed in sheets according to the design specifications of the purchasing company. Stocks of printed tinplate are held for the major customers. The printed sheets are then cut into individual pieces when required and passed onto the production lines.
- Lines producing paint cans (2.5- and 5-litre sizes). The printed container sides are bent into the required round shape by one machine and then automatically passed onto the welder where the ends are welded. The bottoms are next welded to the base and the ring components fixed to the top. Greenwich and Wrexham produce high quality cans to MPMA specifications. Order sizes are generally large (15 000 containers plus) although nowhere near as large as in the case of open top cans, which also differ in another respect – they are not usually printed.
- Lines producing rectangular containers (2.5- and 5-litre sizes). The production process is much the same as that described above and these too are the high volume products of the general line business.
- A line producing 20-litre and 25-litre tinplate drums. These are also standardised relatively high volume products.
- Areas for producing components, e.g. lids, bottoms, handles and rings for container tops.
- Quality control. Samples are regularly checked for strength, leakage and print quality.

Stocks of completed cans are not generally held for any length of time because the space occupied would be considerable. There had been some investment in the previous few years in the facilities at Greenwich, but the drum line at that factory was very old and conditions were very crowded in the factory.

The Shemtec subsidiary has a factory in Leeds which produces paint cans only (0.5, 2.5- and 5-litre sizes). These cans do not conform to MPMA size dimensions and are therefore not usually purchased by the paint company majors. They are not regarded as of the same quality as the Greenwich and Wrexham cans. The Leeds factory has a print facility and a number of paint can production lines. The equipment is considerably older than that at Greenwich and Wrexham. There had been little investment for some years. Components produced here were not compatible with those at the other factories.

The Drummond subsidiary has a factory in Greenock, Scotland. The business of this factory is substantially different from that at the other factories discussed above. The operation here is at the jobbing end of the tinplate business. Order sizes are generally much smaller, less than 10 000 containers. Round cans used to pack powdered food are the only products with order sizes which approach those for rectangular and paint cans. The factory has a good print facility and lines to produce round cans (powdered food), rectangular cans (usually for cooked meats), rectangular tins for shortbread, tins for cigars and small round containers for tobacco. There is also a line for 10-litre paint pails. It should be pointed out that the round and rectangular tins produced at this factory are very different from those produced at the other factories for paint and oil. There had been no investment in this factory for some years; for example, an automatic welder required for top quality cans for the powdered food industry was lacking.

APPENDIX 3F
Summary of the past financial performance of the companies in Suter Packaging Division (£m)

	1980	1981*	1982	1983	1984†	1985‡
Sales						
Francis	14.0	13.4	14.7	16.9	20.8	20.1
Shemtec					4.0	3.4
Francis/Shemtec					24.8	23.5
Drummond		0.8	1.8	1.6	1.8	2.1
Total					26.6	25.6
PBT						
Francis	0.3	0.7	0.9	1.5	0.8	0.6
Shemtec					0.3	0.2
Francis/Shemtec					1.1	0.8
Drummond		0.0	0.1	0.0	(0.1)	0.0
Total					1.0	0.8
Capital employed						
Francis	3.8	3.8	3.8	3.1	6.1	5.8
Shemtec					1.2	1.1
Francis/Shemtec					7.3	6.9
Drummond		0.5	0.3	0.3	0.4	0.5
Total					7.7	7.4
Return on capital employed						
Francis	8	18	24	48	13	10
Shemtec					25	18
Francis/Shemtec					15	12
Drummond		0	33	0	(25)	0
Total					14	11

* Drummond acquired in 1981.
† Shemtec acquired in early 1984.
‡ Companies acquired by Suter in late 1984.

APPENDIX 3G

Market research: composition of Suter Packaging Division's business

At the start of the market research (points from which are summarised in Appendices 3H–M) which Larkfield had undertaken to complete for the Suter Packaging Division, the consultants prepared an analysis of the current composition of the Suter Packaging business. They saw the Suter companies as two distinct businesses.

- Francis Packaging Ltd plus Shemtec Packaging Ltd, whose business is the volume production of standard general-line tinplate containers (round cans, rectangular containers and drums) for the following industries:
  - paint;
  - miscellaneous chemicals (bituminous products, structural and preservative products, paint removers and strippers, putties, fillers, sealers and adhesives, printing inks and insecticides);
  - lubricating oil (largely retail);
  - edible oil for the catering sector.
- Drummond Packaging Ltd, whose business is the short-run production of off-standard, speciality tinplate general-line containers for the cooked meat, powdered food, biscuit and confectionery, and tobacco industries.

The Francis/Shemtec business

The breakdown of Francis/Shemtec business was found to be as follows:

	Sales (£m)		Units (m)		Litres contained (m)	
	1984	1985	1984	1985	1984	1985
Rounds	12.7	11.4			81	83
5 litre			10.5	10.9		
2.5 litre			8.8	8.8		
1 litre			5.1	5.2		
0.5 litre			2.0	2.2		
Rectangulars	6.6	6.5			80	55
5 litre			11.9	8.5		
4 litre			4.2	2.5		
2.5 litre			1.0	1.1		
Drums	5.5	5.6	3.6	3.8	84	88
Total	24.8	23.5			245	226

Francis/Shemtec (FIS) shares of the total tinplate container market (by product) in 1985 were estimated to be as follows:

	Units (m)		Litres (m)		Percentage of
	F/S	Total	F/S	Total	F/S Share
Rounds					
5 litre	10.9	42	55	210	26
2.5 litre	8.8	40	22	100	22
1 litre	5.2	52	5	52	10
0.5 litre	2.2	22	1	11	10
Rectangulars					
5 litre	8.5	30	42	150	29
4 litre	2.5	6	10	24	42
2.5 litre	1.1	2	3	5	55
Drums					
20/25 litre	3.8	13	88	313	28
Total		226		864	26

Using the distribution of deliveries to types of customer for the first nine months of 1985, the consultants made the following analysis (in percentage terms) of the markets into which the products were going:

	Round cans			Rectangular cans			Drums		
	units	litre	value	units	litre	value	units	litre	value
Paint	87	92	89	10	10	10	23	25	24
Chemical	11	6	9	25	25	25	11	11	11
Lubricating oil	–	–	–	54	54	54	25	28	27
Edible oil	–	–	–	7	7	7	39	34	36
Other	2	2	2	4	4	4	2	2	2
Total	100	100	100	100	100	100	100	100	100

The Drummond business

The composition of the Drummond business (percentage of turnover) over the past two years is summarised as follows:

	1984	1985
Tobacco Clipovac tins and cigar ovals	47	28
Oblongs and squares for meat, yeast and Feta cheese	26	56
603 diameter round for powdered food and some chemicals	7	3
Flat rectangular for shortbread	6	5
10-litre pails for paint	4	2
Other	10	6

APPENDIX 3H
Packaging in the paint market

An overview of the paint market in 1985 (millions litres) is given in the following table. The paint market here is defined to exclude paint-related products: structural and preservative products; of bituminous products; putties, fillers and sealers; paint removers and strippers; and printing inks.

Sector	Total	Metal			Plastic				Steel drums bulk containers
		Cans	Rect.	20/25 drum	Tray	Can	Pail	Other	
Decorative									
Trade (water)	92	78				10	4		
Trade (solvent)	70	70							
Retail (water)	82	35			17	30			
Retail (solvent)	46	46							
Total (water)	195	119		6	17	40	5	8	
Total (solvent)	136	125		11					
	331	244		17	17	40	5	8	
Industrial									
Refinishing	24	10	4	10					21
Cars	21								
Commercial vehicles	11								11
Can coatings	18								18
Coil coatings	46								46
Marine	16	7	3	6					
Other/General Industry	129	32	5	12					80
	265	49	12	28					176
Other paint									
Wood finishes	21	5	8				8		
Miscellaneous	8	2	3				1		2
Thinners, etc	7							7	
	36	7	11				9	7	2
Total	632	300	23	45	17	40	14	15	178

The building sectors in which paint is professionally applied (the trade segment) are:

Industro-commercial	17%
New housing – public	7%
New housing – private	25%
Repair and maintenance	51%
	100%

Past trends in the use of paint in the trade segment were:

			Building output			
	Litres	Percentage		New housing		% per annum
Year	(m)	per annum	R&M	Pub.	Priv.	comm.
1980	147	–3	4	–19	–27	2
1981	139	–6	–9	–34	–9	7
1982	146	5	–1	–16	15	14
1983	160	9.5	7	6	20	2
1984	163	2	5	–9	–3	4
1985	162	–1	–4	–23	1	6

The largest manufacturer of paint for the trade sector is ICI. The next three in size are owned by major industrial groupings: Crown owned by Reed International; Berger by Hoecsht; McPhersons by the major Finnish chemical company, Kemira oy. Kalon is an independent company which has been pursuing an aggressive acquisition policy and by this means built up a significant market share. ICI exerts an influence on the market which is far greater than its market share alone would suggest. It is the price leader.

ICI	22%
Crown	16%
Berger	7%
McPherson	9%
Blundell	17%
Kalon	10%
Goodlass Wall	4%
	85%

Over half the paint used by professionals is distributed directly by the paint manufacturers.

	1964	1970	1979	1985
Direct sales	47	49	53	55
Wholesalers/merchants	48	47	43	42
Retail sales	5	4	4	3
	100%	100%	100%	100%

Paint in the trade segment is packaged in round containers up to five litres, with five litres as the predominant size. The decorative quality of the container does have an importance, but not nearly as marked as in the retail market. Concern over corrosion of tinplate containing water-based paint is not marked in this sector, partly because paint stocks move much more quickly. The professional user is generally reported to have a preference for tinplate containers, mainly for strength reasons. The builders merchant consulted in the market research expressed a preference for tinplate, mainly for stacking reasons.

Recent trends in retail paint demand are given below:

Year	Litres (m)	Percentage (pa)	Spending on DIY as percentage (pa)	Home decorating DIY (%)
1980	115	–2.5	–11	45
1981	115	0	–7	44
1982	115	0	–3	43
1983	116	1	–0.5	43
1984	123	6		
1985	128	4		

Market shares in the retail sector are shown below:

	%
ICI	33
Crown	20
Berger	7
McPherson	7
Kalon	10
Goodlass Wall	4
Johnstone	2
	83

Shares of distribution outlets in retail paint (percentage by volume) are shown below:

	1977	1983
Paint and wallpaper specialists	46	35
DIY stores	8	25
Supermarkets	8	15
Woolworths	10	8
Builders merchants	7	5
Other	15	10
	100	100

The market research revealed that paint manufacturers in the decorative sector had the following requirements of packaging.

(a) Service provided by the container manufacturer. This covers reliability in terms of delivery; flexibility in terms of responding at short notice to orders or changes in orders; and communication of any delivery problems which are likely to be encountered. The large paint makers were moving to the 'just-in-time' method of production control.

(b) Responsiveness by the container manufacturer to changes in the requirements of the paint industry in terms of service, quality and marketing.

(c) Package quality: standard dimensions appropriate to filling lines, strength appropriate to warehouse stacking arrangements, a low propensity to leak, dent or corrode.

(d) Appearance and decorative quality so as to enhance the paint product. This is of particular importance in the retail sector.

(e) Container price. The container represents 6 per cent of the final sales price of the paint and it has been increasing much more rapidly than the price of paint.

The requirements of distributors of paint focus primarily on appearance, that is, packaging is very much a marketing factor. As far as they are concerned denting, corrosion and leaking are appearance-related factors, as is the propensity of the package to attract dust.

The requirements of the final user of the package do not seem to attract much attention from either the paint manufacturers or the distributors.

The market research revealed a widespread dissatisfaction with the service provided by the manufacturers of tinplate. The industry was criticised for its lack of flexibility, its poor communication and its old-fashioned attitudes. The lack of response by tinplate manufacturers to the perceived requirements of the paint industry were frequently commented upon. Some of those paint makers currently using plastic regard the service provided by the plastic manufacturers as superior; none thought that it was worse. There was much less of a consensus on the quality of the tinplate product. Some large paint makers did regard leakage as a problem, others thought that the incidence was so low that it was not significant. Denting was also mentioned, but it was not generally seen as a widespread or major problem. There was no unanimity on the view that tinplate is incompatible with water-based materials. Those DIY distributors interviewed did not see corrosion as a problem. There is no readily available information on whether the final user is concerned about corrosion. The price of tinplate containers was not generally regarded as a problem.

ICI had decided to package its emulsion paint in plastic because tinplate corrodes and, despite invitations to address this problem, the tinplate manufacturers had done nothing. ICI introduced the paint tray for solid emulsion and Crown and Berger followed. ICI encouraged Reed Packaging and Mardon Illingworth to develop plastic paint cans with the same dimensions as tinplate cans to avoid investment in filling lines. But some stacking and warehouse rearrangement was still required because of the lower strength characteristics of plastic. These plastic containers are currently sold at the same price as tinplate. The Metal Box, straight-sided plastic can did not meet ICI specifications (overhanging lid). But it is sold at a 10 per cent price discount and is used by some paint manufacturers. The tapered pail had not succeeded in taking market share because of the stacking problems.

Estimates of current plastic can manufacturing capacity are as follows.

	Units 2.5L	5L	End 1985 Litres (m)	End 1986 Litres (m)
Reed Packaging	3	3	22.5	22.5
Mardon Illingworth	3	3	22.5	22.5
Metal Box	2	2	15.0	30.0
Metal Box (new can)	–	–	–	22.5
Total			60.0	97.5

As at November 1985 the market research indicated the following intentions (see table overleaf) by paint makers (millions of litres).

In the longer term there is the strong possibility that solvent-receptive plastic containers will be developed. This might occur through the development of special plastics or, more like, the coating of the interior of plastic containers with a solvent-resistant substance. The overwhelming consensus in the paint industry is that this will occur; developments are already underway. However it is generally regarded as unlikely that this will occur before the 1990s. Another development could be the introduction of

| | 1985 | | | 1986 | | | 1987 | | |
| | Emuls. | Plastic | | Emuls. | Plastic | | Emuls. | Plastic | |
	Total	Tray	Can	Total	Tray	Can	Total	Tray	Can
ICI	54	9	25	55	10	44	57	10	47
Crown	35	5		36	5		37	6	
Berger	14	3		14	3	3	15	3	6
McPherson	16			16			17		
Blundell	16			16			17		
Kalon	19			19			20		
Goodlass	7		5	7		7	7		7
Johnston	4		3	4		4	4		4
Sigma	2		2	2		2	2		2
Others	28		5	30		10	29		15
Total	195	17	40	199	18	70	205	19	81

water-based gloss paints. These already exist and are extensively used in the US. However, they do not display the high gloss characteristics required by the UK market. Further work is proceeding to remedy this and the general consensus is that they will appear on the market in the 1990s.

About two thirds of industrial paint is transported by bulk means. The main categories of industrial paint not transported in this way are:

(a) refinishing paint sold to garages and body shops. The main producers are ICI, followed by Ault and Wiborg. ICI does not exert the dominant role here which it does in the decorative market;
(b) marine paints;
(c) less than 40 per cent of the remaining general industrial paints.

Past trends in some parts of the industrial paint market are summarised below (millions of litres).

Important developments now occurring in the industrial paint segment are the improvement in spraying techniques and the increasing application of

Year	Marine	Other industrial (not bulk transported)
1980	25	65
1981	22	64
1982	22	60
1983	18	68
1984	18	68
1985	16	73

powdered coatings, particularly coil coatings. The increasing import penetration of finished goods also has implications for the industrial paint market. In the longer term there is likely to be a trend towards the gradual reduction of the proportion of aggressive solvents in industrial paints. These paints are also likely to be affected by the development of water-based paints in the 1990s. The appearance of solvent-receptive plastic containers also looks likely.

Current forms of packaging for industrial paint (not bulk transported) are confined to tinplate because of the aggressive solvents used. Packaging is widely spread over the size range with around half in the larger round cans, about one-third in the 20/25-litre drums and the remainder in the larger rectangular containers.

Attitudes to the tinplate are very similar to those held by manufacturers in the decorative paint market.

Customers' opinions of the Suter Packaging companies are varied. None of those interviewed hold the view that either Francis or Shemtec are any worse than the other tinplate manufacturers. A number hold the view that there is nothing to distinguish either Francis or Shemtec from the other tinplate manufacturers. Generally, however, the opinion is that both Francis and Shemtec provide a better service than other tinplate manufacturers in terms of reliability and flexibility. Only a few think that quality is poorer than the competition. But Francis/Shemtec are seen as the number three supplier, mainly on capacity grounds and on the belief that they do not have the resources or the support to function as top suppliers.

APPENDIX 3I
Packaging in the miscellaneous chemicals market

In 1985 some 18 million litres of bituminous product were produced and sold into the DIY and building markets (mainly industrial building) for waterproofing purposes. Both the DIY and building applications have been growing over the past few years. About 300 per cent of these products are water-based. In their packaging, the producers of these products are looking for: reliability; flexibility; modern and appealing design; adequate strength and protection. For the water-based products the manufacturers tend to use plastic because it is cheap (tapered pails), less easily damaged and the decorative qualities are acceptable. For the solvent-based products they use tinplate. The view is that tinplate manufacturers are unreliable and not innovative enough, and in these respects are inferior to the manufacturers of plastic containers. Francis is highly regarded in comparison to other tinplate manufacturers.

An estimated 20 million litres of preservative and structural paint products were produced in 1985. They include wood preservatives and concrete additives. Some of these products (e.g. wood preservatives, are sold into both the DIY and building markets, others (e.g. concrete additives, plasticisers, etc) are sold entirely to building and civil engineering contractors. Some of the products (e.g. wood preservatives) are solvent-based while others (e.g. agents for concrete) have a high proportion of water-based products. A wide range of container sizes is used and the penetration of plastic into the water-based products is heavy because the cheaper, tapered plastic pails are used. Packaging priorities are price and compatibility with the material. The same views as those described above were expressed on tinplate manufacturers.

Paint strippers, fillers, sealers and adhesives are in highly fragmented industries selling mainly into the DIY market, but with an industrial market for adhesives. The DIY products are now almost entirely packaged in plastic and, to a lesser extent, in collapsible aluminium tubes. The main use of tinplate seems to be in 25-litre drums for export.

Demand for printing inks has been growing rapidly over the past few years. Water-based products account for about 30 per cent and plastic-tapered pails are used for packaging because they are cheaper. Requirements of packaging are: strength and compatibility; sales appeal; and price. In future, containers will have to meet United Nations regulations on the carriage of dangerous materials. Sericol import 5-litre tapered tin pails from Holland because they cannot obtain a container of the required quality from UK producers. The views on tinplate versus plastic manufacturers are the familiar ones, as described above.

Insecticides represent a rapidly growing market.

APPENDIX 3J
Packaging in the lubricating oil market

The volume (millions of litres) of lubricating oil supplied to the UK market in 1985 were as follows (see over).

The commercial sector covers all deliveries to vehicle manufacturers, transport authorities, bus companies, nationalised industries and transport companies. While some of the oil is for new cars, the bulk of it is supplied to the operators of commercial transport fleets. The remainder of the transport sector consists of supplies to agricultural machinery, ships and aircraft. The industrial sector includes metal working oils, process oils, greases, fuel oil sold as lubricant and all other oils used in industrial processes.

The demand for lubricating oil for both retail and vehicle servicing is shown below (there are no statistics on the split between them). However, retail demand is probably about 65 per cent of the total and has probably remained a constant proportion of the total over the 1980s.

The decline in lubricating oil demand (despite the slow growth in the vehicle population) in the retail segment has been caused by two factors.

| | | Form of packaging | | |
| | | | | 25L‡ + 205L + |
	Volume	<5L*	5L†	bulk
Transport				
Retail	105	15	90	
Vehicle servicing	65			65
Commercial	170		10	160
Marine/aircraft	70			70
Agriculture	40			40
Industrial	475			475
Total	925	15	100	810

* Predominantly plastic
† Approximately 70 per cent tinplate and 30 per cent plastic
‡ Predominantly tinplate

Year	Total sales litres (m)	Percentage (pa)
1980	195	
1981	182	–7
1982	178	–3
1983	172	–3
1984	170	–1
1985	170	0

(a) Vehicle engines have been improved leading to longer maintenance intervals and thus fewer oil changes. Sumps are also now significantly smaller.
(b) Lubricants themselves have been improved by the addition of additives, also leading to less frequent oil changes.

The retail market can be segmented both by purchasing motivation and by the type of product. By purchasing motivation the market can be divided into:

(a) emergency top up consumers – purchases tend to be in 0.5- and 1-litre packs;
(b) take away consumers, e.g. DIY car servicing – purchases are usually in 5-litre packs.

During the 1970s there was a large shift to DIY car servicing. The proportion of people both topping up and changing their own oil increased from 42 per cent to 60 per cent. During that period the fall in lubricating oil usage in the retail plus vehicle servicing sectors was therefore not reflected in the retail sector – it fell largely on the vehicle servicing sector. It appears that the trend to DIY ceased in about 1980 due to the large proportion of company cars in the UK. The continuing

fall in lubricating oil demand in the 1980s has therefore come to be reflected in retail sales.

By product-type, the market can be segmented into the following.

(a) Multi-grade oils (about 85 per cent of the retail market). The multi-grades subdivide into premium multi-grades and the cheaper multi-grades. The former are the brand leaders and are, technically, superior blends of the latter. The latter tend to be own-brand products and are aimed at the economising motorist. The premium multi-grades tend to be in tinplate at the 5-litre size, while the cheaper multi-grades are in plastic. For both premium and other multi-grades, the smaller packs are almost all now in plastic.
(b) Single-grade oils. These are the old-fashioned oils specific to particular vehicles and seasons. The usage of these oils in the car market is dying out, but they are still important in the high-mileage commercial vehicle sector where oil changes are more frequent. The share of single-grade oils in the retail sector has fallen from 30 per cent in 1970 to around 15 per cent at the present time.
(c) Speciality oils. These are a new generation of high-tech, hyper-grade oils, many of which are synthetic. They can be used in all types of vehicle and in all conditions, although currently they tend to be used only in expensive cars. Speciality oils are available in all retail sizes and are packed in plastic.

Over 70 per cent of retail oil falls into the 5-litre takeaway multi-grade segment.

Castrol and Duckhams have maintained brand leadership in the retail lubricating oil market for many years. The other companies with significant market shares are the major oil companies: Shell, Esso and BP.

	1981 (%)	1983 (%)
Castrol (Burmah)	30	30
Duckhams (BP)	16	15
Shell	10	11
BP	8	7
Esso	8	7
Mobil	4	3
Own label	14	16
Others	10	11

The market has become increasingly competitive with large short-term swings in market shares. Own brands have used price to gain share at the bottom end of the market. The big companies have tended to compete increasingly on promotions, involving free gifts or possible prizes. A major promotion this year, which is viewed as being very successful, was Castrol's offering of 10 per cent extra oil free.

The split between oil distributed by garages and retail outlets is shown below (percentage by volume).

	1971	1979	1981	1985
Garage forecourts	75	50	54	60
Retail shops	25	50	46	40

Within the garage forecourt sector, the relative importance of the major oil companies is shown (percentage shares in the number of garage outlets).

	%
Shell	15
Esso	14
BP/National	12
Texaco	7
Jet/Globe	5
Burmah	4
Mobil	4
Other (50)	39

The major oil companies largely restrict the sale of motor oil on their own forecourt to their own brands. The major brands are also generally not stocked in retail outlets. The exceptions are Castrol and Duckhams, both of which are available over a wide range of garage outlets and retail shops. In the 1970s there was a switch to purchasing oil from retail outlets. This switch has now to some extent been reversed.

The oil companies have all introduced tendering procedures for their supplies from packaging companies.

At present, the oil industry has expressed a preference for 5-litre tinplate rectangles, while at the same time expressing a belief that plastic will take over in the long term. At present, tinplate is seen as having the following advantages:

(a) an up-market connotation;
(b) superior printing qualities;
(c) easier handling and quicker filling times;
(d) greater strength and therefore higher stacking as well as simpler palletisation.

However the oil companies did point to:

(a) the rapid advances in plastic printing technology;
(b) methods of designing production and storage to reduce the costs of using plastic containers without substantial investment.

The oil companies do not have a high opinion of the tinplate manufacturers. They are seen as performing the commercial aspects adequately but they are regarded as highly complacent. There are variations in product quality, reliability and speed of delivery, flexibility and general service. But none of these aspects is considered critical, nor are there differences between suppliers such as to give any of them a major advantage. The oil companies see the tinplate manufacturers as lacking in innovation, product promotion, product differentiation and imagination. While they would like to keep stocks to a minimum, there is not sufficient trust in the suppliers to move to 'just-in-time' production scheduling.

The major distinguishing criterion in placing orders between the four major suppliers (Metal Box, Nacanco, Reads and Francis) is price. Except over very small price variations, differences between the four suppliers on other product/service parameters would need to be much greater if they were to form the basis of contract-placing decisions.

The plastics companies have a much higher reputation in a market which now places so much emphasis on promotions with the consequent requirement for off-standard sizes. Plastic has therefore been making in-roads despite the fact that its products are non-standard and therefore difficult to multi-source. By contrast, both Burmah and BP have been experiencing difficulty in securing the containers they need for their promotions from their tinplate suppliers.

The oil companies regard Francis as the 'best of a bad bunch'. Quality is considered to be about the same as Metal Box. On delivery and flexibility, Francis are considered to be the best in the industry. There is a considerable amount of goodwill towards Francis and they are considered to be the nicest company to deal with. But Francis does not escape the general criticisms of the tinplate industry.

Market shares (as a percentage of litres produced) for competitors in the retail lubricating oil market can be measured in two ways (see table below). The first column shows the share estimates for 1985 as a whole. The second looks at current contracts alone. The share which Francis had of the total retail market over 1985 as a whole is likely to be of the order of 30 per cent. However, if only current contracts are taken into account, then the Francis share of the rectangular 5-litre market falls to 10 per cent. This dramatic fall in share is the consequence of losing the contracts with Castrol, Shell and Esso in the price war instigated by Nacanco. Reads, and to a lesser extent Metal Box, have followed Nacanco in its price cutting.

	1985 (%)	Current contracts (%)
Nacanco	22	35
Metal Box	13	15
Reads	5	10
Francis	30	10
Plastic	30	30

In the garage servicing, commercial transport, agricultural, marine and aviation sectors the increasing efficiency of oils and engines has led to the demand for oil declining at a rate of 1.5 per cent a year. The decline in heavy manufacturing in the UK has resulted in lubricating-oil use in industry falling at a rate of around 2 per cent a year.

The major requirements (for 25-litre drums, used to a considerable extent in the segments given in the above paragraph) are utility and cost. Specification is made according to usage and, within the specification, price is the determinant. Plastic is considered inferior to tinplate because it is not strong enough for required stacking and is unstable for filling and handling. It cannot be multi-sourced because each company's product is different. Plastic has failed to establish a price advantage.

The customers in the other sectors of the lubricating oil market are the same as in the retail market. In these sectors, Nacanco is not a competitor but Van Leer and Tanks and Drums are. With the same customers and mostly the same competitors it is not surprising that customer perceptions of both the tinplate industry and of Francis are the same as they are in the retail sector. Generally, product reliability and flexibility are more important here, while image and other marketing factors are less so.

APPENDIX 3K
Packaging in the edible oil market

The volumes of refined edible oils consumed (000 tonnes) in the UK in 1983, and how they were contained, was as follows.

Manufacture of fats, margarine, etc.	988 Bulk tanker
Bottled oils	70 Glass/plastic
Canned oils	80 Tin/plastic

The product transported by bulk tanker is either transformed into margarine and solid fats or is used by food manufacturers. While imports of edible oils are about 15 per cent of consumption and exports only 3 per cent, in the UK most of the imports are in bulk form and are then packaged for consumption. The recent UK expansion of rape seed production is likely to reverse the adverse import/export balance and, to the small extent that packaged cooking oil is currently imported, growth in production is likely to exceed growth in demand.

The remaining raw edible oil is sold into the domestic and catering markets. Bottled oil roughly equates with the domestic or retail market. Oil here is packaged largely in pack sizes up to three litres and is

mainly in plastic. Canned oils are used mainly in the catering sector and are packaged in tinplate in 5-litre and 20-litre sizes.

Retail demand for edible oil in recent years was as follows.

Year	Tonnes (000)	Litres (m)	Percentage (pa)
1981	52	60	3
1982	55	63	5
1983	59	68	8
1984	64	74	9
1985	70	81	9

The food market is a mature one and growth in most sectors tends to be minimal. But in the case of edible oil the marked shift away from high-cholesterol fats for health reasons has led to the growth trend evident in the statistics shown in the table above.

In the retail sector very little is sold in container sizes above three litres. Only a small proportion of the oil sold in 5-litre sizes in this sector is in tinplate. Plastic is much cheaper than tinplate. Tinplate has an unacceptable image in the retail market because it is not transparent and clean looking.

Recent growth trends in the demand for edible oil in the catering sector were as follows.

Year	Tonnes (000)	Litres (m)	Percentage (pa)
1981	66	76	3
1982	68	78	3
1983	71	82	5
1984	77	89	9
1985	85	95	7

There is no clear distinction between the packers and distributors of edible oil. The packing/distribution structure consists of:

(a) refiners who distribute in bulk to packers, but who also pack for final distribution to caterers, either direct or through wholesalers and specialist catering distributors;

(b) packers who purchase bulk supplies from the refiners and then pack for distribution to caterers either direct or through the wholesalers/distributors;

(c) wholesalers and specialist catering distributors who provide a cash-and-carry service.

Shares of the top refiners in 1985 were:

	%
Acatos and Hutchinson (Pura)	35
Van Den Burgh/Bibby	10
Top Three	50

The top three refiners account for a significantly smaller share of distribution. However Acatos and Hutchinson are aggressively trying to increase their share of both production and distribution. They are pursuing a modernisation and cost-cutting strategy in order to meet foreign competition in a highly price-conscious market. They have taken over a number of other companies recently (e.g. Pura and Britannia) and are engaged in a rationalisation programme. They are talking about the introduction of a just-in-time system to reduce stock holding. They are exploring the possibility of producing their own 20-litre drums, both to cut costs and discourage the specialist packers, and so gain a higher share of distribution. Van Den Burgh regard the edible oil market as a commodity market with margins which are too low to justify an aggressive expansion strategy.

Packing and distribution are fragmented, with the refiners themselves having only a small share. The remainder of packing and distribution includes a large number of ethnic packers who fill by hand.

The largest distributor accounts for about 20 per cent of sales and the next largest for less than 10 per cent. The rest of the distribution network is highly fragmented.

Forms of packaging currently in use in the catering segment of the edible oil market are:

Size	Litre (m)	Material
5-litre	10	Tinplate/plastic
10-litre	–	Tinplate
20-litre	85	Tinplate

Packaging requirements vary to some extent in different parts of the catering market:

(a) at the bottom fragmented end, packers are looking for the cheapest form of packaging;

(b) the larger refiner/packers aim at minimising production and distribution costs. Their emphasis is on a standardised container for automatic filling with good strength characteristics for stacking, handling and transport. Minimising stock holding is of major importance.

Where price is the major factor, plastic has made in-roads and this applies particularly to the 5-litre size. At the 20-litre size the plastic product is not sufficiently technically developed, and is no cheaper than tinplate. At this size plastic is not rigid enough and there are leakage problems.

At the mass production end of the market the tinplate manufacturers are regarded as complacent, spending insufficient time identifying their customers' needs or trying to satisfy them. It is felt that communication is poor.

In terms of quality, reliability and flexibility, Francis are regarded as the best of a bad bunch. But Francis were criticised for poor communication, lack of sales literature and lack of warning on price increases.

Francis has a competitive advantage in terms of location – most of the mass fillers are located in the South East. Francis has a market share of about 30 per cent of the more than four million 2 litre drums used in this market. The competitors are the same as those for 25-litre drums. Francis are in a similar position in the much smaller, 5-litre segment.

APPENDIX 3L
Packaging in the markets for Drummond's products

Drummond sells its products to the fillers of cooked meats requiring non-standard containers, to segments of the powdered beverages markets, confectionery, biscuits, and tobacco.

The 1982 breakdown (£m) of canned meat consumption in the UK is given below. Imports probably account for a small proportion of the 'hot' sector, most of the imports being of 'cold' meats.

Bacon and ham	50
Corned beef	155
Sausages	10
Chopped ham and pork	25
Tongue	10
Poultry	8
Luncheon Meat, other	12
Total cold	**270**
Pies and puddings	20
Mince, stewed steak	25
Pie fillings	15
Casseroles	5
Others	25
Total hot	**90**
Total	**360**

Most of these meat products are contained in open top cans. The sectors of most relevance to Drummond's products are bacon and ham (mostly filled abroad); and pies, puddings, pie fillings and casseroles (mostly filled in the UK).

The UK canned fish market is worth around £130m, but the bulk is of imported filled cans.

Feta cheese is packaged in tinplate since no rectangular plastic cans exist at this time. In the export market the tinplate can be used as a cooking utensil in less developed countries.

Infant milk and instant milk powders constitute an important user of general line containers, but some 25 per cent of their requirement for such containers is manufactured by the users. The UK instant milk market has declined in line with birth rates, but the export market continues to play an important part with a substantial proportion of filled containers going abroad, mainly to third-world countries. In export markets the tinplate container has considerable advantages over its principal domestic competitors – the pouch and lined carton – because of its protective qualities against both climate and impact damage.

The gourmet tea market, characteristically packed in distinct, square, tinplate lever-lid containers and fancy boxes was formerly an important market for the tinplate container. However, rapidly rising tea prices have caused a marked decline. High quality teas are packaged mainly for the export market.

Ground coffee has now followed instant coffee in switching from metal to other forms of packaging – in this case, flexible bags – although an important (but declining) metal container market remains for exports.

For confectionery, the tinplate container is used mainly for exports, specialities and promotions.

The large unit, decorated tinplate biscuit tin market has always been dependent on a few major customers with a quarter of total usage made in-plant. While there is an export element, the substantial seasonal home market is the dominating factor. The biscuit producers seek three suppliers of tins. A few years ago these were Wilkie Paul, Huntley Bourne & Stevens, and Metal Box. Wilkie Paul went bankrupt and Metal Box bought their machinery. Linpac then invested in the necessary machinery. It subsequently bought Huntley Bourne & Stevens. Drummond has just ordered the necessary machinery to become the third biscuit-tin supplier.

For a long time tinplate containers have taken only a small proportion of tobacco packaging and their share has been further eroded by both the decline in smoking and the switch to new packaging materials. The resurgence in demand caused by the cigar, pipe and cigarette hand-rolling markets have now been reversed by the use of polythene pouches and the general fall in demand for all tobacco products. Again, it is the gift and export markets for the premium products (cigars) that offer the most lasting prospect for tinplate sales. Drummond supplies oval cigar tins and Clipovac tins for tobacco. The main tobacco tin alternative is the screw-top tin produced by Metal Box. Gallaher has recently decided to purchase all Clipovac tins from Barnsley Canister, all its oval cigar-tin requirements from Drummond, and all screw-top tins from Metal Box.

Several attributes are important when assessing potential suppliers, varying according to the product being packed:

(a) quality – sizes outside tolerance ranges stop production lines; badly welded cans do not protect the product; the container has to ensure a long shelf-life for products;
(b) consistency of quality in seaming, internal lacquers, size and printing;
(c) sales appeal – the quality of printing is important;
(d) reliable delivery and flexibility – in some markets, producers have to respond rapidly to the demands of retailers or wholesalers for large quantities over short periods of time;
(e) price;
(f) commitment to the user's business;
(g) technical support;
(h) sales contact – regular communication from can makers on availability, problems on the horizon, pricing issues, quality control developments and new ideas.

Drummond's main tinplate competitors are as follows.

● Meat products: Metal Box; American Can; Carnaud; Haustrup; Thomasen & Drijver.
● Biscuits/shortbread: Metal Box; Huntley Bourne & Stevens; Robertson Canisters.
● Tobacco: Metal Box; Huntley Bourne & Stevens.
● Yeast: Cebal.

Customers dual source to give security of supply, ensure a competitive situation (on price, quality and delivery); and encourage more ideas on new developments in packaging. There is no single supplier who meets all of the evaluative assessment criteria discussed earlier, and who produces the full product range required.

Virtually all of Drummond's customers felt that it was falling short of the standards they expect. But customers recognised the efforts which Drummond staff made under difficult circumstances. Although some customers had taken business away from Drummond on quality grounds (seaming was quoted frequently), changing suppliers creates uncertainty and companies do not therefore switch suppliers often. Customers felt that Drummond showed flexibility and willingness to supply smaller volumes, and small company characteristics which enabled the buyer to talk directly to the appropriate person. A notable degree of goodwill was felt towards Drummond. Several customers felt that Drummond took an active interest in how their business is going.

Drummond was criticised in the following respects: quality (cans shorter than specification, wrong tinplate used, seam problems, panels concaving, contents leaking, top and bottom of can printed in different shades); poor quality control; old technology and machinery; little investment, perhaps due to changes in ownership; poor delivery times; few technical support facilities; slow to respond to customer's needs; and a poor response to new business enquiries.

APPENDIX 3M
The views of packaging designers

1 A number of packaging designers were consulted to obtain their views on tinplate as a packaging material, both from the functional and decorative points of view. Their views are set out below.
2 Tinplate is inherently compatible with solvent-based liquids and with foodstuffs where a high oxygen barrier is required or where the container is filled with hot substances. It is not inherently compatible with water-based liquids. Tinplate possesses inherent strength advantages which lead on to lower storage and transport costs. The decorative qualities of tinplate and the high quality of print which it achieves are a major strength which the manufacturers of tinplate have grossly undersold. Tinplate has a quality image and a retention value for uses other than containing the material sold in it. This advantage is not aggressively exploited.
3 The designers suggested going back to how the final user of the container actually uses the container. For example, the lid arrangement of the paint container could be re-designed so that lac-

quer protection is not damaged on opening. The designers who were consulted felt that plastic would ultimately displace tinplate in many uses, leaving a role for tinplate as a specialist, low-volume material in applications where decoration and re-use are important. This view is based on the contention that the cost advantage ultimately lies with plastic. But the time period before the ultimate penetration of plastic is achieved can be greatly extended by the imaginative design of tinplate.

CASE STUDY 4

The Coloroll Group plc*

The Coloroll Group is a good example of those many companies that achieved dramatic growth during the 1980s, and suffered an equally dramatic collapse and break-up at the start of the 1990s.

The company began in London in 1923 as a paper merchant importing rolls of coloured wrapping paper. By the late 1960s, when it moved to Lancashire, the company was also involved in paper bag manufacture. In the 1970s the company was revitalised by Managing Director John Bray who saw an opportunity in the wallpaper market. By 1978, Coloroll was producing 3 million rolls of wallpaper a year and had a turnover of £6m; its UK market share was about 3 per cent. Bray achieved this growth by building up a strong design and management team, including John Ashcroft, recruited from Crown, who succeeded Bray as Managing Director in 1982. That same year the company moved out of family ownership, when it was sold to a group of institutions, including Finance for Industry, Citicorp, and British Rail and National Coal Board pension funds.

Company growth

As soon as Ashcroft arrived in 1978 he began to build a more youthful management team and formulated a business plan which was to be the basis of the company's future development. He identified three critical environmental changes: technological advances in manufacturing, the emergence of out-of-town DIY giants in retailing and the fashion for 'small cottage prints'. Ashcroft mapped out his conclusions in a report, *The White Book*, a corporate plan for Coloroll's development over the next five years. It was accompanied by *The Yellow Book*, a detailed analysis of the marketplace. The company's knowledge of its rivals was helped by the recruitment of managers from major competitors.

One of the objectives stated in the plan was to dominate the wallcoverings market. This was to be achieved by creativity in design and marketing, support for the retailer, and tight financial control. Large retailers were targeted and there was an increased emphasis on quality and product design. Specialist home fashion designers were recruited and ranges of coordinated wallcoverings and fabrics introduced and promoted under the Coloroll brand. The distribution system was reorganised to reduce delivery lead times from one month to two days. On the manufacturing side, computerised production and financial control systems were installed to improve efficiency. The wallpaper plant at Nelson was updated at a cost of £6m, to become the largest and most modern in Europe. The cumulative effect of these changes was that within three years Coloroll had ousted Crown as the market leader in wallcoverings.

This also paved the way for similar service standards following later acquisitions: a seven-day turnaround of orders became the goal for all products absorbed into the home furnishings division, where norms ranged from 21 to 28 days. In ceramics lead times were reduced from 3–4 months to 48 hours !

A second aim was to diversify into other markets to counter dependence on wallpaper sales. In 1980, the home furnishings division was created as the beginning of this diversification programme. Ashcroft's idea was to expand the product range around the unifying concept of 'home fashion', which would enable customers to coordinate their wallpaper, curtains, bed linen, tableware, and eventually furniture and carpets. Fabric design was carried out in-house but most manufacturing was subcontracted. The new range of curtains and bed linen was distributed through department stores as opposed to the traditional DIY outlets used for wallcoverings. In response to the success of 'lifestyle' retailers (Next, Laura Ashley), by 1985 Coloroll was providing retailers with designs for coordinated room settings. During the 1980s the company embarked on an ambitious acquisition programme (see Appendix 4A),

* Copyright © Dorothea Noble (University of Hertfordshire Business School) and Mary Klemm (University of Bradford Management Centre)

culminating in the purchase of the Crowther carpet group in 1989 for £215 million.

In the interests of reducing dependence on the UK market the company began to expand overseas in 1982 by establishing a small distribution outlet in Australia. A more ambitious step was the gradual acquisition of US wallcoverings manufacturer Wall-mates which, when completed in 1985, gave Coloroll an excellent strategic foothold in the huge $500m US wallcoverings market. The Australian operation was not profitable and Ashcroft sent out UK staff in 1987 to effect an expansion and turnaround.

Although the initial expansion had been financed out of profit, one of Ashcroft's long-term aims was to extend the financial base of the company by a stock market flotation. This took place in April 1985, when funds of £8.7m were raised by a share issue. The additional finance enabled the company to continue its expansion by acquiring companies which could be made to fit into the 'home fashion' portfolio. By 1989, these acquisitions represented a dramatic growth, resulting in very high gearing, and concern about the company's indebtedness. In the 1989 annual report, Ashcroft announced his intention to sell off the two Crowther distribution businesses, claiming these disposals would recover more than the purchase price of the whole group.

The retailing experiment

Further expansion of the home fashion theme was envisaged through the development of a series of retail outlets, a so-called 'chintz belt' chain across the country. In 1986, a flagship store was opened in Regent Street and a site purchased in Manchester. The retailers supplied by Coloroll were aghast at the company itself becoming a retailer. Marks and Spencer withdrew £12m worth of orders. Coloroll had no option but to withdraw; the Manchester site was sold, the London store closed and the idea abandoned. Future strategy would have to take account of retailer power, at least in the UK.

Management style

Before Bray and Ashcroft Coloroll had a rigid traditional management style. A former production director said:

> When I first joined the company the management hierarchy ruled with an iron fist but now the atmosphere has entirely changed. (*Management Today*, March 1980)

After Bray, the style and corporate culture developed under the strong leadership of John Ashcroft, a model of the young entrepreneur of the 1980s, and once described by Margaret Thatcher as a shining example of British entrepreneurship. Lancashire born and bred, Ashcroft was educated at the London School of Economics and joined Coloroll at the age of 28. A forceful and flamboyant character, he was often photographed, quoted and featured in the financial media, as well as featuring in the design of company coffee mugs. His management style has been described as ruthless, radical and charismatic. He himself said:

> My style of management provides a clear marketing direction. Mine is a paternalistic, family style of management. (*Superstore Management*, December 1988)

The management team comprised youthful business school types, Ashcroft's ideal executive being 'young, sharp-suited and able to hurl himself over an army assault course at weekends' – the so-called 'MBA barrow boy'. The spirit was jokey but competitive, with skull and crossbones flags marking opportunistic sales zones on the world map, and talk of companies on 'seek and destroy missions' (*Marketing Week*, May 1988).

Under Ashcroft, the company lost traditional status symbols, such as executive dining rooms, and money was spent on facilities for all staff. Various employee-support schemes, such as the Children's Trust, were established to help gifted and handicapped children of Coloroll employees; the 'virtuous circle' was introduced to develop pride and common purpose amongst Coloroll people. Financial incentives operated for all staff via performance bonus, share option and pension schemes. Performance expectations were correspondingly high.

Ashcroft's management philosophy was brought together in 1988 in *The Blue Book*, which supplemented the earlier books of company plans and market analyses. Significant aspects of this philosophy were the interchange of ideas and information at regular Monday morning meetings, where objectives, progress and problems were discussed, and the placement of 'How are we doing?' boards at all Coloroll plants where achievements and shortfalls of performance were reported. The ideas of individuals, both managerial and technical, were tapped through the Coloroll Quality Improvement Scheme (QUIPS).

Structure and control

Divisions were formed and reformed in accordance with acquisitions made. The two UK divisions existing in 1985, Wallcoverings UK and Home Furnishings, had become five autonomous divisions by 1988, including Carpets, Glassware and Ceramics. These were realigned into six divisions in 1989, to absorb the Crowther interests; Glassware and Ceramics combined into a Tableware Division, and Contract Interiors and Furniture made up two new divisions. (Overseas divisions comprised Wallcoverings (USA), and the Australian marketing and distribution business.) Each had a separate management with clear targets and responsibilities; every year divisional heads had to present their own business plans, together with an updated version of *The Yellow Book*. All managers were directly accountable for their own decisions and actions. For senior management as much as 50 per cent of their annual income was bonus-related. In November 1989 Ashcroft, whose salary had trebled in 1988, announced that 'because his pay and that of other directors was "heavily related to profit performance", they would see a significant reduction in remuneration' (*Financial Times*, November 1989).

His concern (some say obsession) with financial control led him, in late 1985, to establish a small central management team, with himself as Managing Director and Chief Executive. This was separate from management of the divisions, which were encouraged to operate autonomously. The divisions were not necessarily represented on the central management team or on the Coloroll Board of Directors. This division of authority within the company left much of the power with Ashcroft himself. On the Crowther acquisition he ignored advice, both from within the company and from city analysts, that this major purchase was too risky at that time.

The company first published annual financial objectives in 1988: 10 per cent return on sales; 25 per cent return on capital; 10–20 per cent growth in earnings per share; 10 per cent dividend growth; and 30–40 per cent gearing. In 1989, the following results were published:

	Target	Actual 1989	1988	1987
EPS Growth	10–20%	11%	26%	23%
Return on Sales	10%	10%	10%	9%
Return on Capital	25%	62%	35%	32%
Dividend Growth	10%	15%	15%	15%
Gearing	30–40%	66%	20%	30%

Marketing strategy

Ashcroft credited Coloroll with the invention of the 'home fashion' concept, a claim backed up by market analysts:

> When Coloroll first started making acquisitions, it came up with the phrase 'home fashion market'. The sector used to be very fragmented, but it created a market for its own purposes, buying up businesses that would fit the mould. (*Marketing Week*, 13 May, 1988)

Coloroll took up the niche 'life style' themes represented by such firms as Next and Laura Ashley and sought to make the idea available to the mass market. Up to the 1980s, the UK home furnishing sector was highly fragmented, tending to be brought together by retailers. Coloroll identified a group of disparate companies and produced a coordinated range of products for distribution through established outlets – 'Now Coloroll is offering one-stop shopping for the retailers' (*Marketing Week*, 13 May 1988). Ashcroft saw home fashion as developing naturally from DIY – once people had fixed the roof and installed central heating, they would move to home enhancement. In his own words:

> Take the trend to home ownership – moving towards 70% – and take the greater emphasis on colour and style and co-ordination for every consumer. Put the two together and you've got a big investment in the home. Even at the most conservative estimate, it's a market that we reckon is going to be worth £5bn by 1990. (*Marketing Week*, 13 May 1988)

The company was very brand conscious. Growth of the wallpaper and soft furnishing business established the Coloroll name with retailers during the early 1980s. Subsequent acquisitions focused on strong brands in various home-related sectors – Denby, Kilncraft, Fogarty, Kossett, etc. A 1986 exhibition was aimed at raising the profile of Coloroll's current brands. A £6m campaign in 1987 sought to increase awareness of the Coloroll brand itself with a wider public, promoting the concept of 'home fashion'. By the late 1980s, full-colour spreads in magazines and colour supplements promoted the individual branded products, linking them to a central home fashion theme under the unifying Coloroll brand. This advertising supported coordinated room-setting displays at retail outlets.

The advertising message was a subtle one. It attempted to appeal to a broad range of taste and income by offering fashionable styles, and what the

marketing press called 'reassurance with slight aspi-
rational value'. It shadowed the offerings of
competitors like Laura Ashley and Next by presenting
similar products and aspirations, but, by linking these
to the improvement of ordinary homes, the target
market was wider, not a specialist niche; the dream
home was made accessible to all. This concept was
embodied in catalogues issued for the Ideal Home
Exhibition, in which room settings were designed for
and photographed in small modern homes – classic
first or second family home – rather than the large
town houses and country settings of their rivals.

The uncertainty and lack of marketing focus evident from this switching between branded product
and corporate advertising perhaps had its roots in
two factors; the closure of access to their own retail
outlets, an obvious means of establishing Coloroll
brand identity; and the autonomy/control dilemma.
Following the retail reversal, advertising concentrated on individual brands. By the late 1980s,
Ashcroft revealed a 60–70 per cent weighting towards
strategic advertising and a 30 per cent allocation for
divisional tactical advertising; 'Obviously, there's a
debate, because the feudal barons in the divisions and
the local marketing directors want to control their
own advertising budget'. It was the residual strength
of individual brands that meant the company
retained some value on break-up in the 1990s.

Acquisitions in the furniture and home furnishings
industries in the late 1980s allowed them to develop
their concept fully over the whole range of household
products. The 1989 Chairman's statement reported
the firm's retention of brand consultants, Interbrand,
'to advise on the value of our principal brands'. Individual brands clearly still held an important place in
their marketing strategy, alongside the 'umbrella'
brand of Coloroll itself.

Performance of the divisions to March 1989

Coloroll had a 40 per cent share of the wallcoverings
market. Although demand increased in the 1980s, the
long-term prospects were not so optimistic. In the
1990s, superstore saturation was expected to lead to a
squeeze on manufacturers' margins.

The UK home furnishings market was worth more
than £1bn at 1988 retail levels. It was no longer a commodity market based on fibre and cloth prices, but
had been transformed into a market where product
differentiation through the home fashion concept was
all important. Even beds responded to the Coloroll

coordinated treatment, allowing the company to
achieve increased margins and nearly 2 per cent
market share; presence in the beds market was short-
lived, however. Production was turned over to
upholstery in a bid to reduce overheads in 1989.

Coloroll was market leader in filled products with
Fogarty's 69 per cent market share. In bed linen and
towels, it was second to Coats Viyella's 25 per cent.
These were mature markets, although vulnerable to
recession, and margins remained good.

With the acquisition of Crowther, Coloroll had
become the main UK carpet manufacturer with a
16 per cent share. The market was growing but a
major feature was increasing import penetration (26
per cent in 1987), resulting in lower margins and
increasing concentration in manufacturing.

In both glassware and ceramics Coloroll had
bought a substantial market share. The product portfolio extended from exclusive lead crystal to basic
pottery mugs. Style and design were increasingly
important and the top end of the market was influenced by the level of inward tourism.

Of the new divisions, Contract Interiors in its first
year of operation took '11 per cent of the public sector
market, 10 per cent of the High Street, and 7.5 per
cent of the hospitality markets'; these last two were
helped by the trend towards shorter renewal cycles.
Furniture Division sales 'were 36 per cent ahead of
prior year' after only 7 months' operation, and substantial growth was expected (*annual report* 1989).
Some of the company's first factory closures started
in this division during 1989.

Overseas activity was restricted to businesses in
Australia and the USA, with limited export sales
within the EC. Turnover and profits in all areas
increased during 1988–9. Coloroll's overseas strategy
had not followed the pattern of its UK expansion, a
policy choice which may be explained by an experience of patchy profitability, and a desire to avoid
currency exposure. As with many UK companies in
the early to mid-1980s, the apparent lack of interest in
the wider European market is very puzzling. Compared with Laura Ashley, Coloroll did not build up a
coherent international business, and in 1989 it still
remained dependent on the UK market for 68 per
cent of its profit and 78 per cent of turnover.

Company crisis

Coloroll's plans were based on a predicted interest
rate peak of 13 per cent in the summer of 1989, followed by an autumn decline.

When they went to 14%, we implemented *condition red*, including a ban on recruitment and tight control of stock.' The response to the 15% rate was an action plan which included factory closures, the possible sale of peripheral businesses, cutting capital spending from £20m this year to less than £10m next and reducing working capital. (*Financial Times*, 17 November 1989)

These increases undermined other predictions: continued market growth and the immediate disposal of unwanted subsidiaries acquired in the Crowther takeover. In May 1989, potential buyers had been found, offering the prospect of a surplus on the total acquisition, and the reduction of gearing to its desired maximum of 40 per cent. By November 1989, these sales had not been realised and buyers for more valued subsidiaries were being sought, as interest payments ate into profits. The deteriorating business climate and the declining value of Coloroll shares (earnings per share) had fallen from 23p in March to 3.2p in September 1989) served to reduce buyer interest in the businesses for sale and to undermine their value.

In addition, interest rates, by causing the collapse of the housing market, destroyed consumer interest in spending on the home:

> Like many retailers, it was caught in the double bind of gearing at a time when high interest rates simultaneously increased costs and reduced demand. But Coloroll also illustrates the sombre truth that when times get hard, assets prove unreliable and liabilities remain unchanged. (*Financial Times*, 8 June 1990)

Growth declined rapidly, affecting all Coloroll's markets; pre-tax profit for the half-year to September 1989 declined from £20.5m to £10.1m (see Appendix 4B). As if this were not enough, Coloroll faced the prospect of having to honour contingent liabilities of up to £40m, incurred in the hurried sale of some businesses in management buy-out arrangements. Ashcroft described the outlook as dour and announced a programme of retrenchment, with factory closures and redundancies. Commentators suggested that divestment could prove difficult:

> In a business which to its credit, has no obvious incongruous part, finding 'peripherals' to sell would be a sign of just how bad things had got. (*Financial Times*, 17 November 1989)

In March 1990, the company's financial position had worsened to the extent that John Ashcroft was forced to resign. The bankers, S G Warburg, arranged a rescue package of £100m, and appointed Kenneth Marks as Chairman, from his recent appointment as non-executive Director; his aim was to keep the company together. He called himself 'Mr Pots & Pans' and favoured a much more subdued style of management. However, only two months later, Coloroll went into full receivership with debts estimated variously at £200m to £400m, depending on source. The break-up value of its businesses was estimated at £200m. Although most of the Coloroll companies were trading profitability, it was a bad time to sell:

> The home products market is still in the doldrums. Many of the likeliest buyers for the businesses are already suffering intense pressure on profitability or they have debt problems of their own. (*Financial Times*, 8 June 1990)

City attitude

Despite strong performance, the City's attitude to Coloroll was wary, particularly following the Crowther acquisition; there were doubts about its growth predictions, as interest rates affected home purchase and expenditure, and therefore raised questions over Coloroll's aim of transforming Crowther's current 5.5 per cent margin on carpets business into their target of 10 per cent. Some reservations were based on its 'rather raffish reputation', and there was great unease at the high gearing involved in that large takeover. According to analysts commentating during Coloroll's last few troubled months, Coloroll had all the signs of a company 'destined for failure'.

> There were gushing profiles in the business press, the chairman with his string of 'young businessman of the year' awards and directors with telephone digit salaries and a penchant for spending weekends on army assault courses. (*Financial Times*, 24 February 1990)

The work of administrators brought in to save the company revealed the extent to which the company had covered up its inefficiencies. Practical problems were aggravated by 'the legacy of the over-optimistic attitude of Coloroll's old management team. Stocks were too high and some factories were operating at over-capacity'. A venture capital company which had announced preliminary rescue proposals withdrew once it discovered 'the full extent of Coloroll's financial and operational problems' (*Financial Times*, 8 June 1990). With this collapse, receivership and the break-up of the company were inevitable, reinforcing the point that 'creative accounting – for which Coloroll had something of a reputation in its heyday – tends to come to grief in bear markets'. The attempted management buy-out at Denby in 1989 serves to indicate that the supposedly autonomous businesses saw opportunities for better returns outside the Coloroll group, although thanks in part to the £3m invested in new equipment by Coloroll following takeover.

APPENDIX 4A
Acquisitions

Year	Company	Price	Activity	Comments
1982	Wallmates (USA)	£10m	Large wallcoverings manufacturer	A phased takeover completed in 1986
1984	Wilmar		Manufacturer of burglar alarms	Synergy of DIY outlet; unprofitable so disposed of
1985	Worley UK	£2m	Vinyl wallpaper manufacturer	
1985	Alexander Drew	£2.5m	Textile printer	One of the largest in UK
1986	Staffordshire Potteries	£15m	Household pottery manufacturer	Strong brands included
1986	Biltons Ceramics	£5.1m	Household pottery manufacturer	Denby, Biltons, Kilncraft, Royal Winton
1986	Fogarty	£31.2m	Major UK manufacturer of duvets, pillows and bed linen	With smaller buys Coloroll became market leader in 'filled products'
1987	Wallbridge	£5m	Small carpet manufacturer	
1987	Crown House	£89m	Glassware and engineering group	Retaining Edinburgh Crystal, Thomas Webb Crystal and Dema Glass; disposed of engineering interests, recovering £57m of purchase price
1988	John Crowther	£215m	Mainly carpet and textile interests	Gave Coloroll UK market leadership in carpets; brands Kossett and Crossley
1988	William Barrett	£15m	Furniture and bed manufacturer	No 2 in UK market
1988	Texture Tex (Europe)	£3.5m	Yarns processing for carpet industry	
1988	Burlington	£7m	Vinyl wall-covering manufacturer	Increased Coloroll share in vinyls

APPENDIX 4B
Interim report for half-year ended 30 September 1989

	Half-year ended 30 September		Year ended 31 March 1989
	1989	1988	1989
	£000	£000	£000
Turnover	283,456	243,778	565,137
Trading Profit	20,077	26,884	72,179
Interest	(10,009)	(6,338)	(16,612)
Profit before Tax	7,752	16,026	43,084
Extraordinary Items	16,825	–	(50)
Profit for Half-year	24,577	16,026	43,034
Dividends to Coloroll Finance Ltd Stockholders	(324)	(257)	(546)
Preference Dividends	(1,125)	–	(1,011)
Attributable to Ordinary Shareholders	23,128	15,769	41,477
Earnings per Share	3.2p	9.8p	23.0p

Notes
1. Extraordinary items comprise cost of closures, plus profits from disposals of two Crowther businesses.
2. EPS calculated on the basis of 198,968,997 Ordinary Shares.

APPENDIX 4C
Financial Analysis
(C=Coloroll, V = Coats Viyella, L=Laura Ashley)

	1984	1985	1986	1987	1988	1989
Actual turnover £m						
C	34.96	37.37	60.83	115.23	257.65	565.14
V	606.9	1695.9	1750	1794.8	1854.9	N/A
L	N/A	96	131	171	201	252
Turnover adjusted for inflation £m						
C	34.96	35.24	55.47	100.83	214.88	437.42
V	606.9	1599.2	1596	1570.5	1546.9	N/A
L	N/A	90.5	119.5	149.6	167.6	195
Real increase in turnover						
C	N/A	0.8	57.4	81.8	113.1	103.6
V	N/A	163.5	−0.2	−1.6	−1.5	N/A
L	N/A	N/A	32	25.2	12	16.3
Profit before tax £m (actual)						
C	2.11	3.81	6.23	10.33	16.09	55.57
V	42.4	149.6	181.7	212.8	135.2	N/A
L	N/A	14	18	22	23	20 ▶

Appendix 4C: Financial Analysis *Continued*

	1984	1985	1986	1987	1988	1989
Profit before tax £m (inflation adjusted)						
C	2.11	3.6	5.68	9.04	21.76	43.01
V	42.4	141.1	165.7	186.2	112.8	N/A
L	N/A	13.2	16.4	19.3	19.2	15.5
Gross profit						
C	29	29	34	31	31	31
Gross profit margin %						
C	6.6	11.8	11.1	10.1	11.2	12.8
V	6.5	9.4	10.7	11.9	7.7	N/A
L	N/A	14.7	13.7	13.1	11.5	8
Ratios						
RONA – return on net assets						
C	19	31	28	17?	24	34
ROCE – return on capital employed						
C	22.4	38.6	31.8	23.3	38.5	71
V	N/A	N/A	25.9	28.4	19.9	N/A
L	N/A	42.2	26	28	27	16
Stock turnover						
C	3.4	4	4.3	2.6?	3.9	4.3
V	N/A	N/A	4.2	4.1	4.2	N/A
Current ratio						
C	1.31	1.4	1.3	1.2	1.5	1.3
Acid test						
C	0.67	0.61	0.61	0.68	0.81	0.72
V	N/A	N/A	1.0	1.0	0.94	N/A
Interest cover						
C	11.4	7.3	12.5	8.6	10.3	4.3
V	N/A	N/A	7.1	8.0	5.2	N/A
Gearing % (ltd/ce+reserves)						
C	2	9.3	5.4	16.1	43.3	91.5
V	N/A	N/A	17.8	17.4	18.5	N/A

CASE STUDY 5

Z Holdings Ltd

Z Holdings is the wholly-owned subsidiary of a major multinational company called Alpha International. It is the vehicle that Alpha International uses to group together a number of companies which it had acquired some time ago and which represent a significant diversification away from its major core businesses. Alpha International controls Z Holdings by appointing a Chairman of the Board of Z Holdings, generally an executive with other responsibilities at the Alpha Head Office. It also appoints the Z Holdings Chief Executive, Finance and Personnel Directors from the ranks of management in its core businesses. The three top Head Office executives generally serve at Z Holdings for periods of three to four years and sometimes for shorter periods than this. Periods at Z Holdings are seen as part of the management development programme of some of Alpha's fast-track managers. Control is also exerted by Alpha in the form of setting return on capital and growth objectives, monitoring against budgets which have to be presented to top Alpha management once a year and also by calling for five-year-plan presentations once a year. In addition, Alpha also imposes stringent safety requirements on Z Holdings and requires it to adhere to other general policies, particularly personnel policies. Z Holdings is required not to undertake activities that might conflict with other Alpha businesses. Within these limits, however, the management of Z Holdings has considerable freedom and for some years now has enjoyed the generous financial support of Alpha for its expansion strategy.

Z Holdings has five major, wholly-owned subsidiaries.

- Company A operates in the building products market in the UK and it controls two fairly recently acquired subsidiaries in the same general markets.
- Company B manufactures road construction products and is organised by region, also with a

recently acquired subsidiary in the same markets. Recently it has undertaken some small road construction projects.
- Company C covers the same market segments as Companies A and B, but in Canada.
- Company D operates mainly in the UK but it also has substantial export business. It manufactures and applies industrial paints.
- Company E covers the same market segments as D but in France and Germany.

The Managing Directors of each of the five major subsidiaries have not come from the ranks of Alpha management. They have all come from the industrial sectors in which their companies operate. They all sit on the Board of Z Holdings, as do the three Head Office Directors and the Chairman. This Board meets every quarter and the same group, without the Chairman, meets once a month as the Management Meeting.

For some time now Z Holdings has been pursuing an active strategy of growth, largely by acquisition. Most of the acquisitions have been put forward by the operating subsidiaries. The normal practice has been for a subsidiary Managing Director and his team to identify and put forward a potential acquisition. This is discussed with the Chief Executive and then reported on to the monthly Management Meeting. If the proposed acquisition is approved by the Chief Executive then Head Office staff prepare a capital requisition for submission to Alpha International. This requisition has to follow a format and meet criteria laid down by Alpha. The requisition is prepared by Z Holdings Head Office staff who also assist the subsidiary Managing Director with the financial and legal aspects of the acquisition. Once the acquisition is made it becomes the clear responsibility of the acquiring subsidiary.

Each of the five major subsidiaries holds a Board Meeting once a quarter, chaired by the Chief Executive of Z Holdings. A typical agenda for one of these meetings is given as Appendix 5A. A significant part of these meetings is taken up with item 2, Last Period Results. A 50-page document is distributed before the meeting. It consists of summary sheets and each item on these summary sheets is then broken down into considerable detail in the rest of the document. Subsidiary management meet on the day before the full Board Meeting to prepare for that meeting at which they report to Z Holdings' Chief Executive, Finance Director and Personnel Director. In between the Board Meetings the management of each subsidiary meets formally on their own each month. A consultant attended a number of the meetings and noted that:

- significant amounts of time were taken up with overlap problems with other subsidiaries and complaints about the policies of Alpha;
- a large loss on a small civil engineering contract was reported on and reasons for it given, but very little discussion took place on what was a relatively new activity for the company.

The monthly Management Meeting of the Head Office Directors and the subsidiary Managing Directors follows a standard agenda, an example of which is given in Appendix 5A. This meeting considers monthly results for the month completed two months before the meeting. A consolidated summary of profits plus total profit for each subsidiary is discussed. A consultant who attended this meeting made the following notes:

- matters arising took up the first hour, of which safety matters accounted for 15 minutes and incentive schemes for employees another 25 minutes;
- discussion on the May financial results took 50 minutes, including some discussion on problems in the building products market and some difficulties on attempts to diversify into small engineering works, and the effects of a government moratorium on local authority spending;
- reports on prospective acquisitions took 30 minutes;
- all afternoon was taken up with reporting on subsidiary company business, as well as highlights and complaints about restrictive Alpha policies.

The Chief Executive has to make a five-year plan presentation to the Chief Executive of Alpha. This occurs in early September and is followed by a more detailed budget presentation in late November. Z Holdings therefore requires submission by its subsidiaries of five-year plans and budgets which allow its timetable to be met. Appendix 5C gives the plan letter sent out and the timetable which subsidiaries are required to follow.

The reward system employed at Z Holdings includes an element which is performance-related and this can amount to 20 per cent of salary. For the subsidiary Managing Directors the bonus is tied to the achievement of target return on capital and profit growth. Subsidiary Managing Directors apply similar schemes to their senior managers.

In early 1988 the board of Z Holdings attended a one-day workshop at which they discussed with consultants the appropriateness of the control style they were employing. They expressed some concern that they had not foreseen in time the deterioration in profitability which had occurred in 1987. This had been due mainly to price cutting to build up volume in Company B. The Management Meeting had been informed that such a price-cutting policy was being employed but had not fully appreciated the consequences. The consultants directed attention to the work which Goold & Campbell (1988) had done on styles of management and the role of the Head Office. The participants of the workshop concluded that the 'strategic control' style of management was appropriate to their business, but that it should be supplemented by an emphasis on financial control. They hired the consultants to assist them to improve the approach of Z Holdings to control and to clarify the role of the top management level of the group as a whole.

At the beginning of the assignment the consultants interviewed all the top managers. The following is a summary of points made during those interviews.

The Management Meeting and the Board are not really consulted on capital expenditure or acquisitions, they are merely informed. They do not generally see the papers submitted to Alpha. Collective responsibility is not exercised. Authority for running the business must be left with the Managing Director of that business. Colleagues on the Board do not know enough to make much contribution to this. The attitudes and values of Alpha conflict with those of the subsidiaries. Is there any point in a Group Board? What are the expectations of Alpha? The Head Office Directors keep changing. Management Meetings and Boards do not provide a forum for input into the development of other Managing Directors' businesses. Should one Board member make comment on and take part in decisions on the business of another Board member? The Management Meetings are a useful forum for discussing overlaps between businesses. Board and Management Meetings are a waste of time. The Chief Executive meets Managing Directors once a month but they rarely talk about the budget.

Reference

Goold, M. & Campbell, A. (1988), *Strategies and Styles*, Oxford: Blackwell.

APPENDIX 5A
Company B Ltd: board meeting agenda

1 Matters arising
2 Period results
3 Capital expenditure
4 Debtors
5 Health and safety
6 Properties
7 Acquisitions
8 Major projects
9 Interface with Alpha
10 Any other business

APPENDIX 5B
Management meeting agenda

1 Matters arising

2 Finance
   (i) Monthly results
   (ii) Acquisition/disposal report
   (iii) Pension

3 Personnel
   (i) Group staff handbook

4 Safety
   (i) Monthly performance
   (ii) Fatality
   (iii) Product safety manual

5 Business highlights/matters of general interest
   (i) Company A
   (ii) Company B
   (iii) Company C
   (iv) Company D
   (v) Company E

6 Central purchasing

7 Internal audit

8 Report on R&D meeting

9 Any other business

APPENDIX 5C
Planning procedures

MEMORANDUM TO: See attached list
FROM: David Douglas
SUBJECT: Business Plan and Budget
DATE: July 1988

There are some general assumptions specific to Z Holdings to which you will wish to refer. A copy of the Z strategy document is enclosed, and you will wish to note:

(a) As a group we must achieve at least 12.5 per cent operating profit improvement in 1989 on the Business Plan for 1988.

(b) We should finance organic growth out of current cash flow, and should expect, in addition, as individual businesses, to be able to pay a dividend out of cash flow of not less than 8 per cent of equity and interest free funding. Actual payment will depend upon financing considerations.

(c) Individual businesses should not include potential acquisitions in their 1989 budget. However, extra resources will be available for expansion through acquisitions.

(d) Health, safety, environment, quality, integrity and honesty will remain our absolute business philosophy.

A Business Plan is not merely a set of numbers. In relation to the business the Management team should discuss and agree:

(a) WHAT IT IS NOW;
(b) WHAT IT SHOULD BE;
(c) HOW WE WILL GET THERE.

The following is a guideline you will wish to use:

1 Outline present business position, including strengths and weaknesses. Compare with previous Business Plan.
2 Identify critical success factors and activities which will influence the successful achievement of your business plans.
3 Agree objectives and timing.
4 Specify assumptions and strategy, both in the long and short terms.
5 Evaluate monthly or quarterly financial plans for 1989 on basis of the agreed objectives. Quantify risk of assumptions being incorrect.
6 Review (5) above. Accept or modify as appropriate.

While we do not require a financial evaluation of the years 1990–94, we wish to fully discuss your five-year strategy. It is only in this context that we can properly consider your plan for the ensuing year. You should therefore, describe how you see your company in 1994 and how you intend to get there.

To meet the enclosed timetable requirements, it will be necessary for you to start the plan process now.

Please would you include a page in the planning package on the use of Information Technology in your business. You should cover:

(a) a statement of your objectives for using IT in your business and the competitive edge you expect this to give you; and
(b) strategies for meeting the objective.

Planning Timetable

1	Managing Directors Outlook Reports	29 August
2	Outline Five-Year Plan to Alpha	9 September
3	Forecasts for 2 years to Alpha	9 September
4	Plan Meetings All data to Head Office 1 week prior to meeting	

Central Office	1 October
Company A	7 October
Company B	11 October
Company C	13 October
Company D	18 October
Company E	21 October

5	First draft budget	31 October
6	Management team Discussion	8 November
7	Final Budget	14 November
8	Presentation to Z Board	21 November
9	Presentation to Alpha Board	24 November

Group Strategy Statement

The Strategy:

- Our group will be operated to the highest standards of safety, honesty and integrity.
- Our products and services will be of a consistently high quality.
- We recognise our responsibility to our customers, the community and our employees.

Our Objective:

- We aim to grow profitably and to maximise our shareholders' interests.

Our targets:

- 20 per cent return on capital at the operating level.
- Sales growth of 12.5 per cent per annum.
- Capital expenditure to be funded from cash flow.
- Recruitment and development of high calibre staff.

Our limits:

- We will concentrate in our existing areas of activity.

PART THREE

Organisational dynamics

The nature of situations far from certainty and agreement and the need for extraordinary management

The purpose of this part is to provide material that it is hoped will provoke you to think about the dynamics of organisational life in a rather different manner than you might have done hitherto. In the interest of our own double-loop learning about the nature of strategic management, we are going to explore in some depth some of the basic assumptions that are made when we think and talk about ordinary management and, therefore, when we extend it over the long term in the hope that we might thereby be able to make intentional strategies. This means that we must consider the systemic nature of an organisation and the fundamental notions about systems upon which ordinary management concepts and prescriptions are built. These fundamental notions are to do with how systems are intentionally driven by negative feedback to produce stable equilibrium adaptation to environments.

Also in the interest of our own double-loop learning about the nature of strategic management, we are going to explore the new science of complexity in the hope of finding new insights, new metaphors and analogies for thinking about strategy in a different manner. That new science indicates that creative systems do not seek stable equilibrium adaptation. On the contrary, such systems spontaneously sustain themselves in a critical state at the edge of disintegration where they are not adapted to their environments: they coevolve with the other systems they interact with and together they create their own new futures. Such systems are dissipative ones that have structure which continually dissolves to be transformed into new states. Such systems spontaneously produce emergent new order out of disorder through a process of self-organisation.

▶

You can see how you will have a complete/y different view of organisational evolution depending upon which of these views of organisational dynamics you take. On the first view, you would conclude that the long-term future of an organisation is currently unknown because we have not gathered enough data or carried out enough analysis: in other words, because we are ignorant. Or you might conclude that the future is currently unknown because incompetent managers cannot be relied upon to gather the facts and carry out the analysis, or because even if they do, the rest of us are so badly behaved that we will block their rational attempts. Armed with these answers you would develop the ordinary management prescriptions of gathering and processing more data, motivating people extrinsically by rewarding them for measured performance, training people to be more competent and converting them to behaviours and beliefs that you think will be more beneficial to the organisation. There will always in this story be a 'you' who can know what will happen and be 'in control' of it all, more or less. In this way the future of a competently managed organisation will be the actualisation of prior shared intention. Order there will be because order has been installed in blueprint form and the only alternative, you will think, is anarchy.

However, if you take the new view of organisational dynamics you will conclude that all of the ordinary management prescriptions, no matter how assiduously applied, will never overcome the currently unknown state of the long-term future simply because it is unknowable. The science of complexity demonstrates convincingly that creative systems evolve into an open-ended evolutionary space so that the future is radically unpredictable. The long-term future of creative systems is thus not simply currently unknown but completely unknowable. It will, therefore, be impossible to plan it or intend it in any way. The future of an organisation, in this view, will emerge without prior intention, through the spontaneous self-organisation of the people who constitute it. Instead of planning their way into the future they will create a future through double-loop learning.

What follows is a long part and sometimes you may not be sure why you are going to all the trouble of understanding it. I believe that it is most important that you should. Without doing so I suspect that you will not fully understand why today's dominant ordinary management prescriptions are so inappropriate for long-term strategy-making, and you will also have a less rich understanding of the alternative, the processes of extraordinary management. We do not have a well-developed language for talking about these processes which is why they have been relatively ignored, perhaps. The new science of complexity provides us with the kind of language, the kind of insight and the kind of metaphor we need to gain a deeper understanding of what we actually do when we face unknowable futures, when we do not know what we are doing or where we are going, but nevertheless produce something quite creative together.

CHAPTER 8

Organisations are feedback systems

Equilibrium and disequilibrium

8.1   INTRODUCTION

The purpose of this chapter is to develop an understanding of the dynamics of organisational life, because without this we cannot really grasp why it does not work when managers extend ordinary management processes into long-term strategic situations far from certainty and agreement. Nor can we fully grasp what processes are actually employed behind the smokescreen created by the apparent application of ordinary management prescriptions in turbulent conditions.

So, what do we mean when we talk about dynamics? When we try to understand the patterns of change that a system displays over time, and when we try to identify the conditions leading those patterns to be stable or unstable, then we are trying to understand the dynamics of a system (see *Key Concept 8.1*).

This matter of the dynamics is of absolutely central importance, because through studying it we come to understand the most fundamental qualities of a system, namely, the nature of causality, the possibility and nature of predictability, and the states of equilibrium or non-equilibrium that a system tends to. It is these qualities of a system that will determine what kinds of prescriptions and approaches to governing it will work and what kinds will not.

The first step in exploring the dynamics is that of defining the kind of system we are concerned with. An organisation is clearly a system in that it consists of a number of interconnected parts. These parts will be called agents from now on and of course the agents in organisations are us. Every organisation is a system consisting of a network of agents all interacting with each other according to some set of rules that each of them uses to examine what their neighbours in the network are up to, then to respond to what they are doing, then to evaluate the reaction of others to their response, then to design a further response, and so on and on.

There are two points to note immediately about the nature of this network system that we humans set up whenever we form a group or an organisation. First, when we join a group or an organisation we join a legitimate system, that is, some existing hierarchy, procedural rules and approved way of behaving. If it is a new group or organisation we bring with us views on these matters and very rapidly establish at least the beginnings of a legitimate system. It is membership of the legitimate system that establishes a clear boundary around an organisation – those who are members of the legitimate system belong to the organisation and those who are not do not belong. Perhaps that is why we so rapidly set up a legitimate system when we begin to form a group or organisation – it contains deep anxieties about belonging and not belonging and by containing such anxieties allows us to begin to work.

However, as soon as we become members of a legitimate system we begin to spin amongst ourselves an informal social system, a learning community of practice, which I will call the shadow system. While the legitimate system has clear, rather permanent

---

Key Concept 8.1

Dynamics

Dynamics is the study of how a system changes over time: classical dynamics establishes laws of motion through time for physical bodies; thermodynamics establishes laws of heat dissipation over time; population dynamics establishes the patterns of change in populations over time; economic dynamics attempts to establish and explain patterns of economic development over time; psychodynamics tries to explain the human behaviour patterns over time that are generated by contradiction and tension, for example by the need to be part of a group and yet be a free individual, by the feeling of love and hate for the same person, and so on. Dynamics is concerned with the effects of tension on a system, with the manner in which contradictions cause tension and so create the energy that drives behaviour.

Dynamics, as we saw in Chapter 1, may be contrasted with statics, the study of states of rest of phenomena, of patterns and positions at a point in time, of snapshots at a point in time.

Dynamics can also be contrasted with comparative statics, the study of change by comparing two snapshots taken at different points in time.

Dynamics is concerned with the path from one state to another, to the next and so on, generated by feedback processes. Amongst the more important questions raised by dynamics are those relating to whether the system being studied is moving from one stable equilibrium state to another, whether the movement is stable and orderly, and whether the movement is predictable. The dynamics is generated by the manner in which a particular system feeds back the information on the outcome of one action to at least partly cause the next one. Dynamics therefore involves the circular causality that flows from feedback systems, matters to be dealt with later in this chapter.

Organisational and managerial dynamics will be concerned with how organisations and managerial actions change over time and with the feedback processes that lead to such changes. The study of dynamics is a difficult matter and therefore tends to be ignored in textbooks. Most of the literature on managing and organising can probably be classified as statics or comparative statics.

boundaries – you are either 'in' or 'out' – the shadow system has fuzzy or fractal boundaries that fluctuate – it is often not all that clear who is 'in' or 'out' and some of those who are 'in' may not even be members of the legitimate system. I will be arguing, particularly in the next chapter and Part Four, that it is the dynamics of this shadow system and its interaction with the legitimate system that is the key to understanding organisational dynamics.

The second key point to note about the network systems that are organisations is that they are feedback systems: that is, information about the consequences of an agent's action just past is fed back into the discovery, choice and action process of that agent to determine the next action. This chapter will focus very much on understanding the nature of feedback because it underlies the dynamics of network systems.

So, turn your mind for a while from how managers make strategies to how managers and members of organisations interact with each other and what the consequences of different kinds of interaction are.

8.2   THE NATURE OF FEEDBACK SYSTEMS

A feedback loop is established as soon as two people interact with each other. Take the following sequence of events as an example. As you walk down a street you may look at an attractive stranger. The stranger may return your admiring glance with an equally appreciative one, prompting you to smile. The stranger may smile too and greet you. So encouraged, you may then stop and find some excuse to start a conversation. That conversation may lead to dinner and that dinner could escalate into many shared meals. The circle of interaction between you and the former stranger could continue for years.

What is happening here is that one action on your part leads to an action on the other's part, which feeds back into a further action on your part. And in this case the feedback is a self-reinforcing amplification of a small chance encounter into a life-long relationship.

Feedback loops are set up whenever one action (event, piece of information) determines some other action (event, piece of information) which then in turn affects the first action (event, piece of information). When an environment causes a decision that in turn affects the environment, then we have feedback. So, when competitors cut their prices, managers in a company have to make a decision as to whether to cut their prices too. If they do, this could prompt the competitors to cut their prices even further and so the pattern of feedback may take the escalating, amplifying form of a price war.

When the output of a machine (or any other system) is monitored back as an information input to regulate or otherwise affect the behaviour of that machine (or system), then we have feedback. When we see managers detecting a negative profit variance, that is profits coming in below target, and then taking positive action to close the gap, we are witnessing feedback at work. This time the feedback is limiting and regulating rather than amplifying and self-reinforcing.

Feedback, a circle of interdependence or mutual causality, is ubiquitous in human systems and in nature's systems too.

Feedback between two individuals

At its most basic, any organisation consists of interactions between individual people (*Weick, 1969/79*). Interactions between people are always, as we saw above, feedback loops. We can represent such interactions in the diagrammatic form shown in *Figure 8.1*, which depicts the following sequence of events:

1 Manager X acts, and draws an accusation of sexual harassment made by employee Z against supervisor Y to the attention of supervisor Y.
2 Supervisor Y listens, so discovering what accusation X is making.
3 Supervisor Y considers what to do and makes a choice to deny the accusation.
4 Supervisor Y acts and denies the accusation.
5 Manager X listens to the denial, so discovering the consequences of the action of making the accusation in the first place.
6 Manager X considers what to do next and chooses to continue with the confrontation by presenting evidence to Y.
7 Manager X acts, setting out the alleged time and place of the incident and asking where Y was at the time and what Y was doing.

And so both X and Y continue to move around a feedback loop in which each acts, discovers the consequences of their action in terms of the other's actions, chooses what to do in the light of the discovery, and then acts once again.

Feedback between three individuals

To illustrate how the web of feedback loops builds up, consider what happens when employee Z is summoned by the manager to a meeting with the supervisor Y. We now need to look at the feedback interactions between three people, each of whom is discovering, choosing and acting. This is illustrated in *Figure 8.2*.

Now when manager X makes a statement – suppose X repeats the accusation – it is heard (discovered) by both Y and Z. Each then considers the available choices for responding. Suppose Y repeats the denial and Z chooses to remain silent. Now X discovers the consequences of acting, namely the denial of Y and the silence of Z, and chooses to take the matter no further. X announces that the matter is closed and asks Y and Z to leave the office. Both Y and Z now discover the consequences of their behaviour. Suppose Z chooses to respond to this discovery and then takes violent action against Y. Now both Y and X discover the consequences of their behaviour. Y chooses to retreat and does so, while X chooses to intervene and tries to restrain Z.

Feedback and the environment

What *Figure 8.2* also depicts is the nature of an environment. Manager X operates in an environment that consists, on this occasion, of two people, Y and Z. We can think of manager X as a feedback loop or system that is part of a web of feedback loops constituting an environment. Note how the environment of manager X is not some 'given' to which X adapts, but a sequence of perceptions and behaviours which X plays a major part, with others, in creating. We create the games we play and many of the rules by which we play them and we change many of the rules, even changing the game itself, as we play.

FIGURE 8.1

Feedback interaction between two people

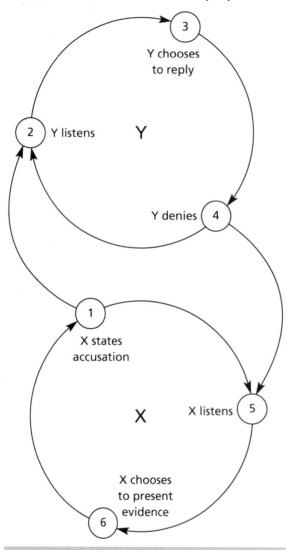

Feedback and groups

We can easily use *Figure 8.2* to describe sequences of interactions between three groups of people in an organisation. For example X can stand for the marketing and Sales Department, Y for the Production Department, and Z for the R&D Department. If we are looking at what happens from the point of view of Marketing and Sales we would see the other departments as its environment. An example of the feedback patterns that might emerge is as follows.

Marketing and Sales might write a memo on a new product idea to R&D. R&D receive it and discuss what it means (discovery). They then choose a response and

FIGURE 8.2
Feedback interaction between three people/ groups/organisations

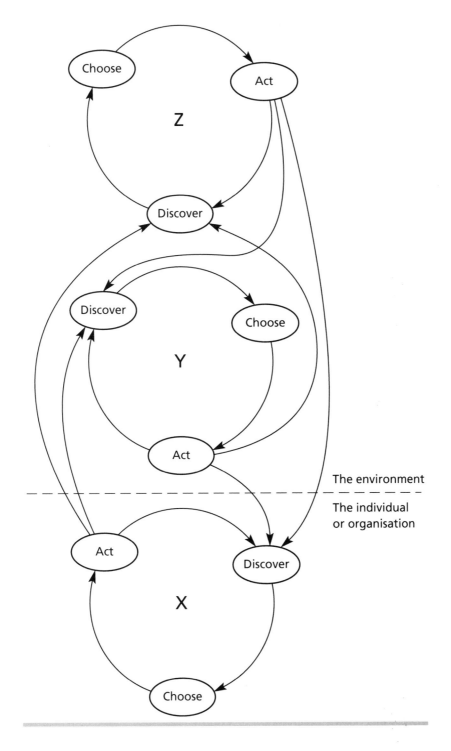

conduct a prototype experiment (action). The Production Department is consulted, considers the production options, and experiments with some of those. The Marketing and Sales Department receives the prototype, chooses some trial customers, and tries them for a response. Marketing and Sales then write a report which they send to R&D and Production.

Feedback and organisations

Alternatively, we could use *Figure 8.2* to follow the evolving pattern of interaction between a whole Organisation X and the Organisations Y and Z that constitute its environment. So Organisation X may decide to boost volumes by severely cutting prices. Organisations Y and Z may respond by even bigger cuts and improvements in product quality as well. This compels X to cut prices even further and so the pattern of feedback takes on the form of a price war. So organisations are components in larger feedback networks that we call industries and markets; and these in turn are part of even larger feedback networks that we call economies, societies and nations; and they in turn are components in global feedback networks.

Positive and negative feedback

As we have already seen in this and previous chapters, feedback may take a negative or damping form, for example when managers use budgets to control the development of their business. When they practise budgetary control, managers react to profit variances by taking action to remove them so that feedback operates in a limiting way to maintain stability – negative feedback. All forms of planning and ideological conformity are essentially negative feedback in form.

However, feedback systems can also operate in a positive, or amplifying manner. For example, central heating and steam engine regulators that operate in a positive feedback manner would take temperature or engine speed further and further away from the desired level. A tiny increase in temperature above the desired level would turn on the heat, so increasing the deviation from the desired level. That deviation would result in continued application of heat so that the room temperature rose even further. Eventually, the inhabitants would die of heat exhaustion. In the case of the steam engine, a small increase in engine speed would partially close the valve, raising steam pressure and thus engine speed. The valve would consequently be closed even further, so increasing the steam pressure and engine speed even more until the engine blew up.

Amplifying feedback here generates a vicious circle that escalates small changes. We would describe the behaviour of the system as 'runaway' or 'explosive'. The operation of the control system is such that fluctuations are amplified, leading to predictable equilibrium behaviour of a highly unstable kind.

No sane engineer designs engine or heating control systems that act in an amplifying manner and set off on predictably unstable paths to explosion. And no sane manager designs business control systems that could lead to increasingly divergent behaviour such that the organisation simply disintegrates. We therefore almost always think of business control systems in terms of negative or damping feedback. In the next section of this chapter we will consider the nature of negative and positive feedback in more detail, and as we proceed through this and later chapters, we will be questioning the notion that control requires that only negative, damping feedback be present.

Feedback and nonlinearity

In addition to their positive and negative properties, feedback systems may be either linear or nonlinear. All the feedback systems we will be talking about in this and later chapters are nonlinear and that nonlinearity has very important consequences for the patterns of behaviour generated by the feedback loops.

Nonlinearity occurs when some condition or some action has a varying effect on an outcome, depending on the level of the condition or the intensity of the action. So the availability of a stock of goods in an inventory affects the shipment rate, but the effect varies. When the stock is close to a desired level, there will be virtually no impact of stock levels on shipment rates. The firm ships according to its order inflow rate. When inventory is very low, stock availability has a powerful constraining effect on shipments.

Another example is where extra labour is hired. At first, extra labour may lead to proportionally extra output but, given fixed equipment, a point will be reached where extra labour adds proportionally less and less to output. Eventually adding extra labour causes output to decline as large numbers interfere with efficient operation. These effects cannot be captured in simple linear relationships where a cause always exerts the same degree of effect on an outcome.

Feedback loops in organisations are nonlinear because of basic economic laws and basic human behaviour. As a firm sells more output its profit levels first rise because it is able to spread fixed cost, but eventually further increases in output lead to falling profit levels as prices have to be cut to sell more. At first demand for a new product rises slowly as a few people try it out. Then the demand may rise very rapidly as more people see that their neighbours have it; the desire for it spreads through the consumer population. But then the demand growth slows as demand reaches saturation levels. Organisational life does not proceed in proportional terms or straight lines; it proceeds non-proportionally, following curves. In this sense organisational life is a consequence of nonlinear feedback.

The important point about nonlinear systems is that they can operate in both negative and positive feedback modes.

Nonlinearity, positive and negative feedback

For example, the behaviour of a population of, say, insects is clearly driven by a feedback system. The size of the population feeds back through the birth and death rates to determine tomorrow's population size. You can see that this feedback system is nonlinear when you consider the two sets of forces driving population changes. The first set of forces is that which generates growth: factors such as better nutrition lead to rising fertility and birth rates as well as declining mortality rates. We can represent this by means of a feedback loop in which population now (P_t) is some multiple (c) of population in the last period (P_{t-1}):

$$P_t = cP_{t-1}$$

This is a positive feedback loop determining that the insect population will grow for evermore. What we are describing is simply the phenomenon of compound growth such as that applied to interest-bearing bank deposits.

But this is not the only set of forces governing the population level. As the population rises, food becomes scarcer and conflict and stress rise as overcrowding increases. In other words, there will also be a negative feedback loop governing population levels at the same time as the positive one. To represent the negative loop we can use the following formula that shows population now (P_t) falling as population of the previous period gets larger:

$$P_t = 1 - P_{t-1}$$

Since both of these sets of forces are acting upon the population level at the same time, we can express the relationship as follows:

$$P_t = cP_{t-1}(1 - P_{t-1})$$

This is the famous logistic difference equation that has been widely used in analyses of populations of all kinds and many other phenomena besides. We can represent it in diagram form as the positive and negative feedback loops shown in *Figure 8.3*.

The reason for going to all the trouble of setting out these equations and loops is the very interesting properties they display, properties we will explore in much greater detail in Chapter 9.

At low levels of the population, the positive growth feedback loop dominates and the population grows. At higher levels, the negative loop dominates and the population declines. Here we have a system with positive and negative loops and loop domination changes because of the nonlinearity in the relationship. A system governed by nonlinear feedback structures, where positive and negative feedback are both present, may move in a regular way to a stable equilibrium when the negative loop dominates. Then it may suddenly flip and operate in a self-reinforcing, explosive direction. After some time it might flip back again. These alterations in behaviour will be due simply to the structure of the system and have nothing to do with changes in the environment. This is a very important difference from the processes of ordinary management which are essentially linear damping loops. As this section will show, adding nonlinearity and positive loops leads to the capture of far more of the complexity of

FIGURE 8.3

Positive and negative feedback in population growth

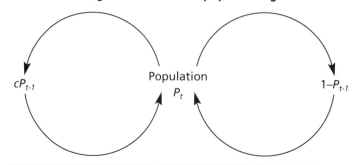

real-life organisational behaviour than a focus on ordinary management processes alone can encompass.

So a human system may be unstable simply because it has a nonlinear, amplifying feedback structure, reasons that have nothing to do with the environment or the competence of individual agents within the system. It will then be rather foolish to look for the cause of failure in some person, some external event, or some scapegoat. It will make little more sense to heap praise on a person or identify the causing event when things go very well.

Feedback, paradigms and perspectives

There is another important point that we need to make about human nonlinear feedback systems. *Figure 8.2* illustrated how the behaviour of each individual in an organisation is a feedback loop connecting discovery to choice, choice to action, and action back to discovery again. You will recall how the process of making sense of Figure 3.1 (the container and the people example in Chapter 3) could also be described as one of discovering, choosing and then acting. The point made in that discussion was this: it is the way we frame our understanding of the world that determines what we perceive or discover. And what we perceive determines what we choose to do. And what we choose to do determines what we actually do. And what we do affects our perceptions and so determines the nature of the further discoveries we make. Feedback loops in human behaviour, then, are heavily conditioned by paradigms and the perceptions those paradigms lead to. When we relate human feedback loops to the impact of paradigms and perceptions we see how environments are social constructions of reality, that is how an environment is a perception that people have woven together through their social intercourse.

Note that the feedback concept is one of a circle and because it is a circle it may be impossible to say what causes what, or what precedes or follows what. We may be acting out part of a sequence of actions before we discover fully what the consequences of those actions will be. If we are considering the feedback loops in the behaviour of groups of people, then in relation to the same issues some groups may be acting before or while other groups are discovering the consequences of those actions. In complex situations it may well be impossible to say whether actions precede or follow choices and discoveries.

Feedback, dynamics, change, control and success

By now enough has been said to make it clear that any group of people, any organisation, is a system consisting of a web of nonlinear feedback loops operating as part of a larger system or environment that is also simply a web of nonlinear feedback loops (see *Key Concept 8.2*).

Why is it so important to base a discussion of strategic management so firmly on what is so simple and obvious a notion?

The reason, as will be made much clearer in later chapters, is that strategic management is, above all, about dealing with change, and the patterns of change a system displays over time depend entirely on the nature of the feedback interaction of that system. It is the nature of the feedback that determines the dynamics of the system and

Feedback systems

A system is an organised body of things, a set of relationships connecting the parts of complex whole together. Whenever humans group they constitute a system in which they are bound together by their interrelated actions and information exchanges.

Perhaps the central feature of human systems is their feedback nature. Feedback is a circle of interaction, a loop connecting one action or piece of information to another that is in turn connected to the first. The patterns of behaviour in such a loop are linked, each influencing the other and in turn responding to the behaviour of the other. The concept of a system in which the connections are feedback loops therefore involves mutual interdependence and circular causality.

In a feedback loop, variable A causally influences variable B, which then causally influences A, in turn feeding back to affect B again, and so on. This feedback connection can be positive in which case the behaviour of A reinforces the behaviour of B, which reinforces the behaviour of A. Feedback here is amplifying and leads to either virtuous or vicious circles of behaviour. Unstable equilibrium is an example of positive feedback.

Alternatively, feedback may be negative in which case the behaviour of A dampens the behaviour of B, which dampens the behaviour of A, and so on. Negative feedback is also self-reinforcing but in a damping way, diminishing and counteracting tendencies to move away from some given position. Negative feedback systems move strongly to stable equilibrium.

Feedback systems may be linear, where one response is proportional to the one which caused it, so keeping the system moving at a regular speed as it were. Or the system may be nonlinear where one response is more (or less) proportional to the one which caused it, so that each response is an increasingly exaggerated one, causing the speed of the system to accelerate or decelerate as it were.

Feedback with its circular causality makes it very difficult to define what is the cause and what is the effect, particularly where the system is nonlinear. An effect may easily be distant from its cause in both time and space and the links between cause and effect may even be lost in the complex detail of what happens.

therefore the nature of the change it has to cope with. When we talk about positive feedback and nonlinear systems, therefore, we are talking about systems in which the potential for under- and over-reaction, the potential for the escalation of tiny changes, are inbuilt characteristics of how the system behaves. What processes of strategic management are possible and effective will depend upon the dynamic and the consequent nature of change. Effective strategic management will take cognisance of the dynamics and the dynamics are a feature of feedback.

It is quite clear how negative feedback controls a system to produce stability. You can also, however, see the connections between feedback, dynamics and control if you consider a price war. The pattern of change, the dynamic, is an escalating vicious circle. It is a sequence of changes that have a predictable outcome – the bankruptcy of the players. That dynamic, or pattern of change, is a consequence of the fact that feedback in this case is positive or amplifying. Feedback has set up a self-reinforcing circle that is having increasingly disastrous consequences. The system is moving along a dynamic path that we may label as explosive equilibrium and it is rapidly heading out of control. This perfectly predictable equilibrium state of explosion and loss of control clearly does not lead to success. So far, it seems that negative feedback produces stability and control, while positive feedback generates instability and a loss of control.

However, to return to the example of positive feedback given above involving feedback loops between Sales & Marketing, Production and R&D departments as they developed a new product: one change led to further amplifying changes, positive feedback, and yet there was control. There was control because there were constraints – each department was significantly constrained by the power of the others. Control then takes on a self-organising form in the sense that the relative power of each department is exercising a controlling influence without anyone directing it. Amplifying feedback within constraints, unstable dynamics within boundaries, can lead to controlled behaviour even though no one party engaged in the interaction is in control. You can see, then, that there is something rather interesting, and rather complicated, about the operation of positive feedback within organisations – something which a focus on ordinary management alone leads us to overlook.

Having outlined the nature of organisations as feedback systems, we are now going to review how the dominant strand of the strategic management literature focuses on negative feedback, while writers who have had much less influence on practitioners have explored the impact of positive feedback. Then we will see how some writers have tried to combine the effects of both positive and negative feedback to provide models of the dynamics of organisational life. So, first consider, now in more detail, the nature and impact of negative feedback on organisational life.

8.3 NEGATIVE FEEDBACK AND EQUILIBRIUM

The concept of negative feedback is set out in *Key Concept 8.3*. To fix ideas on exactly what negative feedback means, consider, first, two commonly quoted examples: a domestic central heating system and the Watt steam engine governor.

A domestic heating system consists of an appliance and a regulator. The regulator contains a device that senses room temperature connected to a device that turns the heating appliance on and off. A desired temperature is set in the regulator. When the room temperature falls below this desired level, the control sensor detects the discrepancy between actual and desired states. The regulator responds to a negative discrepancy with a positive action – it turns the heat on. When the temperature rises above the desired level the opposite happens. By responding to the deviation of actual from desired levels in an opposite or negative way, the control system dampens any movement away from desired levels. The controls keep the room temperature close to a stable level over time utilising negative feedback. *Figure 8.4* illustrates this negative feedback loop.

Negative feedback

Negative feedback simply means that the outcome of a previous action is compared to some desired outcome and the discrepancy between the two is fed back as information that guides the next action in such a way that the discrepancy is reduced until it disappears. Thus when anything at all disturbs a system from its state of equilibrium it will return to that equilibrium if it is governed by some form of negative feedback control. Negative feedback is the process required to produce the dynamics of stability.

The same principle applies to the steam engine governor. As the boiler of the engine is stoked, steam pressure rises causing the engine to speed up. If this speed exceeds a preset desired level, the governor responds by opening a valve to release the steam and so pull the engine speed back to the desired level. As soon as the speed falls below the desired level the valve closes, steam pressure rises, and the engine speed increases to the desired level. Here too the operation of the control system is such that fluctuations around the desired level are damped and predictable. Stable equilibrium behaviour is thus preserved through the use of negative feedback. *Figure 8.4* also illustrates this example.

Negative or damping feedback is the mechanism that is widely used in nature and in engineering for automatic control or regulation. It is also used for this purpose in organisations – as we have already seen, all the processes of ordinary management are essentially negative feedback ones. And the point of central importance about negative feedback is that it is capable of moving a system to a state of stable equilibrium (see *Key Concept 8.4*).

Damping feedback loops and organisational control

The decision-making processes and control systems of an organisation are quite clearly feedback loops and we almost always think about them as negative, damping feedback.

For example, managers fix targets for profits and then prepare annual plans or budgets setting out the time paths for product volumes, process and costs required to yield those profit targets. The plans also establish the actions that are to be taken to secure projected volumes, prices and cost levels. As the business moves through time, outcomes are measured and compared with the plan projections to yield variances or deviations. Frequent monitoring of those variances prompts corrective action to bring performance indicators back into their planned paths. When profits fall below desired levels we take corrective action to increase them – negative feedback. When profits exceed target, then the target may be raised, or more usefully, managers may enquire into why this is happening. It may be that they are exploiting a short-term monopoly advantage, In this case, short-term profit may be high, but competitors will be attracted and customers may be alienated. From a long-term perspective it may there-

FIGURE 8.4
Negative feedback

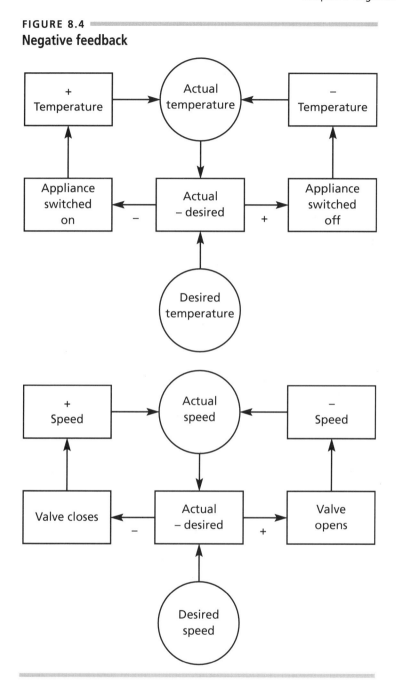

fore be wise to lower prices and pull profits back onto target. Time lags and unforeseen environmental changes will mean that the adjustments are never perfect. But when the control system is operating effectively and actual outcome should fluctuate, in a tightly constrained manner, around the planned levels. The feedback loop is illustrated in *Figure 8.5*.

Key Concept 8.4

Equilibrium

Equilibrium is a possible state of behaviour for a system. It takes a stable form when the behaviour of a system regularly repeats its past and when it is very difficult to change that behaviour to some other state. It requires significant change to shift a system from a state of stable equilibrium. For example, in economic theory markets are assumed always to tend to a state of stable equilibrium. If there is an increase in demand, then prices will rise to encourage an increase in supply to match the demand. If demand then stays constant, so will price and supply. Any chance movement of the price away from its equilibrium level will set in train changes in demand and supply that will rapidly pull price back to its equilibrium level. It will take a noticeable change in demand or supply to alter this behaviour.

Equilibrium can take an unstable form. Here the system will produce behaviour that diverges rapidly from its past state, but in a perfectly regular way. For example, a population may grow at a constant compound rate of growth, say doubling every five years. This is perfectly regular behaviour but it is explosively unstable because it cannot be sustained – sooner or later, the population will run into food constraints and collapse.

Dynamic equilibrium is a state in which a system continuously adapts to alterations in a continually changing environment.

The key point about all forms of equilibrium behaviour is that they are regular, orderly and predictable. Most theories of management and organisation have been developed within an equilibrium framework. Of course, to be regular, orderly and predictable, the links between cause and effect have to be clear cut. In equilibrium there are clear-cut links between cause and effect and consequently behaviour is predictable.

However, scientists are now explaining the functioning of nature in terms of behaviour that is far from equilibrium, a matter we will come to in Chapter 9. We can therefore no longer accept without question explanations that are based on unquestioned assumptions of equilibrium behaviour. Later chapters will explain far-from-equilibrium behaviour and what it might mean for explanations of strategic management.

The scheduling, budgetary and planning control systems of a business utilise negative feedback to operate in a damping manner in exactly the same way as central heating controls or steam engine governors. The outcome is supposed to be the same – the organisation should be kept on its stable, predetermined equilibrium path.

This idea of the dynamics of successful organisations is the most widely accepted one today and it is based upon cybernetics. You may wonder why it is necessary to go back to such basics and review our understanding of cybernetics – the reason is that I am proposing that we reflect at a very deep level on the fundamental way in which we are making sense of life in organisations. We cannot do that unless we understand the

FIGURE 8.5

Negative feedback in business control systems

theoretical foundations upon which today's dominant understanding of organisational life is based, namely, the ordinary management perspective. We are exploring, in some detail, the negative feedback basis of ordinary management so that we may understand clearly what its limitations are.

8.4 NEGATIVE FEEDBACK, CONTROL AND CYBERNETIC THEORY

Cybernetics is an application of the engineer's idea of control to human activity. During the Second World War, the superiority of the German air force led British scientists to consider how they might improve the accuracy of anti-aircraft defences. One of these scientists, Norbert Wiener, saw a way of treating the evasive action of enemy aircraft as a time series that could be manipulated mathematically to improve the gunner's predictions of the enemy plane's future position:

> When we desire a motion to follow a given pattern, the difference between the pattern and the actually performed motion is used as a new input to cause the part regulated to move in such a way as to bring the motion closer to that given pattern. (*Wiener, 1948, p. 6*)

This thought prompted Wiener and his colleagues to see the importance of feedback loops in most human actions – a loop in which the gap between desired and actual performance of an act just past is fed back as a determinant of the next action (see *Figure 8.6*).

If you are trying to hit an object by throwing a ball at it and you miss because you aimed too far to the right, you then use the information from this miss to alter the point at which you aim the next shot: you aim further to the left, trying to offset the last error. In this sense the feedback is negative – it prompts you to move in the opposite direction. You keep doing this until you hit the object. Wiener and his colleagues saw how this negative feedback was essential to controlled behaviour and how breaking the feedback link led to pathological behaviour. Those who do not correct their behaviour in the light of what they have learned about the consequences of such behaviour are in some sense ill.

The systems scientists also realised that when such negative feedback becomes too fast, or too sensitive, the result could be uncontrolled cycles of over- and under-achievement of the desired state. So for example, you may be taking a shower and find the water too hot. This leads you to raise the flow of cold water. If you do not take sufficient account of the lag between your action and the subsequent drop in temperature you may increase the cold water flow again. This may make the water too cold so you raise the flow of hot water which then makes it too hot again. Unless you get the time lag between your action and its consequence right, you may increase the hot water flow until it becomes too hot again. So, if your negative feedback control system is operating too rapidly, the temperature of the water will fluctuate in an unstable manner instead of settling down to a desired level. Negative feedback systems can be highly unstable.

FIGURE 8.6
Negative feedback in cybernetics

Those studying such systems therefore became very concerned to establish the conditions for stability and instability in negative feedback control systems. As a result of this kind of work governments came to accept that their attempts to remove cycles in the level of activity in the economy were usually counterproductive. Just as the economy was recovering from a slump, impatient governments tended to cut taxes and increase expenditure, so fuelling an excessive boom accompanied by rapid inflation. Just as that boom was collapsing on its own, fearful governments increased taxes and cut expenditure, so pushing the economy into a deeper slump than it would otherwise have experienced. To secure stability through negative feedback you must be able to predict not only the outcome of an action but also the time lag between an action and its outcome. The design of a control system that works at the right speed and the right level of sensitivity relies upon such predictions. Given the ability to predict, it is then possible to specify in a precise mathematical way exactly what conditions will produce stability for any negative feedback system.

Having outlined what cybernetics is all about we can now turn to how it has been applied to the control of organisations. Two writers have been of major importance in developing cybernetic theory, particularly as it applies to organisations: *W. Roy Ashby (1945, 1952, 1956)* and *Stafford Beer (1959/67, 1966)*. In this chapter we are trying to identify what those who focus on negative feedback systems have to say about the forces driving such systems and the patterns of behaviour they display. On these matters Ashby and Stafford Beer have made the key points set out in the paragraphs below.

Goal-seeking adaptation to the environment

Cybernetics postulates that two main forces drive an organisation over time. The first force is the drive to achieve some purpose: from this perspective organisations are goal-seeking systems and the goal drives their actions. The second force arises because organisations are connected through feedback links to their environments: they are subsystems of an even larger environmental suprasystem. Reaching the goal requires being adapted to those environments.

Thus, in the cybernetics tradition, organisations are driven by attraction to a predetermined desired state which is equilibrium adaptation to the environment. The state a given organisation comes to occupy is determined by the nature of its environment.

For example, on this view, a company operating in say the electronics industry may be driven by the goal of achieving a 20 per cent return on its capital. In order to achieve this it must deliver what its customers want. If customers have stable requirements for standardised low-cost silicon chips to be used as components in their own products, then our company has to adapt to this environment by employing mass production methods to produce standardised products at lower costs than its rivals. It will have to support these production methods with particular forms of organisational structure, control systems and cultures: functional structures, bureaucratic control systems, and conservative, strongly shared cultures. Our company will look much the same as its rivals in the same market because the overall shape of each is determined by the same environment.

If, however, the electronics market is a turbulent one with rapidly changing technology and many niche markets where customers look for customised chips, then we will get very different kinds of organisation, according to cybernetics theory. Our company will then have to adapt by emphasising R&D and continually developing new products to differentiate itself from its rivals. It will support these production methods with particular forms of structure, control systems and culture: decentralised structures of separate profit centres, greater emphasis on informal controls, and change-loving cultures.

Cybernetics, the reader will by now have recognised, is a contingency theory (see *Key Concept 5.4* in Chapter 5).

But how do organisations come to be adapted to their environments and achieve their goals?

Regulators

According to cybernetics, organisations deploy regulators that utilise negative feedback in order to reach their goals and the desired states of adaptation to their environments. The central problem is how to keep an organisation at, or near to, some desired state and the answer to the problem lies in the design of the regulator, that is, the design of the control system. Cybernetics is the science of control and management is the profession of control. At the heart of that science and that profession lies the design of regulators. You can see how this kind of thinking accords with one of the dominant paradigm's major concerns – that to do with being in control.

There are two types of regulator: the error-controlled regulator and the anticipatory regulator. In Ashby's scheme, disturbances from its environment (D in *Figure 8.7*) impact on the organisation (T in the figure) leading to an outcome (E in the figure). The problem is where to put the regulator (R in *Figure 8.7*).

Anticipatory regulation

If we place the regulator so that it senses the disturbance before that disturbance hits the organisation, then we can take anticipatory action and offset the undesirable impact of the disturbance on the outcome (the top part (A) of *Figure 8.7*).

An immediately recognisable example of this kind of regulator is of course a planning system. Such a regulator takes the form of a sensing device using market research questionnaires or analyses of market statistics. On the basis of these, realistically achievable desired states are established. These desired states are forecasts of sales volumes, prices and costs at some future point; that is, the positions and postures required to achieve the performance target or goal. Action plans to realise these forecasts are also prepared; that is, patterns in future actions are identified. As the company moves through time it continually senses the environment, picks up

FIGURE 8.7
Regulation in control systems

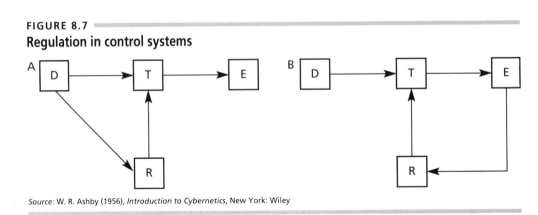

Source: W. R. Ashby (1956), *Introduction to Cybernetics*, New York: Wiley

disturbances before they occur, and prepares planned actions to deal with them before they hit the organisation. This is the ideal control without making mistakes: preventing deviations from plan occurring in the first place. It was referred to as feed forward control in the section on implementing strategic plans in Chapter 5.

Error-controlled regulation

If it is not possible to establish such an anticipatory regulator, or if such a regulator cannot work perfectly, then we have to place a regulator so that it can sense the outcome once that outcome has occurred. This is the classic error-controlled regulator (the lower part (B) of *Figure 8.7*).

An immediately recognisable example of this type of regulator is the monitoring, reviewing and corrective action system of an organisation. It is what a company's board of directors does each month when it meets to review what has happened to the business over the past month, monitors how the performance measures are moving, and decides what to do to correct deviations from plan that have already occurred.

It is clearly preferable to anticipate disturbances as far as possible because there are time lags: first in detecting what is happening; then in deciding what should be done; then in doing it; and then in the outcome materialising from the action. These time lags mean that relying entirely on the error-control system will not produce the intended performance. Since it takes time to correct a deviation, and since time lags can cause instability in performance, we should aim to prevent deviation in the first place. But anticipating disturbances relies on the ability to forecast them and this can never be perfect. Therefore an organisation will have to rely on both anticipatory and error-control regulators. This is exactly what the managers of a business do when they prepare budgets and plans and then monitor and review the environment and the company's performance each month. Note, however, that even error-controlled regulators depend on some form of predictability. When a deviation between a desired and an actual outcome appears, you take action in one period. When the next period comes around and the deviation has still not been removed, do you take further action? You would only do so if the last period's action has already had its effect and that effect was insufficient. You would not do so if the effects were still working their way through. This means that when you take a corrective action you have to be able to predict the timing of its effects if error-controlled control is to be reliable.

Reliance on statistics

An essential requirement for the most effective application of this whole approach to control is the availability of quantitative forecasts of future changes in the organisation and its environment, as well as forecasts of the consequences of proposed actions to deal with these changes. The tools we have for such quantitative forecasts are those derived from statistical theory. Statistical forecasting methods are based on the assumption that the disturbances hitting the organisation from its environment take the form of groupings of large numbers of closely similar events that can be described by a probability distribution. It is implicitly assumed that uniquely uncertain events will be relatively unimportant.

This distinction can be clarified by two examples. An example of a unique event is the Iraqi invasion of Kuwait in August 1990. It is of course unique because it only occurs once. We cannot describe it in terms of an observed probability distribution – either it occurs or it does not. Because of its uniqueness we cannot apply standard statistical techniques to forecast its occurrence. An example of a grouping of events that can be described by a probability distribution is the number of television sets a company sells each month, or the number of faulty television sets customers return to the company each month. By looking at the records for a number of months we will be able to say that the most likely level of demand is say 1000 units and usually some 10 are returned each month. These different possibilities are illustrated in *Figure 8.8*. If the business is primarily affected by events that can be described by probability distributions we will be able to use tried-and-tested statistical techniques to forecast them. Statistical techniques require data generated by many repetitions. If most of the events hitting our business are unique we will not be able to rely on these techniques. If we cannot use these techniques, then practising anticipatory and error-controlled control in the way proposed by cybernetics will not be possible.

FIGURE 8.8
Distribution of events

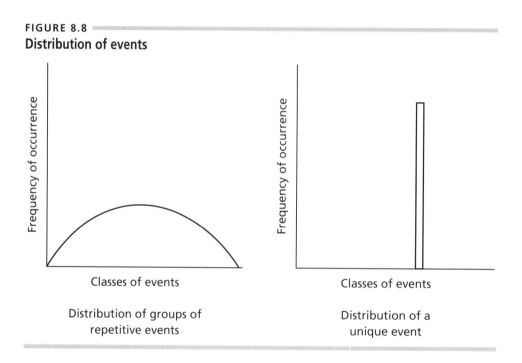

Distribution of groups of
repetitive events

Distribution of a
unique event

The law of requisite variety

However, cybernetics sees the main cause of the difficulty in designing regulators not in terms of the uniqueness of events, but in terms of their variety, or complexity. Variety is the number of discernably different states the environment can present to the organisation and the number of discernably different responses the organisation can make to the environment. It is the function of the regulator to reduce variety so retaining stability within a system, despite high variety outside it. That is, the huge variety of disturbances presented by the environment must be neutralised by a huge number of responses such that the outcome can match the one desirable state selected in advance that will fit the environment. In order to be able to do this, the regulator must be designed to have as much variety as the environment; the number of potential responses must match the number of potential disturbances so that they can cancel each other out and produce a single desired outcome. This is Ashby's Law of Requisite Variety: the complexity and speed of the firm's response must match the complexity and speed of change of the environment. *Key Concept 8.5* gives examples of the forms which requisite variety might take.

In order to see the relevance of this notion of requisite variety to ordinary management models of strategy-making, let us go back to the visionary/ideological model we discussed in Chapter 6.

You will recall from Chapter 6 that these political and cultural processes enable top managers to be 'in control' because they articulate a belief system; that is, a vision for the future and an ideology. Members of the organisation are inspired and persuaded to believe in the vision and ideology that then constitutes a strongly shared culture. Contained by this belief system, people in an organisation then conduct many experimental actions to discover how to reach the vision. Order is sustained by common culture and common intention.

Central to this visionary/ideological explanation of how successful organisations are controlled and developed is the leader as a charismatic political figure who builds and sustains a coalition of supporters. Political activity in this model takes the form of individual product or issue champions who detect, select and build support for particular issues and projects. They use temporary, informal, multi-discipline teams to develop innovative ideas and try them out in experimental form. To keep this overt political activity stable, vested interests must not be threatened. This loop can easily become an amplifying and thus destabilising loop. In the visionary/ideological model of control and development this does not happen because of the strongly shared belief system.

So, in the visionary/ideological scheme, the overt political feedback loop, depicted in *Figure 4.5* in Chapter 4, is kept stable through the way in which the culture and cognition loop is managed. In the visionary/ideological system, strongly shared mental models are promoted and this greatly cuts down on contradiction and conflict. It gives stability to the political system. People are controlled by belief rather than rules and regulations or authority.

This model of strategic decision-making and control retains organisational intention to do with the long-run state managers are trying to achieve but introduces emergent, experimental ways of finding out how to achieve the intended state – Hofstede's trial-and-error control (see *Figure 2.9* in Chapter 2). Those emergent experimental ways are conditioned by managers' mental models or paradigms and how they share these, that is, the culture of their organisation. These emergent experimental ways place particular emphasis on political interaction and upon learning about the outcome of actions.

This model of strategic control and development is fundamental to the popular approach to success prescribed by writers such as *Tom Peters (1982, 1985)*. He presses managers to form a vision, a picture of a future state, and then reach that vision by undertaking hectic trial-and-error actions that satisfy criteria set by shared values and

The law of requisite variety

According to cybernetics an organisation must achieve the goal of continuing adaptation to its environment if it is to survive and succeed. In order to so adapt it has to employ a control system or regulator. It will successfully adapt when the complexity and speed of the responses enabled by its regulator match the complexity and speed of the changes occurring in its environment; that is when it controls its business according to the law of requisite variety.

Suppose an organisation faces a stable environment in which changes follow regular predictable patterns. Then it will succeed when it uses an anticipatory regulator of the comprehensive planning kind. Here it forecasts the changes that will occur and prepares a single comprehensive plan to deal with all the future changes it faces over a given time period: it decides in advance on the sequence of actions it is to follow for a particular time period then it implements that sequence of actions.

In this case we have a simple rather than a complex environment. We also have an environment in which there is little variety: it is regular and we are able to predict the single pattern it will follow in the future. Because the environment is simple and low in variety we can design a regulator that is simple and low in variety; we can establish one single set of intended actions, the comprehensive plan, which we can then follow.

Now suppose that the environment is more complex and displays greater variety. This inevitably means that we have greater difficulty in forecasting what will happen. Using the simple regulator – one plan for the future – is likely to lead to failure because we will not be responding to a great many of the unforeseeable events that are occurring. To succeed, the regulator must be given greater variety. This can be done by preparing a number of different forecast scenarios (see Chapter 5, the section on financial acceptability) and putting together contingency plans for each scenario. As it becomes clearer which scenario is unfolding we can pull the requisite contingency plan from the file and implement it.

In effect we make the whole planning procedure more flexible and keep changing our long-term plans every few months in order to match them to unforeseen changes as those unforeseen changes emerge. So, we may have one plan for an environment in which oil prices are low, exchange rates favourable, rates of growth in demand high, own product prices high, and competitor moves sluggish. We can then develop a different plan for the reverse of all of these environmental conditions, or for only some of them.

Notice how we respond to a higher level of complexity and variety by increasing the complexity and variety of the regulator, in this case the planning system, the range of plans available, and the frequency with which they are changed.

At some point the changes in the environment may become so rapid and unpredictable that we have to give up on even contingency planning; too many contingencies may arise to make it practicable to have a plan ready for all of them. The regulator will therefore no longer take the form of a planning system.

Instead it may take the form of a loose, changing set of project teams or, what Peters and Waterman called skunkworks (Peters & Waterman, 1982). (We discussed this in Chapter 6 under the heading of the visionary/ideological model.) Here each team is working on some project to deal with some possible change in the environment. Each team conducts trials to test out possible market responses. One team will be experimenting with one kind of product that might suit say a rapid-growth low-oil-price environment and another may be experimenting with a product that suits a slow-growth high-oil-price environment. The regulator takes the form of trial-and-error testing of responses that the changing environment might require. The organisation is thus developing a large number of potential responses to a large number of potential environmental changes. Those experiments that succeed are continued with and those that fail are abandoned. The more experiments conducted, the greater and faster the action, the more likely the organisation is to deal with what the environment throws at it.

Here then we have a regulator that has even more variety and complexity built into it so as to match the much higher level of complexity and variety in the environment. The visionary/ideological model of strategic management depends crucially upon the validity of this idea and as we shall see in Chapter 9, in the section on what chaos means for organisations, its validity is questionable.

logical connection to the existing business. But what conditions need to prevail if a process of trial-and-error action according to given criteria is dependably to lead to a vision decided in advance of the action? In other words, what is it necessary to assume about the nature of an organisation and its environment in order to make it sensible to prescribe this form of control and development?

The answer to this question is provided by Ashby's Law of Requisite Variety (see *Key Concept 8.4*). Once again, this law states that a system will remain stable if its control system, or regulator, displays the same level of variety as the environment in which the control is to be exerted. The variety of the environment is simply the number of changes, or random shocks, it generates and the variety of the regulator in a system is simply the number of responses it can make to those changes or shocks. This is a rather elaborate way of saying that the faster the environment changes the faster the system has to respond to stay stable. What is not so obvious, however, is the mechanism that is proposed for responding. Ashby's law says that it is enough to have the same number of responses as environmental shocks, not that each response to each shock has to be the right one. In other words, the mechanism is trial and error and all that is necessary is to get the level or speed of the trial and error right. What is the justification for this?

The justification is the law of large numbers, or probability. If large numbers of random shocks, or unforeseeable changes, keep hitting a system and if that system undertakes large numbers of basically random small trial actions in response, then obviously only some random actions will match some of the random shocks in the sense of being appropriate responses. Most will not but, because of the large numbers involved, the inappropriate responses will tend to cancel each other out – the laws of large numbers. Provided that a system acts fast enough it will maintain stability and move toward its goal but only if shocks and responses are closely similar, or repetitive events of the kind we get, for example, when we toss a coin, where the result always is either heads or tails. It is only with large numbers of repetitive events that we can rely on the cancelling-out of mismatches between random shocks and random actions because it is only then that the law of large numbers works.

It will be shown in Chapter 9 that a nonlinear feedback system may operate in conditions where no specific event is ever repeated in exactly the same way. The probability of any specific event occurring is therefore infinitely small. Each specific event is unique, falling only into general qualitative categories in which items bear a family resemblance to each other. An organisation does not typically get a large number of chances to repeat events that bear a family resemblance close enough to apply probability in even an approximate way. This is essentially what we mean by truly open-ended change.

Under these circumstances there is no guarantee that trial-and-error mismatches with random environmental shocks will cancel out. Large numbers of random actions, even within boundaries set by logical connection with the existing business and core values, cannot be relied on as a search technique that will take the business to its intended vision. The visionary/ideological form of control therefore requires a causal connection between the vision and the actions required to realise it. It can therefore be applied only in situations of closed and contained change and attempts to apply it in other situations are based on unquestioned assumptions that clearly do not apply.

The visionary/ideological approach puts forward a very different mechanism for control, when 'compared to the long-term planning approach – it adds the loop of overt politics and the loop of cognition and culture to the specification of the control system (see *Figure 4.15* in Chapter 4). But both approaches seek to do the same thing. They are both concerned with the intentional adaptation of the business to its environment. Both see success as flowing from the maintenance of order and stability. The one secures order through hierarchy, formal rules, procedures and analytical techniques. The other secures order through ideology and belief. Both proclaim that a system of some sort, bureaucratic or ideological, can be installed to secure success. For both, prior, central intention and uniformity in behaviour provide the constraints that allow top executives to be in control of the outcome of strategic activity. Both propose a negative feedback form of control in which an organisation is kept to a predetermined path of some sort. The dynamic for both is the drive to equilibrium adaptation in which there are clear connections between cause and effect, even though we may not always be aware of what those connections are. Both are concerned with producing regular patterns in behaviour. Both can apply only to closed and contained change situations. Both reflect the paradigm of the stable equilibrium organisation (see *Key Concept 8.6*).

Since neither the planning/monitoring nor the ideological forms of control are practical propositions when managers wish to cope successfully with open-ended change, what is the form of control they will have to rely on? To answer this question we have to develop our model of the organisational control system further and this is what we will do in Chapter 11. Now, however, we return to our examination of cybernetics.

The stable equilibrium organisation

While a system operates in a state of equilibrium it continues to follow exactly the same pattern of behaviour, until some external disturbance promotes a change. That pattern may be a very simple one of sticking to a constant value or it may be one of some kind of regular cycle. So the behaviour of a system in equilibrium may be one of change but that change will be regular and thus perfectly predictable.

A stable equilibrium organisation, therefore, is one where internal behaviour is harmonious, all the elements of the organisation and its strategies are consistent, and the organisation remains fully adapted to its environment. The stable equilibrium organisation follows a predictable course into the future, with no surprises. New developments are dictated by changes in the environment. This idea constitutes a management paradigm in which successful organisations are seen as those moving closer to a state of stable equilibrium, disturbed only by environmental changes that it was not possible to predict. Instability comes from outside and can be reduced by gathering and analysing more data and making more effective forecasts. This represents a particular view of dynamics.

Cybernetics and causality

The law of requisite variety makes it unnecessary, according to the cybernetics tradition, to understand the internal feedback structures of the organisation and the environment. Let me explain.

Cyberneticists recognised that feedback means circular causality – event A causes event B which then causes event A (see *Key Concept 8.7* on the nature of causality). They argued that we can determine the direction this circular causality takes for any pair of events simply by observing which precedes which in a large number of cases. But when we are dealing with large numbers of interconnected pairs it all becomes too difficult. These internal structures are so complex that we cannot hope to understand them – they constitute a 'black box'. Note how an unquestioned assumption is being made here. Those arguing this position are assuming that there is always a specific cause for each specific outcome, the problem being that it is all too complex for us to understand. We will see later in Chapter 9 that there is another way to tackle this difficulty: it may be impossible to reduce our understanding to specific cause-and-effect links because the links themselves are lost in the detail of what happens; the alternative is then to think in terms of patterns in the behaviour of systems as a whole.

The cyberneticists, however, argued that causal connections exist but we do not need to understand them because we can observe a particular type of disturbance impacting on a system and we can observe the outcome of that disturbance, that is, how the system responds. If the regulator has requisite variety, that is, a large enough variety of responses to counteract the variety of disturbances, then it will normally respond to a particular type of disturbance in the same way. From large numbers of observations of such regularities we can establish statistical connections between particular types of disturbance and particular organisational responses.

The importance of this notion of causal connection is that it allows us to use statistical techniques to control in a negative feedback way, despite system complexity so great that we cannot hope to understand it, at least according to the cyberneticists. What matters to them is pragmatic factors such as what we observe and what we do. We do not need to devote much energy to understanding and explaining, they claim, because observing and doing is what matters in a complex world. These writers were not concerned about the dynamic patterns of behaviour that organisations generated or with the complexities of the internal workings of the organisation. No importance is attached to perceptions, to pictures of, or feelings for, the patterns of behaviour generated by systems as a whole.

Note how the law of requisite variety and the view taken of complex causality amount to an assumption that the laws of large numbers, or probability, apply. Large numbers of random disturbances from the environment are to be offset by equally large number of responses from the organisation. But since we cannot know the complex causal relationship between these, according to cybernetic theory, we will have to rely on a process of cancelling out. Because causality is so complex we cannot determine exactly the right response for each disturbance, so some responses will be too weak and others too strong, but taken together the deviations from what is required should cancel out over large numbers.

Now, this is only possible if the disturbances and responses are not unique; that is, they do not take the form of a disturbance requiring one and only one response at a particular point in time if it is to be handled effectively in goal-seeking terms. If amplifying feedback could cause a tiny disturbance to escalate, then it would require an immediate response of exactly the right offsetting nature to stop this happening. If such escalation was not immediately stopped it could swamp the behaviour of the whole system – the cancelling out of inappropriate responses to disturbances would not occur. Without this cancelling out, the law of requisite variety would not be enough to secure control.

This assumption about uniqueness and large numbers is therefore of great significance to the view we have of control, a matter which we will be returning to in Chapters 9 and 11. There we will discover that successful organisations are characterised by amplifying feedback with the result that the law of requisite variety is not a useful way of thinking about control. We have already seen that the law of requisite variety underlies the visionary/ideological approach to strategic management. Its inapplicability therefore undermines the usefulness of that way of thinking about strategic management, at least if that management is to have any relevance to open-ended situations.

Cybernetics, then, is an approach that seeks to control an organisation by using feedback without understanding the feedback structure of the organisation itself. It sees effective regulators as those that cause the system to be largely self-regulating, automatically handling the disturbances which the environment bombards it with. It sees effective regulators as those that maintain continual equilibrium with the environment. The result is stable behaviour, predictable in terms of probabilities of specific events and times.

These aspects of the cybernetic tradition have had an important impact on the prescriptions for designing management control and information systems. The assumptions upon which cybernetics is based are shared by rational, scientific

Key Concept 8.7

The nature of causality

The dominant way of thinking about the relationship between cause and effect in Western culture is what we might call linear and unidirectional. We observe some variable Y whose behaviour we wish to explain. We immediately regard it as dependent and look for other 'independent' variables, X_1, X_2, . . ., that are causing it. We usually reason that more of a cause will lead to proportionally more of the effect.

The usual explanation for success is that it is caused by a particular culture, a particular management style, a particular control system. The more we apply that culture, style, or control system the more successful we will be. We say that the demand for our product depends upon the behaviour of our customers. Opposition parties always say that the government of the day has caused the recession and the inflation. More of the government's policies will, they say, lead to more recession and more inflation. All of this is what is meant by straight-forward unidirectional, linear connections between cause and effect.

Scientists, both social and natural, are increasingly realising that this view of the relationship between cause and effect is far too simple and leads to inadequate understanding of a system's behaviour. Greater insight comes from thinking in terms of the mutual or circular causality we find in feedback loops. The demand for a product does no depend simply on customer behaviour; it also depends upon what the producing firm does in terms of price and quality: the firm affects the customer who then affects the firm. Management style may cause success but success affects the style managers adopt. The government's policies may cause recession and inflation, but recession and inflation may also cause the policies they adopt.

When we think of organisms and organisations as systems then we become aware of more complex forms of causality to do with interconnection and interdependence, where everything affects everything else. In addition to the circular causality and interdependence of feedback systems, there is also nonlinearity. This means that one variable can have a more than proportional effect open another. Nonlinear feedback systems then involve very complex connections between cause and effect, a matter we will discuss in some detail in Chapter 9. It may become unclear what cause and effect mean. The links between them may become distant in time and space and those links may even disappear for all practical purposes. If in these circumstances we proceed as if simple linear links exist even if we do not know what they are, then we are likely to undertake actions that yield unintended and surprising results.

Most managers today think in terms of linear, unidirectional causality; and main-stream strategic management prescriptions are based on this kind of thinking too.

schools of management thought. These assumptions are still the dominant ones in the mental models employed by managers today and they underlie the planning and visionary/ideological approaches to strategic management. But as we shall see in later chapters, what cybernetics omits makes the whole approach of only limited use. In cybernetics:

- Behaviour patterns themselves are thought not to be interesting enough to warrant special comment.
- Circular causation is recognised but then sidestepped by saying it is too complex to understand.
- No particular importance is attached to nonlinearity: that is, the possibility that one even may lead to a more-than-proportional response in terms of the next event is not seen to have any special implications.
- Positive, self-reinforcing or amplifying feedback is largely ignored.

The key points on organisational dynamics made by the cybernetics tradition are summarised in *Figure 8.9*. Whenever managers use planning, monitoring, reviewing and corrective action forms of control, they are making the same assumptions about the world as those made by cyberneticists. Whenever management consultants install such systems they too make the same assumptions. Whenever managers engage in trial-and-error actions in the belief that this will take them to an envisioned end-point in a turbulent environment, that is, whenever they implement the advice of *Peters and Waterman (1982)*, then they are assuming that the law of requisite variety is valid. The problem is that managers and consultants are normally not all that aware of what they are assuming. They hardly ever ask whether their assumptions make sense or not.

FIGURE 8.9

Cybernetics: main points on organisational dynamics

- Organisations are goal-seeking feedback systems adapting to their environments by utilising negative feedback.
- Change is caused by the environment to which the organisation is linked by feedback loops. Instability comes from the environment.
- Feedback links mean circular causality. This makes the relationships so complex that we cannot understand their causal structures. But we can observe statistical links between disturbances and organisational responses.
- Predictability of specific events and their timings is therefore possible in a probabilistic sense. Disturbances coming from the environment are not primarily unique.
- Effective control requires anticipation and a control system that contains as much variety as the environment.
- Nonlinearity and positive feedback are of no particular importance.
- Effective organisations are self-regulating, an automatic mechanical feature flowing from the way the control system is structured.
- Success is a state of stability, harmony and consistency.

8.5 NEGATIVE FEEDBACK AND SYSTEMS ADAPTING TO THEIR ENVIRONMENT: GENERAL SYSTEMS THEORY

Around the same time as the development of cybernetics, there also appeared the closely related ideas of general systems theory. In a number of papers and books between 1945 and 1968 the German biologist *von Bertalanfy* put forward the idea that organisms, as well as human organisations and societies, are open systems. They are systems because they consist of a number of component subsystems that are interrelated and interdependent on each other. They are open because they are connected by feedback links to their environments, or suprasystems of which they are a part (see *Illustration 8.1*).

Each subsystem within a system and each system within its environment has a boundary separating it from other subsystems and other systems. For example, the sales department in an organisation is a subsystem separated by a boundary from the production and accounting departments. One organisation such as IBM is a system separated by a boundary from the other organisations and individuals that form its environment.

Within each system or subsystem, people occupy roles, they conduct sets of activities, and they engage in interrelationships with others both within their part of the system and in other parts or other systems.

Each subsystem within a system and each system within an environment is open in the sense that it imports materials, labour, money and information from other subsystems or systems and in turn exports outputs, money and information to other subsystems and systems.

Open systems explanations of managing and organising therefore focus attention on:

● behaviour of people within a subsystem or system;
● nature of the boundary around a subsystem or system;
● nature of the relationships across the boundaries between subsystems and systems;
● requirements of managing the boundary.

The open system concept provides a tool for understanding the relationship between:

● the technical and the social aspects of an organisation;
● the parts and the whole organisation (for example, the individual and the group, the individual and the organisation);
● the whole organisation and the environment.

Negative feedback

Changing one component in an open system will clearly have knock-on effects in many other components because of the prevalence of interconnection. Changes in the environment will have an impact on changes in the subsystems of an organisation. What happens in one system will affect what happens in another system and that in turn will affect the first.

You can see the importance of the insight provided by open systems theory if you consider how the technical subsystem of an organisation is interconnected with its social subsystem (*Trist & Branforth, 1951*).

Scientific, technically rational management tends to concentrate on the technical subsystem. This system consists of the primary tasks that the organisation is there to carry out: for example, the techniques, technology and sets of tasks required to produce coal in the case of a coal mining business. The prescription for success made by the scientific management school is to make the task subsystem as efficient as possible. So, if you introduce the latest technology for mining coal together with rules and

Illustration
8.1

The organisation as an open system

Kast and Rosenzweig (1970) conceived of the organisation in terms of suprasystems and subsystems:

- *Environmental suprasystem.* This can be divided into general societal and specific task systems. The general environment system covers the culture of the society of which the organisation is a part, its general level of technology, its politics, and so on. The task systems include customers, suppliers, competitors and so on. The more complex and unstable the environmental system, the more complex and differentiated the internal structuring of the organisation will have to be to cope.
- *Goals and values subsystems.* These flow from relationships between five levels: individuals within the organisation; groups of people within the organisation; the organisation as a whole; the task environments; and society at large.
- *Technical subsystem.* This relates to the knowledge required to perform tasks. It includes the technology of production specific to the organisation, the degrees of specialisation and automation required and applied, and the extent to which tasks are routine and non-routine.
- *Psychological subsystem.* This is created by individuals and groups in interaction. Individual behaviour and motivation, status and roles, group dynamics and political interactions are all part of this subsystem. It is clearly influenced by all the other subsystems and suprasystems.
- *Structural subsystem.* This covers the ways in which tasks are divided up and then integrated again. Organisational charts and job definitions, as well as formal communication flows, are the more visible manifestations of this subsystem. It also includes the informal organisation with its networks of personal contacts and casual information flows.
- *Managerial subsystem.* This spans the entire organisation and it relates the organisation to its environment, developing goals and plans, designing structures, and establishing control processes. Its primary role is an integrating one. ∎

regulations about quality and efficiency to govern the work of coal miners, then you should succeed according to scientific management. Success here depends primarily on the technical subsystem.

The behavioural school of management, on the other hand, focuses primarily on the psycho-social subsystem. Its prescriptions for success stress the establishment of a social system in which people are motivated and participate in making decisions about the nature of the tasks and the technology. To succeed you must consult those who perform the organisation's primary tasks, involve them in decision-making, and introduce reward structures that will motivate them to operate efficiently. Success here depends primarily on the social subsystem.

The insight that comes from open systems theory is that the technical and social systems are so interconnected that it makes no sense to regard one as dominant and the other as subordinate. Both subsystems have to be handled together in a manner that takes account of their interdependence.

The importance of this interconnection was demonstrated many years ago in a study of the coal mining industry in the UK by *Trist & Branforth (1951)*. In the late 1940s, the British coal industry introduced the more efficient long-wall method of mining coal. This technology, however, required changes in the set of tasks performed by coal miners. These changes broke up the cooperative teams in which miners were accustomed to working, teams that reflected their social arrangements in the coal mining villages in which they lived. Because of the consequent resistance to working in the new way, the technology failed to yield its technical potential.

The message is that, if changes are to succeed, then they have to be based on a realistic understanding of the interconnection, or feedback, between the social and the technical subsystems. And that interconnection is not simply taken account of by introducing participation or reward schemes for individuals. Instead, general systems theory prescribes a match between the two subsystems, one that establishes stable equilibrium.

Like cybernetics therefore, the general systems strand of thinking sees an organisation as a feedback system. It also sees that feedback system as one that maintains equilibrium with its environment, and between its parts, by utilising the mechanisms of negative feedback.

Paradox and conflict

In general systems theory, open systems are thought of as having maintenance subsystems to sustain orderly relationships between the parts of the system (*Lawrence & Lorsch, 1967*). In an organisation this would be the management information and control systems and the cultures that keep people working harmoniously together. However, it is recognised that these maintenance systems are conservative by nature. They are intended to hold the system together; to prevent it from changing too rapidly; to keep it efficiently carrying out its main tasks. The inevitable consequence of this maintenance form of control is that the overall system and its subsystems become out of balance as time goes by and things change. They become out of balance with each other and with the environment.

Note how close this idea is to that which Miller talks about in describing trajectories that take organisations to excess (see Chapter 4). Also note the similarity to Pascale's idea of organisations moving to a state of 'fit', which was discussed in Chapter 3 and will be reviewed at the end of this chapter.

But organisations also have adaptive mechanisms that promote change so as to keep them in dynamic equilibrium with the environment. These two subsystems, the maintenance and the adaptive, inevitably conflict but successful organisations sustain a stable balance between them, according to general systems theory.

Note that general systems theory recognises fundamental conflict inherent in the structure of the system, the paradox of stability and instability, but assumes that successful systems deal with this by sustaining equilibrium. Recall that Pascale proposes that success occurs when the conflict is sustained and the paradoxical forces rearranged in a dialectical process.

Differentiation and integration

Lawrence & Lorsch (1967) used the conceptual approach of open systems to research the functioning of a number of large organisations. They concluded that as organisations increase in size they differentiate into parts, and the more they differentiate, the more difficult becomes the consequent task of integration.

So as the environment becomes more complex and as they grow in size, companies differentiate into functions – finance, operations, sales and so on. But each part or function then faces the problem of relating to the other parts, if the firm is to operate effectively. Integrating what people in the production department do with what those in the sales or finance departments do then becomes more and more of a problem.

As organisations deal with their external environment they become differentiated into separate units, each dealing with a part of the environment. Think of large multi-national companies, such as ICI or IBM, with perhaps hundreds of different subsidiary companies across the world. They have reached advanced stages of differentiation and face well-known and very difficult-to-solve problems of integrating all their activities.

The authors found a relationship between variables external to the organisation and the states of differentiation and integration within that organisation. They found that organisations become more differentiated as their environments become more diverse.

Citibank operates in a large number of countries, a complex environment, through a great many national subsidiaries. This is a differentiated organisation. Since the environment demands more interdependence and cooperation, the organisation responds with greater integration. So, Citibank superimposes upon its national subsidiaries a central activity to serve its multinational clients wishing to deal with one central point, not hundreds of subsidiaries (*Buzzell, 1984*).

As environments become more diverse and organisations more differentiated, the tasks of integration become greater, leading to a proliferation of complex integrating devices. Citibank finds that conflicts grow up between the national subsidiaries and the central body dealing with multinational clients. It has to set up rules and systems to try to resolve the conflicts.

Lawrence and Lorsch also found that the more unpredictable the environment becomes the more decentralised the organisation becomes, pushing the locus of decision-making down the hierarchy. We encountered this kind of reasoning in Chapter 5 when discussing contingency theory. The general systems approach is also a contingency theory. (See *Key Concept 5.4* in Chapter 5.)

Note how general systems theorists clearly recognise fundamental paradoxes of organising: the need simultaneously to divide tasks up and to integrate them; the need for maintenance control systems for stability but the inevitable drift from the demands of the environment as such maintenance control is applied. Note how they interpret organisations dealing with these paradoxes. They, in effect, see them as solving them, the solutions being dictated by the need to adapt to the environment. As you will see, Pascale suggests a different perspective, one we will be coming back to in Chapter 9.

General systems theory has made an important contribution to our understanding of the nature of managing and organising in a number of ways. It focuses our attention on:

- interdependence, interaction and interconnection between parts of an organisation and between organisations;
- the importance of the boundaries between parts of an organisation and between one organisation and others;
- the roles of people within and across the boundaries and the nature of leadership as management of the boundary.

These ideas have been important in developing our understanding of group dynamics within an organisation (see Chapter 11) and in the discipline of Organisation Development which we reviewed in Chapter 5.

FIGURE 8.10

General systems theory: main points on organisational dynamics

- An organisation is an open system: a set of interconnected parts (individuals, informal groups, formal groups such as departments and business units) in turn interacting with other organisations and individuals outside it.
- Interconnection means that a system imports energy and information from outside itself, transforms that energy and information in some way, and then exports the transformed result back to other systems outside of itself.
- An organisation imports across a boundary separating it from other systems, transforms the imports within its boundary, and exports back across the boundary. The boundary separates a system from its environment but also links it to its environment.
- Relationships across the boundary are always changing, the environment is always changing. The boundary therefore exercises a regulatory function: on the one hand it protects the system from fluctuations in the environment and on the other it relays messages and prompts changes within the boundary so that the system adapts to its environment.
- It is the role of leadership to manage the boundary, to regulate so that the system is protected and changes adaptively.
- Successful management keeps an organisation adapted to its changing environment through a process of negative feedback producing stable equilibrium.
- Adaptation to the environment determines the stable equilibrium balance between differentiation and integration, between maintenance control systems and change, required for success. Organisational paradoxes are thus solved in a unique way determined by the environment.
- Success is therefore a state of stability, consistency and harmony.

The previous two section have demonstrated the major role, played by the concept of negative feedback in the construction of theoretical models of organisations and in the prescriptions for managing them. We turn now to the impact of positive feedback on fit in organisations.

8.6 POSITIVE FEEDBACK AND NONLINEARITY IN ORGANISATIONS

We have already come across amplifying feedback processes at work within an organisation, and between one organisation and the other organisations and individuals that constitute its environment. In Chapter 3 Miller talked about organisations getting caught up in self-reinforcing spirals in which they build on existing strengths to the point of excess and disaster. Consider further important examples of positive feedback in organisations.

Vicious circles

The vicious (or virtuous) circle is a widely used concept and this too is nothing other than a positive feedback loop. An early model of vicious circles in organisations is provided by *Gouldner (1964)*. He studied a gypsum plant in the USA and developed a model to explain what he observed. This is illustrated in *Figure 8.11*.

Senior managers at the gypsum plant were concerned to manage efficiently and believed that this required reduced tension between managers and workers. Such tension could be reduced, they thought, if power relations became less visible and all behaved according to impersonal rules. The intention was to emphasise the 'rationality' of the rules and conceal the fact that power was being exercised. No reasonable

FIGURE 8.11

Gouldner's model of intended and unintended consequences

person could object to rules designed to improve efficiency and those who had to enforce them could deny the personal exercise of power and simply say they were doing their job. Conflicts around the distribution of power would then be removed.

Thus, the demand by senior managers for greater control led to the use of general and impersonal rules intended to decrease the visibility of the power of senior management and hence interpersonal tension. In this way managers hoped to establish a damping, negative feedback loop producing intended consequences of reduced tension.

These actions, however, set up another loop that produced unintended consequences. The rules created norms about minimum performance in terms of time of attendance and output levels. People stuck to the minimum norms, frustrating senior management expectations of increased performance. That led to a call for closer supervision and closer control, which had the effect of increasing the visibility of power and thus increasing the level of tension. More impersonal rules were then required. An unintended positive loop was generating unintended consequences. And that loop came to dominate what was going on, causing a vicious spiralling circle of tighter controls and more tension.

Self-fulfilling prophecies

Merton (1957) developed a model of organisations in terms of self-fulfilling prophecies, another example of positive feedback at work. Many managers argue that most people are not all that competent and cannot be left to make decisions for themselves in relation to their work. They argue that efficiency requires rules. But constant compliance with rules causes individuals eventually to lose the capacity to make decisions for themselves. The constant reliance on rules leads to the rules becoming ends in themselves instead of means to ends. As a consequence of being compelled to obey rules they did not originate, employees lose the capacity for independent thought. The result is trained incapacity. Rule-bound organisations encourage unimaginative people to join them and the imaginative leave. The prophecy that people are incompetent is fulfilled by the means taken to deal with its originally supposed existence.

This is shown in *Figure 8.12*. Managers demand greater control in order to secure reliability in service terms. Employees fulfil the stipulated reliability criteria by sticking to the rules. The result is employees who stick to the rules and supply customers strictly in accordance with them. If this leads to trouble with customers, employees can show how they have kept to the rules. This is the intended feedback loop – negative and damping. But such rigid behaviour and the organisational defences it involves lead to more and more difficulties with clients. Growing customer dissatisfaction leads to top managers calling for greater reliability and more rules. So another positive loop is set up, a vicious circle with unintended consequences.

Bandwagon effects and chain reactions

A bandwagon effect is the tendency of a movement to gain supporters simply because of its growing popularity; or it is the well-observed economic phenomenon of 'keeping up with the Joneses – the demand for a product increases simply because more and more people see that other people have it. This phenomenon of products spreading through consuming populations is another example of a positive feedback loop, this

FIGURE 8.12

Merton's model of intended and unintended consequences

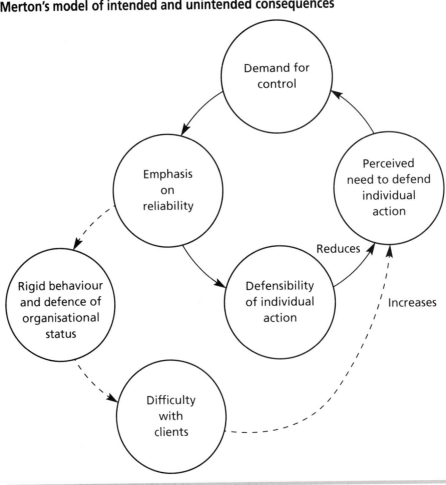

time creating a virtuous circle for the producer of the product. A small gain in market share by one product can, through this spreading and copying effect, be escalated into market domination. So although Sony's Betamax is the technically superior video recorder, Matsushita's VHS recorder obtained a small market lead in the early days of market development. This led to more stores stocking titles in the VHS format. That led to a further increase in VHS recorder market share and therefore more stockists turned to VHS films, and so on.

A similar phenomenon is the chain reaction. Here a positive feedback process escalates a small change into major consequences. Police firing a shot into a demonstrating crowd may touch off a chain reaction which leads to a massive riot or even the overthrow of a government. *Illustration 8.2* gives an example from business.

There is convincing evidence that almost any human system one can think of is characterised by nonlinear relationships and by the powerful effects of positive amplifying feedback, as well as by negative feedback loops. Models that ignore this nonlinearity and the presence of positive feedback must inevitably give a very one-

Changing the Coca-Cola formula

In April 1985, the Chairman of Coca-Cola announced that the original formula for the world-famous soft drink was to be changed to a new sweeter variety to be called 'New Coke'. This announcement followed the two years of research and planning, costing some $4m, that had gone into the development of a new strategy to counter the market share gains being made by Pepsi Cola. Market research had shown that the New Coke would boost Coca-Cola's market share and add some $200m in sales. Taste tests had demonstrated that people preferred the New Coke taste.

New Coke was launched on 23 April 1985 at a press conference attended by 200 newspaper, magazine and TV reporters. They were unconvinced by the New Coke and their stories were generally negative.

The word about the change in Coca-Cola spread quickly. Within 24 hours, 81 per cent of the US population knew about it and early results were encouraging despite the negative media response. About 150 million people tried New Coke and most commented favourably. But the protests were also mushrooming. In the first four hours, the company received 650 calls. By mid May calls ran at 5000 per day, and there was a mass of angry letters – around 40 000 letters were received that spring and summer. The company had to hire new staff to handle the complaints.

People talked about Coke as an American symbol and they felt betrayed. Some threatened to switch to tea or water. Before May, 53 per cent of sample surveys said they liked the New Coke. In July that fell to 30 per cent. Anger spread across the country, fuelled by the media. The Chairman's father threatened to disown him for tampering with a national symbol.

On 11 July 1985 the company acknowledged that it had made a mistake, top executives apologised to the public and announced the restoration of the old Coca-Cola. TV programmes were interrupted to convey the news.

No satisfactory linear cause and effect explanation has been found for this sequence of events. What this demonstrates is how some small change, added sweetness to a soft drink, can escalate into a major consequence through the operation of positive feedback taking the form of herd instinct, bandwagon effects. ■

Source: Hartley (1991)

sided, and therefore suspect, understanding of the dynamics of organising. Such deficient understanding must lead to questionable prescriptions for success. I believe that today's dominant received wisdom on how to practise strategic management is characterised by just this problem of a deficient understanding of positive nonlinear feedback.

The rest of this chapter is devoted to considering what the literature has to say about this matter. Bear in mind that the rest of this chapter covers material that has remained largely outside the mainstream received wisdom on strategic management. It is interesting to note how resolutely the mainstream views on strategic management ignore the widespread prevalence of positive feedback, despite the fact that we are all aware of its manifestations as bandwagon effects and vicious circles, and despite the fact that these phenomena have been written about for at least forty years now. The conventional approach to strategic management says, in effect, that the escalation, the virtuous and vicious circles should not be happening. The prescription is to use rational approaches to remove such phenomena and failing that to use visionary/ideological processes. As we have seen, however, these are all extensions of ordinary management, a model which does not incorporate the impact of positive feedback. The reality is that positive feedback is an inescapable feature, an irremovable structural property of human systems. Instead of building models that suppose we can remove positive feedback phenomena, we need to be building models of how to use and cope with those phenomena.

8.7 POSITIVE FEEDBACKS AND SYSTEMS CREATING THEIR OWN ENVIRONMENT

Karl Weick approaches the understanding of organisations from a psychological and sociological point of view. He analyses the problems of managing and organising at the level of interactions between individuals. He sees those interactions in terms of positive and negative feedback loops. In common with systems models of organisations already discussed in this chapter, Weick explains the operation of the system in terms of feedback interactions. However, his model differs significantly from those so far discussed in two important respects:

- the incorporation of both negative and positive loops in the feedback behaviour; and
- the implicit recognition of nonlinear relationships that cause systems autonomously to change from dominant positive to dominant negative feedback modes.

Weick (1969/1979) invites his readers to see the feedback nature of organisations for themselves by working on the diagram shown in *Figure 8.13.*

This figure depicts a number of variables that affect what happens at a meeting between two or more people in an organisation. The reader is invited to connect the phrases in the diagram with causal arrows showing the effect of one variable on the others, indicating with a plus sign when one variable causes another to increase and with a minus sign when one variable causes another to decrease. The result will be a set of interconnected positive and negative feedback loops. What happens at this meeting will depend upon whether positive or negative loops dominate, and that domination could change during the course of the meeting. The system will be stable or unstable depending upon the dominant form of feedback (see *Illustration 8.3*).

So right at the most basic level of an organisation, that is at the level of interactions between individuals, the unfolding of events will depend upon the nature of the feedback structure that defines these interrelationships.

Because relationships between people in a group inevitably take this complicated, changing feedback form, decision-making cannot be as coherent a process as rational models of any kind would lead us to believe. This becomes even clearer when we take account of the impact of the unconscious on group behaviour. We could add boxes to

FIGURE 8.13

Weick's model: events at a meeting

1. Number of people making comments

2. Variety of ideas suggested

12. My irritation at speaker

3. My fear of embarrassment

11. Amount of group concentration on problem

4. Amount of horsing around in group

10. My feelings of boredom

5. Number of ideas I think of

9. My understanding of material that is presented

6. My willingness to volunteer a comment

8. My self-consciousness

7. Quality of ideas suggested

Source: K. Weick (1979), *The Social Psychology of Organizing*, Reading, Ma: Addison-Wesley

Figure 8.13 to represent the unconscious responses people make to each other and to some situations. For example, when they are confronted by great uncertainty, a group of individuals may regress to infantile defence mechanics that impair their ability to learn, work and make decisions (we will come to this later in Chapter 11).

Tight and loose coupling

Weick points to added levels of complexity in interrelationships and decision making as we move from single groups to the collections of groups that constitute an organisation. Organisations are typically not tightly coupled sets of groups alone. Organisations are more typically sets of groups that are tightly coupled for some purposes, but constitute a loosely coupled system for other purposes.

Groups or systems are *tightly coupled* when there are clear-cut direct connections between them; when they are so closely coordinated that a decision or action in one has immediately apparent implications for decisions or actions in another. So we get tight coupling in an efficient assembly production process, where one group assembling the components on a television set work in a highly coordinated way with another group putting the components into a plastic casing. Any failure in the first assembly operation has an immediate impact on the later operation and vice versa. Tight coupling is highly efficient while all moves according to plan. But unforeseen changes in one area have rapid and major implications for what happens in other

Illustration
8.3

Feedback interactions at a meeting

Suppose we are at a meeting which I am chairing. Suppose that, as my willingness to proffer comments declines, the rest of the group engages in more horseplay (negative link between the boxes 6 and 4 in *Figure 8.13*). Then suppose that, as the level of horseplay increases, it diminishes my understanding of the material being presented at the meeting (negative link between boxes 4 and 9 in *Figure 8.13*). As my understanding falls, my fear of embarrassment rises (negative link). And as my fear of embarrassment rises, my willingness to volunteer comments declines (negative link). The decrease in my comments leads to even more horseplay and so we continue around the amplifying, vicious circle that makes us more and more ineffective as a group. Because we have four negative links, an even number, the feedback loop as a whole is positive. With that kind of structure our meeting is unstable and we will not get much done.

But there could be other links in the loop. Suppose my level of boredom rises as the amount of horsing around increases (positive link). The more bored I become the less self-conscious I become (negative link). This fall in self-consciousness increases my willingness to comment (negative link). That willingness to comment cuts down on the horseplay (negative link). We have here a limiting or self-regulating loop whereby the increase in horseplay sets off automatic responses that tend to hold it in check. This loop has one positive and three negative links. It is therefore a negative feedback loop. It exerts a damping effect, pushing the system towards an equilibrium.

At some point the level of horseplay may become so great that the second loop (the negative one) dominates the first (the positive one) and the meeting will move from a vicious spiral of ineffectiveness onto a path towards more effective communication. Note that the behaviour of the system moves of its own accord, because of its nonlinear feedback structure, from an unstable to a stable state. ∎

areas. A small failure in one small part could bring the whole system down. Tight coupling is characterised by (*Perrow, 1984*):

- no delays in processing;
- no variation in sequences of events;
- only one method of achieving the goal;
- no slack in the flow of activity from one part of the system to another;
- any buffers built in at the design stage;
- possible substitution of supplies or equipment built in at the design stage.

Loose coupling, on the other hand, means that there is a buffer between one group and another. There is the possibility of delays and changes in the sequences of events. Parts of the system can continue to function while failures in other parts of the system are attended to. Alternative methods can be employed and additional resources called upon. Buffers and redundancies are available to deal with the unforeseeable.

Clearly, loosely coupled systems are less efficient, but they are also far safer. The more unpredictable the situation, the more helpful it will be to have a loosely coupled system. So in the assembly operation above we could turn the system into a loosely coupled one by introducing the possibility of building up unplanned inventories at each stage. If the group putting the assemblies into plastic cases fails to maintain its speed, the supervisor of the group assembling the components could decide to continue production and add to inventories, even though there is no plan to do so. Decisions or actions in one group would then not have immediate implications for another.

Because of this possibility of loose coupling, a change in one part of the system need not immediately affect the other parts. Loosely coupled systems are characterised by the possibility of delays and changes in the sequences of events. And because of this we will find it difficult to predict what one group will do when another takes some action. The system becomes safer in the face of uncertainty, but the safety factor itself adds a level of complexity that makes it more difficult to determine how the system will behave or why it is behaving as it does.

Loose coupling means that the connections between decisions and actions in one part of the organisation and decisions and actions in other parts are often obscure. The connections between means and ends, and between problems and solutions, also become less clear. People, problems and choice opportunities are combined in confusing ways that make it difficult to predict agendas of matters to be attended to, and the outcomes of those matters.

When they deal with the ordinary day-to-day management of their existing businesses, successful organisations set up tightly coupled systems. Modern methods of operations management and inventory control, such as Just-in-Time delivery and Materials Resource Programming, are examples of this. But successful organisations always also have to face unpredictable changes to their activities. To deal with this they also evolve loosely coupled systems. Because they face both the predictable and the unpredictable, most organisations are systems that combine tight and loose coupling. The element of loose coupling often makes it very difficult to identify the events in one part of the system that are causing changes in other parts.

Links with the environment

Weick also explains the organisation's links with the environment in terms of feedback loops. The nature of these loops is illustrated in *Figure 8.14*.

First consider what the terms used in *Figure 8.14* mean and then what the loop connections between them signify.

1 *Ecological change* means the changes occurring in the market and wider environments that an organisation operates in. Such changes are primarily the actions undertaken by actors in the environment. These external actions may lead people in an organisation to undertake actions too – hence the arrow and the + sign running from ecological change to enactment.

2 *Enactment* describes what the actors within the organisation itself do; it is the actions they undertake. The term enactment is used rather than the term action, to indicate that people within an organisation do not simply anticipate, react or

adapt to what actors in the environment can be objectively observed to do. Instead, people within an organisation are prompted by their subjective perceptions of what actors in the environment are doing or might do. It is those perceptions that drive their actions.

Furthermore, their actions may lead environmental actors to do what they do. Those within an organisation then perceive this and undertake further action. So they all keep going around a positive feedback loop, represented by the plus signs in the loop shown in *Figure 8.14* between ecological change and enactment. By taking a particular action, people within an organisation may cause people outside it to do what they do – the former are therefore in a real sense creating, or enacting, their own environment. Because they are driven by subjective perceptions it is also quite possible for people within an organisation to invent an environment and then cause it to occur. The reality people within an organisation respond to is being socially constructed by themselves. The question now is this: what causes actors within the organisation to perceive and act in the way they do? The answer lies in what they remember about what they have done before.

3 *Retention* is the process of storing what has been perceived and learned from previous actions. It is the shared memory of the collection of people constituting the organisation, built up from what they have done together over the past, reflecting their perceptions of what has worked and what has not worked. If particular actions worked in particular circumstances before, this will prompt a similar enactment now. So the link running back from retention to enactment can be positive or negative; that is, the organisational memory could prompt an action or stop it. The terms retention and organisational memory as they are used here mean the same thing as the culture of the organisation, its recipe, the paradigm its managers subscribe to, their received wisdom. These terms all have to do with the shared mental models of organisational actors. The next question is this: how does retention come about? The answer lies in a process of selection.

4 Selection is the process through which organisational actors focus on some meanings of what they are doing and some perceptions of what others are doing, while ignoring yet others. What is selected for retention depends upon what has been done or enacted and what has been perceived (the positive arrow running from enactment to selection). And the selection itself is affected by what has been previously retained about how things should be perceived and done (the loop

FIGURE 8.14

Weick's model: links with the environment

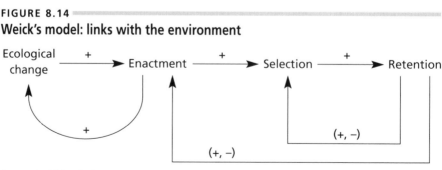

Source: K. Weick (1979), *The Social Psychology of Organizing*, Reading, Ma: Addison-Wesley

running back from retention to selection). What we select to focus on now depends on the mental models we have already built up. These may cause us to accept or reject a perception, hence the positive and negative signs in the retention–selection loop.

By looking at the interactions between an organisation and its environment in this way, Weick clarifies the concept of managers together creating the reality they respond to (see *Key Concept 8.8*).

The social construction of reality

The environment which managers respond to is not a set of independently given, scientifically observable facts. It is a set of perceptions they have. These are determined by the mental models they have built up from previous education and experience and have come to share with each other. They continually amend these models through their ongoing experiences or enactments. In this sense they invent their own environment.

These perceptions are perceptions about the interactions between people inside one organisation and other people outside that organisation. People inside an organisation are taking part in these interactions and in this sense they are creating their environment. Ideas of creating and inventing, that is enacting, environments through interactions across the organisation's boundary are going to be more useful guides to understanding what goes on in organisations than ideas of adapting to an environment.

Since managers are inventing and creating their own environments in conjunction with other actors in the environment in a positive feedback loop, they can easily generate vicious and virtuous circles, self-fulfilling prophecies, chain reactions and bandwagon effects. Because of all this, managers cannot know in advance what they are creating. They have to do something and then understand what they have done before they do the next thing. Here, then, people are attaching meaning retrospectively to what they have done, not deciding in advance what the meaning is of what they will do. In a sense the purpose of actions is defined after the actions have been taken. An organisation does not know what it is about until it looks back and imposes structure and meaning on what it has done.

Self-designing systems

The feedback system view of how an organisation works led *Weick (1977)* to the concept of an organisation as a self-designing system. Rigid rule-bound organisations that spell out exactly how people should behave are incapable of generating new forms of behaviour to meet new situations. To be able to meet the unexpected new situation, organisations need to be loosely coupled, self-designing systems. That requires establishing the following patterns:

Illustration
8.4

Tin cans: inventing the environment

In the mid-1980s the UK manufacturers of tin can emulsion paint containers perceived that the main cause of the decline in the demand for their product was its propensity to rust. Market research at the time indicated that the more important cause was the poor levels of service provided to paint producers. Managers in the tin can firms ignored this and came up with a technical solution to the rust problem. By this time plastic cans backed by design support and high service levels had made major inroads into the market. They have now virtually replaced tin cans in the emulsion packaging market. Managers in the tin can firms were quite clearly enacting an environment, inventing it in fact. Because it bore little relationship to reality, the invention destroyed them.

But note that inventing or creating an environment does not always lead to disaster. Sony created a demand for personal entertainment systems by inventing the Walkman. This turned out to be an invention connected to reality. ∎

- valuing improvisation more than forecasts;
- dwelling on opportunities rather than constraints;
- inventing solutions rather than borrowing them;
- cultivating impermanence instead of permanence;
- valuing argument more highly than serenity;
- relying on diverse measures of performance rather than on accounting systems alone;
- encouraging doubt rather than removing it;
- continuously experimenting rather than searching for final solutions;
- seeking contradictions rather than discouraging them.

Such patterns of behaviour will make organisations less efficient but more adaptable. In the models summarised above, Weick has made a number of key points which have remained largely outside mainstream strategic management, despite the fact that they capture much of what we can directly observe to be happening. These key points are summarised in *Figure 8.15*.

We now turn to another important strand in management literature which has also received very little attention from those concerned with strategic management – system dynamics.

Hamel and Prahalad's analysis

Hamel and Prahalad (1989) also stress the role of organisations in creating their own environments instead of simply adapting to them. They have studied a number of global companies in America, Europe and Japan and they suggest that what distinguishes the noticeably successful (Honda, Komatsu and Canon, for example) from the noticeably less so (General Motors, Caterpillar and Xerox, for example) are the different mental models of strategy guiding their respective actions. This research questions

FIGURE 8.15
Weick's model: key points on organisational dynamics

- Organisations are complex feedback systems, starting right at the fundamental level of interaction between two or more people within the organisation.
- The systematic feedback structure of the organisation itself determines the pattern of behaviour over time. The standard assumption of today's dominant management theory is that the dynamics, the patterns of change, are due mainly to environmental forces outside the organisation. The proposition being made in the Weick models is that patterns of change are determined by the inherent nature of the system structure itself.
- A group of people does not necessarily have to have a shared, common purpose in order to be a group. People form groups before they have a common purpose because they have interdependent needs that require the resources of others. We group because we need each others' support, because of the means not the ends. Purpose comes later. So an organisation is not necessarily driven by goal-seeking behaviour, that is achieving a given goal. It may well be driven by searching for a goal in the first place. This is a very different perspective from today's dominant views on management.
- Meaning for an organisation is retrospective not prospective. We can only understand what we are doing by interpreting what we have done. We impose meaning on what we have done. So a vision would not be a picture of a future state but an interpretation of where we have now got to. Meaning, purpose, vision and mission emerge from what we have done and are doing – they are not prior organisation-wide intentions.
- Organisations create and invent their own environment in the sense that the environment is their perception of what is happening and in the sense that their actions impact on the environment which then impacts back on the organisation. This is different to the simple adaptive view that is common in the dominant received wisdom.
- Predicting what complex feedback systems will do is very difficult. It is difficult to guess what people's preferences will be in the future and it is these preferences that will drive what they do.
- But despite the unpredictability and the complexity, people can operate as part of a system that is too complex for any one person alone to understand. Each plays a part in the complex unfolding of events, understanding only a part, and relies on others to play their parts.
- Loose coupling is important in the ability of such complex systems to remain flexible, but that loose coupling adds to system complexity and makes it even harder to understand and predict its behaviour.
- Such systems are essentially self-designing.
- Positive feedback, self-reinforcing processes play a very important part in what happens. Instability is an essential part of what goes on and we cannot simply ignore it or write it off as something to be banished by negative feedback controls. There is too much evidence that this focus on negative feedback alone leads to unintended positive loops and unintended consequences. People prize improvisation.

one of the basic tenets of the conventional wisdom, namely the notion that successful organisations are those that fit, or adapt to, their environments.

Hamel and Prahalad found that the less-successful companies follow the conventional prescriptions and so seek to maintain strategic fit. This leads them to trim their ambitions to those that can be met with available resources. Such companies are concerned mainly with product-market units rather than core competences, they preserve consistency through requiring conformity in behaviour, and they focus on achieving financial objectives. These companies attempt to achieve their financial objectives by using generic strategies, selected according to criteria of strategic fit, in order to secure sustainable competitive advantage. Hamel and Prahalad report that this approach leads to repetition and imitation.

On the other hand, Hamel and Prahalad found that successful companies focus on leveraging resources, that is using what they have in new and innovative ways to reach seemingly unattainable goals. The main concern of these companies is to use their resources in challenging and stretching ways to build up a number of core competences. Consistency is maintained by all sharing a central strategic intent and the route to this successful state is accelerated organisational learning, recognising that no competitive advantages are inherently sustainable. Here, managers are not simply matching their resources to the requirements of the environment, leaving to others those requirements their resources are incapable of delivering. Instead, managers creatively use the resources they have, they create requirements of the environment which they can then meet, they push to achieve stretching goals, and so they continually renew and transform their organisation.

While these authors question one central assumption of the stable equilibrium model of organisational success, they preserve the other central assumptions. In particular, they continue to see organisational success as flowing from clear, prior organisation-wide intention. They stress what they call strategic intent, a challenging shared vision of a future leadership position for the company. This strategic intent is stable over time. It is clear as to outcome but flexible as to the means of achieving the outcome. It is an obsession with winning and winning on a global scale cannot be secured either through long-term plans or through some undirected process of intrapreneurship or autonomous small task forces. Instead success is secured by discovering how to achieve a broad, stretching, challenging intention to build core competences.

This study questions the idea of adapting to the environment, proposing instead creative interaction. But in other respects – intention, harmony and consistency – it falls within the ordinary management paradigm.

8.8 UNDERSTANDING BOTH POSITIVE AND NEGATIVE FEEDBACK IN ORGANISATIONS: SYSTEMIC THINKING AND ORGANISATIONAL LEARNING

The most important development of complex systems models for application to organisational and social policy issues has been by Jay Forrester. His background is that of a servomechanisms engineer, digital computer pioneer and manager of a large R&D effort. He developed an approach to understanding human systems that is based on concepts of positive and negative feedback, nonlinearity and the use of computers to simulate the behaviour patterns of such complex systems. Feedback is the basic characteristic of his view of the world:

> Systems of information feedback control are fundamental to all life and human endeavour, from the slow pace of biological evolution to the launching of the latest satellite. A feedback control system exists whenever the environment causes a decision which in turn affects the original environment. (*Forrester, 1958, p. 4*)

Here human decision-making is firmly linked to the feedback concept.

Production and distribution chains

Forrester has illustrated his approach by modelling the behaviour of production–distribution chains. A factory supplies a product, say beer, to a number of distributors who then ship it to an even larger number of retailers. Orders for the product flow back upstream from retailers to distributors and from them to the factory. The factory, the distributors and the retailers form a system and the links between them are flows of orders in one direction and flows of product in the other. Each part of the system tries to do the best it can to maintain inventories at minimum levels without running out of product to sell. Each attempts to ship product as fast as possible. They all do these things because that is the way to maximise their individual profits.

But because of its very structure – the feedback and lags in information flows – this system shows a marked tendency to amplify minor ordering disturbances at the retail level. An initial 10 per cent increase in orders at the retail level can eventually cause production at the factory to peak 40 per cent above the initial level before collapsing.

Peter Senge (1990) reports how he has used this example as a game with thousands of groups of managers in many countries. Even when people know about the likely consequences of this system, he has always found that the consequences of a small increase at the retail level is, first of all, growing demand that cannot be met. Inventories are depleted and backlogs grow. Then beer arrives in great quantities while incoming orders suddenly decline as backlogs are reduced. Eventually almost all players end up with large inventories they cannot unload. It is exactly this kind of cyclical behaviour we observe in real-life businesses.

Only by being aware of how the system as a whole functions, rather than simply concentrating on one's own part of it, can the extreme instabilities of the cycles be avoided. It seems, however, that these cycles can never be removed altogether.

The lessons of systems thinking

The lessons of the game are that:

● The structure of the system influences behaviour. The cycles in ordering, inventory levels and production in the game are really the consequence of the structure of the system. But, when people play the game in a classroom, or in real life, they blame others in the system for what is going on. For example, the retailers blame the distributors for running out of stock and not delivering fast enough.

- Structure in human systems is subtle. Structure is the set of interrelationships between people and, because of negative and positive feedback loops, that structure can generate unintended results.
- Coping effectively often comes from a new way of thinking. If one simply focuses on one's own part in the system, thinks for example always as a retailer, then one's behaviour of over- and under-ordering will simply contribute to the system's instability. If, instead, players think in terms of the whole system, they will behave differently. For example, they will realise that widespread over-ordering is likely to occur. They will realise that doing so themselves in this situation will not help them much in the short run, but will eventually lead to stock levels that are too high. They will avoid doing what everyone else is doing, even if this reduces profitability in the short run.

Principles of complex systems

By running computer simulations of a great many different human systems, researchers in the systems dynamics tradition have identified a number of principles about complex human systems. These are set out below.

1 Complex systems often produce unexpected and counter-intuitive results. In the beer game, retailers increase orders above their real need expecting this to lead to bigger deliveries, but because all retailers are doing this, and because of lags in information flows, the unexpected result is lower deliveries. Simulation of other situations suggests that increased low-cost housing in an inner city will exacerbate rather than arrest the decline of inner cities, because it creates ghettoes where social mobility is impossible. Policies of demolishing slum housing and discouraging the construction of cheap housing make the centre more desirable for the better off, but also create a more balanced social system in which there is the opportunity for upward mobility.

2 In complex systems – nonlinear relationships with positive and negative feedback – the links between cause and effect are distant in time and space. In the beer game, the causes of increased demand appeared at the retail end, distant in space from the factory and distant in time because of the lags in order flows. Such distance between cause and effect makes it very difficult to say what is causing what. Those playing the beer game always think that the fluctuations in deliveries are being caused by fluctuations in retail demand when in fact they are due to the manner in which the system operates. The problem is made worse by many coincident symptoms that look like causes but are merely relational. This means that it is extremely difficult to make specific predictions of what will happen in a specific place over a specific time period. Instead, quantitative simulations on computers can be used to identify general qualitative patterns of behaviour that will be similar to those we are likely to experience, although never the same. Simulation here is being used not to capture the future specific outcome within a range of likely outcomes, but to establish broad qualitative features in patterns of behaviour. *Senge (1990, p. 73)* puts it like this:

The art of systems thinking lies in being able to recognise increasingly (dynamically) complex and subtle structures, . . . amid the wealth of details, pressures and cross-currents that attend all real management settings. In fact, the essence of mastering systems thinking as a management discipline lies in seeing patterns where others see only events and forces to react to.

3 Complex systems are highly sensitive to some changes but remarkably insensitive to many others. Complex systems contain some influential pressure, or leverage, points. If we can influence those points we can have a major impact on the behaviour of the system. The trouble is that these are difficult to identify. Note how this concern with leverage points relates to the ideas introduced at the beginning of this chapter on chain reactions, bandwagon effects and virtuous circles of behaviour. In the beer game, the leverage points lie in the ordering practices of retailers and distributors. Unfortunately these pressure points, from which favourable chain reactions can be initiated, are extremely difficult to find. More usually, it seems, complex systems are insensitive to changes and indeed counteract and compensate for externally applied correctives. So when retailers find that deliveries from the distributors are curtailed, they respond by ordering even more and so make the situation worse. When aid programmes provide more dams and water pumps to halt the expansion of the Sahara, tribesmen simply enlarge their herd sizes, leading to overgrazing and the even more rapid encroachment of the desert.

Because of this natural tendency to counteract and compensate, that is to move to stability, it is necessary to change the system itself rather than simply apply externally generated remedies. By their very nature, complex systems often react to policy changes in ways that are the opposite to those which policy makers intend; and complex systems tend to a condition of poor performance because they resist change.

The above points lead inevitably to the conclusion that, because an organisation is a complex system, attempts to plan its long-term future and plan changes in its culture and behaviour patterns are all likely to prompt counter-forces and lead to little change at all or to unexpected and unintended changes. The very structure of a complex system makes it impossible to plan its specific long-term future. We have to operate within the system, in an ongoing way, guided by the general patterns that complex systems display.

Experience supports this conclusion. Individual organisations develop, as we all know, in unforeseen ways. On the national level we have seen the failure of grand design planning systems for whole economies: first in some Western countries such as the UK in the 1960s and 1970s and more recently in the countries of Eastern Europe. However, despite this experience and despite the research done by systems dynamicists, systems thinking attracts very little attention from either researchers into or practitioners of strategic management.

Archetypes of feedback processes

Once the strong possibility that complex systems will counteract correctives and produce unintended consequences is recognised, it becomes essential to analyse and understand the feedback connections in the system, to understand the system as a whole. It becomes vital for effective intervention in the behaviour of the system to understand the dynamics of the system.

Through their simulations, systems dynamicists have built up a set of templates, or archetype feedback processes, that are very commonly found in organisations of all kinds. The purpose of these archetypes is not to make specific predictions of what will happen, but to recondition perceptions so that people are able to perceive the structures at play, to see the dynamic patterns of behaviour, and to see the potential leverage in those structures. The templates are meant to be used in a flexible way to help understand patterns in events. You have to use the template as an analogy with which to build your own explanations of each specific situation you are confronted with. Some examples of these templates are as follows.

1 Limits to growth (Figure 8.16)

Limits to growth occur when a reinforcing positive feedback process is installed to produce a desired result (a positive growth loop) but it inadvertently creates secondary effects (a negative limiting loop) that puts a stop to the growth. We saw this in the discussion on positive and negative feedback in relation to population growth in an earlier section of this chapter, that on nonlinearity, negative and positive feedback. The 'limits to growth' structure is found wherever growth bumps up against limits.

FIGURE 8.16
Limits to growth

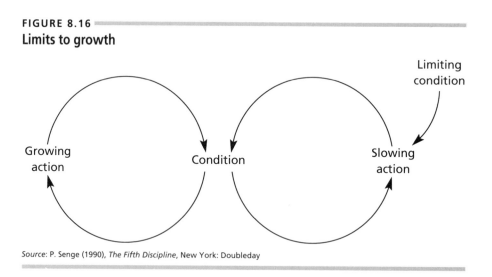

Source: P. Senge (1990), *The Fifth Discipline*, New York: Doubleday

The most immediate response to this structure is that of pushing harder on the factors that cause growth. In fact this is counterproductive because it causes the system to bump even more firmly against the limits. The solution is to work on the negative loop, on relaxing the limits.

For example, a company may grow through introducing new products flowing from its R&D efforts. As it grows it increases the size of the R&D department which becomes harder to manage. Senior engineers then become managers and the flow of new product ideas slows. Pressing for more new product ideas will simply lead to a bigger R&D department and that will exacerbate the management problems, so reducing the flow of new ideas. We need instead to rethink the whole process of developing new products and running R&D activities. The leverage point is the way in which the actual R&D effort is organised and to see how this should be done we need to understand the whole system of which R&D is a part.

2 Shifting the burden (Figure 8.17)

Shifting the burden happens where some underlying problem generates a number of symptoms. Because the underlying problem is difficult to identify, people focus on the symptoms. They look for the quick, easy fix. While these temporarily relieve the symptoms, the underlying problem gets worse. People do not notice at first how the underlying problems are getting worse and as they avoid dealing with these problems the system loses its ability to solve them.

An example is bringing an expert into an organisation to solve a problem. This may leave a manager's ability unaltered and when related problems arise again the manager will be unable to cope without the expert.

FIGURE 8.17
Shifting the burden

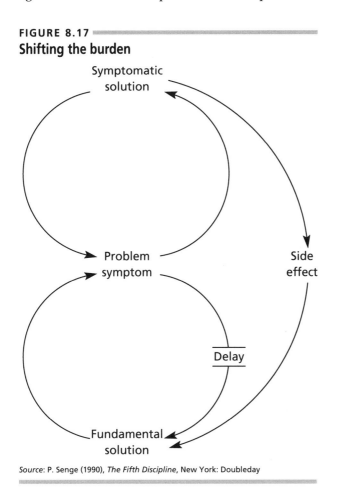

Source: P. Senge (1990), *The Fifth Discipline*, New York: Doubleday

3 Eroding goals (Figure 8.18)

Another template is that of eroding goals, where a short-term solution is effected by allowing fundamental goals to decline. This happens when managers accept a decline in performance standards as a temporary measure to deal with a crisis.

FIGURE 8.18
Eroding goals

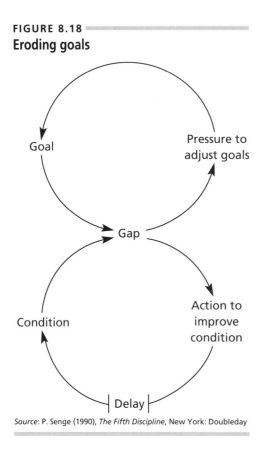

Source: P. Senge (1990), *The Fifth Discipline*, New York: Doubleday

So for example, a company producing a good product attracting high levels of demand increases its delivery time to accommodate a backlog crisis. It then does little to increase production capacity. The next time it goes around the circle, it experiences even bigger backlogs and so it extends delivery time even further. This goes on until customer dissatisfaction suddenly reaches a critical point and demand falls away rapidly.

Simulations show that when firms allow their goals for quality and delivery time gradually to slip it has dramatic effects on their profitability, as shown in *Illustration 8.5*. The message is to beware the symptomatic solution and seek to understand how the system is working.

Illustration 8.5

Peoples Express

Peoples Express provided an innovative low-cost airline service between the US and Europe and within the USA. It was a no-frills service, but it was reliable. However, Peoples Express found that it could not build its service capacity to keep pace with the exploding demand. Instead of slowing its growth (by increasing prices) and focusing on training to increase service capacity, it continued to grow as fast as it could. Service levels declined more and more rapidly, staff morale collapsed, and competition became more fierce. Eventually customers no longer found Peoples Express attractive. ■

Source: Senge (1990)

FIGURE 8.19
Growth and underinvestment

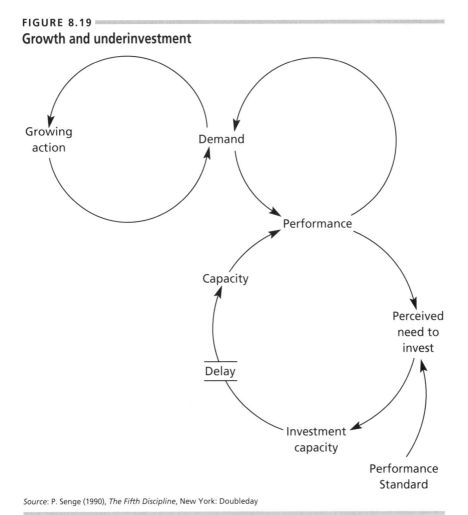

Source: P. Senge (1990), *The Fifth Discipline*, New York: Doubleday

4 Growth and underinvestment (Figure 8.19)

This occurs when new investments in capacity are not made early enough or on a large enough scale to accommodate continuing growth. As growth approaches limits set by existing capacity, the attempts made to meet demand result in lower quality and service levels. The consequence is customer dissatisfaction and declining demand.

The systems dynamics approach to understanding how organisations work makes a number of important key points that are summarised in *Figure 8.20*.

FIGURE 8.20

System dynamics: main points on organisational dynamics

- Nonlinearity and feedback loops are fundamental properties of organisational life, properties we are unused to recognising.
- The feedback structure of the system itself generates patterns of behaviour and we find this confusing because we are accustomed to looking for causes in some discrete event. We believe that something or someone must be to blame when it is really the structure of the system that is leading to what happens.
- In complex systems of the type we are talking about, cause-and-effect links are distant and very difficult to identify.
- Behaviour patterns can emerge without being intended; in fact they often emerge contrary to intention.
- The result is unexpected and counter-intuitive outcomes.
- Forecasting specific sequences of events therefore becomes very difficult and seeing qualitative patterns becomes very important.
- Understanding the structure of the system could lead to the identification of pressure, or leverage, points where efforts to change behaviour have the most effect.
- These pressure points are difficult to find and most changes we try to make to a system simply provoke compensating and offsetting behaviour.
- Consequently, systems have a strong tendency to stabilise and so deteriorate in the face of change. This idea has much in common with that of the forces of differentiation and integration pulling organisations to extremes where they fail. The reader should refer back to Chapter 3 where the ideas of Miller on trajectories to failure are discussed.
- Successful organisations can approach stability and regularity if they understand the system as a whole and if they can identify the leverage points.

Towards a far-from-equilibrium paradigm

The views being put forward by Miller (see Chapter 3) and Pascale contrast starkly with the discussion in Chapter 5 on the criteria for selecting strategies. The latter emphasise stability and harmony, while the former point to the importance of instability, contradiction and rivalry. The reader should also contrast the Miller and Pascale views with the way in which recognised organisational tensions are treated by other writers. For example in Chapter 5 in the section on installing strategic management styles, we saw that Gould and Campbell's styles of strategic management are also based on organisational tensions that are very similar to the ones enumerated by Pascale. But Gould and Campbell's successful organisations are ones that find an equilibrium balance between the tensions. On the Pascale view this leads to failure not success. Also note the difference between Pascale and the Hamel and Prahalad (1989) model discussed earlier: the latter relate success to intention, harmony and consistency, while the former relates success to contention and conflict that leads to emergent strategy.

The Miller and Pascale studies are built on assumptions that are dramatically and fundamentally different to those we identified to be the basis of ordinary management. This is based on an unquestioned assumption that the criteria for success have to do with consistency, regularity and stability – the paradigm of the stable equilibrium organisation. What the studies in this section are suggesting is that we need to revise this view. They point to the conclusions that: continuing movement towards equilibrium is failure; success requires the maintenance of a position away from equilibrium; contradiction between stability and instability, between tight and flexible controls, between centralised and decentralised structures, are all essential to success. Success seems to have something to do with the ability of an organisation to sustain and manage contradiction and tension. And this ability seems to be closely tied to creativity, a point made some time ago by the economist *Schumpeter (1934)*. He pointed out that progress was a process in which companies continually destroyed existing forms of competitive advantage to make way for new ones.

Key Concept 8.9

The far-from-equilibrium organisation

While a system operates in a state far-from-equilibrium it never follows exactly the same pattern of behaviour. It follows complex patterns that are not regular and predictable. Instead, behaviour patterns exhibit features of stability and instability, but not in a predictable manner. A far-from-equilibrium organisation is thus characterised by contradiction and contention, not harmony and consistency. Because of this it generates new perspectives and new forms of behaviour. Such systems have the potential for innovation not possessed by equilibrium systems. They may experience sudden revolutionary changes of direction; they may suddenly move through a crisis to new forms of order.

What the Pascale and Miller studies represent is a move towards a new management paradigm, a different view on the nature of organisational dynamics. We are presented with a picture of patterns of change that are circular, that amplify small changes, that generate vicious and virtuous circles (see Chapter 9). This is in sharp contrast with patterns of change that are orderly, predictable movements towards stable equilibrium. This new view of the nature of organisational dynamics is also very much in evidence in the latest framework developed by Michael Porter (see next section). In Chapter 5 we discussed his industry structure and value chain analyses. In his latest book he has cast these ideas in a more dynamic framework that we now go on to discuss. However, all of this is still only a move towards a new paradigm because these writers still all see management as primarily a process of actualising organisational interaction. In the end this is what keeps their models attached to ordinary management processes. In Part Four, we will be seeking to develop further the notion of the far-from-equilibrium organisation and its extraordinary management processes.

Further developments in systems thinking: Porter's analysis of the competitive advantage of nations

Porter (1990) puts forward an explanation of how nations develop competitive advantage. Since competitive advantage is embedded in organisations and is the consequence of the strategies they pursue, his explanation is also an explanation of strategic change in a single organisation. This approach sees a particular company as part of a complex system consisting of other competing, supplying, supporting, customer and governmental organisations. The pattern of change any one company in this system displays depends upon a self-reinforcing interplay between what all of them are doing. Clusters of supporting and competing companies emerge in particular areas as a result of spreading benefits between them – a form of feedback between them that amplifies advantages and disadvantages and sets off virtuous and vicious circles of development. In this process, partly affected by chance, the cause and effect of individual determinants becomes blurred.

When we discussed Porter's industry structure and value chain analysis in Chapter 5 we painted a picture of managers in an organisation who analyse a given environment and then choose a particular strategy that they then implement. If they choose the right strategy, that is if they formulate the right organisational intention and then actually carry it out, they will succeed. This is a picture of orderly, intentional adaptation to the environment. In the later analysis being discussed here, however, each firm is part of a complex system and therefore what happens to any individual firm will be a consequence, not of the shared intention of its top managers, but of the evolution of the whole system of which that firm and its top managers are a part. This way of looking at the strategic development of a firm is consistent with the approach that Miller and Pascale adopt and like their analysis it represents a decisive break with the conventional wisdom. It is for this reason that we discuss it here.

The analysis is conducted in terms of what Porter calls the 'national diamond' reproduced as *Figure 8.21*. A nation, and therefore any individual firm within it, achieves success in a particular industry when it develops a favourable configuration between the following:

- *Factor conditions* such as skilled labour, the transport and education infrastructure, knowledge resources.
- *Demand conditions* such as the size of markets and the sophistication of buyers.
- *Related and supporting industries*. The point here is that one firm has competitive advantage when it is part of a whole value chain that is competitive. So Italian shoe manufacturers have advantages because they are part of a cluster of industries containing support in the form of leather suppliers and designers. This support industry is made possible by the existence of related firms such as handbag manufacturers.

FIGURE 8.21

Porter's model for analysing the competitive advantage of nations

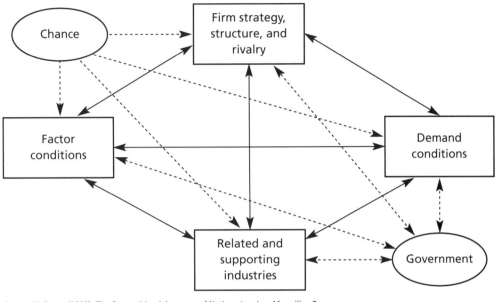

Source: M. Porter (1990), *The Competitive Advantage of Nations*, London: Macmillan Press

● *Firm strategy*, structure and rivalry. The way firms are managed and formulate their strategies affects their competitive advantage. The more intense the rivalry between firms the more effective and efficient they will have to be to survive and therefore the more internationally competitive they will be.

In addition to these four determinants, the development of firms in a cluster depends on chance and on the government. Chance inventions or other events outside the control of companies or their governments create discontinuities that can reshape an industry. Government policies are part of the system too because they can add to or detract from competitive advantage (see *Illustration 8.6*).

These determinants create a system within which the nation's firms are born and develop. They gain advantage when the cluster they are part of is more favourable than competing clusters. This is a self-reinforcing system because the effect of one determinant depends upon the state of the others. Favourable demand conditions only lead to success if the state of rivalry is such that firms respond.

This framework, like the studies by Miller and Pascale, presents a fundamentally different perspective on the dynamics of organisational development to that which has conditioned most of our thinking about the sources of success. Porter is stressing the importance of the notion of an organisation as a complex system within an even larger complex system. He shows how that system develops in an amplifying feedback fashion, where small changes are escalated and generate virtuous and vicious circles (see Chapter 9). He brings in the part played by chance.

Illustration
8.6

Silicon Valley and the Italian shoe industry

Research centres of excellence in microelectronics and information technology at Stanford and Berkeley, together with the availability of skilled labour, played an important part in the development of Silicon Valley in California. The availability of advanced technology made this an attractive location for electronics manufacturers in the early stages of that industry's development. These businesses in turn attracted component suppliers and other support companies. What we can observe is a feedback process through which a particular constellation of industries is built up.

A similar process can be observed around Cambridge in the UK. Once again a research centre of excellence has played an important part in the initial attraction of electronics and information technology firms. Feedback connections attracted others to establish a whole new industrial area. Similar developments are to be observed between Reading and Bristol, for similar reasons.

But the specific composition of the industries, which have grown up around San Francisco, around Cambridge and between Reading and Bristol, are quite different. For example, neither of the two UK areas contains silicon chip manufacturers. These differences may be due to government policies, to some other factor, or even to small chance differences between locations and the way people responded.

Similar patterns of geographic development in fashion clothing and shoes can be observed in Northern Italy around Milan. The process is the same. Some initial advantage attracts a small cluster of companies. Through feedback, support industries are attracted and so the pattern develops.

We can detect and recognise these patterns of geographic economic development, but their specific form seems to be unpredictable, depending to a significant extent on chance. Failed attempt after attempt by governments artificially to establish such geographic concentrations through planned industrial policies attests to this unpredictability. ∎

8.9 SUMMARY

This chapter has shown how the notion of negative feedback processes that move systems toward stable equilibrium adaptation to an environment underlies the tools, techniques and prescriptions of ordinary management. Cybernetic notions of intentionally steering and controlling a system underlie most of the development of systems thinking as applied to organisations. However, this chapter has shown that positive feedback with its amplifying, destabilising impact is a normal and irremovable part of life in organisations. What we do not find in the literature is a well-developed framework for understanding the dynamic consequences of this simultaneous presence of both positive and negative feedback and for understanding how we deal with it when it comes to making strategies. There is no coherent link between systems theory and the descriptive studies of emergent strategy in organisations.

In the next chapter we turn to the modern science of complexity which, I believe, provides us with the kind of coherent framework that allows us to understand the operation of both positive and negative feedback, its link with creativity and the manner in which it can be used to understand the emergence of strategies that we observe in organisations.

Further reading

Richardson (1991) provides an excellent account of the use of feedback thinking in human systems and Senge's (1990) book is an excellent summary of systems thinking. Miller and Rice (1967) is a classic in this area and Turton (1991) provides an excellent discussion in more depth of much of the material in this chapter.

References

Ashby, W. R. (1945), The effect of controls on stability, *Natura*, 155, pp. 242–43.

Ashby, W. R. (1952), *Design for a Brain*, New York: John Wiley.

Ashby, W. R. (1956), *Introduction to Cybernetics*, New York: John Wiley.

Beer, Stafford (1959/67), *Cybernetics and Management*, London: English Universities Press.

Beer, Stafford (1966), *Decision and Control: The Meaning of Operational Research and Management Cybernetics*, London: John Wiley.

Buzzell, R. D. (1984), Citibank: marketing to multinational customers, in Buzzell, R. D. & Quelch, J. A. (Eds.) (1988), *Multinational Marketing Management*, Reading, Ma.: Addison-Wesley.

Forrester, J. (1958), Industrial dynamics: a major break-through for decision-making, *Harvard Business Review*, vol. 36, no. 4, pp. 37–66.

Forrester, J. (1961), *Industrial Dynamics*, Cambridge, Ma.: MIT Press.

Gouldner, A. (1964), *Patterns of Industrial Bureaucracy*, New York: The Free Press.

Hamel, G. & Prahalad, C.K. (1989), Strategic intent, *Harvard Business Review*, May–June, pp. 63–76.

Hartley, R. F. (1991), *Management Mistakes*, New York: John Wiley.

Kast, P. & Rosenzweig, F. (1970), *Management and Organisation*, New York: McGraw-Hill.

Lawrence, P. R. & Lorsch, J. W. (1967), *Organization and Environment*, Cambridge, Ma.: Harvard University Press.

Merton, R. K. (1957), Bureaucratic structure and personality, in *Social Theory and Social Structure*, New York: The Free Press.

Miller, E. J. & Rice, A. K. (1967), *Systems of Organization: The Control of Task and Sentient Boundaries*, London: Tavistock Publications.

Perrow, C. (1984), *Normal Accidents: Living with High Risk Technologies*, New York: Basic Books.

Peters, T. J. (1985), *Thriving on Chaos*, New York: Macmillan.

Peters, T. J. & Waterman, R. H. (1982), *In Search of Excellence*, New York: Harper & Row.

Porter, M. (1991), *The Competitive Advantage of Nations*, London: Macmillan Press.

Richardson, G. P. (1991), *Feedback Thought in the Social Sciences and Systems Theory*, Philadelphia: University of Pennsylvania Press.

Schumpeter, J. A. (1934), *The Theory of Economic Development*, Cambridge, Ma.: Harvard University Press.

Senge, P. M. (1990), *The Fifth Discipline: The Art of Practice of the Learning Organization*, New York: Doubleday.

Trist, E. L. & Branforth, K. W. (1951), Some social and psychological consequences of the long-wall method of coal getting, *Human Relations*, vol. 5, pp. 6–24.

Turton, R. (1991), *Behaviour in a Business Context*, London: Chapman & Hall.

von Bertalanfy, L. (1968), *General Systems Theory, Foundations, Development and Application*, New York: George Braziller.

Weick, K. (1969/1979), *The Social Psychology of Organizing*, Reading, Ma.: Addison-Wesley.

Weick, K. (1977), Organizational design: organizations as self-organizing systems, *Organizational Dynamics*, Autumn, pp. 31–67.

Wiener, N. (1948), *Cybernetics: or Control and Communication in the Animal and the Machine*, Cambridge, Ma.: MIT Press.

CHAPTER 9

System dynamics far from equilibrium

Complex feedback systems coevolving into open-ended evolutionary space

INTRODUCTION

The previous chapter has shown how clearly the literature establishes that organisations are nonlinear feedback systems driven by both positive and negative feedback processes in which small changes can and do escalate into major alterations in patterns of behaviour and in which cause and effect may be very distant from each other. However, this literature has so far developed relatively little insight into the dynamical consequences of these properties. We have no theory of emergence in the literature: there is no coherent framework for understanding the processes that lead to emergent outcomes. We have talked about organisational learning but almost always as a tidy process that produces progressive improvement and that somehow we can always be in control of – signs of the stable equilibrium paradigm at work in our attempts to understand the learning organisation. The systems literature seems to be built on the notion that when we understand the systemic nature of an organisation we will be able to control its behaviour, we will be able to identify the leverage points that will enable us to ensure that an organisation realises someone's vision. Such an approach is based on the assumption that emergence is to be removed rather than understood – if a vision is realised we can hardly say that the outcome emerged. And yet the descriptive literature keeps reporting that strategies very frequently emerge and we will never understand why if we keep building models that have to do with realising an intention of some kind.

It is because of this kind of lack in the management and organisation literature that we must return to the natural sciences from whence organisation theorists ultimately derive today's current theories, because it is the natural scientists who have been constructing a coherent framework for understanding the emergent behaviour of complex systems.

The science of complexity studies the fundamental properties, the dynamics of nonlinear feedback networks – it turns out that most of nature's systems are such systems just as, not surprisingly, most human systems are. Although they have so far focused primarily on the behaviour of systems in nature, those developing the new science have been uncovering the properties of nonlinear feedback itself, properties that are general and apply to all such systems no matter where they are found. In Chapter 8 we have established quite clearly, drawing on a substantial literature in organisational and management theory, that human groups and organisations are nonlinear feedback networks. The discoveries made by complexity scientists must, therefore, have something to say about human systems.

It is the purpose of this chapter to outline what the discoveries of complexity science are and to indicate how they apply to human systems. Part Four of this book will then explore that application in some detail, showing how complexity science gives us a deeper insight into the nature of extraordinary management.

For ease of exposition I am going to divide the science of complexity into two branches – the first will cover the theory of chaos which is concerned with deterministic feedback systems, and the second will cover theories of complexity which are concerned with adaptive systems.

Deterministic nonlinear feedback systems are networks consisting of large numbers of components, or agents, interacting with each other according to certain rules or laws. So, a physical system such as the solar system consists of a number of agents called planets and they interact with each other according to the laws of gravity to produce orbiting patterns of behaviour. The weather is a physical system consisting of air pressure, humidity, wind speed and so on, all interacting with each other at an enormous number of points in the space around the earth. A chemical system consists of a number of molecules of different kinds that interact with each other according to the rules of chemical interaction. All of these are deterministic systems in the sense that the rules which the components follow are precisely defined and fixed over time with no random elements in their formulation at all.

This distinguishes deterministic systems from probabilistic ones. Probabilistic systems have random terms in the laws driving their behaviour to represent:

- exogenous shocks, that is, changes impacting on the system from outside of it that are not driven by its own laws;
- errors in the formulation of the laws;
- noise, or errors in the data being fed into the laws to determine the system's behaviour.

You can see why those studying human systems have normally used probabilistic rather than deterministic formulations. For example, if one is studying a market then one can formulate economic laws governing its behaviour but political forces will have to be represented as exogenous variables, that is, changes impacting from outside the market which cannot be explained by the laws of the market. Also there will have to be terms representing inevitable errors in the formulation of the laws of the market and errors in the data measuring market behaviour.

Furthermore, both deterministic and probabilistic systems must be distinguished from adaptive ones in that the latter consist of agents who change their rules of conduct as the system evolves. Clearly, human system are of the adaptive kind.

So it must be made clear right at the start that any conclusions we derive from the study of the dynamics of deterministic or probabilistic systems cannot be applied directly to adaptive systems, of which organisations are one example. The study of deterministic systems can, however, provide us with metaphors and analogies that might provoke us to see organisational life in a different way – the study of the dynamics of deterministic systems might help us to change our mental model of the nature of management.

In the next section, then, we will explore the dynamics of deterministic systems. After that we will explore the dynamics of adaptive systems and check whether the insights derived from studying deterministic ones apply to adaptive ones too – obviously, I am going to argue that they do, otherwise there would be little point in exploring them further. Having explored both deterministic and adaptive systems we will then be close to making direct connections to human systems because they are adaptive feedback networks.

9.2 THE DYNAMICS OF DETERMINISTIC SYSTEMS: CHAOS THEORY

Since the times of Newton, Bacon and Descartes, scientists have tended to understand the natural world in terms of machine-like regularity in which given inputs are translated through absolutely fixed laws into given outputs. For example, if you apply a force of ten pounds per square inch to a ball weighing fifteen pounds, the laws of motion will determine exactly how far the ball will move on a horizontal plane in a vacuum. Cause and effect are related in a straightforward linear way (see *Key Concept 8.7* in Chapter 8). On this view, once we have discovered the fixed laws and gathered data on the inputs to those laws, we will be able to predict the behaviour of nature's systems. Once we know how the system would have behaved without our intervention, we can then intervene by altering the inputs to the laws and so get nature to do something different, something we want it to do. According to this Newtonian view of the world we will ultimately be able to dominate nature.

This whole way of reasoning and understanding was imported into economics, where it is particularly conspicuous, and also into the other social sciences and some schools of psychology, where it is somewhat less conspicuous. This importation is the source of the stable equilibrium paradigm (see *Key Concept 8.6*) that still today dominates thinking on managing and organising. That thinking is based on the belief that managers can in principle control the long-term future of a human system. Such a belief is realistic only if cause-and-effect links are of the Newtonian type described above, for only then can the future of a system be predicted, and only if its future can be predicted can it be controlled by someone.

Nowadays, complexity scientists make sense of the world by taking a dynamic feedback system perspective. From this point of view, nature is still understood to be driven by laws. The laws, however, are not ones of straightforward unidirectional causality; rather, they take the form of nonlinear feedback loops where causality is circular (see *Key Concept 8.7*)

What the theory of chaos (Gleick, 1988, provides a history of the development of chaos theory) tells us is this: any deterministic nonlinear feedback system (loop, mechanism) can operate in a negative feedback manner to produce stable equilibrium behaviour; or it can be driven by positive feedback to generate explosively unstable behaviour; or finally, it can operate in a mode in which feedback autonomously flips between positive and negative feedback to produce behaviour that is simultaneously both stable and unstable. We have already seen in Chapter 8 that all human organisations are nonlinear feedback systems capable of generating all three of these states and we can see all of them in practice.

More specifically, the theory of chaos says that, when a deterministic nonlinear feedback system is driven away from the peaceful state of stable equilibrium toward the hectic state of explosive instability, it passes through a stage of *bounded instability* in which it displays highly complex behaviour, in effect the result of the system flipping randomly between positive and negative feedback. We might think of this stage as a border area between stable equilibrium and explosive instability; that is, a state of paradox in which two contradictory forces, stability and instability, are operating simultaneously, pulling the system in opposing directions. While the system is in this border area neither of these contradictory forces can ever be removed; instead, the forces are endlessly rearranged in different yet similar patterns. When the system is in the border area it never behaves in a regular way that leads to equilibrium. Instead, it generates patterns of behaviour that are not only irregular but also absolutely unpredictable. Nonetheless, such behaviour has an overall, 'hidden', qualitative pattern. The technical name for what I am here calling 'bounded instability' is 'low dimensional deterministic chaos', but for our purposes we do not need to be so precise – we are interested in the qualitative insight which chaos theory yields rather than its precise mathematical properties.

These conclusions are fundamental properties of nonlinear feedback systems no matter where they may be found; they are consequences of the nonlinear structure of the system itself, not due to any environment the system may operate in. Since, as we have already seen organisations are nonlinear feedback systems, these specific properties indicate something about human organisations. It will be useful, therefore, to understand these properties somewhat more fully.

Bounded instability far-from-equilibrium

The key discovery that chaos theorists have made about the operation of deterministic nonlinear feedback systems is that stable equilibrium and explosive instability are not the only *attractors*, or end points, of behaviour open to such systems. Nonlinear systems have a third choice: a state of bounded or limited instability far from equilibrium in which behaviour has a pattern, but it is irregular. This kind of instability is produced because the system's structure is such that, when the system is far enough away from equilibrium, it continually flips between negative and positive feedback. This means that the choice of far-from-equilibrium behaviour is a *both/and* one because the system is driven alternately by both positive and negative feedback and the outcome is both stable and unstable. And it is so driven, not because some agent within or outside it applies first one kind of feedback and then the other, but because the nonlinear structure of the loop causes this to happen autonomously in an apparently random way. Nonlinearity is in a sense its own constraint and stable instability is one of its fundamental properties. The choice of equilibrium behaviour, on the other hand, is an *either/or* one. Either the system is driven by negative feedback and then it tends to stable equilibrium, or the system is driven by positive feedback and then it tends to explosive instability. If that instability is to be removed, then some agent or condition outside the system would have to 'step in and put a stop to it'. In other words, when systems are held far from equilibrium, they automatically apply internal constraints to keep instability within boundaries. This is so because of the nonlinear structure of the system. Once such a system moves into an unstable position, however, any constraint has to come from outside the system.

When it operates in the border between stability and instability, the behaviour of the system unfolds in so complex a manner, so dependent upon the detail of what happens, that the links between cause and effect are lost. We can no longer count on a certain given input leading to a certain given output. The laws themselves operate to escalate small chance disturbances along the way, breaking the link between an input and a subsequent output. We have come across all these points in Chapter 8 in relation to organisations, but the conclusion we now reach is stronger, clearer and more definite: *deterministic nonlinear feedback systems generate completely unpredictable behaviour at a specific level over the long-term.* The long-term future of such a system operating in the borders between stability and instability is not simply difficult to see: it is inherently unknowable. And it is so because of the feedback structure of the system itself, not simply because of changes going on outside it and impacting upon it. Nothing can remove that unknowability. If this were to apply to an organisation operating in the border area between stability and instability, then any decision-making process that involved forecasting, envisioning future states, or even making any assumptions about future states would be ineffective. Those applying such processes in conditions of bounded instability would be engaging in fantasy activities. In other words, ordinary management would be completely ineffective and would be being used a cover up.

Although deterministic nonlinear feedback systems may generate unpredictable specific behaviour, that behaviour nevertheless has an overall qualitative pattern to it. Perhaps the easiest way to think of this is as follows. Dynamic feedback systems generate sequences of specific behaviours or events that fall into categories recognisable by 'family resemblance' type features which the behaviour or events share with each other. But within those very general, rather vague and irregular categories, each piece of behaviour or event is different. What we have is endless individual variety within broad categories – the templates or archetypes developed in the Forrester-type models, for example (see Chapter 8). If this applied to organisations we would have to abandon all decision-making techniques that involved step-by-step reasoning from assumptions about the future. We would have to rely instead on using qualitative patterns to *reason by analogy and intuition*. Those who succeeded in the borders between stability and instability would be those who saw patterns where others searched for specific links between causes and events.

This discovery, the very surprising one that perfectly deterministic laws can yield behaviour that is in a sense random, has been called deterministic chaos. Note that low dimensional deterministic chaos has a precise mathematical meaning – it is not utter confusion but a combination of qualitative patterns and specific randomness; a combination of fuzzy categories within which there is endless variety. The shape of a snowflake, for example, is generated by the feedback loop between it and its environment as it floats to the ground; it quite clearly belongs to the category 'snowflakes', but it is different from all other snowflakes and it is different because positive feed-back loops have amplified tiny chance differences in the environment it experienced as it floated to earth, making it a product of its precise history.

So far we have been discussing how order (fixed laws) leads to disorder (random patterns of behaviour and completely unpredictable long-term futures). Now consider how disorder leads to unexpected new forms of order. Nonlinear feedback systems have also been discovered to possess another surprising and important property. Such systems are capable of spontaneously producing unpredictable, more complex forms of behaviour. They do this when they are pushed far from equilibrium, near to or into chaos; and they do it through a process of self-organisation. This means that, in nonlin-ear feedback systems, continuously novel behaviour emerges. Such innovation is not the result of any prior intention or purpose on the part of the system and it cannot be planned in advance. Experimenters seeking to provoke such unpredictable behaviour have to operate on the boundary conditions. They cannot determine what the system will do in specific terms but they can bring about some general patterns of behaviour if the right surrounding conditions are created. In these circumstances the system may be creative (see *Key Concept 9.1*).

Let me emphasise this point. The theory of chaos is a tremendously important analogy to use in thinking about organisational life because it is telling us that systems are cap-able of variety and novelty (creativity and innovation in organisational terms) only when they are pushed far from equilibrium to the edge of disintegration. Keeping a system in the orderly equilibrium zone is the same as trapping it in endless repetition of its past and destroying its creativity. This suggests that negative feedback controls and ordinary management processes trap organisations into repeating their past and destroying their creativity. Creative organisations will require something that works against this.

Key Concept 9.1

Systems and creativity

At the border between stability and instability nonlinear feedback systems generate a whole world of forms that are neither stable nor unstable but a paradoxical combination of both. Their variety and beauty are such that we can describe such mathematical systems as ones that are continuously creative. If a system is not conscious and yet produces an endless stream of new and beautiful forms, it might be argued that it is just as creative as a conscious system doing the same thing. In the old mechanistic mind-set of the scientist, nature's systems were thought to behave in absolutely predictable, predetermined ways. From this perspective it would be absurd to talk about a natural system choosing to behave in a particular way or creating something new. Choice and creativity are, from this perspective, confined to consciousness and any order would be there by prior design. The new understanding is that nature's systems are driven by nonlinear feedback and the understanding of how these systems function changes the whole mind-set. We can now see that inanimate systems can choose and be creative; order can emerge unpredictably from chaos without prior design. In this way, nature produces the beautiful and the surprising.

These discoveries, therefore, have extremely important implications for the way in which we think about creativity and about control. If systems are developing along inherently unpredictable specific paths, and if they spontaneously produce innovative forms through a process of self-organisation, then no one can be in control of such a system. It is totally impossible for humans to be in control of, or to dominate, systems such as this. The discoveries also mean that creativity arises out of instability. Looking at the world in this new way helps us to see why instability and unpredictability are essential to innovation and creativity. You can begin to see how this might provide us with a theory to explain the observation made by Mintzberg and others (*Mintzberg & Waters, 1982–1985*) that strategies often emerge without intention in organisations.

The properties of low dimensional deterministic chaos and self-organisation have been found to apply to nonlinear feedback systems in meteorology, physics, chemistry and biology (*Gleick, 1988*). Economists and other social scientists are now exploring whether these discoveries are relevant to their disciplines (*Baumol & Benhabib, 1989; Kelsey, 1988; Anderson, Arrow & Pines, 1988*). There are strong indications that chaos explanations apply to foreign exchange markets, stock markets and oil markets (*Peters, 1991*). Some have also applied these ideas to theories of managing and organising (*Nonaka, 1988; Stacey, 1991; Zimmerman, 1991*). However, before returning to the world of organisations we will continue to explore what bounded instability and self-organisation mean. It is worth doing this because the implications for decision making and control are so important.

The nature of deterministic chaos

In the discussions on organisational dynamics in the last chapter we have seen how:

- organisations are sets of nonlinear feedback loops;
- organisations are capable of generating stable equilibrium behaviour and also explosively unstable behaviour;
- nonlinear systems containing both positive and negative loops can, simply because of their structure, flip from stability to instability and back again;
- most organisations seem to be in a state that has characteristics of stability and instability, a state away from equilibrium that seems to be in the borders between stability and instability.

The theory of chaos explains the nature of this border area between stability and instability for a deterministic system: it is a state in which a system combines both stability and instability to generate patterns of behaviour that are irregular and inherently unpredictable, but yet have a structure. This theory might therefore provide us with rich metaphors for organisational life.

Mapping chaos

To illustrate the state of deterministic chaos consider the following famous feedback loop. It is the equation that generates what is called the Mandelbrot set, named after its discoverer, Benoit Mandelbrot (*Mandelbrot, 1982; Gleick, 1988; Stewart, 1989*):

$$Z_t = Z_{t-1}^2 + c$$

This is a feedback loop because event Z now at time t is determined by event Z last time at time $t - 1$ and it will determine event Z next time at time $t + 1$. Starting with any Z event, this feedback relationship will generate a whole sequence of subsequent Z events over time; each Z event is simply fed back into the loop to generate the next Z event. Precisely what that sequence will look like will depend upon the parameter c. If we start with a Z and some value for c, we get one sequence of events. Change the Z keeping the same c and we get another sequence. If we start with the same Z but another c we will get yet another sequence of events.

Some of the sequences will be stable and orderly, settling down into predictable patterns over time. The patterns may be ones of constancy or of perfectly regular cycles. This is the equilibrium of stability. Yet other Z events will generate sequences that grow explosively to infinity in a perfectly predictable way – the equilibrium of explosive instability.

If we take many thousands of Z events and c parameters, examining them to see if they generate stable or unstable sequences, we will be able to draw a map of all the starting conditions leading to stability and all the starting conditions leading to instability. This will be a map of the two final states to which this particular nonlinear feedback system is attracted. It will be a map of the two attractors for the system.

A computer program (*Peitgen & Richter, 1986*) can be written to calculate sequences of Zs from the above equation (Z is a complex number, but it does not matter for our purpose what a complex number is) and that program plots a black point for all Zs that produce stable sequences and a white point for all Zs that generate unstable sequences. The result of doing this is shown in *Figure 9.1* and there is nothing at all surprising about it: there is a black blob in the middle representing all combinations of starting events that yield stable outcomes (attraction to stable equilibrium) and outside this blob there is a large white area for all events that lead to instability (attraction to explosively unstable equilibrium).

According to this map, this particular feedback system has a choice between being attracted to stability or instability. If this is the only choice we are aware of, we will quite naturally conclude that successful systems must be stable systems.

The surprise comes, however, when we start to look closely at the border between stability and instability, for we discover that the border is not the clean-cut clear line dividing stability from instability that we might have expected. Instead we discover that this border area is a completely different form of behaviour that scientists knew little about until the last twenty years or so. The discovery means that nonlinear feedback systems are not confronted by a simple choice between stability and instability – they could choose to operate in the third state, one of bounded instability. This is qualitatively different behaviour from either stability or instability.

We can see what this third attractor looks like on our computer map by taking smaller and smaller intervals between the Z events and the c parameters at the border line and plotting their resulting stability or instability. When we do this we find, as shown in *Figure 9.2*, that the borders are complex, highly irregular, wispy lines.

Now examine one of these wispy lines in more detail and your computer will draw a complex pattern of the kind shown in *Figure 9.3*. These patterns in the figure are in black and white, but you could instruct the computer to use different colours according to how long it takes to identify whether an initial point will end up as an unstable sequence. With these instructions, the computer will draw a contour map of the strength

FIGURE 9.1

A map of stability and instability

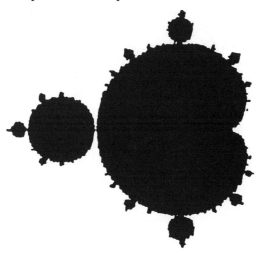

Source: R. Penrose (1989), *The Emperor's New Mind: Concerning Computers, Minds and the Laws of Physics*, Oxford: Oxford University Press

FIGURE 9.2

Mapping the borders between stability and instability

Source: R. Penrose (1989), *The Emperor's New Mind: Concerning Computers, Minds and the Laws of Physics*, Oxford: Oxford University Press

of the pull to infinity or instability and the result is patterns of great beauty (see for example, *Peitger & Richter (1986)* or *Gleick (1988)*). Part of the pattern in *Figure 9.3* can now be blown up and you will see other patterns embedded in it. What you see depends each time on how closely you look and it is always different. But it is also always similar – recognisable irregular patterns always appear. Tiny differences in your perspective, tiny differences in the range of events or numbers you are concerned with, lead to very different, yet recognisably similar patterns, with the original shape, islands of stability, popping up over and over again. These patterns are constant only in the degree of their irregularity. Tucked between stability and instability, at the frontier, nonlinear feedback systems generate a whole world of creative, exciting, beautiful forms of behaviour that are neither stable nor unstable but continuously new and creative.

What this discovery, made only some thirty years ago, amounts to is this. There is no clear-cut border between stability and instability for a deterministic nonlinear feed-

FIGURE 9.3
A closer look at the border

Source: R. Penrose (1989), *The Emperor's New Mind: Concerning Computers, Minds and the Laws of Physics*, Oxford: Oxford University Press back system. Instead there is an infinitely intricate border that is neither stable nor unstable, but a state of bounded instability, an intertwining of order and disorder. Perhaps one can think of it as a state of inherent contradiction between stability and instability in which order and disorder cannot be separated.

In this border area we cannot make clear-cut distinctions between stability and instability because the starting conditions that lead to one are so close to the starting conditions that lead to the other. They are so close, in fact, that we could never measure or act upon the differences between them; we could never determine in advance which end condition was going to occur because we are incapable of infinite precision. For all practical purposes, then, instability and stability, irregularity and regularity, are hopelessly intertwined with each other here and, because of this, the specific future of the system is inherently unpredictable.

Ideas of this kind are certainly not new concepts. Many ancient mythologies incorporate them and artists and philosophers have spoken in these terms for a very long time. Jungian analytical psychology is built on the notion of contradictory opposites generating the tension that creates psychic energy from which the endless variety of human behaviour patterns emerges. What is astonishing, however, is that very simple, absolutely fixed mathematical equations can generate the kind of behaviour we have just discussed. What is equally astonishing is that such equations describe how a great many of nature's systems behave. These ideas are no longer confined to the realms of mythology, art, philosophy and psychology, but have potentially moved to the centre of all sciences, even though those proposing them are still at the fringes of the scientific community. If managers wish to adopt a scientific approach to understanding organisations, they must now take account of these properties of nonlinear feedback systems. *Illustration 9.1* provides some examples of chaos in nature's systems.

Illustration 9.1

Chaos in nature's systems

Chaos exists, outside abstract mathematical equations, in the earth's weather system. The weather is patterns in interdependent forces such as pressure, temperature, humidity and wind speed which feed into each other and thence back into themselves. The weather is generated by a nonlinear feedback system.

To model its behaviour, the forces have to be measured at a particular point in time, at regular vertical intervals through the atmosphere from each of a grid of points on the earth's surface. Rules are then necessary to explain how each of the sets of interrelated measurements, at each measurement point in the atmosphere, move over time. This requires massive numbers of computations. When these computations are carried out they reveal that the weather always follows what is called a *strange* attractor, another name for a chaotic pattern. The shape of that attractor is shown in *Figure 9.4*.

What this shape means is that the weather follows recognisably similar patterns, but those patterns are never ever exactly the same as those at any previous point in time. The system is highly sensitive to some small changes and blows them up into major alterations in weather patterns. Chaotic dynamics mean that we will never be able to forecast the weather for more than a few days ahead. The theoretical maximum for accurate forecasts is two weeks, one meteorologists are nowhere near reaching yet.

FIGURE 9.4
The strange attractor for the weather system

Source: R. Stacey (1991), *The Chaos Frontier: Creative Strategic Control for Business*, Oxford: Butterworth-Heinemann

Throughout the 1970s and the 1980s the principles of chaos have been explored in one field after another and found to explain turbulence in gases and liquids, certain pathological conditions of the heart, the eye movements of schizophrenics, the spread of some diseases, and the impact of some inoculation programmes against some diseases. The body's system of arteries and veins follows patterns determined by feedback rules with chaotic properties. The growth of insect populations has chaotic characteristics. The leaves of trees grow through a process of iterating deterministic rules contained in their spores; they are fractal and self-similar enough to allow us to distinguish one kind from another but no two of a kind are ever exactly the same. You can reproduce similar individuals, clearly belonging to one category, on a computer using the rules and iteration. Human cells divide in the same way following rules encoded in the DNA. The reason for no two snowflakes ever being the same can be explained using chaotic dynamics. The orbit of the moon Hyperion around Saturn follows a path which can be explained using the principles of chaos as can the Great Red Spot of Jupiter. Water dripping from a tap has been shown to follow a chaotic time pattern, as does smoke spiralling from a cigarette. ∎

At this stage, note from our map in *Figure 9.2* that the particular system we are talking about there will find it most easy to be attracted to explosive instability – most Z events and *c* parameters produce this result. The next easiest option will be stability because large numbers of Z events and *c* parameters lead to this eventual outcome. The most difficult option to follow will be that of bounded instability because the range of Z events and c parameters leading to it is so much smaller. Indeed the area over which chaotic behaviour applies is so small that for centuries scientists did not notice its existence.

It is useful to reflect upon how the relative ease of reaching stability, explosive instability and chaos relate to the findings of Miller and Pascale discussed in Chapter 3. They too found that organisations seem to be attracted most easily to states of stability and explosive instability. What organisations seem to find most difficult is sustaining a state of contradiction, a state between the extremes of differentiation and integration, the extremes of instability and stability. The lesson seems to be that staying in the border area is a difficult task that requires continuing energy and attention.

Illustration 9.2 gives another way of looking at this important border area between stability and instability.

Illustration 9.2

Chaos and the logistic equation

In Chapter 8, Section 8.8, we examined the operation of negative and positive feedback in the logistic equation. Now consider how much further the theory of chaos takes our understanding of this system.

Suppose that the profit level P of a particular company in a time period t depends exactly upon its advertising outlay in that period. Suppose further that there is a simple nonlinear relationship between profit and advertising. This means that increased advertising has a diminishing impact on consumers until eventually some increase in advertising brings in a profit which is smaller than the outlay, so that the total profit falls. Therefore, sometimes profit follows an amplifying feedback loop and sometimes it follows a damping feedback loop. To represent this behaviour in mathematical terms we can use the logistic difference equation already encountered in Chapter 8.

$$P_t = cP_{t-1} (1 - P_{t-1})$$

This nonlinear feedback loop will generate a sequence of profits over time for any value of c. The question is what patterns will profit follow as you raise the value of the parameter c (bigger impact of advertising on profit and/or bigger proportion of profit devoted to advertising).

At low levels of c, profit will settle into stable equilibrium paths of straight lines over time (values for c between 0 and 3), or of regular, repetitive cycles (values for c between 3 and 3.5). At high values for c (above 4), profits will show an unstable but uniform pattern of explosive growth to infinity. As with the Mandelbrot equation, therefore, we have states of stable equilibrium at first and later on states of unstable equilibrium, and we want to know what happens at the borders between them (values for c between 3.5 and 4).

To see this we have to perform thousands of calculations on a computer, gradually increasing the value of c. For example, at $c = 3.2$, we find that profits fluctuate along a regular two-period cycle with one peak and one trough. At a value for c of 3.5, a period four cycle appears – two peaks and two troughs. If you tune the parameter up to 3.56 the period doubles again and you get a period eight cycle. By 3.567 the cycles are to period 16. Thereafter there are rapid period doublings until you reach a value for the parameter c of 3.58 *(Stewart, 1989)*.

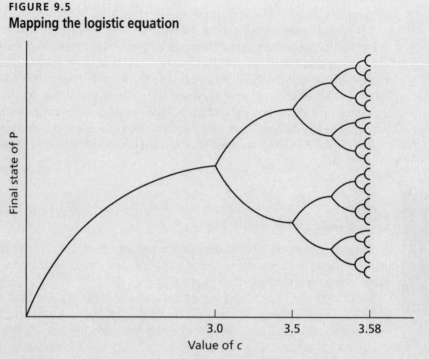

FIGURE 9.5
Mapping the logistic equation

Source: R. Stacey (1991), *The Chaos Frontier: Creative Strategic Control for Business*, Oxford: Butterworth-Heinemann

This pattern is shown in *Figure 9.5.* Here the final values reached by profit are plotted (on the vertical axis) against the value of the parameter *c* (on the horizontal axis). So for each value of *c* between 0 and 3 we have a single stable point, a higher point for each value of the parameter shown by the rising curve from 0 to 3. At 3 we have two final values for profit: the peak and the trough of the cycle. The line splits into two, or bifurcates. And the peaks and troughs diverge as we go from 3 to 3.5. At 3.5 we get a further bifurcation to show two peaks and two troughs. They in turn bifurcate and soon at 3.58 there are infinitely many bifurcations. This diagram has been called a figtree diagram, showing how, at successive values of the parameter, the trunk of final values splits into boughs, the boughs into branches, the branches into twigs, the twigs into twiglets and so on. The behaviour of the system is far more complicated than we could have imagined.

What happens as we continue to tune up the parameter *c*? At the parameter value of 3.58 the behaviour of the system becomes random (instability), within fixed boundaries (stability). There are no regular cycles; the values from each iteration shoot all over the place (within boundaries) and never return to any value they previously had. No matter how many thousands of iterations you try this remains true. There are cycles that you can recognise as cycles, but they are always irregular. This is chaos, also known as a strange attractor. There is no way you could ever forecast what will happen to profit if the parameter value is 3.58 – and that has nothing to do with environmental changes or random shocks. Nothing changes outside the equation, you follow the same constant rules as before and the parameter value sticks at 3.58, but the consequence is totally unpredictable disorder in the path of profit over time.

Figure 9.6 shows a representation of many thousands of iterations for parameter values between around 3.3 and 4. The black areas are chaos and the white stripes within chaos are windows of order.

You can now examine the first white stripe in the top part of *Figure 9.6* by iterating for very small intervals of the parameter value which yields that white stripe. In effect, you 'blow up' the picture within the window of order, and you find that this magnified portion resembles the whole diagram. This is shown in *Figure 9.7*. If you repeat the blow-up procedure for the first white stripe in *Figure 9.7* you will once again find a picture that resembles the whole diagram as shown in *Figure 9.6*. The structure is infinitely deep; there are pictures within pictures forever and they are always similar.

FIGURE 9.6
Further map of the logisitic equation

Source: R. Stacey (1991), *The Chaos Frontier: Creative Strategic Control for Business*, Oxford: Butterworth-Heinemann

FIGURE 9.7

Yet another map of the logistic equation

What we have, then, is a very simple nonlinear feedback relationship, or decision-making rule, that produces a highly complex pattern of results over time. Between stability and instability there is a complex border that combines both stability and instability. ■

Source: R. Stacey (1991), *The Chaos Frontier: Creative Strategic Control for Business*, Oxford: Butterworth-Heinemann

The properties of chaos

The discovery of the state of bounded instability is of such great importance because of what it means for the nature of cause and effect. Since, as we have seen in Chapter 8 there are reasons for believing that organisations might be operating in states like those of deterministic chaos, these important conclusions about cause and effect might apply to organisations, in effect helping us to understand just what the open-ended change facing organisations is.

Cause and effect

In a state of deterministic chaos a system operates to amplify tiny changes in starting conditions into major alterations of consequent behaviour. This is called *sensitive dependence on initial conditions*. That sensitivity is so great that differences in the value of a variable or parameter to the thousandth or even the millionth decimal point can eventually alter the complete behaviour of the system. Tiny changes that we could not possibly hope to detect, measure or record could lead the system to completely different, qualitatively different, states of behaviour. This means that the links between cause and effect are lost in the detail of what happens. For all practical purposes the links have disappeared and we will therefore not be able to identify the specific consequences of a specific action nor will we be able to identify the specific cause of a specific event. Any claim that we have so done will simply be our own fantasy. To be connected to reality we will have to think instead in terms of general qualitative patterns related to the system as a whole.

The system dynamics we surveyed in the last chapter recognised that the links between cause and effect become distant in complex systems and are hard to detect. We can now see that it might be more extreme than that – the links can disappear altogether if the system operates in the area of bounded instability.

Chaos, cybernetics and statistical relationships

You will recall that those who developed cybernetics (see Chapter 8) were also concerned with what feedback meant for cause-and-effect links. They sidestepped the problem by saying that a feedback system is so complex that we cannot establish what the causal links are. But the way cybernetic models operate is based on the assumption that the links are still there, even though we cannot identify them. Those links are assumed to generate clear connections between inputs to the system and outputs from it. It is only because of this assumption that cybernetic control can be based on statistical relationships. We can now see that this connection is broken when a system operates in deterministic chaos and that must make cybernetic control absolutely impossible. When the cause-and-effect links are in effect lost in the complexity of specific experience we may detect a strong statistical association in data from the past, but that association will not continue into the future.

Going back in time

Consider what this breakdown of cause-and-effect links means. Suppose a system has moved from a particular state A many periods ago and now occupies another state B. Could we take control of this system and take it back to state A? We could, if it were possible to identify the links between the causes and effects of its behaviour and we had a record of those causes over the past periods. We could then simply make the system retrace its steps and go back into its own history. If we did not have perfectly accurate records of past causes, and if we had not specified the causal links absolutely precisely, we could still hope to get the system back to a position approximating A, provided that the system does not escalate tiny differences in an unpredictable way. So we could only take a system back to some previous state if it is operating in equilibrium, either stable or explosively unstable. Only then are there the required clear-cut connections between cause and effect and only then do tiny differences not escalate in an unpredictable way.

If, however, the system operates in bounded instability it will be completely impossible to make it retrace its steps. For, on its journey through time from state A to state B, it will have lost some information (the law of entropy). It will have been impossible to keep infinitely accurate records of everything that happened to it, to measure with infinite accuracy to the millionth decimal place. This inability to retain every single scrap of information as the system moves from A to B is of great importance when the system operates in deterministic chaos. For, as we try to take the system backwards, we inevitably make a tiny mistake in reproducing what happened to it. Before long that tiny mistake takes over and we completely miss the state A that we are trying to take the system back to. Time is irreversible (because of the law of entropy and the nature of feedback) and we can never give an entirely accurate explanation of why the system now is where it now is *(Prigogine & Stengers, 1984)*. (As an aside, in a world of nonlinear feedback systems operating in bounded instability, the law of entropy makes it impossible for time machines to take us back into history. If this is how our world operates, and many scientists think it is, then time machines will always remain fiction.)

Going forward in time

The same points apply if we want to control the movement of a system to a fixed point in the future. There is no fundamental problem of principle in doing this if the system is an equilibrium one. But, to control movement to a future point when the system is boundedly unstable, we would have to specify with infinite accuracy each event, each action, required to reach that future state. If we make some tiny error in our specification the system could well amplify this and end up somewhere completely different. We cannot then decide on some future state for the system, say C, and identify the events required to take it there. We cannot measure or record in the infinitely accurate detail required to allow this to happen. The tiniest error could escalate and swamp the behaviour of the system. Nor could we fix on some future point and then get there by trial-and-error action because our errors would not cancel out.

We could imagine this desirable state C and stipulate that that is where we wish to go, but there is an infinitely small chance that we will actually reach it. Stipulating the future state is then an illusion, a waste of time, when the system is operating in bounded instability. Making some assumptions about what that future state might be is also rather pointless because we will have to keep changing those assumptions. If we make an assumption about the specific future of a chaotic system, then the only useful thing we can say about that assumption is that it will not happen. It then becomes difficult to see how the assumption helps one to make a decision. The real drivers of behaviour become what has just happened, not some hypothetical and unrealisable assumption about what might (see *Illustration 9.3*). There is no option but to create where the system is going through action and discovering where it is going as it is going there. This is a process of learning in real time, provoked by paradox and conducted through reasoning by analogy.

It follows that we cannot be 'in control' of a system that is far from equilibrium in the way we normally think about control. We cannot be in control because we cannot forecast the specific future of a system operating in bounded instability – it moves randomly at a specific level. We cannot envision it either, unless we believe in clairvoyance or prophecy. We cannot establish how the system would move before we make a policy change and then how it would move after the policy change. We have no option but to take a chance, make the change and see what happens. The future of a chaotic system is open-ended and inherently unknowable: it moves in a random way over the long term affected by small chance disturbances. Note that the future of the system is inherently unpredictable. It is unknowable. It is not just that it is difficult to forecast accurately. It is utterly impossible to do so. Such systems are an unravellable record of their own histories. This means that we have seriously to question any prescriptions based on assumptions that long-term futures can be forecast to any extent at all.

Making assumptions about the future

Take a very abstract case. Suppose we have to decide now whether we are going to invest in a particular project or not. The project will make a lot of money if certain conditions prevail in five years time but lose a great deal if certain other conditions prevail then. We decide that we cannot forecast what the situation is likely to be in five years time because of the level of uncertainty, but we believe that we must at least make some assumptions before we can take the decision and that we should make the decision on the basis of these assumptions.

Suppose that after much research and discussion we decide that the most reasonable assumptions are that conditions ABCD will prevail. On this basis we decide that the project will make money and we go ahead, even though we know that ABCD will not be what actually materialises. We believe we can live with that if we keep updating our assumptions as time passes. So we make the investment.

Nearly a year later, some way through to completion of the project, we review the situation and find that we need to change the basic assumptions – ABCZ is now a much more reasonable scenario, we think. But three months later the project runs into a hitch and we review the situation again. Now we think that conditions XBCW make a more reasonable scenario. Even if these conditions indicate that we are unlikely to make much money, the project is now almost complete so we continue. Some three months later the project is complete and further reviews reveal that YPCW is now the likely scenario. This looks better so we set the project running. A month later we review the first month of full-scale operation and find that the situation likely to prevail at the end of our original five-year period is now assumed to be ZPNX.

Two years ago we decided to go ahead on the basis of assumptions ABCD, knowing that they would not actually prevail. Now, looking three years ahead, we are saying that the conditions will be ZPNX, completely different as we suspected all along. And no doubt we will continue to change the assumptions during the next three years. When we look back we have to admit that we decided to do something for reasons that were completely invalid and furthermore, we knew we were doing this at the time.

In what possible sense can we say that it was sensible or reasonable to make the decision on the basis of ABCD in the first place? The answer must be none. If we know that a set of conditions will not prevail it makes no sense at all to make a decision on the basis of such a fantasy. Yet this is exactly what boards of directors do when they use discounted cash flow calculations to make investments. ∎

The properties of a system operating in deterministic chaos mean that we have to abandon hope of being in control of its long-term future. We will not be able to plan its long-term future nor envision it; but in the short term, because it takes time for small changes to build up, it is possible to forecast how the system will behave. It is therefore perfectly possible to be in control, to plan the short-term development of such a system.

When it comes to the longer term, chaotic systems do have a property in addition to inherent unpredictability, one that enables us to cope. Systems operating in bounded instability always follow recognisably similar patterns, similar but always different too. The patterns are recognisable in terms of their similarity and their irregularity. *Illustration 9.4* provides an example of what is meant by this in a system in nature.

Low dimensional deterministic chaos

Chaos is, in one sense, an inherently random pattern of behaviour generated by fixed inputs into deterministic (that is, fixed) rules (relationships), taking the form of nonlinear feedback loops. Although the specific path followed by the behaviour so generated is random and hence unpredictable in the long term, it always has an underlying pattern to it, a 'hidden' pattern, a global pattern or rhythm. That pattern is self-similarity, that is, constant degree of variation, consistent variability, regular irregularity, or more precisely, a constant fractal dimension. Chaos is therefore order (a pattern) within disorder (random behaviour).

To see what the property of self-similarity, or recognisably similar patterns, means for an organisation, recall the templates or archetypes described in Chapter 8 in the section on Forrester's models: for example, patterns of shifting the burden, patterns of pushing the growth factors instead of relaxing the limiting factors. We can detect similar patterns of this type in one organisation after another, but they are never exactly the same. In Chapter 1 we talked about categories of patterns in actions – we called them strategies. One category is differentiation. We can observe many companies carrying this strategy out, but it is never the same from one company to the next. Chapter 1 also described categories of positions in markets; market leaders constitute a category but individuals within the category are always different. We also discussed categories of postures adopted by organisations. Chapter 5 discussed configurations and Chapter 3 reviewed the ultimate states typical trajectories led to from these configurations. In these cases too we were talking about rather loose categories, ones with similarities and differences, ones we would be able to recognise when they occurred although we could not necessarily predict their specific nature. Chaos is endless individual variety within recognisably similar, irregular categories.

We humans do not find it all that difficult to cope with chaos in the scientific meaning applied to it above. We saw in the section in Chapter 2 how humans store their perceptions of the world in terms of family resemblance type categories rather than precise details. Humans cope with the unfamiliar through reasoning by analogy with other situations that bear some similarity to new ones, just as coping with chaos requires.

The weather system

Although the specific path of behaviour in chaos is random, that behaviour does have a 'hidden' pattern, a qualitative shape. *Figure 9.4* in *Illustration 9.2* above gave a simplified picture of that shape, the strange attractor which the weather follows.

That figure shows how the weather, described in terms of air pressure, humidity and temperature and so on, varies over time, moving around one of the lobes of the shape and then suddenly switching to the other. The weather system moves endlessly around this shape, never once returning to any point it previously occupied; the lines never intersect. (They appear to do so in *Figure 9.4* only because this is a two-dimensional representation of a three-dimensional figure.)

So the specific path of the weather is totally unpredictable in the long term, but it always follows the same global shape. There are boundaries outside which the weather system hardly ever moves and, if it does so, it is soon attracted back to the shape prescribed by the attractor. Some weather conditions are not allowed – snow storms in the Sahara desert or heat waves in the Arctic. There is an overall shape to weather behaviour because it is constrained by the structure of the feedback mechanisms generating it.

Because of this 'hidden' order, the system displays typical patterns, or recognisable categories of behaviour. Even before we knew anything about the shape of the weather's strange attractor, we always recognised patterns of storms and sunshine, hurricanes and calm, and seasonal patterns. These recognisable patterns are repeated in an approximate way over and over again. They are never exactly the same, but there is always some similarity. They are similar to what went before and similar to what is occurring elsewhere in the system.

The category winter follows the category autumn and within a particular winter we find typical patterns of temperature, rainfall and wind speed. As we enter a particular winter, we do not know whether the temperature will be very low or very high for that time of the year, the rainfall heavy or light, the wind speed moderate or at gale force.

This means that we cannot identify specific causes that yield specific outcomes, but we know the boundaries within which the system moves and the qualitative nature of the patterns it displays. We know that the very irregularity of the weather will itself be regular because it is constrained in some way – it cannot do just anything. We can use the resulting self-similar patterns of winter weather to prepare appropriate behaviour. We can buy an umbrella or move the sheep off the high ground. We can cope with the uncertainty and the lack of causal connection because we are aware of self-similar patterns and use them in a qualitative way to guide specific choices. ■

9.3 THE DYNAMICS OF DETERMINISTIC SYSTEMS: SELF-ORGANISATION

The chemist Illya Prigogine has shown how nonlinear feedback systems develop unpredictable new forms of behaviour when they are pushed far from equilibrium. There is a fundamental relationship between states of bounded instability or chaos on the one hand and innovation or creativity on the other: systems can only be creative through experiencing instability.

The state of chaos performs the important task of amplifying small changes in the environment, causing the instability necessary to shatter existing behaviour patterns and make way for the new. Creative systems pass through states of instability or crisis and reach critical points where they may spontaneously self-organise to produce some new structure or behaviour. The choice made at such critical points is unpredictable. The new more complex structure is dissipative because it takes energy to sustain the system in that new mode.

For example, as energy is pumped into a particular gas the molecules are put into a more and more excited state. They all move randomly in different directions – a state of instability or chaos. This instability is performing the function of amplifying or spreading the energy or information around the molecules in the gas. The instability is also shattering any relationship the molecules bore to each other before the energy was pumped in. In this state the gas emits a dull glow. As further energy is pumped into this system, it reaches a critical point. At this point the molecules appear to communicate with each other and suddenly they spontaneously organise themselves to all point in the same direction. The result is a laser beam casting its light for miles. The sudden choice of molecules all to point in the same direction is not predictable from the laws of physics. There is no central intention or law prescribing this behaviour; it emerges out of instability through a self-organising creative process.

Key Concept 9.3

Self-organisation

Self-organisation is a process in which the components of a system in effect spontaneously communicate with each other and abruptly cooperate in coordinated and concerted common behaviour.

Applying these ideas to an organisation we get a picture of the creative organisation as one that continually confronts instability and crisis, out of which it creates new order in spontaneous emergent ways. The studies of Miller and Pascale presented in Chapter 3 describe just such a development pattern for organisations.

Pascale (1990) was involved in and has sought to explain how Ford was transformed from a loss-making company that focused primarily on low costs in the late 1970s into a profitable quality-conscious concern by the late 1980s. He shows how this process was not the consequence of some master plan established early on in the period of transformation. Instead the changes came about as a large number of independently-started change initiatives built into a major movement. The at-first unconnected initiatives included schemes for employee participation, the use of multi-discipline teams to design the new Taurus, setting up various informally operating committees to examine how to break down barriers to change and extensive bureaucracy, the establishment of many task forces, and the use of training and development programmes. All of this did not happen as the result of some central intention, corporate plan or culture change programme. *Pascale (1990, p. 122) concludes:*

> The remarkable occurrence at Ford was that, somewhat mysteriously, a set of independent initiatives flowed together and became mutually reinforcing.

This is what is meant by self-organisation in human systems. The existence of such processes in successful organisations is also supported, as we have seen in Chapter 5, by studies of the political process in organisations. These studies depict stages close to the instability, crises, amplification and self-organisation described above.

Successful organisations seem to show the same temporal patterns of creative change as do systems in nature and the reason they do is that they too are nonlinear feedback systems.

What self-organisation means for organisations

Self-organisation theory provides an explanation of the stages a system passes through as it develops new, more complex forms of order. In organisational terms it establishes patterns in the change process through which new strategic directions or innovations emerge. This way of understanding human organisations makes it clear that new strategic direction can only emerge; it cannot be planned. And it makes it clear that the processes through which emergence occurs are ones of political interaction and group learning.

First, in what sense does self-organisation mean political interaction?

The way for spontaneous self-organisation is opened up by the manner in which nonlinear feedback systems amplify small changes in their environments. In human systems this happens when individuals detect some issue and then build support for it. The building of coalitions around issues, persuading and negotiating with others to support an idea, is clearly a political process. It requires the deployment and use of power. Innovations in organisations always begin with individuals and they can go no further than the individual unless the awareness of the issue is spread and commitment to it developed through the organisation. It is this political process that gets the issue onto the organisational agenda in the first place.

The importance of political interaction also clearly continues throughout the life of an issue. Politics is the process through which managers make and enact strategic choices. Whether an issue continues to sustain attention, what kind of attention it receives, whether it is ever tried out in the form of some experiment, and whether it is finally invested in or not, all depend on how its supporters use their power and sustain the support.

It is accurate to call the political processes we have been talking about self-organising. This is so because no-one centrally organises the support groups around particular lines.

Nor can anyone because no one knows what the issues are until some coalition is formed around them. Whether an issue is ever noticed or not is self-organising in the sense of spontaneously gathering support or failing to.

Second, in what sense is spontaneous self-organisation in an organisation a learning process?

Nonlinear systems amplify changes and in so doing they shatter old patterns, making way for the new through a process of correlation or communication between components or agents of the system. In human systems this process of shattering the old and developing the new applies in the first instance to perceptions; only later on does it apply to structures, roles and so on. When we question and throw out old perceptions and then replace them with new ones we are learning. In organisations this kind of learning is done in groups. Group learning is thus the essence of strategic discovery and choice. The effectiveness with which groups in an organisation learn is the major determinant of whether that organisation takes effective strategic actions or not. But groups are affected by unconscious process as well as the primary learning tasks they have come together to perform. No-one can make a group learn. Whether or not it does depends upon its own spontaneous behaviour. That behaviour is all the more spontaneous because it is affected by unconscious processes, as we will see in Chapter 11. These unconscious processes make its behaviour patterns and what will emerge from its learning activities unpredictable.

We can interpret self-organisation in an organisation as the process of political interaction and group learning from which innovation and new strategic directions for the organisation may emerge. These processes are themselves nonlinear feedback ones. They too are only effective when they are held far-from-equilibrium in states of contention, contradiction and paradox. The outcome therefore emerges without central intention and is unpredictable.

Note that self-organisation is not the same thing as self-managing teams nor is it the same thing as democracy. A self-managing team or a democratic group is one that makes choices by some kind of majority vote, without being instructed what to do by its leaders or from outside its ranks. Self-organisation can and will occur even in a dictatorship: revolution may be a form of self-organisation and that is how dictatorships are overthrown. Self-organisation may well occur in bureaucratic organisations if managers from different hierarchical levels or different parts of the bureaucracy come to find themselves supporting and working together on some common issue. Self-organisation does not mean that job definitions are loose and overlapping. It can occur even when jobs are rigidly defined. Self-organisation is an irregular pattern of collaborative interaction: it can take many forms.

It is not a predictably mechanistic process as automatic control is in cybernetics. Weick's views on self-designing systems are a form of self-organisation, but so is a revolution or a coup.

Self-organisation occurs when people form a group that produces patterns of behaviour, despite the absence of formal hierarchy within that group or authority imposed from outside it. Such groups could behave in what we would describe as a completely uncontrolled way, for example a mob, but such groups may also behave in a way that we would have to describe as self-controlled.

As soon as a collection of people begin to interact with each other, say at a party, we find that particular attitudes, ideas, enthusiasms, propositions and issues emerge

Self-organisation in human systems

In organisations, self-organisation is the spontaneous formation of interest groups and coalitions around specific issues, communication about those issues, cooperation and the formation of consensus on and commitment to a response to those issues. The term spontaneous communication arenas, that is, meetings and document exchanges, may be used to describe the occasions on and the means through which this occurs.

Controlled behaviour consists of sequences of words and deeds over time that have some kind of pattern; that is, words and deeds that are not haphazard. The patterns in controlled behaviour do not have to be regular; they might be irregular but, nevertheless, recognisable as patterns and so still constitute controlled behaviour. Patterns will be generated when sequences of words and deeds are constrained in some way. The feedback connections and the constraints may take different forms; hence, control may take different forms. Negative feedback and constraint by intention give the planning/monitoring form of control. Feedback that flips from negative to positive, constrained by the need to persuade others and sustain support, results in self-organising political and learning forms of control.

spontaneously within a very short time. People form themselves into groupings around say, some issue. One group may be for the issue and another against it. Soon the conversation will switch spontaneously to another issue and the groupings will spontaneously reform. No-one directs this process, nor does it move to a plan: it is a self-organising process. That process of spontaneous self-organisation can be seen quite clearly at a party, but it is also evident in all other human systems, including business organisations. It happens because of the intrinsic property of human systems to self-organise.

Informal groups and networks of managers within an organisation clearly form and conduct themselves through self-organising processes: no central authority organises the network of informal contacts and coalitions that develop in an organisation and yet that network can behave in a controlled way and become a vital part of the organisation's control system. Most managers are not used to the idea that a system, that is, a set of interactions, can control itself. For them, control requires some individual to take charge.

Self-organisation differs from self-managing teams (to be discussed in Chapter 11) in the following important ways:

- Self-organisation is a fluid network process in which informal, temporary teams form spontaneously around issues, while self-managing teams are permanent or temporary but always formally established parts of a reporting structure.
- While top managers cannot control self-organising processes – they can only intervene to influence the boundary conditions around them – they can install a structure of self-managing teams and control them through the rules that govern how they are to operate.

- Participants decide on who takes part in self-organisation and what the boundaries around their activities are, while top managers make these decisions with regard to self-managing teams.
- Self-organising networks operate in conflict with and are constrained by the hierarchy, while self-managing teams replace the hierarchy.
- Unequal power energises networks through conflict but also operates as a constraint, while dispersed power is supposed to lead to self-managing teams and consensus.
- In self-organising processes, people empower themselves while, in self-managing teams, the top empowers people.
- The self-organising process is both provoked and constrained by cultural difference, while the self-managing process is based on strongly shared culture.

In Chapters 10 and 11, we will discuss the behaviour of self-organising small groups of people within organisations.

9.4 THE DYNAMICS OF ADAPTIVE SYSTEMS: COMPLEXITY THEORY

In the last two sections we have seen that many physical and chemical systems in nature are nonlinear feedback networks driven by a small number of deterministic rules, that is, rules which remain the same over time. We also saw that:

- these systems are capable of operating in a stable ordered zone, in an unstable completely disordered zone, between the two. That zone transition, or border area, is a completely different kind of behaviour in that it is paradoxically both stable and unstable at the same time. Such paradox is to be found at the edge of system disintegration;
- it is only when a system is in the border area that it is endlessly variable;
- when a system is in this creative phase transition its specific future is inherently unpredictable but it nevertheless displays archetypal patterns;
- although the long-term future is unknowable the short-term future is more or less predictable;
- the system evolves dialectically rearranging fundamental paradoxes rather than resolving them;
- outcomes emerge spontaneously through self-organisation rather then as the result of some intention or blueprint.

Probabilistic feedback systems are not different in any fundamental way from deterministic ones, so the above properties apply to them too (*Kelsey, 1988*).

As we noted earlier, however, human systems are adaptive in the sense that agents in the system do not just blindly follow the same set of rules but change their rules as they go along. In other words, they engage in double-loop rather than simply single-loop learning. Furthermore, instead of a system with a small number of rules, human systems contain a large number of agents all with their own rules so that we have a system with a huge number of rules. Complexity theory is about just such systems – systems with huge numbers of agents and rules who double-loop learn to change the rules and through their interaction with each other create emergent futures.

As we shall see in what follows, the above properties of deterministic systems continue to apply even when we are dealing with complex adaptive system. Complex adaptive system:

- evolve to the edge of chaos or system disintegration where they display recognisable archetypal patterns of behaviour but with specific actualisations that are radically unpredictable;
- are creative only when they operate at the edge of disintegration;
- evolve dialectially;
- produce emergent outcomes through a process of spontaneous self-organisation.

We turn now to a survey of complexity theory.

Complex adaptive systems

A complex adaptive system (*Gell-Mann, 1994*):

- consists of large numbers of agents interrelated in a nonlinear way, that is, a way in which the action of one agent can provoke more than one response from other agents;
- interacts with other complex adaptive systems and together they constitute the environment to which each must respond;
- acquires information about the systems constituting its environment and information about the consequences of its own interaction with those systems. In other words, complex adaptive system employ feedback;
- identifies regularities in the feedback information it acquires and then condenses those regularities into a schema or model, in effect selecting one of a number of competing models which might 'explain' the regularities;
- acts in relation to the systems that are its environment on the basis of the schema it has developed;
- observes the responses its actions provoke, as well as the consequences of those responses and uses this information to revise its schema, in other words, it employs feedback to learn or adapt. This is rather complex learning because it involves adjusting both the behaviour and the schema driving that behaviour.

So, a complex adaptive system consists of a number of components interacting with each other according to sets of rules in such a manner as to improve their behaviour and thus the behaviour of the system which they comprise. In other words, in a complex adaptive system, agents interact in a manner that constitutes learning. Since any complex adaptive system operates in an environment that is also, for the most part, characterised by the above features, the system and its environment together form a coevolving supra-system that, in a sense, learns its way into the future. In this coevolving supra-system, individual subsystems or agents learn, that is, they alter their schemes during their own individual lifetimes and the system as a whole learns, that is, it evolves.

Such network systems are ubiquitous in nature and, not surprisingly, since we too are a part of nature, human interaction sets up such systems too. So, each of us has a brain that is a complex adaptive system in which the neurons that make up our brains are the agents. Each of us has a mind that is a complex adaptive system in which symbols and images are the agents. As a group we constitute a complex adaptive system. So do all organisations. Organisations interact to form a national economic, societal and political system and those national systems interact to form a global one, which interacts with natural systems to form an interconnected ecology, which now seems to be warming up. All are complex adaptive systems, one fitting into the other.

Complexity theory has so far focused primarily on the evolution of life and the behaviour of chemical and physical systems. It has been developed by mathematicians and computer scientists, physicists and biologists such as Murray Gell-Mann, Stuart Kauffman (1993, 1995), Christopher Langton and John Holland at the Santa Fe Institute in New Mexico, others at the Centre for Complex Studies at the University of Illinois, and Brian Goodwin (1994) in the UK at the Open University. However, it is not only to natural systems that this science applies, because as we have seen humans too constitute such systems.

So, what does the science of complexity have to say and how does it study these complex adaptive systems that we find all over the place?

How complex adaptive systems are studied

The most important method of studying complex adaptive systems is to simulate their evolution on a computer. We can quite plausibly think of members of an organisation, or members of an ant colony, as agents whose behaviour is driven by a set of rules. Some of those rules are conscious and explicit, while others are implicit and unconscious, at least in the case of humans. Nevertheless we can, by observing a person, draw out the regularities in that person's behaviour and then articulate a set of rules which produces such regularities – this is, after all, what psychologists and psychoanalysts do. In other words, it is perfectly reasonable to regard each of us as:

- firstly, a set of operating rules driving how we perform the tasks necessary for survival; plus
- secondly, a set of rules for evaluating our operating performance; and
- thirdly, a set of rules for changing both the operating and evaluating rules, that is, for learning; and
- finally, and most importantly, a set of rules for copying ourselves to the next generation, rules about selecting a mate and what to do with that mate.

A computer program is a set of operating rules and instructions and it is perfectly possible to add a set of rules for evaluating those operations, and for changing the rules of operation and evaluation in the light of their performance, and also a set of rules for copying the whole computer program which could quite easily consist of rules for finding another computer program for a mate and then doing something with that mate. Such a program could quite realistically be regarded as an agent if some of its rules required it to examine the state of other computer programs and adjust its rules in the light of the state of those other programs. In this way we could build up a population of computer programs that could interact with each other, breed, and so evolve and learn. We would then have a complex adaptive system in our computer consisting of a collection of agents, each of which is a computer program.

Furthermore, each computer program would be made up of a bit string, a series of 0s and 1s, because that is how computer programs are coded. The analogy with our rules of conduct is still very close because our rules of conduct are coded, not into 0s and 1s it is true, but into symbols taking the form of words and images; and the analogy with our bodies is even closer, perhaps, since our physical code consists of genes that can be on or off, more or less. It is therefore quite legitimate to use such simulations to try to uncover the fundamental properties of complex adaptive systems everywhere, whether physical or mental. We will of course have to check whether human characteristics such as consciousness, whatever that is, and emotion and so on alter the conclusions we reach, but as a first step, the simulations on a computer may, and I suggest do, yield some very important insights.

The importance of mess

Those who have developed the study of complex adaptive systems have been most interested in this analogy between the digital code of computer program agents and the chemical code in the genes of living creatures. One of their principal questions has been this: if in its earliest days the earth consisted of a random soup of chemicals, how could life have come about? You can simulate this problem if you take a system consisting of computer programs with random bit strings and ask if they can evolve order out of such random chaos. The amazing answer to this question is that such systems can indeed evolve order out of chaos, and even more amazingly this chaos, or mess, is essential to the process.

Contrary to some of our most deep-seated beliefs, mess is the material from which life and creativity are built and it turns out that they are built, not according to some prior design, but through a process of spontaneous self-organisation that produces emergent outcomes. If there is a design, it is the basic design principles of the system itself, a system that produces patterns in behaviour, namely, a network of agents driven by iterative nonlinear feedback to produce unknowable outcomes which do have pattern. There is inherent order in complex adaptive systems simply waiting to unfold through the experience of the system, but no one can know what that experience will be until it does unfold in real time. There are deep reasons why, in certain conditions, agents interacting in a system can produce, not anarchy, but creative new outcomes that none of them ever dreamt of, if they are left to self-organise in what looks like a mess most unlikely to contain within it an implicate order. It is simply not true that if we cannot know the outcome and if no one can be 'in control' we are doomed to anarchy. On the contrary, these are the very conditions required for creativity, for the exciting journey into open-ended evolutionary space with no fixed, predetermined destination. The whole universe, it seems, is indeed lawful and yet it has freedom of choice – the price for the freedom of choice is an inability to know the final destination and an inability to be in control of the journey.

I would now like to make these points a little more specific by taking you through one of the simulations that has excited me most – it was developed by Thomas Ray (1992) in the United States and he called it Tierra.

The Tierra simulation

The environment in this simulation consists of a computer's Central Processing Unit (CPU), that is, a computer operating software system and a memory. Each agent in this environment is a string of digits making up a set of instructions read directly by the CPU. Each agent's code is:

- an operating program to carry out a task for which it is rewarded with points based on how effectively it carries out that task; and
- a replicating program according to which it copies its code to the next generation, its chance of using that program being dependent upon the number of points it earns in carrying out the task.

In order to carry out their operational instructions agents need CPU time. They are therefore lined up in a circular queue and each in turn receives its slice of CPU time. Agents are also lined up in a linear queue according to their age and a 'reaper' lops off some of these, generally the oldest. However, by successfully executing their programs, and so increasing their fitness, agents can slow down their move up the linear queue while flawed agents rise quickly to the top.

So, the experimenter sets a general task, defines the fitness function and sets the initial replication rules, a schema common to all. The experimenter also introduces constraints in the form of scarcity (available CPU time) and agent life span, and determines that the evolution of this system is initially to be driven by random mutations in the replication process and the operational instructions, that is, by noise, or random flipping of bits in agents' code. The agents, as parts of a system, are then left to learn how to perform the task. In other words, they must develop their own survival strategies. The learning occurs first at a system level through the feedback of successful performance into an increased probability of replicating. Later, as the system develops, there is learning at the level of differentiated groupings of agents, in the sense that they change their rules in the course of their lifetimes. This simulation is thus probabilistic and adaptive rather than mechanically deterministic.

The simulation was set off by introducing a single agent consisting of 80 instructions. In order to replicate this agent, obviously, had to use the method of cloning with random variations, and it had to execute these replication instructions 8000 times. Within a short time the CPU space was 80 per cent occupied by agents, but then the reaper took over and prevented further population growth. After a while mutants consisting of 79 instructions replaced the original agents. In other words, the system had discovered that smallness was a criterion for survival or fitness – smaller agents used up less CPU time and so became more successful at replicating. Later, agents consisting of 45 instructions appeared but they were too short to replicate. They overcame this problem by attaching themselves to longer agents and borrowing some of their code in order to replicate. This strategy increased their fitness because in their normal operations they needed less CPU time and so had more time for replication using borrowed code. In other words, parasites had emerged.

However, if the parasites destroyed too many hosts in order to replicate then they destroyed their own ability to replicate and so declined. In the simulation the parasites suffered periodic catastrophes. One of these catastrophes occurred because the hosts mutated to make life more difficult for the parasites: normal procedure was for the hosts to post their locations in the CPU on a public notice board, but some hosts developed an immunisation to parasites by evolving instructions to stop posting their positions and in effect hide – camouflage then became a criterion or strategy for fitness. Although the parasites could then not find the hosts, those hosts had to examine themselves each time their turn to operate came because in hiding they had not retained any note on their positions. This increased the time hosts needed for normal operation and reduced the time they had available for replication. While not perfect, the strategy worked in a good enough way so that the parasites were nearly wiped out. Then, however, the parasites developed their own memories and did not need to consult the public posting board. Once again it was the parasites' turn to succeed. Later on cooperative strategies were developed in which the hosts examined themselves and swopped instructions with each other to shorten their use of CPU time.

Later still, hyper-parasites appeared to feed off the parasites – these were 80 instructions long just like hosts, but they had developed instructions to examine themselves for parasites and feed off the parasites by diverting CPU time from them. These hyper-parasites worked symbiotically by sharing reproduction code – they could no longer reproduce on their own but required cooperation. Cross-over replication had thus emerged spontaneously as a strategy for survival without anyone programming it in. This 'sexual' cooperation was then exploited by opportunistic mutants in the form of tiny intruders who placed themselves between replicating hyper-parasites and intercepted and used hyper-parasite code for their own replication – what a horrible image! These cheaters could then thrive and replicate although they were only 27 instructions long. Then the hyper-parasites found a way to defeat the cheats, but not for long. The story has no end.

Insights into the dynamics of adaptive systems

I would now like to draw your attention to some of the major insights that this simulation provides on the nature of complex adaptive systems.

First, this system produces order of a changeable and diverse kind, that comes about in a spontaneous, emergent way – it has not been programmed in, there is no blueprint, grand design, or plan. There is neither mission statement, nor vision, nor even a charismatic leader in sight. Furthermore, this spontaneous self-organising activity, with its emergent order, is vital for the continuing evolution of the system and its ability to produce novelty. However, what form that order takes – that is, the global pattern of behaviour, the system-wide strategies – cannot be predicted from the rules driving individual agent behaviour. In that sense the system is disorderly. This system continuously operates in a state of bounded instability: periods of stability are followed by upheavals as particular strategies for the survival of both hosts, and parasites emerge from spontaneous self-organising processes that appear to be so close to market competition. The experimenter is not introducing them and neither is an agent taking over and formulating the strategy.

The strategies are emerging unpredictably in a coevolutionary arms race occurring in a dynamical, somewhat disorderly environment, driven partly by chance. First the strategy is small size, but then parasites change the rules and the most successful strategy becomes feeding off others. Then the hosts change the rules and the better strategy is camouflage. But the parasites change the rules of the game again and the best strategy becomes the development of a local memory. Competition and conflict emerge and the evolution of the system is driven by agents trying to exploit each other, but the game can go on only if neither side succeeds completely, or for long, in that exploitation.

What we see is self-organisation, or the collapse of chaos, in that the environment was at first random but as soon as an agent is introduced the collapse begins. The evolution of life in the universe, and life in organisations, does not occur primarily through random mutations selected for survival by the forces of competition, but primarily through an internal, spontaneously self-organising, cooperative process that presents orderly forms for selection by the forces of competition. Selection is not made by freely operating competition that chooses between random little pieces, but by a competitive process constrained to choose between new forms emerging from a cooperative process. Life in the universe, and life in organisations, arises from a dialectic between competition and cooperation, not from an unconstrained free market! The implications are both profound and, of course, contentious.

Second, this system has discovered, quite spontaneously, the importance of competition. But not competition all on its own, rather competition in tension with cooperation. Through an internal process of spontaneous self-organisation this system produces an emergent predator–prey dynamic, behaviour that is, paradoxically, both cooperative and competitive.

Third, this system has discovered, all on its own, the importance of sex, that is, in more technical language the superiority of cross-over replication over cloning. Such cross-over replication of course takes two, and like the predator–prey dynamic it is also paradoxically both cooperative and competitive at the same time, as we all know only too well.

Note the common thread running through these three insights about complex adaptive system dynamics – each is a paradox, each is the simultaneous presence of stability and instability, order and disorder, tidiness and mess. Take the first – there is emergent order but it is unpredictable. Take the second – there is the tidy harmony of cooperation but it operates in tension with the dissonance of destructive and messy competition. Take the third – sexual reproduction certainly requires cooperation and without doubt it is messy, because it involves mixing up the code, digital, or genetic, or mentally symbolic. Why is this? Well, in cloning an agent gets to copy itself only if it is relatively successful, so that less successful code is incrementally weeded out and the system moves progressively in the direction of improvement. In cross-over replication, however, one agent copies half his code and splices it to a copy of half of her code, thus mixing up the code. This makes it possible for some inefficient and ineffective code to be passed on to the next generation, as well as effective code. Evolution is, then, not an incrementally progressive affair, but a rather stumbling sort of journey in which a system moves both forwards and backwards. And this, as we shall now see, is the most effective way to proceed.

Fitness landscapes

You can see why this is so if you think in terms of fitness landscapes, a concept *Stuart Kauffman (1993, 1995)* has used to give us new insights into the evolutionary process. Picture the evolution of a particular species, say leopards, as a journey across a landscape characterised by hills and mountains of various heights and shapes, and valleys of various depths and shapes. Suppose that movement up a hill or mountain is equivalent to increasing fitness and moving down into a valley is equivalent to decreasing fitness. Deep valleys would represent almost certain extinction and the high peaks of mountains would represent great fitness for the leopards. The purpose of life is then to avoid valleys and climb peaks.

What determines the shape of this landscape, that is, the number, size, shape and position of the peaks and valleys? The answer is, the survival strategies that other species interacting with leopards are following. So, leopards could potentially interact with a large number of species in order to get a meal. They could hunt elephant, for example. However, the elephant has a survival strategy based on size and if leopards go the elephant-hunting route they will have a tough time surviving. Such a strategy, therefore, is a move down into a rather deep and dead-end sort of valley. Another possibility is to hunt rather small deer. In order to achieve this the leopard might adopt the strategy of speed, competing by running faster than the deer. To the extent that this works it is represented by a move up a fitness hill. Or, the leopards may specialise in short distance speed plus a strategy of camouflage. Hence their famous spots. This strategy seems to have taken them up a mountain to a reasonably high fitness peak.

The evolutionary task of the leopard, then, is to journey across the fitness landscape in such a manner as to reach the highest fitness peak possible, because then it stands the greatest chance of surviving. To get caught in a valley is to become extinct and to be trapped in the foothills is to forego the opportunity of finding one of the mountains.

So, how should the leopards travel across their landscape to avoid these pitfalls, given that they cannot see where the high peaks are? They can only know that they have reached a peak when they get there. Suppose the leopards adopt what strategy theorists call a logically incremental strategy. That is, they adopt a procedure in which they 'stick to the knitting' and take a large number of small incremental steps, only ever taking a step that improves fitness and avoiding, like the plague, any steps that diminish fitness. This rational, orderly procedure produces relatively stable, efficient, progressive movement uphill, consistently in the direction of success. Management consultants and academics in the strategy field would applaud leopards following this procedure for their eminent common sense. However, a rule which in essence says 'go up hills only and never downwards' is sure to keep the leopards out of the valleys, but it is also almost certain to get them trapped in the foothills, unless they start off with a really lucky break at the base of the highest, smoothest mountain, with no crevices or other deformities. This is highly unlikely, for a reason we will come to.

The point to note here is that the rational, efficient way to move over the short term is guaranteed, over the longer term, to be the most ineffective possible. What is the alternative? This is where the mess comes in. The alternative is to abandon this nice, neat strategy of logically incremental moves and travel in a somewhat erratic manner that involves sometimes slipping and tumbling downhill into valleys out of which a desperate climb is necessary before it is too late. This counterintuitive and somewhat inebriate method of travelling across their fitness landscape makes it likely that the leopards will stumble across the foothills of an even higher mountain than the one they were climbing before. So the mess of cross-over replication, sex to us, makes it more likely that we will find higher mountains to climb than, say, bacteria who replicate by cloning precisely because of the disorder of mixing the genetic code rather than incrementally improving it. So, we do actually learn from suffering as the ancient wisdom teaches us.

The whole picture becomes a great deal more interesting when you remember that the fixed landscape we have been considering for the leopard is in fact a fiction, because the survival strategies of the other species determine its shape and they are not standing still – they too are looking for peaks to climb and every time they change their strategy then what was a peak for the leopard is deformed and could become a valley. So, if the leopard increases its short distance speed and improves its camouflage then it moves up towards a fitness peak on its landscape. But, if the deer respond by heightening their sense of smell, then that peak certainly subsides and may even turn into a valley.

The evolutionary journey for all of us, therefore, is across a constantly heaving landscape and it is heaving about because of another mess, namely, competition. The mess of competition ensures that life itself never gets trapped – species come and go but life itself carries on, becoming ever more complex. It is this mess of competitive selection that is one of the sources of order, the other being the cooperative, internal process of spontaneous self-organisation.

The insight is this. Systems characterised by dynamics that combine order and disorder, that operate at the edge of disintegration, are capable of learning faster than those that are purely orderly, those that operate well away from the edge of chaos in the stable zone. At the edge of chaos, at the edge of disintegration, systems are capable of endless variety, novelty, surprise, in short, creativity. Systems that get trapped on local fitness peaks look stable and comfortable, but they are simply waiting for destruction by other species following messier paths.

Redundancy or loose coupling

Another insight follows from the study of complex systems. Life survives at the edge of disintegration because of massive inbuilt redundancy. It is redundancy flowing from self-organising cooperation that is the source of constancy and order. Some kind of mess, or inefficiency, is required to enable faster discovery and other kinds of mess, redundancy, are required to be able to survive that disorder. The human brain, for example, is characterised by redundancy in that one part of it is capable of carrying out functions normally carried out by some other parts. We can, therefore, survive the destruction of fairly large parts of our brain. Slack resources, multi-tasking, overdeterminancy, loose coupling – these are what make systems resilient enough to cope with the pressures of creativity at the edge of system disintegration. I find this a chilling thought when I remember the huge drive over the past decade to remove redundancy in our organisations.

Dominant and recessive schemes

Now consider how and where complex adaptive systems use the mess, the disorder, the unpredictability, the randomness. Each agent in a complex adaptive system interacts with the others comprising that system according to a set of rules, a schema, unique to that individual agent, and according to a set of rules, a schema, which that agent shares with other agents. It is according to these rules that each agent adjusts its behaviour to that of others, that is, according to which it learns in a simple way. Agents also learn in a complex way when they change the rules to make their behaviour more beneficial to themselves and to the system as a whole. Now the rules are expressed in code – in the case of a computer simulation the code is digital, a sequence of 0s and 1s, or electrical, a sequence of 'on' and 'off' positions. In the human brain the code is a sequence of electrical impulses that pass across synaptic connections between neurons, the agents of the brain. In the human mind the code is symbols, such as words, images, thoughts.

And the important point about all this code is that part of it is arranged into that set of rules governing an agent's current engagement with its primary tasks – part of the code takes the form of rules governing the stable, predictable conduct of everyday tasks, the implementation of the current survival strategy. We may call this the dominant schema. However, the dominant schema does not use up all the available code – there is part left over constituting what we might call a recessive schema. We can study what happens to this recessive schema in computer simulations as a system evolves and that study yields what is to my mind a very exciting discovery. While the agent and the system it is contributing to move in a stable, more or less steady fashion from iteration to iteration, from day to day as it were, following its dominant schema, the recessive schema is more or less randomly rearranging itself. The recessive schema is in a continual state of flux and it is evolving a replacement for the dominant schemes. What then happens is that the dominant schema is quite suddenly replaced by a new one that has quietly accumulated in the recessive symbol system. It looks as if the system is jumping from one stable equilibrium position to another, but in fact this is only apparent, because the replacement has been gradually prepared, behind the scenes, subversively, in the recessive schema.

While part of the system is getting on with the serious task of carrying out its day-to-day survival in a stable manner, another part is engaged in play. Play without a clear purpose, play that is spontaneously self-organising, and this ultimately can lead to a kind of coup d'état in which the dominant schema is replaced by a new one – innovation in the dominant schema follows creative activity, play, in the recessive one. The important point is that these two systems are working in tension with each other and creativity is intimately linked to destruction.

This links to Prigogine's important notion of dissipative structures. He has shown how certain chemical systems, certainly those upon which life is based, have a structure but one that continually dissolves. Take our bodies – over a two-year period every cell in my body, so I am told, is replaced with others and yet the structure, me, is preserved, although unfortunately in a subtly altered, increasingly aged form. I read recently that cancer is not caused by the excessive growth of malformed cells, as had been previously thought, but by the suppression of the instruction to die. Survival, it seems requires death as well as birth – death is indeed a part of life as the ancient wisdom teaches us.

The link to human systems

It is time now to return to the world of human organisation, carrying with us some very profound insights about the fundamental nature of the feedback networks we set up when we interact with each other. Let me summarise those key insights and make some quick links with us.

First, feedback networks are creative only when they operate right at the edge of disintegration, in a kind of phase transition between stability and instability.

In human terms, the old wives' tale about genius being close to madness then turns out to have a solid scientific basis which we share with the universe – we are creative when we manage to move away from the stability of neurotically defensive behaviour but avoid the disintegration of psychotic episodes. Melanie Klein called this place at the edge of mental disintegration, the depressive position, the place where we are able to hold the ambiguity and paradox of life and contain the anxiety they generate. She showed how this depressive position was the ground from which we make reparation for our destructiveness, the foundation of creative behaviour. Donald Winnicott called this space the Transitional Phase between the real world outside the mind and the inner fantasy world, and located creative behaviour there, the world of mythologising and play, that is, the foundation of creativity. We will discuss these matters in Chapter 11.

In groups we mostly operate in a state in which we utilise structures and processes, covert politics and game-playing to block anxiety-provoking complex learning – the stable zone for a group. Alternatively we find ourselves tipped into shared psychotic fantasies, what Wilfred Bion called the basic assumption behaviour of dependency, fight, flight and so on – the unstable zone for a group. But at the edge of such disintegration we are able to contain the anxiety provoked by complex learning and then we are able to question the fundamental assumptions we are making about our world and so engage in true dialogue, an exciting journey of discovery. We will also discuss these matters in Chapter 11.

In other words, we are a part of nature and so, not surprisingly, we are not all that different from it – we too are creative when we operate at the edge of disintegration.

Second, the creative process that takes place at the edge of disintegration is inherently destructive – it is messy and fundamentally paradoxical. It involves cross-fertilisation, and that can take place with mental symbols as well as with genetic material or digital code – true dialogue between human beings is just such cross-fertilisation and we all know that true dialogue is at least uncomfortable, which is why we so rarely practise it. The messy creative process at the edge of disintegration involves competition and this, as we know only too well, takes place in the medium of ideas, power, products and services as well as genetic material and computer code. The creative process in human systems, therefore, is inevitably messy: it involves difference, conflict, fantasy and emotion; it stirs up anger, envy, depression and many other feelings. To remove the mess by inspiring us to follow some vision, to indoctrinate us to share the same culture, to sing off the same hymn sheet and pull together, is to remove the mess that is the very raw material of creative activity. Instead of killing creativity in this way, we might try to work out how to contain, rather than avoid, the high levels of anxiety that it inevitably arouses.

Third, neither the messy creative processes at the edge of system disintegration, nor their outcomes, can be planned or intended because long-term outcomes are truly unknowable at the edge of chaos. In fact, the links between our next actions and their long-term outcomes disappear so that no-one can be 'in control'. This becomes far less anxiety provoking once we accept it, and understand that when a system is held at the edge of disintegration, the consequence is not necessarily randomness and anarchy.

This is because at the edge there is also inherent order brought about by redundancy and cooperation. And that cooperation does not occur according to some blueprint, some prior intention of the most powerful. It is true empowerment, it is a truly bottom-up process in which agents get on with their own thing without waiting to be told that they may. Such spontaneous self-organisation produces emergent strategies, that is, the interaction itself creates patterns that no agent individually intends or can foresee. Emergence means that it is not possible to foresee the global outcome of inter-action between individuals, it is not possible to reduce the global pattern to the behaviour of the agents. This is not some kind of mysticism, but a hard, demonstrable property of interactive nonlinear feedback.

So, when you insist on your vision, when you try to stick to your blueprint when you cling with so much determination to control, are you destroying the capacity of your organisation for complex leaning? When you expel the redundancy from your organisation out into the community, have you become more efficient but also so brit-tle that you cannot survive turbulence? Is there time left for the play and the dialogue without which nothing truly new can happen?

Fourth, one part of the schema's driving agent and system behaviour is dominant in the sense that it drives day-to-day performance of the current primary task, the imple-mentation of the existing strategy for survival. But there is also another part, the recessive symbol system which is continuously evolving in a spontaneously self-organising manner that may ultimately produce a replacement for the current dominant schema. In other words, one part of the total symbol system operates in ten-sion with the other, ultimately to undermine and destroy it in the interests of a fitter replacement. This is the very process of complex learning itself, the messy process of one subsystem subverting another in an ongoing act of creative destruction.

Now, as I have said, this fits with our understanding of the human mind. There is a part of our mental capacity, a part of the repertoire of symbols, words, images and so on, that are arranged into rules driving our daily engagement with reality – a stable system carrying out our primary task in a given manner. But there is more to our mental contents than this. There is a whole repertoire of thoughts and images and fan-tasies engaged in the imaginative mental play of day dreaming and night dreaming too. And it is in this playful imaginative part, the transitional space of Winnicott, that our creativity develops.

Furthermore, it is not hard to see the equivalent in organisations. Whenever we become a member of an organisation we in fact join its legitimate system. This is the formal network of agents whose behaviour is driven by the currently dominant schema – the hierarchy, bureaucracy and officially approved ideology. But, as soon as we join the legitimate system we engage with, and take part in, the creation of a shadow system – the informal links we spontaneously establish amongst ourselves in a self-organising manner, the social and friendship links, the political and conflictual encounters, the personal networks we build and maintain to enable us to do our jobs and to advance in the world.

Now, what goes on in this shadow system? I suggest that it is a form of play that is sometimes bizarre, sometimes cruel and quite destructive, but also sometimes very exciting and quite creative. I would argue that it is in the shadow system that we carry out complex learning together and it is in the shadow system that we simultaneously try to kill that learning. It is in the shadow system that we engage in covert politics and game-playing to advance our careers and enhance our power, but also progress our ideas and build support for new things to do and new ways of doing them. In other words, the shadow system is the equivalent of the recessive symbol system – it works subversively to prepare replacements for currently dominant schemes. This is what we mean by innovation.

However, this messy process of creative destruction in the shadow system gives rise to great anxiety and so we normally conceal what we are up to in it. And there is no better way of doing this than pretending that we are following some charismatic leader's vision, or following some mission statement. There are few more effective cover-ups than long-term plans, long-term strategy statements, missions and the latest 'Saviour' recipes of the most fashionable guru.

Because of this kind of cover-up we can avoid reflecting upon what we do in the shadow system, the place where creativity really occurs and innovation is born. This, I believe, makes it extremely difficult to make sense of our experience of life in organisations. It preserves the appearance of rational order, but makes it so difficult to comprehend the real, messy processes.

The message of complexity theory

For me the key message coming from the science of complexity is this. It is possible, with much effort, for someone, or some small group of powerful people, to predict the outcomes of group, organisational and societal systems and, therefore, to remain 'in control' of them. But this is possible only if such systems are held well within the stable zone of operation, far away from the edge of chaos. The result will be stability, perhaps for a long time, but it will be the death of creativity and innovation and hence, ultimately, the death of the system. If it is to survive every human system must return to the edge of chaos, where outcomes are unknowable and no one can be 'in control'. So, the system cannot move according to some blueprint, but it will produce emergent new outcomes and it will be controlled through the process of spontaneous self-organisation itself, unless we, in our desperate attempts to stay 'in control', cause it to tip over into the unstable zone. For managers it is a message about having the courage to let go and let it happen, while vigilantly seeking to avoid tipping an organisation into the unstable zone. It is a message for members of organisations to reflect publicly on their own processes while they act, in order better to understand the operation of their organisation's shadow system The key seems to lie, not in preparing blueprints, but in trying to understand how to contain the anxiety of operating at the edge of chaos. The true role of the leader of a creative system is, not to foresee its future and take control of its journey, but to contain the anxiety of its members as they operate at the edge of chaos, where they are creating and discovering a new future that none could possibly foresee.

By now it is clear, I hope, how the science of complexity is a new frame of reference for understanding literally the whole world in a different way. From a Newtonian perspective we are nothing, unexplained specks on a vast, predictable machine that is the universe. From a Darwinian perspective we are an accidental cobbling together of attributes that were selected by the survival of the fittest. From the complexity perspective the archetype of life was always immanent within the laws governing nonlinear feedback networks, an archetype waiting to be unfolded by experience in a unique, unpredictable way that combines both lawfulness and free choice.

Down at the level of organisations the perspective is totally different too. The machine perspective of organisations has it that human agents are there to process information and obey the rules embodied in hierarchies and bureaucracies, in information and control systems. At the top a few of the powerful design the machine of which we are simply components – they do the thinking and we do the doing. The adapting organism view of organisations leads to two possible views. On the one hand we could see successful organisations as chance survivors who happened to have the attributes required by their environment, as the ecology school of strategic management would have it. Or we can see successful organisations as the intentional creation of charismatic leaders who somehow managed to foresee the environment that they had to fit into and persuaded the rest of us to do what was required in order to realise that fit, as the strategic choice school has it. All of these views assume that organisations survive when someone has at least some idea of where they are going and preserves some measure of control, in other words, when things are orderly and efficient, when redundancies are removed.

The science of complexity leads to a diametrically opposed perspective in which disorder plays a vital role, in tension with order; in which people do not know where they are going over the long term, but through interaction develop, discover and create a new direction through their self-organising interaction. The result emerges without prior shared intention. This is a never-ending process in which we all play a part, and in which the role of our leader is much more to contain the anxiety it generates than to tell us what to do.

9.5 SUMMARY

The Miller/Pascale studies reviewed in Chapter 3 and 7 show that successful companies are those that avoid stable equilibrium and operate in a state of contradiction and creative tension. This is essentially about the order of new strategic direction emerging from the disorder of contradiction and contention. The fundamental reasons why this should be so are however not made clear, nor is there a framework to understand why orderly organisational systems following rather simple decision rules should generate instability. There is no explanation of how disorder flows from order.

Approaching the matter from another angle, others have constructed complex feedback system models. They have shown that the connections between cause and effect are distant in these systems and that this leads to unintended and unexpected consequences of actions. Successful action then has to depend on an understanding of the system as a whole, seeing qualitative patterns and using archetypes and templates to reason by analogy. The models explain the instability of the dynamics in terms of the complexity of the system, but they do not explain how such instability is essential to success. They explain how disorderly behaviour flows from orderly organisational systems, but they do not explain how new order flows from that disorder.

The theories of complexity, chaos and self-organisation provide the links. Disorderly dynamics are fundamental properties of nonlinear feedback systems wherever they are found. Such systems generate patterns of behaviour over time that are jagged or fractal. They display cycles of irregular periods and trends with sudden discontinuities. They move within irregular but recognisably similar categories, providing the archetypes and templates we observe. Orderly nonlinear feedback systems are structured so as to be capable of generating disorderly changes. Such systems use the disorder to destroy old behaviour patterns allowing the new to emerge through spontaneous self-organisation. This is why unstable dynamics are essential to success and how such dynamics may produce such success. This is the link back from disorder to order.

In addition to providing a coherent framework within which all the models of managing and organising discussed in Chapter 8 can be incorporated, the theories of complexity chaos and self-organisation focus attention more clearly on certain important features of the dynamics. When you think within the framework provided by modern nonlinear dynamics you cannot escape the essential unknowability of the long-term future of any organisation. Once you accept this essential unknowability you have to reject a great deal of the received wisdom on strategic management and control. You have to accept the importance, instead, of forms of spontaneous self-organisation.

This chapter has been concerned with the basic forces driving organisations over time – the dynamics of organising. The reason for this concern is that what managers implicitly believe about these matters will determine how they make sense of what is going on and therefore what they do.

The dynamics of organising can most usefully be understood by looking at the properties of feedback systems. Feedback in an organisational system can be negative or positive, or it can flip from one to the other to create complex patterns of behaviour. An organisation is a system that operates in some conditions in a manner that is well explained by the idea of stable equilibrium. Here it utilises negative feedback to limit its behaviour to predetermined patterns. It is also capable of operating in an explosively unstable manner where vicious and virtuous circles are generated by positive feedback. Where they are used exclusively, both of these modes of equilibrium behaviour lead ultimately to failure.

Successful organisations operate in states of bounded instability, using positive and negative feedback to create complex new patterns of behaviour – innovations and new strategic directions. Because they operate in this state they face reasonably predictable short-term futures but totally unknowable long-term ones. This requires us to review carefully what we mean by decision-making and control, and how we practise both, a task to be pursued in the next two chapters.

This chapter is a pivotal one in that it is concerned with scientific explanations of how and why nonlinear feedback loops, of which human organisations are composed, operate when they are creative and innovative. The conclusion we arrive at is that organisations must operate in states at the edge of chaos if they are to transform themselves and that the process of transformation is a spontaneously self-organising one. These properties lead us to see that the conventional wisdom on strategic management is a limited special case applicable only to the short-term control of an organisation or to the strategic development of organisations required simply to repeat their past. In all other cases the conventional wisdom cannot apply and thinking in those terms is a harmful fantasy escape from reality. Instead we need to think of an organisation as a learning community out of which new strategic directions may emerge.

A complexity theory of organisation

A complexity theory of organisation is built on the following propositions:

- *All organisations are webs of nonlinear feedback loops connected to other people and organisations (its environments) by webs of nonlinear feedback loops.*
- *Such nonlinear feedback systems are capable of operating in states of stable and unstable equilibrium, or in the borders between these states, that is far-from-equilibrium, in bounded instability at the edge of chaos.*
- *All organisations are paradoxes. They are powerfully pulled towards stability by the forces of integration, maintenance controls, human desires for security and certainty, and adaptation to the environment on the one hand. They are also powerfully pulled to the opposite extreme of unstable equilibrium by the forces of division and decentralisation, human desires for excitement and innovation, and isolation from the environment.*
- *If the organisation gives in to the pull to stability it fails because it becomes ossified and cannot change easily. If it gives in to the pull to instability it disintegrates. Success lies in sustaining an organisation in the borders between stability and instability. This is a state of chaos, a difficult-to-maintain dissipative structure.*
- *The dynamics of the successful organisation are therefore those of irregular cycles and discontinuous trends, falling within qualitative patterns, fuzzy but recognisable categories taking the form of archetypes and templates.*
- *Because of its own internal dynamic, a successful organisation faces completely unknowable specific futures.*
- *Agents within the system cannot be in control of its long-term future, nor can they install specific frameworks to make it successful, nor can they apply step-by-step analytical reasoning or planning or ideological controls to long-term development. Agents within the system can only do these things in relation to the short term.*
- *Long-term development is a spontaneously self-organising process from which new strategic directions may emerge. Spontaneous self-organisation is political interaction and learning in groups. Managers have to use reasoning by analogy.*
- *In this way managers create and discover their environments and the long-term futures of their organisations.*

Further reading

For those who wish to understand more fully how the concept of feedback systems is used in the social sciences, Richardson (1991) is an excellent source. On chaos there is the classic account of how chaos was discovered and what it means by Gleick (1988). Also Briggs & Peat (1989) and Kellert (1993). A more mathematical but accessible treatment is Stewart (1989). On self-organisation it is useful to read Prigogine & Stengers (1984), Davies (1987) Nicolis &

Prigogine (1989). On complexity theory there is Waldorp (1992), Casti (1994), Cohen & Stewart (1994), Goodwin (1994), Kauffman (1993, 1995), Levy (1992). How chaos and self-organisation may apply to organisations can be explored further in Nonaka (1988), Goldstein (1994), Wheatley (1992), Zimmerman (1991, 1992) Anderson, Arrow & Pines (1988), Parker & Stacey (1994), and Stacey (1991, 1995, a, b, c, 1996).

References

Anderson, P. W., Arrow K. J. & Pines, D. (1988), *The Economy as an Evolving Complex System*, Menlo Park, Ca.: Addison Wesley.

Baumol, W. J. & Behabib, J. (1989), Chaos: significance, mechanism and economic applications, *Journal of Economic Perspectives*, Winter, vol. 3, no. 1, pp. 77–105.

Bion, W. R. (1961), *Experiences in Groups and Other Papers*, London: Tavistock Publications.

Briggs J. & Peat, F. (1989), *The Turbulent Mirror*, New York: Harper & Row.

Casti, J. (1994), *Complexification: Explaining a Paradoxical World through the Science of Surprise*, London: Harper Collins.

Cohen, J. & Stewart, I. (1994), *The Collapse of Chaos: Discovering Simplicity in a Complex World*, New York: Viking.

Davies, P. (1987), *The Cosmic Blueprint*, London: William Heinemann.

Gell-Mann, M. (1994), *The Quark and the Jaguar*, New York: Freeman & Co.

Gleick, J. (1988), *Chaos: The Making of a New Science*, London: William Heinemann.

Goldstein, J. (1994), *The Unshackled Organization: Facing the Challenge of Unpredictability through Spontaneous Reorganization*, Portland, Oreg.: Productivity Press.

Goodwin, B. (1994), *How the Leopard Changed its Spots*, London: Weidenfeld & Nicolson.

Kauffman, S. A. (1993), *Origins of Order: Self Organization and Selection in Evolution*, Oxford: Oxford University Press.

Kauffman, S. A. (1995), *At Home in the Universe*, New York: Oxford University Press.

Kellert, S. H. (1993), *In the Wake of Chaos*, Chicago: University of Chicago Press.

Kelsey, D. (1988), The economics of chaos or the chaos of economies, *Oxford Economic Papers*, vol. 40, pp. 1–31.

Klein, M. (1975), *The Writings of Melanie Klein*, London: Hogarth Press.

Levy, S. (1992), *Artificial Life*, New York: First Vintage Books.

Mandelbrot, B. (1982), *The Fractal Geometry of Nature*, New York: W. H. Freeman.

Mintzberg, H. & Waters, J. A. (1985), Of strategies deliberate and emergent, *Strategic Management Journal*, vol. 6, pp. 257–72.

Nicolis, G. & Prigogine, I. (1989), *Exploring Complexity: An Introduction*, New York: W. H. Freeman & Co.

Nonaka, I. (1988), Creating organizational order out of chaos: self-renewal in Japanese firms, *California Management Review*, Spring, pp. 57–73.

Parker, D. & Stacey, R. (1994), Chaos, management and economics: the implications of nonlinear thinking, *Hobart Papers 125*, Institute of Economic Affairs, London.

Pascale, R. T. (1990), *Managing on the Edge: How Successful Companies Use Conflict to Stay Ahead*, London: Viking Penguin.

Peitgen, H. -O. & Richter P. H. (1986), *The Beauty of Fractals: Images of Complex Dynamical Systems*, Berlin: Springer-Verlag.

Penrose, R. (1989), *The Emperor's New Mind: Concerning Computers, Minds and the Laws of Physics*, Oxford: Oxford University Press.

Peters, E. E. (1991), *Chaos and Order in the Capital Markets: A New View of Cycles, Prices and Market Volatility*, New York: John Wiley.

Prigogine, I. & Stengers, I. (1984), *Order out of Chaos: Man's New Dialogue with Nature*, New York: Bantam Books.

Ray, T. S. (1992), An approach to the sythesis of life, in Langton, G. C., Taylor, C., Doyne Farmer, J. & Rasmussen, S. (Eds), *Artificial Life II, Santa Fe Institute, Studies in the Sciences of Complexity, Vol. X*, Reading, Mass: Addison-Wesley.

Richardson, G. P. (1991), *Feedback Thought in the Social Sciences and Systems Theory*, Philadelphia: University of Pennyslvannia Press.

Stacey, R. (1990), *Dynamic Strategic Management for the 1990s*, London: Kogan Page.

Stacey, R. (1991), *The Chaos Frontier: Creative Strategic Control for Business*, Oxford: Butterworth-Heinemann.

Stacey, R. (1992), *Managing the Unknowable: The Strategic Boundaries Between Order and Chaos*, San Francisco: Jossey Bass. Also published in the UK as *Managing Chaos*, London: Kogan Page.

Stacey, R. (1995a), Creative organisations: the relevance of chaos and psychodynamics systems, in Montuori, A. & Purser, R. E. (Eds), *Social Creativity*, Hampton Press.

Stacey, R. (1995b), The role of chaos and self organisation in creative organisations, in *Proceedings of the University of Hull at Quebec Conference on Chaos and Society*.

Stacey, R. (1995c), The science of complexity: an alternative perspective for strategic change processes, *Strategic Management Journal*, August.

Stacey, R. (1996), *Complexity and Creativity in Organizations*, San Francisco: Berrett-Koehler.

Stewart, I. (1989), *Does God Play Dice? The Mathematics of Chaos*, Oxford: Blackwell.

Waldorp, M. M. (1992), *Complexity: The Emerging Science at the Edge of Chaos*, Englewood Cliffs, NJ: Simon & Schuster.

Wheatley, M. J., (1992), *Leadership and the New Science: Learning about Organization from an Orderly Universe*, Berrett-Koehler.

Zimmerman, B. J. (1991), *Strategy, Chaos and Enquiry: A Case Study of Federal Metals Inc.*, unpublished doctoral dissertation, York University, Toronto, Canada.

Zimmerman, B. J. (1992), The inherent drive towards chaos, in Lorange, P., Chakravarthy, B., Van de Ven, A. & Roos, J. (Eds), *Implementing Strategic Processes: Change, Learning and Cooperation*, London: Blackwell.

Sociocracy in Endenburg Elektrotechniek*

In the early 1970s Gerard Endenburg, a trained engineer and the general manager of Endenburg Elektrotechniek, started to experiment with the so-called sociocratic model of organisation. He was especially inspired by earlier efforts by Kees Boeke, a famous Dutch educator and social theorist, to adapt Quaker consensus decision-making methods to secular organisations. The term 'sociocracy' was adopted because it is associated with administering an organisation by all its members on the basis of equivalence.

In practical operation since the mid-1970s, the sociocratic model has progressed beyond the experimental stage and is being used rather successfully in organisations as diverse as a technical contracting company (Endenburg Elektrotechniek), municipal police department, management consulting firm, primary school, high school, chain of hairdressing shops and several health organisations. All these have reported productivity increases of 30 to 40 per cent, and both workers and managers (or students and teachers) seem to like working in them. In addition, the sociocracy model has been tested in organisations up to 1,300 people and is being tried out on a limited basis in substantially larger organisations in the Netherlands, Brazil, Canada and the USA. This case describes the development of the sociocratic model in Endenburg Elektrotechniek.

Endenburg Elektrotechiek B.V.

Endenburg Elektrotechniek was founded in 1950 by Gerard Endenburg's parents. Both Endenburg senior, who was interned in a German concentration camp during World War II, and his wife were idealistic individuals who came very disappointed out of the war period. They set out to influence these developments from what they thought was one of the key positions in Dutch society, the business owner. In their view, the business owner's 'side of the line ' was where the power is and where therefore most problems arise.

Over the years, Endenburg Elektrotechniek's products became well known for their quality and reliability. Endenburg Elektrotechniek now specialises in designing, producing, installing and renovating electro-technical installations, control systems, switching boards and electronic instruments. Its most important customers are companies in the manufacturing, ship-building, offshore, housebuilding and utility-building industries.

In 1968 Gerard Endenburg took over his father's position as managing director of the company. Gerard Endenburg had been educated in an extraordinary Dutch high school, founded by Kees Boeke, which was quite famous for its success with students who failed to perform adequately in the regular schools system. Inspired by Quaker consensus principles, this school dealt with its students as responsible partners in the design of their own curriculum. After high school Endenburg obtained a master's degree in electrical engineering. By comparing his experiences in high school with those in university, he discovered that the ruling structure of a school system to a large extent determines student behaviour. He found that when students are not given the responsibility for their own schooling process, they will focus on norms, goals and criteria that are imposed by others (e.g. teachers, examiners). Endenburg observed that this kind of school system tends to inhibit the ability to learn *how* to learn, which requires an open dia-

* This case study was written for educational and training purposes rather than to illustrate effective or ineffective handling of an administrative situation. The case was written with the help of the Harald Burmeister Scholarship, created by the Centre for Organisational Studies, Barcelona. The kind cooperation of Endenburg Elektrotechniek B.V. is gratefully acknowledged. Copyright © A.G.L. Romme & A. Reijmer, 1994. Address correspondence to A.G.L. Romme, Department of Management Sciences, University of Limburg, P.O. Box 616, 6200 MD Maastricht, Netherlands; or to A. Reijmer, Sociocratic Center, IJsclubstraat 13, 3061 GR Rotterdam, Netherlands.

logue between teachers and students on the basis of equivalence in decision-making.

After completing his university training in electrical engineering and radar technology, Endenburg was recruited by the Dutch army, where he developed steering processes on the basis of radar technology. To resolve radar problems Endenburg used the method of analogy: translate a radar problem into an electrical problem for which the solution is known, and translate this solution back into radar technology. After his military service Endenburg became the owner of a small, loss-making electrotechnical company, bought by his father. After a year this company was turned around into a profitable company, and was integrated into Endenburg Elektrotechniek. Around the same time, Endenburg took over the ownership and the position of general manager of Endenburg Elektrotechniek.

In the late 1960s, Endenburg decided to stop further growth of the company, in order to be able to focus on organisational change and renewal. He thus started to experiment with some of the ideas he had about remuneration, decision-making and organisational structure. On the basis of his experience with the method of analogy, he tried to learn from the solutions of steering problems in radar and electrical technology, in order to solve organisational problems. First, he adapted the Quaker consensus principle of full agreement to consent, which he defined as the 'absence of any argued objection'. In other words, where a consensus decision is arrived at when all say yes, for a consent decision it is sufficient than no-one says no. From an engineering viewpoint, the consent principle would give each individual employee the power to influence and control his or her own work environment, which would in turn motivate employees. The emphasis on argued objections was meant to stimulate creative solutions Moreover, Endenburg assumed that this way stalemate win–lose positions could be avoided and damaging processes of 'losers' could be stopped.

Other elements of sociocracy were derived by analogy from cybernetic concepts. Cybernetics distinguishes between linear and dynamic systems. In linear systems power and information flow in one direction only. Dynamic systems are more complex because they contain feedback and control loops, and thus a complexity of interrelated 'circle' processes. All living systems, such as individual human beings or human organisations, are dynamic systems able to evaluate and adjust their position in a continuously changing environment.

Organisations are typically viewed with a linear image in mind; for example, we tend to assume that power flows from top to bottom. Endenburg found that from an engineering standpoint organisations are severely hampered by their fundamentally linear management structure. He therefore decided to create a cybernetically dynamic structure, in which feedback rather than power was the basic organising principle.

The experiments with these ideas in Endenburg Elektrotechniek have led to an organisation in which every sub-part has a sovereign voice in the management of the organisation. At a later stage, the label 'sociocracy' was adopted because it refers to administering an organisation by every member of the organisation on the basis of equivalence. Endenburg's model of sociocracy relies on the following four ground rules:

1. *Consent.* Decision-making is governed by consent ('no argued objection'). The reasons and arguments offered are of prime importance; the decision is made when each participant gives his or her consent. Day-to-day decisions about policy implementation are not made by consent.

   Note that the consent rule allows the application of other decision methods, as long as this is agreed by consent. Thus, decisions about implementation of policy are generally made by line managers or supervisors, but other methods such as democratic majority can also be used.

2. *Circle.* Every member of the organisation belongs to at least one circle, a functional work unit (e.g. department). A circle is a group of people with a common work objective whose basic mode of policy decision-making is consent. The circle includes the functional leader (supervisor). Consent decision-making normally occurs in specially scheduled meetings. Circle meetings decide about policy decision topics which are relevant to the work objectives of the circle, within the limits of their authority.

3. *Double linking.* A larger organisation is normally subdivided into a hierarchy of circles. When a hierarchy of circles exists, each circle is represented in the next higher circle by the functional leader (supervisor or manager) and one or more additional representatives chosen from the circle by consent.

4. *Election of persons.* A circle assigns its members to the functions and tasks required by the

common work objective via consent after open discussion. (Appendix 6A provides a more detailed explanation of these four rules.)

The implementation of these rules has left the traditional hierarchical structure of Endenburg Elektrotechniek largely unchanged. In this respect, the hierarchy is integrated into the sociocratic model. *Exhibit 6.1* shows the company's administrative hierarchy in the early 1990s. The sociocratic circle structure of the company is superimposed over the hierarchical structure (see *Exhibit 6.2*). The staff of a department makes up the membership of each departmental circle. The general management circle includes the general manager, the unit managers and department supervisors, and one or more representatives chosen from each unit or departmental circle by consent. The members of the top circle are the general manager, another representative from the general management circle chosen by consent, a representative of the stockholders, and three outside experts.

Early experiments

In the late 1960s the works council (*Ondernemingsraad*) was the central place where employees attempted to influence company policy. The installation of a works council was required by Dutch laws on organisational democracy. The works council in Endenburg Elektrotechniek at that time did, however, not perform according to expectations. Instead of providing an opportunity for effective consultation between management and employees, discussions in the works council frequently generated conflicts. Thus, Gerard Endenburg decided to look for other ways to provide space for participation by employees. Inspired by the idea of sociocracy, he started to develop the model of sociocratic circles. In 1970 the first actual experiments with circles were set up. A circle hierarchy was formed, representatives were chosen, and the first circle meetings were held. At that time, the sociocratic model involved three basic rules: consent decision-making, double linking, and election of persons by

EXHIBIT 6.1

Administrative structure of Endenburg Elektrotechniek in 1993

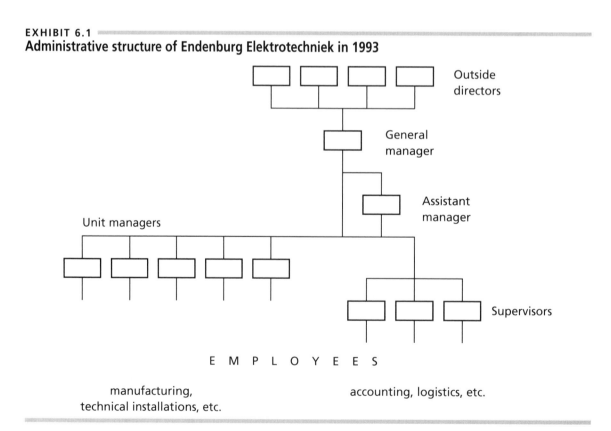

EXHIBIT 6.2
Sociocratic circle structure of Endenburg Elektrotechniek in 1993

consent. The first departmental circle to apply the consent principle included employees with quite different personalities, and in addition, two members were reputed to be rather 'difficult' persons in meetings. Before the first circle meeting, most circle members did therefore not expect this meeting to go smoothly. They thought the consent principle would remove all traditional instruments to make the two 'difficult' employees go along with any collective decision. In the usual system based on authority, they thought, the supervisor of the department would have the authority to do so.

When the first meeting of this circle started, the two 'difficult' employees behaved as expected. By their interventions, they tried to undermine the discussion. However, after a short while their initial resistance appeared to dissolve and the nature of the discussion changed towards a collective attempt to find solutions for the problems that were being dis-

cussed. The kind of undermining behaviour typically observed from two of the circle's members had simply disappeared without any deliberate interventions from the chairperson or any other participant. The success of this first meeting stimulated the circle to arrange for a new meeting in order to solve several complex problems. Moreover, this initial success also stimulated other circles to start working with the sociocratic principles.

Payment and compensation

In the same period, Gerard Endenburg started applying his ideas about new forms of payment and compensation. These new forms were derived from the idea of risk-sharing, and, in addition, the idea of providing an adequate mix of fixed and variable rewards to both the suppliers of labour and the suppliers of financial capital. Endenburg had been discussing these ideas in the late 1960s with the employees of his company, representatives of labour unions, and the Dutch government. This proposal for a new payment and compensation system involved three components: a base payment, short-term incentive, and long-term incentive. The base payment, or 'subsistence guarantee', was at that time largely determined by collective agreements between labour unions, employers and the Dutch government. This kind of payment would under normal circumstances allow each employee to have an acceptable standard of living.

Both the short-term and long-term incentives were based on financial accounting. The short-term incentive was meant to provide immediate feedback on the contribution of individual employees in a given project. Thus, each participant in a project received a percentage of the net result of the project, or if the net result was negative all participants contributed to the loss on the project. The percentage was calculated on the basis of their individual salary relative to the turnover of the project. The reactions to this kind of compensation, from both insiders and outsiders, varied from extremely positive to extremely negative. Positive reactions expressed appreciation of the way in which this system gave individual employees greater insight into and control over their compensation. However, employees as well as representatives from labour unions wondered whether the short-term incentive did not in fact boil down to a traditional kind of pay system. These critics feared it might in fact involve a new technique of manipulation, similar to the traditional piece-work system in which employees are paid according to how much they produce regardless of how long is spent completing jobs. The discussions in most circles showed that this fear of being manipulated was deeply rooted. By the mid-1970s, the short-term incentive did nevertheless result in greater personal commitment to projects. It appeared that the sociocratic principles and the base payment to a large extent alleviated the fear of manipulation.

The long-term financial incentive was in effect a profit-sharing plan. Thus, managers, employees and stockholders received a share in the net profit of the company. On the basis of the result shown in the annual accounts the top circle decided what amount was to be distributed. This might in principle be the entire annual profit, the entire profit less reserves, an appropriation from reserves, or nothing at all (if the company made a loss). Salary or stock in relation to turnover was used to calculate how much each participant received. This long-term incentive did not necessarily need to be in the form of money, but might also be distributed in the form of, for example, stock or stock certificates.

In the early 1970s the experiences with the sociocratic circle organisation and experiments with the new compensation system were quite positive. Circle members participated in a serious manner in circle meetings, and most circles developed into increasingly cohesive work groups. The sociocratic way of working appeared to provide an opportunity to deal with issues and problems that would otherwise have been avoided.

In the meantime the company also showed a steady pattern of turnover growth. Thus, in addition to the experiments with the sociocratic model, the company had to face problems raised by continuous growth. The top circle especially felt it necessary to broaden their expertise by recruiting a third external member. As a result, the top circle in the mid-1970s was composed of three external members, an accountant, a stockholder, two general managers, and two chosen representatives from the general circle.

The crisis of 1976

In 1976 the company ran into a crisis situation which, in retrospect, can be seen as one of the most critical incidents in the development of the sociocratic model. A few local shipyards suddenly shut down, not being able to deal with foreign competition. These shipyards accounted for more than one-third of the business of Endenburg Elektrotechniek. This had several consequences for the Technical Installations department, which built heavy-duty electrotechnical equipment for ships. Gerard Endenburg believed that there was no choice but to lay off 60 workers from this department. Because this kind of decision fell within the limits of his authority, he announced the intended layoff to the members of the general circle and others in the company. The day after the decision was announced, one of the fitters in the Manufacturing department, Jan De Groot, asked the secretary of his circle to call a meeting as quickly as possible in order to discuss an idea he had for a better way to handle the sudden crisis. De Groot felt the traditional way of laying off employees just did not fit into sociocracy. The circle secretary was able to arrange a meeting for the next day, when everyone was gathered, De Groot explained his idea.

'It seems to me,' he said, 'we'd do a lot better if we delayed the layoff for a few weeks and shifted everyone who would be laid off into a concentrated marketing effort. The overall development in our kind of business is not as worse as it seems. There has got to be more business out there! I would much rather spend my time wiring generators than knocking on doors with a suit and tie on, but I'll do it if it means keeping my job.'

The circle members then started to discuss Jan De Groot's, proposal and after about half an hour the circle seemed to fall in behind his proposal.

The circle's chair, who was also the chosen representative in the general circle, summarised the picture that apparently had emerged.

'It sounds like this is what we want to do: we appoint Jan as a temporary second circle representative to the general management circle. He will propose that we delay the layoff for one month while everyone in the company who can be spared concentrates on marketing. The marketers will have to give us a crash course and run the show.'

The chairman glanced at the circle's secretary who was scribbling in the official circle notebook. The secretary responded by nodding to indicate that he did not need him to repeat the proposed decision.

'OK,' the chair continued, 'let's go around the circle to see if anyone has objections.'

No one did. As the meeting broke up, the supervisor of the manufacturing department said he would report the decision to the general manager, Gerard Endenburg, at once and request the general circle's secretary to call a meeting for the next afternoon.

The next day the general circle met and started to discuss the proposal presented by Jan De Groot. After some initial reservations, including those of Gerard Endenburg, the general circle decided to support De Groot's initiative. Thus, in subsequent meetings the general circle developed a new layoff procedure which implied that most layoffs were postponed. All 'spare' workers would spend most of their time acquiring new projects. A final decision could not be made because of policy limitations on their authority to spend the company's reserve fund. This kind of decision could only be made by the top circle, and Jan De Groot was designated as the temporary second representative to the top circle.

In the same period, the top circle had met several times on its own accord to discuss the crisis situation. In these meetings two external members of the top circle expressed serious concerns with the operation of the sociocratic model in a crisis. They argued sociocracy now had to be set aside: 'There is a crisis, and, therefore things have to be reorganised without sociocracy. '

Alarmed, the representatives of the general circle had refused to go along with this kind of crisis management: 'Precisely in this situation, sociocracy has to prove itself. All creativity available in the company is needed to ensure the continuity of the company, and therefore we cannot give consent to your proposal. '

As a consequence, the two external members decided to resign from their membership of the top circle.

Several days later the top circle, with De Groot as the new second representative of the general circle, met and discussed the general circle's proposal. The top circle quickly gave its consent to spending part of the company's reserve fund for this purpose, which allowed the general circle to launch the plan into action. Within several weeks, enough new projects were acquired to justify further postponement of the layoff. Only a few workers were laid off some months later. The Technical Installations department was sized down, but several other treatments started to grow and since the late 1970s the company has started to develop a much more diversified customer base.

Starting anew

In the late 1970s several evaluation studies of the sociocratic process in Endenburg Elektrotechniek were conducted. One of these studies was performed by a university professor who concluded that both the top circle and general management circle met on a frequent basis, but that this was certainly not so for the departmental circles. In fact, several departments appeared to have lost all interest in circle meetings. One of the explanations given at that time was that the need to hold circle meetings decreases when the company functions relatively well. In addition, in discussions with members of the department circles it appeared that they were not or were barely aware of the opportunities provided by the sociocratic way of organising.

However, in several meetings in which these opportunities were discussed, it quickly became clear that there were other problems apart from a need for information. It seemed many workers had been confronted with sociocracy too abruptly, and needed a more gradual introduction into the sociocratic principles.

After extensive discussions in the top and general circle, the decision was made to implement sociocracy anew, as if nothing was known about it. This implementation process was not supervised by Gerard Endenburg, but by staff from the Sociocratic Center, a foundation that had been established to supervise and support the introduction of sociocracy in other organisations (see Appendix 6B).

A company without owners

Endenburg's ideas about sociocracy implied that the company could not be 'owned' in the traditional manner. He felt that external owners, such as stockholders, would not be interested in any other commitment to the company than by their share in the company's equity.

In a traditionally structured company, the stockholders or owners have the right, by virtue of the capital they provide, to decide what proportion of the profit is to be distributed to them. Their remuneration is dependent on the profit level, and is thus variable. By contrast, workers receive a remuneration which is largely fixed (e.g. salary), and they do not have a substantial impact on how profit is distributed. This picture is summarised in *Exhibit 6.3*.

Endenburg argued that the traditional ownership situation 'constitutes a threat to the sociocratic nature of Endenburg Elektrotechniek, because it allows outside meddling based on stock ownership. Consent decision-making presupposes that the nature of one's function in the organization, and not the amount of stock held, determines what a person gets to consent to.'

The profit and compensation system in Endenburg Elektrotechniek tried to solve this problem by

- separating purely financial interests from power in the company by

- subjecting the financial stakeholders to decisions by consent by members of the company (including a representative of the stockholders at the board level); and
- giving the employees opportunities for financial participation.

The remuneration system in Endenburg Elektrotechniek is summarised in *Exhibit 6.4*.

Dutch corporate law, however, did not support these principles, because all existing legal forms were based on the concept of ownership. This problem was solved by constructing a legal structure out of two conventional legal forms, the corporation and foundation. The foundation now is the owner of all stock in the corporation, and as such controls the company. The constitution of this foundation is based on sociocratic ground rules, and the top circle of the corporation also acts as the top circle of the foundation. Thus, the company is not owned by external persons or organisations.

This legal structure also appears to provide an effective protection against hostile takeover attempts. Nevertheless, the company's management thought it was extremely important to operate in a sociocratic circle organisation without jeopardizing the beneficial properties of the free market economy. Although profit was no longer seen as the primary purpose of the company, it still served as a yardstick. In this respect, the top and general circles used profit and other competitive information exclusively for measurement, feedback and control.

Some external observers claim that the profit and compensation system used in Endenburg Elektrotechniek is not a key element of sociocracy. In this respect, applications of the sociocratic model in organisations such as a high school suggest that other

---

EXHIBIT 6.3

Position of stockholder and employee in a traditional company

	Fixed remuneration	Variable remuneration	Participation in decision-making
Providers of capital	–	X	X
Providers of labour	X	–	–

Source: G. Endenburg (1988) *Sociocracy: The Organization of Decision-making*, Rotterdam: Sociocratic Center.

EXHIBIT 6.4
Position of stockholder and employee in Endenburg Elektrotechniek

	Fixed remuneration	Variable remuneration	Participation in decision-making
Providers of capital	X	X	–
Providers of labour	X	X	X

Source: G. Endenburg (1988) *Sociocracy: The Organization of Decision-making*, Rotterdam: Sociocratic Center.

compensation systems are also compatible with sociocracy. Moreover, the short-term incentive has been evaluated by some as inadequate because it is derived from financial accounting data. An adequate response by individual employees to this kind of incentive, by maximising certain financial accounting data, can be suboptimal for the company as a whole.

Sociocratic elections

In the course of the 1980s and early l990s, participants in circle meetings at all levels in the company found that the transition from familiar autocratic or democratic methods to sociocratic procedures deeply affected each member of the organisation. This transition became most evident in sociocratic elections.

Important elections involve the circle's chair, representative(s) to the upper circle, supervisors of the unit or departmental circles, and the general manager(s). Although election of persons by consent logically follows from the first three rules (consent, circles, and double linking), practical experience underscores the importance of adding this fourth rule. Most people are very reluctant about discussing other people in public, especially when they are present. Through our experiences in democratic systems we have been programmed with the message that secret voting is the best way to deal with elections.

A sociocratic election places a great deal of weight on the arguments raised in favour of certain candidates. Speaking openly about the potential of circle members is an essential step in getting the right person to the right position. If after some time the circle finds that the 'wrong' member has been chosen, the procedure can be repeated. In order to prevent some individuals routinely holding on to their positions in Endenburg Elektrotechniek, each position is

re-elected at least once every two years.

What actually happens in an election procedure? Before the election meeting, the circle members are informed in writing about the election (as an item on the agenda). During the meeting they are asked to write the name of anyone they wish to propose as a potential candidate on a special form. Exhibit 6.5 shows a typical ballot form used in elections. Using this ballot form, it is immediately clear who is proposing a certain candidate.

EXHIBIT 6.5
Ballot form used in sociocratic elections

I, ...

(your name)

CHOOSE:

. . . .

(name of candidate)

At the meeting, the chair will ask each member to state the arguments which prompted him or her to nominate this particular candidate, for example by asking: 'John, you voted for Muriel. Would you give your reasons for choosing her?' The chair makes sure there are no discussions during the presentation of arguments. Only after all members have made their arguments clear may an open discussion develop. At some point, the chair may go around with the question: 'Do you want to change your candidate, in view of the arguments you have heard?' When the chair feels that a certain candidate has been most emphatically nominated – which need not be the candidate with a majority support – he or she will ask if there is anyone who wishes to withhold consent from this particular candidate. If there are no objections to this candidate, he or she is elected by consent. In case anyone withholds consent, he or she is asked to put forward arguments for doing so. If after the discussion which follows the objector still withholds consent, the chair will move to the next candidate. Note that the chair's role is crucial in this process. Most circles therefore give much attention to electing their chair.

New circle members who are unfamiliar with this procedure tend to be reluctant to talk about others during an election, but their insecurity is often soon overcome. Through the process of argument and open discussion, circles learn to use their collective wisdom in delegating functions and tasks to circle members. Thus, as one of the participants after a circle meeting expressed it: 'To my surprise we do not have any winners or losers after the election, but instead I feel we have done a good job together.'

A new general manager

One of the most important election procedures in the company's history was started in 1993, when the general circle decided to elect a new general manager who would replace Gerard Endenburg. The recruitment procedure was started by setting up a support circle of the general circle. This support circle first formulated a set of criteria (profile), and then developed a recruitment procedure. The initial profile required the new manager, amongst other things to have a technical background and to be familiar with sociocracy. The general circle gave its consent to this proposal and then delegated its execution to a special committee. The committee first tried to find an appropriate candidate within the company. Initially, these attempts failed and the support circle tried to recruit an outside candidate. Several people were invited for a meeting with the committee, but no one was evaluated as a good candidate. External recruitment and selection agencies were consulted, but again without success. These external agencies also had a hard time in defining and understanding the 'strange' nature of their client.

With these experiences in mind the committee decided to look again for an internal candidate. The top and general circle organised an election in a joint meeting. After a short introduction by the chairman, each participant was asked to write the name of a candidate on a ballot form. When the ballot forms were handed over to the chairman, he started to ask each participant for the reasons behind his or her vote. Of a total of sixteen participants, seven did not come up with a candidate; five voted for Piet Slieker, a unit manager without a technical background; two participants voted for a general management team of two persons (including Slieker); and the two remaining votes were for other internal candidates. In the subsequent discussion, it became clear that the position of general manager had to be redefined. At the end of the meeting, the chairman proposed Piet Slieker for the position of general manager. Two participants did not give their consent to this proposal because they wanted to wait for the results of a psychological assessment test.

Two months later, during a second joint meeting of the top and general circle, the test results were discussed (after Slieker had agreed to the report's being distributed). The candidate was again carefully evaluated in an open discussion, and subsequently all participants gave their consent to the decision to appoint Piet Slieker as the new general manager. This implied Piet Slieker would replace Endenburg after a period of transition.

All participants were quite positive about the election process. Piet Slieker felt his candidateship had been carefully evaluated, which gave him company-wide support in his new position. One of the consequences of the decision to elect Piet Slieker is that the top structure had to be redefined, especially in view of Piet Slieker's background in business administration rather than technical engineering.

The idea of quality

Recently, the company has started to integrate quality management concepts (ISO) into sociocratic practice. In 1993 the general management circle set up a temporary 'support circle' to implement the ISO-9000 norms in one or two units of the company. This support circle develops policy proposals and consists of the general manager, all unit managers and department supervisors, an internal expert, and a quality consultant from the Sociocratic Center. The general circle discusses the proposals, takes the key decisions, and delegates implementation to managers or supervisors.

A crucial element in applying quality management in Endenburg Elektrotechniek is the logbook system, the key information system for all participants in the sociocratic circle structure. This information system contains both general and specific information for all circles and individuals in the company. Everyone in the company has free access to any information, except for those pieces of information which are established by consent as exceptions. The logbook system has been implemented on a general, computerised information system. For specific norms such as those to do with ISO or health and safety, a small handbook is currently being drafted.

Most employees feel that their long experience with working in sociocratic circles gives them a headstart in applying quality management ideas. Moreover, it is clear that the sociocratic approach of quality management goes beyond the approach adopted in other companies, where circles are introduced merely in order to foster employee involvement, awareness of product quality, and so forth. Working with the idea of quality in sociocratic circles involves a continuous process in which all employees and managers produce, create, repair and re-create the company on the basis of the consent principle.

In order to measure the quality of the sociocratic conditions in the company, a social accountancy report is made each year by a social accountant from the Sociocratic Center. This report measures if individuals and circles are able to use the sociocratic method in a correct manner.

Outlook

Since its foundation in 1950, Endenburg Elektrotechniek has gradually developed from a manufacturing company towards a company offering a complete package of designing, producing, installing, renovating and servicing a variety of systems and installations for industrial customers. Most of the company's customers are located in (western) Europe, although it also has important customers in countries such as Tanzania and Indonesia. In this respect, the large-scale production of electrical installations increasingly is moving to less developed parts of the world. This development has recently been extensively discussed in several circles, and some participants regard it as a threat to the company's continuity.

Piet Slieker, the new general manager, does not see this development as a fundamental threat:

> The relocation of industrial activity especially concerns large series production. Our strength is in small series and custom-made products. We have developed a core technology with a lot of opportunities to tailor the product to the needs of the customer. Thus, we provide tailor-made products at the price level of large scale work. Moreover, the sociocratic principles appear to provide the ideal vehicle to respond in a timely fashion to any external development.

Reference

Endenburg, G. (1988) *Sociocracy: The Organization of Decision-Making*, Rotterdam: Sociocratic Center.

APPENDIX 6A
Sociocracy: The organization of decision-making

In 1981 Gerard Endenburg published the book *Sociocratic: Het Organiseren van de Besluitvorming*, which was later translated as *Sociocracy: The Organization of Decision-Making* (1988). This book describes in detail the principles of the sociocratic circle model, and also provides several examples of how this model can be applied in companies, non-profit organisations, schools and families. A few excerpts from the first part of this book, describing the basic rules of sociocratic circle organisation, are reproduced here.

Sociocracy is relevant to every organization, regardless of its object

The society which has to create the conditions necessary to make our life possible is a complex of organizations, each striving to achieve a particular objective. Each individual is part of some of these organizations and tries to make a personal contribution to the achievement of the objectives in question. Generally speaking, it is necessary to make certain agreements and establish certain rules in order to achieve together the objective which has been set. This is true of all organizations, regardless of their objectives. In this context I am thinking not only of the obvious organizations such as company, school, hospital and government agency, but also such organizations as the family and the individual. The number of people making up the organization is not important here, because the way in which the agreements are made and the rules are established and the way in which they can be amended and compliance with them supervised is the same for every organization.

The decision-making process governed by the principle of concent

Until quite recently, it was common practice to establish rules in an authoritarian fashion. Even in the case of the family, this procedure was embodied in the law. The main feature of the authoritarian approach is that the will (i.e. the interest) of an individual or small group governs the making and implementation of decisions and the supervision of compliance with them.

Nowadays, however, there is a growing movement away from the authoritarian approach towards a more democratic method of working.

The mean feature of the democratic approach is that the will (i.e. the interest) of the majority governs the making and implementation of decisions and the supervision of compliance with them. The authoritarian approach is still possible, but the principle of decision-making by the majority predominates. The great virtue of the democratic process is that reversing to authoritarian decision-making is prevented by the 'threshold' or safeguard formed by the majority principle. In practice, however, we find that that threshold requires constant supervision. The space created above the threshold is the space which we, both as individuals and as a group, are free to use to arrange our lives and the life of our community. Whether we are willing or able to do so depends on many different factors, but at least democracy allows the necessary space.

The great disadvantage of democracy is that majority decisions can evoke the same reaction as authoritarian decisions, because the power of the majority can, strictly speaking, be described as the dictatorship of numbers.

In order to win over a majority, one can use argument, but one can also resort to other means. The minority is defeated, not convinced. The minority's reaction may be to reject or to accept with reluctance the decision reached in this way, and may have recourse to other means in an attempt to reverse their defeat, none of which is beneficial to the decision's effectiveness. The more or less serious consequences of this kind of reaction are evident every day in what we learn from newspapers, radio and TV.

This disadvantage is, furthermore, a fatal flaw in this organizational model. For, just as there are always forces within an autocracy or dictatorship which are working towards democratization, so there are always forces within a democracy urging regression to an authoritarian process. The resulting swing to and fro of the pendulum is obvious all around us.

Sociocracy should be seen as the next phase in the development of the organizational forms of our society. And with sociocracy, the swing of the pendulum disappears.

The main feature of the sociocratic process is that the will (i.e. the interest) of both the individual and the group of which he is a member governs the making and implementation of decisions and the supervision of compliance with them, through the principle of consent (principle of no objection). Both democratic and authoritarian decision-making processes remain as 'normal' possibilities, but they are controlled by the principle of consent. Compared with the democratic model, the threshold in the sociocratic model makes available more space for both individual and group to arrange their lives in accordance with their own wishes and needs.

Sociocracy does not, therefore, create a new ideal, but a new basis. The sociocratic circle organization guarantees an equal basis for each individual within the organization of the society. The equality of each individual in the decision-making process within the sociocratic society is guaranteed by the way in which the individual is able to take part in the decision-making process and help to control it. In applying the principle of consent, sociocracy does not ask for a 'yes' but does provide an opportunity to give a reasoned 'no'.

Sociocracy does not require solidarity

Sociocracy does not require solidarity, does not require unanimity, does not demand a 'yes' – it provides the opportunity to give a reasoned 'no'.

That does not mean solidarity, unanimity and affirmation are not possible within sociocracy, nor that they are forbidden, but they are *not a prerequisite*, and that is very important.

Every day we hear that things would be a lot better if people showed a little more solidarity. To put it mildly, this is a most unrealistic view.

To feel solidarity with a cause, a person or a group implies a feeling of unity, of being at one with the other, a subjugation of your interest to the general interest, suppression of yourself for the sake of the community. This is clearly an example of an either/or situation: either I or the group. The self can perhaps be suppressed for a short period, but certainly not in the longer term.

The sociocratic model gives scope to the individual, based on a both and relationship – both my interest and the interests of the group – thus making possible the interplay between the two. And obviously, in certain situations people can act in solidarity with one another for a short period.

In the case of unanimity and the seeking of affirmation, there is potentially an extra unreasonable demand, the demand for understanding. After all, the voter should know why he votes in favour of a particular course of action. But this is an unreasonable demand – the voter should have the freedom to decide whether a particular matter is sufficiently important for him to want to understand it, and thus also the freedom to choose whether or not to leave the decision-making to someone else. The principle of consent (principle of no objection) gives him this freedom. It follows that, for example, 'compulsory' attendance at meetings (solidarity) should be unnecessary – you attend a meeting when there are items on the agenda which might be of interest to you. On the other hand, it is essential that you know that meetings exist as a tool and that you are free to use this tool whenever you consider it necessary.

The double link as the safeguard for the circle process

The number of people making up an organization determines to some extent whether a particular decision-making process is suitable. If the principle of consent is to be applied consistently, large organizations will have to be broken down into smaller units, which I described as *circles*. A circle is a group of people who are *functionally related*, such as a department, a class or a team.

The important thing is that the circles should be interlinked in such a way that the sociocratic prin-

ciple, the circle process, can continue to operate. Accordingly, each circle is linked to the next higher circle by a double link consisting of at least two persons, one an elected representative and the other the functional leader of the circle. This way of linking circles is new and it is one of the essential elements of the sociocratic model. Likert's single link, the 'linking pin', is well-known. However, the double link is not simply a doubling of the single link or an addition of an extra person, it is an innovation which is of fundamental importance. What it does is to create feedback, the essential feature of the circle process . . . In practice it has been found that this double link has much more than simply organizational consequences, not only in the interlinking of circles within a single organization but also in the linking of different organizations with common interests. One consequence, for example, is that the traditional function of the supervisory board or committee takes on a completely new meaning.

The four basic rules

The four rules on which the sociocratic circle organization is founded are:

I   The principle of consent governs the decision-making process (consent = no objection). This means that a decision can only be taken when no-one has any reasoned objection to it.

II   A sociocratic circle has its own objective, delegates the three functions of directing, operating and measuring/feedback to its own members and maintains its own memory system through integral education.

III The connection between two circles takes the form of a double link. This means that at least two people from one circle take part in the decision-making in the next higher circle: the functional leader and one or more elected representatives.

IV People are elected exclusively by consent after open discussion.

It will be clear from the foregoing that the first three of these rules are fundamental to sociocratic organization. The fourth rule has been added because it has been found repeatedly in practice that, although this rule follows on logically from the first three, we have been so strongly conditioned that we still tend to select people by counting votes, rather than by argument. Sociocracy is the power of argument.

Applying the four basic rules

Despite the fact that this model was constructed on the assumption that it would have universal application – in other words, that it could be applied irrespective of the objectives of the organization concerned – it is still something of a surprise to discover in practice that this is in fact so.

The model can be applied irrespective of the objective of the organization and irrespective of whether it is, in the current terminology, a profit-making or non-profit making organization. However, it must be noted that it is not simply a matter of introducing the four rules. Each organization has its own specific problems, and as soon as the sociocratic circle model is introduced it will be found that these problems can no longer be resolved in the ways we have become used to: the solutions have to be sought in the sociocratic way.

Examples of such problems might be establishing rules concerning the limits within which an executive is allowed to exercise his power, policy decisions, dismissal and recruitment procedures, investment policy, profit distribution, in short all rules which are essential to the proper functioning of an organization. In principle, everything can be open to discussion. What is remarkable is how greatly we are hampered in our search for new rules and procedures by our conditioning. The result of adopting a new approach is that in most cases the solution we arrive at is not the one we would have chosen under our traditional approach. Frequently solutions come from people whom 'no-one would have thought of'.

Once again, the importance of the circle structure is apparent, as is the importance of not requiring solidarity. A circle holds a meeting on a particular subject, and only those who have an interest in the decision under discussion need to be present at the meeting.

To avoid any misunderstanding, I would once again stress that the sociocratic circle organization is not intended to replace a particular organizational structure, but that it is an addition to that structure.

One fact which has consistently been apparent since the early days (1970) of the experiments with sociocracy is that one can work according to the four basic rules irrespective of the level of intellectual development of the individuals involved in the decision-making process. Generally speaking, the function which one performs within an organization is determined to some extent by natural aptitude, intellectual development and/or technical skill. However, the 'tools', the four basic rules on which the community is organized, are the same for all the members of the organization: each individual is entitled to live his or her own life. Experience has shown that decisions are always made in the same way in every circle. There are, of course, differences between the circles in the type of problem encountered, the terminology used and in numerous other respects, but in every circle the people concerned make use of the power of argument to find the best possible solution for the problems which arise.

APPENDIX 6B
Sociocratic Center

The Sociocratic Center (Sociocratisch Centrum), located in Rotterdam, was founded in 1978 on the basis of Endenburg's vision of a society in which people live together as different, unique people respecting their mutual equivalence. The Center tries to realize this equivalence by means of the sociocratic method. The Center's mission statement is to provide support for processes that guide society toward the equivalent community. In doing so, the Sociocratic Center intends to:

(1) develop and motivate the use of sociocracy, and protect and improve the quality of existing sociocratic organisations;
(2) integrate organisations using the sociocratic model into a global network.

The Sociocratic Center is involved in educational activities, management consultancy, social accountancy, legal and financial consultancy, research and development, and publishing reports on sociocracy. It has also set up a network of circles all over the Netherlands, in order to facilitate the exchange of experiences with the sociocratic model.

The Center has developed an implementation strategy for small and large organisations, based on especially education. In addition, a method to measure the sociocratic quality of an organisation (social accountancy) has been developed. Moreover, the Center is currently developing a sociocratic quality system, the so-called Sociocratic Quality Method. In addition, the Center stimulates consultancy firms, high schools and universities to use sociocracy. A special network is set up for consultants using the sociocratic method, and for general managers of sociocratic organisations.

Finally, similar Centers have been set up in Canada, the US and Brazil in order to be able to serve local organisations interested in the sociocratic philosophy and method.

CASE STUDY 7

The European Technology Transfer Committee*

The 'official' version

During the late 1960s and early 1970s international policy makers were seeking ways of aiding the less developed countries through the transfer of appropriate, intermediate technology. Members of the European Community established a European Technology Transfer Committee (ETTC) to address this issue from a European perspective. The role of the ETTC was to identify technology projects for funding from European Community sources and then monitor the execution of those projects. The ETTC consisted of members nominated by the relevant government department in each member country, with a chairman and executive committee drawn from that membership.

Administrative support for the ETTC a provided by a Division of the European Commission, call it the Technology Division. The Head of this Division, a civil servant, also acted as the Executive Secretary of the ETTC. The ETTC projects were run, as were projects in all other international aid agencies at that time, by project directors supported by project teams and responsible to the Head of Division. The expense of ETTC meetings and the fund for ETTC projects were met by a Technical Fund contributed by member countries and administered by the Commission.

By the mid-1980s the concern with appropriate and intermediate technology transfer had diminished and attention was refocused on the globalisation of industry, as well as the spreading trend to deregularising industry and privatising the public sector. These changes in the environment within which the ETTC worked called for some further changes. The Head of the Technology Division at that time appointed a review group to examine the

role of the ETTC and the Technology Division which serviced it. This report recommended a number of specific industries and geographic areas in which to concentrate European technology assistance. It also recommended a restructuring of the ETTC, changes in the way that the Division worked and initiatives to improve the overall management of technology in the developing countries, including more effective prioritisation of technology project.

A series of workshops and discussions took place over the subsequent five years or so, culminating in the setting up of a Technology Management Network (TMNET). By early 1993 TMNET was well into the implementation of its vision of becoming a major agent for change through technology transfer. TMNET operates through cooperative networking and resourcing to provide advisory services to governments on technology management.

The continuing pressures of globalisation, privatisation and deregulation made it a matter of great importance for public and private sectors to cooperate in the development of technology. To respond to these needs TMNET launched its Public–Private Sector Partnership in 1993.

The above constitutes a 'linear', formal account of how TMNET was set up and how it now operates: changes in the external environment meant that globalisation and privatisation became more important issues than appropriate technology transfer, and this required more effective management and prioritisation of technology projects. To meet this need a report reviewing the role of the ETTC as commissioned and on it recommendations the TMNET was set up. As environmental demands continued to develop TMNET established a partnership with the private sector.

---

* Copyright © Michaela Smith and Ralph Stacey

The 'participant–observer' version

Now consider how individuals involved in the above developments tell the story.

In the years after 1945 a number of individuals in European countries found themselves taking up roles, both formal and informal, which involved advising their governments on scientific matter. Many of these individuals increasingly came across each other when they represented their governments at international scientific gatherings, particularly gatherings of international bodies charged with promoting and allocating funds to the development and transfer of technology. Their European links created a natural could improve their bargaining position by mutually supporting each other. This practical issue of improved negotiating strength provided the focus around which an informal club of European government scientific advisors evolved. Having evolved, the informal club then performed other cooperative functions as well. Gradually, however, this informal club developed a number of formal aspects until it became an official body with its own chairman and executive committee: the European Technology Liaison Committee.

By 1975 this Liaison Committee was caught up in the increasing institutionalisation of links between European countries and became the ETTC. Thus, the loose club composed of individuals self-selected to support each other in their own work had gradually been replaced, first by a more formalised collection of individuals and then by an institutionalised collection of formally appointed representatives of government departments. That institutionalised body then exercised the primarily formal functions of legitimating the allocation of funds to technology projects but the work and the real decision-making power had passed to a Division of the European Commission.

In the mid-1980s Jose Fonseca became the Executive Secretary of the ETTC and Head of the Technology Division. He had been the director of research for a large multinational corporation and his appointment was part of a programmme to swop executives between industry and the Commission. Fonseca was concerned with breaking down the technology divide that existed between the developed and developing countries – he wanted to introduce greater team efforts and quality controls into technology development in the developing countries, and felt that this was not assisted by the domination which the Division exerted over the ETTC. He therefore set up a review group of formally nominated ETTC members headed by someone brought in from outside the organisation to find out what the developing countries were really looking for with regard to technology, and to review how effectively the ETTC and the Division were meeting those needs. The purpose of this review group was also to identify priority areas for future technology effort.

The resulting report identified a number of key areas for technological developments in developing countries and it made recommendations for reforming the ETTC and the Division. However, the difficulty in getting a group of formally appointed government representatives to agree upon any order of technology development priority convinced Fonseca that the prime need was for member countries to learn how to manage and prioritise their own technology development efforts.

Efforts to reorganise the ETTC and the Division along the lines recommended in the report ran into difficulties which were unavoidable given the different perspective of Fonseca, the newcomer, and the civil servants in the Commission. Fonseca saw the purpose of the ETTC as one of assisting countries to prioritise their technology efforts and so wanted it to consist of individuals selected on the basis of their expertise. The civil servants, however, saw the ETTC as a legitimating body and so wanted to continue with appointments on a representative basis. Furthermore, the areas identified for top priority by the report did not attract projects because of funding and political difficulties.

The report came out in late 1984. At its meeting in 1986 the ETTC was still arguing about the recommendations. At the end of 1986 Fonseca's contract was not renewed and in early 1987 a civil servant took over. He had a different set of priorities which did not include the ETTC reform programme. At a 1988 ETTC meeting the argument about reform continued, as it also did in 1989 and 1990.

All attempts at implementing the comprehensive formal programme of change for the ETTC and the Division, as well as the attempt to form a rational plan for prioritising and allocating technical assistance, failed to materialise. Instead, assistance continued to be allocated largely on the basis of political pressure and changes in the methods of cooperation in technology development happened in a completely different way. It is to this different way that we now turn.

After the publication of the report in late 1984 Fonseca hired a temporary aide, called Johnson, who had worked previously with Fonseca in his multinational days. Johnson was brought in to deal with the recommendations on managing, organising and prioritising technology development efforts. When he arrived, Johnson found that a Workshop had already been set up for early 1985 in Mauritius to initiate the 'management of technology' programme, and he was asked to organise it. For this Workshop, Johnson developed an expert system which he called VALTEC (short for technology evaluation). This expert system incorporated a number of principles, suitably weighted according to expert opinion, to do with prioritising research. The system made it possible for policy makers to ask a number of questions about a specific set of research projects presented to them and be guided by the system in the making of priority judgements. Johnson and not been trained in running Commission-style conferences so, instead of concentrating on the presentation of official papers, he arranged for delegates to work on the VALTEC system using their own research programmes and then to discuss the problems raised with each other.

The 50 people attending the Mauritian Workshop had all been nominated by their government departments – they were a mixture of scientists and civil service bureaucrats, some at very high levels in their departments. Their response to the interactive event which Johnson had organised was to form themselves into teams, first to understand what an expert system was and then to work with the system on common sets of problems. In doing to, the apparently fixed developing–developed country divide seemed to melt and delegates began to realise that they could work out their own science and technology spend priorities themselves, without hiring consultants. The effect of working on the expert system was to make clear to delegates that no rational set of techniques for determining priorities existed – instead, they saw each set of circumstances as unique and so requiring the exercise of expert judgement, which might be assisted by using broad principles extracted from judgements previously made in analogous situations.

The Workshop was particularly important to members from a number of small African countries. Each of these small countries had been pursuing its own attempts to manage its science and technology programmes in isolation from the others. At the Workshop, however, they had spontaneously formed a team, without realising that they were doing so, to work jointly on VALTEC. In doing this they discovered how similar their problems were. After the

Workshop they asked Johnson for further help in using the expert system. He applied, in his personal capacity, to the Hatfield Fund, a private research foundation, for a research grant to conduct research into prioritising projects. It so happened that the Hatfield Fund managers were themselves facing this problem. Johnson was therefore given a substantial personal research grant, while he continued to get short-term renewals of his employment contract with the Division.

Johnson then assembled about 20 senior managers of research institutions and departments in the small African countries. Each of these came with their own problems and the aim of developing generic methods for evaluating projects in small countries. It was their intention to apply such methods over the three years of the research grant and observe how effective they were – the classic observer–participant approach of action science. They named this the VALTEC project and during the life of that project they established a working network amongst themselves which still exists.

These developments had to be reported to the ETTC and the Division and the response was largely critical – critics could not see what useful purpose was served by this informal getting together to discuss the principles of prioritising projects. To deal with this criticism, Johnson approached individual members of the ETTC and invited them to attend meetings of the African VALTEC network. The civil servants in the Division objected to the breaking of protocol when a very junior and temporary member of the Division personally approached very senior civil servants without using the proper channels. However, the VALTEC project attracted a trickle of important visitors despite the opposition.

Then, having heard about VALTEC, the government scientific advisor in Canada invited Johnson and his colleagues to attend a conference he was organising in Vancouver. One of the most immediately interested delegates to this conference was an Indonesian Permanent Secretary, who asked Johnson to return home via Jakarta to discuss the problems his department faced in electing and prioritising research projects for which they had been allocated a large budget – if they could not rapidly come up with a sensible priority likely to attract political agreement, the Treasury might well remove that budget. On arrival in Jakarta, Johnson was taken to see the scientific advisor to the Prime Minister. It was easy for this to happen because Johnson had no official standing and therefore no official channels had to be followed to arrange for his visit.

This discussion was followed by another when the scientific advisor was on a visit to Brussels in early 1981. On that occasion they sat down with the country's five-year plan and within two days had come up with prioritisation principles which could be defended in debate with the Treasury and other departments. Johnson described the African network to the Indonesian scientific advisor and indicated how a similar network of research institution leaders in Indonesia could be used to apply the prioritisation principles to identify a set of projects on which they could all agree to spend the research budget. Shortly thereafter Johnson was invited once more to Jakarta, this time to assist in setting up an African-style network. During this week Johnson helped to set up PAT (Prioritizing Applied Technology) which consisted of an informal network of selected individuals from the Treasury, the Economic Planning Ministry and 40 research institutes and universities. This network was centred around the scientific advisor and it still functions today.

By June this network had completed the budget exercise and it was shown to be a success – the rather informal network had indeed produced an agreed set of priorities and the budget had been approved.

In the meantime, Johnson brought network members from Canada, Africa and Mauritius to PAT meetings in Indonesia. What was developing was a system in which people in one network could call on people in another geographic area to provide consulting services drawing on their experience of similar problems. The prioritisation project had started with attempts to set up a system, but had evolved into a judgemental procedure for applying some very general principles with a mutually cooperative setting. The scientific establishments in other countries too began to take up this mutual self-help idea.

The Commission back in Brussels did not, however, approve. Johnson was told that he was working outside his brief – he was contacting very senior people without going through the proper hierarchical channels and he was engaged on personal consulting work rather that on the training programmes he had been hired for. His explanation that he was training people to act as consultants to each other and that he was facilitating the setting up of links between people were not accepted as satisfactory. The notes continued telling him that he should not be talking to the senior people he was in touch with. He was able to continue with his way of working, however, because he had Fonseca's support within the Division, and influential support outside of it. He also had money from his own research contract and various overseas supporters were paying for air tickets – he therefore did not have to make applications for resources for every activity through formal Commission channels.

By early 1987 there were about 80 individuals actively participating in a worldwide network of technology policy makers assisting each other on issues of mutual concern – the network operated on a system of bartering favours. However, the problems with the official structure of the ETTC and the Commission were multiplying. Johnson was now a full-time employee of the Technology Division and the members of the network were members of, or associated in some way with, the ETTC. However, while the network was thus related to the formal ETTC and Divisional structures in many ways, it as also clearly in opposition to it in many others.

The dilemma was as follows. On the one hand, the relationship with Commission institutions was important to members of the network because it provided something they could identify with and it provided some visible structure, some way of demonstrating accountability and legitimacy. But on the other hand, in order to carry on assisting each other in practical, flexible ways, they were having, in a sense, to flout the rules of the ETTC and the Commission. For example, the official view was that ETTC and Division work should focus on technology proper rather than multidisciplinary policy matters. Network members, however, were working in a multidisciplinary way across government departments trying to integrate technology development budgets into national plans. Also, within the Commission, Johnson's work cut across Divisions.

So, in mid-1988 the 80 or so members of the informal network, together with the head of the Commission's Technology Division, established a body they called TMNET (Technology Management Network) to formalise to some extent the consulting assistance they were providing each other in relation to the management of science and technology. TMNET elected a chairman and an advisory group and appointed Johnson to provide a central communication node. It was hoped that this formalisation would meet objections to the work of the network within the Commission, but this was not to be the case. The visibility of the network created by this formalisation did, however, increase interest in it and ETTC members now seemed more interested in TMNET than in the ETTC itself.

During the course of 1991 some kind of structure and routine was installed in TMNET. For example, when members wanted consulting assistance on some issue they made a formal application to the unit, which would then pass it on to other TMNET members judged likely to be able to assist and in this way an informal project would be set up. Some 230 projects of this kind were carried out between 1991 and 1994 – this must be seen in relation to the TMNET's budget of under £200 000 per annum.

An example of the initiative generated by TMNET is the following. A network of senior scientists and public administrators in Indonesia, Mauritius and Africa are cooperating in projects which address the problems of watershed management and the management of mineral natural resources. As do other TMNET project, this one works by initiating a task-oriented informal group to define problems and issues and identify ways of dealing with them likely to attract sufficient support. This is based on the assumption that improvements in outcome are best sought within the management process itself rather than hiring external consultants. Issues are handled through a process in which an individual, called the team leader, serves as a catalyst and is supported by a local project advisory group, and together they facilitate the development of a local network around the problem.

One of the most important recent development of TMNET has been its Public–Private Sector Partnership launched in early 1993. This is a response to the problem of commercialising technology projects and it aims to promote trade and investment flows through the transfer of best practice in technology management. The Partnership also operates on a largely informal network basis, meant to foster both national and international public–private sector cooperation. The networks are self-organising systems used to identify and exploit investment opportunities through commercialisation of critical technologies. These initiatives reflect the conviction that science is incorporated most effectively into the economic life of a country when there is a successful partnership between government and industry to develop business opportunities through the exploitation of technology. These partnerships are seen as practical means of facilitating the widespread transition to more market-oriented economies.

In the first year after the Partnership's formation, TMNET facilitated the carrying out of 30 tasks involving cooperation with the private sector. The formation of public–private sector partnerships is not without difficulties, however. Each side tends to be suspicious of the other – the private members think that the public sector members are bureaucrats and the public sector regard the private sector members as out to use contacts with government to secure favours.

By late 1993 TMNET consisted of a self-organised network of over 400 senior executives, technology managers and other professionals from both the private and public sectors, who provide each other with technology management advisory services. This largely informal organisation had a chairman who was one of its members and was supported by an executive group drawn from the membership. TMNET was administered by a small unit of five people provided by the Commission.

This loose structure, however, continued to cause concern in the ranks of the Commission. Many had difficulty in getting to grip with the idea of a self-organising network and so they created pressure for formalisation. They were not the only one: the extension of the networks of private sector bodies also had organisational implications in that private sector members were used to ventures carried out in companies – they too applied pressures for greater formalisation. The difficulty of formalising TMNET however, is that its resources lie in its members' skills traded on a favour-by-favour basis – formalisation could well destroy this. Despite this difficulty, it was decided in early 1994 to set up a limited liability company to run TMNET and its Private–Public Sector Partnership. A formal strategy document was prepared setting out the company's mandate as well as its vision, mission, goals and strategy.

Small firms in a Swedish context: Målerås, Pilgrimstad and Söderhamn*

Sweden, the largest country in Scandinavia, has a population of about nine million distributed quite unevenly over an area of 450 000 square kilometres. Sweden's government promotes a viable private business sector through industrial and regional policies and maintains its position as a welfare state with social services organised mainly through the public sector. The result is that general living conditions in terms of basic infrastructure and social services are about the same all over Sweden. Access to qualified business services, however, varies considerably between metropolitan areas and peripheral regions.

The Swedish small business sector is of considerable importance to its economy; as many people are employed in firms with less than 20 employees as in corporations with 200 employees or more. Furthermore, in spite of the increasing internationalisation of the relatively small Swedish economy and the higher level of merger activity, the small business sector has increased in importance. Over the period 1983 to 1988 the increase in the number of jobs in firms with less than 20 employees was 16 per cent while the larger firms provided only an additional 6 per cent of jobs.

In 1978 a structure for implementing small business policy was set up, consisting of 24 regional development funds jointly financed by the state and the regional county councils. Each regional development fund included representatives from industry and the Unions and was run by a Board appointed by the county councils. Development Funds provided loans to supplement bank loans, services such as training to supplement private services, and technology-transfer assistance. In 1990 the government reduced the financing role of the regional development funds, transferring these functions to six new regional venture capital companies.

The Swedish government therefore recognises the importance of the small business sector in its sectoral, industrial and regional policies, but it sees general measures, such as providing an appropriate infrastructure, as its major contribution to the promotion of small businesses. Thus, out of total direct state financial support to industry in 1987/88, only 2 per cent was explicitly directed to small firms. Swedish municipalities are restricted in terms of the financial support they may provide to individual companies: basically, they are limited to the provision of liaison services and premises. The government also promotes specific initiatives from time to time: for example the targeting of women through special start-up groups, selective measures to improve design, assistance in dealing with environmental issues, etc.

The creation of science parks, i.e. industrial and commercial complexes focusing on high-technology activities and usually located close to a university, is a consequence of a national technology policy. But local economic development also occurs more or less spontaneously as 'industrial districts' evolve in the absence of any specific policy initiative. In the Swedish context, the success of any of these local development efforts is conditioned by the ability to cope with four important power centres. Very few local initiatives, either planned science parks or spontaneously developing industrial districts, can succeed without building alliances with one or several of the four cornerstones of Swedish society, namely, the large corporations which dominate the markets, the political system, the public administrative machine, and the powerful interest groups, such as the centralised labour movement, the large-scale Cooperative Societies, and the traditional Agricultural Associations.

Local economic development strategies are affected by the Swedish municipalities who are subject to strict legal limits but may use their financial resources to cope with the consequences of decreasing population and increasing unemployment. Also, task forces, usually including Union or Cooperative Society representatives, are often specially set up to cope with realised or expected unemployment. The need for modernisation of industry is especially prevalent in central Sweden, dominated as it is by one-company towns based on iron manufacturing. Unions and Cooperative Societies often play a major role in dealing with the decline in a town's main industry. Finally, there is the part played by the local inhabitants themselves and this obviously varies from case to case. Three specific examples are provided below that illustrate typical processes of local entrepreneurial development in Sweden.

Målerås

At the end of the 1970s the small community of Målerås had a population of 300 that had declined by two-thirds over a 30-year period. The dominant glassworks had come under external control and had shrunk to a fraction of its former size. However, a strong local identity had survived, due to geographic isolation and to kinship ties among the inhabitants reaching back several generations.

One of the 300 inhabitants, Mats Jonasson, was active in various local arenas such as the sports association, the local orchestra and the village committee. He recognised the potential of the social resources of Målerås and perceived that they could be mobilised to create businesses and jobs. So, Mats founded a local organisation, Project Målerås. People taking part in this project collectively approached banks, local authorities and various other organisations for venture capital, inexpensive premises and professional advice. Mats supplied ideas and designs for new products to the local leather industry, to a small iron foundry and to a trading company. The iron foundry and a local metal manufacturing company became sub-contractors to the glass works. Mats also formulated the idea of taking over the local glass works.

Once the project gained momentum, however, it became difficult to control and it proved impossible to provide facilities for all the new projects that were created in Målerås or were attracted to the community.

Over a period of five years the number of companies and the number of locally employed workers more than doubled in Målerås and the number of inhabitants increased slightly. The glass works became a local company owned by employees and the local people. But it was not all plain sailing: there were close-downs and bankruptcies; the second largest company in the community came under external control and its work force was reduced. The commercial success of the glass works provoked a hostile takeover bid from one of the major corporations in the glass industry and this led Mats Jonasson to acquire the majority of the stock. Local ownership was thus retained but Målerås is again approaching the status of a one-company town.

Pilgrimstad

Pilgrimstad is located in the centre of Sweden and has a population of 3500. In 1986 it was economically completely dependent on an externally controlled fibreboard plant built in the early 1950s. At the beginning of 1986 the plant owners decided to concentrate production in another unit located on the Baltic Sea.

Pilgrimstad is located in the municipality of Bracke and one of the main political leaders in Bracke was Erik Magnusson: he was the Chairman of the Municipal Board for the district that included Pilgrimstad. In addition he was a Union representative on the Board of the company that owned the fibreboard plant. Professionally, he was in charge of the maintenance of the plant. In January 1986, when the company had announced that it would close the plant in six months' time, he had organised a project-group to cope with the situation. That group's ambition was either to rescue the factory or to find alternative products for the plant. For this mission, Erik used his contacts in the Unions and also in the political sector and the public bureaucracy. Despite all his work, however, the plant was closed down.

When the 90 employees of the plant were laid off, about one-third were interested in participating in local efforts to create new jobs locally. Another third of the previous work force was granted early retirement and the youngest third preferred to move immediately to jobs in adjacent villages. For the first-mentioned third, a training programme was organised and it attracted 19 persons.

Erik Magnusson's strategy was, first, to make sure that his former workmates got jobs and social security, even if it meant commuting to a nearby town, Ostersund. Second, he recognised the need to guarantee the maintenance of private and public community services. Third, he wanted to initiate a self-supporting local business development programme. At first, therefore, he focused on finding large external companies that could fill the employment gap quickly. The local group even suggested appropriate ventures. However, it was impossible to find a suitable prospect for the available premises.

In 1987 the new management of the parent company of the fibreboard plant dismantled the machinery and virtually donated the premises to the community early in the following year. The premises were then managed by the municipality's technical department. These changes forced Erik Magnusson to re-define the economic development concept in line with an alternative plan he had mentally been preparing since 1986. He thought of attracting small firms that could not pay high rents but wanted to operate close to the regional centre of Ostersund. Erik and two other colleagues set up a task force to prepare the premises provisionally and offer them to prospective tenants. They restructured the factory into what they called an 'industrial hotel'. They shaped the areas tenants wanted in consultation with them so as to meet their requirements. Erik had great difficulty persuading his political colleagues that this project was viable – many wanted to tear down the factory or at least employ a recognised consultancy agency to do the job professionally. Many referred to Erik as the 'village idiot'.

By the end of 1990, however, more than half of the potential premises had been put to use. About a dozen companies were active within the premises and all the original 90 jobs had been replaced.

Söderhamn

Söderhamn is located in north Sweden on the Baltic Sea. The municipal area has for centuries been dominated by large corporations exploiting the rich natural resources of the hinterland: iron ore, timber and hydropower. However, all of these companies have for a long time been externally controlled by national corporations within the private as well as the state sectors. Until 1975 huge production units, mainly within the forest and engineering industries, provided the town with increasing employment. But in the late 1970s several major plants were closed down due to changed business conditions and restructuring because of ownership changes. In less than one decade employment was reduced by more than 2500 and the population decreased from 32 000 to less than 30 000 between 1976 and 1984. In 1989

about 30 per cent of the remaining jobs were in the manufacturing industry (the national average is 21 per cent).

Towards the end of the 1970s Söderhamn's town authorities mobilised administrative resources to deal with the increasing problems. A development corporation was established and an industrial liaison officer engaged. The focus was then on various defensive operations such as lobbying for state money and revitalising companies in crisis. The most speculative move was the acquisition of a company that manufactured heavy chain cables, mainly for oil platforms. The company was at that time a subsidiary of a state-owned conglomerate within the steel industry. The local development corporations took over ownership under pressure from the employees and their Unions. When the oil extrusion industry stagnated after some successful years, the company went bankrupt. Municipal involvement in individual business is illegal in Sweden and indirect ownership through development companies is questionable. Therefore, Söderhamn and its politicians had to face media scrutiny when the company went bankrupt. The effect of this was to tarnish the image of Söderhamn nationally and spread a negative self-image among the local populace.

Under pressure from the Ministry of Industry, another local development company was set up, this time by the large, private cooperative and state corporations. But by 1989 this company had invested only 20 per cent of its original capital and contributed little to job generation.

In 1983 three businessmen organised a planning committee for a local trade show in order to counteract the emerging defeatism in the community. Later the same year, the local authorities, in their capacity as owners, planned to demolish the premises sold off by a major, shrinking engineering company. Sven-Mikael Mickelsson, who had worked for the factory for 16 years, organised a protest movement for the preservation of the abandoned premises. He argued that these should be used for a revitalisation of the indigenous local, small business sector.

Mickelsson and a partner had for several years run a company in another municipality 50 kilometres from Söderhamn. This firm, with fifteen employees, specialised in the development of new machinery for the major manufacturing corporations. Together, Mickelsson and his partner had more than one hundred patents. In 1984 Mickelsson started an inventors' workshop on the rescued premises. He also conducted other educational activities on how to start a business and set up an inventions competition for all ages.

Also in 1983, Ingvar Oremark, the Chief Executive Personnel Officer of the major regional forest industry, retired. In the 1970s he had organised the resistance to the closure of the local hospital and was very highly regarded by members of the community. In 1984, Oremark joined the task force that Mickelsson had set up. He organised special days when potential 'returnees' were persuaded to return to the community. On the 1985 and 1986 days Söderhamn was invaded by returning 'emigrants' and they were registered for future contacts by what had now become known as the 'Söderhamn Spirit Task Force'. The task force set about changing the negative image of Söderhamn by systematically informing the national media about developments in the local community.

Then the 'Söderhamn Spirit' was formally organised as an association with about 1000 members including local firms. Ingvar Oremark became the Chairman and the purpose was to mobilise the inventiveness of the community in both the technical and the business senses.

In 1983, Hans-Olof Olsson, in charge of the finance of the local public administration, was recruited to the Board of 'Söderhamn Spirit'. Then in 1986, Hans-Olof Olsson was appointed mayor in Söderhamn in charge of industrial issues and had to resign his position on the 'Söderhamn Spirit' Board. However, he moved his office from the town hall to the Development Centre as a symbol of support. He was also in a position to supply practical support through his department's budget. By 1990 the Development Centre included an inventors' workshop, an exhibition hall, a restaurant and training facilities. Sven-Mikael is consultant to the Centre and he organises courses on how to transform technical ideas into business ventures.

The decline of Söderhamn's population has slowed and the image of Söderhamn has improved.

PART FOUR

Extraordinary management far from certainty and agreement

Self-organisation and the emergence of new strategic direction in the shadow system

Part Two of this book surveyed the processes of ordinary management. These are practised within an organisation's legitimate system and applied to the management of situations close to certainty and agreement. Ordinary management within the legitimate system, that is, operation within a shared paradigm, is how groups of people find it possible to take coherent, efficient joint action to perform their current day-to-day primary tasks. The negative feedback, single-loop learning processes of ordinary management enable groups of people to realise prior shared intention and produce stability, regularity and harmony in their behaviour.

However, none of the techniques of ordinary management can be applied far from certainty and agreement, simply because in such conditions it is necessary to change rather than sustain the shared paradigm. In the interest of understanding this point and in appreciating the nature of situations far from certainty and agreement, Part Three of this book examined, in some detail, the dynamics of nonlinear feedback networks, since this is what organisations are.

The key insights that we now have about such systems are that they are creative when they operate at the edge of disintegration. To be far from certainty and agreement, but not too far, means being at the edge of disintegration but not disintegrating. It means being ▶

375

neither stable nor unstable alone but both at the same time. Such a situation involves the simultaneous operation of both positive and negative feedback and when a system operates at the edge its long-term future is radically unpredictable, although it does display recognisable, archetypal patterns. It is this characteristic of situations far from certainty and agreement that makes it impossible to apply the techniques of ordinary management.

We saw, in the last Part, that when a system is far from certainty and agreement, at the edge of disintegration, it creates new futures through a process of spontaneous self-organisation. This means that the agents making up a system interact with each other according to their own local rules of conduct to produce emergent global patterns that cannot be reduced to the behaviour of any of the agents. In fact, the agents and the system as a whole perform double-loop learning, changing rules of behaviour as they evolve. They all learn in real time as they act.

It is the purpose of this Part of the book to translate these insights, about spontaneous self-organisation leading to emergent behavioural strategies for a system into human organisation terms. I will argue that human organisations also evolve creatively through a process of spontaneous self-organisation to produce emergent new strategic directions without any blueprint, or plan, or any prior intention of any or all of the members of that organisation. I will argue that this process takes place, not in the legitimate system, but in an organisation's shadow system.

Chapter 10 will examine the nature of this shadow system and Chapter 11 will explore the extraordinary management processes that occur within it. Extraordinary management is the process of organisational learning out of which creative new directions and innovations emerge. This learning process is a double-loop one in which individuals, at first, and then groups, change their mental models. This process of learning provokes great anxiety because it is destructive as well as creative. It therefore immediately gives rise to unconscious processes and covert politics, game-playing and organisational defence routines that have the effect of blocking the double-loop learning process. If the anxiety and fear of failure can be contained rather than avoided or completely submitted to, then groups of people can learn in a complex manner. Extraordinary management processes can, therefore, be thought of as:

- behaviour to do with defending against and containing the anxiety that people experience as they approach the task of questioning deeply held beliefs;

- dialogue, discussion and conflict through which they explore alternative positions to gain insight, a step they can only accomplish to any useful extent if they succeed in holding the anxiety already referred to;
- negotiation with, persuasion and conversion of powerful others so as to amplify new belief systems through an organisation.

Together, when they are not internally blocked, these processes create new knowledge and so it is that an organisation learns. That new knowledge, or learning, is then institutionalised or embodied in the legitimate system.

All of these learning processes are self-organising and they take place in the shadow system in a manner that is inevitably subversive of the legitimate system, in that they seek to destroy parts of the legitimate system, replacing them with more useful alternatives. Extraordinary management is thus not a bag of tools or techniques and it cannot be installed. The shadow system and its processes can, however, be blocked or encouraged, they can be shaped by interventions. The key role of leadership in this system is not to be 'in control' since that is impossible, but to act as a container of anxiety and to create the conditions and to make the interventions that will encourage the self-organising process and assist to shape strategic patterns as they emerge.

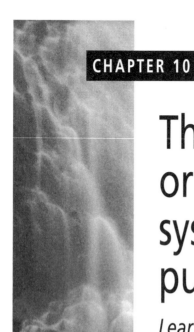

CHAPTER 10

The nature of an organisation's shadow system and its primary purpose

Learning far from certainty and agreement

10.1   INTRODUCTION

In the last chapter we saw that nonlinear feedback network systems, such as human organisations, must be far from certainty and agreement if they are to be changeable and thus capable of novelty and surprise. One form of novelty is creativity and innovation and another, of course, is crisis and disaster. The state far from certainty and agreement is a paradoxical place because it is both stable and unstable at the same time, it is capable of producing what we afterwards call the creative and the disastrous. For humans this state is characterised by anxiety but also the containment of that anxiety. At this paradoxical edge of disintegration agents interact with each other in a system to create unknowable futures, but futures that do have recognisable patterns. To do this they utilise a spontaneously self-organising process of double-loop learning out of which futures emerge without intention. It is clear that this does not happen in the legitimate system of an organisation. Indeed, it is anathema to the legitimate system and that system therefore seeks to block and remove any destabilising, self-organising complex learning. Legitimate systems seek to curb and block creativity in the interests of safety and efficiency.

The destabilising creative process occurs within an organisation's shadow system. All members of an organisation are members of its legitimate system and all of those members also take up any number of roles in the shadow system too. Generally speaking, the higher up in the legitimate hierarchy the more skilled a person is likely to be in the shadow system – it is the skilled operation in the shadow system that ensures a rise up the legitimate hierarchy, hence the saying, 'it's not what you know, but who you know that counts'.

It is the purpose of this chapter to explore the nature of the shadow system and the next will examine what members of this shadow system get up to with each other.

10.2 THE NEED FOR A SHADOW SYSTEM

It has been recognised for a long time that bureaucratic control is an essential part of ordinary management, is neither rational nor efficient outside certain limited conditions and that it produces a number of negative behavioural consequences that undermine its effectiveness. The need for an informal organisation arises, then, simply because the formal bureaucracy often cannot work. It is the part of this informal organisation which operates without the approval of the legitimate system that I call the shadow system. This distinguishes it from an organisation's legitimate system, which could include officially sanctioned informal links. There are two major reasons why a bureaucracy fails so frequently to produce what it is supposed to.

1 Adverse human reactions to bureaucracy

There is a considerable literature that identifies the adverse impact and consequent reaction of people to working in bureaucracies:

- Bureaucracies have an alienating impact on people. By definition, in a bureaucracy, people are allocated to narrowly defined roles and repetitive tasks and are thus treated as the means to some end (for example, profit). People are consequently separated from their own creativity and from social contact with their fellow human beings. This leads to feelings of powerlessness, isolation, frustration, dissatisfaction and aggression (*Blauner, 1964*).
- Bureaucracies tend to make people subordinate, passive, dependent, and lacking in self-awareness. Rule-regulated work limits people's behavioural repertoire, and confines them to interests that are superficial and cover short time spans. These are all the exact opposite of the characteristics of maturity and will therefore reduce motivation and efficiency (*Argyris, 1957*).
- Bureaucracies may lead to work that has lost its moral character and cultural significance. People then perform according to rules they do not believe in. Without shared values to govern their work, their behaviour and the sharing of rewards, people feel that their work has no meaning – a state of anomie. In this normless state, some will behave in ways that others regard as unacceptable. For example, the salaries that some company top executives pay themselves lead to envy and public outcries that escalate into strikes and other forms of disruption.
- Bureaucracies can deskill people, leading to trained incapacity (*Merton, 1957*). Merton's study, already referred to in Chapter 8, shows how exclusive reliance on bureaucratic systems develops trained incapacity so that people cannot make decisions to cope with the unforeseen.
- The operation of bureaucracies can contravene or provoke certain kinds of social behaviour and so touch off vicious circles. For example, in Chapter 8 we saw how an attempt to impose bureaucratic control can lead to unintended consequences in which people stick legalistically to the rules and are therefore less efficient; or they resist and so undermine the bureaucratic controls (*Gouldner, 1964*).

2 The bureaucracy's inability to handle ambiguity and uncertainty

Even if the operation of a bureaucracy does not itself provoke adverse human reactions that limit its operation, there are situations where the bureaucratic form of control cannot hope to work at all.

● Bureaucracies cannot cope with complex, unstable, unpredictable environmental and working conditions because they are inevitably too inflexible and slow to respond to change (*Burns & Stalker, 1961*). Rules and regulations cannot be established in advance to deal with the unforeseen. Chapters 2 and 3 were particularly concerned with this point and with the reasons why technically rational decision-making and control processes, an essential part of bureaucracy, cannot work in open-ended situations.

● Bureaucracies are filled with other functions and by their nature avoid the ambiguous. To see this consider what the functions of a bureaucracy are and on what basis people are supposed to perform those functions. The function of a bureaucracy is to divide up tasks in a predetermined way and ensure that those tasks are performed to a prearranged standard. To do this, task performance has to be regularly reported up the hierarchy and compared against standards at prescribed levels in the hierarchy. Instruction for action, or legitimation of decisions taken, has to be passed down the hierarchy. These flows of information, decisions, and instructions require a set of communication arenas (meetings, telephone calls, document circulations) to review what has just happened in the performance of current tasks, make decisions on how to respond, legitimise any deviation from the rules, policies and plans and perform symbolic functions to generate loyalty and security (for example, appearing to be in control even when events are occurring unpredictably). Who is to take part in each arena is determined by position in the hierarchy.

The people taking part in any one arena have many tasks and so the capacity of any one arena will be limited. It will tend to fill with its obvious and primary functions of reviewing the past, legitimising decisions, and discussing symbolic actions. The higher up the hierarchy, the more this is likely to happen. Ambiguous issues with consequences that will probably not be felt for some time, that is the real strategic issues, will inevitably therefore be delayed, if they are ever accorded any attention in the first place. This will be most true of the board of directors and other formal top executive meetings. Some other type of communication arena will therefore have to deal with open-ended issues if they are to be dealt with at all and those other arenas will be the informal ones (*Stacey, 1991*).

People deal with these shortcomings of the bureaucratic system by colluding to operate a 'mock' bureaucracy (*Gouldner, 1964*) and acting instead within an informal organisation that they set up themselves (*Blauner, 1964*). The 'mock' bureaucracy is one in which all pay lip service to the rules but tacitly agree not to enforce them. The appearance of rationality and order is thus maintained, and any conflict that might have been generated by the application of inappropriate rules is avoided.

Since they are not actually using the bureaucracy to control and develop their organisation in these particular conditions, people have to turn to something else and that something else is the informal organisation that they spontaneously develop amongst themselves (see *Key Concept 10.1*). When they operate through the informal organisation, people are practising extraordinary management – they are undertaking activities that threaten, potentially at least, the operation of the bureaucracy and the paradigm it reflects.

Key Concept 10.1

The shadow network system of an organisation

Those who share similar experiences and expectations, who are affected by and take an interest in similar matters, who resent and try to offset the alienating, anomic and deskilling consequences of bureaucracy, form social groupings. People develop networks of contacts and relationships within their own department, across other departments, and even across other organisations that they then use in both social and work senses.

The groups are essentially political in nature; that is, people handle conflicting interests through:

- *persuasion and negotiation;*
- *implicit bargaining of one person's contribution or interest for another's;*
- *the application of power that takes the form of influence rather than authority; that influence is derived from personal capability and the breadth of other network contacts.*

There are a number of important points to notice about this network organisation. The first is that it is self-organising in a rather obvious way. It is not established by some central, prior intention or design. Instead, it emerges from the interaction of people as they come into contact with each other and work together. It is self-organising too in the sense that the groups that result are governed by norms that emerge from the way people in those groups interact. What they do and how they do it is determined jointly by the people within the group, not by some hierarchical authority either within or outside the group. Networks, then, are not self-managing teams, but self-organising small groups of people.

Second, those self-organising groups are not formal or legitimate in the sense that they have received any kind of seal of approval from the formal organisation.

Third, the groups that form may be fairly long-lasting social groups or they may be very-short-lived groups that come together to pursue a particular issue. The shadow network organisation has a fluid, shifting aspect.

Fourth, the shadow system, or network of political contacts, is the mechanism which people in an organisation use to deal with the highly complex, the ambiguous, the unpredictable, the inconsistent, the conflicting, the frustrating and the alienating. They use it to satisfy social and motivational needs, as the means of operating organisational defences, as a means of dealing with conflicting demands placed on the organisation, and as the tool to promote innovation and change. ▶

> **Key Concept 10.1 continued**
>
> *Fifth, it follows that the shadow system is essentially destabilising. It exists, sometimes in place of the formal organisation and sometimes in competition with it, but always because the formal is defective in some way.*
>
> *Sixth, the shadow system organisation is the way in which the formal organisation is changed and it is so changed in the most fundamental way by altering the existing paradigm.*
>
> *Another way of conceptualising the informal organisation is to think of it as a 'community of practice'; that is, a spontaneous grouping of people who carry out the same task and use their social network to learn informally from each other.*

We are now going to look at the shadow system and what it does from a number of different angles. The purpose will be to understand more fully what the shadow system is, before we turn to the functions it performs. We are therefore going to consider the shadow system as a communication and social network, and a learning community of practice.

10.3   COMMUNICATIONS AND SOCIAL NETWORK

When people work together they establish social relationships and customary ways of doing things – they form a social group (*Stewart, 1983*). Such groups will tend to develop their own aims and these may or may not coincide with those of the formal organisation. The informal group can often exert sanctions – the fear of rejection – that are stronger than those of the formal organisation. The great advantage of such groups is that they are self-disciplining and self-checking and therefore do not require superior management supervision for work to be carried out satisfactorily; indeed, their nature is such that they cannot be supervised. On the other hand, such groups could undermine and impede what superior managers want to do and they may protect the inefficient and ineffective.

The importance of social groups has been recognised for a long time; for example, in the 1930s, *Chester Barnard (1938)* stated that their function was the communication of intangible facts, opinions, suggestions, and suspicions that could not pass through the formal channels without giving rise to public conflict. He said that social groups made it possible for individuals to exercise influence far greater than the position they held in the hierarchy might indicate. The web of social groups was described as a hidden communication and operating structure. Thus, although four managers may all report directly to the managing director, one may be more important than the others because of close personal ties with the managing director. Another may have very little importance because the managing director in fact does not delegate any authority to that manager. What the managing director learns about the organisation will therefore come primarily from the personally closest manager. All those formally passing information will be sifting it and passing on only what they think the managing director should hear. It may well be the informal rather than the formal organisation, then, that determines actual communication flows.

The social system in multinationals

Interest in the functioning of the informal organisation has continued. For example, a study of multinational companies in the early 1980s found that they develop internal groups that allow the organisation to sense, analyse and respond to a far wider range of environmental factors than the formal organisation could (*Bartlett, 1983*). The web of informal groups across these companies allowed multiple perspectives to develop and it allowed greater flexibility in making decisions. The advice of the author of this study was that multinational companies should step off the endless merry-go-round of reorganisation in reporting structures and place greater reliance on the informal organisation. He did not, however, see the informal organisation as an uncontrollable by-product of the formal organisation. Instead, he maintained that top managers could influence the development of informal communication channels by overcoming barriers between operating units and building bridges between them. He recommended the greater use of temporary task forces and workshops. He stressed that these more informal mechanisms were to supplement not replace the formal organisation.

Social networks

More recently the informal organisation is frequently referred to as the network organisation. The network is an internal web of floating teams that work across functions and manoeuvre through the bureaucracy (*Charan, 1991*). It is also defined as the web of contacts managers in one firm have with managers in other organisations; or as a set of external relationships, alliances and joint ventures between one firm and other organisations. (Note that a computer network is one of the tools of the bureaucracy and is therefore fundamentally different to the way in which the word is being used here.) Networks have been described as the fundamental social architecture of the organisation, the mechanism through which key managers communicate, exert power, build trust, and make the trade-offs that shape the formal organisation (*Charan, 1991*).

Networks and networking cohabit with hierarchy and bureaucracy and should be identified and encouraged because this is how to make organisations more flexible and faster-acting (*Mueller, 1986*). Networks are like wild flowers – they cannot be cultivated, only permitted to grow – you cannot install them but you can create a favourable environment for them. For example, organisations that set up social occasions create the possibility of networks developing.

> Networks are informal systems where dissonance is encouraged and consensus a common goal. The nature of networks is that they are short-lived, self-camouflaging and a disciplinary. They are invisible, uncountable, unpollable, and may be active or inactive. In practical terms, networks nurture spontaneous feedback via telephone, mail, meetings, computers or a shout across the room.
> (*Mueller, 1986, p. 155*)

Mueller goes on to describe networks as independent, self-reliant groups of interdependent participants, where the border between one group and another is fuzzy and indistinct. Network groups tend to have many leaders. He claims that networking is vital to the introduction of novel products and processes and to the acceptance of other changes in an organisation.

There are, as we noted above, other ways of conceptualising the informal organisation.

Illustration
10.1

The French bread industry

There are 50 000 bread bakeries employing 80 000 people in France, one bakery per thousand people. Typically these bakeries are run by a baker, his wife and sometimes an apprentice or two. The organisational unit is in fact a married couple with the husband taking the role of artisan and his wife the role of shopkeeper – little has changed for a century. This is in marked contrast to other developed countries such as Germany, the United Kingdom and the United States where bread production is dominated by a small number of very large baking companies, in turn part of large food conglomerates. Why is it that France, operating in much the same environment as its industrial neighbours, has never developed a modern bread industry?

It turns out that the answer is more complicated than simply one of cultural differences in eating habits. The answer has to do with the nature of the self-perpetuating social system to be found in the French bread industry. In the late nineteenth century, peasants stopped baking their own bread as large numbers of rural bakeries developed, drawing on the surplus labour of the French peasantry. The culture of the baking industry was, like that of the peasantry, based on fierce individualism and hard work. The large rural community in France still continues to supply apprentices to the bakeries. Typically a young man becomes apprenticed between the ages of 15 and 17 to learn the arduous trade. Then, at an early age, he seeks to set up independently as a baker, buying a business from a retiring couple. Since it is unlikely that the young purchaser will be able to raise the money to buy the bakery, the retiring couple lend it to him, using the repayments as a pension. To ensure the reliability of their pension, they first interview the purchaser's wife, since she is seen as the key to a successful bakery.

Large companies have made attempts to break up this system that brings in its recruits at one end and provides them with a pension at the other. In 1966, for example, the largest flour-milling group in France was rumoured to be preparing to build a large bakery on the outskirts of Paris. The flour company then changed its terms of trade with the small bakers so that only full truck loads of flour would be delivered. This threatened the bakers with serious storage problems and so they identified some smaller flour millers that were about to close down in response to the growing monopoly position of the large flour miller. News of flour suppliers available in the required quantities soon spread around the bakery network, demand was switched to smaller flour millers and the large company had to abandon its plans for a modern baking factory. ■

Source: Clegg, 1990

10.4   LEARNING COMMUNITY OF PRACTICE

Another way of conceptualising the shadow system is as a community of practice that performs learning functions (*Brown & Duguid, 1991*). A community of practice is a group of people who carry out similar tasks. So, physicists studying turbulence, the geography teachers at a school, the nurses on a ward, the managers on the executive team of a company, or the service technicians who repair the machines their company has sold (see *Illustration 10.2*) are all communities of practice. People performing closely similar tasks always form informal social groups in which they discuss what they are doing and the environment they are doing it in. They gossip, repeat anecdotes, and tell war stories. They recount the difficulties they have experienced in carrying out particular tasks and others compare these with similar experiences they have had. What is going on when this happens is, however, far more important than pleasant social exchange. What is going on is in fact a vitally important form of learning.

There have always been communities of practice and they have always played a major part in learning. The men of a primitive clan constitute a community of practice and it is by joining this that the boys learn to hunt. Apprentices join the communities of practice of craftsmen and that is how they learn. It is no different for managers. The method of learning such communities employ is embodied in their story telling. It is through telling stories that the knowledge required to deal with difficult situations is passed on. The stories are a rich source of analogies that people can subsequently draw upon to design new responses in unique situations. Furthermore, it is not just managers who learn in this way, but people at all other levels too, as *Illustration 10.2* shows.

Organisations can deal with the predictable using systems, procedures, rules and regulations, but when it comes to the unique, ambiguous, uncertain situation never before encountered, whether organisations cope well or badly depends upon how effective their communities of practice are. For predictable situations, people can be prepared by formal training and development courses, but for the unpredictable they have to learn by being members of a community of practice. Complex double-loop learning takes place informally in organisations through political and social interaction within a community of practice, often in conflict with the formal organisational procedures. Organisations are simply communities of such communities of practice and they develop in innovative new directions when the collection of communities of practice that constitute them are actively learning. Informal collaboration and social construction are essential aspects of this learning process. Furthermore, complex learning takes place at all hierarchical levels. It is not the hierarchical level that determines whether or not complex learning is required, but the level of uncertainty and ambiguity in the situations people are confronted with. Anything that obstructs complex learning at any level cuts down on the amount of uncertainty and ambiguity an organisation as a whole can cope with.

Illustration
10.2

Non-routine repairs

In a large company in the United States, service technicians (reps) answer customer calls for the service and repair of the sophisticated machinery supplied by their company. The procedures for servicing and repairing the machinery are set out in great detail in manuals and rep training programmes are provided so that reps can learn to follow the directive procedures set out in the manuals. Those training programmes stress that any departure from the recognised procedures is to be regarded as deviant, unacceptable behaviour.

When they actually carry out repairs, however, the reps find that the mechanistic procedures and training programmes often obstruct rather than help. For example. the prescriptive documentation does not cover all the faults that arise in practice. When a problem arises that is not covered by the manuals, the reps improvise and then conceal what they were doing; they make it look as though they are employing the legitimate procedures because this is what they have been instructed to do.

For example, on one service call a rep dealt with a defective machine that produced the error codes upon which standard repair procedures were based. But the error codes did not match the nature of the machine fault and the repair manuals therefore provided no assistance. The correct procedure according to the manual would have been to replace the machine. The rep was reluctant to do this because he and his company would lose face and the disruption to the customer's work would damage relationships, endanger the rep's bonus, and make life more difficult in the future. He ignored the procedures, and since he had not encountered this particular problem before, he sent for a technical specialist who acted as a supervisor. The supervisor too had not encountered this problem before and was also reluctant to assign the machine to the scrap heap.

The rep and his supervisor then began to question the users and to swop stories about similar malfunctions each had encountered before or heard about from colleagues – they approached the task of diagnosis through a story-telling procedure that had nothing to do with formal manuals. Eventually the stories and anecdotes of similar experiences, conducted while the rep and his supervisor tried one experiment after another on the faulty machine, led to a correct diagnosis and repair.

Subsequently when they met with other colleagues they recounted the story of the repair and that story then became a part of the folklore of the rep community, folklore that would later be used to provide analogies that would assist in diagnosing unpredictable machine failures on future occasions. The reps were dealing with unpredictable problems using a process of narration through which they explored analogies and so jointly discovered an explanation of what had gone wrong. They constituted a community of practice and what they were doing was learning. What they learned was then embodied not in a rigid manual but in a loose story that would be remembered by others. ∎

Source: Brown & Duguid (1991)

10.5   SELF-ORGANISATION AND THE SHADOW SYSTEM

Self-organisation theory provides an explanation of the stages a system passes through as it develops new, more complex forms of order. In organisational terms it establishes patterns in the change process through which new strategic directions or innovations emerge. This way of understanding human organisations makes it clear that new strategic direction can only emerge; it cannot be planned. And it makes it clear that the processes through which emergence occurs are ones of political interaction and group learning.

First, in what sense does self-organisation mean political interaction?

The way for spontaneous self-organisation is opened up by the manner in which nonlinear feedback systems amplify small changes in their environments. In human systems this happens when individuals detect some issue and then build support for it. The building of coalitions around issues, persuading and negotiating with others to support an idea, is clearly a political process. It requires the deployment and use of power. Innovations in organisations always begin with individuals and they can go no further than the individual unless the awareness of the issue is spread and commitment to it developed through the organisation. It is this political process that gets the issue onto the organisational agenda in the first place.

The importance of political interaction also clearly continues throughout the life of an issue. Politics is the process through which managers make and enact strategic choices. Whether an issue continues to sustain attention, what kind of attention it receives, whether it is ever tried out in the form of some experiment, and whether it is finally invested in or not, all depend on how its supporters use their power and sustain the support.

It is accurate to call the political processes we have been talking about self-organising. This is so because no-one centrally organises the support groups around particular lines. Nor can anyone because no-one knows what the issues are until some coalition is formed around them. Whether an issue is ever noticed or not is self-organising in the sense of spontaneously gathering support or failing to.

Second, in what sense is spontaneous self-organisation in an organisation a learning process?

Nonlinear systems amplify changes and in so doing they shatter old patterns, making way for the new through a process of correlation or communication between components or agents of the system. In human systems this process of shattering the old and developing the new applies in the first instance to perceptions; only later on does it apply to structures, roles and so on. When we question and throw out old perceptions and then replace them with new ones we are learning. In organisations this kind of learning is done in groups. Group learning is thus the essence of strategic discovery and choice. The effectiveness with which groups in an organisation learn is the major determinant of whether that organisation takes effective strategic actions or not. But groups are affected by unconscious process as well as the primary learning tasks they have come together to perform. No-one can make a group learn. Whether or not it does depends upon its own spontaneous behaviour. That behaviour is all the more spontaneous because it is affected by unconscious processes, as we will see in Chapter 11. These unconscious processes make its behaviour patterns and what will emerge from its learning activities unpredictable.

We can interpret self-organisation in an organisation as the process of political interaction and group learning from which innovation and new strategic directions for the organisation may emerge. These processes are themselves nonlinear feedback ones. They too are only effective when they are held far-from-equilibrium in states of contention, contradiction and paradox. The outcome therefore emerges without central intention and is unpredictable.

Note that self-organisation is not the same thing as self-managing teams nor is it the same thing as democracy. A self-managing team or a democratic group is one that makes choices by some kind of majority vote, without being instructed what to do by its leaders or from outside its ranks. Self-organisation can and will occur even in a dictatorship: revolution may be a form of self-organisation and that is how dictatorships are overthrown. Self-organisation may well occur in bureaucratic organisations if managers from different hierarchical levels or different parts of the bureaucracy come to find themselves supporting and working together on some common issue. Self-organisation does not mean that job definitions are loose and overlapping. It can occur even when jobs are rigidly defined. Self-organisation is an irregular pattern of collaborative interaction: it can take many forms.

It is not a predictably mechanistic process as automatic control is in cybernetics. Weick's views on self-designing systems are a form of self-organisation, but so is a revolution or a coup.

Self-organisation occurs when people form a group that produces patterns of behaviour, despite the absence of formal hierarchy within that group or authority imposed from outside it. Such groups could behave in what we would describe as a completely uncontrolled way, for example a mob, but such groups may also behave in a way that we would have to describe as self-controlled.

As soon as a collection of people begin to interact with each other, say at a party, we find that particular attitudes, ideas, enthusiasms, propositions and issues emerge spontaneously within a very short time. People form themselves into groupings around, say, some issue. One group may be for the issue and another against it. Soon the conversation will switch spontaneously to another issue and the groupings will spontaneously re-form. No-one directs this process, nor does it move to a plan: it is a self-organising process. That process of spontaneous self-organisation can be seen quite clearly at a party, but it is also evident in all other human systems, including business organisations. It happens because of the intrinsic property of human systems to self-organise.

Informal groups and networks of managers within an organisation clearly form and conduct themselves through self-organising processes: no central authority organises the network of informal contacts and coalitions that develop in an organisation and yet that network can behave in a controlled way and become a vital part of the organisation's control system. Most managers are not used to the idea that a system, that is a set of interactions, can control itself. For them, control requires some individual to take charge.

Self-organisation differs from self-managing teams in the following important ways:

- Self-organisation is a fluid network process in which informal, temporary teams form spontaneously around issues, while self-managing teams are permanent or temporary but always formally established parts of a reporting structure.
- While top managers cannot control self-organising processes – they can only intervene to influence the boundary conditions around them – they can install a structure of self-managing teams and control them through the rules that govern how they are to operate.
- Participants decide on who takes part in self-organisation and what the boundaries around their activities are, while top managers make these decisions with regard to self-managing teams.
- Self-organising networks operate in conflict with and are constrained by the hierarchy, while self-managing teams replace the hierarchy.
- Unequal power energises networks through conflict but also operates as a constraint, while dispersed power is supposed to lead to self-managing teams and consensus.
- In self-organising processes, people empower themselves while, in self-managing teams, the top empowers people.
- The self-organising process is both provoked and constrained by cultural difference, while the self-managing process is based on strongly shared culture.

10.6 SUMMARY

This chapter has reviewed what the management and organisation literature has to say about the nature of the shadow system.

First, we saw that the importance of a shadow system was recognised decades ago, at least, but it has hardly featured in mainstream theorising and prescribing. Its function was seen primarily in terms of alleviating human reactions to the alienating and anomic nature of bureaucracy. It was also quite clearly seen as a system that could either powerfully assist or terminally block the operation of the legitimate system. Its central role in organisational learning and creativity, its self-organising and emergent properties, have not been accorded all that much attention until quite recently.

We then went on to see how shadow systems emerge as members of a legitimate system engage with each other socially and we saw the important role that this plays in communication – the 'grapevine'. The more recent conceptualisation of the shadow system as a learning community of practice was described and then the self-organising nature of that system was considered.

We now go on to see what people do when they take up their roles in the shadow system, the processes they use and are used by.

Further reading

Brown and Duguid (1991) is an important paper that is well worth reading. Charan (1991) and Mueller (1986) provide a useful understanding of the role of informal networks in organisations.

References

Argyris, C. (1957), *Personality and Organization,* New York: Harper & Row.

Barnard, C. I. (1938), *The Functions of the Executive,* Cambridge, Ma.: Harvard University Press.

Bartlett, C. A. (1983), MNLs: get off the reorganisation merry-go-round, *Harvard Business Review,* March–April.

Blauner, R. (1964), *Alienation and Freedom,* Chicago: University of Chicago.

Brown, J. S. & Duguid, P. (1991), Organisational learning and communities of practice: toward a unified view of working, learning and innovation, *Organisational Science* vol. 2, no. 1, Feb., pp. 40–57.

Burns, T. & Stalker, G. M. (1961), *The Management of Innovation,* London: Tavistock Publications.

Charan, R. (1991), How networks reshape organizations for results, *Harvard Business Review,* Sept–Oct.

Clegg S.R. (1990), *Modern Organizations: Organizational Studies in the Post-Modern World,* London: Sage Publications.

Gouldner, A. (1964), *Patterns of Industrial Bureaucracy,* New York: The Free Press.

Merton, R. K. (1957), Bureaucratic structure and personality, in *Social Theory and Social Structure,* New York: The Free Press.

Mueller, R. K. (1986), *Corporate Networking: Building Channels for Information and Influence,* New York: The Free Press.

Stacey, R. (1991), *The Chaos Frontier: Creative Strategic Control for Business,* Oxford: Butterworth-Heinemann.

Stewart, R. (1983), *The Reality of Management,* 2nd edn, London: Heinemann.

CHAPTER 11

Decision-making and control processes employed in the shadow system

Effective and ineffective learning in organisations

11.1 INTRODUCTION

Extraordinary management is the manner in which people make decisions and the way in which behaviour is controlled in the shadow system of an organisation. Just as the ordinary processes of decision-making and control practised in the legitimate system amount to a form of learning – single-loop learning – so too do the decision-making and control processes of extraordinary management amount to a form of learning – double-loop learning.

It is the task of this chapter to examine how this double-loop learning takes place, or fails to take place, in organisations. We first examine how people employ covert politics to protect themselves against the fear of failure and embarrassment that is aroused when they try to learn in a complex manner far from certainty. Notions of how these defences may be overcome are presented. Then we look at how groups of people employ unconscious processes to protect themselves against the anxiety aroused by creative double-loop learning and thereby avoid having to carry out that learning. Some suggestions for how this might be avoided by providing containment for the anxiety are described.

Then we turn to how overt political processes are required to amplify any destabilising questioning of assumptions and to convert others to an acceptance of new beliefs flowing from creative complex learning. This leads into a consideration of the nature of leadership and the role of groups in the shadow system.

11.2   COVERT POLITICAL PROCESSES AND THEIR IMPACT ON ORGANISATIONAL LEARNING

Extraordinary management begins when people question their own unique mental models and when together they start questioning the mental models they share with each other. As soon as they do this they arouse fears to do with failing to produce anything that functions in place of what they are destroying, as well as the fear of embarrassing themselves and others with questioning and discussion that may appear incompetent, or threatening, or even crazy. As soon as such fears are aroused we automatically defend ourselves against them by activating defence routines of one kind or another. The raising of such defensive routines in an organisational setting is what I mean by covert politics. It is a form of game-playing that all are aware is going on but all agree, tacitly, not to discuss.

Figure 4.15 in Chapter 4 summarised the ordinary management processes. We are now going to add to this the processes of extraordinary management and explore the impact that they have on what happens to an organisation. So, *Figure 11.1* adds a loop to those depicted in *Figure 4.15*, a loop to take account of the feedback effect of covert politics. This shows that as soon as people engage in double-loop learning they focus upon the anomalies and contradictions that the real world presents to their mental reconstructions of it. This is what it means to double-loop learn. If the effect of focusing on the gap between what we expect and what happens to us is predominantly to raise fears of failure, then it is protected against by the organisational defence routines that we will discuss in the rest of this section. However, if this fear of failure can be recognised and held rather than avoided, if, that is, it can be perceived primarily as a challenge, then the emotion actually reinforces the double-loop learning process. Challenge and the containment of fear leads to reflection and learning. Avoidance of the challenge and the fear leads to defensive routines that block learning. Leaders cannot direct people to perform complex learning, but they can try to create conditions where anomalies are perceived as challenges rather than giving rise to fear.

Note how all the processes I have described in this regard are self-organising and how their outcomes emerge without prior shared intention. There is no blueprint, no plan, no powerful agent instructing people to fear, contain their fear, perceive a challenge or not. It does not work to instruct people to stop playing political games – they simply deny that they are doing it. Whether people do these things or not and how they interact with each other to provoke or put a stop to what happens all emerges out of their own self-organising propensities. Leaders are prime players in this process, not controllers of it. Note too how all these processes take place in the shadow system. Furthermore, you can see right at the start how problematic extraordinary management is and how the key question about what to do about it has nothing to do with installing some technique, or structure, or preparing some blueprint, or setting objectives, or measuring anything. The question of what to do has, rather, to do with how we might together create conditions of an emotional kind that will enable rather than cripple us in the process of complex learning.

We now turn now to an examination of the covert politics people employ in organisations to block their own creative complex learning.

FIGURE 11.1
Fear of failure and the impact of covert political processes

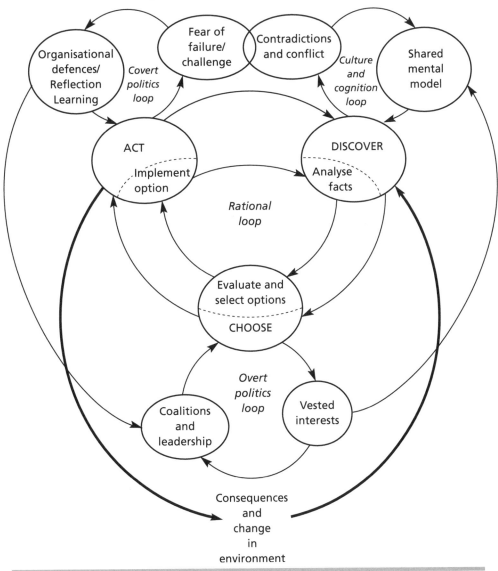

Organisational defence routines

One of the main reasons for the failure of groups of people to engage in complex learning is that the questioning of deeply held individual and shared assumptions about the world they are operating in may well provoke and reinforce powerful organisational defence routines that are very difficult to identify and even more difficult to deal with effectively (*Argyris, 1990*). The activation of such defence routines is a specific example of a general point: namely that complex systems tend to counteract planned changes to the system because they also unintentionally provoke positive feedback loops called organisational defence routines.

For example, top managers may try to abandon a command and control model of managing in the belief that this will make their organisation more flexible and entrepreneurial. This may be an example of double-loop learning if they are genuinely trying to question the assumptions underlying their currently shared mental model of management – the command and control one. Consider first what is meant by a command and control model of managing. It is one in which:

- the manager's power is derived from position in the hierarchy;
- people are motivated by the task; and
- people respond most to short-term rewards in relation to task achievement.

These beliefs about the source of power and the way to motivate people are closely associated with the suppression of negative feelings and judgements about people's performance. Such judgements are usually not publicly exposed and tested in case they upset and demotivate others, so reducing levels of task performance. Instead evaluations are made privately and covered up in public – covert politics. All understand that this is what is happening but they accept it as a necessary defence against hurting people's feelings and against the consequent organisational inefficiency.

When a manager is fired, this is frequently presented as a resignation due to health reasons or some other factor. Memoranda are distributed thanking the fired person for years of valued contributions. All know that this is a tissue of lies but none publicly says so. This is an example of a defence routine, a game people play to protect each other from having to face unpleasant organisational truths in public. As a result, the real reason for firing the person, a judgement that the person is incompetent, is never properly examined; it could well have been unjustified and turn out to be harmful to the performance of the organisation.

These kinds of beliefs about control lead to win/lose dynamics in which people adopt tactics of persuasion and selling, only superficially listening to others. People driven by win/lose behaviour also tend to use face-saving devices for themselves and each other. They save face by avoiding the public testing of the assumptions they are making about each other's motives or statements. This behaviour produces what has been called skilled incompetence: skilled in that the behaviour is automatic; incompetent in that it produces obstacles to work, real learning, effective decision-making. These obstacles take the form of organisational defence routines that become embedded in behaviour and are extremely difficult to change (see *Key Concept 11.1*).

Defence routines become so entrenched in organisations that they come to be viewed as inevitable parts of human nature. Managers make self-fulfilling prophecies about what will happen at meetings, because they claim it is human nature; they indulge in the game playing, so confirming their belief in human nature. The defence routines, game playing and cover-ups can become so disruptive that managers actually avoid discussing contentious open-ended issues altogether. Even if this extreme is not reached, the dysfunctional learning behaviour blocks the detection of gradually accumulating small changes, the surfacing of different perspectives, the thorough testing of proposals through dialogue. When they use the control management model with the organisational defence routines it provokes, managers struggle to deal with strategic issues. They end up preparing long lists of strengths and weaknesses, opportunities and threats that simply get them nowhere. They produce mission statements that are so bland as to be meaningless, visions not connected to reality, and long-term plans that are simply filed. Or they may decide on an action and then not implement it.

Organisational defence routines

Organisational defence routines are patterns of behaviour that people in an organisation deploy to protect themselves and others from embarrassment and anxiety.

The prime defence routine is to make matters undiscussable and to make the fact that they are undiscussable itself undiscussable. So subordinates refrain from telling their superiors the truth if those superiors are thought likely to dislike it. Subordinates do not publicly admit that they are doing this and of course superiors know that this is going on because they do it themselves. The result is an undiscussed game of pretence in which all indulge and all know they are doing it. The pretence enables all involved to avoid confronting embarrassing or potentially explosive behaviour.

Defence routines take the form of bypasses cover-ups and games. For example, a manager may ask a colleague with whom there is disagreement for comprehensive proof of a proposal outcome when it is quite clear to all that such proof is impossible to provide.

A well-known game is to prevent a decision one dislikes by repeatedly calling for more reports and research on the grounds that a rational decision can only be made on the basis of the facts. For example, one company played the following game for over a year. One faction in the top management team thought that the company should diversify the range of its activities. Another faction led by the chairman thought that it should not. However the chairman did not openly quash the idea. He called for a paper setting out general diversification principles. After discussion at the formal executive meeting specific proposals were called for – the principles paper was held to be too general. When the specific proposals were discussed the chairman called for a discussion of the general principles. So it went on and needless to say, no diversification occurred. All involved knew it was a game and while they admitted this to each other in groups of twos or threes, no one ever raised it at the full meetings.

Long-term plans mission statements and visions could well be games of a similar kind. They are usually abstract statements without operational content simply to convey an impression of rational decision-making and to keep people quiet or feeling more secure.

Perhaps the most popular cover up, mostly unconscious, is to espouse a different style of management while actually continuing to use the control model. A manager ostensibly looking for team decision-making and open to different views can become visibly annoyed when such views are put forward. That manager makes it clear, by behaving in a particular manner, that team decision-making is not actually to occur despite any statements made to the contrary.

Managers collude in this behaviour and refrain from discussing it. They then distance themselves from what is going on and blame others, the chief executive, or the organisational structure, when things go wrong. They look for solutions in general

Illustration
11.1

The Challenger disaster

In 1986 a Presidential Commission enquired into the disaster that had occurred when the Challenger shuttle had crashed soon after launching. It concluded that NASA had sound structures, policies and rules to secure safety. What had gone wrong was that those most intimately involved with the launch had focused so heavily on the launch itself that they neglected safety matters. The conclusion was that there was nothing wrong with the organisation: the disaster was due to human failures. These were to be addressed in the future by making it compulsory for all launch constraints, and waivers of launch constraints, to be considered by all levels of management. In other words there was to be more referral up the management hierarchy.

Argyris (1990) analyses this episode to show how the disaster was actually due to organisational defence routines, which both NASA and the Presidential Commission were unwittingly covering up. The recommendation of more referral to higher management levels would do nothing to remove those organisational defence routines. It would therefore most probably be ineffective in preventing another accident.

Using the testimony presented to the Commission, Argyris shows the following. Before the launch, engineers had indicated that the launch should be delayed because of problems with rings, problems that ultimately caused the disaster. At a meeting with the engineers, one manager understood them to be advising a delay, but his superior concluded that they were simply raising some questions. The two managers did not explore their different understandings with each other; they did not test them publicly. The superior manager decided, without discussing it with anyone, not to report on the meeting with the engineers to higher levels of management. The engineers sounded a number of warnings and then stopped when they realised that no-one would listen. Engineers never questioned management as to why they would not listen; that would have been regarded as an affront to management capability.

At each level, the engineers and managers were covering themselves. The engineers raised the problem, but the next level did not heed them. Engineers were defending themselves by drawing attention to a problem and then giving up when it became clear that the next level would not listen. Engineers would not themselves take the matter further up the hierarchy because they knew that this would antagonise their immediate superiors. So they adopted the routine of raising the matter, knowing it would be ignored, and then dropping it, all in order to defend themselves – if anything went wrong, they would not be to blame. The first manager heard the message but bowed to his superior. He was covered because he was doing what the superior wanted. The superior was covered because he interpreted the points made by the engineers as simply raising questions and no-one contradicted him. He probably made this interpretation because he knew that those above him did not want bad news that they would have to convey to the President. In the end the disaster was due to all of these organisational defence routines and cover-ups. All knew that what was being covered up was important. They do not need rules to tell them this. Introducing rules is therefore unlikely to prevent this kind of thing from happening again. No rule can stop some manager from interpreting a warning as a question. If it is a warning it has to be conveyed up the hierarchy. If it is a question it does not. The only way around this is to require everything to be conveyed up the hierarchy and that is impossible. The real solution is to uncover the defences and discuss them, despite the anxiety and difficulty this involves. Argyris (1990, p. 43) concludes:

> Organizational defence routines make it highly likely that individuals, groups, intergroups, and organizations will not detect and correct the errors that are embarrassing and threatening because the fundamental rules are to (1) bypass the errors and act as if that were not being done, (2) make the bypass undiscussable, and (3) make its undiscussability undiscussable.
>
> These conditions, in turn, make it difficult to engage the organizational defence routine in order to interrupt them and reduce them. Indeed, the very attempt to engage them will lead to the defensive routines being activated and strengthened. This, in turn, reinforces and proliferates the defensive routines. ■

models, techniques, visions and plans. All the while the real causes of poor strategic management – the learning process itself, the political interaction and the group dynamic – remain stubbornly undiscussable.

People within an organisation collude in keeping matters undiscussable because they fear the consequences if they do not. Consultants too find themselves sucked into defence routines because they are nervous of the consequences of exposing them – they may be fired. The result of the defence routines we have been talking about is passive employees and managers, highly dependent upon authority, who are not well equipped to handle rapid change. In these conditions, managers produce vague, impractical prescriptions as a defence against having to do anything in difficult situations, such as 'we need more training' or 'we need a vision'. The organisation loses out on the creativity of people because of the management model it uses.

The way out of this impasse is for managers and managed to reflect jointly, as a group, on the processes they are engaged in. It they can perceive this is a challenge rather than a potential source of embarrassment and fear, then they are able to engage in complex, double-loop learning: that is, in extraordinary management. For example, joint reflection might lead them to consider the extent to which:

- power flows from expertise and contribution, not simply position in the hierarchy;
- people are motivated primarily by their own internal commitment; and
- people respond to long-term rewards.

These beliefs about power and motivation tend to encourage the public exposure and testing of relevant feelings and judgements, even if they are negative, in order to ensure that decisions are being taken on valid data. Behaviour according to such a 'commitments' model should lead to cooperative dynamics and mutual control, allowing people to put their own creativity to use for the organisation.

The problem is that the attempt to move to such a 'commitment' model is itself likely to provoke the damping feedback loops of organisational defences. When people behave according to the control model, they set off damping loops of organisational defence which have the effect of blocking the complex learning process, so trapping an organisation in a state of stable equilibrium, that is, within the same mental model.

One of the main fears touching off such damping loops is the fear managers have of losing control. This can quite easily completely immobilise learning, decision-making and action.

The fear of losing control

If people are to engage in complex learning then they must expose relevant negative feelings, the basis of the judgements they make on the performance of others, the cover-ups and games they are playing.

Such learning is therefore bound to upset people and to arouse management fears of losing control. Such fears will reduce commitment to complex learning, and consistent with the control model they are still using, even though they are trying to get away from it, people will also tend to conceal the diminishing commitment. The effect is to reduce the effectiveness of any attempt to engage in complex learning and the possibility of switching to some other model of control. The harder they try, the more it provokes the fears that impede it.

What we have then is a positive feedback loop running from the control mental model to anomalies and contradictions which weaken the control model and build up an alternative model. But movement around this loop itself touches off movement around another loop too. This is a negative, damping loop that undermines the complex learning process and therefore strengthens the control model. This is depicted in *Figure 11.2*.

FIGURE 11.2
Fear of losing control

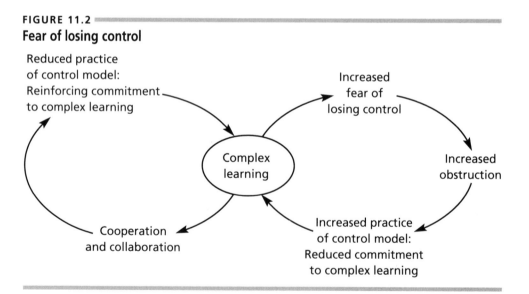

The problems we have been talking about in this section are primarily due to the fact that all of us try to hang onto our existing model of how to learn as we learn: we all try to kill our own learning for one reason or another. How can we overcome thus? Well, one popular prescription for promoting the learning organisation is that of empowering people throughout the organisation; where empowerment is equated with democracy, dispersed power and widespread participation. However simply dispersing power, inviting widespread participation, is no guarantee whatsoever that the organisation will function more effectively or make better decisions. First, widespread participation means that, although more people are being invited to take part in decision-making, they are all still using the control model. We simply have more people behaving incompetently. There is no guarantee that lower managers or employees behave better than top executives. While the larger number involved in decision-making continue to use the control model they simply spread the win/lose dynamics more widely. The negative damping loops of organisational defences will be reinforced. Widespread participation is no guarantee of more effective learning or better decision-making at all. People first have to learn how to operate on the basis of continuing complex learning and that is very difficult to achieve. Simply inviting people to do so will not have the required result. Widespread participation is no guarantee of better learning.

So, managers and members of an organisation are agents in a complex system that is coevolving with a number of other complex systems it interacts with. This evolutionary interaction inevitably generates conditions far from certainty and agreement and in all complex adaptive system agents cope with this by adapting the rules driving their behaviour to make that behaviour more beneficial to themselves, that is, to develop superior survival strategies. In other words, all surviving complex adaptive systems practise double-loop learning. Human organisations are no different to the other complex adaptive systems we find in nature – organisations also survive in the evolutionary game they play with each other through processes of double-loop learning that may lead to creative new survival strategies. This is a self-

---

FIGURE 11.3

Defence routines and covert politics: main points on organisational dynamics

- The behaviour of people in organisations is dominated by what Argyris has called the control model of management. This is usually operated within a pluralistic political system, in which a number of groupings have countervailing power.
- Use of the control model, the existence of different power groups, leads to win/lose behavioural dynamics. Here people employ a number of organisational defence mechanisms to protect themselves and others from the consequences of the win/lose pressures. They play games and make matters undiscussable. Consequently, decisions are often not made on valid data, implementation of decisions is often obstructed, small changes go undetected for lengthy periods. In short the ability of the organisation to develop strategically is severely impaired.
- But movement from the control model/pluralistic political system is fraught with difficulty. The most widespread idea of what to move to is a commitment model of control operating within a collegiate political system. This is the OD programme (and also the prescriptions of writers such as Peters, discussed in Chapter 6). Movement away from the control model, and particularly movement to the collegial model, touches off many positive amplifying feedback loops which undermine that movement.
- These positive feedback loops are activated because any attempt to change an organisation in a fundamental way upsets the balance and nature of power and raises the levels of uncertainty and ambiguity. All of these changes increase anxieties of one kind or another. And it is the anxiety that provokes positive feedback loops.

organising process out of which effective survival strategies will emerge for some but not all of the players.

In the case of humans, emotion plays a major role in this double-loop learning process. As soon as the human agents of an organisation embark upon double-loop learning they must confront their own fear of failing. This gives rise to something like a bifurcation point: people could avoid the fear, and hence the learning, altogether by engaging in organisational defence routines, or they could hold the fear, see it as a challenge and proceed with the double-loop learning as long as they can hold the fear and not be swamped by it.

There is no general set of prescriptions that can be taught to a group of people so that they can perceive threats to their current ways of making sense of the world as a challenge in which fear can be held, as opposed simply to a source of fear that must be defended against. There are no simple techniques or tools that a group of people can practise so as to become expert double-loop learners. There is no system that we can install, no identifiable list of new behaviours that we can learn over a weekend course and take back to apply to our workplace on a Monday morning. What then are we to do about complex learning in organisations? The truth is that no-one really knows in a precise way and yet it is clear that, from time to time, we do succeed in doing it. What I think flows from the recognition that organisational learning must be accompanied by the fear of failure and that, therefore, it is automatically defended against is this: while there is nothing that we can install, there are ways that we can intervene to help create the conditions in which complex learning is perceived more as a challenge and less as a fear. Such conditions have to do with the manner in which the most powerful exercise their power and with the atmosphere of trust and support that groups of people manage to build amongst themselves in the shadow system. We will return to these matters later on in this chapter.

We turn now to a further examination of the extraordinary management processes involved in complex learning in an organisation.

11.3 UNCONSCIOUS PROCESSES AND THEIR IMPACT ON ORGANISATIONAL LEARNING

The last section considered how complex learning provokes fears of embarrassing and being embarrassed, fears of failing and losing control, all rather conscious reflections of a much more general anxiety. A deeper understanding of the processes of extraordinary management, that is, of complex organisational learning, requires a deeper understanding of group responses to anxiety, including responses that are unconscious.

An unconscious group process is one in which a group of people engage without consciously agreeing to it or even realising that they are doing it. When groups of people are in this state they find what is happening to them both puzzling and upsetting and it makes it impossible for them to engage in complex learning. Covert politics is a defence against anxiety that people are more or less conscious of practising but unconscious processes are defences they indulge in quite automatically without being aware of what they are doing.

So, anxiety triggers an automatic negative feedback loop, a damping process that inhibits movement away from a currently shared mental model so trapping a group of people in stability. A group of people can only learn in a complex way when they are able to hold the anxiety such learning provokes, as opposed to avoiding it through covert politics, on the one hand, or becoming overwhelmed by it in the form of unconscious processes, on the other hand.

Figure 11.4 adds a further loop to the diagram in *Figure 11.1*, this time to take account of the feedback loop to do with unconscious processes. This shows that when people focus on the contradictions between their mental representation of the world and their experience of it, they become anxious. That anxiety may rise to such high levels that people swing into automatic basic assumption behaviour. This is a notion developed by Wilfred Bion that we are going to consider in some detail in this section. When groups are dominated by basic assumption behaviour they cannot learn and therefore their organisation cannot develop new strategic direction. On the other hand, if there is a good enough holding environment so that people can contain rather than submit to or avoid the anxiety, then insight and creativity may be generated by and accompany the anxiety of complex learning.

You can see once again how the complex learning process that is extraordinary management is a self-organising one. It is not possible for a leader to instruct people to contain their anxiety. Leaders cannot simply legislate away basic assumption behaviour. No one puts such behaviour in place and no one can install any system to remove it, simply because it is self-organising. Patterns of basic assumption behaviour, and patterns of holding it at bay so that work is possible, all emerge from a spontaneously self-organising process that takes place in the shadow system of an organisation. Once again, however, it is possible for leaders, members and outsiders to intervene in the shadow system to affect what is going on and perhaps shape it to some extent. Most importantly, however, it is possible to create a good enough holding environment. Leaders do this when they are able to articulate what is happening to those that they lead, when they are able to inspire confidence and to challenge and provoke people to learn. Once again the extraordinary management task has nothing to do with instructing or installing and everything to do with contributing to productive emotional atmospheres.

We now go on to consider the work of Bion, and others, on the nature of unconscious group processes.

Bion's models: unconscious group processes

The nature of interaction between people depends upon the extent to which those people are aware of the nature of their own and each other's behaviour. This point is made in *Figure 11.5*, a diagram known as JOHARI's window.

When people are aware of their own behaviour and those with whom they are interacting are also aware of that behaviour, then interaction between them takes on a Public form – we all know what we are doing together and why. But one group of people may be doing something that they are completely aware of to others who are unaware of what is going on. Such behaviour is labelled Hidden in *Figure 11.5*; some of us are manipulating others. Again, one group may be performing in a particular way, for reasons that they are unaware of, but their behaviour is transparent to others. Such behaviour may be called Blind: we may pretend we are doing one thing while we do another, but other people can see through this. The figure also shows a quadrant that is cross-hatched, depicting behaviour where those behaving and those responding are unaware of the true nature of their interaction. This is unconscious behaviour.

FIGURE 11.4

Anxiety and the impact of unconscious group processes

FIGURE 11.5
JOHARI window

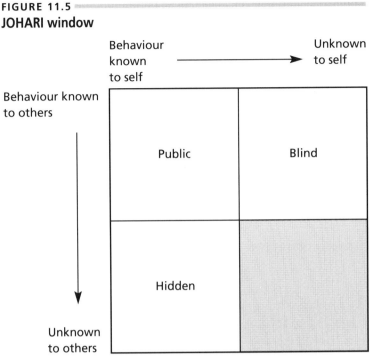

Source: P.B. Smith (1969), *Improving Skills in Working with People: The T Group*, London: HMSO

When individuals behave in such a way that they are not explicitly aware of the nature, or the quality, or the causes of that behaviour, then we can say that they are behaving unconsciously. For example, when we react in a hostile manner to a total stranger we have never heard about or met before, then we are behaving unconsciously – there is no obvious reason, no clear connection with external reality, to explain our reaction. The reason for our reaction probably lies in the unconscious mind; the particular person has activated a response from some other experience in the past that has been pushed into the unconscious. Whenever we react to some stimulus in a manner which others, and later we ourselves, perceive to be out of all proportion to the stimulus, then in all probability the cause of that behaviour lies in our unconscious.

When you lose your temper at a typist for making a small spelling error, the true source of the anger is most probably not the typist at all; you are simply projecting anger felt for someone else, who might well be yourself, onto the unfortunate typist. This kind of projection is an unconscious process in which all humans regularly indulge.

Since all of us as individuals behave in ways that are directed by unconscious as well as conscious processes, it is inevitable that, when we come together as a group, at least part of what we discover and choose to do in that group will be determined by those unconscious processes. In other words, unconscious group process will inevitably be an inextricable part of most decision-making processes in an organisation.

This is an obvious proposition, but one not recognised in most explanations of managing, organising and decision-making. The role of unconscious processes is also firmly denied any explicit attention by the great majority of management practitioners.

Such considerations tend to be dismissed as peripheral concerns for mature managers who are supposed to make decisions in largely technically rational ways. When unconscious processes are discussed they are normally seen as peripheral influences on a decision, usually adverse influences, which must and can be removed.

More careful reflection, however, makes it clear that unconscious processes are so deeply embedded in human behaviour that it is only some completely inhuman, and therefore non-existent, decision-making process that can occur in the absence of unconscious processes, or with those processes occupying a position of only peripheral importance. Unconscious processes are at the heart of the decision-making processes managers actually employ. It is therefore a matter of great importance for the effectiveness of strategic management to explore what impact these processes have and how they come about. First consider one way of becoming aware of what the processes we are talking about actually are.

Group relations conferences

A very powerful way of experiencing what unconscious group processes actually feel like is provided by what is known as Group Relations Conferences, or Tavistock Conferences (*Miller, 1989*). This approach to training in group awareness was popular in the 1960s but fell from favour largely because it did not produce predictable, long-lasting changes in people's skills in building cohesive teams. Since we are here questioning whether that is a valid aim, the criticism need not deter us from learning what we can from this approach and I would therefore like to describe some of the kinds of behaviour that always emerge in such events and then outline the explanations that have been put forward to account for it.

What I am going to describe is based on three separate conferences, each lasting two days over a weekend. The participants on each occasion were about thirty part-time MBA students, average age around thirty-five. Some points on the composition of these groups are as follows: about 15 per cent were female; perhaps 10 per cent of the total were from minority groups; about 70 per cent of the total were from the commercial and industrial sector and the remainder from public sector and charitable bodies; over 90 per cent had degrees or professional qualifications. All of these intelligent people held responsible managerial positions in their organisations.

Participants arrived at the residential weekend with some feelings of apprehension because they had heard rumours from others about the strange happenings likely to occur. At the start of the weekend, all of the participants met in a plenary session with the staff who were to act as consultants to groups of participants. The staff consisted of three visiting consultants with considerable experience in running such conferences and two teachers from my own institution who played a relatively minor consulting role. The task of the weekend was briefly outlined: it was to study group processes, particularly unconscious processes, so enabling each individual to examine the part he or she plays in those processes, including the exercise of authority.

Participants were then divided into Study Groups of 10–12 members each and the task of the Study Group was stated to be that of studying intra-group processes in the here and now, when they happen and as they happen. It was clearly explained to the participants that each Study Group would be attended by a consultant, who would not be there to teach, but to provide working hypotheses about the processes occurring in groups. It was quite clearly stated that participants must take responsibility for their own learning.

The Study Groups were therefore set up in such a way that there was nothing that the managers involved recognised as the kind of objective and task they were used to. Managers do not normally simply examine their own behaviour in a group – the behaviour normally lies in the background of dealing with an objective and a task. Here the behaviour itself is brought out of the background to actually provide the, rather unfamiliar, objective and task. The role that the consultants steadfastly occupy is also not one that the participants are used to. The consultant clearly occupies some position of authority as far as the participants are concerned, but that consultant abandons the participants in the sense that the consultant refuses to occupy the expected role of teacher, expert or leader. Then, however, having abandoned them in this sense, the consultant nevertheless keeps intruding in the role of consultant to offer interpretations of what the participants are doing (*Gustafson & Cooper, 1978*).

These two changes, the removal of what is normally regarded as a task and the removal of what is normally regarded as a teacher or leader, always provoke high levels of anxiety in the participants, anxieties which they are reluctant to recognise. Those anxieties find expression in all manner of strange behaviours. Group discussions may take on a manic form with asinine comments and hysterical laughter. In a remarkably short space of time the participants attack the visiting consultant for not playing a more usual and active role and openly question whether they are earning their consulting fees. Participants become incredibly rude to the consultants, behaviour they would not normally display to a visitor, no matter how poor the visitor's performance might be. Significantly, however, participants never attack my colleague and myself, perhaps because we represent the ongoing authority figures for the MBA course.

Members of Study Groups might try to find a leader to replace the non-functioning consultant but they rarely seem to be successful in this endeavour for very long. They begin to pick on an individual, usually some highly individualistic or minority member of the group, and then treat this person as some kind of scapegoat. They all become very concerned with remaining part of the group, greatly fearing exclusion. They show strong tendencies to conform to rapidly established group norms and suppress their individual differences, perhaps because they are afraid of becoming the scapegoat.

The Study Group events are followed by the Inter-Group Event. Here the participants are invited to organise themselves into groups and then study inter-group behaviour in the here and now as it happens. The sight of these mature people organising themselves into groups is quite astonishing. They do so without any forethought, all seemingly in a panic at the thought of being left out of a group. Within seconds the room is cleared of people who have all rushed off, away from the consultants, in one group or another. Then they begin to interact and within minutes the win/lose dynamic takes powerful hold. Even though there is no specific objective, other than studying behaviour, even though the groups have formed without any common purpose whatsoever, some groups at least start to talk about dominating the others. They then proceed to try to do so, brushing aside any quiet, puzzled voice that might ask why they are doing this. In their pursuit of domination, group members lie to each other, spy on each other, and play one deceitful game after another.

The one thing they hardly do at all is examine the behaviour they are indulging in, the task they have actually been given. Individuals and whole groups become scapegoats, set up by others and collaborating in that set-up. Very real emotions of anger and fear are evoked by what goes on, despite the fact that all know that this is 'only a training weekend'. Rumours spread about what other groups are doing, fantasies that participants afterwards realise are completely false. But at the time little effort is made to check on the data: all is wild assertions, building up fantasies of attacking and being attacked, rejecting and being rejected. People talk all the time about the group as some real thing separate from themselves as individuals. They place enormous store on being part of the group and on the group being cohesive. They talk about belonging to the strongest, most cohesive group, the best group, in a fantasy-like neurotic manner.

I personally found it most surprising that undoubtedly competent, mature people in responsible managerial positions react so strongly to two rather small changes from the normal. After all, there is a task: it is to study group processes as they happen and there is certainly much happening. There is assistance in performing the task in the form of comments and guidance from the experienced consultants, even though they refuse the role of teacher. But it seems that the original stimulus of two rather unusual changes sets off some kind of amplifying feedback loop in the behaviour of the groups of participants from which they seem incapable of escaping during the whole week-end. They, and even I as a rather peripheral consultant, become totally caught up in very strong and difficult-to-understand amplifying processes. The fact that the magnitude of the response is out of all proportion to the stimulus is a sign that we are dealing with unconscious processes. Throughout the experience it becomes apparent to many participants that processes of this kind occur every day within their own real life organisation, although usually at a much lower level of intensity.

How are we to explain the nature and cause of these unconscious processes that make it virtually impossible for a group of intelligent and competent managers to work on a task for a whole weekend? The most useful explanation seems to be that, when humans are confronted by high levels of anxiety provoked by unfamiliar tasks and lack of leadership, they revert very easily to infantile mechanisms. They begin to behave according to patterns they learned as infants. So first let us look briefly at what seems to be the most useful explanation of how infants cope with their world (*Klein, 1975*).

Infantile mechanisms

According to Melanie Klein's explanation (1975), infants are born with two powerful drives: the libido, or life force, which is the drive to love; and the morbido, or death wish, which is the fear of death and destruction, the feeling of persecution. The inner life of the infant is very simple – it is dominated by these two extremes of love on the one hand and persecutory fear on the other.

The infant's perception of its external world is also very simple, consisting of two part objects: a good part of the mother that feeds and comforts it and a bad part that denies it food and comfort.

The infant copes with this simple and also powerfully distressing world by splitting its inner life into a loving part that is projected onto the good part of the mother. The infant then identifies itself with that good part and in projects it back into itself. The same thing is done with the persecutory feelings and the aggression and hatred they arouse. These are all projected onto the bad part of the mother, and the infant identifies its own violent impulses with that bad part – it in projects that bad part of the mother back into itself.

This process of splitting, followed by projective identification and introjection, amounts to setting up feedback loops. The infant projects its feelings and then perceives those feelings as coming from the outside object. It therefore reacts to the object in a manner provoked by the feelings which originally come from itself. So it projects its own fears of persecution and then reacts to the object projected upon as if that object is actually persecuting it. This leads to a reaction of hate and aggression, strengthening the feeling of persecution. If the projection affects the behaviour of the object, then the whole feedback process becomes even stronger. It is through this feedback that the character of the infant is formed. If it experiences loving responses to its loving projections then the loving side of its character is strengthened. If the persecutory projections are reinforced by lack of love and actual persecution then this side of the character is reinforced. Right at the earliest stages of behaviour, then, positive and negative feedback loops play major parts in the development of each of us.

This first stage of infantile development is known as the paranoid–schizoid position. It is schizoid because the infant splits the external world and it splits its own internal world too. It is paranoid because of the persecutory fears of the infant. The infant deals with these fears by using the mechanisms of splitting and projective identification, putting what is inside its own mind out into some external object or person and then identifying with and reacting to what it has projected. It copes with harsh reality by creating an external fantasy world of separate objects, some of which are persecuting it. It is idealising the good parts and denying its own bad parts by projecting them, so building the external bad into a demon.

The infant who develops normally works through this position and comes to realise that the bad and good objects in its external world are really one and the same whole person. But having learned how to defend ourselves against the earliest anxieties, we lay those lessons down in the unconscious. In later life when we confront anxiety again, we are highly likely to regress to the infantile mechanisms of splitting the world and ourselves into extreme and artificial categories of the good and the bad, projecting the parts of ourselves we do not like onto others, so creating fantasies that have little to do with reality.

Once the infant realises that it loves and hates the same person it is filled with anxiety because of the feelings of anger and hatred previously projected into the mother. This causes the depressive position. The normal infant works its way through this position too, developing strong feelings of love and dependence on the mother, while seeking to make amends for previous bad feelings. It experiences hope from the maturer relationship with the mother. Once the infant can hold the depressive position, that is, hold in the mind the paradox of simultaneously loving and hating, then that child can go on to make reparative acts and have reparative feelings. If these are responded to with love then a life-long cycle of experiencing guilt, making reparation and receiving forgiveness is put in place. Melanie Klein saw this as the basis of all later creative behaviour. So, it is when we are in the depressive position, when we can hold in our minds the paradoxes and ambiguities of organisational life, that we are able to engage in complex learning. When we regress from that depressive position to the psychotic paranoid–schizoid position we become trapped in primitive ways of thinking and behaving. And this happens to all of us when we cannot contain the anxiety of learning and when our environment provides us with no anxiety containment either.

Transitional objects, learning and play

Winnicott's (1971) work gives us a further insight into the development of the ability to learn and be creative. He identified child development with a process of separation from the carer and he stressed the vital importance of 'good enough holding' by the carer in this process. He defined the good enough carer as one with a fine judgement of just how much to gratify the child to sustain a sufficient degree of security, and just how much to frustrate that child to provoke exploration of and relation to the environment: that fine balance constitutes 'good enough holding' and comes from the instinctive empathy the carer has with the child. Good enough holding enables children to cross the boundary of their own minds and begin to explore, relate to and manipulate the real world outside their minds.

However, eventually the child has to develop its own holding mechanisms as it were, since reliance cannot be placed on the carer to do this all the child's life. Winnicott proposed that such holding mechanisms take the form of what he called transitional objects. As they mature children develop the ability to compensate for short absences of their carer by developing a very powerful relationship with some special object such as a blanket or a teddy bear. Winnicott suggested that this object stands for the carer: it is treated for short periods as if it were the carer and so it provides enough security for the child to continue exploring the environment. In this sense the object is a transitional one: it is a transition from a present carer to an absent carer; it stands for the carer although it is not the carer. This is how the child begins to use symbols, the beginning of all language and reasoning powers.

In fact the teddy bear soon comes to stand for anything the child wants it to be, providing experiences of play which develop the imagination and the ability to manipulate symbols. It is through this experience of play that the child learns and develops imaginative, creative powers. The child discovers how to control and manipulate objects outside the mind, first by manipulating the transitional object and then by controlling real objects. The play takes place in a transitional space between the inner fantasies of the mind and the outer reality of a concrete world, as depicted in *Figure 11.6*. Here the child holds ambiguity and paradox: the transitional object is one thing but stands for something else. In this sense the transitional space is close in meaning to the depressive position (*Miller, 1983; Gordon, 1993*).

Play continues to be a major source of learning and it continues throughout life to be closely associated with creativity. It is when individuals are able to play, when they are able to manipulate symbols, when they are able to occupy the illusionistic world, that they are able to be creative. Winnicott argued that the transitional space continues throughout life to be the area in which people develop cultures, myths, art and religion. So, the extraordinary management processes of complex learning in organisations have to do with creating the space for play and with creating the conditions that will hold the anxiety such creative play arouses.

Groups and infantile mechanisms

When mature, competent managers come together as a group, each brings along the infantile mechanisms of dependence, idealisation, denial, splitting, projection and fantasising which have been learned as an infant and laid down in the unconscious.

FIGURE 11.6
The creative space

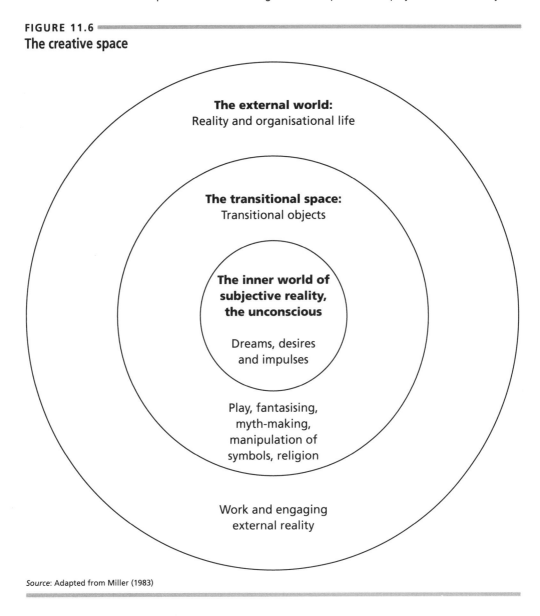

Source: Adapted from Miller (1983)

Anything that raises uncertainty levels and thus anxiety levels could provoke regression to those infantile mechanisms.

Bion has provided the most insightful explanation of how these mechanisms are manifested in group behaviour, leading to the kinds of behaviour at the group relations conferences described above (*Bion, 1961*).

Bion distinguishes between two important aspects of any group of people. The first aspect is the sophisticated work group. This is the primary task that the group has come together to perform. So a team of top executives has the primary tasks of controlling the day-to-day running of the business of the organisation and also the strategic development of that organisation.

All groups are also at the same time what Bion called 'basic assumption groups'. A basic assumption group is one that behaves as if it is making a particular assumption about required behaviour. The assumption becomes most apparent when uncertainty and anxiety levels rise. What Bion is talking about here is the emotional atmosphere, the psychological culture, of the group. All groups of people have these two aspects: some task they are trying to perform together, accompanied by some emotional atmosphere within which they are trying to perform their task. That atmosphere can be described in terms of a basic assumption they are all making.

So, at any one time, a group of people may constitute a sophisticated work group characterised by a basic assumption on behaviour that occupies a kind of low-level background position, influencing the conduct of the primary task but not dominating or blocking it. Then when uncertainty and anxiety levels rise markedly the group can become suffused with and dominated by the basic assumption; a strong emotional atmosphere, or group culture, that blocks the group's ability to function as a sophisticated work group. The primary task will not be carried out, or it will be carried out in an ineffective manner.

Bion distinguished between three basic assumptions:

1 **Dependence.** Here the group behaves as if it has come together to depend on some leader. The members of the group seek a leader on whom they can depend. They abandon their individuality and critical faculties in favour of some kind of adoration of a charismatic leader. They actively seek a charismatic person who will tell them what to do. Charisma lies not in the person of the leader but in the interrelationship between the followers and the leader.

In this state, members of a group will idealise the leader, expecting completely unrealistic performance from the leader. Groups working on this assumption are destined to be disappointed and will quickly abandon the leader. This dependence is an infantile mechanism because the members of the group are projecting their requirements for something to depend upon onto someone else. This projection will in effect select the leader. Note how this raises a possibility we do not normally think of. When a group is behaving in this mode it is creating its own leader through projecting demands on to a person – it is not the leader who is creating the group. If the person selected for this projection does not cooperate or disappoints, then members of the group project their frustration and fear onto that person and begin to attack. This brings us to the second basic assumption.

2 **Fight/flight.** Here it is as if the group has come together for the purpose of fighting some enemy or for the purpose of fleeing from some enemy. Members project their desire for fight or flight onto someone to lead them in fight or flight. Once again they may rapidly become disappointed with and attack the leader. Groups in this state invent fantasy enemies in some other department or some other organisation. The energy goes into competition and win/lose dynamics.

3 **Pairing.** Pairing is another mode a group might operate in. Here it is as if the group has come together to witness the intercourse between two of their number which will produce the solution to their anxieties. The atmosphere here is one of unrealistic hope that some experts will produce all the answers.

Turquet (1974) has added a fourth basic assumption.

4 Oneness. Here it is as if the group has come together to join in a powerful union with some omnipotent force which will enable members to surrender themselves in some kind of safe passivity. Members seem lost in an oceanic feeling of unity.

The dynamics

The explanation presented so far is summarised in *Figure 11.7.*

FIGURE 11.7
Unconscious group processes

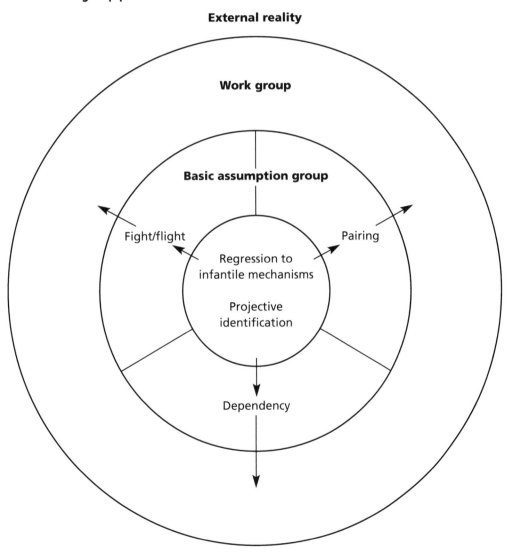

Source: R. de Board (1978), *The Psychoanalysis of Organizations*, London: Tavistock Publications

Once a group of people come to be dominated by one of the basic assumptions, they enter into volatile dynamics in which they switch, for apparently no reason, from one basic assumption to another. While people in a group are behaving like this they are incapable of performing the primary task or acting as a work group. They cannot remember what they have just discussed; they go around and around in incompetent circles; they suck unsuitable people into leadership positions; they create scapegoats; they act on untested myths and rumours; they build fantasies and lose touch with reality. Individuals sink their individuality in group uniformity and become deskilled. The organisational defence routines and game playing discussed in the last section provide examples of this in real-life organisations.

What provokes the switch from a work group with some background basic assumption, being used in a sophisticated way to support their task, to a group dominated by a basic assumption? The provocation seems to have a great deal to do with levels of ambiguity and uncertainty on the one hand, and with certain styles of exercising power on the other. If leaders abandon groups in times of great uncertainty and ambiguity then they will develop into basic assumption groups and become incapable of handling the uncertainty and ambiguity.

But note that we are not talking about clear-cut causality between a specific action, say the withdrawal of power, and specific outcomes in behavioural terms. All we can say is that, when the nature of power in a group is changed so that people's requirement for dependency is frustrated, we will be able to observe general patterns of behaviour, archetypes, that we can label as fight/flight or some other label. We will not be able to say what form such fighting or such flight may take, or when it will occur.

Another point to make now, the relevance of which will become clearer later in this chapter, is this. When the nature of power and authority, the boundary conditions of the group, are changed, the group spontaneously displays a form of self-organisation. It spontaneously operates in fight/flight patterns for example. More supportive, more containing boundary conditions could result in a spontaneous switch to a serious work group. Forms of self-organisation may then be prompted by unconscious processes.

Implications for strategic management

Some important points follow from this analysis. Normally the role of power in the strategic management of organisations is discussed as one of the factors influencing the implementation of a strategy. There is also a quite separate literature, one taking a psychoanalytic view of organisations, where the possibilities and consequences of leaders becoming neurotic are discussed (*Kets de Vries & Miller, 1987*). But mainstream views on strategic management do not relate to this at all. Leaders are assumed to be perfectly healthy, balanced people, who set the direction of the organisation for others to follow. However, as soon as we recognise that basic assumption groups can very quickly emerge from work groups, we have to recognise that leaders can also be the creations of the group. It is quite possible that leaders are vainly trying to act out the fantasies that those in the management team are projecting. Reality is once again a feedback loop. Leaders affect what groups do, but groups also affect what leaders do through processes of unconscious projection.

The group relations approach also opens up these insights:

- Charismatic leaders and the strong cultures of dependence they provoke in followers may well be extremely unhealthy for organisations. Researchers (for example, *Peters & Waterman, 1982*) may therefore note the presence of charismatic leaders and superficially conclude that this is the reason for success, when it might well be a neurotic phenomenon that is about to undermine the company.
- A cohesive team of managers may not be a healthy phenomenon at all. It may be an unhealthy and unproductive reflection of the fantasy of basic assumption groups acting out dependence or oneness assumptions. Again researchers not considering an organisation from a psychoanalytic point of view may well conclude that such neurotic cohesion is a reason for success.
- The idea of the group or the management team may itself be a defence mechanism. So, faced by high levels of strategic uncertainty and ambiguity, managers may retreat into the 'mother figure' of the team for comfort and in so doing fail to deal with the strategic issues.
- Groups clearly do not have to have a purpose or even a task to function very tightly as a group, even if it is a misguided one. Again, signs of close teams should provoke suspicion, not praise.
- Groups or teams are a two-edged sword. We need them to establish our identity. We need them to operate effectively. But they can also deskill us.
- The desire for cohesion may well be a neurotic phenomenon.
- Plans and rigid structures and rules may all be defences against anxiety instead of the rational way of proceeding we usually think they are. The way we cling to the dominant paradigm of strategic management, despite all the evidence to the contrary, is a sign of this.
- One aspect of culture is the emotional atmosphere, the basic assumption, that a group of people create as they interact.

Implications for complex learning and extraordinary management

Unconscious group processes will have an effect on the possibility of complex learning since that learning will inevitably raise anxiety levels simply because existing mental models are threatened. Perhaps even the behaviour of the consultants hired to assist the complex learning process could create the conditions in which the work groups set up by their programme could be swamped by basic assumption behaviour. For example, consultants could encourage client dependence. If this happens then of course we will get a negative damping feedback loop that will offset the positive amplifying loop of the complex learning process itself. This possibility is depicted in *Figure 11.8*.

The most important strategic issues, the response to which could alter the direction of the organisation, are by definition ambiguous with highly uncertain consequences. Such issues threaten the stability of how people work and their power positions. When teams of managers deal with strategic issues it is therefore inevitable that the basic assumption aspect of any work group should come to occupy a more prominent role and even threaten to swamp the work group. This means that we have to see unconscious group process as an integral part of the process of making strategic choices, a part which is deeply embedded in human nature and cannot be removed. Inevitably, the handling of strategic issues activates positive feedback loops of unconscious behaviour.

FIGURE 11.8

Unconscious group processes and organisation development

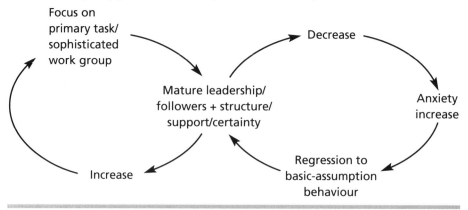

FIGURE 11.9

Unconscious group processes: main points on organisational dynamics

- Positive feedback loops are activated by any attempt to change an organisation in a fundamental way. This is because change upsets the balance and nature of power and raises the levels of uncertainty and ambiguity. Consequent anxiety provokes positive feedback loops.
- Increased anxiety unleashes unconscious processes of regression to infantile behaviour. Work groups become swamped with basic assumption behaviour in which they are incapable of undertaking strategic developments.
- A group of managers facing strategic issues is, by definition, tuning up the levels of uncertainty and ambiguity since these are characteristics of strategic issues. Such issues, by definition, threaten power positions. It is therefore inevitable that strategic issues themselves will touch off the positive amplifying loops of basic assumption behaviour. Such behaviour is an inevitable part of the process of making strategic decisions.
- In these circumstances it is quite likely that long-term plans, mission statements, visions and the like are simply being used as defence mechanisms. Perhaps we cling to today's dominant paradigm despite all the evidence to the contrary because it is our main defence mechanism against anxiety.
- The dynamics of any real life organisation are inevitably unstable, unless they are completely dominated by rules, fears or force, in which case they will atrophy and die. Strategic management proceeds as part of this unstable dynamic.
- Success has to do with the management of the context or boundary conditions around a group. The main factors that establish the context are the nature and use of power, the level of mutual trust, and the time pressures on people in the group. The purpose of managing the context, or the boundaries, is to create an emotional atmosphere in which it is possible to overcome defences and to test reality rather than indulge in fantasy. In other words, the context must be managed to create an atmosphere that enables complex learning.

The conclusion is that the basic OD model and mainstream models of strategic management with their emphasis on negative feedback do not take adequate account of the complex dynamics of organisations and will therefore not work. The consequence is that large-scale culture change programmes are highly unlikely to go according to plan, as *Illustration 11.2* shows.

Illustration 11.2

The culture change programme

In early 1988, the senior managers at Apex Engineering were driven by increased international competition to find significant and permanent cost reductions. The management team examined the problem and decided to reorganise from a functional structure to one of profit-responsible business units. They employed consultants to identify international cost standards and set benchmarks relating to the level of inventories, product completion times, sales per employee, added value per square metre of space occupied, and people employed per project. They also employed consultants to develop a strategy to achieve the cost standards by 1994.

In early 1989, the management team in conjunction with the consultants, set out its mission. That mission was to become the prime world-class manufacturer of its main product and the strategy to achieve this consisted of installing just-in-time inventory control systems and cellular manufacturing; that is, small multidiscipline teams responsible for clearly specified parts of the total product. In addition, a leaner, flatter organisation was to be created by removing a rung of middle management.

The senior managers recognised that the strategy represented a major change in the way people worked and therefore it set up a culture-change programme. A change champion was appointed and management groups set up to deal with initiatives, problems and issues. The intention was to promote collective problem-solving and decision-making. But the role of the change champion was specified as that of ensuring that key people did in fact attend the groups. No-one seemed to think it odd that managers were to be compelled to cooperate. Right at the beginning a control model was to be used to install a commitment model.

The result was a network of people who were committed to the change but they tended to be located in the former department of the change champion – the personnel and purchasing functions. Little real support existed in the manufacturing function because so many managers stood to lose power from a switch to cellular manufacturing.

Senior management in discussion with each other stated that, without careful communication and selling to the workforce as a whole, the strategy would be viewed with scepticism, mistrust and outright rejection. So the managing director gave propaganda talks to people, a three-dimensional model of the new site configuration was built for all to see and questions were invited. This whole exercise might be viewed as a defence routine: senior managers are making presentations calling for group problem solving, but they are presenting a solution that has not been arrived at in this way. Those listening to the presentation know this but do not point it out.

▶

The next step was to negotiate changes in work practice with the trade unions. When the unions asked what the mission and cost standards set for 1994 meant for work practices, the senior managers said that they could not readily be translated into specific work practices. They also said that the vision did not allow specific savings to be identified and so they could not identify any rewards for introducing new work practices. Managers are promoting a commitment model, but they are not being open with the unions. Or they are telling the truth and their missions and plans are so general and vague as to be meaningless.

In view of this the unions would not support the change programme and a small pilot programme was mounted instead. This was supposed to emphasise management commitment (but in fact the managing director showed little interest in it) and to test the cellular method of manufacturing. The pilot team was set up and received awareness training, diagnostic skills training and teamwork skills training. The pilot project was said by many to be a success, but no hard evidence to support this was produced and it did not run for its full time period – it was halted by a strike. Nine months later the unions agreed to cellular manufacturing but by this time, late 1990, the economy was in recession and the whole project was petering out. ∎

11.4 AN INTEGRATED MODEL OF EXTRAORDINARY MANAGEMENT PROCESSES

We are now in a position to look at the model we have been building throughout this book. This is a model of what seem to be the key processes we must incorporate if we are to understand how people in organisations both conduct their day-to-day affairs in an efficient and predictable manner and transform their organisation, producing new strategic directions in an inevitably creative and destructive manner. If an organisation is to survive longer than others then its members must be more adept than others at both efficient day-to-day performance and at transformational complex learning, at both ordinary and extraordinary management. The key process in this combined model are shown in *Figure 11.10*.

This figure shows the technically rational processes of planning in the middle and the political processes expressing vested interests supporting it, all within a shared mental model. When they are close to certainty then this is what managers are able to focus upon and they can forget about the other feedback loops. However, as soon as they move far from certainty and become aware of discrepancies between the world they operate in and the world they have constructed in their minds, the other loops are activated and what then happens to an organisation depends predominantly upon how managers and members cope with the loops so activated.

The processes at the centre of the diagram takes place within the legitimate system and those at the periphery take place in the shadow system.

What this diagram depicts is a complex web of feedback loops. They could be joined to each other at any point – the arrangement in the figure is simply one possibility. All

FIGURE 11.10
An integrated model of decision-making and control

the loops are connected through some loop to all others. When people in an organisation deal with closed and contained change, that is when leaders can be relied on to exert authority and people carry out repetitive tasks to achieve known objectives, then decision-making and control can quite adequately be described by the rational loop in the middle of the diagram. It is as if the other loops all fade into the background and become of little consequence. Or in such closed and contained conditions we may find political activity kept stable by shared cultures. The control system model above has planning and ideological forms as special cases applicable to closed and contained change.

However, as soon as open-ended issues present themselves to people in an organisation, the level of ambiguity and uncertainty rise dramatically and leaders can no longer deal with the situation by applying their authority. We can think in terms of the level of ambiguity being tuned up while the level of applied power is tuned down. These inevitable consequences of the open-ended issues that are so characteristic of strategic management mean that the political, cognitive and unconscious loops that we previously ignored as background now become very important; they are activated to become major parts of the process of decision-making and control. The loops are not activated in any set order – each new situation provokes a new specific way of moving around the loops. In this system of feedback loops, some will inevitably operate in amplifying ways, opening up the possibility that the system will become explosively unstable, that is uncontrolled. The key question then is under what conditions we can expect such a complex system to generate controlled behaviour. The first general condition for controlled behaviour is still present: there is a feedback loop connecting discovery, choice and action as there was before; it is simply that the elements are defined in far more complex ways. The problem is that we can no longer rely on organisational intention to provide constraint. If the system is to be controlled we have to look for some other form of constraint.

It is important to note how the processes of extraordinary management are directly opposed to those of ordinary management. Management is a paradoxical process requiring people dialectically to rearrange contradictory processes. The shadow system seeks to subvert and undermine the legitimate system in the interests of changing it. These points are summarised in *Figure 11.11*.

11.5 OVERT POLITICS AND THEIR IMPACT ON ORGANISATIONAL LEARNING

The integrated model of decision-making and control put together in the last section shows a feedback loop depicting overt politics. In Chapters 4 and 5 we discussed political processes from an ordinary management point of view. There, politics is conducted within a shared paradigm to realise the pattern of vested interests – it is vested interests that determine the outcome of any conflict between objectives and so restore agreement. Far from certainty, when the processes of the shadow system are activated, however, politics takes on a different aspect and plays a different part.

The process of complex learning inevitably threatens the pattern of vested interests and the overt response of the most powerful; the manner in which they employ their power comes to have a major impact on the process of complex learning. We will see in this section how the use of power impacts on the group dynamic, either assisting or blocking the process of complex learning. Overt politics is therefore also an extraordinary management process and it can play a major part both in containing the anxiety of complex learning and, paradoxically, also in amplifying and spreading the disturbances created by such learning so that they ultimately alter the pattern of vested interests. Good enough exercise of power is thus a vital part of the constructive learning process. We go on to explore this matter in the present section.

FIGURE 11.11
Relationship between ordinary and extraordinary management

	Legitimate system and ordinary management	*Shadow system and extraordinary management*
Stable equilibrium	Integrated hierarchy and bureaucracy Negative feedback control systems	Conformist risk averse dependent culture Strongly shared vision and culture
(Functioning formal systems supported by informal systems)		
Instability/ randomness/ fragmentation	Too decentralised Ineffective control systems	High cultural diversity, conflict, widespread political activity
(Malfunctioning formal systems aggravated by subversive informal systems)		
Chaos/ at the edge	Integrated hierarchy and bureaucracy Negative feedback control systems	High cultural diversity, conflict, widespread political activity, dialogue Weakly shared vision, ambiguity, learning
(Functioning formal systems subverted and so changed by informal systems)		

Source: Stacey (1995c)

The dynamics in a political system (*Stacey, 1991*) are determined by the relationship between leaders and followers. Leaders derive power either from hierarchical position or from the contributions they are able to make to the group. Furthermore, leaders may or may not choose to exert that power. These sources of leaders' power and their willingness to exert it are set out on the horizontal plane in *Figure 11.12*.

Illustration
11.3

Imperial Industries

One of the largest divisions of a company I will call Imperial Industries consists of two main UK subsidiaries, as well as subsidiaries in the US and Sweden. Subsidiary A in the UK designs and installs information technology systems. It manufactures a few of the components required for these systems, but mostly buys them from other companies and assembles them. One of A's suppliers is its sister subsidiary in the UK, company B, which manufactures components which it sells to A and to A's competitors for integrated systems contracts.

The division therefore has a direct route to the end-user market and an indirect route through Own Equipment Manufacturers (OEM). Operating these two routes is a source of conflict between A and B in the marketplace because A demands preferential treatment from B, but B resists this pointing to the damage it does to its business with A's competitors. The difficulties are magnified when account is taken of export business since both A and B are trying to sell components to overseas OEMs.

The Swedish company also gets involved in the conflict because it operates in the same way and supplies components to A and to A's competitors. The company in the US combines both routes to market in one company, but conflict occurs where the UK and US companies appear in the same export market. The strategic issue then is which route to market is to be chosen: one or both? Is there to be an emphasis on one rather than the other? If both routes are to be retained and no particular emphasis laid on either, then what policies are to govern relationships between the companies? What organisational structure is likely to reduce conflict to manageable levels? This has all the hallmarks of the strategic issue: it is ambiguous; the outcomes of different solutions are uncertain; it is difficult to structure the problem; any change affects some power position; different people have different perspectives; it is characterised by paradox or dilemma; levels of anxiety are raised.

To deal with these issues, the Chief Executive arranged a one-day workshop with his executive team, the managing directors of the subsidiaries. Each of the four MDs was a powerful and ambitious figure intent on winning out in the battle. They all had considerable talent and the CEO did not wish to see any of them leave. For most of the day the workshop focused on general market conditions and how they were likely to develop in the future. They talked a lot about future market position. Then they turned to putting together a mission statement or a vision. After much amicable discussion they agreed that it was impossible to make a choice at this stage between one route to market and the other – the future of the IT industry was too uncertain. They agreed on a vision 'to be a leading player in the worldwide IT market'.

Then towards the end of the day they turned to the question of how the division might be organised to reduce levels of conflict in the marketplace. The meeting immediately broke into acrimonious bickering as each MD fought in a highly personalised way to preserve his power.

What emerges quite clearly from this is the following. Those managers were using a friendly discussion about the future marketplace and about a vague general vision to flee from dealing with the real issue of how to organise themselves in a sensible way. In this sense a focus on the future and on vision was simply a defence mechanism to keep conflict and anxiety at bay. When they did confront the real issue, the group became dominated by the fight basic assumption. What this workshop on strategic management clearly shows is that the covert and overt political loops as well as the unconscious group process loop explain what is going on. The rational loop in the middle of *Figure 11.10* plays the part simply of a smokescreen.

The CEO then invited a distinguished consultant to yet another workshop which was to address the issue. That consultant identified the key problem to do with relationships between the subsidiaries and their MDs and the need for policies and structures. But he said the first step was to form a dream or vision. This then let everyone off the hook again. They discussed the potential vision and decided that the one they had come up with before was the best they could do. Was this hiring of a consultant another example of flight behaviour? Did the consultant collude in this by providing another opportunity for flight in his insistence on a vision?

Yet another consultant was then employed. This time an attempt was made to unblock the political obstacle at the top by bringing together a working group of middle managers and asking them to propose policies and structures. They after all were at the forefront of the conflict. The idea was that pressure from their subordinates would move at least some of the MDs.

The proposals of the middle managers were presented to the MDs at a board meeting. Apparent peace prevailed while there was a discussion of the general principles of the restructuring proposed, but when it got close to anything specific a number of things tended to happen. The CEO chairing the meeting would get up and leave the room to attend to something urgent. The discussion would then peter out as soon as he left. On other occasions one of the MDs in particular would keep making personal remarks that he was quite aware would antagonise his colleagues. In this way he could sidetrack the meeting away from the real issue.

Once again, the point is that this process of making a strategic decision is characterised far more by covert political behaviour and unconscious group processes of flight and fight, than it is by analytical reasoning.

A few months later, the CEO built up enough support to implement a number of the proposals the middle management group had put forward and one of the MDs left. Had that MD been fired early in the process, a number of managers may well have left with him and, even if they did not, there would probably have been continuing covert opposition to the reorganisation. It happened, however, that no-one else left and there was considerable support for the new structure.

Clearly the outcome of this strategic issue emerged; it was not the consequence of organisational intention. It emerged from a complex process of moving around a number of interconnected feedback loops that had to do with overt and covert political behaviour and with unconscious group processes. It would be naive to believe that it is possible to remove these processes from an organisation. The behaviour of those involved was controlled in a self-organising manner, although no one was in control. Although the MDs conflicted, they did so within the boundaries set by each other's power. ∎

Followers may consent to be led because they believe in the ideology propounded by their leaders, or because they accept the hierarchical authority of those leaders. Furthermore, followers too may withhold their consent to be led. These factors are set out in the vertical axis of *Figure 11.12*.

When these factors are combined in different ways, they lead to different forms of power and these in turn provoke different typical patterns of group dynamic, so creating a context within which a group works on its tasks. Five typical contexts are depicted in *Figure 11.12*:

FIGURE 11.12

Determinants of the form of power

Exertion of power based on:

Consent to power based on:	Power not exerted	Contribution/ gain	Structure/ rules
Duty, obligation, strong belief	Vacuum	Authority	Authority
Contribution + gain	Vacuum	Influence	Force
Fear No consent	Impotence	Impotence	Force

Source: R. Stacey (1991), *The Chaos Frontier: Creative Strategic Control for Business*, Oxford: Butterworth-Heinemann

1 Authority and compliance. Here both leaders and followers operate on the basis of their hierarchical position and shared ideology. The result is the exercise of authority and a group dynamic of compliance where followers suspend intellectual and moral judgements about the appropriateness of the superiors' choices and actions and willingly and unquestioningly do what the leaders want (*Bacharach & Lawler, 1980*).

2 Influence and volatile group dynamics. When both leader and followers work on the basis of their own personal skills and experience, then they influence each other by offering advice, entering into discussions, making suggestions, and persuading. A whole range of dynamics can emerge, from conflict to cooperation, from avoidance to commitment, from compliance to dissatisfaction with the leader, from questioning and consensus seeking to game playing and making issues undiscussable.

3 Force, submission and rebellion. Where leaders apply force, the dynamic is either submission or rebellion. Force and its consequent dynamics are clearly not conducive to ordinary or extraordinary management, but may nevertheless be necessary in extreme circumstances.

4 Impotence. Where neither leader nor followers are willing to use or consent to power, there is a state of impotence. The typical group dynamic here is intense rivalry.

5 Power vacuum. Finally, where the leader is unwilling to apply power while followers are willing to consent, we get a power vacuum. Typical group dynamics here are passive loyalty, searching for a new leader, frustration.

Which of these five states prevails will depend upon the extent to which people share the culture and how power is distributed:

- When people in a group strongly share the same cultural norms and power is highly concentrated in clear hierarchies, then they will be willing both to exert and consent to the use of power. It follows that the context they will operate in will be that of authority and compliance. This is a psychologically secure state and it is highly appropriate for ordinary management. Consequently, all organisational political systems will be powerfully pulled to this state. As organisations try to take advantage of synergy and interconnection, as they drive towards commonly accepted goals and build shared cultures, they move to political systems where authority is the predominant form of power and compliance the predominant group dynamic.

- When people in a group do not share the same cultural norms and power is widely dispersed, there will be a low willingness to exert power and to consent to it. The result will be a state of political impotence in which the predominant group dynamic is one of intense rivalry. Since all organisations are powerfully pulled towards disintegration by the forces of division and differentiation, all political systems in business organisations will be pulled towards this state. As the organisation tries to deal with high levels of uncertainty and benefit from the division of tasks and the segmenting of markets, it develops many different units with different cultures. The power of the centre weakens and rivalry breaks out between the units.

- Organisations and their leaders may respond to weak sharing of values by imposing greater order and concentrating power at the top. Willingness to exert power is thus great but willingness to accept it is low. Power then takes the form of force and the predominant group dynamic is either submission, or resistance, or alternation between the two.

- Another response to the consequences of division and differentiation may be to offset the effects of widespread distribution of power by promoting the strong sharing of cultural norms over a wide range. Ability and willingness to exert power are then low and willingness to consent is high. This creates a power vacuum in which the typical dynamics are ones of passive loyalty, or frustration, or search for leadership.

Figure 11.13 depicts these four final states.

The political system of an organisation is therefore pulled in four different directions toward four different equilibrium states. It is very difficult to move an organisation away from any of these equilibrium states. It requires some political coup

FIGURE 11.13
Equilibrium states for an organisation's political system

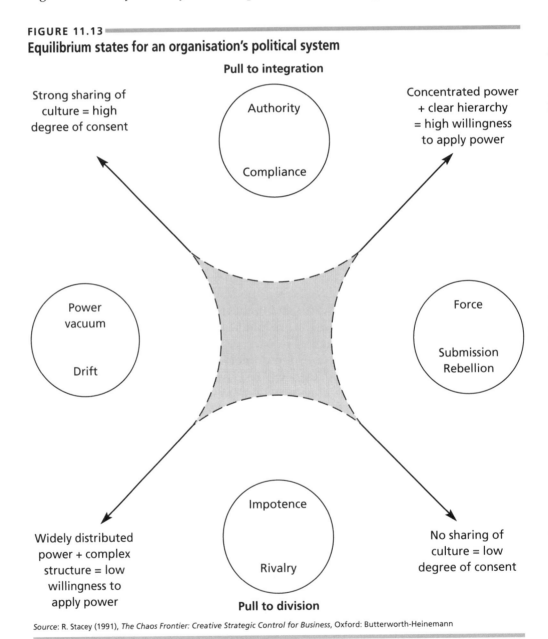

Pull to integration

Strong sharing of culture = high degree of consent

Authority

Compliance

Concentrated power + clear hierarchy = high willingness to apply power

Power vacuum

Drift

Force

Submission
Rebellion

Impotence

Rivalry

Widely distributed power + complex structure = low willingness to apply power

No sharing of culture = low degree of consent

Pull to division

Source: R. Stacey (1991), *The Chaos Frontier: Creative Strategic Control for Business*, Oxford: Butterworth-Heinemann in which the leader is removed, or some major restructuring of the hierarchy, or alterations to systems and procedures. Furthermore, none of these equilibrium states can successfully deal with open-ended change because the group dynamics provoked by all of them simply obstruct questioning and complex learning.

Successful political systems are therefore those that are sustained far-from-equilibrium, by preventing:

- Strong sharing of cultural norms over a wide range and avoiding a state in which they are hardly shared at all. Organisational political systems are sustained far-from-equilibrium by weak sharing of cultural norms that occurs when people make different unconscious assumptions on what and how to learn. Differences in culture are essential to change.
- Widespread distribution of authority over strategic resource allocation and the confusion of hierarchical structures. The far-from-equilibrium state is one where authority is distributed, but not widely, and where hierarchies are clear, not confused. Difference in power distribution is also essential to change.

Successful political systems are those that enable people to cope with open-ended change and that can only happen when the political system allows and encourages questioning and the exposure of new perspectives. Clearly, people are not open to persuasion and new perspectives when they strongly share a wide range of cultural norms and when they share none at all. They are also clearly not open to persuasion when power is so highly concentrated that those at the top do not need to listen, or when it is so widely distributed that there is not much they could do even if they did listen. Cultural difference and differences in power distribution therefore create the conditions in which people influence and are influenced. In other words, power is not continuously applied as authority or force, and continuous power vacuums and impotence are also avoided. It is in the border area between the equilibrium states of authority, force, power vacuum and impotence that we find power in its form of influence and that is what change requires.

The impact of overt political activity on the complex learning process

Highly authoritian political systems based on mechanistic rules and completely impotent ones riven by rivalry are, however, rather rare in practice. There is far more likely to be a complex pluralistic political system in which power is already spread around an organisation in groups with vested interests (*Greiner and Schein, 1988*). Thus, the typical modern corporation does not have a political system in which one or two powerful executives at the top control what goes on throughout the company. Instead we find powerful subsidiary companies and powerful departments in many different parts of the organisation and those at the top have to sustain enough support to govern. Any change of any significance is going to affect the balance of power, making one department, subsidiary company or management grouping weaker or stronger than it was before. Any sign of change will touch off fears that such power shifts might occur even before it is clear what they might be. People and groups will therefore start taking protective action as soon as they get wind of any possible change.

Any attempt to engage in complex learning, to change mental models, is likely to be just such a change, one that is directly concerned with changing power positions. It is therefore highly likely to touch off damping feedback loops of a political nature that will undermine and perhaps eventually destroy it. The more people are persuaded to move to a consensus collegiate way of making choices, the more powerful groups with vested interests are threatened and the more likely they are to put a stop to the programme. The more managers try to head off this threat, the more they have to play by the rules of the political system they are trying to replace. If they do this they simply reinforce what they are trying to remove. This is shown in *Figure 11.14*.

Once again, initiatives will fail if they do not recognise and deal with the damping feedback loops that are always present in organisations. And how to deal with these loops is far from clear.

Power vacuums and organised anarchies

If managers do succeed in installing a collegiate political system and the commitment management model, yet other damping feedback loops may be activated by the shift in the distribution of power.

As authority and other forms of power are dispersed, as organisational structures are flattened, as job descriptions become looser, and as the establishment of widespread consensus comes to be required before decisions are possible, so the likelihood of a power vacuum at the centre increases. It becomes more and more difficult for anyone to exercise much authority; more and more people have to be able to handle their own independence. In situations in which most people seek the comfort of dependency this could create serious difficulties. We will explore what group relations theory has to say about this in a later section. Another way of understanding the consequences of changes in power distribution is provided by *Greiner* and *Schein (1988)*.

Greiner and Schein use the device given in *Figure 11.15* to relate changes in willingness to assert and to accept power to the consequent group dynamic. When both leaders and followers consent freely to the exercise of power, there is a high probability of active consensus. When the leader exerts power but the followers do not consent, then we get the behaviour of covert resistance. You will see from *Figure 11.15* that as the leader becomes less able or willing to exert power, while followers still look for a

FIGURE 11.14
Threats to vested interests

FIGURE 11.15
Power and group dynamics

Source: L. E. Greiner & V. E. Schein (1988), *Power and Organization Development: Mobilizing Power to Implement Change*, Reading, Ma: Addison-Wesley

lead, then we get the behaviour of passive loyalty. If, in the same circumstances, the followers too become less willing to accept the exercise of power, the group's behaviour is characterised by peer rivalry.

What we see, then, is that the dispersal of power and the spread of participation could set off feedback loops in which declining central power leads to greater rivalry throughout the organisation, or to passive loyalty, both of which will block the creativity that complex learning is supposed to unleash. Indeed events could be much more complex than this if at the same time we raise levels of uncertainty and ambiguity by loosely defining people's jobs.

Others have studied the decision-making processes in organisations such as universities, hospitals, as well as other public sector and professional bodies, that are characterised by the collegiate-type political system. They have described these organisations as organised anarchies and their decision-making processes as 'garbage can' decision-making (*Cohen, March & Ohlsen, 1972*).

The point to be made here is this. When decision-making procedures are highly unstructured, as they tend to be when power is dispersed and widespread participation invited, then the particular decision taken on a particular occasion will depend almost entirely on the detailed context at the time. Here context means details such as: who attended the meeting at which the decision was taken; how important those attending were; what other matters they had on their minds. In this sense the particular decision made comes to depend upon chance. And in these circumstances there is a high level of probability that decisions will be postponed and, even if made, not implemented.

FIGURE 11.16

Vested interests and political interaction: main points on organisational dynamics

- Positive feedback loops are activated by any attempt to change an organisation in a fundamental way. This is because change upsets the balance and nature of power and raises the levels of uncertainty and ambiguity. Consequent anxiety provokes off-setting negative feedback loops.
- One feedback loop has to do with the fears of existing power groups that they will lose control. As change programmes are pushed, so these fears are increased, leading usually to covert undermining of the programme. Organisational defence routines are then strengthened rather than weakened.
- Dispersing power and weakening central authority can set off loops leading to peer rivalry or passive loyalty. Both determine creativity and decision-making ability.

11.6 LEADERSHIP AND THE ROLE OF GROUPS IN EXTRAORDINARY MANAGEMENT

In the last chapter, we saw that the shadow system present in every human society and organisation is a fluid network of contacts, nodes, links and interactions between people both within that society or organisation and across its boundaries with other societies and organisations. That network has many facets that can be explained and described in terms of:

- a social system that meets people's needs for mutual support and meaning in their work; and
- a communication system that enables rapid and sensitive flows of information; and
- a political system that deals with conflicting interests through persuasion, negotiation, bargaining, compromise, and the application of power; and
- a vehicle for hypocrisy and irrationality: in other words, a decision-making process that allows people to say one thing while doing another in the interests of mobilising concerted action; and
- a set of interactions through which people may learn.

Whatever facet of the shadow systems focuses on, however, there is one property common to them all – they are all aspects of the behaviour of a shifting set of small groups of people that are self-organising. How the shadow system actually works, whether its consequences help or hinder the organisation, all depend upon the behaviour of people in small groups. Ultimately, whether an organisation is able to change its shared mental models, and therefore innovate and develop new strategic directions, and what changes, innovations and new strategic directions it develops, all depend upon how the network of informal small groups of people in the organisation behaves.

We have already discussed formal groups in Chapter 4 and the important distinction between the work and basic assumption aspects of any small group in an earlier section of this chapter on Bion's models. We may think of small groups in terms of a paradoxical constellation of behaviour that constitutes work on the one hand, and basic assumption behaviour that makes work impossible on the other. The dynamic development of a group is a dialectical process in which these contradictory forces are continually rearranged. We now turn to a more detailed exploration of how small groups develop.

Patterns in small group development

Gibbard, Hartman & Mann (1974) distinguish between three models of group development: linear progressive, life-cycle, and pendular models. They describe each of these types of models in the following terms.

Linear progressive models

In this kind of model the explanations of group behaviour run in terms of progressive stages that the members of a group pass through and the resolutions they achieve in each stage before they can work effectively together. One of the best known descriptions of group development (*Tuckman, 1965*) identifies the four sequential steps that all groups are claimed to follow during the course of their development:

- *Forming.* When people first come together to form a group, they go through a hesitant testing stage in which they begin to identify their task, form relationships, and develop roles. It is a stage in which people are typically dependent and look for guidance.
- *Storming.* Having acquired some sense of security, the members of a group then conflict over what it is they should be doing, how they should do it, and what roles each should occupy. This is a stage of emotional expression.
- *Norming.* The next stage is that of working through the conflict and developing shared values or norms to govern how they are to operate together. The outcome is conformity and cohesion.
- *Performing.* This is the stage in which the group produces what it has gathered together to produce; it performs its primary task.

You will recall from Chapter 4 that Lewin described the stages of change in an organisation and a group in terms of a period of 'unfreezing' (similar to forming and storming), followed by a period of 'reformulation' (similar to norming), followed in turn by 'refreezing' (similar to performing). Another model identifies two phases in group development, each of which consists of a number of subphases (*Bennis & Shepard, 1956*):

- *The authority phase.* When people first come together to form a group they are preoccupied with the question of authority; that is, who is to be in charge, who is to be looked to for guidance, who is to be depended upon in performing the primary task. This phase is typically divided into subphases. First, people in the group behave in a submissive way, looking for and being willing to take guidance on what to do and how to do it. The hope is that some leader will provide the solutions that will allow the group to work. This is followed by the next subphase in which people rebel against those they have at first depended upon, hoping that conflict will provide a solution to the problems of group life. The third subphase is one in which members find a compromise solution and partial resolution of the dependency-authority/submission- rebellion issue, one that accepts their simultaneous presence.

● *The interpersonal phase.* Once the group has at least partially worked through the questions of authority and dependence, submission and rebellion, the concern then becomes that of interdependence between the members of the group. The first subphase here is one in which members of the group identify with each other, the subphase of 'enchantment'. The psychological force here is a desire on the part of individuals to find the security that comes from fusing themselves into the group. This is a primitive defence in which members seek the route to performing their primary task through group cohesion. This gives way to the second subphase in which members of the group experience 'disenchantment' with their interdependence and seek to establish their own individuality and independence of the group. The third subphase here is one in which there is some resolution of the fusion–individuation tension, one in which fusion and individuation are both present.

It is easy to see how these models are part of the stable equilibrium organisation paradigm – they seek ways of solving the paradox. These models appear to assume that a group reaches a peak of efficient work and then ends or continues at that level.

Life-cycle models

These models are an elaboration of the linear progressive models, the principal addition being the emphasis on the terminal phase for small groups. Thus *Mills (1964)* adds a stage of 'separation' in which the group begins to face and cope with its own death and members assess the success or failure of their efforts.

Pendular or recurring-cycle models

These models describe group development in terms of recurring cycles of issues or pendular oscillations between them. You will recall the description of Bion's theory of groups in which he describes groups moving between the primary task and various basic assumptions. Here there is no predetermined progression from one stage to another until the group functions properly. Groups may perform their primary task quite adequately for a time and then some event may provoke basic assumption behaviour that interrupts efficient performance. Bion sees groups as perpetually trying to resolve their difficulties, endlessly rearranging their basic assumption behaviour, but never succeeding in removing that behaviour completely for any length of time. Here the development of a group is seen in continuing efforts to deal with anxiety provoked by psychic non-equilibrium – tension between the pull to fuse with the group and the pull to develop as an individual (*Jacques, 1955*).

This view of group development is more realistic and fits well with the far-from-equilibrium organisation paradigm. Having discussed how small groups develop, we now turn to the roles people take up in those small groups.

Roles and leadership in small groups

In ordinary management, leaders are appointed to an office in a bureaucracy, or perhaps elected to a position in some representative body, where they take charge of a group of people who have also been appointed or elected in some formal way. People come to their roles in a formal fashion in groups that already have structures, procedures, norms, cultures, systems, goals and relatively clear primary tasks. In these circumstances the important question quite clearly is one of identifying how groups can most effectively and efficiently perform the task and reach the goal. When we observe that people have a natural tendency to develop informal social groupings as they work together in addition to the formal, the concern becomes one of harnessing that informal group to support and not obstruct the performance of the main task. The concern is with motivation and the prime role of the leader is to motivate, form the vision and clarify the cultural values. We then look to personality traits, styles and skills as the determinants of good leaders. We reach the conclusion that we can install techniques and programmes to develop good leaders and cohesive groups, ones that are aware of social and psychological self-realisation needs of individuals.

The extraordinary management perspective on roles and leadership is, as we have seen, a very different one. Here the point is to destroy the existing paradigm and the structures, cultures and styles that embody it, as the essential prelude to change. And the instrument organisations require to do this is the informal organisation. That informal organisation is the spontaneous emergence of small groups – the same groups we talked about as shadows to the formal in Chapter 4 – but now we see them not as purely social and psychological phenomena required to keep individuals healthy and motivated, but as instruments of change with vital tasks of their own. These groups are informal and unstructured, without a task or an objective – the task is to find and structure tasks and objectives.

People arrive at informal groups without roles and there are no leaders, the task is to develop these. Such groups do not relieve anxiety, they create it, and the group has to find out how to defend itself against that anxiety. When an organisation is able to produce such groups that do keep performing their obscure unstructured tasks then it is innovative and develops new strategic directions. If the organisation fails to produce such groups it is incapable of change.

The questions of interest are very different from this perspective to those that interested us from the ordinary management perspective. Now we want to know how such groups evolve, in other words how they develop differentiated roles and leaders, how they identify and structure their tasks. (See *Key Concept 11.2.*)

Key Concept 11.2

Roles and leadership in informal groups

Unconscious group processes produce informal roles in unstructured groups. The leader may well not create the group, but rather be the creature of the group. Leadership is the ability to interpret the processes of the group without being sucked into them, so as to help the group identify its task. From this perspective we can see how an organisation can quite easily become neurotic if its leaders produce or get sucked into neurotic processes.

Leadership

Bales (1970) identified the emergence of two kinds of leaders in small task-oriented groups: the task leader who gives suggestions, shows disagreement and presses the group to focus on task completion; and the social–emotional leader who asks for suggestions, shows solidarity, and soothes tempers by encouraging tension release. (The leadership theories discussed in Chapter 4 also focused on this dilemma of the task and the people.) These leadership roles are mutually supportive in that each helps the group solve different problems, provided that the role occupants can work together. Sometimes one person can combine both roles – the 'great man' leader (*Borgatta, Couch & Bales*, 1954). When specialist leaders of this kind do not emerge or cannot work together, then members begin to deal with their frustration in unconscious ways that lead to the emergence of scapegoat roles, enemy roles, messiah roles and so on. *Bion (1961)* distinguishes between different types of leader in the basic assumption group: the fight leader, the flight leader, the dependency leader, and the leader who symbolises some unrealistic utopian, messianic, or oceanic hope. Bion points to the precarious position these leaders occupy. The important point here is that the leader is sucked into that position by the group and is controlled by the group, not the other way around as we usually believe.

An important distinction is that between the leader of a work group and a basic assumption leader. An effective leader is one who maintains a clear focus on and definition of the primary task. That task determines the requirements of the leader, who must continually struggle to synthesise, participate, and observe. The effective leader operates on the boundary of the group, avoiding both emotional immersion and extreme detachment. Leaders are there to regulate transactions between their groups and other groups. Both immersion and distance make this impossible. When a group is dominated by basic assumption behaviour it sucks into the leadership position one who is completely immersed in the emotional atmosphere, the basic assumption behaviour of the group. This leader is subjected to conflicting and fundamentally impossible roles – to provide unlimited nurturance, to fight and subdue imaginary enemies, to rescue the group from death and dissolution, to fulfil utopian or messianic hopes.

> One of the most intriguing aspects of relatively unstructured and ego-involving small groups is the evolution of a constellation of informal roles that serve important social and psychological functions for the group. Most small-group research has addressed itself to groups that do not have formal statuses and ascribed social positions. The roles that emerge are usually described as 'behaviour patterns,' 'individual roles,' or 'interpersonal styles.' Under relatively unstructured conditions, psychological factors, conscious and unconscious, become increasingly important as determinants of role structure . . . Explicit and formal social prescriptions are replaced by fantasy conceptions of norms and sanctions. At the same time, it is assumed that such roles are not simply expressive of idiosyncratic needs but perform necessary and recurrent functions for the social system – such functions as impulse expression, group maintenance, tension release.
>
> (*Gibbard, Hartman & Mann, 1974, p. 179*)

The kinds of roles that have been distinguished are those of the aggressor, the seducer who tries to seduce people into exposing their feelings and positions, the scapegoat, the hero, the resistors, the anxious participators, the distressed females, the respected enactors, the sexual idols, the outsiders, the prophets (*Dunphy, 1968*). These informal roles develop in order to contain and deal with internal conflict, the tension of fusion and individuation. One of the key roles is that of leader.

Since strategic issues are ambiguous, ill-structured issues that usually start small and get bigger, it is the informal organisation that has to deal with them until they reach an advanced state of definition, at least. It follows that strategic choice and action will have more to do with these unconscious processes than any rational consideration. The example given in *Illustration 11.4,* based on actual events, demonstrates what is meant.

Illustration 11.4

Choosing a training programme

David, the manager of a particular department, met with Judy, the personnel director, to talk about a possible training programme for his department. The idea had arisen casually before that in a conversation between David and Judy. David wanted to mount a team development weekend similar to one that he and his senior management colleagues had been on. During that weekend they had operated competitively in teams to win points in each of a series of events such as rock climbing, finding their way back to base over rough terrain and so on. He and his colleagues had enjoyed the event and felt that it had increased the team spirit among them.

Judy was supportive and so they involved David's secretary and the most senior supervisor in his department, Chris. As soon as he became involved, Chris suggested that they use a firm set up by his friends to run team training events on a yacht – crewing together develops team spirit. David opposed the idea on the grounds that many of the staff in the department were women who would not want to spend the weekend on a yacht. Privately he told Judy that Chris was an accomplished yachtsman and was pressing his idea simply so that he could win, something not all that good for the rest of the department.

In the end the yacht idea was dropped for what sounded like fairly rational reasons. However, frank discussions with David revealed completely different reasons. David was a sensitive, rather individualistic person who felt somewhat guilty about not being an enthusiastic member of the team who worked for him. Chris, on the other hand, was a boisterous, outgoing, macho man who was quite clearly a full member of the team. David felt threatened by Chris and his real reason for ensuring that the yacht weekend idea was quashed had to do with fears, probably about his own sexual prowess, in relation to Chris. In this way conscious and unconscious processes covered over with rational sounding reasons often determine what happens. ∎

To summarise, we have discussed patterns of small group behaviour as the consequences of social interaction, the development of norms or a culture through the experience of being and working together – a behaviourist approach (see Chapter 4). We have also just been discussing patterns of small group behaviour as the consequences of unconscious processes – a psychodynamic approach that derives from

Freud. Now we turn to another explanation that derives from Jung. While the Freudian approach tends to focus on drives and phases common to all of us, Jung stressed the differences between people that flow from the many instincts (archetypes) that drive us. He identified a number of common psychological types, preferred ways of behaving, or temperaments. From this perspective, patterns in the behaviour of small groups would be explainable from the manner in which different temperaments typically interact.

The impact of personality

Jung distinguished between preferences that go to make up different temperaments (*Kiersey & Bates, 1978*). First, people express preferred modes of behaviour somewhere between extroversion (E) and introversion (I). The E person derives energy from contact and interaction with others, while the I person is exhausted by such contact and seeks energy from internal, reflective sources.

Secondly, people have a preference along a spectrum that stretches from sensation (S) at one end to intuition (N) at the other. The S person prefers facts and knows through experience; such a person is firmly anchored to reality. The N person lives in anticipation and looks for change, skipping from one activity to another; such a person values hunches and prefers speculation.

The third pair of preferences are thinking (T) and feeling (F). The T person prefers the logical, impersonal basis for choice, while the F person prefers the personal, emotional basis.

Finally, there is the spectrum running from perceiving (P) to judging (J). The P person prefers to keep options open and fluid, seeing things from different points of view, while the J person prefers closure, that is narrowing choices down and reaching solutions.

The four pairs of preferences lead to sixteen possible temperament types and the possibility of having evenly balanced preferences adds a further 32 combinations to these. All these temperaments, however, can be sorted into four broad categories:

- **The Dionysian or SP person.** As a manager this type of person prefers not to be tied down by routine, but focuses on the present, seeks action, and tends to be impulsive.
- **The Epimethean or ST person.** As a manager this type of person is dutiful and desires to belong to the organisation. Such a manager is careful, thorough and accurate, a giver rather than a taker.
- **The Promethean or NT person.** As a manager this personality type is interested in power, control and predictability. They avoid the personal and emotional and want to be competent and in charge.
- **The Apollonian or NF person.** As a manager this type makes intuitive decisions, seeks to be unique, and finds it difficult to take negative criticism.

When people come together, their temperamental differences lead to misunderstandings and the widest gulf is that between the sensing and the intuitive types – the one insisting on logic and the facts, the other pushing proposals based on intuition and experience. People with the same personality type can also clearly have difficulties – a whole group of NT types all trying to control the group, for example, is a recipe for destructive conflict and inactivity. But differences bring contributions to relationships that would otherwise be lacking and some similarity provides the basis of understanding each other.

The behaviour patterns of groups of people would on this view be driven by the understanding and misunderstanding generated by the range of temperaments of the people constituting the group. The implication is that effective groups can be designed if we find out enough about the personality composition of sets of people, or group functioning can be improved by becoming more aware of the difficulties and contributions flowing from temperamental preferences.

Belbin's classification

Belbin has used teams of managers playing business games to identify the effects on group performance of different personality types (*Belbin, 1981*). He showed how some types work effectively together while others do not and that this has a greater impact on performance than the individual abilities of the people involved. Teams made up of people simply on the basis of their ability – how clever they are – do not make winning teams. Teams designed to include a balance of different personality types are much more likely to win even if they do not contain the most able individuals; it is actual contribution and interdependence that determines performance.

In Belbin's terms the basis of a good team is the Company Worker types – the conservative, dutiful and predictable, even if inflexible people (much the same as the Epimethean manager above). These Company Workers are the basis of a good team because of the stability they provide and the steady work contributions they make.

This is not enough for superior performance, however. In addition a team needs members paired into the 'Chairman' (Promethean) and the 'Shaper' (Apollonian) types. The 'Chairman' is calm, self-confident and controlled, arouses the contributions of many types, has a strong sense of objectives, but is average in creative ability. The 'Chairman' therefore needs to be balanced with a 'Shaper' who is highly strung and dynamic, challenges complacency and self-deception, and is impatient and irritable. The team is strengthened by the addition of the 'Plant' (Apollonian) and the 'Resource Investigator' (Dionysian). The 'Plant' is an unorthodox individualist who contributes new ideas but is apt to be 'up in the clouds'. The 'Resource Investigator' is an enthusiastic extrovert, eager for challenge but apt to lose interest quickly. These two types need to be balanced with sober and prudent 'Monitor Evaluators' and the orderly, conscientious 'Completer Finishers' (both Epimethean). Finally, superior teams contain 'Team Workers' who are socially oriented but tend to be indecisive in times of crisis (Apollonian, perhaps).

Neurotic forms of leadership

So far, we have been trying to understand what leadership means when it is functioning well, but of course leaders often do not function all that well and quite often they are definitely dysfunctional. Such dysfunctional leadership has not attracted all that much attention, but it occurs frequently and it is therefore a matter of great importance to understand something about it. Functional leaders assist in the containment of anxiety and thus help to create the possibility of complex learning, but dysfunctional, neurotic leaders may well get caught up, and drive others to get caught up, in neurotic defences that will block such learning.

Kets de Vries (1989) explains the nature of neurotic leadership in the following way. All of us behave in a manner that is affected by what we might think of as an inner theatre. That theatre consists of a number of representations of people and situations, often formed early in childhood, and those that have come to play the most important roles are core conflictual relationships. It is as if we spend much of our lives re-enacting conflicts that we could not understand in childhood, partly because they are familiar to us, and partly, perhaps, because we are always seeking to understand them. What we do, then, is to project this inner play with conflictual situations out onto the real world we have to deal with. Leaders do this just as we all do, the difference being that they project their inner conflicts onto a much larger real world stage that includes their followers. A leader projects internal private dialogues into external public ones and these dialogues are about core conflictual themes from childhood. The particular neurotic style a leader practises will be determined by the nature of these core conflicts.

Followers also project their inner plays onto the leader and these leader/follower projections create a feedback loop that keeps leaders and followers engaged with each other in a particular manner. Followers project their dependency needs into leaders and displace their own ideals, wishes and desires into them too.

The inner theatre in which leaders and followers join each other contains scenarios which are the basis of imagined, desired and feared relationships between them. There are typical scenarios that we find over and over again and they constitute typical dispositions, typical ways of defending against, repressing, denying and idealising particular leader/follower relationships. Everyone uses such devices and everyone has a number of prominent dispositions that constitute that person's neurotic style. This is quite normal and it becomes a problem only when we massively, compulsively and habitually use a rather small number of defences. This blocks our ability to relate to reality effectively and it is then that we might label ourselves or someone else as 'neurotic'.

Kets de Vries (1989) distinguishes between a number of such dispositions or neurotic styles as follows. Every leader will display a combination of some of these styles and it becomes a problem only when a rather small number of these come to dominate the behaviour of the leader and the followers.

1 The **aggressive** disposition tends to characterise many who become leaders and rather fewer who are followers – aggression is often acceptable in leaders but creates problems for followers. Tough chief executives who are socially forceful and intimidating, energetic, competitive and power oriented fall into this category. People are not important to them and they want to dominate. They tend to be impulsive and to believe that the world is a jungle. They expect people to be hostile to them and they become aggressive in advance to counteract such expected hostility. Of course their behaviour may well provoke the hostility they expect. Such leaders probably experienced parental rejection or hostility.

2 The **paranoid** disposition is found frequently amongst leaders and less amongst followers. Such people are always looking for hidden motives and are suspicious of others. They are hypervigilant, keep scanning the environment and take

unnecessary precautions. They deny personal weakness and do not readily accept blame. They tend to be restricted and cold in relationships with little humour. They are fond of mechanistic devices to measure performance and keep track of people. Such people may have had intrusive parents and may feel uncertain of themselves.

3 The **histrionic** disposition is characterised by a need to attract the attention of others at all costs. Such people are alert to the desires of others, they are sociable and seductive with their sense of self-worth heavily dependent on the opinion of others. They love activity and excitement and tend to overreact to minor incidents, often throwing tantrums. Such people may have had difficulty attracting the attention of parents.

4 The **detached** disposition is displayed when people find it difficult to form close relationships. They tend to be cold and aloof and this may be a response to parental devaluation.

5 The **controlling** disposition is high in leaders and low in followers and it is displayed by people who want to control everything in their lives. They have an excessive desire for order and control. This is a way of managing hostile feelings that may have arisen from the behaviour of controlling parents. The resultant hostility may emerge as tyrannical ways of behaving or its opposite of submission.

6 The **passive–aggressive** disposition tends to be found more in followers than in leaders. Such people are highly dependent but tend to attack those they depend upon. They resist demands for performance, they are defiant, provocative and negative, complaining all the time and demanding much from their leaders. They tend to blame others all the time, they are ambivalent and pessimistic. This difficulty might arise because such people find it difficult to assess what is expected of them. They are likely to have parents who presented them with conflicting messages.

7 Other dispositions are the **narcissistic** one when people see themselves as exceptional and special; the **dependent** disposition in which people are excessively dependent upon others; and the **masochistic** disposition.

It is not just the style of the leader or the style of the followers on their own that determines how their joint behaviour unfolds. It is how the styles engage each other that will create the environment within which they have to work. So, an aggressive, controlling leader interacting with dependent, masochistic followers will produce a rather different context and pattern of behaviour compared to such a leader interacting with, say, passive–aggressive followers. These patterns of interaction will have a powerful impact on how effectively an organisation learns. Such neurotically based interactions, therefore, have to be understood as processes of extraordinary management.

11.7 SUMMARY

In this chapter we have reviewed what happens to managers when they engage in, or are affected by, extraordinary management processes. What all those processes have in common is that they either block or assist the performance of complex learning. That complex learning and all the extraordinary management processes involved in it are self-organising and they produce emergent patterns taking the form of change first in shared mental models, and then in joint action that changes the legitimate system in some way. Complex learning and its extraordinary management processes lead to creativity and innovation, to new strategic directions and different survival strategies. Whether they work or not depends upon what the other organisations who are the environment are doing.

We have seen how covert politics can trap an organisation in stability and that complex learning can occur only if those covert politics are brought into the open and publicly reflected upon. We have seen how unconscious processes may plunge groups of people into psychotic fantasies where they are incapable of learning. Once again it is public self-reflection that can mitigate this and it is containing leadership and good enough holding environments that can enable people to hold the anxiety of learning. This led us to explore how the exercise of power affects the group dynamic and thus the learning process, and how the nature and exercise of leadership has a similar kind of impact. In the next chapter we are going to examine the outcome of complex learning when it overcomes the obstacles and some ways in which managers might intervene to assist the process.

Further reading

Hirschorn (1990) provides an important exposition of the role of the informal organisation as a defence against anxiety. Rush, White & Hurst (1989) explain how personality types affect decision-making, as does Belbin (1981). Kiersey & Bates (1978) give a questionnaire that you can use to identify your own personality type. I would also strongly recommend Carr & Shapiro (1995) and Kets de Vries (1989), as well as Miller (1993) and Oberholzer & Roberts (1995). They all give deeper insight into the psychodynamics of organisations. Winnicott (1971) is also well worth reading. Stacey (1996) develops ideas in this chapter.

References

Argyris, C. 1990, *Overcoming Organizational Defenses: Facilitating Organizational Learning*, Boston: Allyn & Bacon, Prentice-Hall.

Bacharach, S. B. & Lawler, E. J. (1980), *Power and Politics in Organizations*, San Francisco: Jossey-Bass.

Belbin, R. M. (1981), *Management Teams: Why They Succeed or Fail*, Oxford: Heinemann.

Bales, R. F. (1970), *Personality and Interpersonal Behaviour*, New York: Holt.

Bennis, W. G. & Shepard, H. A. (1956), A theory of group development, *Human Relations*, vol. 9, pp. 415–57. [Republished in Gibbard, G. S., Hartman, J. & Mann, R. D. (Eds.) (1974), *The Analysis of Groups*, San Francisco: Jossey-Bass.]

Bion, W. R. (1961), *Experiences in Groups and Other Papers*, London: Tavistock Publications.

Borgatta, E.F., Couch A. S. & Bales, R. F. (1954), Some findings relevant to the great man theory of leadership, *American Sociology Review*, vol. 19, pp. 755–59.

Carr, Wesley A. & Shapiro, E. R. (1995) *Lost in Familiar Places*, New Haven, Mass: Yale University Press.

Cohen, M. D., March, J. G. & Ohlsen, J. P. (1972), A garbage can model of organizational choice, *Administrative Science Quarterly*, vol. 17, pp. 1–25.

Dunphy, D. C. (1968), Phases, roles and myths in self analytic groups, *Journal of Applied Behavioural Science*, vol. 4, pp. 195–226.

Gibbard, G. S., Hartman, J. J. & Mann, R. D. (Eds.) (1974), *Analysis of Groups*, San Francisco: Jossey-Bass.

Gordan, R. (1993) *Bridges: Metaphors for Psychic Processes*, London: Karnac Books.

Greiner, L. E. & Schein, V. E. (1988), *Power and Organization Development: Mobilizing Power to Implement Change*, Reading, Ma.: Addison-Wesley.

Gustafson, J. P. & Cooper, L. (1978), Toward the study of society in microcosm: critical problems of group relations conferences, *Human Relations*, vol. 31, pp. 843–62.

Hirschorn, L. (1990), *The Workplace Within: Psychodynamics of Organizational Life*, Cambridge, Ma.: MIT Press.

Jacques, E. (1955), Social systems as a defence against persecutory and defensive anxiety, in Klein, M., Heinmann, P. & Money-Kyrle, P. (Eds.) (1955), *New Directions in Psychoanalysis*, London: Tavistock Publications. (Also published in Gibbard, G. S., Hartman, J. J. & Mann, R. D. (1974), *Analysis of Groups*, San Francisco: Jossey-Bass.)

Kets de Vries, M. F. (1989), *Prisoners of Leadership*, New York: John Wiley.

Kets de Vries, M. F. R. & Miller, D. (1987), *The Neurotic Organization*, San Francisco: Jossey-Bass.

Kiersey, D. & Bates, M. (1978), *Please Understand Me: Character and Temperament Types*, Del Mar, Ca.: Prometheus Nemesis Books.

Klein, M. (1975), *The Writings of Melanie Klein*, London: Hogath Press.

Miller, E. H. (1983), *Work and Creativity*, Occasional Papers, London: Tavistock Publications.

Miller, E. H. (1993), *From Dependency to Autonomy: Studies in Organization and Change*, London: Free Association Books.

Miller, E. J. (1989), *The Leicester Conference, Occasional Papers*, London: Tavistock Publications.

Mills, T. M. (1964), *Group Transformation: An Analysis of a Learning Group*, Englewood Cliffs, NJ: Prentice-Hall.

Oberholzer, A. & Roberts, V. Z. (1995), *The Unconscious at Work: Individual and Organizational Stress in the Human Services*, London: Routledge.

Peters, T. J. & Waterman, R. H. (1982), *In Search of Excellence*, New York: Harper & Row.

Rush, J. C., White R. E. & Hurst, D. C. (1989), Top management teams and organizational renewal, *Strategic Management Journal* vol. 10, pp. 87–105.

Schwartz, H. S. (1990), *Narcissistic Process and Organizational Decay: The Theory of the Organization Ideal*, New York: New York University Press.

Smith, P. B. (1969), *Improving Skills in Working with People: The T Group*, London: HMSO.

Stacey, R. (1991), *The Chaos Frontier: Creative Strategic Control for Business*, Oxford: Butterworth-Heinemann.

Stacey, R. (1995a), Creative organisations: the relevance of chaos and psychodynamics systems in *Social Creativity*, Montuori, A. & Purser R. E. (Eds.), Hampton Press.

Stacey, R. (1995b), The role of chaos and self organisation in creative organisations, in *Proceedings of the University of Hull at Quebec Conference on Chaos and Society*.

Stacey, R. (1995c), The science of complexity: an alternative perspective for strategic change process, *Strategic Management Journal*, August.

Stacey, R. (1996), *Complexity and Creativity in Organisations*, San Francisco: Berrett-Koehler.

Tuckman, B. W. (1965), Developmental sequences in small groups, *Psychological Bulletin*, vol. 63, pp. 384–99.

Turquet, P. (1974), Leadership: the individual and the group, in Gibbard, G. S., Hartman, J. J. & Mann, R. D. (Eds.), *Analysis of Groups*, San Francisco: Jossey-Bass.

Winnicott, D. W. (1971), *Playing and Reality*, London: Tavistock Publications. Reprinted 1993 by Routledge.

CHAPTER 12

Extraordinary management in the shadow system:

How managers create knowledge and intervene far from certainty

INTRODUCTION

So far in this Part of the book we have considered what the shadow system of an organisation is and what the processes are that people use, either consciously or unconsciously, both to learn in a complex way and to block that learning. We now go on to describe how managers use, and how they are affected by, these processes to progress issues and to bring about joint action. We then go on to review the functions of the shadow system, demonstrating that it is a highly complex system that produces patterns of behaviour which are both beneficial and harmful. Finally some tentative suggestions are made on how managers might intervene in the shadow system to try to increase the outcomes that are beneficial and reduce those that are not.

WHAT MANAGERS DO FAR FROM CERTAINTY AND AGREEMENT

The model of an organisational decision-making and control system depicted in *Figure 11.10* in the last chapter is a web of nonlinear feedback loops that will operate in both damping and amplifying modes. When faced with clear, familiar tasks, leaders are likely to exert their authority and followers are likely to comply. In these conditions, the organisational feedback system will be close to stable equilibrium and operate in a negative feedback mode. The system will, in effect, be dominated by the rational loop at the centre of *Figure 11.10* and the other loops will fade into the background.

There are other conditions in which the organisational feedback system depicted in *Figure 11.10* will operate in an amplifying way leading to explosively unstable equi-

441

librium. For example, confronted by the need to perform tasks that are ambiguous with outcomes that are uncertain, leaders may exert their power in the form of force and followers may rebel. The result is a highly unstable revolution. Again, leaders may not know what to do and in the ensuing power vacuum intense rivalry amongst followers might break out. The result is likely to be highly unstable conflict.

There are, however, other conditions in which the feedback control system depicted in *Figure 11.10* will operate in an alternately damping and amplifying manner to produce bounded instability. This is controlled behaviour because it is coherent and has a pattern that we can recognise when we encounter it even if it is irregular and we cannot predict its specific form. Control in this state of bounded instability takes on a self-organising form just as it does in the nonlinear feedback systems to be found in nature.

You will recall from Chapter 9, how nonlinear feedback systems amplify small changes to break the symmetry of existing patterns of behaviour and then self-organise to form new patterns. This process of symmetry-breaking and spontaneous self-organisation can be observed in organisations too. It takes the form of a rhythm to, a number of phases in, the behaviour of managers as they handle open-ended issues. These phases are depicted in *Figure 12.1* and briefly summarised below (*Stacey, 1991 & 1992*).

FIGURE 12.1

Political and learning processes: self-organising control

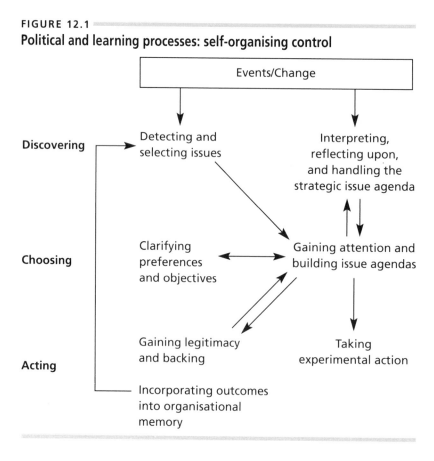

Detecting and selecting open-ended issues

Open-ended change is typically the accumulating result of many small events and actions. Since what is going on is unclear, ambiguous and confusing, with consequences that are unknowable, the key difficulty is that of identifying what the real issues, problems and opportunities are. The challenge is to find an appropriate and creative aspiration or objective. In these circumstances an organisation has no alternative but to rely on the initiative of individuals to notice and pursue some issue, aspiration or challenge. In order to do this, those individuals have to rely on their experience-based intuition and ability to detect analogies between one set of ambiguous circumstances and another. This activity on the part of an individual is spontaneous and self-organising in the sense that no central authority can direct anyone to detect and select an open-ended issue for attention, simply because no-one knows what it is until someone has detected it.

Gaining attention and building issue agendas

After some individual, at some level in the hierarchy, has detected some potential issue, that individual begins to push for organisational attention to be paid to that issue. A complex process of building special interest groups or coalitions around an issue is required before that issue can be said to have gained organisational attention. This political activity of building support for attention to some detected issue is also clearly self-organising and spontaneous in the sense that it is informal and not part of the normal rules and procedures. No-one is centrally organising the factions and coalitions that form around detected issues. Once an issue has gained sufficient support, in the sense that it is being discussed by those with sufficient power to do something about it, then that issue becomes part of the organisation's strategic issue agenda. The agenda is a list of issues, aspirations and challenges that key groups of managers are attending to and it is always changing in a manner that reflects what is being detected, how the pattern of political interplay is developing, and what managers are learning. Once issues arrive on the agenda, some are attended to while others drop off the list without ever being acted upon, yet others are successfully enacted, and still others lead to actions that fail. There is no overall framework or grand design to which managers can refer before they decide how to tackle any issue on this agenda because they are unique and cannot be foreseen. Instead, managers discover what objectives they should pursue and what actions might work through discussion with each other and with customers, suppliers and even rivals. In this sense they are learning what to do as they progress the issue. They are in effect altering old mental models, existing company and industry recipes, to come up with a new way of doing things. Thus, when managers deal with the issues on their strategic agenda they are performing a real-time learning activity. The communication that this involves is spontaneous in the sense that it is not directed by some central authority, but depends upon the personalities of the individuals involved, on the context provided by the dynamic of their interaction with each other, and by the time they have available given all the other issues requiring their attention.

Interpreting, reflecting upon, and handling the strategic issue agenda

When managers deal with the strategic issue agenda of their organisation, they are performing a vitally important destabilising function. Open-ended strategic issues, by definition, threaten existing work patterns, organisational structures and power positions. Strategic issues are about new and different ways of doing things and different things to do. One issue has to compete with other issues for attention and scarce resources. Progressing open-ended issues through discussion, conflict and dialogue changes perceptions and is an activity that activates the covert political and unconscious process loops shown in *Figure 11.10* This instability and confusion, or bounded instability, performs the function of shattering the existing order to make the new possible. In handling issues on the agenda, building support is an activity that amplifies this instability through the system. Instability breaks the existing order, making way for the new.

Clarifying preferences and objectives

Some issues on the agenda may be dealt with very quickly. Others may attract attention, continuous or periodic, for a very long time. How quickly an issue is dealt with depends upon the time required to reach enough consensus and commitment to proceed to action. It depends upon the course which the political and learning interaction takes. At some critical point, some external pressure, or some internal pressure arising from power, personality or group interaction, in effect forces a choice. The outcome on whether and how to proceed to action over the issue is unpredictable because it depends upon the context of power, personality and group dynamic. The result may or may not be some action. The point about this consensus required to proceed to action is that it is temporary, fragile and related to a specific issue. When the group of managers turns to the next issue, consensus has to be established anew. In a dynamic organisation, one dealing with an active, ever-changing issue agenda, consensus will be the exception, not the norm. It requires continuing inputs of energy and attention to sustain consensus – what scientists call a dissipative structure.

Taking experimental action and feedback

Action will usually be experimental at first, so providing a vehicle for further learning.

Gaining legitimation and backing

Building and handling strategic issue agendas proceeds largely outside the formal structures and procedures of the organisation. At various points in this largely spontaneous and self-organising process, however, the formal bodies and procedures of an organisation are required to legitimise the choices being made and to allocate resources to the exploration of, and experimentation with, issues. Although the support and interest of the formal bodies in the organisation are vital to the effective building and progressing of strategic issues, such bodies are essentially peripheral. They provide the boundaries within which the self-organising process of dealing with strategic issues occurs. As unclear open-ended issues proceed through learning and experimentation to emerge as potentially successful new strategies, the formal bodies of the organisation play a more prominent role. New strategies will emerge only if those bodies back potential success with sufficient resource to allow the new strategy to emerge.

Incorporating outcomes in organisational memory

Managers in a business come to share memories of what has worked and what has not worked in the past. In this way they build up a business philosophy for their company; they establish a company recipe and in common with other rivals they build industry recipes too. All of this is the same as developing a culture or a retained organisational memory. An organisation's memory has a powerful effect on what issues will subsequently be detected and attended to. It constitutes the frame of reference within which managers interpret what to do next – we have completed the circle and are back to individuals detecting issues. The retained memory provides a boundary around the instability of the political and learning processes through which strategic issues are handled. It is, however, a boundary that can easily become inappropriate to new circumstances. An essential part of the complex learning process required to handle strategic issues is the continual questioning of the organisation's retained memory.

An example of the process we have just considered is given in *Illustration 12.1*.

Spontaneous self-organisation produces controlled behaviour

In the paragraphs above we have described people spontaneously interacting to form a self-organising system that often amplifies their behaviour, leading to overt and covert political actions, unconscious processes, organisational defences and the questioning of shared mental models. That is, we have described the operation of a destabilising system that shatters existing structures and perspectives. It is nevertheless a system in which people sometimes spontaneously follow the phases described above to produce coherent patterns in behaviour that lead to new forms of order, given a favourable context. So, faced with open-ended situations, people in an organisation amplify small changes to form different patterns of behaviour that are irregular and unpredictable, but they are nonetheless coherent because we can recognise them when we encounter them even if we cannot predict their specific form.

The kind of self-organising behaviour described above is therefore controlled behaviour because it has a pattern and it satisfies the same general criteria for control as the planning/monitoring and ideological forms did, but in a different way:

- The first general criterion of controlled behaviour is satisfied because there is feedback connection between discovery, choice and action. It is simply that the feedback connection is a good deal more complex than it is when planning/monitoring or ideology is the form of control. The elements in the feedback loop are simply defined in a different, far more complex way – discovery involves questioning existing mental models and bringing unconscious processes to the surface; choice involves overt and covert politics; and action involves exploration.

Illustration
12.1

Amstrad

In the 1970s Alan Sugar noticed that it would be much cheaper to make plastic covers for record players by injection moulding rather than vacuum forming and this led to his first successful product. Later, he became aware that, while people liked the fashionable appearance of a hi-fi set, they did not want to assemble a number of different units. This led him to market the highly successful tower system consisting of one unit that looked like a number of different ones. After that, he perceived the needs of potential customers for personal computers. Those potential customers knew too little about computers to be able to assemble a number of different units and load software onto them. Alan Sugar turned that perception into a low-cost product that could be taken from the store, plugged in and used immediately.

So one new product idea succeeded the other over the years, but at any one time managers at Amstrad were having to deal with a great many issues. For example, in the mid-1980s there were issues to do with different computer products, sourcing components in the Far East, manufacturing and assembly, setting up distribution channels in Europe, organisational structures and control systems, and many more. Which of those issues was attended to at any one time depended heavily on the political process in the organisation – in this case on the power of Alan Sugar himself.

Action on these issues took an experimental form: for example, Amstrad first set up agents in France, Spain and Germany. These operations all developed in different ways from which Amstrad learned, finally selecting the more successful French model to redesign operations in Spain and Germany. Only after it had learned from this experience did it set up subsidiary companies in those countries.

But Amstrad did not simply settle into a fixed mould. In the 1980s Alan Sugar abandoned crucial ingredients of the ultra-entrepreneurial, small business ethos and set in train the installation of structures more appropriate for the day-to-day management of a large company. ∎

Source: Thomas, 1990

- The second general criterion for control is constraint. In the system we have just been considering, however, constraint cannot take the form of organisational intention or strongly shared ideology because intention has to be discovered and ideology questioned if issues are to be surfaced and dealt with. Instead, constraint is provided by the boundaries around the amplifying manner in which the system operates.

Control through context

The most obvious boundaries around the instability created by the political amplification of issues are the legitimate formal bodies of the organisation needed to legitimise what is going on and to allocate resources on the one hand, and the retained memory, culture or ideology that must be questioned on the other. But less obvious boundaries are even more important.

The first of these less obvious boundaries arises from the very nature of a group of people who actually pursue a learning task. In such a group, individuals discover small changes, anomalies and ambiguities. They reflect upon these and push others to attend to them, so giving rise to conflict, contradiction, contention, dialogue and exploratory action – all essentially destabilising activities. However, behaviour is constrained partly by individual differences in culture and perceptions, by disagreements preventing a single view from dominating. Behaviour is also partly constrained by the shared views that groups working together come to acquire, but constantly have to question if they are to learn. Constraint then is a consequence of the tension between the simultaneous presence of both sharing and difference. The extremes of either sharing or difference both remove the constraints and lead to uncontrolled behaviour.

The second of these less obvious boundaries, context factors or constraints arises from the very nature of political activity. People interacting politically form factions and build support through persuasion and negotiation. Their behaviour is constrained by the unequal distribution of power, by the existence of hierarchy, by the need to sustain sufficient support for the progress and enaction of issues. It is the tension inherent in an unequal distribution of power that acts as a boundary on what people can do in a political system. If power is not distributed at all but concentrated in the hands of one or two, the boundary is removed; those few can do whatever they wish and we get potentially explosive instability. If power is equally distributed, the constraint is also removed; there is no power grouping capable of restraining any individual from doing whatever that individual chooses to do and the result is once again potentially explosive behaviour. A context in which power is either concentrated or equally shared provides little control, but one in which power is both concentrated and shared – that is, unequally distributed – does provide the constraints necessary for controlled behaviour.

Note how it is uniformity that provides the constraint necessary for control in the planning/monitoring and ideological forms of control: uniform intention, uniform ideology. In the self-organising form, however, it is the tension created by difference that provides the constraint.

Top management and self-organising control

Top management exerts an influence on the learning and political form of coherent behaviour that is just as important as the influence it exerts through plans and ideologies – the area of influence is simply different. Instead of influencing through fixing intentions and establishing predetermined rules to yield an outcome, top management exerts its influence in open-ended change by operating on the boundary conditions surrounding the learning process in the organisation. In open-ended change there can be no central control over the choices made or their outcomes, but through operating on the boundary conditions, top managers determine whether learning occurs at all, how widespread that learning is, and what quality it displays. They operate on the boundary conditions (context) through the manner in which they use their power; in this way they provoke group dynamics that either help or hinder. Top managers allocate resources and so determine the time pressures learning groups face: if the pressures are too tight learning will not occur.

Note that central, shared intention is not an essential requirement for there to be controlled behaviour. We can intend explosive instability and that is not controlled. Behaviour may be chaotic, without central shared intention, and yet it is controlled. Predictability and stability are also not essential requirements for control. Explosive instability follows a perfectly predictable course and yet it is not controlled. Chaotic behaviour is unpredictable and unstable, but still controlled, simply because it is constrained and does display patterns even though they are irregular.

12.3   ENSURING JOINT ACTION

Ultimately, the purpose of every organisation is to enable its members to take some joint action together – to take organisational, or concerted, action. People will act in a concerted way only if they have expectations in common, and they are motivated and committed to action (*Brunson, 1985*). To act in concert, people must:

- expect that their individual action will be accompanied by the actions of others aimed at the same end result: these expectations are the individual cognitive requirements for concerted action;
- be motivated by having made a judgement as to whether the action and its intended end result are good or bad: such judgements are the basis of enthusiasm for action or the lack of it. This motivation is an individual emotional requirement for concerted action;
- be committed to the action in the sense that they can rely on others: this commitment is a social requirement for concerted action.

These three factors are interdependent and mutually reinforcing. Thus when a number of people in a group can rely on each other's commitment, this will reinforce individual expectations that it is worth performing the action, and this in turn will increase individual motivation. It is a strongly shared paradigm or ideology that provides the most important condition for self-reinforcing expectations, motivation, and commitment, and therefore for concerted action. This condition is met by ordinary management through the formal organisation, and such management therefore consistently produces organisational action.

However, when anomalies and uncertainties lead managers to question the current paradigm, they have to express their doubts through the social network and begin their manoeuvres in the political system – the formal organisation does not allow the questioning of the very basis upon which it is built. Furthermore, the discussions that occur in the informal organisation cannot be governed by the paradigm, since that is what is under question. The very framework that determines clear objectives and fixes the logical rules of discussion, reasoning, option generation, and evaluation is therefore suspended.

In other words, the basis for technical rationality is destroyed and it follows that, when they operate in the informal organisation, people have to use some 'irrational' way of conducting their discussions, making decisions, and eventually undertaking some concerted action to change the existing paradigm and the bureaucracy upon which it is built.

The extraordinary management task of changing the paradigm is, in the first place, one of destruction and, in the second place, it is one of one group persuading others to believe in a replacement paradigm. In other words, the task is first one of generating a variety of perspectives and beliefs, and in the second place the task is to reduce that variety enough to allow a new direction in organisational action to be taken. The rational decision-making process cannot help in the destruction phase because rationality is built on that which is being destroyed. Rationality also cannot help in the second phase, the reducing of variety to the point where action is possible, because of the effect it has on expectations, motivation and commitment (*Brunson, 1989*). Consider why this is so.

An essential part of the technically rational decision-making process is that of generating as many different options for action as possible for rational evaluation. When this is done in conditions where people are not sharing the same ideology, the variety of options simply increases subjective feelings of uncertainty and confusion. That leads to conflict. Confused, uncertain, conflicting people are not motivated to act because:

- they quite rightly do not expect that others are likely to join them in action;
- since they are conflicting they, by definition, do not feel jointly committed to action;
- individual motivation to act is consequently greatly lowered.

The more technically rational people try to be in these circumstances, the less likely they are to take action. A divide therefore opens up between decision rationality and action rationality.

What kind of decision process is likely to promote concerted action in these circumstances? It will be one in which a particular group, the dominating group, has already made a choice by some means – probably intuitive and political – and then takes steps to reduce uncertainty and conflict in the wider group as part of persuading that wider group to adopt its choice.

The irrational decision process

This can be done, first, by avoiding the formulation of clear objectives in advance since people will simply disagree with whatever objectives are formulated. Indeed, given the uncertain conditions, the dominating group may not be sure what the objectives should be; it may simply have judged that some attributes of the action it is proposing are, in some sense, good. Objectives can be formulated later when it is clearer what they should be. Instead of trying to motivate by setting objectives, the dominant group focuses on bargaining and compromise about proposed actions – one group commits to action now in return for a favour later (*Lindblom, 1959*). The choice made by the dominant group is not a statement of preference but a commitment to action.

Second, the dominant group will be more persuasive if it reduces the number of options presented for consideration. The technique is not to generate as many options as possible for rational evaluation because this simply sows confusion, but to present the favoured action option together with one alternative. Only the advantages of the favoured option will be mentioned, with perhaps a few disadvantages that are obviously most unlikely to occur. The alternative option will be one that is quite clearly inferior or impossible to carry out and its presentation is weighed down with disadvantages.

Third, action is more likely to follow, when the paradigm is under attack, if managers suppress disturbing information, create illusions of unanimity, and take big risks. If action is the required outcome, these steps are not stupid, as they may seem to be from a technically rational decision point of view, but realistic ways of securing organisational action.

What has been described above is a decision process that is only apparently concerned with making a choice but is really about persuading others to accept a new paradigm embodied in the action being preached – the decision process follows the choice and is being used as propaganda. The irrational decision process maintains the pretence of being rational; it goes through the same steps of setting out objectives and options, but these are 'cooked' or 'fixed', and because of this it gives surface legitimacy to what is going on. It allows all the participants to pretend that they have not abandoned rationality. *Illustration 12.2* gives an example of the irrational decision process and the positive role it plays in generating concerted action.

According to the above analysis, attempts to make rational decisions when the paradigm is under question will simply destroy the organisation's ability to take concerted action. Here decision rationality would lead to action irrationality. Furthermore, when managers use the rational decision-making process in conditions of uncertainty, they try to reduce the risks to their organisation and to themselves by a number of means:

- refraining from action altogether;
- looking for less risky actions;
- breaking the action down into smaller steps;
- trying to forecast the outcome and then later arguing that none could have foreseen what happened;
- trying to reduce their stake in the action by diluting personal responsibility in a group decision or by involving other groups and organisations in the action.

All these responses reduce the likelihood of concerted action. Higher commitment to action flows from irrational decision processes.

It is only once the process of conversion to a new paradigm has been accomplished that technical rational decision-making which produces concerted action will once again be possible.

Note the role that technical rationality plays in the informal organisation: it is a front used to reduce embarrassment by covering up what is really going on; it is a defence against anxiety because it preserves fantasies of control and rationality that cover up the extent of the uncertainty faced.

Defective learning

There is an alternative to this analysis and its conclusion that irrationality is required to generate concerted action. According to that alternative analysis, the irrational processes just described are the consequences of an inappropriate learning model (*Argyris & Schon, 1978*). The argument here is that because the participants in the process are employing the win/lose unilateral control learning model in conditions of uncertainty, they end up playing games and using organisational defence routines. Thus the whole pretence of using a rational decision process, while actually employing an irrational one and then never discussing this, is a typical defence routine. The result will be an inferior choice because it is never exposed to wide-ranging questioning. The prescription then is not to accept decision irrationality for the sake of action rationality, but to educate people into using a more appropriate learning model in which they first question the choices and then commit to action. Those who propose the improved learning route admit, however, that this is a difficult task and that people keep slipping back into the old learning model (*Argyris, 1990*). Whatever we prescribe, we quite clearly have to base it on an explanation that is built on irrational, defective learning behaviour.

You can see from this that it is possible to understand the processes of extraordinary management in the shadow system of an organisation from many different perspectives, each of which may be 'true' at some point in time in some context. So extraordinary management may be

- a constructive process in which people engage in complex learning to produce creative new outcomes, albeit a process that is necessarily also anxiety provoking and destructive;
- a defensive process in which people engage in covert politics and unconscious processes to avoid complex learning and creativity. In this way they protect themselves from anxiety but potentially trap themselves in a highly stable system that they cannot meet changing demands;
- a destructive process in which people undermine the legitimate system without any constructive outcome, intentionally or unintentionally;
- a hypocritical process in which people pretend they are doing one thing while they are actually doing another in the interests of securing joint action;
- an ethical process in which people seek to subvert and destroy an oppressive legitimate system;
- a completely unethical, dishonest process in which people engage in bribery and corruption to subvert the legitimate system to their own ends.

The role that the shadow system plays in the evolution of human systems depends, then, on how we use those shadow systems.

12.4   THE FUNCTIONS PERFORMED BY THE SHADOW SYSTEM

We have seen, then, that we can think of an organisation's shadow system as a political system, a learning community of practice, a shifting set of small groups employing un-conscious processes and fantasies, an irrational decision-making process, and a communication and social network. We will see later how people develop roles in the shadow system's informal networks that are very different to the ones they play in the legitimate systems of their organisation, and we will also see how the nature of leadership changes when it is exercised in the shadow system. The result is a many-faceted self-organising system that coexists with the legitimate system, but that is far more flexible and therefore much more capable of dealing with the unexpected and the unknowable.

Illustration
12.2

The Swedish Steel Corporation

In 1975 there were three steel corporations in Sweden. One was the State-owned NJA situated at Luleå, the others were privately owned, one situated at Oxelösund and the other at Borlänge. At that time, the steel industry was in deep recession, profits had fallen for all, and NJA and Oxelösund were making losses. A government commission was set up to investigate whether the steel industry could be restructured and if so how. Its report was published in 1977 and its proposals were based on an analysis of the ways in which profitability could be achieved, irrespective of the employment consequences, in an industry that had a production capacity double what the market could bear. The principal proposal was to concentrate crude steel production at Luleå and Oxelösund, and close down crude steel capacity at Borlänge. The commission compared this solution with the alternative of maintaining crude production at all three plants. Calculations were not presented for other alternatives.

As a result of the report, merger discussions were initiated. At this stage the unions requested and were granted representation at the negotiations and consideration of the employment effects. They hired consultants to work on other alternatives, this time to minimise unemployment. The unions at Borlänge claimed that correct calculations would show that the best alternative was to keep crude production at all plants. But in the meantime, in order to proceed with the mergers, the negotiators had to agree on the size of the future government investment and that would depend on which plants were kept open. For the purpose of this calculation, all agreed to use an option that was much the same as the commission's report, but it was stressed that this was simply a 'forecast', without practical implications, that would allow negotiations to proceed.

The result was the creation of the Swedish Steel Corporation, partly State and partly privately owned, to be run on a commercial basis. It was agreed that the structure of the company was to be decided by negotiation between management and unions.

In January 1978 unions and management met, together with an army of experts, in negotiations that were to last for five months. The first task was to estimate the future volume of sales and then the size and distribution of production. The primary alternative was the 'forecast' used as an illustration case in the merger negotiations. The unions put forward an alternative that retained all sites – the 'reference' alternative. Seven variants of the forecast were proposed but eventually dropped. Most of the discussion concentrated on ways of calculating costs and prices. The two main alternatives were subjected to discounted cash flow calculations (see section on financial acceptability in Chapter 5) and at first there was no significant difference between them. Later calculations showed the 'forecast' alternative to be slightly better. The advocates of the 'forecast' now shifted ground and pointed out that Borlänge was an old plant not near the coast, a location essential to cut imported iron ore transport costs. This had been known all along and required no calculation. Calculations proceeded, while management and government supported the 'forecast' and unions the 'reference' alternative. Then the unions met for two days and agreed to the 'forecast' alternative provided that the employment situation was not allowed to deteriorate (but remember that the 'forecast' is based on the closure of Borlänge). Consultants were studying the effects of the proposals on employment but their findings were ignored.

After the decision had been made it was clear that the decision-makers did not agree on its interpretation. Unions at Borlänge mounted a strike and a new commission was appointed, but eventually the original 'forecast' alternative was implemented.

Thus, the proposal made in 1977 was eventually implemented. The decision-making process was presented throughout as the means of making the choice. The choice, however, had already been made, informally out of the gaze of the formal organisation. The 'decision' process was really a way of gradually persuading people to accept the decision, while allowing action to proceed. The process was decision irrational but action rational. ■

Source: Brunson (1985)

Beneficial functions

Our discussion so far indicates that an informal organisation performs some functions that are beneficial to both the organisation and its members:

- It enables more rapid responses to unforeseen changes than a formal organisation because it is inherently flexible.
- It generates change and new knowledge. It is the vehicle for political interaction and organisational learning out of which innovation and new strategic direction may emerge.
- It provides important psychological and social relief to individuals who have to operate in a bureaucratic system or have to confront great ambiguity and uncertainty. The consequence is that members are more motivated and psychologically able to operate effectively.

Harmful functions?

An informal organisation, however, also functions in ways that are quite clearly harmful to both members and the organisation as a whole; or are harmful to the organisation, in appearance at least, but are perhaps needed by the members of the organisation in some way; or that are quite difficult to draw immediate conclusions about. These judgements about the possible harmfulness of informal organisations are based on observing how people use informal groups to:

- achieve their own personal aims in conflict with the good of their organisation;
- practise hypocrisy in that they claim to be taking decisions in a rational manner in order to gain the support of, say, shareholders and bankers, when in fact they are taking decisions and acting on 'irrational' beliefs;
- operate organisational defence routines, to defend themselves and protect their colleagues in embarrassing and anxiety-laden situations;

● build symbols, practise rituals, develop ideologies, generate rumours, myths, dreams, visions, conscious and unconscious fantasies and other forms of irrational belief that then determines what they do; unstructured small groups with unstructured tasks, the inevitable consequence of vague and ambiguous strategic issues, have been shown to be prolific generators of collective fantasy.

The dominant paradigm of the stable organisation predisposes us to reach the conclusion that all of the above factors are bad for an organisation and must be removed, or at least damped down if that organisation is to be successful. This is the dominant impression one is left with after reading most textbooks on strategic management, organisational behaviour and change management. A more careful review of the nature of the informal organisation, however, makes it clear that we cannot reach such easy judgements. To be sure, there are circumstances where most would agree that it is harmful to satisfy self-interests, practise hypocrisy, operate defence routines, and fabricate fantasies. But mostly it is not at all clear that this is the case.

We have seen, for example, that the practice of organisational hypocrisy may be required in the interests of concerted action. Such hypocrisy may also be required to deal with the inconsistent requirements of the environment. For example, when an organisation finds it impossible to predict events for more than about a year ahead, it clearly cannot prepare meaningful five-year plans. If its bankers nevertheless demand such plans to justify their financial support, then it is necessary to prepare fantasy plans to satisfy this demand. The decisions and actions, however, must be taken on some basis other than the rational to satisfy the requirements of unpredictable reality. Of course, the bankers will not believe the plans any more than the organisation's managers really do, but they will later be able to use them to demonstrate the rational basis of their lending decisions should anything go wrong. Those to whom they have to justify their decisions will also know that the plans are meaningless, but they will have some supposedly rational basis for judging what the bankers have done.

So, widespread hypocrisy of this kind can oil the wheels of action. We can no longer be so sure, therefore, that we need to banish it. Indeed as far as the managers of any single enterprise are concerned, they would be most unwise to try unilaterally to banish hypocrisy for reasons that are quite obvious.

Much the same point can be made about the pursuit of self-interest and the practice of organisational defence routines. A manager who really adopts a posture of altruism, avoids engaging in defence routines, and honestly exposes the routines others are engaged in will soon become an ineffective outcast. Changing patterns of behaviour is far more complex than simply recognising and confronting them.

Fantasy in organisations

Even the most 'hard-nosed' business people engage in fantasy activity: sometimes this is clearly an obstacle to effective management, but at other times it is a benefit. Mostly, however, fantasies have a paradoxical mixture of beneficial and harmful consequences. Consider some fantasy activities that have harmful aspects because they promote self-deception, but on the other hand may encourage and motivate people in situations that might otherwise be so depressing as to remove the incentive to act.

One frequent fantasy is the utopian one. When managers and their financial advisers prepare five-year projections of sales and profits, they generally make reasonable estimates for the next year or so, but almost always show massive improvements occurring after year three – the well-known 'hockey stick effect'. Also, it is not at all uncommon to hear managers describing their organisation's strengths and weaknesses, or the opportunities open to them, in terms that an uninvolved observer can see are grossly over-optimistic. Managers frequently have exaggerated ideas of the importance and standing of their organisation – they state that they are the best and the strongest without ever looking at any data to see if this is so.

Again, managers may blow out of all proportion some perceived threat presented by some other department and come to see that department as an enemy. On some occasions managers may develop messianic fantasies around some new chief executive appointed at a time of crisis. Chief executives can quite easily develop fantasies of deification with which their subordinates collude. Subordinates use terms such as the 'inner sanctum' to describe the executive suite consisting of a room for the secretary, leading to a room for the personal assistant, leading finally to a 'holy-of-holies' that contains the chief executive.

Fantasies come to be expressed in rituals such as the annual sales meeting in which people whip each other up to create a myth of invincibility in the marketplace. Or managers may go away for action-packed weekends to develop myths about their cohesiveness and fantasies about how good a team they are.

Why do we all engage in these activities and are they necessarily as dysfunctional as at first they sound? Fantasy activity in groups is thought to derive from:

- Individual intrapsychic and psychological sources: on this explanation, the social structure and fantasy activities of a group flow from what happens within individual psyches and how they are projected into group life.
- Group-based and sociological factors: here it is the social system that determines individual functioning and the social structure and fantasy activities of the group take the forms they do because they are acceptable to the group and fulfil some group need at the time.

Some writers adopt the psychoanalytic approach and others adopt the sociological approach. It would be more realistic, however, to see fantasy activity in a group as the consequence of a feedback loop that connects the intrapsychic with the social. We develop fantasies when we come together in a group for reasons that have to do with both individual psychological needs and social needs that operate in a circular self-reinforcing way. The consequence is that unpredictable variety in specific behaviour that nevertheless falls into recognisable categories – chaos.

From the psychoanalytic perspective, fantasy activity is usually seen as a defence against anxiety (see the section on Bion's models). However, some psychologists have stressed the additional role of fantasy activity in integrating people into a group and in the ability of the group to cope with the world it operates in (*Dunphy, 1968*). It has been argued that fantasy activity is an alternative form of planning and imaginative thought that often plays an important part in problem solving just as dreams and daydreams are known to do (*Singer, 1966*). Others have described group fantasies as an intermediate area between inner and outer reality, an area of illusion on the way from hallucination and delusion to reality, that is vital for creativity (*Gibbard, Hartman &*

Mann, 1974). But myths and fantasies are irrational and may easily become highly unrealistic, thus serving as a hindrance to the tasks of a group.

The conclusion, then, is that the capability for creativity and flexibility provided by an organisation's shadow system is inextricably wound up with its function as a vehicle for self-interest, hypocrisy, defence routine and fantasy. Trying to remove these manifestations would destroy the creativity and flexibility. Instead, it is necessary to create an emotional atmosphere in which self-interest, defence and fantasy activity might turn out to be primarily beneficial rather than harmful. Note that all we can hope for is that network activity might turn out to be primarily beneficial. In other words, there can be no prior guarantee that it will, nor is there any way of separating what we might regard as the harmful from the beneficial. The informal organisation is inherently unstable and this instability is the reason for its creative potential: it is the tension created by the paradoxical nature of informal networks of small groups that drives organisational creativity.

We turn now to the manner in which the informal organisation is creative and then to how it contains the instability that is so essential a part of that creativity.

Creating new knowledge

The practice of ordinary management through the instruments of hierarchy, bureaucracy and Management Information and Control Systems is all about the processing of information, primarily quantitative information. The practice of extraordinary management, on the other hand, is above all else concerned with the creation of new knowledge, largely of a qualitative kind – it is only through new knowledge that an organisation can innovate and develop new strategic directions. The informal organisation is the instrument managers have to use if they wish to create new knowledge. We can see why this must be so if we consider the nature of new knowledge, succinctly set out in an article by *Ikujiro Nonaka (1991)*.

New knowledge is created when the tacit is made explicit and crystallised into an innovation, that is, a re-creation of some aspect of the world according to some new insight or ideal. New knowledge comes from tapping the tacit, subjective insights, intuitions and hunches of individuals and making them available for testing and use by the organisation as a whole.

Key Concept 12.1

Tacit knowledge

Tacit knowledge is personal and hard to formalise. It is rooted in action and shows itself as skill, or know-how. In addition to technical skills, tacit knowledge lies in the mental models, beliefs and perspectives ingrained in the way people understand their world and act in it (see Chapter 3.) Tacit knowledge is below the level of awareness and is therefore very difficult to communicate. The nature of explicit knowledge, however, is easy to understand: it is the formal and systematic knowledge that we express and communicate clearly, for example product specifications or computer programs.

Tapping tacit knowledge

Nonaka gives an example of how tacit knowledge is tapped. In 1985, product developers at Matsushita could not perfect the kneading action of the home bread-baking machine they were developing. After much unhelpful analysis, including comparison of x-rays of dough kneaded by the machine and dough kneaded by professionals, one member of the team proposed a creative approach. She proposed using a top professional baker as a model, so she trained with a top baker to acquire his kneading technique and after a year of trial and error she was able to help her colleagues reproduce a mechanical kneading action that mimicked that of the professional. This example describes a movement between different kinds of knowledge, the tacit and the explicit:

- tacit to tacit as the product developer acquires the skill of the professional baker through observation, copying and practising, so internalising it and learning;
- tacit to explicit as the product developer articulates the foundations of her newly acquired tacit knowledge to her colleagues;
- explicit to tacit as the colleagues internalise the knowledge made explicit by the product developer and use it to alter their own tacit knowledge or mental models – in other words, they learn;
- explicit to explicit as the newly formulated product specifications are communicated to the production department and embodied in working models and final production processes.

Innovation then flows from a form of learning, that is, new knowledge creation, that in turn flows from moving knowledge between one type and another.

New knowledge starts with an individual and its production cannot be centrally designed because no-one can know what will be produced until it is produced. Tacit knowledge has to travel from one person to another, also in a way that cannot be centrally intended because no-one knows what is to travel, or to whom, until it has travelled. New knowledge can therefore only be created when individuals self-organise into the unstructured small groups that make up the informal networks.

A key difficulty in the creation of new knowledge is that of bringing tacit knowledge to the surface of individual awareness, conveying tacit knowledge from one person to another, and finally making it explicit. This is so difficult because it requires expressing the inexpressible and this needs figurative rather than literal language.

Metaphors Metaphors have to be used to link contradictions to each other and express paradoxes. It is when we juxtapose seemingly illogical and contradictory things that we are stimulated to look for multiple meanings, to call upon our tacit knowledge, and so develop new insights. The ambiguity of metaphors provokes and challenges us to define them more clearly. Metaphors are formulated through intuition, a form of tacit reasoning that links images that may seem remote from each other. Nonaka describes how, in 1978, top management at Honda inaugurated the development of a new car concept with the slogan 'Let's gamble', indicating the need for a completely new approach. The development team expressed what they should do to deal with this metaphor in the form of another slogan: 'Theory of Automobile Evolution' (a contradictory idea of a car as both a machine and an organism). This posed the question: if a car was like an organism how would it evolve? The designers discussed what this might mean and produced another slogan: 'Man–maximum, Machine–minimum'. This conveyed the idea that the car should focus on comfort in an urban environment. The idea of evolution prompted the designers to think of the car as a sphere, a car that was 'short' and 'tall'. This gave birth to the idea of a 'Tall Boy' car, eventually called the Honda City.

Analogy Once metaphors have provoked new ideas, analogies between one thing and another can then be used to find some resolution (perhaps only temporary) of the contradictions that have provoked us into thinking new things. Analogy is a more structured process of reconciling opposites and making distinctions, clarifying how the opposing ideas are actually alike or not alike. To illustrate this, Nonaka recounts the story of Canon's development of the mini-copier. To ensure reliability, the developers proposed to make the copier drum disposable – the drum accounted for 90 per cent of maintenance problems. Team members were discussing, over a beer, the problem of how to make the drum easily and cheaply, when the team leader held up his beer can and asked how much it cost to make one. This led the team to examine the process of making cans to see if it could be applied to the manufacture of photocopier drums. The result was lightweight aluminium copier drums.

Models Finally, models are used actually to resolve the contradiction and crystallise the new knowledge: for example, a prototype kneading machine, or a prototype small photocopier.

As purported new knowledge is dispersed through a group and an organisation, it must be tested – that means that there must be discussion, dialogue and disagreement. The dispersion of purported new knowledge threatens people's existing perceptions and positions, raising anxiety levels and perhaps provoking strange groups dynamics. Insecurity, anxiety, conflict and confusion must be accepted as inevitable factors in the process of new knowledge creation; they can be removed only by stamping out the creation of new knowledge. It is the function of the informal organisation to use this chaos to generate new perspectives, learn, destroy existing paradigms and lead to the new. But it is also the role of the informal organisation to contain the instability, to keep it bounded, for without this we get utter confusion, not chaos – remember chaos is bounded instability.

Providing the boundaries around instability

For the creation of new knowledge, top managers must rely upon the development of a shadow system and accept the consequent instability. Indeed, they must add to that instability by challenging and provoking people, so destroying belief systems. They must also intervene in order to affect the boundaries around the self-organising processes and consequent instability that produce unpredictable new strategic direction.

While no-one can control the shadow network system, managers can affect the boundaries around that system, boundaries which affect the formation, activity levels and degree of stability of the networks (*Stacey, 1992*). It is possible for managers to intervene in such a way as to tighten the boundaries; they may become so tight that networks become relatively inactive and thus stable, or active in a covert way and thus unstable. Or it is possible to intervene so as to loosen the boundaries so much that networks become hyperactive and produce organisational anarchy. Yet other interventions can produce states of chaos in which instability is constrained and organisations can function creatively. What are these interventions and boundaries? The boundaries are provided on the one hand by hierarchical structure and the distribution of power, and on the other hand by organisational culture. Let us consider the sense in which each of these constitutes a boundary around self-organising processes and instability.

Hierarchy and power

The instability of the network organisation is constrained, first, because networks exist in contradiction and tension with the hierarchy and, second, because of the way networks operate. The manner in which network systems are constrained by the hierarchy is obvious: hierarchical authority confers important advantages to particular players in the network system and choices emerging from network operation have to be legitimised by those with hierarchical authority. However, the network system is a political one where power derives only partly from authority; influence derived from others' judgements of one's ability to contribute is just as important. Such a system produces sequences of behaviour and choice that are constrained by the need to convince, persuade and maintain political support.

The boundary is thus provided by the fact that different people have different levels of power, but none is too powerful. Wild swings in behaviour and choice are not produced unless the boundaries around this political activity, that is, the need to obtain and sustain support, are either too tight or too loose. That tightness and looseness will be determined by the manner in which managers, especially those at the top, intervene to use their power. The choice for managers lies in when to use their authority derived from hierarchy, when to rely instead on their influence, and when to refrain from exerting their power at all. If managers always apply their authority no matter what the situation, they in effect intervene in the network system to establish very tight boundaries. They ensure a political system in which people are either dependent and submissive, or rebellious; that is, the self-organising networks are either largely dormant or operating in a covert manner. Perhaps surprisingly, the charismatic leader tends to have much the same effect. The followers of charismatic leaders are also dependent, willingly surrendering their critical faculties in the utopian hope that the leader will produce what is required. Such an emotional climate does not encourage the active operation of networks. Even more harmful, however, is that it greatly reduces the need to work at sustaining political support. The result is that it is much easier for top managers to pursue either haphazard sequences of decisions or to go off in one direction to disaster.

If, instead of a few at the top using their authority all the time, we have managers frequently using only their influence, or even making space for those lower down to take the initiative, then we have a different kind of boundary condition, a different context for the operation of the networks.

Culture and learning capability

Next, consider how conflicting cultures constitute a boundary around network operations and thus constrain instability. When managers explore open-ended issues in groups, they are in fact learning. Through this learning they discover how to frame issues and what to do about them. If they all share the same culture they will all reach much the same conclusions about how the issue should be framed and what should be done about it. If this consensus is wrong, as it often will be in a rapidly changing environment, then the whole group will pursue a given sequence of decisions for a long time before they realise their error. If, however, they all do not share the same culture, they will approach the issue from different perspectives and frame it in different ways. The conflict that this generates will prevent the group from pursuing one line of reasoning for lengthy periods. This constraint provides a boundary around learning and decision-making.

If on the other hand a group of people trying to learn together share almost nothing in cultural terms, they will do little but conflict. However, strong sharing and the failure to share culture at all both have the effect of creating boundaries that are too tight or too loose; that is, a context that is inappropriate to complex learning. Weakly shared, multiple cultures, on the other hand, both generate instability and provide a boundary around that instability. The boundary is provided by the need to convince and persuade others to follow a line of reasoning. There is a boundary when a group acts as a learning group and that happens when it is not swept along by a strongly shared emotional atmosphere, or shared culture, of fighting, fleeing from the issues, depending heavily on leaders, or indulging in unrealistic utopian fantasies. An effective learning group has its own inbuilt limits to instability and the more effective the people constituting the group are at complex learning the more they will be able to contain the instability their learning itself inevitably generates.

12.5   INTERVENING IN THE SHADOW SYSTEM

Mainstream prescriptions on organisational success largely ignore the shadow system of organisation and many practitioners, as we have seen, cover up its use with a 'mock' bureaucracy. Those who have recognised the major part that the shadow system plays in successful organisational development, and in obstructing all change, seem to have adopted one of two approaches:

- installing the flexible aspects of the shadow system in place of the rigid aspect of the legitimate one;
- creating an atmosphere in which the shadow systems can function and then participating in that functioning.

Installing flexibility

The most frequent prescriptions flowing from a recognition of the importance of the informal organisation have been about building the flexibility of networks into the formal organisation. What is envisaged is:

- first, the removal of the demotivating, frustrating and ossifying aspects of hierarchy, bureaucracy and Management Information and Control Systems; and
- second, the installation of approaches that motivate and increase flexibility.

Thus, the earliest response to the deficiencies of scientific management and its bureaucracy was the 'human relations' movement (*Mayo, 1945*) that sought to empower people, enrich jobs, and create more democratic, autonomous work groups (referred to in Chapter 4). Job enlargement schemes have sought to reduce the demotivating effects of extreme specialisation by rotating people between tasks and expanding the number of operations any one worker performs. These ideas were developed into those of job enrichment in which opportunities are designed into the work for achievement, recognition, responsibility and advancement. The idea is to design jobs that give people higher degrees of responsibility for their own work. A natural extension of this idea is that of an autonomous team of workers that jointly take responsibility for the effective design of their own tasks. Here the group manages itself to achieve targets set for it.

These ideas were extended to an organisation-wide level by *Burns & Stalker (1961)* who distinguished between mechanistic (bureaucratic) organisations and organic (flexible network-type organisations) and prescribed the former for stable environments and the latter for volatile ones. Since dependence is a major cause of alienation, some (for example, *Argyris 1957*) saw participation in decision-making, based on trust between superiors and subordinates, as one way of improving organisations. More recently, Ouchi has developed the idea of the 'theory Z organisation' which largely replaces control by rules with cohesion brought about through socialisation, that is sharing the same beliefs (*Ouchi, 1981*). This is the idea of an organisation as a clan rather than a bureaucracy. All of these ideas have found expression in the prescriptions of popular writers such as *Tom Peters (1982,1985)* and *Rosabeth Moss Kanter (1985, 1989)*.

Over the past decade there has been growing concern about the ability of rigid organisational hiererachies to cope with increasingly complex and turbulent business conditions. That concern has led to more and more top management interest in installing 'flexible organisational structures' and mounting 'culture change' programmes to empower people throughout an organisation. The aim of both the restructuring and the culture change is the same: to free employees and those below the top in the management hierarchy from instructions and controls, and allow them to take decisions themselves. It is believed that this approach will make organisations more responsive to the marketplace, encourage people to be more innovative, reduce administration costs by cutting out layers of management, and improve collaboration by making it easier for people to communicate horizontally from one business function or unit to another.

The mainline response to the drawbacks of the bureaucratic form of control has therefore been to try to replace it with some other kind of structure, that is, replacing a structure of hierarchy with a structure of belief. More recently this idea of replicating some of the aspects of the network organisation into the formal one has been carried further to the point of a direct replication. Here it is proposed that Chief Executives set up teams of senior managers with the task of acting like a network (*Charan, 1991*). *Mueller (1986)* too talks about designing the networks by deciding on the purpose to be achieved, preparing an inventory of networking skills, and so on. What is being sought then is a solution to, a resolution of, the paradox of freedom and control. The solutions are reflections of the dominant paradigm, in that they seek to establish cohesion and teamwork and so avoid conflict.

However, the attempt to install and institutionalise the informal runs the serious risk of damaging both the bureaucracy and the self-organising networks:

- Flexible structures and empowered people intentionally weaken the hierarchy and thereby destroy the short-term control system.
- The flexible organisation seeks to resolve the paradox of flexibility and control by choosing a balance that favours flexibility, but flexibility by design so as to reduce the tension. It is this very tension, however, that provides the creative drive of the informal organisation.

In the flexible organisation concept, therefore, managers face the choice of either tight short-term control or flexibility through what might be called 'self-managing teams' (dispersed power, widespread participation, wide spans of control, supportive supervision) and they make a choice that favours the latter. In the approach we have been following in this book, successful managers choose both strong hierarchies for short-term control and self-organising processes of political interaction and learning out of which new strategic direction may emerge.

A flexible organisation, then, consists of a particular constellation of self-managing teams that are a permanent part of a centrally installed structure. Self-managing teams have formal leaders, either appointed or elected, who have formally agreed, permanent roles defined as supportive rather than controlling. Self-managing teams also consist of permanent members formally appointed to the team with roles defined by loose job descriptions and rights to make suggestions and participate in what is probably meant to be democratic decision-making. What decisions they are to participate in, and how, is formally established when their team is set up. The climate the team is to operate in, is one that is set by the shared vision and values, and by the financial controls. That climate is intended to be one of stability with a state of consensus as the norm – the 'tight' property. It is also intended to be a climate of freedom – the 'loose' property.

Flexibility and short-term control

When one considers what is necessary for the operation of an effective planning/monitoring control system, however, it becomes dear that 'loose–tight' control is not a paradox, but a logical inconsistency. The essence of tight planning/monitoring control is the clear allocation of responsibility for carrying out predetermined tasks having reasonably predictable results to which rewards are tied. We cannot allocate clear responsibility for predetermined tasks unless those tasks are clearly defined. Loose role and job definitions accompanied by unclear hierarchies and organisational structures are completely incompatible with tight planning/monitoring control. Such control is essentially management by rules and manuals. Tearing them up simply destroys the system. The essence of this form of control is frequent and regular formal review and reporting. The operation of an effective short interval control system therefore requires managers to collect and present information, to attend review meetings, and promptly carry out corrective action. If stripping out layers of middle managers is carried too far, it will damage the ability to carry out tight short-interval control.

Widespread participation in decision-making and the dispersal of power to allocate resources are also incompatible with tight planning/monitoring control. The whole system is essentially a top-down one in which top management sets targets, after some negotiation with those lower down, and retains the power to allocate resources. It is through power to allocate resources that the top maintains short-term control and stability. Furthermore, the point of distributing power to allocate resources is to empower people to take action to deal with turbulent and complex environments; in other words, with events that have not been foreseen, whereas the essence of planning/monitoring control is to delegate power to use resources in predictable circumstances for predetermined purposes only. Allocating power to use resources in unforeseen circumstances would undermine the whole system.

Flexible structures and tight planning/monitoring control are thus completely incompatible and the choice is an either/or one. Either you have clear hierarchies with clear job definitions and power increasing markedly as you move up the hierarchy, or you have much diminished short-term financial control. The approach developed in this book advocates choosing quite clearly in favour of hierarchies and short-term control, thereby rejecting the idea of a comprehensive structure of loosely controlled self-managing teams.

Flexibility and strategic issues

On the face of it, widespread participation and more equally shared power should lead to more people detecting changes that occur in the environment and taking trial actions to deal with the uncertainty those changes provoke. However, as we have seen in Chapter 6, this does not guarantee that decision-making or organisational learning will improve. Dispersing power can lead to 'garbage can' decision-making and since almost everyone uses a mental model that blocks double-loop learning, opening up participation in the learning process to larger numbers of people simply means many more people performing learning tasks ineffectively. If managers wish to improve the ability of an organisation to learn, and thus to develop emergent new strategic direction, then the first step must be that of tackling ineffective learning models at the individual and small group levels. If participation is widened before this is done, the result is likely to be the spreading of organisational defence routines and game-playing and that will harm rather than help the business.

Flexible structures and dispersed power, then, tend to lead to decision-making processes in which the sequence of choices depends primarily on chance and to the spreading of organisational defence routines and game-playing rather than learning. They thus lead to potentially explosive instability (checked only by the extent to which people share a culture and a 'vision') rather than stability or bounded instability.

Elliot Jacques (1991) makes the point that it is a delusion to believe that a company's management can be improved simply by doing psychotherapeutic work on personalities and attitudes of managers. Insight into psychodynamics and small group functioning on their own will fail to produce much change. This is because of the employment contract. Organisations do not employ groups, they employ individuals. It is individuals who have responsibility and authority. And large numbers of individuals have to be organised into hierarchies unless there is to be complete disorder. Attempts to replace hierarchy with groups will not work. Any use of informal groups has to proceed alongside clear hierarchies and effective bureaucracies and Management Information and Control Systems. Just as we cannot replace the bureaucracy with informal groups, so we cannot turn the self-organising network into a self-managing team where the hierarchy sets the goals. All we then do is set up an appendage to the hierarchy. The formal has to stay formal and the informal has to be really self-organising if they are to make their distinctive contributions to the organisation. So what, if anything, can managers do to improve the informal organisation?

Intervening rather than installing

The informal and self-organising nature of the network makes it impossible to formalise and install the fluid patterns of small groups that constitute the network and then control it and determine its outcome. As soon as we try to formalise, install and control it, we destroy it. It is possible, however, to say something about the contexts within which self-organising groups are: highly unlikely to form; likely to form and operate in a dysfunctional manner; and likely to form and operate in a helpful manner, although even then we will not be able to predict or control what they do. Our inability to predict and control the behaviour of the network, together with our ability to understand something about the impact of context on behaviour, allows us to make partial interventions only, so creating an atmosphere in which the networks might generate change.

A number of writers have set out measures that managers can take to create a context favourable to self-organisation. *Nonaka (1991)* sees senior managers managing the chaos generated by the informal organisation by articulating ideals, challenges, umbrella concepts and metaphors to guide the thinking and acting of people in the organisation. He sees it as vital for senior managers to present people with challenges that are open to many conflicting interpretations. For example, senior managers presented their people at NEC with the challenge of 'Computers and Communication' and Sharp presented people with the concept of 'Optoelectronics'. He advises senior managers to build redundancy into their organisations because the overlapping responsibilities and activities, the internal competition, encourage communication and provoke new perspectives, even if it all appears to be wasteful. He advises that people be rotated to create counter-cultures and he advises that access to information should be freed up.

Some of the key intervention steps that can be undertaken to create a context favourable to the functioning of networks as engines of enquiry and learning are listed below (*Stacey, 1992*).

1 Developing new perspectives on control

Many managers fear that piecemeal interventions in the context without much knowledge of the consequences amounts to an abdication of control. Either newly freed managers will enthusiastically undertake high volumes of inconsistent and duplicated actions that expose the business to unacceptable levels of risk; or managers exposed to the uncertainty accompanying the absence of clear organisational intention will focus excessively on the short term and avoid strategic thought and action altogether.

Establishing the conditions in which managers at different levels can create and discover emergent strategy does not necessarily amount to an invitation to people to do whatever they like, provided that there are boundary conditions. As we have seen earlier in this chapter, clear hierarchies of managers in which power is by definition unequally distributed provides an important boundary condition. Managers will then not do whatever they like because they know that they will need to build appropriate levels of support before they embark on any new direction. They will know that their proposals have to be legitimised, and resources allocated to carrying them out, according to the standard procedures in the organisation. In other words, the distribution of power and the operation of the political system of the organisation will perform control functions even where there is no prior intention or clear direction.

The first essential step toward creating a context for effective networking is the changing of the mental models of managers at the top. Without this, inappropriate forms of control will continue and they will block the emergence of effective networks.

2 Designing the use of power

The manner in which power is used has a direct impact on the dynamics of group interaction and group dynamics have a powerful effect on how managers in that group work together and what they learn. What they learn together determines the strategic choices they make and the actions they take.

If power is highly concentrated and always applied as force of authority, we get a very stable organisation in which very little complex learning occurs – the boundary conditions are too tight. The organisation can then only deal with whatever open-ended change the most powerful notice and are capable of dealing with. Strategy is the result of the intention of the top executive and, unless that executive is exceptionally talented, the organisation will fail to develop sufficiently creative new strategic directions to survive.

If power is widely distributed and hardly ever used as authority, we get conditions of organised anarchy in which there is also very little complex learning – the boundary conditions are too loose. The result is very little in the way of new strategic direction for the organisation as a whole. Instead we find fragmented individual strategies resulting from individual intentions which rarely converge because the group dynamics are those of continual conflict or avoidance.

If power is unequal, but distributed and applied in forms which alternate according to the circumstances, we find a flexible, fluctuating boundary around the political process that enables complex learning. But the important point is that establishing such a boundary does not ensure that such learning will occur or that it will produce some outcome that can be predetermined or guaranteed to be successful. The political and learning activity that may produce creative choices is spontaneous and self-organising. We cannot instruct anyone to have a creative idea in an open-ended situation. We cannot orchestrate factions and coalitions between people guaranteed to support the right idea, because when the situation is open-ended we cannot know what the right idea is. All we can do is control the boundaries within which behaviour favourable to the emergence of an innovative choice might occur. We have to leave the choice and the culture to the spontaneous self-organising ability of people in groups operating in favourable conditions.

3 Establishing self-organising groups

Top management can establish groups of key managers to operate in a spontaneous and self-organising manner. Workshops around issues or processes in general, or multi-discipline task forces set up to explore particular issues, are examples. For a team of managers to be self-organising, it has to:

- *have freedom to operate* as its members jointly choose, within the boundaries provided by their work together. This means that when they work together in this way, the normal hierarchy has to be suspended for most of the time. Members are there because of the contributions they have to make and the influence they can exert through those contributions and their own personalities. This suspension of the normal hierarchy can take place only if those on higher levels behave in a manner which indicates that they attach little importance to their position for the duration of the work of the group.
- *discover its own challenges, goals and objectives.* This means that top managers setting up such a team must avoid the temptation to write terms of reference, set objectives, or prod the group to reach some predetermined view. Top managers have to take the chance that the group will produce proposals of which they may not approve. Instead of terms of reference, targets and agendas, top management establishing a self-organising team will present it with some ambiguous challenge. There is no point in setting up such a group unless those at the top are genuinely looking for a new perspective. The ambiguous challenge may be to find a better organisational structure; or it may simply be to identify strategic issues and choices the organisation should be attending to; or it may be to produce proposals for a new product or promotional campaign. The task is to work at contradictions and anomalies.
- *have a membership drawn from a number of different functions, business units and hierarchical levels.* The purpose is to generate new perspectives and this requires new groupings of people. Middle management is a much under-utilised resource in most companies when it comes to developing new strategic directions. These managers are closer to the action and more likely to be detecting contradictions, anomalies and changes from which new strategic direction is born. By drawing people from different levels and units, we widen perspectives and overcome the inherent inflexibility of existing structures and systems.

However, beware! It is quite possible for managers to use task forces and workshops as a defence mechanism. By setting up vast numbers of task forces and action teams, facilitated by armies of consultants, all of whom produce analyses and recommendations that are never acted upon, managers can create the illusion of action to cover up a determination, perhaps unconscious, to change nothing.

4 Developing multiple cultures

New perspectives are blocked when people strongly share the same culture. There are a number of ways in which management can develop counter-cultures. The first is to rotate people between functions and business units. The motive for doing this is usually one of developing wider experience in executives. It is usually seen as a method of management development, in which a cadre of managers with the same management philosophy is built up throughout the organisation. This tendency needs to be over-come by the design of development programmes that stress the importance of cultural diversity rather than uniformity.

A more effective way of promoting counter-cultures is that practised by Canon and Honda. Here managers are hired in significant numbers, mid-way through their careers in other organisations. The intention is the explicit establishment of sizeable pockets of different cultures that conflict with the predominant culture. It is important that this should be done at different levels in the hierarchy, not confined to one or two top executives.

A third possibility is to use outsiders on some of the self-organising teams in the organisation.

5 Presenting challenges and taking risks

Active strategic issue agendas evolve out of the clash between different cultures in self-organising teams. Top management can provide this activity by setting ambigu-ous challenges. Instead of trying to set clear objectives, top management should throw out half-formed issues for others to develop. Problems without objectives should be posed intentionally to provoke emotion and conflict, leading to active search for new ways of doing things.

This activity of presenting challenges should also be a two-way one. Top execu-tives should hold themselves open to challenge from subordinates. General Electric has developed this into a regular process that it calls the 'work-out'. Here business leaders outline their views to a small group of employees drawn from all levels. The employees think about the ideas and about issues around their own jobs. They then reconvene to discuss the issues with the manager, who can accept or reject the ideas for improvement thrown up in the discussion, or can promise to think about them. If such a promise is made, the manager must report back to the group with a final deci-sion within 30 days. This process is applied rigorously across the company, from top to bottom. It is structured so that managers cannot get away with doing nothing. Independent experts act as facilitators. They sit in on the sessions, make sure man-agers do not bully those who speak their minds, and check that they are sticking to their promises. The aim is to create an atmosphere where it is acceptable to speak out, where telling the truth is rewarded, and where bosses who yell at people for speaking out are not.

Provoking challenges and holding oneself open to challenge involves taking bigger personal risks; but taking chances and enabling creative strategies to emerge are closely intertwined. This applies not only at the personal level of the manager, but at the organisational level too. Some managers react to the idea that the future is unknowable and that the setting of prior organisational intention is impossible, by concluding that the organisation must avoid taking risks as much as possible. It should stick to the business it knows best and avoid uncertain long-term investments at all costs. The reaction amounts to saying, 'if you can't manage the outcome, don't do anything'.

6 Improving group learning skills

The role of top management in the strategic learning process is an enabling and provoking one. It is necessary to create the opportunities for, and the atmosphere of openness in which, many small changes and different perspectives may be surfaced. The role of top management is to create the context and provide challenges. Creating the context means identifying and overcoming the obstacles to complex learning. These obstacles take the form of unconscious and thus unquestioned assumptions about how groups should learn together. These assumptions generate organisational defences, game playing and cover-ups. It is these that have to be surfaced and worked on. Obstacles to learning also take the form of managers focusing their concerns on their own position without perceiving how they interact within the whole system of which they are a part. Obstacles take the form of managers distancing themselves from responsibility for the way they are interacting and so blaming others or the system.

In practical terms these obstacles can be overcome only by managers in groups actually working on them. This will require a programme of frequent workshops. *Peter Senge (1990)* recounts the story of the insurance company Hanover. Here a continuing, long-term programme was instituted for managers to work on their learning models and expose their defensive routines. That company has consistently outperformed the industry averages for profitability.

7 Creating resource slack

The creative work to deal with open-ended issues takes time and management resource, and investment in this resource has an unpredictable return. For lengthy periods it is quite possible that little will emerge from a great deal of discussion and experimentation. But without this investment in what appears to be management resource slack, new strategic directions will not emerge. A vital precondition for emergent strategy is thus investment in management resource to allow it to happen. This runs counter to the requirement for short-term profit and short-term efficiency, but it is a price which has to be paid if new strategic directions are to emerge. The current fashion for cutting out layers of middle management, for reducing numbers of senior executives and loading them up with day-to-day duties, can easily be taken so far that it destroys the ability of a company to attend to open-ended issues. Executives who work 12 or 14 hour days are unlikely to have the mental resources to attend to such issues. A careful judgement therefore has to be made on the amount of management resource slack required to enable emergent strategy.

12.6 SUMMARY

This chapter has shown how managers operate when they find themselves far from certainty. They detect and select issues, they attract attention for such issues and build support for something to be done about them. This is an amplifying, destabilising political process that is intimately tied up with the questioning and undermining of existing mental models and existing vested interest. It is in fact complex learning and raises the defences, both conscious and unconscious, that we considered in the last chapter. Frequently therefore, managers may try to practise some form of organisational hypocrisy in order to ensure joint action. This runs the danger, however, of becoming dysfunctional learning. We should now be familiar with the notion that much of what goes on in the shadow system is counterproductive – it may block learning in a defensive manner, and of course it may be used for all manner of unethical purposes such as bribery and nepotism. However, the shadow system also makes a highly positive and constructive contribution to the development of an organisation. In the right conditions it is the system that managers employ to create new knowledge, the creative act that leads to innovation. It is the conditions created by uses of power and by leadership style, the amount of time and resource slack available for creative play, that will determine whether the uses the shadow system are put to are primarily harmful to organisational survival or primarily beneficial.

Further reading

Nonaka (1988), Brunson (1985, 1989), Senge (1990), Pascale (1990) and Stacey (1992) all provide useful perspectives for the reader to consider how managers might usefully intervene in the shadow system to create largely beneficial conditions for its operation.

References

Argyris, C. (1957), *Personality and Organization*, New York: Harper & Row.

Argyris, C. 1990, *Overcoming Organizational Defenses: Facilitating Organizational Learning*, Boston: Allyn & Bacon, Prentice-Hall.

Argyris, C. & Schon, D. (1978), *Organizational Learning: A Theory of Action Perspective*, Reading, Ma.: Addison-Wesley.

Brunson, N. (1985), *The Irrational Organisation*, Chichester: John Wiley.

Brunson, N. (1989), *The Organisation of Hypocrisy*, Chichester: John Wiley.

Burns, T. & Stalker, G. M. (1961), *The Management of Innovation*, London: Tavistock Publications.

Charan, R. (1991), How networks reshape organizations – for results, *Harvard Business Review*, Sept–Oct.

Dunphy, D.C. (1968), Phases, roles and myths in self analytic groups, *Journal of Applied Behavioural Science*, vol. 4, pp. 195–226.

Gibbard, G. S., Hartman, J. J. & Mann, R. D. (Eds.) (1974), *Analysis of Groups*, San Francisco: Jossey-Bass.

Jacques, E. (1991), In praise of hierarchy, *Harvard Business Review*, Jan–Feb.

Kanter, R. M. (1985), *The Change Masters: Innovation and Entrepreneurship in the American Corporation*, Englewood Cliffs, NJ: Simon & Schuster.

Kanter, R. M. (1989), *When Giants Learn to Dance: Mastering the Challenge of Strategy Management and Careers in the 1990s*, Englewood Cliffs, NJ: Simon & Schuster.

Lindblom, L. (1959), The science of muddling through, *Public Administration Review*, vol. 19, pp. 79–88.

Lindblom, L. & Norstedt, J. (1971), *The Volvo Report*, Stockholm: Swedish Employers Confederation.

Mayo, E. (1945), *The Social Problems of an Industrial Civilization*, Cambridge, Ma.: Harvard University Press.

Mueller, R.K. (1986), *Corporate Networking: Building Channels for Information and Influence*, New York: The Free Press.

Nonaka, I. (1988), Creating organizational order out of chaos: self-renewal in Japanese firms, *Californian Management Review*, Spring, pp. 57–73.

Nonaka, I. (1991), The knowledge-creating company, *Harvard Business Review*, Nov–Dec., pp. 96–104.

Ouchi, W. (1981), *Theory Z : How American Business Can Meet the Japanese Challenge*, Reading, Ma.: Addison-Wesley.

Pascale, R.T. (1990), *Managing on the Edge: How Successful Companies Use Conflict to Stay Ahead*, London: Viking Penguin.

Peters, T. J. (1985), *Thriving on Chaos*, New York: Macmillan.

Peters, T. J. & Waterman, R. H. (1982), *In Search of Excellence*, New York: Harper & Row.

Senge, P. M. (1990), *The Fifth Discipline: The Art and Practice of the Learning Organization*, New York: Doubleday.

Singer, J. L. (1966), *Daydreaming: An Introduction to the Experimental Study of Inner Experience*, New York: Random House.

Stacey, R. (1991), *The Chaos Frontier: Creative Strategic Control for Business*, Oxford: Butterworth-Heinemann.

Stacey, R. (1992), *Managing the Unknowable: The Strategic Boundaries Between Order and Chaos*, San Francisco: Jossey-Bass. Also published in the UK as *Managing Chaos*, London: Kogan Page.

Thomas, D. (1990), *Alan Sugar: The Amstrad Story*, London: Century Hutchinson.

Enigma Chemicals (A)

Enigma Chemicals is a large company producing a limited range of chemical products from three sites in the UK, mostly for the domestic market, although it does export about 20 per cent of its output. The chemicals that Enigma produces are important inputs into the production processes of a number of other major companies. Although the Enigma products are important to its customers' production processes, they do not constitute a major cost component in the final products of those customers. Furthermore, through control over a vital raw material and through various patent arrangements, Enigma occupies an almost monopoly position in the UK and has done so for many years.

Another fact about Enigma's products is also important; they are of a hazardous, environmentally threatening nature and this makes Enigma an ideal target for environmental pressure groups. The company is frequently attacked by the media, despite the fact that it has, on the whole, a rather good safety record – its policies and monitoring systems certainly place tremendous importance on these matters. However, over the past few years there have been two serious incidents of a rather dramatic nature: in one of these incidents pollutants were accidentally released into the atmosphere causing health problems for people living in the vicinity of the plant concerned; and in another serious incident pollutants leaked into a river, killing fish, birds and other wild life over an area of many miles. Periodically, there were fires in the manufacturing plants and some former employees were suing the company on the grounds that the manufacturing process had damaged their health. These incidents had created a public image that Enigma was experiencing great difficulty in changing.

The patents that afforded Enigma a near monopoly position were due to expire in ten years' time, after which Enigma could expect fierce competition to cause a dramatic decline in its sales. Over the past

few years, Enigma's managers and employees had experienced a foretaste of what this might be like: the long recession of the early 1990s had caused a significant decline in sales and for the first time in its 30-year history Enigma had been forced to reduce its work force. Although the reduction in the numbers of both managers and employees had been accomplished entirely through early retirement and voluntary redundancy, it had unsettled people at Enigma, the great majority of whom had come to believe that they had 'jobs for life'.

As part of the strategy for coping with the new commercial realities, the management reporting structure of Enigma had been reorganised. Before the reorganisation, there had been a monolithic functional structure: main Board Directors were responsible for personnel, R&D, health and safety, finance, engineering and production. The production function, by far the largest employer, was subdivided according to geographic sites, each of which was run by a General Manager to whom a number of works managers reported. These works managers were responsible for a number of plant managers; in turn responsible for supervisors, to whom foremen reported. After the reorganisation, Enigma consisted of five divisions, each responsible for its own profitability and having a wide range of its own functional activities such as personnel and engineering. The corporate level still had functional responsibilities, but in theory at least, much of the responsibility and the authority had been devolved to the divisions.

At the time of the reorganisation, the Board had also reviewed its strategic planning process and decided to devolve much of the responsibility for this to the divisions. Whereas the central planning function had in the past prepared five- and ten-year plans with little involvement of managers at the site level, it was now to act more as an adviser to divisional management which was charged with preparing the five-

and ten-year plans for the approval of the main Board. In future, the Chief Executive would lay down a general framework to establish future direction and he would articulate some important strategic thrusts, but then it would be up to divisional managers to develop the strategy.

The Chief Executive, Harry Bream, had spent his entire career at Enigma and consequently knew it well. He could recall previous reorganisations and previous attempts to change strategic direction, none of which had actually done a great deal to change the way people at Enigma worked. He knew from experience, therefore, that simply reorganising and pushing strategic responsibility further down the hierarchy would not necessarily lead to the strategic actions that a more hostile world and the eventual running out of the patents would create. He therefore contracted with a team of consultants to advise how the inevitable obstacles to implementation might be removed. The consultants conducted a series of interviews with a sample of managers and staff at all levels in order to identify what the issues were and what sort of company Enigma was. The notes that follow on three of these interviews turned out to be rather typical of all of those conducted with top management and the views of supervisory and middle management are indicated in a summary of interview notes prepared by one of the consultants, which is given below after the interview notes. The consultants now faced the task of formulating an approach to assisting their client.

Notes on an interview with Adrian Sinclair, Director of Division X

Adrian Sinclair had been with Enigma since he left university with an engineering degree some twenty years ago. In his interview with the consultant he started by describing how the organisation had changed since he joined it. Twenty years ago it had been an extremely bureaucratic, status-conscious organisation. Thus, there had been a sharp divide between the shop-floor workers on the one hand, and the staff on the other. Staff in turn were divided into professional and scientific streams; people entered the company either as a technician or as an administrator and tended to remain in the stream they had joined, moving regularly up the strictly graded structure. Relationships between people at different levels were very formal – you always addressed a more

senior person as 'Mr', and you always communicated in strict hierarchical order. No one ever went around their boss to a higher level.

The system had changed when the distinction between the professional and the scientific grades was abolished. All new entrants now came into a unified stream and then progressed up the grades according to experience. As they progressed, they encountered two important break-points in the pay grading structure. At the first of these points, those promoted were given significantly better terms and conditions. So, when entrants joined from university, they had terms and conditions set out in a staff handbook with a brown cover and at the first important break-point, the ranks of middle management, they acquired the terms and conditions set out in a green staff handbook. Then, when a person reached senior management status, the terms and conditions changed once more and this time they were set out in a blue staff handbook. Managers therefore came to be classified into clear-cut groups known as 'Greens' and 'Blues'. Everyone knew to which group a manager belonged and every year there were separate conferences for 'Greens' and 'Blues'.

One thing had not changed, however, and that was the open-interview procedure for promotions up the grade structure. Competent people could expect promotion as a matter of course. All openings were publicly advertised throughout the company and applications were invited from anyone with the right qualifications. Those selected had to attend a Promotions Committee consisting of three people, two of whom were outside the department in which the promotion was to be made. In this way, said Adrian, 'We can be seen to be fair and it prevents people from promoting their blue-eyed boys'. With this system, everyone got a fair chance and the company benefited when new talent was unearthed.

Adrian outlined how it was everyone's ambition to reach 'Blue' status and how he had thought of the 'Blues' as a kind of 'club' or 'secret society' until he had joined it. Once one reached the 'Blue' level, one was entitled to the BMW grade of car, a secretary, personally selected office furniture, private medical assurance and other benefits.

Adrian reiterated how the company had changed, how people had become much more flexible and less status-conscious than they were, but he did say that there were 'many images of old ways of behaving still lurking about', and it was these that he saw as the major obstacles to achieving the low-cost regimes and the entrepreneurial behaviour that were called for in the ten-year corporate plan.

According to Adrian, one of the principal images of the past, which were still 'lurking about', related to the manner in which managers at Enigma typically handled poor performance. There was a system in which people's performance was appraised each year. Although the system allowed people to be placed into one of five performance categories, ranging from the 'completely unsatisfactory' to the 'excellent', in fact managers tended to put almost everyone into the average performance category. Most people consequently got the average level of bonus and incentive pay. It was very difficult to fire non-performers because of agreements with powerful unions and because of the complex procedures that had to be followed before anyone could be fired. But quite apart from this, managers did not like to apply sanctions to anyone anyway. There was therefore a widespread perception that managers avoided tough decisions and personal confrontation. 'We do not like to go home at night feeling that we have been unpleasant to people', is how Adrian put it. He also felt that if managers lower down were suddenly given the right to appoint and fire staff without going through all the laborious procedures, they would simply not take up that responsibility.

Adrian did point out, however, that if he was determined to do something, then the bureaucratic systems simply did not stop him. He got around the bureaucracy through his informal contacts. He felt that those who complained that they could not manage because of bureaucratic systems imposed on them by the corporate centre, were simply using this' as an excuse for not managing. When he had a staff member who did not perform he usually managed to find someone inexperienced enough to take that person, or he privately convinced the non-performer to go, or he just found the non-performers something else to do, usually a promotion that got them out of the way. He felt that managers at Enigma did not sack people because they had not got the stomach for it. They all felt that they had a job for life and if that was changed in one case, who knew where it might stop. Anyway, it was a bad idea to do anything that would provoke a strike because that would simply attract media attention and the old environmental scares would simply be revived.

Notes on an interview with Adam Frusquin, Director of Division Y

Adam had joined the company 25 years ago after completing his doctorate in chemistry. He described how for years people at Enigma had seen their company as a good employer operating in a stable industry, giving people jobs for life. He described the family atmosphere that prevailed and gave examples of the caring attitude the company adopted to its people. He also described Enigma as a not particularly demanding employer.

In his view this was a company in which, even nowadays, 'people tended to know their place' in a clearly structured hierarchy. It was also a company in which everything was done by negotiation rather than instruction. The result was a relatively comfortable, conflict-free and content organisation. However, Adam was convinced that these attitudes would have to change and he talked about the need 'to be seen to be more commercially aggressive'. Instead of operating strictly according to hierarchical position and following well-established negotiating procedures, Adam believed that people at all levels would have to be empowered to take their own decisions. But he recognised that many managers would find this threatening and would not want the responsibility.

Notes of an interview with Anita Cummings, Director of Human Relations

Anita was a highly unusual manager at Enigma: first, she was the only woman in a senior position; and second, she had been at Enigma for only year. Harry Bream had brought Anita on to the Board as his way of signalling that he wanted change in behaviour throughout the organisation and that personnel practices and systems were going to change to bring this about. He 'was tired of having everything he tried to do disappearing into a fog'. Anita's arrival had caused quite a stir because she had previously been the Personnel Director of AMR, a ruthless conglomerate, and in that position she had acquired a reputation for being tough with non-performing managers.

In the interview with the consultant, Anita confessed that she was still surprised at the lack of focus on costs and financial performance generally. She found the style of management to be highly bureaucratic, proceduralised and very slow-moving. As far as she was concerned, people did not seem to recognise any pressures for change, but channelled much of their energies into what she called 'sibling rivalry'. She explained how people tended to form fairly cohesive teams in the department or immediate project group they worked in, but built up animosities against other groups and did their best not to cooperate with them. She spoke with some amusement about the classification of managers into the 'Greens' and the 'Blues'. As far as she was concerned these were secretive 'men's clubs' that were not open to her and were, anyway, irrelevant as far as the business was concerned. She said that people at Enigma 'react to newcomers with fear'. She said that managers felt that 'they had to be seen to be members of the "Blue" club'.

She still found it surprising that senior managers kept starting new initiatives that somehow always required a committee, a task force or a workshop and often the assistance of consultants. There was so much activity examining everything and suggesting changes in everything and yet so little change itself.

She described the culture of the organisation as a comfortable family atmosphere in which people saw their roles in terms of the pay grade they had reached.

Summary notes on interviews with middle managers

In almost all the interviews managers stated their support for the company which they viewed as a good employer that provided them with job security. However, they were also critical of more senior managers who, they said, avoided tough decisions. Senior managers tended to communicate with them using memos rather than walking around. Despite all the efforts to promote participation, most middle managers saw it as a sort of front – they believed that decisions were really taken in a rather autocratic way. Middle managers complained about communication with higher levels where they had to rely on the grapevine and they thought this was wrong. They called for more detailed and precise information on the company's objectives and strategies. When the consultant pointed out that they had been sent summary copies of the ten-year plan, some said they could not remember what it said, others said it was in a drawer somewhere, others said it was not detailed and precise enough. They claimed that top managers had no sense of direction and they, at the middle level, needed to be told what this direction was before they could function properly.

As far as the outside world was concerned, few middle managers talked about the prospects facing the company as its monopoly hold on its chief product weakened. But they all mentioned the unreasonable way in which pressure groups and the media pilloried them for what they felt were imaginary environmental dangers.

Apex Engineering Plc*

Apex plc is an internationally diversified corporation with a portfolio of activities in the heavy engineering, control systems and information technology markets. The corporation has undergone many transformations during the past twenty years as a result of mergers and acquisitions as well as organic growth. One of the larger subsidiaries, the one in the heavy engineering industry, is called Apex Engineering Ltd and it operates from a number of factory sites in the UK.

In 1988 a new Chief Executive was appointed to run Apex plc and one of his first steps was to announce a rationalisation strategy for Apex Engineering Ltd: this would involve closing three sites and reducing costs by 30 per cent within four years at the remaining three sites. Between 1988 and 1990 those three sites were indeed closed and, in accordance with the cost-cutting strategy, many thousands of people were made redundant at the others.

The recession of the early 1990s made life even more difficult and by mid-1992 it was clear that a further site would have to be closed. Sites at Warrington, Newcastle and Birmingham were therefore vying to secure a position as one of the survivors.

This case is concerned with events at the Warrington site, the principal activity of which was the manufacture of heavy equipment. In 1988 the production process was one of batch manufacture of components and flowline assembly. The site was run by a General Manager and reporting to him there were a number of Directors of support functions (Finance, Engineering and Personnel) and also a Production Director. The General Manager and the Directors together formed an Operations Executive Committee (OEC). A number of Production Managers reported to the Production Director and to each of them, a number of works managers reported. Each works manager had a number of product managers reporting to them and they in turn had supervisors to whom foremen reported.

*Copyright © Christine Czyzewska

The Warrington strategy

In 1988, in response to the Apex Chief Executive's strategy on rationalisation, Warrington's OEC appointed consultants to assist in formulating a strategy for the survival of the Warrington site. About a year later, the strategy agreed upon was that of dividing the operations function at Warrington into smaller, more manageable units, flattening the reporting structure of the manufacturing activity by reducing the levels of management to three and empowering people at lower levels to make decisions and become accountable for their actions. The new organisational structure was therefore to be one in which a number of work shop managers were to report to the Production Director. Each work shop was to consist of a number of cells, each with its own cell supervisor, and each manufacturing cell was to be given responsibility for a section of the final product. Each cell would include staff from the support function and they would report to the cell supervisor, retaining only a functional link to the old support function departments, which would become advisory in nature. So, instead of some people manufacturing parts of a component while others assembled them all, components would in future be manufactured and put together into subassemblies before going on to a higher-level assembly operation. In addition, the manufacturing cells were to operate just-in-time (JIT) inventory policies, pulling their supplies from other units as they needed them. And the way accountants, controllers and personnel people would work would, of course, be significantly changed because they would now relate to cell teams.

The old performance reporting system

These changes in work practices in turn required changes in the way that performance was measured, controlled and rewarded. Under the batch production and flowline assembly system, performance measures were built up from data collected at the level of the individual operator to construct manhour and cost indicators for batches of components. Reporting for monitoring and control purposes was against batch cost standards and the performance measures were therefore cost accounting measures. It was, consequently, the function of the site's Finance Department to set the standards, collect the cost data and report on performance.

In 1988, the key performance measures were:

- batch delivery times to outside customers;
- manhour costs per batch;
- actual hours against standard;
- numbers of quality defects per batch.

Although these measures were generally considered adequate, it was known that the reporting system was not distributing costs into the right cost categories, but because the interest was only in cost at a higher level of aggregation, the system was not changed.

Throughout the history of the Warrington plant the accounting system measured shop floor workers' output against standard packages of work and the individual bonus schemes and payments by results systems were tied to this. Both shop floor operators and managers were thus interested in maintaining 'accurate' data. Although the data was perceived to be 'accurate', the operators' bonuses grew each year until in 1978 they had become unacceptably high. The bonus payment system had then been replaced with one based on components delivered to outside customers and applied to all people in the company. This meant that operators away from the final assembly activity could not relate their performance to the final product and so they had lost the incentive to work against target. They also lacked the motivation to collect accurate data since they could not see what purpose it served. The recorded manhours against the job increased and performance deteriorated.

The project to develop and apply new performance measures

Operating a strategy of cellular manufacturing and JIT would clearly require a different system for measuring performance and monitoring and controlling it. It would be essential to measure not the batch cost, but the cost of each item that a manufacturing cell

produced. Without this information, cell team members would not be able to identify areas for improvement. In the new system information would not simply be reported up the hierarchy for attention by senior managers. Instead, cell team members would monitor their own performance and decide how to keep to target. For this new method of control to work faster information feedback to team members themselves would have to be ensured.

OEC members recognised the pivotal importance of performance measures for the new manufacturing strategy and so appointed a project leader to design a new set of performance measures. The project leader appointed consultants to design appropriate new performance measures and the consultants' proposals for a new set of six measures was accepted.

The pilot cell

The first step in implementing the new manufacturing strategy was to set up a pilot manufacturing cell. A joint Union/Management committee was set up to monitor the progress of this pilot over a three-month period, after which the committee was to review the conditions under which the trial would continue. The trial was to include a shift from an external department, measuring individual performance, to the cellular team, measuring themselves and then doing what was needed to improve performance. It was necessary, however, to ensure that links were maintained between the old method of measuring performance and the new one during the trial period. Therefore, an informal management review board, including representatives of all site functions, was set up to monitor the use of the new performance measurements. This board sent a project leader into the pilot cell to work with the cell team to design and implement new performance measures.

Before the three-month trial was up, however, the Unions withdrew their support, ostensibly because of a disagreement on overtime in another part of the site, and the informal board refused to approve the specific performance measures that cell members proposed. The operators in the trial cell then withdrew their cooperation with the engineers and controllers who had been allocated to the team from the site's support functions. The operators continued to produce the performance data in the form they had recommended to the informal board, but of course, the data was not used for anything.

Six months later, the objection to the pilot cell was withdrawn and the trial continued. A formal initiative called Performance Management and Reporting (PMR) was established to look at performance reports. A new project leader was appointed and he set up an informal working group, consisting of the support departments. A number of meetings were held but little progress was made because individuals had other priorities. One meeting resulted in a slanging match between Finance and Operations – both complained about each other's ability: Finance accused Operations of not managing its people, while Operations claimed that financial reporting was useless because it was so out of date and not at the level of detail required to understand the problems. The informal group was also criticised for not including operators and cell supervisors. In the end the frustrated project leader defined his own set of performance measures, but these too failed to secure senior management approval.

Shortly after this, senior Apex Engineering Ltd management arranged for a group of experts to present their ideas on performance to the management of all sites in the company. The presenters were highly critical of the Apex approach to performance measurement and those attending reacted with disbelief to the adverse comparisons made with their competitors. When the Apex Finance Director arrived to close the day's event, he presented a message that conflicted with the presenters' emphasis on long-term thinking – the Finance Director stressed the importance of short-term financial results.

By late 1990 the Operations function at Warrington had initiatives of one kind or another running into double figures. Senior managers became concerned at the number of changes that were being examined and the PMR board was called together to try to obtain an understanding of what all these initiatives were and what they were supposed to achieve. A small working group was asked to define a ten-point plan to prioritise the initiatives. When this plan was discussed it was decimated and no action was taken. Instead people said things like, 'This topic is already covered by another initiative', or 'That has already been completed', or 'This topic is something that needs to be looked at in the future'.

After these failed PMR meetings, Operations circulated a list of performance measures defined by an engineering support function leader. In response to this, a number of memos were issued by the Finance Department on cell accounting. Operations did not respond to these memos – they said the memos were not comprehensible – and so Finance let the matter drop.

Consultant intervention

Then in January 1991, the Managing Director of Apex Engineering Ltd suggested that consultants be appointed to define performance measures at the Warrington site. A joint Consultant-Operations team was set up and, after eight weeks' work, the following set of performance measures, to be taken at the manufacturing cell level, was agreed by the PMR board, with the exception of the cost statement that required the agreement of the Finance Department and this was not forthcoming:

- delivery time compared to plan;
- order-delivery response time;
- capacity utilisation against plan;
- stock levels;
- costs.

These were designed to be simple measures that operators and management could understand at a glance. The measures were to be displayed on charts on the wall for all to see. The data for the charts was to be collected by team members themselves. Problems were to be reported up the hierarchy only on an exceptions basis.

A senior Operations Manager then requested that an analysis be made of all current performance reports so that some could be dropped when the new measures came into force. The consultant did not want to be involved in a discussion of what were the best measures so the analysis was conducted by another group. This analysis showed that 90 people in Operations and Finance were generating data in 85 reports coming mostly from support departments that had no relevance to the manufacturing cells. The reports were too complex to understand quickly and were the result of years of *ad hoc* accumulation. This confirmed what had been known for years – that there was too much irrelevant information.

Implementation

The next step was that of setting up a Performance Reporting Board to manage the implementation phase of the now agreed performance measures. The consultant left and a new project manager was appointed. Implementation was seen as the joint responsibility of Operations and Finance, but gradually Finance withdrew and eventually the Finance Director stopped attending meetings of the Performance Reporting Board. The fifth agreed performance measure, the cost statement, was therefore not developed further or applied.

In the meantime, as we have seen, Union resistance to cell manufacturing had been overcome and a number of Manufacturing Centres and their constituent cells had been set up. In the absence of site-wide agreed performance measures, each cell was using its own.

CASE STUDY 11

Managing Creativity in the Pharmaceutical Industry*

Pharmex Research plc[†] is the research and development arm of Pharmex Products, a highly profitable transnational pharmaceutical organisation. The Pharmex group has grown rapidly in recent years from a middle-sized company to one of the largest in the world. Pharmex Products has a strong research and development orientation and this has been concentrated almost exclusively within Pharmex Research plc (PR plc), a multidivisional organisation with the role of discovering, developing and carrying out clinical trials upon new pharmaceutical products. Reflecting the organisation of the rest of the Pharmex group, PR plc has sites in the UK, throughout Europe and in the USA.

Within the UK PR plc has concentrated its operations in the southeast of England on the sites of pharmaceutical companies taken over during the apparently inexorable rise of Pharmex Products to its current position. The recent growth of the company has meant that operations are now constrained by lack of space and several years ago a decision was taken to move them to a single site. After considerable research into suitable sites had been undertaken, Greenfields was chosen – a previously undeveloped 100 acre area about 60 miles away from the existing London head office. There are four major subdivisions within PR plc in the UK (two on each of the existing main sites) and these represent the traditional divisions within scientific disciplines, although changes in the nature of science brought about by developments in scientific understanding and in biotechnology have begun to blur the edges of these functional divisions.

The existing sites

A visit to the laboratories at either of the main Pharmex Research sites is revealing. The white-coated scientists working at their rather cramped, equipment-covered benches are young and casually dressed, giving the laboratories the feel of those in the Universities many will have recently left. Pharmex's growth, much of it during periods of high demand for well-qualified scientists, means that some 60 per cent of the workforce have been in the company for five years or less. Many of the buildings are old and consist of long corridors with laboratories leading off on both sides. The size of the laboratories to a large extent determines the size of the research teams based within them. Generally there will be a team of six in each laboratory supervised by a research leader.

During periods of high employment Pharmex could expect an annual labour turnover of between 10 and 14 per cent, although this was always highest amongst the less well-qualified ancillary and technician staff. By spring 1993 average labour turnover had dropped to around 3–4 per cent and growth in staff had largely come to an end. Pharmex was seen as a good employer in terms of pay, deliberately placing itself in the top quartile.

Industry analysts have identified three key strategic considerations which are seen as acting upon Pharmex (as well as upon other companies in the sector) and which appear to have contributed to the decision to develop Greenfields:

† A pseudonym.

1 Increasing competition in the world pharmaceutical industry

The time taken to discover, develop and carry out clinical trials on a drug before it can be marketed widely is lengthy. After a drug is patented there is a time limit, after which competitors are free to develop the 'generic' product (i.e. the chemical substance which is the drug's active component). In order to recoup the investment made at the research and development stage, aggressive marketing is important to convince medical practitioners to prescribe the product. Increasingly, however, the most successful companies will be those able to shorten the development period of a product and hence exploit the longer period before the generic drug can be manufactured by others in the industry. Where all of those involved in the design of a new drug can be gathered together Pharmex management believes that the discovery process can be expedited.

2 Changes in pharmaceutical technology

The traditional division in pharmaceutical science is based on the separation of biology and chemistry. Developments in, for instance, biotechnology have begun to break down these divisions. There is a developing understanding of cell biology due to improved biotechnology. At a senior level Pharmex is keen to encourage scientists from different disciplines to talk to each other and separation of the disciplines on several sites militates against this.

3 The need for greater efficiency in the process of drug discovery

A squeeze on profits over the next few years seems inevitable with the tightening on price controls by governments and public health authorities across the globe.

A fourth consideration, specific to Pharmex, was identified by senior managers within the company:

4 Recent growth of the company has put pressure on laboratory space

Growth in employee numbers has led to cramped working conditions with a number of scientists, for instance, sharing a fume cupboard in each laboratory and having to search for bench space to write up reports.

There are now some 1500 employees of PR plc. Over 50 per cent are graduates and one in six has a doctorate. One looming problem lies in the impact the combined problem of rapid growth and low labour turnover will have upon perceptions of career opportunities for younger scientists.

The Greenfield site

The new site will cater for the increased numbers of staff and a tour reveals a development on an impressive scale. The architect's design documents make reference to a 'campus-style' development. Asked what kind of an image Pharmex wished to promote on its newest site the Human Resource Director replied, 'something modern, young, not a factory, not an office, something that looks exciting to go to . . . the sort of thing that reflects what we're trying to do, what we are as a company, modern, flexible, innovative.'

The electronic attendance monitoring machines apparent on the walls of each floor at the existing sites and essential to the current flex-time system will not be used at Greenfields. Members of the senior management of Pharmex have been consulted during the design process in the hope that the resulting site will meet the needs of a modern scientific research organisation into the twenty-first century. The result is a set of buildings designed to promote interaction between its occupants. There will be 'nodal points' (coffee machines and informal seating areas) and each laboratory can be approached from two sides; from one side a 'clean corridor' will lead into the office side of the work space containing each researcher's desk. From the other side a 'dirty corridor' used for the transportation of materials and equipment will lead into the laboratory. This half of the work space will contain the fume cupboards where experiments are carried out. Each scientific worker will have a fume cupboard to him/herself – a major improvement upon the situation at the existing sites.

Management of innovation

At Pharmex the management of research rests in the hands of highly qualified scientists with good track records in research themselves. Gary Brice, Head of Research, argued:

> Most of our management is done through science. You don't want a heavily structured or heavily organised environment if you want people to be creative. I always

say its like running an opera house. You've got to make sure that the toilets are clean, you've got to make sure that the tickets are sold, the ice creams are there in the interval, your gin and tonics are available, but if the fat lady don't sing, it's all a waste of time. And what is important is generating an environment where the prima donnas perform, because it's the prima donnas who actually make the invention, who take you to places you couldn't otherwise go. There's a few people out there who are really a bit special, who put things together in a different way. What we've got to create is something that allows them to perform, not something that necessarily satisfies the aspirations of the masses, because you can do that by making it run very smoothly. Everyone will say 'it's a fantastic place to work', but you never make inventions. What the hell good's that?

The impending move to Greenfields had prompted a new approach to the management of working time which is currently being piloted in certain divisions. Gary Brice put it as follows:

When you move house you are awfully conscious of the fact that you've got a lot of things in the loft or in the top of the garage that you don't actually have a use for any longer and you get shot of them, or you take them down to the tip, or you send them to a jumble sale. . . I'm quite keen on looking at flextime. Twenty years ago we adopted flextime as a liberalising influence. Prior to that everybody was getting in at 8.45 and signing in before the line was drawn across the page. Flextime was a big step forward, but then we had the whole business of time recorders and people signing that they had done so many hours and then had not had the opportunity to have the days off that they had accumulated over the flex period. What I'm saying is do you really, as creative people, as professional people at the beginning of the twenty-first century, want all this paraphernalia associated with time, because it doesn't get us any new drugs and I'm not bothered about it. What I want is for people to feel committed and I want to work towards this end.

'Flexible working', the new system, is based on self-management in which scientific staff will be expected to be present at work during core hours of 10.00–12.00 and 2.00–4.00, but this is not formally monitored. They are not expected to account formally for the remaining seventeen and a half hours attendance per week for which they are contracted. Managers believe the flextime system encouraged an instrumental approach to work where employees who needed to put in hours to meet the system's requirements simply clocked in early for a day or two but might not then spend the time engaged in useful activity. Clocking in and flextime were con-

cerned with 'control' and 'bureaucracy'. This was not an appropriate or fruitful way to encourage well-qualified people to make use of their creative ability. As another senior manager said:

We don't want to have clocks in our new environment, in Greenfields, because we don't think it's compatible with a professional environment, and also it makes people conscious of time, and they should really be conscious of what they are doing and how they're doing it. Time management is really irrelevant to research when you think about it. It's the management of ideas, and how you produce them in practice and the quality of your goals, and whether they are practical or not or how innovative they are, things like that, those are key issues.

What was required, it was felt, was to make maximum use of the commitment to the process of scientific innovation which the young scientists brought with them from their universities and which led them not to count hours at work but to concentrate on achieving scientific goals. Under the old system employees were allowed up to 12 'flex' days per year off if they built up time credits. Under the new system such credit could not be 'banked', as such, but line managers had the ability to award days off to employees who they felt had done something to deserve it.

Pharmex operate a performance-related pay system, but the scheme has not been popular with staff and both this and a high degree of stress were identified during attitude surveys carried out during 1992. A human resource manager asserted:

Most people say they like performance-related pay, but they never seem to like it when it is applied to them . . . PRP is a very hot area for discussion at the moment.

Much of the work carried out by scientific staff necessarily involves significant individual autonomy within a teamworking environment. Measuring the output from work is extremely difficult, as only a tiny proportion of compounds created ever reach the market. A human resource manager commented on the problem of rewarding performance in a research environment:

You find that in research targets are much woollier than they are, say, in IT. In research you might have a target today of finding a new nasal spray to prevent the common cold, and two months later Wellcome publish a patent and there's no point in doing it anymore. Your entire project switches to something new and, of course, many researchers are in a position year in, year out where they produce a whole bunch of failures. I mean, when you think that one compound makes it to the market out of every 10 000 compounds, one each year, and we've got 3700 research scientists across the globe pursuing it, it's not surprising that you get a lot of people whose life is a whole bunch of failures, and the supervisor has the job of subjectively assessing how good they were at getting those failures out. It's quite a difficult task. How do you assess someone's innovation or motivation or energy or drive? It's not all about how many hours they've spent at the bench, because you've got some people who can spend twelve hours a day at the bench and get a 'fair' appraisal ranking and you can get someone else who can spend six hours there but the way their brain and luck works they can achieve a 'special award'.

The pay review system involves line managers in judging their staff as performing somewhere on a scale from 'poor' to 'exceptional' without many formal guidelines as to what constitutes each category.

Taken together the PRP system and flexible working appeared to be putting a high degree of subjective power in the hands of line managers. The result was a heightened awareness amongst research workers of the need to convince line managers of the value of the work that they were doing. Line managers were not necessarily project leaders and so did not always have direct evidence of an employee's day-to-day performance. One scientist put it this way:

> We're very task orientated here and we're working towards goals. Maybe there isn't so much freedom because I think we all spend a lot of time communicating what we are doing and making sure that, if you like, our managers and bosses can see the positive aspects of our work.

Good employee relations at Pharmex Research were seen as achievable by senior managers without recourse to recognising trade unions. A significant proportion of employees (about 1 in 4) were members of MSF (the Manufacturing, Science and Finance union), but this was recognised only for the purposes of representation of employees in, for instance, grievance procedures. Collective bargaining did not occur. However, at Greenfields Pharmex was intending to withdraw recognition for even this limited purpose. On the whole derecognition seemed unlikely in itself to represent an issue with research staff. Salaries were good, conditions at Greenfields were likely to be an improvement on the existing sites, jobs were seen as being secure and staff still had a high degree of autonomy about how they carried out their work. Indeed, there was some degree of freedom to choose *where* work was carried out and in many respects sci-

entists were expected to operate like their peers who had chosen to remain in an academic environment. As a senior manager pointed out:

> You must remember that scientific grades are contracted to work $37\frac{1}{2}$ hours per week and we would expect employees on average to be sorting their lives out such that they work those hours. But that doesn't necessarily mean at the bench, that just means contributing to GGR for $37\frac{1}{2}$ hours on average a week, and there's a hint that it doesn't have to therefore even be in the building. It can be contributing elsewhere in a library, in an institution somewhere else, whatever. But overall, contribution will not be measured on the hours you have your card in the machine in the future, but on the part that you play in achieving the objectives of the company.

However, the road to drug discovery is not an easy one, or one which has guaranteed success at its end. In many ways it is a game of chance. Pharmex has been seen as overdependent on one or two very successful products, so-called 'blockbuster drugs', and with nothing of the same magnitude yet in the pipeline to replace these when the patents expire. The increasingly competitive nature of the industry means that whilst resources will be put behind potential scientific leads by investing in projects likely to lead to new products, those that are seen as unlikely to give competitive advantage are shut down promptly and their members integrated into new or continuing projects. This can be a source of frustration to project team members as there may be knowledge of scientific interest still to be gained from the work. This market orientation can clearly be seen to differentiate work in the industrial and academic environments and to a significant number of scientists working at the bench the attempt to make the new site 'more like a university' was viewed with cynicism.

Greenfields, then, represents an attempt by Pharmex management to develop an environment conducive to the needs of the new product discovery side of the pharmaceutical industry as it approaches the twenty-first century. In order to work creatively scientists are seen as needing a degree of autonomy, and managers, nearly all of them accomplished scientists in their own right, appear to recognise the need to build this into working practices. However, it is possible to identify tensions in the company arising out of the necessity of directing activity towards the production of a marketable product. The question remains whether such a tension can be managed in a way which can ensure Pharmex a continuing place amongst the leading companies in the industry.

CASE STUDY 12

British Airways and Virgin Atlantic:
David and Goliath in the Civil Aviation Industry[*]

In January 1993 British Airways ended a libel case brought against them by Richard Branson's company, Virgin Atlantic, by apologising unreservedly for any 'injury caused to the reputation and feelings of Richard Branson and Virgin Atlantic' and particularly for questioning the good faith and integrity of Mr Branson. The judge ordered BA to pay legal costs (approximately £3 000 000) and Mr Branson was awarded £610 000 in damages.

This case was widely seen as a humiliating climb down for BA, especially for Lord King, Chairman of the Board, and Sir Colin Marshall, Chief Executive of the company. BA were labelled as a company which would stoop to any level of dirty trickery to get rid of competition. The shock waves from this case will reverberate around the halls of big business and government for some time.

The case involves several strands of interest to students of business ethics. The clash between BA's carefully crafted image as the world's favourite airline and its publicly pronounced customer culture and its actions in this case is one such theme. The avoidance of responsibility by senior executives and board members is another. The logic of free-market competition and effects on business behaviour is a third. The consequences of unethical behaviour constitute a fourth.

This case study examines the background to the case, the details of BA's behaviour and the consequences which flowed from the discovery of unethical business behaviour.

Background

Competition

Competition between airline companies is fierce. Much of the competitive action revolves around pricing, flexibility of flight arrangements, customer convenience, quality of service at airports and on the plane. There is another side to the battle between airlines of which most air travellers are not aware.

This relates to slots. A slot represents the right of an airline to take off or land at a given airport. Slots can be 'arrival' or 'departure' slots. They are allocated by the hour so that a slot in the 0800 hour may be from 0800 to 0855.

Each airport has an Airport Coordinator responsible for allocating slots. This can be either an individual or a group or committee consisting of airline representatives. Airlines make seasonal submissions to the Coordinator at each airport which they wish to use. This is a submission for a whole season – summer (April to October) or winter (November to March). Clearly the greater the congestion at an airport and the greater the demand for slots, the more difficult the role of the Coordinator become.

Airlines compete for the most lucrative slots and the process of slot allocation can be crucial for the success or failure of the competitive strategies of individual airlines. From one season to the next, airlines are able to rely on their historical allocation. Any planned growth in activity requires new slots.

[*] This case was written by *Alan Kitson*, Bolton Business School, Bolton Institute, as a basis for classroom discussion rather than to illustrate either effective or ineffective handling of a management situation. The case has been compiled from published sources. Copyright © 1993 A Kitson, Bolton Institute.

Slot planning is affected by some unpredictability in the environment. This might consist of announcements about enhanced runway capacity by the British Airports Authority (as happened in 1992) or changes in the Traffic Distribution Rules by the Department of Transport (as happened in 1991 enabling 17 new airlines to operate in and out of Heathrow).

Virgin Atlantic has long been campaigning to be allowed more slots (i.e. take-off and landing times). Their longstanding ambition is to fly to the world's 12 largest cities from Heathrow. In 1993 Virgin had 3000 slots per year and had been offered a further 1000 slots. This gave Virgin a 1 percent share of total available slots. This can be compared with 5 per cent for Lufthansa which was Heathrow's third largest carrier (*Guardian*, 18.1.93).

Size

The relative sizes of the two protagonists in this case were remarkably disparate. Virgin Atlantic employed 2400 people, whereas BA employed 48 450; Virgin had 8 aircraft, BA had 227; Virgin carried approximately 1 million passengers a year, BA carried 25 million; Virgin made a loss of £3 million in 1991, BA made over £300 million profit; BA had a turnover approximately 14 times greater than that of Virgin (*Guardian*, 12.1.93).

Previous cases

The Virgin Atlantic case is the latest in a series of controversial cases involving British Airways and smaller competitors.

In 1985 Freddie Laker alleged that BA had conspired with a group of other airlines to put Laker out of business and to remove the threat created by the novel and popular Skytrain operation which made air travel more convenient for the regular traveller. The case against BA was settled out of court, with significant payments being made to the Laker organisation, its creditors, pension fund and staff.

Sir Michael Bishop, the chairman of British Midland, also considers his company to have been the victim of sharp practice by BA. British Midland has a small sister airline, Loganair. Sir Michael claims that he was approached during 1992 by Liam Strong, then BA's marketing director. BA was interested in a joint venture serving the Scottish highlands and islands. They had some problems with their own service in

this area and approached Sir Michael because of the Loganair connection. Loganair was involved in this area also.

Sir Michael states that letters of confidentiality were drafted and had to be signed by both companies. These letters were designed to protect the commercial secrets of both organisations and to prevent either side using any confidential information to its advantage. Sir Michael signed his, BA management did not sign theirs. Sir Michael trusted them and proceeded with the exchange of information about passenger numbers and began negotiations. As the time approached to sign a final deal, Sir Colin Marshall, BA's Chief Executive, called the whole thing off.

Six months later BA had established new flights from Manchester to Edinburgh which happened to be Loganair's most profitable route. Sir Michael took the view that BA extracted useful commercial information from him and then withdrew from a possible agreement to take commercial advantage of the information which they had been given in confidence (*Independent on Sunday*, 17.1.93).

The political dimension

BA is clearly the dominant player in the British civil aviation industry. It also makes strenuous attempts to maintain strong links with important political and governmental decision-makers.

The House of Commons publishes annually a list of members' interests. This is a list, declared by MPs themselves, of any outside interest they have with external bodies including trade unions, charitable organisations, pressure groups and businesses. It is common for MPs to indicate the financial aspects of any relationship which may exist. The list of members' interests published in early January 1993 indicates that BA appears as a donor more often than any other company. At least 14 MPs received free flights or other benefits during 1992. Angela Rumbold, Deputy Chairman of the Conservative Party, and Alan Haselhurst, a member of the House of Commons Select Committee on Transport, were among the beneficiaries. Select Committees can exert some influence on government policy and the practices of the departments which they scrutinise.

BA decided to stop making payments to the Conservative Party in 1991, after Mrs Thatcher was ousted as party leader.

Two members of Parliament registered that they had received free flights from Virgin.

BA's corporate culture and management style

BA was privatised in 1985. It had been prepared for privatisation by Sir John (now Lord) King and Colin (now Sir Colin) Marshall who launched a series of major training events and reorganisations within the business to enhance the quality of customer service.

There is considerable evidence to show that the changes brought about by BA management have led to a clear customer service focus. BA's Annual Report for 1991/92 describes the company as being 'Committed to quality with every one of its 50 000 staff participating in its new customer service programme, Winning with Customers.' David Young (1989), in a report for the Ashridge Strategic Management Centre, indicates that employees generally recognise that considerable changes had taken place between 1983 and 1989. BA managers interviewed in 1988 saw the organisation as being more professional, customer-led, adapting, innovative and more purposive. This change is further underlined by customer reaction. The airline has regularly won awards for good customer service voted by the customers themselves.

The BA Mission Statement (British Airways Report and Accounts, 1991–92) contains a series of value-statements which are meant to guide the operations of the company. The Mission Statement declares that the overall mission is 'To be the best and most successful company in the airline industry' and the goals which stem from this mission are:

- to be a safe and secure airline;
- to deliver a strong and consistent financial performance;
- to secure a leading share of air travel business worldwide with a significant presence in all major geographical markets;
- to provide overall superior service and good value for money in every market segment in which we compete;
- to excel in anticipating and quickly responding to customer needs and competitor activity;
- to sustain a working environment that attracts, retains and develops committed employees who share in the success of the company;
- to be a good neighbour concerned for the community and the environment.

In addition to introducing a strong customer culture within the company, Sir Colin Marshall also made fundamental changes to the management style within BA. The emphasis has shifted from decision by committees and the avoidance of individual responsibility to an approach which stresses urgency, the need for individual managers to take decisions and to accept responsibility. There is also an expectation that managers will be visible. David Young (1989) describes the style thus:

> At all levels it is clearly about 'putting the customer first', the customer service focus established by Marshall back in 1983. At a management level it appears to be about getting things done, responding to the business challenges, and not standing on ceremony in doing it. (See also *Bruce, 1987* and *Höpfl, Mith & Spencer, 1992.*)

In discussing the reasons for BA's success in creating a sense of mission within the organisation, Young identifies the following 'keys to this success'

- the selection of simple and appropriate themes encouraging care for people and personal accountability;
- a context of uncertainty to make change possible;
- consistent, persistent, courageous, visible and open leadership;
- focus on the practicalities;
- formal programmes which reinforced the messages of the new management style.

Sir Colin Marshall, according to a former BA manager Michael Levin, is recognised by the staff as a decent human being who projects caring, concern and moral probity, and Young asserts that this is an important factor in BA's success. Michael Levin reappears below.

The story

The activities of BA which came to light as a result of the court case brought by Mr Branson could be taken straight from any novel about big business. All it appears to lack is a sex theme. Searching through journalists' rubbish, phone-tapping, people attending meetings with hidden microphones secreted about their person, attempts to hide trails and shuffle off responsibilities to others are all aspects of this bizarre case.

There are three main components to BA's campaign against Virgin Atlantic. First, there is the attack on Virgin's Atlantic operations. This consisted of persuading Virgin passengers at airports to switch to BA, cold-calling Virgin customers and alleged hacking into computers to discover sensitive commercial information.

Secondly, there was a report on Virgin produced by Brian Basham, a public relations consultant hired by BA. This was presented to the Chief Executive in the form of a slide show.

Finally, there was operation Covent Garden, which began in 1991 as a response to worries within BA that it had a mole in its midst.

The first campaign, the so called switch-selling campaign, was allegedly backed up by hacking into Virgin's computers. Former BA employees reported on television in January 1992 that they had accessed Virgin's computerised reservations service. They had subsequently telephoned passengers to tell them that their flights had been cancelled and offer them flights with BA.

This may be in breach of the Data Protection Act which seeks to establish certain basic principles about the fairness and legality with which personal information is obtained. The Computer Misuse Act 1990 makes it a crime to access other people's computers.

The second component consisted of the report produced by Brian Basham. This component was known as Operation Barbara. Estimates as to its costs vary from £40 000 to £50 000. That it was sanctioned by the Chief Executive, Sir Colin Marshall, seems to be not in doubt. This report was selectively leaked to parts of the press and resulted in items appearing which were critical of Richard Branson personally and made allegations about the weaknesses of Virgin as a company. The report was produced in April 1991 and authorisation for the project was needed from the Chief Executive's office because it cost more than the Director of Public Relations, Mr David Burnside, was able to approve.

The report summarises financial, personal and operational aspects of Mr Branson's businesses. It identifies popular misconceptions about Virgin, draws attention to Mr Branson's personal style of management and his highly experimental strategy. It also comments on the fact that he owns a nightclub about which there have been allegations of crime, drug-peddling and homosexuality. The report states that this ownership 'seems to be high risk in terms of his all-important image' (*Guardian*, 15.1.93).

The third component is known as Operation Covent Garden. The court case made it clear that Mr Branson had not attempted to discredit BA or its busi-

ness, but BA executives became convinced during their attempts to undermine Virgin that Virgin was organising industrial espionage against BA.

It was towards the end of 1991 that BA became worried about possible spying by Virgin. Ian Johnson Associates were hired by Sir Colin Marshall and David Hyde, BA's head of security (*Independent on Sunday*, 17.1.93). Such was the paranoia at this time that when Mr David Burnside, BA's Director of Public Relations, went for dinner with a mutual friend of Mr Branson he was wired for sound and the conversation was recorded. Staff from Ian Johnson's organisation were also keeping watch. As it happened, this meeting had been arranged by the mutual friend so that Mr Burnside could meet with the person who had indeed been hired by an organisation other than Virgin to investigate Mr Burnside.

The report produced by Mr Johnson details phone-tapping of BA's senior executives. An executive's car was broken into and details of BA's UK management were taken. Informants told BA senior staff that informants had been planted at one of their offices and that a secretary at headquarters was feeding information to Virgin.

The report strung together a series of unconnected events to support a claim that Virgin was spying on BA. However, the report concluded that the investigators were not able to substantiate the claim. The report recommended that senior executives should be very cautious when using mobile telephones, fax machines and engaging in conversations which could be heard (*Guardian*, 15.1.93).

The court case showed conclusively that Virgin had not been investigating BA.

Consequences

The consequences flowing from the court case and judgement made can be categorised as follows:

- consequences for BA as a business;
- consequences for individuals within BA;
- consequences for Virgin.

Consequences for BA as a business

Clearly BA's image has been tarnished. Press and other media coverage was generally unfavourable to BA. What effect this will have on customer loyalty and confidence in BA is difficult to identify clearly.

This Opposition Spokesman on Transport, Mr John Prescott, called for resignations from Lord King and Sir Colin Marshall for what he labelled their 'disreputable campaign of deceit, lies and illegal activities' (letter to John MacGregor, Minister of Transport). He refused to accept the attempt made by BA to dissociate the Board from the actions taken.

Following the court case, Mr Branson demanded a concrete expression of good faith from BA and negotiations began between the two companies focusing on slot allocation and financial compensation for Virgin.

On 27 January 1993, Mr Prescott wrote again to Mr MacGregor protesting at the way in which airline slots were being traded by BA as part of the negotiations between BA and Virgin. His criticism was that such private deals should not be the way in which slot allocation is made and he urged the minister to intervene.

Other airlines have watched with some apprehension as negotiations between BA and Virgin have proceeded. These negotiations have been seen as an attempt by BA to buy off Virgin and to encourage them not to take the threatened legal action against BA in the US courts. On 15 February l993, Sir Michael Bishop, Chairman of British Midland, said:

> It has to be nipped in the bud that BA has the power to pass over slots other than the ones that they own. If BA want to settle their dispute with Virgin by trading slots they can only trade the ones they already own (*Guardian*, 16.2.93).

Further political pressure was brought to bear when Peter Mandelson, MP for Hartlepool, urged the Transport Secretary to arrange for the Office of Fair Trading to investigate the 'commercial bullying and political manipulation' allegedly practised at British Airways (*Guardian*, 8.2.93).

The Data Protection Registrar, established by the Data Protection Act, began investigations into possibilities of breaches of the law by BA and asked for details of allegations and information from Virgin. If a case is brought and proven against BA then this will further damage its reputation as a business.

The outcome of the libel case could have serious implications BA's activities in the USA. Shortly after the court case BA acquired a 19.9 per cent shareholding in US Air, which is America's sixth largest carrier. On 1 February 1993 the three biggest US airlines formally lodged a petition with the US Department of Transportation in an attempt to overturn this arrangement. Previous bids by BA had been received with hostility by the US authorities and the three US airlines were now arguing that the deal between BA and US Air was substantially the same as an earlier plan from which BA had been forced to withdraw.

Much will depend on the reaction of American politicians and media. Mr Branson has appeared on US television and is very widely admired as an entrepreneur. The new American President, Mr Clinton, may adopt a more protectionist approach to industrial policy than his predecessor and the three airlines are pressing the Administration to form a definitive policy regarding foreign investment in the US airline industry.

Press coverage in Britain has been generally damning of BA. Jeremy Warner in the *Independent on Sunday* (17.1.93) writes of a company driven by deep paranoia operating a no-holds-barred approach to business. Will Hutton writing in the *Guardian* (12.1.93) says, 'Competition British Airways style seems to include personalised attacks, systematic campaigns of denigration and even, abusing commercial privacy – not what the enterprise culture was supposed to be about.'

The boardroom changes which took place on 5 February 1993 were unsympathetically covered by the media, with prime time news broadcasts showing an angry and somewhat harassed Lord King responding aggressively to loud press questioning.

Further image and public relations difficulties for BA arose from the awards of the *Executive Travel* magazine. Its readers voted Virgin Atlantic 'Airline of the Year' and best transatlantic carrier, best business class, cabin staff, food and wine, in-flight entertainment and airport lounges.

Despite the generally unsympathetic media coverage, BA's customers show no signs of deserting them as a result of the 'dirty tricks' case. The *Financial Times* reviewed customer reaction (22.1.93) and found that factors other than BA's guilt in conducting 'dirty tricks' were foremost in travellers' minds. The quality of customer service on BA flights and its safety record were important factors in retaining customer loyalty. Even customers of Virgin stated that BA's behaviour would not stop them using BA in future.

Shareholders (see *Appendix 12B*) were reported in the press to be alarmed at the extent of 'the dirty tricks' campaign and the prospects of Sir Colin Marshall taking over as Chairman and retaining his Chief Executive position, contrary to the recommendations of the Cadbury Committee. They were, however, unwilling to press Sir Colin too hard on this issue as he had let be known that he would resign if he were not made Chairman and they were impressed by his performance as Chief Executive.

Some shareholders were concerned that the board had not tried hard enough to get to the bottom of the case. BA's solicitors had conducted an investigation a year before and found nothing. Sir Michael Angus, non-executive Deputy Chairman, emerged as a pivotal figure during January and February. He ordered a second full investigation, the report of which was highly critical of aspects of the 'dirty tricks' campaign. The *Financial Times* stated (21.1.93) that this report 'confirmed that the campaign was carried out by a few individual employees and did not involve the highest levels of management'.

Shortly after the court case was closed BA published a new code of business conduct for all its staff (see *Appendix 12D*).

Consequences for individuals within BA

Calls for the resignations of Lord King and Sir Colin Marshall quickly followed in the wake of the outcome of the court case. BA insisted that no director was involved in the case. The claim by the company is that no director – including Lord King and Sir Colin – knew anything about the activities alleged to have taken place despite the fact that substantial sums were spent and the activities lasted for almost a year. Also, Richard Branson claims that a member of the Board, Mr Michael Davies, who is also a friend of Mr Branson's father, was sent as an emissary from the board of BA to ask Virgin to drop its libel case.

Mr Basham, the public relations consultant who produced the report on Virgin Atlantic which was selectively leaked to the press, has signed a sworn statement insisting that everything he did was with the full approval of the Board (*Guardian*, 12.1.93).

It had been planned that Lord King would take up the position of President, an honorary position, during the summer of 1993 and that Sir Colin Marshall would take on the role of Chairman and Chief Executive. There was much media speculation about boardroom manouevrings during January and February 1993. Finally, after strong intervention from non-executive directors on the BA Board, Lord King became President on 5 February and Sir Colin became Executive Chairman. Robert Ayling was appointed as Group Managing Director.

Lord King's remuneration package as President was a subject of press articles. He was said to be receiving £200 000 per year, plus a contribution to his pension, a central London office and secretary, use of a limousine and chauffeur free first-class air travel for himself and his family, free air travel for his staff. This could amount to £600 000 per year for life. Lord King is also Chairman of Babcock International.

Sir Colin will be responsible for corporate strategy, finance, legal and company secretary affairs, safety, security, public relations, the environment, health and medical matters. Mr Ayling will add to his previous portfolio of marketing and operations, responsibility for engineering, flight crews, information services, and human resources (*Independant*, 6.2.93).

The changes in the boardroom also resulted in Sir Michael Angus agreeing to give more time to his role as Deputy Chairman of the Board. In addition, two further non-executive board members were to be appointed.

Mr Basham's public relations contract has not been renewed. Mr Burnside resigned on the day the board changes were announced.

Michael Levin, who was quoted above, provides a curious postscript to the discussion of consequences for individuals in BA. The *Guardian* reported on 28 January 1993 that confidential papers collected by a former aide of Sir Colin Marshall had been offered for auction by a New York lawyer. This former aide was Michael Levin, who had acted as a management consultant for BA between 1983 and 1989 when he was dismissed. He died in 1991. The contents of the papers have yet to be revealed.

Consequences for Virgin

The winning of the case and the positive publicity for Virgin Atlantic resulting from it should help Virgin in its campaign to open up competition in the civil aviation industry.

Mr Branson divided up the damages paid by BA amongst his workforce at Virgin Atlantic in an action which received widespread press coverage. In a letter to his staff he wrote, 'Thank you all for your help in our defence. After all a Virgin's honour is her most prized possession.'

Mr Branson indicated that he expected an expression of good faith from BA.

He also put his case to the Secretary of State for Transport that more slots should be released at Heathrow generally. The official government view is that the court case and the slots issue are unconnected. Slots are agreed by an independent committee made up of the airlines.

Clearly, the outcome of the case has opened up some possibilities for Virgin. Its ability to exploit whatever commercial advantage might accrue is, however, limited by the structure of the industry and by the system of public regulation and control.

Postscript

Protracted negotiations between Virgin and BA aimed at settling the dispute between them came to halt on 19 March 1993. They had started in January, immediately after the court case. They focused on demands by Virgin for compensation from BA for business lost by Virgin during the 'dirty tricks' period.

Mr Branson claimed that BA had insisted on demanding a commitment from Virgin not to refer again to the dirty tricks campaign. He was prepared to accept the £9 million financial compensation, but not to accept a clause in the draft agreement which he claimed would 'gag' Virgin and restrict 'its ability to refer to the case in any further actions or to provide information to anyone else in a similar dispute' (*Guardian*, 18.1.93).

BA's Group Managing Director, Mr Robert Ayling, said, 'We have simply asked them not to rake over the events of the past. The fundamental point on which we cannot agree with Virgin is their requirement to reopen past events' (*Guardian*, 18.1.93).

BA published the controversial clause. It reads:

British Airways and Virgin Atlantic agree that they shall each use their best endeavours to discourage media coverage or comment about the past relationship between BA and VA and the matters covered by this agreement (*Independent*, 20.3.93).

Virgin instructed its lawyers to consider all the remedies available to it, including UK legislation concerning the misuse of computer information, (The Data Protection Act and the Computer Misuse Act), US anti-trust laws and the competition rules of the Treaty of Rome through the European Commission.

Whichever route was finally chosen by Virgin, it was likely to be a very costly and prolonged business with no certainty of a successful outcome for Mr Branson.

The British government was said to be unhappy about the prolonged dispute. Adverse publicity, especially in American courts, would damage its position in discussions with the US government about aviation deregulation (*Financial Times*, 20.3.93).

References

Bruce, M. (1987) Managing People First – Bringing the Service Concept to British Airways, *Industrial & Commercial Training*, Mar/April.

Höpfl, H., Mith, S. & Spencer, S. (1992) Values and Valuation: The Conflicts between Culture Change and Job Cuts, *Personnel Review*, Vol. 21 No. 1, pp. 24–38.

Young, D. (1989) *British Airways – Putting the Customer First*, Ashridge Strategic Management Centre, July.

Further reading

Clutterbuck, D. et al. (1992) *Actions Speak Louder: A Management Guide to Corporate Social Responsibility*, London: Kogan Page.

Donaldson, J. (1989) *Key Issues in Business Ethics*, Academic Press, Harcourt Brace Jovanovich.

Shaw, W. & Barry, V. (1989) *Moral Issues in Business*, Wadsworth.

APPENDIX 12A
BA Annual Report 1991–92, Chairman's Statement

I BEGAN my annual report to you a year go by describing the preceding 12 months as among the most volatile in the history of our industry. Times since then have been little, if any, easier. The effects of the Gulf war persisted well into the financial year ended 31 March 1992.

In fact, 1991 has been described as the most difficult year since records began. ICAO, the International Civil Aviation Organisation has reported the first ever annual fall in international scheduled passenger traffic down overall by six per cent, with IATA, the industry association estimating combined losses on international scheduled services alone of some $4 billion.

Against this background, I think we may fairly describe British Airways' performance as highly creditable.

Profits are up 119 per cent to £285 million at the pre-tax level and turnover up six per cent, leading the Board to recommend a final dividend of 7.24 pence a share, against the 6.05 pence in each of the past two years. This would give dividends for the full year of 10.18 pence a share, a rise of 15 per cent.

To accomplish this, your company had to call upon its considerable store of talent, skill, ingenuity and sheer determination as never before. The World's Biggest Offer, our imaginative and bold promotion, which took off on 23 April last year, jumpstarted the world travel market after the slump caused by the Gulf war. Besides creating immense goodwill towards British Airways, this daring promotion attracted publicity worth tens of millions of pounds. More importantly, it ensured that we recovered from the downturn faster than our rivals. Meanwhile we have had to contend with economic recession in our main markets, which has meant that a return to more normal trading conditions has not happened as speedily as we would have wished.

As expected, we have also faced increasingly tough competition, particularly at our Heathrow home base. Following changes in the government's traffic distribution rules controlling access to the airport, the number of carriers competing with us there last summer increased by 17, to 87. They include some of the largest and most competitive airlines in the world. We have responded strongly, with a whole host of marketing initiatives and product enhancements. The result has been an increase in our market share at London.

Within the company, we have acted energetically in the past 12 months to reduce our costs, with the support of our employees and trade unions. The contraction in the size of our workforce has been achieved through early retirement, voluntary severance and the disposal of certain activities, with a consequent increase in productivity of almost 12 per cent.

We have made some important changes in the structure of our business. In order to liberate resources for the development of the airline, we sold the business formerly carried on by British Airways Engine Overhaul Limited to a subsidiary company of General Electric Company of the USA. We believe that the new owners, as engine manufacturers, will be able to invest further resources in the development of this

excellent business, while allowing us to get on with what we do best. We also contracted out our property maintenance and parts of our security functions

We have carried out in-depth reviews of our operations at Gatwick and in the UK regions, to ensure that these activities have the best opportunities to reach adequate levels of profitability.

We exceeded our initial targeted savings of £200 million in the initial phase of our three-year Gap Closure programme by £65 million. We are aiming to trim a further £150 million from our costs in the 1992–93 financial year.

What we shall not trim, however, is the quality of our customer service. In our determination to build on this principal underlying strength of British Airways we recently launched "Winning for Customers", the latest and most extensive in our series of customer service development initiatives. Every employee will take part in its corporate event called "Winners". Our intention is that this programme should gain us as much of a competitive edge in the 1990s as did our original "Putting People First" initiative in the 1980s.

There has been a great deal of media speculation in the past year regarding British Airways' globalisation plans. Although we remain committed to the concept of a global airline, and while we believe our long-term future may be bound up with worldwide alliances, we are still in a position of strength which many would envy. We will not act in haste and repent at leisure. Finding the right partner remains high on our agenda, but there is much else besides. Until the right deal presents itself, we will continue to operate a highly successful, profitable business achieving exceptional levels of customer satisfaction.

Growth prospects for this industry remain sound. British Airways is in a good position to take advantage of the opportunities afforded by the liberalisation of the industry provided the playing field is level and "competition" is not misinterpreted to mean "substitution". We are encouraged by the support of the UK's newly-elected Government for opening the skies of Europe and for examining the role of state subsidies enjoyed by some continental carriers – particularly as the United Kingdom holds the presidency of the European Community in the six months leading up to 1993 and the dawning of the single European market.

We now have our own first platform on the continent, with the establishment of the new German airline Deutsche BA, in which we hold a 49 per cent stake. We are also progressing the development of Air Russia, working with our partners in Russia.

The Company's Directors have for many years

benefited from the counsel of Robert Ayling, in his capacity as Company Secretary, Legal Director and Director of Human Resources. Following his appointment as Director of Marketing and Operations, we were pleased to welcome him in December as a full member of the Board.

British Airways is now firmly on its flightpath to recovery after the turbulence caused by the Gulf conflict and recession in many countries. We have demonstrated our ability to manage this business effectively during the most severe downturn it has experienced. In doing so, we have earned the admiration of the industry.

For this, the employees of your Company deserve a substantial vote of thanks reflected by my Board's decision to increase the level of their profit sharing bonus from the formula driven 1.4 weeks to two weeks' basic pay. Their contribution in a trying, often unsettling and constantly challenging 12 months cannot be overstated.

Nonetheless, they and I are only too well aware that there is still much to achieve if we are to accomplish our mission of becoming the undisputed best and most successful company in the industry – to which we remain committed.

Lord King of Wartnaby *Chairman*

BOARD MEMBERS AND EXECUTIVE MANAGEMENT

BOARD MEMBERS

Lord King of Wartnaby (74) *Chairman*
Chairman since 1981. Chairman, Babcock International PLC since 1972. Director, Daily Telegraph plc. (B)

Sir Colin Marshall (58) *Deputy Chairman and Chief Executive*
Chief Executive since 1983. Director, Grand Metropolitan PLC, IBM United Kingdom Holdings Limited, Midland Group plc and British Tourist Authority. (B)

Sir Michael Angus (62) *Deputy Chairman and Chairman of the Audit and Remuneration Committees*
Deputy Chairman, Whitbread PLC and National Westminster Bank PLC. Director, Thorn EMI plc. President, Confederation of British Industry. (A, C)

Robert Ayling (45) *Director of Marketing and Operations*
Joined the Board of British Airways in December 1991 after his appointment as Director of Marketing and Operations in September. Joined the airlines Legal Director in 1985 and subsequently took on the duties of Company Secretary and, later, Director of Human Resources. Formerly Under Secretary at the Department of Trade.

Derek Stevens (53) *Chief Financial Officer*
Chief Financial Officer since 1989. Formerly Finance Director, TSB Group plc.

Captain Colin Barnes (58) *Chairman of the Air Safety Review Committee*
Joined the Board of British Airways in 1991 after 36 years flying with the airline as a pilot, the last ten as Chief Pilot and a final five as Director of Flight Crew. (A, B)

Michael Davies (57)
Chairman, Calor Group PLC, Wiltshire PLC and Perkins Foods PLC. Deputy Chairman, TI Group Plc. (A, B, C)

Sir Francis Kennedy KCMG CBE (66) *Special Advisor to Chairman and Board*
Diplomatic Service, 1964–86. Director, Fluor Daniel Corp. and Smith and Nephew plc. (B)

The Hon Charles H. Price II (61)
Former United States Ambassador to the UK. Chairman, Mercantile Bank of Kansas City. Director, Hanson Plc, Texaco Inc, Sprint Corporation and New York Times Company Inc. (A, B, C)

Lord White of Hull KBE (69)
Chairman, Hanson Industries. (A, C)

The letters in brackets indicate membership of the following committees of the Board:
(A) Audit Committee, (B) Air Safety Review Committee, (C) Remuneration Committee

EXECUTIVE MANAGEMENT
David Burnside (40) *Director of Public Affairs*
Alistair Cumming (57) *Director of Engineering*
Dr Michael Davies (54) *Director of Health Services*
Tony Galbraith (53) *Treasurer*
David Holmes (57) *Director of Government and Industry Affairs*
David Hyde (55) *Director of Safety, Security and the Environment*
Captain Jock Lowe (48) *Director of Flight Crew*
Clive Mason (48) *Director of Purchasing and Supply*
Roger Maynard (49) *Director of Corporate Strategy*
Gail Redwood (43) *Company Secretary*
Mervyn Walker (33) *Legal Director*
John Watson (48) *Director of Human Resources and Information Management*

APPENDIX 12B
BA Annual Report 1991–92, Shareholder information and directors' interests

SHAREHOLDERS

As at 15 May 1992 there were 265,819 shareholders. An analysis is given below.

Size of shareholding	Percentage of shareholders	Percentage of shares	Classification shareholding	Percentage of shareholders	Percentage of shares
1 – 1,000	95.59	9.11	Individuals	98.33	12.21
1,001 – 5,000	3.77	2.70	Nominee companies	1.02	77.15
5,001 – 10,000	0.24	0.61	Insurance companies	0.03	3.72
10,001 – 50,000	0.18	1.57	Banks	0.14	1.52
50,001 – 100,000	0.05	1.43	Pension funds	0.02	0.90
100,001 – 250,000	0.07	4.47	Other corporate holders	0.46	4.50
250,001 – 500,000	0.05	6.36			
500,001 – 750,000	0.01	2.99			
750,001 – 1,000,000	0.01	3.06			
Over 1,000,000	0.03	67.70			
	100.00	100.00		100.00	100.00

The following have holdings in the Company in excess of 3 per cent of the total shares issued:

	Percentage of shareholding
Templeton Investment Management Limited	5.53
Fidelity Investments	4.52
Schroder Investment Management	3.96

Morgan Guaranty Trust Company of New York, the Company's ADR Depositary, has a non-beneficial interest in 17.68 per cent of the shares in the name of Guaranty Nominees Limited. British Airways is not aware of any other interest in its shares of three per cent or more.

DIRECTORS' INTERESTS
At 31 March 1992

	Ordinary shares subject to no restrictions		Ordinary shares subject to restrictions		British Airways Plc Options Executive and SAYE Share Schemes		Options exercised during year·	British Airways Capital Ltd Convertible Capital Bonds	
	31 March 1992	1 April 1991	31 March 1992	1 April 1991	31 March 1992	1 April 1991		31 March 1992	1 April 1991
Lord King	105,000	35,084	–	316	296,809	853,330	556,521	13,332	13,332
Sir Colin Marshall	25,836	25,520	–	316	485,436	710,155	224,719	11,304	11,304
Sir Michael Angus	3,000	3,000	–	–	–	–	–	1,333	1,333
R J Ayling**	4,459	3,485	744	1,718	215,261	334,224	187,938	–	–
D M Stevens	5,050	5,050	3,403	3,403	337,254	337,254	–	109	109
A M Davies	5,060	5,060	–	–	–	–	–	2,221	2,221
Captain C A Barnes	7,983	831	4,723	6,875	69,976	208,334	135,692	644	644
Sir Francis Kennedy	5,250	5,250	1,860	1,860	166,666	166,666	–	1,421	1,333
Hon Charles Price II	10,000*	10,000*	–	–	–	–	–	–	–
Lord White	–	–	–	–	–	–	–	–	–
	171,638	93,280	10,730	14,488	1,571,402	2,609,963	1,104,870	30,364	30,276

* Held in American Depositary Receipts
** R J Ayling was appointed to the Board on 16 December 1991.

The Directors' interests set out above are in each case beneficial. The options under the Executive Share Option and Savings Related Share Options Schemes are at prices varying between 135p and 210p per share. No Director has any beneficial interest in shares in any subsidiaries of the company other than those shown above in the 9.75 per cent Convertible Capital Bonds 2005 in British Airways Capital Limited. There have been no changes in the interests set out above between the end of the financial year and 18 May 1992.

APPENDIX 12C
BA Annual Report 1991–92, Principal investments

At 31 March 1992

SUBSIDIARY UNDERTAKINGS
Principal subsidiary undertakings are all wholly-owned direct subsidiaries except where indicated

	Principal activities	Country of incorporation and principal operations
Air Miles Travel Promotions Ltd	Airline marketing	England
(51 per cent of ordinary shares owned)		
Bedford Associates Inc	Specialist computer reservations software	USA
(a subsidiary undertaking of BritAir Acquisition Corp Inc)		
BritAir Acquisition Corp Inc	Holding company	USA
British Airways Associated Companies Ltd	Airline management services	England
British Airways Australia (Holdings) Pty Ltd	Holding company	Australia
British Airways Capital Ltd	Airline finance	Jersey
(89 per cent of founders' shares owned)		
British Airways Finance BV	Airline finance	Netherlands
British Airways Holidays Ltd	Package holidays	England
Caledonian Airways Ltd	Airline operations	England
Chartridge Centre Ltd	Airline training services	England
Speedbird Insurance Co Ltd	Airline insurance	Bermuda
Travel Automation Services Ltd *(trading as Galileo UK)*	Computer reservations systems	England

ASSOCIATED UNDERTAKINGS

	Percentage of equity owned	Principal activities	Country of incorporation and principal operations
Air Russia	31	Airline operations	Russia
Concorde International Travel Pty Ltd	50	Airline marketing	Australia
Deutsche BA Luftfahrtgesellschaft mbH	49	Airline operations	Germany
Euro-Hub (Birmingham) Ltd	21	Airport terminal services	England
G B Airways (Holdings) Ltd	49	Airline holding company	Jersey
The Galileo Company Ltd	24	Computer reservations systems	England
World Aviation Systems (Australia) Pty Ltd	50	Airline marketing	Australia

TRADE INVESTMENTS

	Percentage of equity owned	Principal activities	Country of incorporation and principal operations
Covia Partnership	11.0	Computer reservations system	USA
Hogg Robinson plc	12.4	Travel, transport and financial services	England
Ruby Aircraft Leasing and Trading Ltd	19.3	Aircraft leasing	England
Sapphire Aircraft Leasing and Trading Ltd	19.3	Aircraft leasing	England
The Plimsoll Line Limited	49.9	Airline holding company	England

(Holding company of Brymon Aviation Ltd and Birmingham European Airways Ltd. The investment is equivalent to 14 per cent of the voting rights.)

APPENDIX 12D
BA's Code of business conduct

The success of British Airways is dependent on the quality of the decisions and the behaviour of individuals at all levels throughout the organisation. The code has been developed to provide guidance and assistance to both managers and staff in their dealings with all those with whom we do business, with our customers and suppliers, and with each other.

Adherence to the principles will help ensure that our reputation and success that has been built up over the years through the dedicated hard work of you and your colleagues will continue to grow.

Judgement and discretion will need to be exercised in applying the principles where, at first sight, they appear to be at variance with local custom and practice or commercial common sense.

It is not the intent of the code to anticipate and provide a framework of governing values and advice on how to proceed when making difficult decisions namely to establish the norms of business behaviour throughout the company.

General Standards

Compliance: Comply with all the laws that regulate and apply to the company, its systems and the conduct of its business.

Fairness: Treat all groups and individuals with whom we have a business relationship in a fair, open and respectful manner.

Integrity: Show respect for the individual, treating each in a consistent way and honouring commitments made.

Openness: Share and declare information on personal and corporate conflicts of interest (political, financial, relationship) including the offer or acceptance of gifts or hospitality of significant value. Seek guidance and where appropriate confirmation from a higher authority before acting.

Honesty: This goes beyond simply telling the truth to ensuring that any misrepresentation is quickly corrected. Do not allow people to be misled. Where there are valid reasons for withholding information, be clear about the motives and if possible explain why you are doing so.

Fair Competition: Ensure comparisons drawn with competitors and working partners are based on fact and avoid innuendo. Competition should be based on the quality value and integrity of British Airways' service and products.

Determination: Demonstrate a sense of purpose and commitment to achieving the optimum even in adversity.

Responsiveness: Recognise changes in the business environment and use a creative flexible style to respond to them.

Enablement: Provide sufficient guidance to enable individuals to act upon their own initiative to solve problems and grow in their role.

Conformity: Promote corporate values and competitive edge through the established performance systems of performance and appraisal.

Through employing these practices and behaviours, staff should:

- Use British Airways' stated goals and objectives as guidance, using your values and judgement to interpret against the principles of this code.
- Treat others as you would like to be treated.
- Be prepared to solicit views as to whether something would be appropriate before action, rather than after.
- Discuss difficult decisions with those whose values and judgement you respect. Use company process to earn respect.
- Ask whether you would feel comfortable explaining your decision or behaviour to your boss, your family or the media.
- Be prepared to challenge if you believe others are acting in an unethical way. Create the climate and opportunities for people to voice genuinely held concerns about behaviour or decisions that they perceive to be unprofessional or inappropriate.
- Do not tolerate any form of retribution against those who do speak up. Protect individuals' careers and anonymity if necessary. Encourage an environment of learning from mistakes and mutual trust in each others' motives and judgements.
- Treat the assets and property of British Airways and its customers and its suppliers with the same respect as you would your own. Apart from tangible assets this would include company information as well as the name, image and reputation of British Airways.

The Cooperative Alliance between the Bank of St Hellier of the UK, and Banco Real of Spain*

In late 1988, the UK bank the Bank of St Hellier (BSH)[†] and Banco Real of Spain[†] announced plans for a wide-ranging commercial cooperation, backed by a cross-holding of shares of an equivalent market value in each other's organisation.

This alliance was intended to be the backbone of EC strategy for both banks. Real was already well established in Latin America, and both banks had some presence in the USA. Both felt unable to develop a Europe-wide strategy of their own, when faced with the established presence and resources of the larger EC banks. For BSH particularly, the possibility of takeover could not be ignored; substantial family ownership and strong liquidity served to protect Real from that threat.

The banking environment

Until the country became an EC member in 1985, Spanish banking was closed to non-Spanish banks, with the exception of very few with a long history of banking in the territory, pre-dating Franco. The need to make the sector more competitive in the early 1980s encouraged the Spanish government to stage-manage the takeover of some weaker institutions by foreign banks. However, with the issue of the Second Banking Coordination Directive in 1988, a single market in EC banking came closer, and those not positioned to compete at this level could prepare for takeover. The directive provides for a 'single banking licence' whereby any credit institution authorised to act as such in one EC market is automatically qualified to carry out those same activities in any other member state.

This, controversially, applied to non-EC financial institutions too. The directive also changes, among other things, minimum capital requirements and capital adequacy arrangements by stating minimum levels to be met by all, in part to avoid use of the least strictly regulated country as the channel for entry by non-EC firms.

Given these changes, financial institutions throughout Europe were conscious of the need to build a position in the EC that would be of sufficient substance to meet the growing competition from outside the region, as well as maintain their relative position vis-à-vis local rivals. Hence the search by BSH and Real, both smaller European operators with limited non-domestic presence, for partners in a European growth strategy.

Reaching agreement

One executive commented on the apparent mismatch of image between the 'careful' north European banker counting and protecting his reserves, and the dashing Spanish patron taking care of his friends and leaving everything to mañana However, both banks had carried out a structured search for potential partners in the four main EC banking countries; they had found banks too large, and too politically influenced, to be considered potentially 'equal' partners. Real as a family-owned bank was freer from political influence than many Spanish institutions, and participation in the market was attractive because of its recent liberalisation, the dynamism of the national industry, and the continuing availability of high margins; the Spanish are accustomed to paying for their banking services.

---

* Copyright © Dorothea Noble, University of Hertfordshire Business School

[†] Not the companies' real names

From the Spanish perspective, the UK was attractive as an advanced competitive market, open to international competition on many fronts for a long time and with a reputation for product developments that could have immediate application in Spain. Also links between the north of Spain and the UK are long-established, through trade mainly, and the more recent developments of emigration and tourism. 'When we chanced upon the BSH it seemed to fit, happily.'

BSH was in the final phase of restructuring in the UK at the time; its position was fragile and it was vulnerable to hostile takeover; BSH needed to have 'a good friend on board' according to one manager at Real. With an important presence in the UK, and an international outlook, it was an attractive target at a time when all EC banks were on the acquisition trail. Real's 10 per cent holding in BSH gave something of the 'white knight' role to the alliance, 'giving them time to get to know each other and see whether merger may eventually be a good thing'. The bank stressed that this was a secondary motive, however, with the main focus on the benefits of joint action in specific areas.

The banks were about the same size at the time, with just over £1 billion equity each, and profits of £200 million. Assets were valued at approximately £15 billion for Real and £20 billion for BSH, according to an BSH press release at the time. Market valuation for Real was higher, so equivalent financial investment would eventually give BSH 5 per cent of Real and Real 10 per cent of BSH, the exchange to be phased over an agreed period.

Their motives were based on the realisation that increasingly their existing customers' market would be Europe, and that both banks would have to be able to provide those services currently available at home in other EC markets. By each giving immediate access to the other's domestic branch networks their range was greatly extended. In addition, BSH bought 50 per cent of the equity of two small banks in Belgium and Germany that Real had acquired the previous year from Bank of America, and they became 50 per cent partners in operations in Gibraltar and Portugal. Each of these joint ventures was to be managed under the leadership of either BSH or Real to simplify reporting structures and to exploit the most appropriate experience. BSH had concluded that parity and the existence of complementary skills and opportunities would be essential to the success of the alliance; these projects seemed to be prime examples of that.

The nature of the agreement developed through a series of conversations between the presidents and chief executives of the two banks. From discussion of the theme of providing services to each other's customers as a starting point one executive reported how other ideas came, and some have flown, and others have not flown as we've talked and come together'. The alliance 'wasn't set up with any particular structured plan in mind; it was very much set up to be in a position to cooperate, to jointly take advantage of opportunities as they came along'. (One manager likened it to the Treaty of Rome – 'designed to accommodate every eventuality'.) The discussions threw up broad areas of interest, in addition to those of servicing each other's customer base through existing branch networks, and specialist subsidiaries. Prospective areas included technology development, the consideration of joint acquisitions, exploration of ways to improve cross-border financial services, and possible joint action in the Far East. The resulting agreement was 'something looser than acquisition, with the potential to be something else, as and when it became necessary'.

The press reported the scoffing of securities analysts: 'How will it benefit shareholders; when will they see a return on their investment?' The straight-talking chairman of BSH, tired of being quizzed on the relationship's bottom line, has repeatedly stated: 'We are taking a 10-year view. This is not about making profits 12 months from now! '

Some have viewed it more favourably. 'They are starting out small with broad objectives rather than attempting to instantly smash themselves together. . . I think that has a better chance of success. One manager queried the validity of other banks' strategies:

> We've just sold two of Real's secondary bank brands to a major French institution [Crédit Lyonnaise] for a massive premium. I'm intrigued to know how they expect to recoup that investment. They would say the same as us – that they take a long-term view – but the bill they're facing is substantially larger than the one we face.

Getting organised

Initial contacts and negotiations had involved the most senior executives of the banks, and their involvement continued to be of major importance once the agreement became official. Their stated objective was to allow the development of both groups throughout Europe to proceed more rapidly than either could achieve alone by:

- developing profitable customer bases in Europe;
- marketing improved cross-border financial services;
- providing services to corporate and personal customers of both Groups through a larger number of locations in Europe (press release, 1988).

Interpreted by one of their managers three years later, these become:

- To serve our domestic customer bases in foreign countries through close cooperation with our respective partner.
- To look for opportunities and approaches to the rest of Europe to achieve that service to our domestic customer base in the other European countries too.
- To jointly cooperate to take advantage of niche opportunities that may arise in third countries.
- Where possible, to transfer product ideas, technological ideas, management ideas between ourselves in order to position ourselves better in our domestic markets.

These reflect the two banks' philosophy that banking is essentially local in each market. Their need for EC-wide presence was based on their domestic customers' interest in receiving services over a wider geographic area than previously, not on the belief that they could offer domestic banking to the nationals of each country where they had a presence. Their expansion would therefore be by acquisition of small banks serving local niches, and offering some established branch network which could be accessed straight away for the partners' own customers, and which would continue to operate locally for its existing customer base. These would subsequently gain access to the wide service base offered by the alliance and its network throughout the EC. 'Any commercial customers of ours should know that we can service them anywhere in Europe.' This contrasts with the strategies of other UK clearing banks, Barclays and National Westminster for instance, who have expanded under their own names in all EC markets, often gaining access by initial acquisition, and subsequently expanding organically.

Certain ground rules were established for the alliance partners to follow too. Both banks were committed to remaining independent, therefore share holdings would not be increased by either party without prior reference to the other bank. Shares would not be sold without offering the partner bank first refusal on the holding; and each would support the other's strategy by voting the shares it holds according to the recommendation of the other's Board (press release, 1988). These developed to include giving each other first refusal on sharing any further investments either may wish to make in any other European country; and that alliances with other banks from their respective territories would only be undertaken with the full knowledge of their partner.

Development of the alliance became the responsibility of a surveillance committee, which met every six weeks and was made up of the chief executives and presidents of the two banks, and several senior managers. Their initial role was to identify the broad areas of greatest potential for commercial cooperation and operationalise the process of investigating them. Six broad areas of interest were defined:

- Access for all customers to services via each other's branches.
- Shared ownership of operations in other EC countries.
- Collaboration between the two investment banking arms of each group.
- Technology development, with priority for electronic home banking, self-service terminals, and enhanced branch technology.
- Joint acquisitions in countries where neither bank has access to a branch network, with one of the partners being designated in each case as lead management.
- Exploration of ways to enhance service to customers in the Far East.

This committee set a framework for the alliance, formed a hub for the exploration of ideas and the identification of those to receive priority treatment. The seeds of cooperation and trust would be nurtured and spread from this centre, as these were the senior people who had sensed the initial rapport, and had had confidence in the ability of the two organisations to collaborate.

Audit teams were proposed for each of the areas of interest, with representatives from each partner; they would work with internal teams in the partners' offices to discover specific systems, products and techniques that could be applicable in the operations of the other partner; identify areas of development where work was complementary and worth coordinated action; and report back to the surveillance committee with recommendations for priority attention. Overall priorities and budget allocations were approved by the committee, with operations managers ensuring that appropriate task forces and project teams would take up the agreed actions.

In addition to these meetings, the chief executives and presidents of the two banks were members of the other's Board, so information exchange at the strategic level was formally well established.

As one manager put it: 'We are trying to build a flexible management structure, a flexible branch network, a flexible management information system, in order to be able to compete in whatever situation arises.'

Operation of the alliance: making it work

The technological audit jointly carried out in both banks generated many opportunities for shared development; the most notable to the international customer must be their work on speeding international movements of money.

The inter-bank transaction network

A senior manager described how this idea developed in the following terms:

> We had had this idea floating around for a while to link our computer systems in order to provide same day transactions, real time transactions between Spain and Britain. We looked at that idea and thought about it, referred it to various technological bods in Spain and in the UK, who talked together and reported to the surveillance committee; I wonder if it would work – but maybe it won't; I tell you what, we'll try it with our cash point network first. So this time last year [1990] we linked the two computers together and now you can withdraw money from your UK account here in Spain just using your BSH card in a Spanish machine.[*] Right; that works so can we extend it to provide a similar service, or even a more complicated one to medium-sized corporate customers? And we examined that idea and eventually decided it was feasible; and now [1991] we're launching an inter-bank system and will be grafting on more complicated corporate-oriented products as we check that it works. . . This has allowed us to do things today in a way that was impossible just a few months ago.

Since 1991, this inter-bank transaction system has expanded steadily. It moved from project status with four-month exchanges of IT staff, to become a joint venture between the two alliance banks, the joint venture being charged with the responsibility of developing the service and marketing it to other interested parties. The service offered the virtually instant transfer of funds among banks who are members of the network, without reference to existing financial infrastuctures; initially it was targeted at small transfers, but established operators in the transfer of large sums saw this as the first step in a progress towards competing for large transfers.

At first the network was extended to link BSH and Real to their other joint ventures; subsequently, they envisaged that one bank in each EC country could join and be the access point for all national subscribers; by mid-1993 they were having some difficulty in deciding how best to extend the network. Five US banks were showing interest in joining. Limiting access meant that competitor products were being developed, not only by alternative EC bank networks, but also by the 'American interlopers', Visa and American Express. It seemed that the two banks' resources were not sufficient to tackle its further expansion alone.

The alliance partners had drawn on British Telecom and Digital Equipment Corporation for support with the initial phase of development. Early in 1994 a US computer services giant took a 30 per cent share in the network, bringing in expertise to boost its expansion – a digital superhighway for the banking industry. With a director of global business in place, and letters of intent from a further eight international banks wanting to join the network by the end of 1994, the venture's goal was to capture 10 per cent of the international payments market by the end of the decade, and have a customer base of 500 banks.

Additional technological benefits

Other areas were identified for transfer between the banks, and adaptation to suit other markets or internal systems. Real were seen to be 'leading the pack' with management information systems, particularly for tracking the profitability of individual branches, customers and products; BSH's insurance technology system, telephone insurance, was seen as having great potential in Spain; and both studied the German joint venture's practice on consumer credit products

---

[*] For Spanish people operating in the UK it was slightly more difficult because exchange controls were still in place, but it was still technically possible for them to access Spanish accounts from the UK.

to exchange ideas on applications over a wider market. 'We're promoting interchange of people at the technology level, and looking for every single opportunity where we can do technological or product transfers.'

Despite the potential from their shared ideas, both banks were convinced that at the individual and small corporate customer level, products and services would be different from one country to another.

> There will be a natural process of convergence as we put new products on the market, as they do the same, as we gain each other's ideas, and as products across Europe become more standardised. But I think we'll see two different sets of products for the foreseeable future. As we go up the tree in terms of customer size, you'll see an increasing convergence and standardisation of the products that both banks provide, but we're always independently seeking UK solutions to UK problems, and Spanish solutions to Spanish problems. That's one advantage we have from this alliance format – no-one at the top, as head of European branch banking, has any crazy idea that we should be able to standardise lending products for all customers across Europe.

International expansion

On setting up the alliance, BSH had bought into existing branch networks that Real already owned in Portugal, Germany and Belgium, and Real had bought into BSH's existing operation in Gibraltar. These continued therefore as joint ventures with one of the partners being lead management in each case. 'We have representatives on the boards of all of them and each is confident that the other can manage the day to day operational management as well as anyone else – and we talk very openly'. The plan was to continue to expand through the acquisition of small branch networks, with the initial focus being on France and Italy.

As other developments take place, consideration is given to the possible benefits of joint action. Both banks had investments in the USA, not originally planned as an area for co-operation, but 'these things get talked about, is there anything we can do together in America? There's no formal consultation structure, there's just lots of chat.'

New product development

The same applied to the development of banking products; the UK had more experience of interest bearing current accounts in 1988, 'so there were conversations between the consumer people here and the consumer people in the UK about the pitfalls and possibilities of that; we're bringing experience to bear in each other's marketplace and we hope there will be opportunity for product interchange.'

Evidence of the influence exists: Real is attributed with starting the war of the 'supercuentos' when it sought to expand its domestic customer base by announcing interest-bearing current accounts in 1990, causing something of a shake-up in traditional Spanish personal banking. The press in 1994 talked also of how Real had 'built up an international reputation for innovation – in fields such as telephone banking, a probable offshoot of BSH's long experience in the direct selling of financial services.

The City's questioning of BSH's dual strategy in direct and branch banking is enlightening. According to an analyst at SG Warburg quoted in the *Financial Times*:

> Doubts about it having overlapping distribution methods. . .are easing. As more banks reduce their branches and turn to telephone and direct selling methods, BSH's dual delivery approach appears increasingly sensible. BSH's ability via direct selling to attract reliable, well-off customers means they can take market share cheaply, and with little risk. 'People do not realise the value of having more than one brand.' BSH has the ability via direct selling to price personal loans differently according to its assessment of how credit-worthy the borrower is. The branch bank could not do it because it would be socially unacceptable.

Day-to-day operation

Management information systems tend to be applied to the overall management of branch networks within each bank separately, with adaptations to suit each other where interactive systems are necessary. The operation of the alliance itself relies on informal contacts and conversations that tap into the experience of project team members, staff exchanges – anyone that has had contact with the partner organisation.

> We have continuous contacts at the highest levels, at levels lower down it's not so well developed yet; it's more difficult to talk to our colleagues where the levels of confidence and trust aren't there yet. We would tend to route through those channels where we have confidence. If someone here in the retail banking side wants to know something about some bit of technology or some work going on in the UK, it will generally get passed up the

line, until we find some point where 'oh yes, I know that guy in London, he's good, he'll help us with that', and it will be done by phone. There's not much need for formal information flows. . .the channels are found on a very *ad hoc* basis. Because we're not a subsidiary, we don't have the fall-back position of saying 'we're the boss – do it!' We have to make personal contacts. We're finding an advantage here through this structure that we wouldn't have if we had direct ownership.

One of the things that developed from the exchange of expert teams to carry out audits, working on identified projects, was the idea of exchanging staff simply with the idea of getting to know each other.

> This was a specific idea, that we should get to know each other at the strategic level and we should let people have a broad idea of what their partners were doing; so we got swapped. One of the problems for staff interchange is that everyone in Spain's head office speaks English, but no-one in the UK speaks Spanish.

They have got round this by having someone from Spain in the UK while projects are going on; he can speak to counterparts in both offices and problems can be solved that way.

Visits to each other's territory automatically mean visiting partner offices.

> I've done a survey and there's someone here [Madrid] from BSH virtually every day; the marketing people come, the technology people, and you'll bump into somebody in the corridor because they're doing a presentation on information systems, or mortgage products, or we're sharing ideas on branch networks.

Management opinion

Managers interviewed expressed a range of views regarding the benefits of the alliance, its success, difficulties associated with it, and perceptions of its value.

Benefits

From the point of view of jointly developed products, and of building up the customer base, there were examples of a high level of success either achieved already, or with increasing potential as time goes by:

> The alliance has created opportunities for differentiating our product that didn't exist before. For example, the ability to make same-day transfers, with fixed fees quoted in advance and the absolute certainty that it's

going to arrive that same day is an incredible new product for the European market; I can't see anyone doing the same thing. Banking though is more than simply the products; it's very much a question of building relationships with clients, but we believe that the technological base that we're building will provide an excellent foundation for gaining new customers and also developing new products for those customers. We'll be able to do – no-one really knows, it's like trying to take a crystal ball.

Its role in the expansion of both banks within the EC remains:

> We believe that the alliance is a key building block in the strategy of maintaining a profitable operation here in Spain, and looking for niches in the rest of Europe; the alliance is key to that.

The value of London as a financial centre, and of an experienced presence there for intelligence about what is going on across Europe, was acknowledged:

> London is for the time being the most important financial market in Europe; what is most important are the informal flows of information – people coming, talking; by just being here you hear things, know what's going on.

Success factors

The significance of an intuitive sense of being able to do business together was repeated often:

> So much of establishing the alliance has really been down to the chemistry between the two sides. The alliance probably wouldn't have happened if the two managements hadn't hit it off; we've been very lucky and the chemistry worked.

The importance of top-level support was indicated too:

> In our bank there's only one person that really matters and that's the Chairman – it's not very democratic.

A manager with Real saw the alliance in 1991 as having worked out well for BSH; it had given them the chance to focus on their restructuring without concern for a hostile takeover, although he questioned whether they could be giving time to European expansion, while preoccupied with restructuring at home. For Real he was not so sure:

> It's hard to say; the intangibles that are building up can't be measured in NPV terms; but at senior level it is taking up a lot of time; however, things may develop over the long term.

Difficulties

Managers repeated the advantage of the alliance in representing a much lower financial commitment, and therefore exposure, than is involved in merger or acquisition:

> There have been painful moments, and pleasant ones, but we're not carrying the same risk, we're not carrying the same weight of expectations.

Even with that, however, the attitude of city analysts has not been helpful; they have criticised the high premiums paid to acquire financial services companies, seeing little prospect of an appropriate return to shareholders in the short term. Yet the lesser commitment of the alliance is viewed with suspicion:

> If there's been one disadvantage of doing it so early, it's been that everyone said great, now what are you going to do, let's see some results, some numbers; let's see your increased profits, and as time goes by analysts say we haven't seen any benefit from this, when are we going to see something credible from the alliance; so if there's a problem it's the perceptions of the market in the very short term.

A manager with Real had a problem in believing the partners would cooperate in areas of strength; in his view, people would only want to cooperate in areas of weakness that they could not progress alone. This demonstrated a lack of trust and confidence in the partnership – it was not easy for him to believe that a good opportunity would be shared: 'Why are they going to give you a piece of their business – only if it is bad!'

Perceptions

A manager with BSH agreed that within the two organisations there was some scepticism about the alliance and its significance. He felt there were two main reasons for this:

> One is that the European market isn't developing quite how we saw it in 1988; it's not developing as fast as we thought, and we realise that cultural factors and national boundaries are still going to play an enormous part in business post-1992. So there aren't the opportunities to gain massive amounts of new business that maybe we thought were there in 1988, which we were afraid of losing. The other reason is that working across borders within whatever structure, be it acquisition or through an alliance, is a lot more difficult that anyone can ever tell you in advance, and it does take time; it takes time to build the trust, it takes time to build the communications. For example, no-one in the BSH speaks Spanish. So, OK, we can do business at the highest level with people who speak English, and we can use people from Spain who can speak English to speak to the BSH; but at the computer level, for example, it takes time for the right people to do the jobs.

The same manager had experienced a conversion regarding face-to-face contact with colleagues and collaborators.

> One thing I was sceptical about when I was working in London was the value of personal contacts. 'What are these people doing, jetting off to Spain, going there for a three-day meeting; I'm sure that isn't necessary, we need to control costs!' What I realise now is that in this kind of business, this kind of structure, personal contact, personal confidence is a number one priority.

As one of the directors exchanged to encourage alliance contacts, he felt there was wide optimism about the alliance, and a strong conviction as to its value:

> We're definitely satisfied with the way it's progressing, despite internal questioning and the scepticism of the analysts; we're satisfied that we're building something quite special and unique, and we're reaching those targets that exist.

PART FIVE

Creativity and tension between legitimate and shadow systems

The paradox of ordinary and extraordinary management

This is a very short part of the book which presents a brief summary of the main points about the management process as a whole, the combination of both ordinary and extraordinary management that is required if an organisation is to be capable of both day-to-day task performance and of new survival strategy generation. The key point it seeks to underline is one that is by now very clear: management is a paradox and that which is required for ordinary management actually blocks that which is required for extraordinary management and vice versa. Creative development flows from the tension between the two systems, not the victory of one over the other. The management of an organisation is a continual process of rearranging this basic paradox.

CHAPTER 13

Strategic management and organisational dynamics in perspective

In Chapter 1 the field of study that we call strategic management was first described in terms of a number of elements. The first element is the feedback loop running from discovery, to choice, to action, and back to discovery again; that is, the process of strategic management which in turn generates the second element of the field of strategy study, namely patterns in organisational action that we may perceive either before or after the event. Those patterns in action continually alter the position of an organisation in relation to actors in its environment and its posture or internal shape. Position and posture determine the final element of the strategy field of study, namely performance. The task of students of management is to identify what kinds of circular feedback processes of strategic management generate patterns, positions, postures and levels of performance that are in some sense successful. In Chapter 1 it was stated that this would require consideration of nine important questions.

The first three of these questions had to do with the dynamics of organisational development: the stability or otherwise of the patterns associated with those dynamics; the kinds of feedback systems that generate those patterns; and the effect of uncertainty and ambiguity on the operation of those feedback systems. In relation to these questions we have discovered that:

- Organisations are systems that take the form of webs of nonlinear feedback loops connecting the individuals, groups, functions, tasks and processes within an organisation to each other, and connecting an organisation to those other systems that are its environment.
- As soon as we put forward prescriptions on how an organisation is to achieve long-term success, we make assumptions about the nature of those feedback loops, the state they operate in when successful, and the dynamics or patterns of change they generate over time.
- The prescriptions will succeed only if our assumptions about the dynamics are a useful simplification of the world we have to operate in.
- Those prescriptions that the great majority of practitioners find acceptable, espouse and believe in are all derived from the assumption that successful organ-

isations are dominated by negative feedback loops that keep them close to states of stable equilibrium where patterns of change in behaviour are regular and predictable. It is implicitly assumed that systems affected by positive feedback loops, apart from steady growth, will be explosively unstable and thus fail and that it is possible to remove or greatly reduce the impact of positive feedback loops in human systems.

- However, the closeness to reality of these assumptions and the usefulness of the prescriptions they lead to has been questioned for a long time. Systems dynamics, as well as models developed by social psychologists, have all pointed to the irremovable presence in real life human systems of amplifying, positive feedback loops leading to unexpected and unintended outcomes. More recently, studies have shown that companies moving to either stable or unstable equilibrium fail, that successful organisations operate in some state of non-equilibrium. That state is one of contradiction and continuing paradox which produces dynamics of irregular changes in behaviour that are difficult to predict.

- The modern science of complex dynamics, the theories of chaos, complexity and self-organisation, explains such states of non-equilibrium and the dynamics they generate. These scientific developments show that nonlinear feedback systems have a choice between operation in stable equilibrium, or unstable equilibrium, or the border between stability and instability. The border between stability and instability is a far-from-equilibrium state of chaos where specific long-term outcomes are unknowable, but they always display recognisable qualitative patterns that humans are capable of using to think by analogy.

- Since organisations are nonlinear feedback systems they must be capable of operating far from equilibrium, a paradoxical state that combines both stability and instability. For a long time now organisational theorists have pointed to the contradictory nature of organising. They have pointed to the diametrically opposed requirements to integrate and divide up tasks, to maintain the system and yet change it, and many others. It has been clear that a position in which one of these sets of forces dominates leads to failure. It is therefore clear that innovative organisations operate far from equilibrium.

- The very structure that causes long-term unpredictability also makes it possible for far-from-equilibrium systems to be continually creative. Such systems create variety, they innovate, through a process of self-organisation that also involves instability and destruction.

Returning to the questions identified in Chapter 1, we can now see that in the ensuing chapters we also developed some insight into those questions concerned with the roles of shared beliefs and intentions in driving organisational strategy, the impact of group behavioural dynamics, and the relationships between the formal and informal systems of an organisation. This insight has been achieved through comparing and contrasting two fundamentally different ways of conceptualising the process of strategic management.

On the one hand you can think of the successful organisation as the one that forms a clear intention of the future state it is to occupy and then intentionally follows a predetermined route to that state. Here the successful organisation is pulled by prior shared intention to an approximately known point in the long-term future. The strategic management task is then to identify the future state and take control of the path the organisation is to follow to reach it. This would be the task of managers at the top of the hierarchy and the more stable the organisation the more likely it would be to succeed in identifying and reaching the future point.

On the other hand, you can think of the successful organisation as one that is propelled from its current state to create and discover a long-term future that its managers cannot now foresee. Here the successful organisation is driven by contradiction and conflict in the here-and-now to develop new ways of understanding what it is doing, new ways of more usefully rearranging the paradoxical forces of organising. The strategic management task is then itself a paradoxical one. It is, firstly, to promote and protect order and stability in the day-to-day conduct of the existing business and in its existing strategic direction; in other words to practise ordinary management which is the operation of an efficient bureaucracy. But, if this is all that managers ever did, then their organisation would simply repeat its past or imitate what others had already done. So the strategic management task is also, secondly, to create an atmosphere of questioning and contention, disorder and chaos, that threatens the bureaucracy, and then manage the boundaries around the instability that has been generated. In other words, the second task, in direct opposition to the first, is to nurture an informal network of managers that in effect invites and encourages them to self-organise spontaneously to destroy the bureaucracy. This second task is what opens up the possibility of innovation.

Through such spontaneous self-organisation managers may identify small ambiguous strategic issues, build dynamic agendas of such issues, and continually experiment with responses to those issues. Such responses will inevitably undermine the bureaucracy. Successful organisations have vibrant issue agendas frequently leading to exploratory actions from which new strategic directions may or may not emerge. Here organisations do not know where they are heading and no-one can be in control of the journey, but the behaviour of the organisation may nevertheless be controlled and creative new strategic directions may emerge, although there can be no guarantee of that.

Let me underline the point this book has been making. One approach to strategy is based on the idea that successful organisations are pulled to an identified future point. The task of management would then be relatively simple: it would be to maintain order in all time frames across all issues. However, this book has argued that the dynamics of organising make this an impossible approach to apply in practice and succeed. Those that do apply it are ultimately led to failure. To succeed, managers must practise the other approach, the one based on the idea that successful organisations are driven from where they are now to a destination that they create and discover. And this process of creation and discovery is paradoxical management; that is to say, the simultaneous application of two contradictory forms of management – ordinary management and extraordinary, revolutionary management.

Ordinary management preserves, protects and enacts the existing paradigm. That existing paradigm is the same thing as the culture or the business philosophy; that is, the shared framework that managers use to make sense of their world. The paradigm is a shared repertoire of examples, images, understandings and ways of acting. The paradigm is used by managers in an automatic unquestioning way that binds them together. It enables them to explain their world to each other without having to justify each step in the argument. The paradigm enables managers to agree relatively rapidly on actions to deal with their environment. The objectives managers set, the actions they design, the outcomes they expect all flow from the paradigm. The paradigm is expressed, is made particular, in the hierarchical structure of the organisation, the shape that managerial roles display, the control systems managers employ, the management styles they adopt, the strategies they are pursuing, and the manner in which they manifest a common culture in their physical environment and through the stories they tell.

For example, the core of the paradigm may be the belief that success flows from providing mass-produced low-cost products to customers. This will probably be reflected in the primacy of the financial function that exerts its power through tight financial control systems, so managing the business by cost objectives. Or the core belief may be that success is reaped from high-quality products for selected niche markets. Here it may be the marketing and sales functions that exert the most power, so managing the business according to prescribed quality measures.

Ordinary management is the process of finding out how to achieve known objectives and expected outcomes; it is all about finding solutions to organisational puzzles within the existing paradigm. Ordinary management solves the puzzle of how to achieve the low-cost or the high-quality targets in the above example. Ordinary management is the enactment of the organisational intention set by the paradigm.

The more effectively managers carry out the ordinary management of their existing business, the more they will identify the excesses such beliefs take them to: the more, in other words, they will uncover anomalies to the existing paradigm. So, as managers in the first company pursue their low-cost targets, they will find that quality deteriorates and sales decline; or the other company focusing on quality will find that this leads them to higher and higher cost levels, also causing a loss of sales. This will make it harder for managers to continue sharing the paradigm in an unquestioning way. The paradigm, anyway, is hardly ever a clear-cut, monolithically shared set of beliefs. It is the sharing of a few key beliefs about what is important to the successful conduct of the organisation's business accompanied by conflicting interpretations of other matters: a mixture of stability and instability. Eventually these conflicting interpretations will spill over to undermine the core beliefs. The paradigm is essentially paradoxical: it is both stable and unstable.

That extraordinary or revolutionary management that questions and threatens the existing paradigm therefore flows quite naturally from the effective conduct of ordinary management, unless obstacles both structural and behavioural are put in the way. For example, the doubts raised about the low-cost paradigm in the above example could lead to its replacement by a paradigm of high quality and this will occur through the processes of extraordinary management, unless people's roles are so constrained and they are so demotivated that they cannot be bothered. Extraordinary management produces emergent new strategic direction.

Figure 13.1 summarises the differences between ordinary and extraordinary management.

FIGURE 13.1 ▬▬▬▬▬▬▬▬▬▬▬▬▬▬▬▬▬▬▬▬▬▬▬▬▬▬▬▬▬▬▬▬▬▬▬

Comparison between ordinary and extraordinary management

Ordinary management	Extraordinary management
There are stages: (a) formulation of desired action at the top – preparing the blueprint; (b) implementation down the line – actualising the blueprint; (c) monitoring as top calls line to account – measuring outcome, comparing with policy prediction, damping the difference. Essence is that learning is done before doing and embodied in documents.	There are no clearly distinguished stages. Ideas pop up from many sources and are pursued in many different ways depending on the people and circumstances at the time. The process is political. Deviations from the expected are not dampened, rather, new ideas are amplified through the institution. Essence is that learning is done in the action. It is real time reflection-in-action.
Mechanism is an institution's legitimate system and thus: – comprehensive information is collected and funnelled to the centre for analysis and use in policy formulation at the top.	Mechanism is an institution's shadow system, its informal networks, and thus: – information is localised in the minds, actions and interactions of members, that is, agents of the institution. There is, too much information, it is changing too fast and its meaning is too ambiguous to make it possible or worth centralising.
Essence is the focus on comprehensive and centralised information – explicit knowledge of the institution to be found in its systems and procedures.	Essence is the focus on localised information – implicit knowledge of the institution to be found in the different experiences of agents, who cannot all know and experience the same things. The 'grapevine' is the key information system and the institution's knowledge is contained in myths, stories and rumours.
Mechanism is an institution's legitimate system and thus: – instructions for implementation are passed down the hierarchy for implementation in accordance with bureaucratic rules. Essence is the transparent use of the recognised hierarchy and bureaucracy.	Mechanism is an institution's shadow system and thus: – it is self-organising with suggestions being made at many points as agents avoid the normal hierarchical and bureaucratic channels. Essence is the use of personal networks in a much less transparent way relying on chance encounters.
Legitimate authority drives interactions.	Interpersonal relationships, trust and respect drive interactions.
Outcome is thus the realisation of prior, intention on the part of the most powerful.	Outcome emerges without prior, widely shared intention and is later articulated and incorporated as a change to the legitimate system.

▶

Fig 13.1 continued

Those in charge of the legitimate system are 'in control'.	Behaviour is controlled by the need to sustain support but no one is 'in control'.
Relationships are contractual, particularly between public and private sectors and between one country and another.	Relationships are based on trust, honour, friendship, fear of retribution etc.
Ethical conduct is explicitly prescribed by rules.	Ethical conduct flows from interaction, from ongoing conversation between the parties.
In principle the link between policy and implementation is not problematic – the blueprint establishes local rules of conduct for agents of the institution to follow. These have been designed to produce global pattern, or strategy. We can therefore reason from global causes (e.g. current economic scenario) to requisite policy (e.g. means of exploiting an opportunity) and thence to a strategy, or global pattern (e.g. cooperative alliance) of action. Difficulty is seen as lying at level of policy formulation, not level of joint action. Here the local behaviour of agents that comes between stating a strategy and implementing it is assumed to be unimportant.	Uncertainty, ambiguity, disagreement, complexity all make it impossible to start with intentional policy. Problem is to develop joint action out of which policy, and strategy, can emerge. It is the joint action, or implementation, that is problematic, not the policy formulation. It is the local behaviour of the agents that creates an emergent strategy, or global pattern of action, and this is later legitimised. Tendency is to rationalise this after the event to make of it sound like traditional governance.
Failure to secure predicted outcomes is thus seen as consequence of – – –	No attempt is made to predict outcome. Outcome is articulated and interpreted ignorance; as it occurs. incompetence; bad behaviour.
Consequently, we do not need to distinguish between behaviour at the level of the agent and at the level of the institution or system. We need not tell the personal stories of individuals in order to understand what happened. Instead we can talk about abstract causes such as an economic scenario leading to a strategy.	Consequently we do need to distinguish behaviour at the level of the agent and at the level of the institution or system. We need then to tell the personal stories of individuals if we are to understand how patterns of global behaviour, that is, strategies, came about. The link between one pattern, a global scenario, and another, a strategy, depends upon personal stories as one pattern emerges from another through the personal stories.
Sustains the status quo.	Operates in tension with the legitimate system and provokes change in that legitimate system.

At this point we can return to the key questions posed in Chapter 1 – question 8 had to do with the relationship between success and stability and we can now see how previous chapters have dealt with this.

There has been little attempt so far to define success – it has simply been argued that success requires an organisation to be innovative. For most organisations this is so obviously true today that there is little need to justify the assertion. It is, however, not universally so and we can see this if we consider how we might define success. A sensible definition of success might be as follows: an organisation can be judged successful if it reasonably consistently sustains the support of its environment for lengthy periods of time. Organisations exist because people within them and outside them are willing to support them in financial, political and legal terms. Successful organisations are those that do reasonably enough what those inside and outside principally expect from those organisations or will accept from them. Success can then be judged only in terms of the nature of the primary task that the community sets for an organisation. Failure at that task leads to the withdrawal of support.

If an organisation is a commercial enterprise operating in a fiercely competitive international market, its primary task is quite clear and that is to innovate. If those who constitute such an organisation fail to innovate then they will fail simply because customers withdraw their support. This book has argued that such an organisation can succeed only if it sustains itself far from equilibrium with all that this means about instability, unpredictability and self-organising creativity.

At the other extreme, people in a community may want some organisations that operate in stable equilibrium. Those who support religious institutions, for example, set a primary task, not of innovating but of preserving age-old beliefs. Much the same point may apply to other organisations whose primary tasks have to do with security and safety. For example, the primary task of an army or a police force is that of protecting a community.

However, even for these organisations, some form of innovation seems to be connected to their primary tasks. When this is the case, extraordinary management becomes of major importance. For extraordinary management, a dialectical, paradoxical and chaotic conceptualisation of the strategic management process, in which strategy emerges, is far more useful than is the received wisdom, derived as it is from the stable equilibrium paradigm. This conclusion is supported by studies showing that those who try to practise according to the intentional conceptualisation eventually fail. Those who practice according to the emergent conceptualisation may succeed, although success is not guaranteed. The intentional approach leads to the certainty of eventual failure. The emergent approach leads to the possibility, but not the certainty, of success.

Finally, question 9 in Chapter 1 is all about paradox and how managers cope with it. The fundamental paradox is expressed in the need to sustain and manage the continuing tension created by simultaneously practising two diametrically opposed forms of management: one that sustains the paradigm and the other that destroys it and creates a new one. We have seen in previous chapters how managers often deal with the anxiety such paradoxes and tensions bring by colluding among themselves, often unconsciously, to erect defences against their anxiety, that is, all manner of games and cover-ups. One such defence may well be the insistent claim that the conventional wisdom on strategic management is applicable to innovative situations. It is so much easier to sustain the fantasy that we can plan the unknowable than it is to delve into the group processes that obstruct complex learning in organisations. The question nowadays, however, is whether we can afford such protection from anxiety. If we become convinced, however, that we cannot afford the price, care must be taken in removing organisational defences. If the primary task of an organisation is that of safety, it may be disastrous to strip away the apparently rational procedures people are using to defend themselves against their anxiety, at least without being satisfied that the boundaries around any consequent instability are manageable.

Index